WARNE'S EFFICIENT RECKONER

Warne's
EFFICIENT RECKONER

FREDERICK WARNE & CO LTD
LONDON AND NEW YORK

© FREDERICK WARNE & CO LTD
LONDON, ENGLAND 1970

Reprinted 1970
Reprinted 1971

Whilst the Publishers have endeavoured to ensure the accuracy of these tables, they cannot hold themselves responsible for any inconvenience or loss occasioned by any error therein.

ISBN 0 7232 1332 1

Printed in Great Britain by William Clowes and Sons, Limited London, Beccles and Colchester

1760.371

NOTES ON THIS RECKONER AND ITS USE

In general the usefulness of any reckoner lies in the speed of accurate calculation which it allows and the ease with which rapid verification and checking can be accomplished. Every effort has been made to present the tables in this book in the clearest possible way. The following notes may be helpful.

Multiplication: The left-hand column in the currency tables shows the 'units' and there is a page for each different rate. Thus to find the value of 112 units at £0.0005 each, turn to the page for £0.0005 and read off the value opposite 112. If the number of units to be valued does not appear in the table (e.g. 630) divide it up into two parts which *do* appear in the table and then add the two corresponding values together. Thus 630 can be taken as 625+5. The values of both 625 and 5 can be read straight from the table. The value of 630 is then the sum of these two values added together.

Similarly, if there is no page for the exact *rate* at which items are to be charged (as for example where fractions of 1p are involved) the rate should be divided into parts for which tables *do* exist. Thus the rate 4.7p (£0.047) may be taken as 4p plus 0.7p (£0.0070) for both of which tables are provided.

For rates of more than £1 the whole pounds should be calculated separately and added. This can be done easily from the tables, for example £4=£0.40×10 so look up the answer for £0.40 and shift the decimal point one place to the right. Other even easier ways of calculating the whole pounds will of course often suggest themselves.

Division: If one wants to find, for example, how many items can be bought at 5p (£0.05) out of a total sum of £750, turn to the page for 5p and find the number of units corresponding to the value of £750. If the exact figure does not appear in the table, use the same procedure as for multiplication but in reverse. Thus £520 can be regarded as £500 plus £20, both of which values do appear in the table. If one wants to find the single unit value knowing that, for example, a batch of 900 items costs £140, turn over the pages looking at the 900 units entry until the corresponding money value approximates to £140. The single unit value wanted is then the rate shown on the top of this page.

Discount or Commission: Turn to the page for the relevant percentage rate. The table gives the actual discount or commission in pounds and decimals of pounds on money values ranging from $\frac{1}{2}$p to £1000. The percentages range from $1\frac{1}{4}$% to $97\frac{1}{2}$%. If the exact figures wanted do not appear in the table, use the same procedure of dividing into parts as for multiplication, i.e. £157.25 may be taken as £150+£7+£0.25 and the corresponding three commissions are added together.

General Information: In the currency table the units column has been specially designed to contain values which are likely to be needed in everyday practice both before and after the change to decimalization. Tens are emphasized by bold type and dozens and their multiples by an asterisk. The money rates given range from 1/20p to £1.

The Decimal Currency Board has recommended that fractions of a new penny must be expressed as a decimal of a pound and *not* of a penny. To comply with this recommendation the fractional tables in this reckoner, i.e. 1/20p to 19/20p, have been computed as four-figure decimals of a pound.

To extend a sum involving a four-figure decimal to pounds, new pennies and decimal parts of a new penny:

1 All figures before the decimal point are pounds.

2 The first two figures AFTER the decimal point are pennies.

3 The third and fourth place decimals are tenths and hundredths of a penny respectively.

Thus for £123.8525

pounds	=	123.
new pennies	=	0.85
parts of a new penny	=	0.0025 (= $\frac{1}{4}$p)

£123.8525

During the period of change to decimal currency and for several years subsequently it will frequently be necessary to convert values expressed in decimals to £SD and vice versa. Suitably designed Conversion Tables are included in this book to meet this need.

CONVERSION TABLE

NEW p		ROUNDED s.d	s.d	NEW p		ROUNDED s.d	s.d
½	..	1¼	1·2	25½	..	5 1¼	5 1·2
1	..	2½	2·4	26	..	5 2½	5 2·4
1½	..	3½	3·6	26½	..	5 3½	5 3·6
2	..	4¼	4·8	27	..	5 4¼	5 4·8
2½	..	6	6·0	27½	..	5 6	5 6·0
3	..	7¼	7·2	28	..	5 7¼	5 7·2
3½	..	8½	8·4	28½	..	5 8½	5 8·4
4	..	9½	9·6	29	..	5 9½	5 9·6
4½	..	10¾	10·8	29½	..	5 10¾	5 10·8
5	..	1 0	1 0	30	..	6 0	6 0
5½	..	1 1¼	1 1·2	30½	..	6 1¼	6 1·2
6	..	1 2½	1 2·4	31	..	6 2½	6 2·4
6½	..	1 3½	1 3·6	31½	..	6 3½	6 3·6
7	..	1 4¼	1 4·8	32	..	6 4¼	6 4·8
7½	..	1 6	1 6·0	32½	..	6 6	6 6·0
8	..	1 7¼	1 7·2	33	..	6 7¼	6 7·2
8½	..	1 8½	1 8·4	33½	..	6 8½	6 8·4
9	..	1 9½	1 9·6	34	..	6 9½	6 9·6
9½	..	1 10¾	1 10·8	34½	..	6 10¾	6 10·8
10	..	2 0	2 0	35	..	7 0	7 0
10½	..	2 1¼	2 1·2	35½	..	7 1¼	7 1·2
11	..	2 2½	2 2·4	36	..	7 2½	7 2·4
11½	..	2 3½	2 3·6	36½	..	7 3½	7 3·6
12	..	2 4¼	2 4·8	37	..	7 4¼	7 4·8
12½	..	2 6	2 6·0	37½	..	7 6	7 6·0
13	..	2 7¼	2 7·2	38	..	7 7¼	7 7·2
13½	..	2 8½	2 8·4	38½	..	7 8½	7 8·4
14	..	2 9½	2 9·6	39	..	7 9½	7 9·6
14½	..	2 10¾	2 10·8	39½	..	7 10¾	7 10·8
15	..	3 0	3 0	40	..	8 0	8 0
15½	..	3 1¼	3 1·2	40½	..	8 1¼	8 1·2
16	..	3 2½	3 2·4	41	..	8 2½	8 2·4
16½	..	3 3½	3 3·6	41½	..	8 3½	8 3·6
17	..	3 4¼	3 4·8	42	..	8 4¼	8 4·8
17½	..	3 6	3 6·0	42½	..	8 6	8 6·0
18	..	3 7¼	3 7·2	43	..	8 7¼	8 7·2
18½	..	3 8½	3 8·4	43½	..	8 8½	8 8·4
19	..	3 9½	3 9·6	44	..	8 9½	8 9·6
19½	..	3 10¾	3 10·8	44½	..	8 10¾	8 10·8
20	..	4 0	4 0	45	..	9 0	9 0
20½	..	4 1¼	4 1·2	45½	..	9 1¼	9 1·2
21	..	4 2½	4 2·4	46	..	9 2½	9 2·4
21½	..	4 3½	4 3·6	46½	..	9 3½	9 3·6
22	..	4 4¼	4 4·8	47	..	9 4¼	9 4·8
22½	..	4 6	4 6·0	47½	..	9 6	9 6·0
23	..	4 7¼	4 7·2	48	..	9 7¼	9 7·2
23½	..	4 8½	4 8·4	48½	..	9 8½	9 8·4
24	..	4 9½	4 9·6	49	..	9 9½	9 9·6
24½	..	4 10¾	4 10·8	49½	..	9 10¾	9 10·8
25	..	5 0	5 0	50	..	10 0	10 0

CONVERSION TABLE

NEW p	ROUNDED s.d	s.d	NEW p	ROUNDED s.d	s.d
50½ ..	10 1¼	10 1·2	75½ ..	15 1¼	15 1·2
51 ..	10 2½	10 2·4	76 ..	15 2½	15 2·4
51½ ..	10 3½	10 3·6	76½ ..	15 3½	15 3·6
52 ..	10 4¾	10 4·8	77 ..	15 4¾	15 4·8
52½ ..	10 6	10 6·0	77½ ..	15 6	15 6·0
53 ..	10 7¼	10 7·2	78 ..	15 7¼	15 7·2
53½ ..	10 8⅛	10 8·4	78½ ..	15 8½	15 8·4
54 ..	10 9½	10 9·6	79 ..	15 9½	15 9·6
54½ ..	10 10¾	10 10·8	79½ ..	15 10¾	15 10·8
55 ..	11 0	11 0	80 ..	16 0	16 0
55½ ..	11 1¼	11 1·2	80½ ..	16 1¼	16 1·2
56 ..	11 2½	11 2·4	81 ..	16 2½	16 2·4
56½ ..	11 3½	11 3·6	81½ ..	16 3½	16 3·6
57 ..	11 4¾	11 4·8	82 ..	16 4½	16 4·8
57½ ..	11 6	11 6·0	82½ ..	16 6	16 6·0
58 ..	11 7¼	11 7·2	83 ..	16 7¼	16 7·2
58½ ..	11 8½	11 8·4	83½ ..	16 8½	16 8·4
59 ..	11 9½	11 9·6	84 ..	16 9½	16 9·6
59½ ..	11 10¾	11 10·8	84½ ..	16 10¾	16 10·8
60 ..	12 0	12 0	85 ..	17 0	17 0
60½ ..	12 1¼	12 1·2	85½ ..	17 1¼	17 1·2
61 ..	12 2½	12 2·4	86 ..	17 2½	17 2·4
61½ ..	12 3½	12 3·6	86½ ..	17 3½	17 3·6
62 ..	12 4¾	12 4·8	87 ..	17 4¾	17 4·8
62½ ..	12 6	12 6·0	87½ ..	17 6	17 6·0
63 ..	12 7¼	12 7·2	88 ..	17 7¼	17 7·2
63½ ..	12 8½	12 8·4	88½ ..	17 8½	17 8·4
64 ..	12 9½	12 9·6	89 ..	17 9½	17 9·6
64½ ..	12 10¾	12 10·8	89½ ..	17 10¾	17 10·8
65 ..	13 0	13 0	90 ..	18 0	18 0
65½ ..	13 1¼	13 1·2	90½ ..	18 1¼	18 1·2
66 ..	13 2½	13 2·4	91 ..	18 2½	18 2·4
66½ ..	13 3½	13 3·6	91½ ..	18 3½	18 3·6
67 ..	13 4¾	13 4·8	92 ..	18 4¾	18 4·8
67½ ..	13 6	13 6·0	92½ ..	18 6	18 6·0
68 ..	13 7¼	13 7·2	93 ..	18 7¼	18 7·2
68½ ..	13 8½	13 8·4	93½ ..	18 8½	18 8·4
69 ..	13 9½	13 9·6	94 ..	18 9½	18 9·6
69½ ..	13 10¾	13 10·8	94½ ..	18 10¾	18 10·8
70 ..	14 0	14 0	95 ..	19 0	19 0
70½ ..	14 1¼	14 1·2	95½ ..	19 1¼	19 1·2
71 ..	14 2½	14 2·4	96 ..	19 2½	19 2·4
71½ ..	14 3½	14 3·6	96½ ..	19 3½	19 3·6
72 ..	14 4¾	14 4·8	97 ..	19 4¾	19 4·8
72½ ..	14 6	14 6·0	97½ ..	19 6	19 6·0
73 ..	14 7¼	14 7·2	98 ..	19 7¼	19 7·2
73½ ..	14 8½	14 8·4	98½ ..	19 8½	19 8·4
74 ..	14 9½	14 9·6	99 ..	19 9½	19 9·6
74½ ..	14 10¾	14 10·8	99½ ..	19 10¾	19 10·8
75 ..	15 0	15 0	100 ..	£1 0 0	£1 0 0

Section 1

DECIMAL CURRENCY RECKONER FOR NEW PENNY (p) RATES

No.	£	No.	£	No.	£	No.	£
1	0·0005	38	0·0190	76	0·0380	114	0·0570
1½	0·00075	39	0·0195	77	0·0385	115	0·0575
2	0·0010	40	0·0200	78	0·0390	116	0·0580
3	0·0015	41	0·0205	79	0·0395	117	0·0585
4	0·0020	42	0·0210	80	0·0400	118	0·0590
5	0·0025	43	0·0215	81	0·0405	119	0·0595
6	0·0030	44	0·0220	82	0·0410	120	0·0600
7	0·0035	45	0·0225	83	0·0415	128	0·0640
8	0·0040	46	0·0230	84	0·0420	130	0·0650
9	0·0045	47	0·0235	85	0·0425	140	0·0700
10	0·0050	48	0·0240	86	0·0430	144	0·0720
11	0·0055	49	0·0245	87	0·0435	150	0·0750
12	0·0060	50	0·0250	88	0·0440	156	0·0780
13	0·0065	51	0·0255	89	0·0445	160	0·0800
14	0·0070	52	0·0260	90	0·0450	168	0·0840
15	0·0075	53	0·0265	91	0·0455	170	0·0850
16	0·0080	54	0·0270	92	0·0460	180	0·0900
17	0·0085	55	0·0275	93	0·0465	190	0·0950
18	0·0090	56	0·0280	94	0·0470	196	0·0980
19	0·0095	57	0·0285	95	0·0475	200	0·1000
20	0·0100	58	0·0290	96	0·0480	220	0·1100
21	0·0105	59	0·0295	97	0·0485	224	0·1120
22	0·0110	60	0·0300	98	0·0490	256	0·1280
23	0·0115	61	0·0305	99	0·0495	280	0·1400
24	0·0120	62	0·0310	100	0·0500	300	0·1500
25	0·0125	63	0·0315	101	0·0505	365	0·1825
26	0·0130	64	0·0320	102	0·0510	400	0·2000
27	0·0135	65	0·0325	103	0·0515	480	0·2400
28	0·0140	66	0·0330	104	0·0520	500	0·2500
29	0·0145	67	0·0335	105	0·0525	516	0·2580
30	0·0150	68	0·0340	106	0·0530	560	0·2800
31	0·0155	69	0·0345	107	0·0535	600	0·3000
32	0·0160	70	0·0350	108	0·0540	625	0·3125
33	0·0165	71	0·0355	109	0·0545	640	0·3200
34	0·0170	72	0·0360	110	0·0550	700	0·3500
35	0·0175	73	0·0365	111	0·0555	750	0·3750
36	0·0180	74	0·0370	112	0·0560	800	0·4000
37	0·0185	75	0·0375	113	0·0565	900	0·4500

No.	£	No.	£	No.	£
1000	0·5000	1760	0·8800	6000	3·0000
1016	0·5080	2000	1·0000	7000	3·5000
1094	0·5470	2240	1·1200	7500	3·7500
1120	0·5600	2500	1·2500	10000	5·0000
1250	0·6250	3000	1·5000	15000	7·5000
1500	0·7500	4000	2·0000	20000	10·0000
1750	0·8750	5000	2·5000	30000	15·0000

No.	£	No.	£	No.	£	No.	£
1	0·0010	38	0·0380	76	0·0760	114	0·1140
1½	0·0015	39	0·0390	77	0·0770	115	0·1150
2	0·0020	40	0·0400	78	0·0780	116	0·1160
3	0·0030	41	0·0410	79	0·0790	117	0·1170
4	0·0040	42	0·0420	80	0·0800	118	0·1180
5	0·0050	43	0·0430	81	0·0810	119	0·1190
6	0·0060	44	0·0440	82	0·0820	120	0·1200
7	0·0070	45	0·0450	83	0·0830	128	0·1280
8	0·0080	46	0·0460	84	0·0840	130	0·1300
9	0·0090	47	0·0470	85	0·0850	140	0·1400
10	0·0100	48	0·0480	86	0·0860	144	0·1440
11	0·0110	49	0·0490	87	0·0870	150	0·1500
12	0·0120	50	0·0500	88	0·0880	156	0·1560
13	0·0130	51	0·0510	89	0·0890	160	0·1600
14	0·0140	52	0·0520	90	0·0900	168	0·1680
15	0·0150	53	0·0530	91	0·0910	170	0·1700
16	0·0160	54	0·0540	92	0·0920	180	0·1800
17	0·0170	55	0·0550	93	0·0930	190	0·1900
18	0·0180	56	0·0560	94	0·0940	196	0·1960
19	0·0190	57	0·0570	95	0·0950	200	0·2000
20	0·0200	58	0·0580	96	0·0960	220	0·2200
21	0·0210	59	0·0590	97	0·0970	224	0·2240
22	0·0220	60	0·0600	98	0·0980	256	0·2560
23	0·0230	61	0·0610	99	0·0990	280	0·2800
24	0·0240	62	0·0620	100	0·1000	300	0·3000
25	0·0250	63	0·0630	101	0·1010	365	0·3650
26	0·0260	64	0·0640	102	0·1020	400	0·4000
27	0·0270	65	0·0650	103	0·1030	480	0·4800
28	0·0280	66	0·0660	104	0·1040	500	0·5000
29	0·0290	67	0·0670	105	0·1050	516	0·5160
30	0·0300	68	0·0680	106	0.1060	560	0·5600
31	0·0310	69	0·0690	107	0·1070	600	0·6000
32	0·0320	70	0·0700	108	0·1080	625	0·6250
33	0·0330	71	0·0710	109	0·1090	640	0·6400
34	0·0340	72	0·0720	110	0·1100	700	0·7000
35	0·0350	73	0·0730	111	0·1110	750	0·7500
36	0·0360	74	0·0740	112	0·1120	800	0·8000
37	0·0370	75	0·0750	113	0·1130	900	0·9000

No.	£	No.	£	No.	£
1000	1·0000	1760	1·7600	6000	6·0000
1016	1·0160	2000	2·0000	7000	7·0000
1094	1·0940	2240	2·2400	7500	7·5000
1120	1·1200	2500	2·5000	10000	10·0000
1250	1·2500	3000	3·0000	15000	15·0000
1500	1·5000	4000	4·0000	20000	20·0000
1750	1·7500	5000	5·0000	30000	30·0000

No.	£	p	£	No.	£	p	£
$\frac{1}{16}$	0	00	0·0001	34	0	04½	0·0425
$\frac{1}{8}$	0	00	0·00015	35	0	04½	0·04375
$\frac{1}{4}$	0	00	0·0003	36	0	04½	0·0450
$\frac{1}{2}$	0	00	0·00065	37	0	04½	0·04625
$\frac{3}{4}$	0	00	0·00095	38	0	05	0·0475
1½	0	00	0·0019	39	0	05	0·04875
2	0	00½	0·0025	40	0	05	0·0500
3	0	00½	0·00375	41	0	05	0·05125
4	0	00½	0·0050	42	0	05½	0·0525
5	0	00½	0·00625	43	0	05½	0·05375
6	0	01	0·0075	44	0	05½	0·0550
7	0	01	0·00875	45	0	05½	0·05625
8	0	01	0·0100	46	0	06	0·0575
9	0	01	0·01125	47	0	06	0·05875
10	0	01½	0·0125	48	0	06	0·0600
11	0	01½	0·01375	49	0	06	0·06125
12	0	01½	0·0150	50	0	06½	0·0625
13	0	01½	0·01625	51	0	06½	0·06375
14	0	02	0·0175	52	0	06½	0·0650
15	0	02	0·01875	53	0	06½	0·06625
16	0	02	0·0200	54	0	07	0·0675
17	0	02	0·02125	55	0	07	0·06875
18	0	02½	0·0225	56	0	07	0·0700
19	0	02½	0·02375	57	0	07	0·07125
20	0	02½	0·0250	58	0	07½	0·0725
21	0	02½	0·02625	59	0	07½	0·07375
22	0	03	0·0275	60	0	07½	0·0750
23	0	03	0·02875	61	0	07½	0·07625
24	0	03	0·0300	62	0	08	0·0775
25	0	03	0·03125	63	0	08	0·07875
26	0	03½	0·0325	64	0	08	0·0800
27	0	03½	0·03375	65	0	08	0·08125
28	0	03½	0·0350	66	0	08½	0·0825
29	0	03½	0·03625	67	0	08½	0·08375
30	0	04	0·0375	68	0	08½	0·0850
31	0	04	0·03875	69	0	08½	0·08625
32	0	04	0·0400	70	0	09	0·0875
33	0	04	0·04125	71	0	09	0·08875

No.	£ p	£	No.	£ p	£
1000	1 25	1·2500	1500	1 87½	1·8750
1016	1 27	1·2700	1750	2 19	2·1875
1094	1 37	1·3675	1760	2 20	2·2000
1120	1 40	1·4000	2000	2 50	2·5000
1250	1 56½	1·5625	2240	2 80	2·8000

No.	£	p	£	No.	£	p	£
72	0	09	0·0900	110	0	14	0·1375
73	0	09	0·09125	111	0	14	0·13875
74	0	09$\frac{1}{2}$	0·0925	112	0	14	0·1400
75	0	09$\frac{1}{2}$	0·09375	113	0	14	0·14125
76	0	09$\frac{1}{2}$	0·0950	114	0	14$\frac{1}{2}$	0·1425
77	0	09$\frac{1}{2}$	0·09625	115	0	14$\frac{1}{2}$	0·14375
78	0	10	0·0975	116	0	14$\frac{1}{2}$	0·1450
79	0	10	0·09875	117	0	14$\frac{1}{2}$	0·14625
80	0	10	0·1000	118	0	15	0·1477
81	0	10	0·10125	119	0	15	0·14875
82	0	10$\frac{1}{2}$	0·1025	120	0	15	0·1500
83	0	10$\frac{1}{2}$	0·10375	128	0	16	0·1600
84	0	10$\frac{1}{2}$	0·1050	130	0	16$\frac{1}{2}$	0·1625
85	0	10$\frac{1}{2}$	0·10625	140	0	17$\frac{1}{2}$	0·1750
86	0	11	0·1075	144	0	18	0·1800
87	0	11	0·10875	150	0	19	0·1875
88	0	11	0·1100	156	0	19$\frac{1}{2}$	0·1950
89	0	11	0.11125	168	0	21	0·2100
90	0	11$\frac{1}{2}$	0·1125	196	0	24$\frac{1}{2}$	0·2450
91	0	11$\frac{1}{2}$	0·11375	200	0	25	0·2500
92	0	11$\frac{1}{2}$	0·1150	220	0	27$\frac{1}{2}$	0·2750
93	0	11$\frac{1}{2}$	0·11625	224	0	28	0·2800
94	0	12	0·1175	256	0	32	0·3200
95	0	12	0·11875	280	0	35	0·3500
96	0	12	0·1200	300	0	37$\frac{1}{2}$	0·3750
97	0	12	0·12125	365	0	45$\frac{1}{2}$	0·45625
98	0	12$\frac{1}{2}$	0·1225	400	0	50	0·5000
99	0	12$\frac{1}{2}$	0·12375	480	0	60	0·6000
100	0	12$\frac{1}{2}$	0·1250	500	0	62$\frac{1}{2}$	0·6250
101	0	12$\frac{1}{2}$	0·12625	516	0	64$\frac{1}{2}$	0·6450
102	0	13	0·1275	560	0	70	0·7000
103	0	13	0·12875	600	0	75	0·7500
104	0	13	0·1300	625	0	78	0·78125
105	0	13	0·13125	640	0	80	0·8000
106	0	13$\frac{1}{2}$	0·1325	700	0	87$\frac{1}{2}$	0·8750
107	0	13$\frac{1}{2}$	0·13375	750	0	94	0·9375
108	0	13$\frac{1}{2}$	0·1350	800	1	00	1·0000
109	0	13$\frac{1}{2}$	0·13625	900	1	12$\frac{1}{2}$	1·1250

No.	£	p	£	No.	£	p	£
2500	3	12$\frac{1}{2}$	3·1250	7500	9	37$\frac{1}{2}$	9·3750
3000	3	75	3·7500	10000	12	50	12·5000
4000	5	00	5·0000	15000	18	75	18·7500
5000	6	25	6·2500	20000	25	00	25·0000
6000	7	50	7·5000	30000	37	50	37·5000

No.	£	No.	£	No.	£	No.	£
1	0·0015	38	0·0570	76	0·1140	114	0·1710
1½	0·00225	39	0·0585	77	0·1155	115	0·1725
2	0·0030	40	0·0600	78	0·1170	116	0·1740
3	0·0045	41	0·0615	79	0·1185	117	0·1755
4	0·0060	42	0·0630	80	0·1200	118	0·1770
5	0·0075	43	0·0645	81	0·1215	119	0·1785
6	0·0090	44	0·0660	82	0·1230	120	0·1800
7	0·0105	45	0·0675	83	0·1245	128	0·1920
8	0·0120	46	0·0690	84	0·1260	130	0·1950
9	0·0135	47	0·0705	85	0·1275	140	0·2100
10	0·0150	48	0·0720	86	0·1290	144	0·2160
11	0·0165	49	0·0735	87	0·1305	150	0·2250
12	0·0180	50	0·0750	88	0·1320	156	0·2340
13	0·0195	51	0·0765	89	0·1335	160	0·2400
14	0·0210	52	0·0780	90	0·1350	168	0·2520
15	0·0225	53	0·0795	91	0·1365	170	0·2550
16	0·0240	54	0·0810	92	0·1380	180	0·2700
17	0·0255	55	0·0825	93	0·1395	190	0·2850
18	0·0270	56	0·0840	94	0·1410	196	0·2940
19	0·0285	57	0·0855	95	0·1425	200	0·3000
20	0·0300	58	0·0870	96	0·1440	220	0·3300
21	0·0315	59	0·0885	97	0·1455	224	0·3360
22	0·0330	60	0·0900	98	0·1470	256	0·3840
23	0·0345	61	0·0915	99	0·1485	280	0·4200
24	0·0360	62	0·0930	100	0·1500	300	0·4500
25	0·0375	63	0·0945	101	0·1515	365	0·5475
26	0·0390	64	0·0960	102	0·1530	400	0·6000
27	0·0405	65	0·0975	103	0·1545	480	0·7200
28	0·0420	66	0·0990	104	0·1560	500	0·7500
29	0·0435	67	0·1005	105	0·1575	516	0·7740
30	0·0450	68	0·1020	106	0·1590	560	0·8400
31	0·0465	69	0·1035	107	0·1605	600	0·9000
32	0·0480	70	0·1050	108	0·1620	625	0·9375
33	0·0495	71	0·1065	109	0·1635	640	0·9600
34	0·0510	72	0·1080	110	0·1650	700	1·0500
35	0·0525	73	0·1095	111	0·1665	750	1·1250
36	0·0540	74	0·1110	112	0·1680	800	1·2000
37	0·0555	75	0·1125	113	0·1695	900	1·3500

No.	£	No.	£	No.	£
1000	1·5000	1760	2·6400	6000	9·0000
1016	1·5240	2000	3·0000	7000	10·5000
1094	1·6410	2240	3·3600	7500	11·2500
1120	1·6800	2500	3·7500	10000	15·0000
1250	1·8750	3000	4·5000	15000	22·5000
1500	2·2500	4000	6·0000	20000	30·0000
1750	2·6250	5000	7·5000	30000	45·0000

No.	£	No.	£	No.	£	No.	£
1	0·0020	38	0·0760	76	0·1520	114	0·2280
1½	0·0030	39	0·0780	77	0·1540	115	0·2300
2	0·0040	40	0·0800	78	0·1560	116	0·2320
3	0·0060	41	0·0820	79	0·1580	117	0·2340
4	0·0080	42	0·0840	80	0·1600	118	0·2360
5	0·0100	43	0·0860	81	0·1620	119	0·2380
6	0·0120	44	0·0880	82	0·1640	120	0·2400
7	0·0140	45	0·0900	83	0·1660	128	0·2560
8	0·0160	46	0·0920	84	0·1680	130	0·2600
9	0·0180	47	0·0940	85	0·1700	140	0·2800
10	0·0200	48	0·0960	86	0·1720	144	0·2880
11	0·0220	49	0·0980	87	0·1740	150	0·3000
12	0·0240	50	0·1000	88	0·1760	156	0·3120
13	0·0260	51	0·1020	89	0·1780	160	0·3200
14	0·0280	52	0·1040	90	0·1800	168	0·3360
15	0·0300	53	0·1060	91	0·1820	170	0·3400
16	0·0320	54	0·1080	92	0·1840	180	0·3600
17	0·0340	55	0·1100	93	0·1860	190	0·3800
18	0·0360	56	0·1120	94	0·1880	196	0·3920
19	0·0380	57	0·1140	95	0·1900	200	0·4000
20	0·0400	58	0·1160	96	0·1920	220	0·4400
21	0·0420	59	0·1180	97	0·1940	224	0·4480
22	0·0440	60	0·1200	98	0·1960	256	0·5120
23	0·0460	61	0·1220	99	0·1980	280	0·5600
24	0·0480	62	0·1240	100	0·2000	300	0·6000
25	0·0500	63	0·1260	101	0·2020	365	0·7300
26	0·0520	64	0·1280	102	0·2040	400	0·8000
27	0·0540	65	0·1300	103	0·2060	480	0·9600
28	0·0560	66	0·1320	104	0·2080	500	1·0000
29	0·0580	67	0·1340	105	0·2100	516	1·0320
30	0·0600	68	0·1360	106	0·2120	560	1·1200
31	0·0620	69	0·1380	107	0·2140	600	1·2000
32	0·0640	70	0·1400	108	0·2160	625	1·2500
33	0·0660	71	0·1420	109	0·2180	640	1·2800
34	0·0680	72	0·1440	110	0·2200	700	1·4000
35	0·0700	73	0·1460	111	0·2220	750	1·5000
36	0·0720	74	0·1480	112	0·2240	800	1·6000
37	0·0740	75	0·1500	113	0·2260	900	1·8000

No.	£	No.	£	No.	£
1000	2·0000	1760	3·5200	6000	12·0000
1016	2·0320	2000	4·0000	7000	14·0000
1094	2·1880	2240	4·4800	7500	15·0000
1120	2·2400	2500	5·0000	10000	20·0000
1250	2·5000	3000	6·0000	15000	30·0000
1500	3·0000	4000	8·0000	20000	40·0000
1750	3·5000	5000	10·0000	30000	60·0000

No.	£	p	£	No.	£	p	£
1/16	0	00	0·00015	34	0	08½	0·0850
1/8	0	00	0·0003	35	0	08½	0·0875
1/4	0	00	0·00065	36	0	09	0·0900
1/2	0	00	0·00125	37	0	09	0·0925
3/4	0	00	0·0019	38	0	09½	0·0950
1½	0	00	0·00375	39	0	09½	0·0975
2	0	00½	0·0050	40	0	10	0·1000
3	0	00½	0·0075	41	0	10	0·1025
4	0	01	0·0100	42	0	10½	0·1050
5	0	01	0·0125	43	0	10½	0.1075
6	0	01½	0·0150	44	0	11	0.1100
7	0	01½	0·0175	45	0	11	0·1125
8	0	02	0·0200	46	0	11½	0·1150
9	0	02	0·0225	47	0	11½	0·1175
10	0	02½	0·0250	48	0	12	0·1200
11	0	02½	0·0275	49	0	12	0·1225
12	0	03	0·0300	50	0	12½	0·1250
13	0	03	0·0325	51	0	12½	0·1275
14	0	03½	0·0350	52	0	13	0·1300
15	0	03½	0·0375	53	0	13	0·1325
16	0	04	0·0400	54	0	13½	0·1350
17	0	04	0·0425	55	0	13½	0·1375
18	0	04½	0·0450	56	0	14	0·1400
19	0	04½	0·0475	57	0	14	0·1425
20	0	05	0·0500	58	0	14½	0·1450
21	0	05	0·0525	59	0	14½	0·1475
22	0	05½	0·0550	60	0	15	0·1500
23	0	05½	0·0575	61	0	15	0·1525
24	0	06	0·0600	62	0	15½	0·1550
25	0	06	0·0625	63	0	15½	0·1575
26	0	06½	0.0650	64	0	16	0·1600
27	0	06½	0·0675	65	0	16	0·1625
28	0	07	0·0700	66	0	16½	0·1650
29	0	07	0·0725	67	0	16½	0·1675
30	0	07½	0.0750	68	0	17	0·1700
31	0	07½	0·0775	69	0	17	0·1725
32	0	08	0·0800	70	0	17½	0·1750
33	0	08	0·0825	71	0	17½	0·1775

No.	£	p	£	No.	£	p	£
1000	2	50	2·5000	1500	3	75	3·7500
1016	2	54	2·5400	1750	4	37½	4·3750
1094	2	73½	2·7350	1760	4	44	4·4400
1120	2	80	2·8000	2000	5	00	5·0000
1250	3	12½	3·1250	2240	5	60	5·6000

No.	£	p	£	No.	£	p	£
72	0	18	0·1800	110	0	27½	0·2750
73	0	18	0·1825	111	0	27½	0·2775
74	0	18½	0·1850	112	0	28	0·2800
75	0	18½	0·1875	113	0	28	0·2825
76	0	19	0·1900	114	0	28½	0·2850
77	0	19	0·1925	115	0	28½	0·2875
78	0	19½	0·1950	116	0	29	0·2900
79	0	19½	0·1975	117	0	29	0·2925
80	0	20	0·2000	118	0	29½	0·2950
81	0	20	0·2025	119	0	29½	0·2975
82	0	20½	0·2050	120	0	30	0·3000
83	0	20½	0·2075	128	0	32	0·3200
84	0	21	0·2100	130	0	32½	0·3250
85	0	21	0·2125	140	0	35	0·3500
86	0	21½	0·2150	144	0	36	0·3600
87	0	21½	0·2175	150	0	37½	0·3750
88	0	22	0·2200	156	0	39	0·3900
89	0	22	0·2225	168	0	42	0·4200
90	0	22½	0·2250	196	0	49	0·4900
91	0	22½	0·2275	200	0	50	0·5000
92	0	23	0·2300	220	0	55	0·5500
93	0	23	0·2325	224	0	56	0·5600
94	0	23½	0·2350	256	0	64	0·6400
95	0	23½	0·2375	280	0	70	0·7000
96	0	24	0·2400	300	0	75	0·7500
97	0	24	0·2425	365	0	91	0·9125
98	0	24½	0·2450	400	1	00	1·0000
99	0	24½	0·2475	480	1	20	1·2000
100	0	25	0·2500	500	1	25	1·2500
101	0	25	0·2525	516	1	29	1·2900
102	0	25½	0·2550	560	1	40	1·4000
103	0	25½	0·2575	600	1	50	1·5000
104	0	26	0·2600	625	1	56	1·5625
105	0	26	0·2625	640	1	60	1·6000
106	0	26½	0·2650	700	1	75	1·7500
107	0	26½	0·2675	750	1	87½	1·8750
108	0	27	0·2700	800	2	00	2·0000
109	0	27	0·2725	900	2	25	2·2500
No.	£	p	£	No.	£	p	£
2500	6	25	6·2500	7500	18	75	18·7500
3000	7	50	7·5000	10000	25	00	25·0000
4000	10	00	10·0000	15000	37	50	37·5000
5000	12	50	12·5000	20000	50	00	50·0000
6000	15	00	15·0000	30000	75	00	75·0000

No.	£	No.	£	No.	£	No.	£
1	0·0030	38	0·1140	76	0·2280	114	0·3420
1½	0·0045	39	0·1170	77	0·2310	115	0·3450
2	0·0060	40	0·1200	78	0·2340	116	0·3480
3	0·0090	41	0·1230	79	0·2370	117	0·3510
4	0·0120	42	0·1260	80	0·2400	118	0·3540
5	0·0150	43	0·1290	81	0·2430	119	0·3570
6	0·0180	44	0·1320	82	0·2460	120	0·3600
7	0·0210	45	0·1350	83	0·2490	128	0·3840
8	0·0240	46	0·1380	84	0·2520	130	0·3900
9	0·0270	47	0·1410	85	0·2550	140	0·4200
10	0·0300	48	0·1440	86	0·2580	144	0·4320
11	0·0330	49	0·1470	87	0·2610	150	0·4500
12	0·0360	50	0·1500	88	0·2640	156	0·4680
13	0·0390	51	0·1530	89	0·2670	160	0·4800
14	0·0420	52	0·1560	90	0·2700	168	0·5040
15	0·0450	53	0·1590	91	0·2730	170	0·5100
16	0·0480	54	0·1620	92	0·2760	180	0·5400
17	0·0510	55	0·1650	93	0·2790	190	0·5700
18	0·0540	56	0·1680	94	0·2820	196	0·5880
19	0·0570	57	0·1710	95	0·2850	200	0·6000
20	0·0600	58	0·1740	96	0·2880	220	0·6600
21	0·0630	59	0·1770	97	0·2910	224	0·6720
22	0·0660	60	0·1800	98	0·2940	256	0·7680
23	0·0690	61	0·1830	99	0·2970	280	0·8400
24	0·0720	62	0·1860	100	0·3000	300	0·9000
25	0·0750	63	0·1890	101	0·3030	365	1·0950
26	0·0780	64	0·1920	102	0·3060	400	1·2000
27	0·0810	65	0·1950	103	0·3090	480	1·4400
28	0·0840	66	0·1980	104	0·3120	500	1·5000
29	0·0870	67	0·2010	105	0·3150	516	1·5480
30	0·0900	68	0·2040	106	0·3180	560	1·6800
31	0·0930	69	0·2070	107	0·3210	600	1·8000
32	0·0960	70	0·2100	108	0·3240	625	1·8750
33	0·0990	71	0·2130	109	0·3270	640	1·9200
34	0·1020	72	0·2160	110	0·3300	700	2·1000
35	0·1050	73	0·2190	111	0·3330	750	2·2500
36	0·1080	74	0·2220	112	0·3360	800	2·4000
37	0·1110	75	0·2250	113	0·3390	900	2·7000

No.	£	No.	£	No.	£
1000	3·0000	1760	5·2800	6000	18·0000
1016	3·0480	2000	6·0000	7000	21·0000
1094	3·2820	2240	6·7200	7500	22·5000
1120	3·3600	2500	7·5000	10000	30·0000
1250	3·7500	3000	9·0000	15000	45·0000
1500	4·5000	4000	12·0000	20000	60.0000
1750	5·2500	5000	15·0000	30000	90·0000

No.	£	No.	£	No.	£	No.	£
1	0·0035	38	0·1330	76	0·2660	114	0·3990
1½	0·00525	39	0·1365	77	0·2695	115	0·4025
2	0·0070	40	0·1400	78	0·2730	116	0·4060
3	0·0105	41	0·1435	79	0·2765	117	0·4095
4	0·0140	42	0·1470	80	0·2800	118	0·4130
5	0·0175	43	0·1505	81	0·2835	119	0·4165
6	0·0210	44	0·1540	82	0·2870	120	0·4200
7	0·0245	45	0·1575	83	0·2905	128	0·4480
8	0·0280	46	0·1610	84	0·2940	130	0·4550
9	0·0315	47	0·1645	85	0·2975	140	0·4900
10	0·0350	48	0·1680	86	0·3010	144	0·5040
11	0·0385	49	0·1715	87	0·3045	150	0·5250
12	0·0420	50	0·1750	88	0·3080	156	0·5460
13	0·0455	51	0·1785	89	0·3115	160	0·5600
14	0·0490	52	0·1820	90	0·3150	168	0·5880
15	0·0525	53	0·1855	91	0·3185	170	0·5950
16	0·0560	54	0·1890	92	0·3220	180	0·6300
17	0·0595	55	0·1925	93	0·3255	190	0·6650
18	0·0630	56	0·1960	94	0·3290	196	0·6860
19	0·0665	57	0·1995	95	0·3325	200	0·7000
20	0·0700	58	0·2030	96	0·3360	220	0·7700
21	0·0735	59	0·2065	97	0·3395	224	0·7840
22	0·0770	60	0·2100	98	0·3430	256	0·8960
23	0·0805	61	0·2135	99	0·3465	280	0·9800
24	0·0840	62	0·2170	100	0·3500	300	1·0500
25	0·0875	63	0·2205	101	0·3535	365	1·2775
26	0·0910	64	0·2240	102	0·3570	400	1·4000
27	0·0945	65	0·2275	103	0·3605	480	1·6800
28	0·0980	66	0·2310	104	0·3640	500	1·7500
29	0·1015	67	0·2345	105	0·3675	516	1·8060
30	0·1050	68	0·2380	106	0·3710	560	1·9600
31	0·1085	69	0·2415	107	0·3745	600	2·1000
32	0·1120	70	0·2450	108	0·3780	625	2·1875
33	0·1155	71	0·2485	109	0·3815	640	2·2400
34	0·1190	72	0·2520	110	0·3850	700	2·4500
35	0·1225	73	0·2555	111	0·3885	750	2·6250
36	0·1260	74	0·2590	112	0·3920	800	2·8000
37	0·1295	75	0·2625	113	0·3955	900	3·1500

No.	£	No.	£	No.	£
1000	3·5000	1760	6·1600	6000	21·0000
1016	3·5560	2000	7·0000	7000	24·5000
1094	3·8290	2240	7·8400	7500	26·2500
1120	3·9200	2500	8·7500	10000	35·0000
1250	4·3750	3000	10·5000	15000	52·5000
1500	5·2500	4000	14·0000	20000	70·0000
1750	6·1250	5000	17·5000	30000	105·0000

No.	£	p	£	No.	£	p	£
$\frac{1}{16}$	0	00	0·00025	34	0	13	0·1275
$\frac{1}{8}$	0	00	0·00045	35	0	13	0·13125
$\frac{1}{4}$	0	00	0·00095	36	0	13½	0·1350
$\frac{1}{2}$	0	00	0·0019	37	0	14	0·13875
$\frac{3}{4}$	0	00½	0·0028	38	0	14½	0·1425
1½	0	00½	0·00565	39	0	14½	0·14625
2	0	01	0·0075	40	0	15	0·1500
3	0	01	0·01125	41	0	15½	0·15375
4	0	01½	0·0150	42	0	16	0·1575
5	0	02	0·01875	43	0	16	0·16125
6	0	02½	0·0225	44	0	16½	0·1650
7	0	02½	0·02625	45	0	17	0·16875
8	0	03	0·0300	46	0	17½	0·1725
9	0	03½	0·03375	47	0	17½	0·17625
10	0	04	0·0375	48	0	18	0·1800
11	0	04	0·04125	49	0	18½	0·18375
12	0	04½	0·0450	50	0	19	0·1875
13	0	05	0·04875	51	0	19	0·19125
14	0	05½	0·0525	52	0	19½	0·1950
15	0	05½	0·05625	53	0	20	0·19875
16	0	06	0·0600	54	0	20½	0·2025
17	0	06½	0·06375	55	0	20½	0·20625
18	0	07	0·0675	56	0	21	0·2100
19	0	07	0·07125	57	0	21½	0·21375
20	0	07½	0·0750	58	0	22	0·2175
21	0	08	0·07875	59	0	22	0·22125
22	0	08½	0·0825	60	0	22½	0·2250
23	0	08½	0·08625	61	0	23	0·22875
24	0	09	0·0900	62	0	23½	0·2325
25	0	09½	0·09375	63	0	23½	0·23625
26	0	10	0·0975	64	0	24	0·2400
27	0	10	0·10125	65	0	24½	0·24375
28	0	10½	0·1050	66	0	25	0·2475
29	0	11	0·10875	67	0	25	0·25125
30	0	11½	0·1125	68	0	25½	0·2550
31	0	11½	0·11625	69	0	26	0·25875
32	0	12	0·1200	70	0	26½	0·2625
33	0	12½	0·12375	71	0	26½	0·26625

No	£	p	£	No	£	p	£
1000	3	75	3·7500	1500	5	62½	5·6250
1016	3	81	3·8100	1750	6	56½	6·5625
1094	4	10½	4·1025	1760	6	60	6·6000
1120	4	20	4·2000	2000	7	50	7·5000
1250	4	69	4·6875	2240	8	40	8·4000

No.	£	p	£	No.	£	p	£
72	0	27	0·2700	110	0	41½	0·4125
73	0	27½	0·27375	111	0	41½	0·41625
74	0	28	0·2775	112	0	42	0·4200
75	0	28	0·28125	113	0	42½	0.42375
76	0	28½	0·2850	114	0	43	0·4275
77	0	29	0.28875	115	0	43	0·43125
78	0	29½	0·2925	116	0	43½	0·4350
79	0	29½	0·29625	117	0	44	0·43875
80	0	30	0·3000	118	0	44½	0·4425
81	0	30½	0·30375	119	0	44½	0·44625
82	0	31	0·3075	120	0	45	0·4500
83	0	31	0·31125	128	0	48	0·4800
84	0	31½	0·3150	130	0	49	0·4875
85	0	32	0·31875	140	0	52½	0·5250
86	0	32½	0·3225	144	0	54	0·5400
87	0	32½	0·32625	150	0	56½	0·5625
88	0	33	0·3300	156	0	58½	0·5850
89	0	33½	0·33375	168	0	63	0·6300
90	0	34	0·3375	196	0	63½	0·6350
91	0	34	0·34125	200	0	75	0·7500
92	0	34½	0·3450	220	0	82½	0·8250
93	0	35	0·34875	224	0	84	0·8400
94	0	35½	0·3525	256	0	96	0·9600
95	0	35½	0·35625	280	1	05	1·0500
96	0	36	0·3600	300	1	12½	1·1250
97	0	36½	0·36375	365	1	37	1·36875
98	0	37	0·3675	400	1	50	1·5000
99	0	37	0·37125	480	1	80	1·8000
100	0	37½	0·3750	500	1	87½	1·8750
101	0	38	0·37875	516	1	93½	1·9350
102	0	38½	0·3825	560	2	10	2·1000
103	0	38½	0·38625	600	2	25	2·2500
104	0	39	0·3900	625	2	34½	2·34375
105	0	39½	0·39375	640	2	40	2·4000
106	0	40	0·3975	700	2	62½	2·6250
107	0	40	0·40125	750	2	81½	2·8125
108	0	40½	0·4050	800	3	00	3·0000
109	0	41	0·40875	900	3	37½	3·3750

No.	£	p	£	No.	£	p	£
2500	9	37½	9·3750	7500	28	12½	28·1250
3000	11	25	11·2500	10000	37	50	37·5000
4000	15	00	15·0000	15000	56	25	56·2500
5000	18	75	18·7500	20000	75	00	75·0000
6000	22	50	22·5000	30000	112	50	112·5000

No.	£	No.	£	No.	£	No.	£
1	0·0040	38	0·1520	76	0·3040	114	0·4560
1½	0·0060	39	0·1560	77	0·3080	115	0·4600
2	0·0080	40	0·1600	78	0·3120	116	0·4640
3	0·0120	41	0·1640	79	0·3160	117	0·4680
4	0·0160	42	0·1680	80	0·3200	118	0·4720
5	0·0200	43	0·1720	81	0·3240	119	0·4760
6	0·0240	44	0·1760	82	0·3280	120	0·4800
7	0·0280	45	0·1800	83	0·3320	128	0·5120
8	0·0320	46	0·1840	84	0·3360	130	0·5200
9	0·0360	47	0·1880	85	0·3400	140	0·5600
10	0·0400	48	0·1920	86	0·3440	144	0·5760
11	0·0440	49	0·1960	87	0·3480	150	0·6000
12	0·0480	50	0·2000	88	0·3520	156	0·6240
13	0·0520	51	0·2040	89	0·3560	160	0·6400
14	0·0560	52	0·2080	90	0·3600	168	0·6720
15	0·0600	53	0·2120	91	0·3640	170	0·6800
16	0·0640	54	0·2160	92	0·3680	180	0·7200
17	0·0680	55	0·2200	93	0·3720	190	0·7600
18	0·0720	56	0·2240	94	0·3760	196	0·7840
19	0·0760	57	0·2280	95	0·3800	200	0·8000
20	0·0800	58	0·2320	96	0·3840	220	0·8800
21	0·0840	59	0·2360	97	0·3880	224	0·8960
22	0·0880	60	0·2400	98	0·3920	256	1·0240
23	0·0920	61	0·2440	99	0·3960	280	1·1200
24	0·0960	62	0·2480	100	0·4000	300	1·2000
25	0·1000	63	0·2520	101	0·4040	365	1·4600
26	0·1040	64	0·2560	102	0·4080	400	1·6000
27	0·1080	65	0·2600	103	0·4120	480	1·9200
28	0·1120	66	0·2640	104	0·4160	500	2·0000
29	0·1160	67	0·2680	105	0·4200	516	2·0640
30	0·1200	68	0·2720	106	0·4240	560	2·2400
31	0·1240	69	0·2760	107	0·4280	600	2·4000
32	0·1280	70	0·2800	108	0·4320	625	2·5000
33	0·1300	71	0·2840	109	0·4360	640	2·5600
34	0·1360	72	0·2880	110	0·4400	700	2·8000
35	0·1400	73	0·2920	111	0·4440	750	3·0000
36	0·1440	74	0·2960	112	0·4480	800	3·2000
37	0·1480	75	0·3000	113	0·4520	900	3·6000

No.	£	No.	£	No.	£
1000	4·0000	1760	7·0400	6000	24·0000
1016	4·0640	2000	8·0000	7000	28·0000
1094	4·3760	2240	8·9600	7500	30·0000
1120	4·4800	2500	10·0000	10000	40·0000
1250	5·0000	3000	12·0000	15000	60·0000
1500	6·0000	4000	16·0000	20000	80·0000
1750	7·0000	5000	20·0000	30000	120·0000

No.	£	No.	£	No.	£	No.	£
1	0·0045	38	0·1710	76	0·3420	114	0·5130
1½	0·00625	39	0·1755	77	0·3465	115	0·5175
2	0·0090	40	0·1800	78	0·3510	116	0·5220
3	0·0135	41	0·1845	79	0·3555	117	0·5265
4	0·0180	42	0·1890	80	0·3600	118	0·5310
5	0·0225	43	0·1935	81	0·3645	119	0·5355
6	0·0270	44	0·1980	82	0·3690	120	0·5400
7	0·0315	45	0·2025	83	0·3735	128	0·5760
8	0·0360	46	0·2070	84	0·3780	130	0·5850
9	0·0405	47	0·2115	85	0·3825	140	0·6300
10	0·0450	48	0·2160	86	0·3870	144	0·6480
11	0·0495	49	0·2205	87	0·3915	150	0·6750
12	0·0540	50	0·2250	88	0·3960	156	0·7020
13	0·0585	51	0·2295	89	0·4005	160	0·7200
14	0·0630	52	0·2340	90	0·4050	168	0·7560
15	0·0675	53	0·2385	91	0·4095	170	0·7650
16	0·0720	54	0·2430	92	0·4140	180	0·8100
17	0·0765	55	0·2475	93	0·4185	190	0·8550
18	0·0810	56	0·2520	94	0·4230	196	0·8820
19	0·0855	57	0·2565	95	0·4275	200	0·9000
20	0·0900	58	0·2610	96	0·4320	220	0·9900
21	0·0945	59	0·2655	97	0·4365	224	1·0080
22	0·0990	60	0·2700	98	0·4410	256	1·1520
23	0·1035	61	0·2745	99	0·4455	280	1·2600
24	0·1080	62	0·2790	100	0·4500	300	1·3500
25	0·1125	63	0·2835	101	0·4545	365	1·6425
26	0·1170	64	0·2880	102	0·4590	400	1·8000
27	0·1215	65	0·2925	103	0·4635	480	2·1600
28	0·1260	66	0·2970	104	0·4680	500	2·2500
29	0·1305	67	0·3015	105	0·4725	516	2·3220
30	0·1350	68	0·3060	106	0·4770	560	2·5200
31	0·1395	69	0·3105	107	0·4815	600	2·7000
32	0·1440	70	0·3150	108	0·4860	625	2·8125
33	0·1485	71	0·3195	109	0·4905	640	2·8800
34	0·1530	72	0·3240	110	0·4950	700	3·1500
35	0·1575	73	0·3285	111	0·4995	750	3·3750
36	0·1620	74	0·3330	112	0·5040	800	3·6000
37	0·1665	75	0·3375	113	0·5085	900	4·0500

No.	£	No.	£	No.	£
1000	4·5000	1760	7·9200	6000	27·0000
1016	4·5720	2000	9·0000	7000	31·5000
1094	4·9230	2240	10·0800	7500	33·7500
1120	5·0400	2500	11·2500	10000	45·0000
1250	5·6250	3000	13·5000	15000	67·5000
1500	6·7500	4000	18·0000	20000	90·0000
1750	7·8750	5000	22·5000	30000	135·0000

No.	£	p	No.	£	p
$\frac{1}{16}$	0	00	34	0	17
$\frac{1}{8}$	0	00	35	0	17½
$\frac{1}{4}$	0	00	36*	0	18
$\frac{1}{2}$	0	00	37	0	18½
$\frac{3}{4}$	0	00½	38	0	19
1½	0	01	39	0	19½
2	0	01	40	0	20
3	0	01½	41	0	20½
4	0	02	42	0	21
5	0	02½	43	0	21½
6	0	03	44	0	22
7	0	03½	45	0	22½
8	0	04	46	0	23
9	0	04½	47	0	23½
10	0	05	48*	0	24
11	0	05½	49	0	24½
12*	0	06	50	0	25
13	0	06½	51	0	25½
14	0	07	52	0	26
15	0	07½	53	0	26½
16	0	08	54	0	27
17	0	08½	55	0	27½
18	0	09	56	0	28
19	0	09½	57	0	28½
20	0	10	58	0	29
21	0	10½	59	0	29½
22	0	11	60*	0	30
23	0	11½	61	0	30½
24*	0	12	62	0	31
25	0	12½	63	0	31½
26	0	13	64	0	32
27	0	13½	65	0	32½
28	0	14	66	0	33
29	0	14½	67	0	33½
30	0	15	68	0	34
31	0	15½	69	0	34½
32	0	16	70	0	35
33	0	16½	71	0	35½

No.	£	p	£	No.	£	p	£
1000	5	00	5·0000	1500	7	50	7·5000
1016	5	08	5·0800	1750	8	75	8·7500
1094	5	47	5·4700	1760	8	80	8·8000
1120	5	60	6·6000	2000	10	00	10·0000
1250	6	25	6·2500	2240	11	20	11·2000

Continued on facing page

No.	£	p	No.	£	p
72*	0	36	110	0	55
73	0	36½	111	0	55½
74	0	37	112	0	56
75	0	37½	113	0	56½
76	0	38	114	0	57
77	0	38½	115	0	57½
78	0	39	116	0	58
79	0	39½	117	0	58½
80	0	40	118	0	59
81	0	40½	119	0	59½
82	0	41	120*	0	60
83	0	41½	128	0	64
84*	0	42	130	0	65
85	0	42½	140	0	70
86	0	43	144*	0	72
87	0	43½	150	0	75
88	0	44	156	0	78
89	0	44½	168	0	84
90	0	45	196	0	98
91	0	45½	200	1	00
92	0	46	220	1	10
93	0	46½	224	1	12
94	0	47	256	1	28
95	0	47½	280	1	40
96*	0	48	300	1	50
97	0	48½	365	1	82½
98	0	49	400	2	00
99	0	49½	480	2	40
100	0	50	500	2	50
101	0	50½	516	2	58
102	0	51	560	2	80
103	0	51½	600	3	00
104	0	52	625	3	12½
105	0	52½	640	3	20
106	0	53	700	3	50
107	0	53½	750	3	75
108*	0	54	800	4	00
109	0	54½	900	4	50

No.	£	p	£	No.	£	p	£
2500	12	50	12·5000	7500	37	50	37·5000
3000	15	00	15·0000	10000	50	00	50·0000
4000	20	00	20·0000	15000	75	00	75·0000
5000	25	00	25·0000	20000	100	00	100·0000
6000	30	00	30·0000	30000	150	00	150·0000

No.	£	No.	£	No.	£	No.	£
1	0·0055	38	0·2090	76	0·4180	114	0·6270
1½	0·00825	39	0·2145	77	0·4235	115	0·6325
2	0·0110	40	0·2200	78	0·4290	116	0·6380
3	0·0165	41	0·2255	79	0·4345	117	0·6435
4	0·0220	42	0·2310	80	0·4400	118	0·6490
5	0·0275	43	0·2365	81	0·4455	119	0·6545
6	0·0330	44	0·2420	82	0·4510	120	0·6600
7	0·0385	45	0·2475	83	0·4565	128	0·7040
8	0·0440	46	0·2530	84	0·4620	130	0·7150
9	0·0495	47	0·2585	85	0·4675	140	0·7700
10	0·0550	48	0·2640	86	0·4730	144	0·7920
11	0·0605	49	0·2695	87	0·4785	150	0·8250
12	0·0660	50	0·2750	88	0·4840	156	0·8580
13	0·0715	51	0·2805	89	0·4895	160	0·8800
14	0·0770	52	0·2860	90	0·4950	168	0·9240
15	0·0825	53	0·2915	91	0·5005	170	0·9350
16	0·0880	54	0·2970	92	0·5060	180	0·9900
17	0·0935	55	0·3025	93	0·5115	190	1·0450
18	0·0990	56	0·3080	94	0·5170	196	1·0780
19	0·1045	57	0·3135	95	0·5225	200	1·1000
20	0·1100	58	0·3190	96	0·5280	220	1·2100
21	0·1155	59	0·3245	97	0·5335	224	1·2320
22	0·1210	60	0·3300	98	0·5390	256	1·4080
23	0·1265	61	0·3355	99	0·5445	280	1·5400
24	0·1320	62	0·3410	100	0·5500	300	1·6500
25	0·1375	63	0·3465	101	0·5555	365	2·0075
26	0·1430	64	0·3520	102	0·5610	400	2·2000
27	0·1485	65	0·3575	103	0·5665	480	2·6400
28	0·1540	66	0·3630	104	0·5720	500	2·7500
29	0·1595	67	0·3685	105	0·5775	516	2·8380
30	0·1650	68	0·3740	106	0·5830	560	3·0800
31	0·1705	69	0·3795	107	0·5885	600	3·3000
32	0·1760	70	0·3850	108	0·5940	625	3·4375
33	0·1815	71	0·3905	109	0·5995	640	3·5200
34	0·1870	72	0·3960	110	0·6050	700	3·8500
35	0·1925	73	0·4015	111	0·6105	750	4·1250
36	0·1980	74	0·4070	112	0·6160	800	4·4000
37	0·2035	75	0·4125	113	0·6215	900	4·9500

No.	£	No.	£	No.	£
1000	5·5000	1760	9·6800	6000	33·0000
1016	5·5880	2000	11·0000	7000	38·5000
1094	6·0170	2240	12·3200	7500	41·2500
1120	6·1600	2500	13·7500	10000	55·0000
1250	6·8750	3000	16·5000	15000	82·5000
1500	8·2500	4000	22·0000	20000	110·0000
1750	9·6250	5000	27·5000	30000	165·0000

No.	£	No.	£	No.	£	No.	£
1	0·0060	38	0·2280	76	0·4560	114	0·6840
1½	0·0090	39	0·2340	77	0·4620	115	0·6900
2	0·0120	40	0·2400	78	0·4680	116	0·6960
3	0·0180	41	0·2460	79	0·4740	117	0·7020
4	0·0240	42	0·2520	80	0·4800	118	0·7080
5	0·0300	43	0·2580	81	0·4860	119	0·7140
6	0·0360	44	0·2640	82	0·4920	120	0·7200
7	0·0420	45	0·2700	83	0·4980	128	0·7680
8	0·0480	46	0·2760	84	0·5040	130	0·7800
9	0·0540	47	0·2820	85	0·5100	140	0·8400
10	0·0600	48	0·2880	86	0·5160	144	0·8640
11	0·0660	49	0·2940	87	0·5220	150	0·9000
12	0·0720	50	0·3000	88	0·5280	156	0·9360
13	0·0780	51	0·3060	89	0·5340	160	0·9600
14	0·0840	52	0·3120	90	0·5400	168	1·0080
15	0·0900	53	0·3180	91	0·5460	170	1·0200
16	0·0960	54	0·3240	92	0·5520	180	1·0800
17	0·1020	55	0·3300	93	0·5580	190	1·1400
18	0·1080	56	0·3360	94	0·5640	196	1·1760
19	0·1140	57	0·3420	95	0·5700	200	1·2000
20	0·1200	58	0·3480	96	0·5760	220	1·3200
21	0·1260	59	0·3540	97	0·5820	224	1·3440
22	0·1320	60	0·3600	98	0·5880	256	1·5360
23	0·1380	61	0·3660	99	0·5940	280	1·6800
24	0·1440	62	0·3720	100	0·6000	300	1·8000
25	0·1500	63	0·3780	101	0·6060	365	2·1900
26	0·1560	64	0·3840	102	0·6120	400	2·4000
27	0·1620	65	0·3900	103	0·6180	480	2·8800
28	0·1680	66	0·3960	104	0·6240	500	3·0000
29	0·1740	67	0·4020	105	0·6300	516	3·0960
30	0·1800	68	0·4080	106	0·6360	560	3·3600
31	0·1860	69	0·4140	107	0·6420	600	3·6000
32	0·1920	70	0·4200	108	0·6480	625	3·7500
33	0·1980	71	0·4260	109	0·6540	640	3·8400
34	0·2040	72	0·4320	110	0·6600	700	4·2000
35	0·2100	73	0·4380	111	0·6660	750	4·5000
36	0·2160	74	0·4440	112	0·6720	800	4·8000
37	0·2220	75	0·4500	113	0·6780	900	5·4000

No.	£	No.	£	No.	£
1000	6·0000	1760	10·5600	6000	36·0000
1016	6·0960	2000	12·0000	7000	42·0000
1094	6·5640	2240	13·4400	7500	45·0000
1120	6·7200	2500	15·0000	10000	60·0000
1250	7·5000	3000	18·0000	15000	90·0000
1500	9·0000	4000	24·0000	20000	120·0000
1750	10·5000	5000	30·0000	30000	180·0000

No.	£	p	£	No.	£	p	£
$\frac{1}{16}$	0	00	0·0004	34	0	21½	0·2125
$\frac{1}{8}$	0	00	0·0008	35	0	22	0·21875
$\frac{1}{4}$	0	00	0·00155	36	0	22½	0·2250
$\frac{1}{2}$	0	00½	0·00315	37	0	23	0·23125
$\frac{3}{4}$	0	00½	0·0047	38	0	24	0·2375
1½	0	01	0·0094	39	0	24½	0·24375
2	0	01½	0·0125	**40**	0	25	0·2500
3	0	02	0·01875	41	0	25½	0·25625
4	0	02½	0·0250	42	0	26½	0·2625
5	0	03	0·03125	43	0	27	0·26875
6	0	04	0·0375	44	0	27½	0·2750
7	0	04½	0·04375	45	0	28	0·28125
8	0	05	0·0500	46	0	29	0·2875
9	0	05½	0·05625	47	0	29½	0·29375
10	0	06½	0·0625	48	0	30	0·3000
11	0	07	0·06875	49	0	30½	0·30625
12	0	07½	0·0750	**50**	0	31½	0·3125
13	0	08	0·08125	51	0	32	0·31875
14	0	09	0·0875	52	0	32½	0·3250
15	0	09½	0·09375	53	0	33	0·33125
16	0	10	0·1000	54	0	34	0·3375
17	0	10½	0·10625	55	0	34½	0·34375
18	0	11½	0·1125	56	0	35	0·3500
19	0	12	0·11875	57	0	35½	0·35625
20	0	12½	0·1250	58	0	36½	0·3625
21	0	13	0·13125	59	0	37	0·36875
22	0	14	0·1375	**60**	0	37½	0·3750
23	0	14½	0·14375	61	0	38	0·38125
24	0	15	0·1500	62	0	39	0·3875
25	0	15½	0·15625	63	0	39½	0·39375
26	0	16½	0·1625	64	0	40	0·4000
27	0	17	0·16875	65	0	40½	0·40625
28	0	17½	0·1750	66	0	41½	0·4125
29	0	18	0·18125	67	0	42	0·41875
30	0	19	0·1875	68	0	42½	0·4250
31	0	19½	0·19375	69	0	43	0·43125
32	0	20	0·2000	**70**	0	44	0·4375
33	0	20½	0·20625	71	0	44½	0·44375

No.	£	p	£	No.	£	p	£
1000	6	25	6·2500	1500	9	37½	9·3750
1016	6	35	6·3500	1750	10	94	10·9375
1094	6	84	6·8375	1760	11	00	11·0000
1120	7	00	7·0000	2000	12	50	12·5000
1250	7	81½	7·8125	2240	14	00	14·0000

No.	£ p	£	No.	£ p	£
72	0 45	0·4500	110	0 69	0·6875
73	0 45½	0·45625	111	0 69½	0·69375
74	0 46½	0·4625	112	0 70	0·7000
75	0 47	0·46875	113	0 70½	0·70625
76	0 47½	0·4750	114	0 71½	0·7125
77	0 48	0·48125	115	0 72	0·71875
78	0 49	0·4875	116	0 72½	0·7250
79	0 49½	0·49375	117	0 73	0·73125
80	0 50	0·5000	118	0 74	0·7375
81	0 50½	0·50625	119	0 74½	0·74375
82	0 51½	0·5125	120	0 75	0·7500
83	0 52	0·51875	128	0 80	0·8000
84	0 52½	0·5250	130	0 81½	0·8125
85	0 53	0·53125	140	0 87½	0·8750
86	0 54	0·5375	144	0 90	0·9000
87	0 54½	0·54375	150	0 94	0·9375
88	0 55	0·5500	156	0 97½	0·9750
89	0 55½	0·55625	168	1 05	1·0500
90	0 56½	0·5625	196	1 22½	1·2250
91	0 57	0·56875	200	1 25	1·2500
92	0 57½	0·5750	220	1 37½	1·3750
93	0 58	0·58125	224	1 40	1·4000
94	0 59	0·5875	256	1 60	1·6000
95	0 59½	0·59375	280	1 75	1·7500
96	0 60	0·6000	300	1 87½	1·8750
97	0 60½	0·60625	365	2 28	2·28125
98	0 61½	0·6125	400	2 50	2·5000
99	0 62	0·61875	480	3 00	3·0000
100	0 62½	0·6250	500	3 12½	3·1250
101	0 63	0·63125	516	3 22½	3·2250
102	0 64	0·6375	560	3 50	3·5000
103	0 64½	0·64375	600	3 75	3·7500
104	0 65	0·6500	625	3 90½	3·90625
105	0 65½	0·65625	640	4 00	4·0000
106	0 66½	0·6625	700	4 37½	4·3750
107	0 67	0·66875	750	4 69	4·6875
108	0 67½	0·6750	800	5 00	5·0000
109	0 68	0·68125	900	5 62½	5·6250
No.	£ p	£	No.	£ p	£
2500	15 62½	15·6250	7500	46 87½	46·8750
3000	18 75	18·7500	10000	62 50	62·5000
4000	25 00	25·0000	15000	93 75	93·7500
5000	31 25	31·2500	20000	125 00	125·0000
6000	37 50	37·5000	30000	187 50	187·5000

No.	£	No.	£	No.	£	No.	£
1	0·0065	38	0·2470	76	0·4940	114	0·7410
1½	0·00975	39	0·2535	77	0·5005	115	0·7475
2	0·0130	40	0·2600	78	0·5070	116	0·7540
3	0·0195	41	0·2665	79	0·5135	117	0·7605
4	0·0260	42	0·2730	80	0·5200	118	0·7670
5	0·0325	43	0·2795	81	0·5265	119	0·7735
6	0·0390	44	0·2860	82	0·5330	120	0·7800
7	0·0455	45	0·2925	83	0·5395	128	0·8320
8	0·0520	46	0·2990	84	0·5460	130	0·8450
9	0·0585	47	0·3055	85	0·5525	140	0·9100
10	0·0650	48	0·3120	86	0·5590	144	0·9360
11	0·0715	49	0·3185	87	0·5655	150	0·9750
12	0·0780	50	0·3250	88	0·5720	156	1·0140
13	0·0845	51	0·3315	89	0·5785	160	1·0400
14	0·0910	52	0·3380	90	0·5850	168	1·0920
15	0·0975	53	0·3445	91	0·5915	170	1·1050
16	0·1040	54	0·3510	92	0·5980	180	1·1700
17	0·1105	55	0·3575	93	0·6045	190	1·2350
18	0·1170	56	0·3640	94	0·6110	196	1·2740
19	0·1235	57	0·3705	95	0·6175	200	1·3000
20	0·1300	58	0·3770	96	0·6240	220	1·4300
21	0·1365	59	0·3835	97	0·6305	224	1·4560
22	0·1430	60	0·3900	98	0·6370	256	1·6640
23	0·1495	61	0·3965	99	0·6435	280	1·8200
24	0·1560	62	0·4030	100	0·6500	300	1·9500
25	0·1625	63	0·4095	101	0·6565	365	2·3725
26	0·1690	64	0·4160	102	0·6630	400	2·6000
27	0·1755	65	0·4225	103	0·6695	480	3·1200
28	0·1820	66	0·4290	104	0·6760	500	3·2500
29	0·1885	67	0·4355	105	0·6825	516	3·3540
30	0·1950	68	0·4420	106	0·6890	560	3·6400
31	0·2015	69	0·4485	107	0·6955	600	3·9000
32	0·2080	70	0·4550	108	0·7020	625	4·0625
33	0·2145	71	0·4615	109	0·7085	640	4·1600
34	0·2210	72	0·4680	110	0·7150	700	4·5500
35	0·2275	73	0·4745	111	0·7215	750	4·8750
36	0·2340	74	0·4810	112	0·7280	800	5·2000
37	0·2405	75	0·4875	113	0·7345	900	5·8500

No.	£	No.	£	No.	£
1000	6·5000	1760	11·4400	6000	39·0000
1016	6·6040	2000	13·0000	7000	45·5000
1094	7·1110	2240	14·5600	7500	48·7500
1120	7·2800	2500	16·2500	10000	65·0000
1250	8·1250	3000	19·5000	15000	97·5000
1500	9·7500	4000	26·0000	20000	130·0000
1750	11·3750	5000	32·5000	30000	195·0000

No.	£	No.	£	No.	£	No.	£
1	0·0070	38	0·2660	76	0·5320	114	0·7980
1½	0·0105	39	0·2730	77	0·5390	115	0·8050
2	0·0140	40	0·2800	78	0·5460	116	0·8120
3	0·0210	41	0·2870	79	0·5530	117	0·8190
4	0·0280	42	0·2940	80	0·5600	118	0·8260
5	0·0350	43	0·3010	81	0·5670	119	0·8330
6	0·0420	44	0·3080	82	0·5740	120	0·8400
7	0·0490	45	0·3150	83	0·5810	128	0·8960
8	0·0560	46	0·3220	84	0·5880	130	0·9100
9	0·0630	47	0·3290	85	0·5950	140	0·9800
10	0·0700	48	0·3360	86	0·6020	144	1·0080
11	0·0770	49	0·3430	87	0·6090	150	1·0500
12	0·0840	50	0·3500	88	0·6160	156	1·0920
13	0·0910	51	0·3570	89	0·6230	160	1·1200
14	0·0980	52	0·3640	90	0·6300	168	1·1760
15	0·1050	53	0·3710	91	0·6370	170	1·1900
16	0·1120	54	0·3780	92	0·6440	180	1·2600
17	0·1190	55	0·3850	93	0·6510	190	1·3300
18	0·1260	56	0·3920	94	0·6580	196	1·3720
19	0·1330	57	0·3990	95	0·6650	200	1·4000
20	0·1400	58	0·4060	96	0·6720	220	1·5400
21	0·1470	59	0·4130	97	0·6790	224	1·5680
22	0·1540	60	0·4200	98	0·6860	256	1·7920
23	0·1610	61	0·4270	99	0·6930	280	1·9600
24	0·1680	62	0·4340	100	0·7000	300	2·1000
25	0·1750	63	0·4410	101	0·7070	365	2·5550
26	0·1820	64	0·4480	102	0·7140	400	2·8000
27	0·1890	65	0·4550	103	0·7210	480	3·3600
28	0·1960	66	0·4620	104	0·7280	500	3·5000
29	0·2030	67	0·4690	105	0·7350	516	3·6120
30	0·2100	68	0·4760	106	0·7420	560	3·9200
31	0·2170	69	0·4830	107	0·7490	600	4·2000
32	0·2240	70	0·4900	108	0·7560	625	4·3750
33	0·2310	71	0·4970	109	0·7630	640	4·4800
34	0·2380	72	0·5040	110	0·7700	700	4·9000
35	0·2450	73	0·5110	111	0·7770	750	5·2500
36	0·2520	74	0·5180	112	0·7840	800	5·6000
37	0·2590	75	0·5250	113	0·7910	900	6·3000

No.	£	No.	£	No.	£
1000	7·0000	1760	12·3200	6000	42·0000
1016	7·1120	2000	14·0000	7000	49·0000
1094	7·6580	2240	15·6800	7500	52·5000
1120	7·8400	2500	17·5000	10000	70·0000
1250	8·7500	3000	21·0000	15000	105·0000
1500	10·5000	4000	28·0000	20000	140·0000
1750	12·2500	5000	35·0000	30000	210·0000

No.	£	p	£	No.	£	p	£
1/16	0	00	0·00045	34	0	25½	0·2550
1/8	0	00	0·00095	35	0	26	0·2625
1/4	0	00	0·0019	36	0	27	0·2700
1/2	0	00½	0·00375	37	0	27½	0·2775
3/4	0	00½	0·00565	38	0	28½	0·2850
1½	0	01	0·01125	39	0	29	0·2925
2	0	01½	0·0150	**40**	0	30	0·3000
3	0	02	0·0225	41	0	30½	0·3075
4	0	03	0·0300	42	0	31½	0·3150
5	0	03½	0·0375	43	0	32	0·3225
6	0	04½	0·0450	44	0	33	0·3300
7	0	05	0·0525	45	0	33½	0·3375
8	0	06	0·0600	46	0	34½	0·3450
9	0	06½	0·0675	47	0	35	0·3525
10	0	07½	0·0750	48	0	36	0·3600
11	0	08	0·0825	49	0	36½	0·3675
12	0	09	0·0900	**50**	0	37½	0·3750
13	0	09½	0·0975	51	0	38	0·3825
14	0	10½	0·1050	52	0	39	0·3900
15	0	11	0·1125	53	0	39½	0·3975
16	0	12	0·1200	54	0	40½	0·4050
17	0	12½	0·1275	55	0	41	0·4125
18	0	13½	0·1350	56	0	42	0·4200
19	0	14	0·1425	57	0	42½	0·4275
20	0	15	0·1500	58	0	43½	0·4350
21	0	15½	0·1575	59	0	44	0·4425
22	0	16½	0·1650	**60**	0	45	0·4500
23	0	17	0·1725	61	0	45½	0·4575
24	0	18	0·1800	62	0	46½	0·4650
25	0	18½	0·1875	63	0	47	0·4725
26	0	19½	0·1950	64	0	48	0·4800
27	0	20	0·2025	65	0	48½	0·4875
28	0	21	0·2100	66	0	49½	0·4950
29	0	21½	0·2175	67	0	50	0·5025
30	0	22½	0·2250	68	0	51	0·5100
31	0	23	0·2325	69	0	51½	0·5175
32	0	24	0·2400	**70**	0	52½	0·5250
33	0	24½	0·2475	71	0	53	0·5325

No.	£	p	£	No.	£	p	£
1000	7	50	7·5000	1500	11	25	11·2500
1016	7	62	7·6200	1750	13	12½	13·1250
1094	8	20½	8·2050	1760	13	20	13·2000
1120	8	40	8·4000	2000	15	00	15·0000
1250	9	37½	9·3750	2240	16	80	16·8000

No.	£	p	£	No.	£	p	£
72	0	54	0·5400	110	0	82½	0·8250
73	0	54½	0·5475	111	0	83	0·8325
74	0	55½	0·5550	112	0	84	0·8400
75	0	56	0·5625	113	0	84½	0·8475
76	0	57	0·5700	114	0	85½	0·8550
77	0	57½	0·5775	115	0	86	0·8625
78	0	58½	0·5850	116	0	87	0·8700
79	0	59	0·5925	117	0	87½	0·8775
80	0	60	0·6000	118	0	88½	0·8850
81	0	60½	0·6075	119	0	89	0·8925
82	0	61½	0·6150	120	0	90	0·9000
83	0	62	0·6225	128	0	96	0·9600
84	0	63	0·6300	130	0	97½	0·9750
85	0	63½	0·6375	140	1	05	1·0500
86	0	64½	0·6450	144	1	08	1·0800
87	0	65	0·6525	150	1	12½	1·1250
88	0	66	0·6600	156	1	17	1·1700
89	0	66½	0·6675	168	1	26	1·2600
90	0	67½	0·6750	196	1	47	1·4700
91	0	68	0·6825	200	1	50	1·5000
92	0	69	0·6900	220	1	65	1·6500
93	0	69½	0·6975	224	1	68	1·6800
94	0	70½	0·7050	256	1	92	1·9200
95	0	71	0·7125	280	2	10	2·1000
96	0	72	0·7200	300	2	25	2·2500
97	0	72½	0·7275	365	2	73½	2·7375
98	0	73½	0·7350	400	3	00	3·0000
99	0	74	0·7425	480	3	60	3·6000
100	0	75	0·7500	500	3	75	3·7500
101	0	75½	0·7575	516	3	87	3·8700
102	0	76½	0·7650	560	4	20	4·2000
103	0	77	0·7725	600	4	50	4·5000
104	0	78	0·7800	625	4	68½	4·6875
105	0	78½	0·7875	640	4	80	4·8000
106	0	79½	0·7950	700	5	25	5·2500
107	0	80	0·8025	750	5	62½	5·6250
108	0	81	0·8100	800	6	00	6·0000
109	0	81½	0·8175	900	6	75	6·7500

No.	£	p	£	No.	£	p	£
2500	18	75	18·7500	7500	56	25	56·2500
3000	22	50	22·5000	10000	75	00	75·0000
4000	30	00	30·0000	15000	112	50	112·5000
5000	37	50	37·5000	20000	150	00	150·0000
6000	45	00	45·0000	30000	225	00	225·0000

No.	£	No.	£	No.	£	No.	£
1	0·0080	38	0·3040	76	0·6080	114	0·9120
1½	0·0120	39	0·3120	77	0·6160	115	0·9200
2	0·0160	40	0·3200	78	0·6240	116	0·9280
3	0·0240	41	0·3280	79	0·6320	117	0·9360
4	0·0320	42	0·3360	80	0·6400	118	0·9440
5	0·0400	43	0·3440	81	0·6480	119	0·9520
6	0·0480	44	0·3520	82	0·6560	120	0·9600
7	0·0560	45	0·3600	83	0·6640	128	1·0240
8	0·0640	46	0·3680	84	0·6720	130	1·0400
9	0·0720	47	0·3760	85	0·6800	140	1·1200
10	0·0800	48	0·3840	86	0·6880	144	1·1520
11	0·0880	49	0·3920	87	0·6960	150	1·2000
12	0·0960	50	0·4000	88	0·7040	156	1·2480
13	0·1040	51	0·4080	89	0·7120	160	1·2800
14	0·1120	52	0·4160	90	0·7200	168	1·3440
15	0·1200	53	0·4240	91	0·7280	170	1·3600
16	0·1280	54	0·4320	92	0·7360	180	1·4400
17	0·1360	55	0·4400	93	0·7440	190	1·5200
18	0·1440	56	0·4480	94	0·7520	196	1·5680
19	0·1520	57	0·4560	95	0·7600	200	1·6000
20	0·1600	58	0·4640	96	0·7680	220	1·7600
21	0·1680	59	0·4720	97	0·7760	224	1·7920
22	0·1760	60	0·4800	98	0·7840	256	2·0480
23	0·1840	61	0·4880	99	0·7920	280	2·2400
24	0·1920	62	0·4960	100	0·8000	300	2·4000
25	0·2000	63	0·5040	101	0·8080	365	2·9200
26	0·2080	64	0·5120	102	0·8160	400	3·2000
27	0·2160	65	0·5200	103	0·8240	480	3·8400
28	0·2240	66	0·5280	104	0·8320	500	4·0000
29	0·2320	67	0·5360	105	0·8400	516	4·1280
30	0·2400	68	0·5440	106	0·8480	560	4·4800
31	0·2480	69	0·5520	107	0·8560	600	4·8000
32	0·2560	70	0·5600	108	0·8640	625	5·0000
33	0·2640	71	0·5680	109	0·8720	640	5·1200
34	0·2720	72	0·5760	110	0·8800	700	5·6000
35	0·2800	73	0·5840	111	0·8880	750	6·0000
36	0·2880	74	0·5920	112	0·8960	800	6·4000
37	0·2960	75	0·6000	113	0·9040	900	7·2000

No.	£	No.	£	No.	£
1000	8·0000	1760	14·0800	6000	48·0000
1016	8·1280	2000	16·0000	7000	56·0000
1094	8·7520	2240	17·9200	7500	60·0000
1120	8·9600	2500	20·0000	10000	80·0000
1250	10·0000	3000	24·0000	15000	120·0000
1500	12·0000	4000	32·0000	20000	160·0000
1750	14·0000	5000	40·0000	30000	240·0000

No.	£	No.	£	No.	£	No.	£
1	0·0085	38	0·3230	76	0·6460	114	0·9690
1½	0·01275	39	0·3315	77	0·6545	115	0·9775
2	0·0170	40	0·3400	78	0·6630	116	0·9860
3	0·0255	41	0·3485	79	0·6715	117	0·9945
4	0·0340	42	0·3570	80	0·6800	118	1·0030
5	0·0425	43	0·3655	81	0·6885	119	1·0115
6	0·0510	44	0·3740	82	0·6970	120	1·0200
7	0·0595	45	0·3825	83	0·7055	128	1·0880
8	0·0680	46	0·3910	84	0·7140	130	1·1050
9	0·0765	47	0·3995	85	0·7225	140	1·1900
10	0·0850	48	0·4080	86	0·7310	144	1·2240
11	0·0935	49	0·4165	87	0·7395	150	1·2750
12	0·1020	50	0·4250	88	0·7480	156	1·3260
13	0·1105	51	0·4335	89	0·7565	160	1·3600
14	0·1190	52	0·4420	90	0·7650	168	1·4280
15	0·1275	53	0·4505	91	0·7735	170	1·4450
16	0·1360	54	0·4590	92	0·7820	180	1·5300
17	0·1445	55	0·4675	93	0·7905	190	1·6150
18	0·1530	56	0·4760	94	0·7990	196	1·6660
19	0·1615	57	0·4845	95	0·8075	200	1·7000
20	0·1700	58	0·4930	96	0·8160	220	1·8700
21	0·1785	59	0·5015	97	0·8245	224	1·9040
22	0·1870	60	0·5100	98	0·8330	256	2·1760
23	0·1955	61	0·5185	99	0·8415	280	2·3800
24	0·2040	62	0·5270	100	0·8500	300	2·5500
25	0·2125	63	0·5355	101	0·8585	365	3·1025
26	0·2210	64	0·5440	102	0·8670	400	3·4000
27	0·2295	65	0·5525	103	0·8755	480	4·0800
28	0·2380	66	0·5610	104	0·8840	500	4·2500
29	0·2465	67	0·5695	105	0·8925	516	4·3860
30	0·2550	68	0·5780	106	0·9010	560	4·7600
31	0·2635	69	0·5865	107	0·9095	600	5·1000
32	0·2720	70	0·5950	108	0·9180	625	5·3125
33	0·2805	71	0·6035	109	0·9265	640	5·4400
34	0·2890	72	0·6120	110	0·9350	700	5·9500
35	0·2975	73	0·6205	111	0·9435	750	6·3750
36	0·3060	74	0·6290	112	0·9520	800	6·8000
37	0·3145	75	0·6375	113	0·9605	900	7·6500

No.	£	No.	£	No.	£
1000	8·5000	1760	14·9600	6000	51·0000
1016	8·6360	2000	17·0000	7000	59·5000
1094	9·2990	2240	19·0400	7500	63·7500
1120	9·5200	2500	21·2500	10000	85·0000
1250	10·6250	3000	25·5000	15000	127·5000
1500	12·7500	4000	34·0000	20000	170·0000
1750	14·8750	5000	42·5000	30000	255·0000

No.	£	p	£	No.	£	p	£
1/16	0	00	0·00055	34	0	30	0·2975
1/8	0	00	0·0011	35	0	30½	0·30625
1/4	0	00	0·0022	36	0	31½	0·3150
1/2	0	00½	0·0044	37	0	32½	0·32375
3/4	0	00½	0·00655	38	0	33½	0·3325
1½	0	01½	0·01315	39	0	34	0·34125
2	0	02	0·0175	**40**	0	35	0·3500
3	0	02½	0·02625	41	0	36	0·35875
4	0	03½	0·0350	42	0	37	0·3675
5	0	04½	0·04375	43	0	37½	0·37625
6	0	05½	0·0525	44	0	38½	0·3850
7	0	06	0·06125	45	0	39½	0·39375
8	0	07	0·0700	46	0	40½	0·4025
9	0	08	0·07875	47	0	41	0·41125
10	0	09	0·0875	48	0	42	0·4200
11	0	09½	0·09625	49	0	43	0·42875
12	0	10½	0·1050	**50**	0	44	0·4375
13	0	11½	0·11375	51	0	44½	0·44625
14	0	12½	0·1225	52	0	45½	0·4550
15	0	13	0·13125	53	0	46½	0·46375
16	0	14	0·1400	54	0	47½	0·4725
17	0	15	0·14875	55	0	48	0·48125
18	0	16	0·1575	56	0	49	0·4900
19	0	16½	0·16625	57	0	50	0·49875
20	0	17½	0·1750	58	0	51	0·5075
21	0	18½	0·18375	59	0	51½	0·51625
22	0	19½	0·1925	**60**	0	52½	0·5250
23	0	20	0·20125	61	0	53½	0·53375
24	0	21	0·2100	62	0	54½	0·5425
25	0	22	0·21875	63	0	55	0·55125
26	0	23	0·2275	64	0	56	0·5600
27	0	23½	0·23625	65	0	57	0·56875
28	0	24½	0·2450	66	0	58	0·5775
29	0	25½	0·25375	67	0	58½	0·58625
30	0	26½	0·2625	68	0	59½	0·5950
31	0	27	0·27125	69	0	60½	0·60375
32	0	28	0·2800	**70**	0	61½	0·6125
33	0	29	0·28875	71	0	62	0·62125

No.	£	p	£	No.	£	p	£
1000	8	75	8·7500	1500	13	12½	13·1250
1016	8	89	8·8900	1750	15	31½	15·3125
1094	9	57½	9·5725	1760	15	40	15·4000
1120	9	80	9·8000	2000	17	50	17·5000
1250	10	94	10·9375	2240	19	60	19·6000

No.	£	p	£	No.	£	p	£
72	0	63	0·6300	110	0	96½	0·9625
73	0	64	0·63875	111	0	97	0·97125
74	0	65	0·6475	112	0	98	0·9800
75	0	65½	0·65625	113	0	99	0·98875
76	0	66½	0·6650	114	1	00	0·9975
77	0	67½	0·67375	115	1	00½	1·00625
78	0	68½	0·6825	116	1	01½	1·0150
79	0	69	0·69125	117	1	02½	1·02375
80	0	70	0·7000	118	1	03½	1·0325
81	0	71	0·70875	119	1	04	1·04125
82	0	72	0·7175	120	1	05	1·0500
83	0	72½	0·72625	128	1	12	1·1200
84	0	73½	0·7350	130	1	14	1·1375
85	0	74½	0·74375	140	1	22½	1·2250
86	0	75½	0·7525	144	1	26	1·2600
87	0	76	0·76125	150	1	31½	1·3125
88	0	77	0·7700	156	1	36½	1·3650
89	0	78	0·77825	168	1	47	1·4700
90	0	79	0·7875	196	1	71½	1·7150
91	0	79½	0·79625	200	1	75	1·7500
92	0	80½	0·8050	220	1	92½	1·9250
93	0	81½	0·81375	224	1	96	1·9600
94	0	82½	0·8225	256	2	24	2·2400
95	0	83	0·83125	280	2	45	2·4500
96	0	84	0·8400	300	2	62½	2·6250
97	0	85	0·84875	365	3	19½	3·19375
98	0	86	0·8575	400	3	50	3·5000
99	0	86½	0·86625	480	4	20	4·2000
100	0	87½	0·8750	500	4	37½	4·3750
101	0	88½	0·88375	516	4	51½	4·5150
102	0	89½	0·8925	560	4	90	4·9000
103	0	90	0·90125	600	5	25	5·2500
104	0	91	0·9100	625	5	47	5·46875
105	0	92	0·91875	640	5	60	5·6000
106	0	93	0·9275	700	6	12½	6·1250
107	0	93½	0·93625	750	6	56½	6·5625
108	0	94½	0·9450	800	7	00	7·0000
109	0	95½	0·95375	900	7	87½	7·8750

No.	£	p	£	No.	£	p	£
2500	21	87½	21·8750	7500	65	62½	65·6250
3000	26	25	26·2500	10000	87	50	87·5000
4000	35	00	35·0000	15000	131	25	131·2500
5000	43	75	43·7500	20000	175	00	175·0000
6000	52	50	52·5000	30000	262	50	262·5000

No.	£	No.	£	No.	£	No.	£
1	0·0090	38	0·3420	76	0·6840	114	1·0260
1½	0·0135	39	0·3510	77	0·6930	115	1·0350
2	0·0180	40	0·3600	78	0·7020	116	1·0440
3	0·0270	41	0·3690	79	0·7110	117	1·0530
4	0·0360	42	0·3780	80	0·7200	118	1·0620
5	0·0450	43	0·3870	81	0·7290	119	1·0710
6	0·0540	44	0·3960	82	0·7380	120	1·0800
7	0·0630	45	0·4050	83	0·7470	128	1·1520
8	0·0720	46	0·4140	84	0·7560	130	1·1700
9	0·0810	47	0·4230	85	0·7650	140	1·2600
10	0·0900	48	0·4320	86	0·7740	144	1·2960
11	0·0990	49	0·4410	87	0·7830	150	1·3500
12	0·1080	50	0·4500	88	0·7920	156	1·4040
13	0·1170	51	0·4590	89	0·8010	160	1·4400
14	0·1260	52	0·4680	90	0·8100	168	1·5120
15	0·1350	53	0·4770	91	0·8190	170	1·5300
16	0·1440	54	0·4860	92	0·8280	180	1·6200
17	0·1530	55	0·4950	93	0·8370	190	1·7100
18	0·1620	56	0·5040	94	0·8460	196	1·7640
19	0·1710	57	0·5130	95	0·8550	200	1·8000
20	0·1800	58	0·5220	96	0·8640	220	1·9800
21	0·1890	59	0·5310	97	0·8730	224	2·0160
22	0·1980	60	0·5400	98	0·8820	256	2·3040
23	0·2070	61	0·5490	99	0·8910	280	2·5200
24	0·2160	62	0·5580	100	0·9000	300	2·7000
25	0·2250	63	0·5670	101	0·9090	365	3·2850
26	0·2340	64	0·5760	102	0·9180	400	3·6000
27	0·2430	65	0·5850	103	0·9270	480	4·3200
28	0·2520	66	0·5940	104	0·9360	500	4·5000
29	0·2610	67	0·6030	105	0·9450	516	4·6440
30	0·2700	68	0·6120	106	0·9540	560	5·0400
31	0·2790	69	0·6210	107	0·9630	600	5·4000
32	0·2880	70	0·6300	108	0·9720	625	5·6250
33	0·2970	71	0·6390	109	0·9810	640	5·7600
34	0·3060	72	0·6480	110	0·9900	700	6·3000
35	0·3150	73	0·6570	111	0·9990	750	6·7500
36	0·3240	74	0·6660	112	1·0080	800	7·2000
37	0·3330	75	0·6750	113	1·0170	900	8·1000

No.	£	No.	£	No.	£
1000	9·0000	1760	15·8400	6000	54·0000
1016	9·1440	2000	18·0000	7000	63·0000
1094	9·8460	2240	20·1600	7500	67·5000
1120	10·0800	2500	22·5000	10000	90·0000
1250	11·2500	3000	27·0000	15000	135·0000
1500	13·5000	4000	36·0000	20000	180·0000
1750	15·7500	5000	45·0000	30000	270·0000

No.	£	No.	£	No.	£	No.	£
1	0·0095	38	0·3610	76	0·7220	114	1·0830
1½	0·01425	39	0·3705	77	0·7315	115	1·0925
2	0·0190	40	0·3800	78	0·7410	116	1·1020
3	0·0285	41	0·3895	79	0·7505	117	1·1115
4	0·0380	42	0·3990	80	0·7600	118	1·1210
5	0·0475	43	0·4085	81	0·7695	119	1·1305
6	0·0570	44	0·4180	82	0·7790	120	1·1400
7	0·0665	45	0·4275	83	0·7885	128	1·2160
8	0·0760	46	0·4370	84	0·7980	130	1·2350
9	0·0855	47	0·4465	85	0·8075	140	1·3300
10	0·0950	48	0·4560	86	0·8170	144	1·3680
11	0·1045	49	0·4655	87	0·8265	150	1·4250
12	0·1140	50	0·4750	88	0·8360	156	1·4820
13	0·1235	51	0·4845	89	0·8455	160	1·5200
14	0·1330	52	0·4940	90	0·8550	168	1·5960
15	0·1425	53	0·5035	91	0·8645	170	1·6150
16	0·1520	54	0·5130	92	0·8740	180	1·7100
17	0·1615	55	0·5225	93	0·8835	190	1·8050
18	0·1710	56	0·5320	94	0·8930	196	1·8620
19	0·1805	57	0·5415	95	0·9025	200	1·9000
20	0·1900	58	0·5510	96	0·9120	220	2·0900
21	0·1995	59	0·5605	97	0·9215	224	2·1280
22	0·2090	60	0·5700	98	0·9310	256	2·4320
23	0·2185	61	0·5795	99	0·9405	280	2·6600
24	0·2280	62	0·5890	100	0·9500	300	2·8500
25	0·2375	63	0·5985	101	0·9595	365	3·4675
26	0·2470	64	0·6080	102	0·9690	400	3·8000
27	0·2565	65	0·6175	103	0·9785	480	4·5600
28	0·2660	66	0·6270	104	0·9880	500	4·7500
29	0·2755	67	0·6365	105	0·9975	516	4·9020
30	0·2850	68	0·6460	106	1·0070	560	5·3200
31	0·2945	69	0·6555	107	1·0165	600	5·7000
32	0·3040	70	0·6650	108	1·0260	625	5·9375
33	0·3135	71	0·6745	109	1·0355	640	6·0800
34	0·3230	72	0·6840	110	1·0450	700	6·6500
35	0·3325	73	0·6935	111	1·0545	750	7·1250
36	0·3420	74	0·7030	112	1·0640	800	7·6000
37	0·3515	75	0·7125	113	1·0735	900	8·5500

No.	£	No.	£	No.	£
1000	9·5000	1760	16·7200	6000	57·0000
1016	9·6520	2000	19·0000	7000	66·5000
1094	10·3930	2240	21·2800	7500	71·2500
1120	10·6400	2500	23·7500	10000	95·0000
1250	11·8750	3000	28·5000	15000	142·5000
1500	14·2500	4000	38·0000	20000	190·0000
1750	16·6250	5000	47·5000	30000	285·0000

No.	£	p	No.	£	p	No.	£	p	No.	£	p
$\frac{1}{16}$	0	00	34	0	34	72*	0	72	110	1	10
$\frac{1}{8}$	0	00	35	0	35	73	0	73	111	1	11
$\frac{1}{4}$	0	00½	36*	0	36	74	0	74	112	1	12
$\frac{1}{2}$	0	00½	37	0	37	75	0	75	113	1	13
$\frac{3}{4}$	0	01	38	0	38	76	0	76	114	1	14
1½	0	01½	39	0	39	77	0	77	115	1	15
2	0	02	40	0	40	78	0	78	116	1	16
3	0	03	41	0	41	79	0	79	117	1	17
4	0	04	42	0	42	80	0	80	118	1	18
5	0	05	43	0	43	81	0	81	119	1	19
6	0	06	44	0	44	82	0	82	120*	1	20
7	0	07	45	0	45	83	0	83	128	1	28
8	0	08	46	0	46	84*	0	84	130	1	30
9	0	09	47	0	47	85	0	85	140	1	40
10	0	10	48*	0	48	86	0	86	144*	1	44
11	0	11	49	0	49	87	0	87	150	1	50
12*	0	12	50	0	50	88	0	88	156	1	56
13	0	13	51	0	51	89	0	89	168	1	68
14	0	14	52	0	52	90	0	90	196	1	96
15	0	15	53	0	53	91	0	91	200	2	00
16	0	16	54	0	54	92	0	92	220	2	20
17	0	17	55	0	55	93	0	93	224	2	24
18	0	18	56	0	56	94	0	94	256	2	56
19	0	19	57	0	57	95	0	95	280	2	80
20	0	20	58	0	58	96*	0	96	300	3	00
21	0	21	59	0	59	97	0	97	365	3	65
22	0	22	60*	0	60	98	0	98	400	4	00
23	0	23	61	0	61	99	0	99	480	4	80
24*	0	24	62	0	62	100	1	00	500	5	00
25	0	25	63	0	63	101	1	01	516	5	16
26	0	26	64	0	64	102	1	02	560	5	60
27	0	27	65	0	65	103	1	03	600	6	00
28	0	28	66	0	66	104	1	04	625	6	25
29	0	29	67	0	67	105	1	05	640	6	40
30	0	30	68	0	68	106	1	06	700	7	00
31	0	31	69	0	69	107	1	07	750	7	50
32	0	32	70	0	70	108*	1	08	800	8	00
33	0	33	71	0	71	109	1	09	900	9	00

No.	£	p	No.	£	p	No.	£	p
1000	10	00	1760	17	60	6000	60	00
1016	10	16	2000	20	00	7000	70	00
1094	10	94	2240	22	40	7500	75	00
1120	11	20	2500	25	00	10000	100	00
1250	12	50	3000	30	00	15000	150	00
1500	15	00	4000	40	00	20000	200	00
1750	17	50	5000	50	00	30000	300	00

1½p $\quad$ £0·015

No.	£	p	No.	£	p	No.	£	p	No.	£	p
1/16	0	00	34	0	51	72*	1	08	110	1	65
1/8	0	00	35	0	52½	73	1	09½	111	1	66½
1/4	0	00½	36*	0	54	74	1	11	112	1	68
1/2	0	01	37	0	55½	75	1	12½	113	1	69½
3/4	0	01	38	0	57	76	1	14	114	1	71
1½	0	02½	39	0	58½	77	1	15½	115	1	72½
2	0	03	40	0	60	78	1	17	116	1	74
3	0	04½	41	0	61½	79	1	18½	117	1	75½
4	0	06	42	0	63	80	1	20	118	1	77
5	0	07½	43	0	64½	81	1	21½	119	1	78½
6	0	09	44	0	66	82	1	23	120*	1	80
7	0	10½	45	0	67½	83	1	24½	128	1	92
8	0	12	46	0	69	84*	1	26	130	1	95
9	0	13½	47	0	70½	85	1	27½	140	2	10
10	0	15	48*	0	72	86	1	29	144*	2	16
11	0	16½	49	0	73½	87	1	30½	150	2	25
12*	0	18	50	0	75	88	1	32	156	2	34
13	0	19½	51	0	76½	89	1	33½	168	2	52
14	0	21	52	0	78	90	1	35	196	2	94
15	0	22½	53	0	79½	91	1	36½	200	3	00
16	0	24	54	0	81	92	1	38	220	3	30
17	0	25½	55	0	82½	93	1	39½	224	3	36
18	0	27	56	0	84	94	1	41	256	3	84
19	0	28½	57	0	85½	95	1	42½	280	4	20
20	0	30	58	0	87	96*	1	44	300	4	50
21	0	31½	59	0	88½	97	1	45½	365	5	47½
22	0	33	60*	0	90	98	1	47	400	6	00
23	0	34½	61	0	91½	99	1	48½	480	7	20
24*	0	36	62	0	93	100	1	50	500	7	50
25	0	37½	63	0	94½	101	1	51½	516	7	74
26	0	39	64	0	96	102	1	53	560	8	40
27	0	40½	65	0	97½	103	1	54½	600	9	00
28	0	42	66	0	99	104	1	56	625	9	37½
29	0	43½	67	1	00½	105	1	57½	640	9	60
30	0	45	68	1	02	106	1	59	700	10	50
31	0	46½	69	1	03½	107	1	60½	750	11	25
32	0	48	70	1	05	108*	1	62	800	12	00
33	0	49½	71	1	06½	109	1	63½	900	13	50

No.	£	p	No.	£	p	No.	£	p
1000	15	00	1760	26	40	6000	90	00
1016	15	24	2000	30	00	7000	105	00
1094	16	41	2240	33	60	7500	112	50
1120	16	80	2500	37	50	10000	150	00
1250	18	75	3000	45	00	15000	225	00
1500	22	50	4000	60	00	20000	300	00
1750	26	25	5000	75	00	30000	450	00

No.	£	p	No.	£	p	No.	£	p	No.	£	p
$\frac{1}{16}$	0	00	34	0	68	72*	1	44	110	2	20
$\frac{1}{8}$	0	00½	35	0	70	73	1	46	111	2	22
$\frac{1}{4}$	0	00½	36*	0	72	74	1	48	112	2	24
$\frac{1}{2}$	0	01	37	0	74	75	1	50	113	2	26
$\frac{3}{4}$	0	01½	38	0	76	76	1	52	114	2	28
$1\frac{1}{2}$	0	03	39	0	78	77	1	54	115	2	30
2	0	04	40	0	80	78	1	56	116	2	32
3	0	06	41	0	82	79	1	58	117	2	34
4	0	08	42	0	84	80	1	60	118	2	36
5	0	10	43	0	86	81	1	62	119	2	38
6	0	12	44	0	88	82	1	64	120*	2	40
7	0	14	45	0	90	83	1	66	128	2	56
8	0	16	46	0	92	84*	1	68	130	2	60
9	0	18	47	0	94	85	1	70	140	2	80
10	0	20	48*	0	96	86	1	72	144*	2	88
11	0	22	49	0	98	87	1	74	150	3	00
12*	0	24	50	1	00	88	1	76	156	3	12
13	0	26	51	1	02	89	1	78	168	3	36
14	0	28	52	1	04	90	1	80	196	3	92
15	0	30	53	1	06	91	1	82	200	4	00
16	0	32	54	1	08	92	1	84	220	4	40
17	0	34	55	1	10	93	1	86	224	4	48
18	0	36	56	1	12	94	1	88	256	5	12
19	0	38	57	1	14	95	1	90	280	5	60
20	0	40	58	1	16	96*	1	92	300	6	00
21	0	42	59	1	18	97	1	94	365	7	30
22	0	44	60*	1	20	98	1	96	400	8	00
23	0	46	61	1	22	99	1	98	480	9	60
24*	0	48	62	1	24	100	2	00	500	10	00
25	0	50	63	1	26	101	2	02	516	10	32
26	0	52	64	1	28	102	2	04	560	11	20
27	0	54	65	1	30	103	2	06	600	12	00
28	0	56	66	1	32	104	2	08	625	12	50
29	0	58	67	1	34	105	2	10	640	12	80
30	0	60	68	1	36	106	2	12	700	14	00
31	0	62	69	1	38	107	2	14	750	15	00
32	0	64	70	1	40	108*	2	16	800	16	00
33	0	66	71	1	42	109	2	18	900	18	00

No.	£	p	No.	£	p	No.	£	p
1000	20	00	1760	35	20	6000	120	00
1016	20	32	2000	40	00	7000	140	00
1094	21	88	2240	44	80	7500	150	00
1120	22	40	2500	50	00	10000	200	00
1250	25	00	3000	60	00	15000	300	00
1500	30	00	4000	80	00	20000	400	00
1750	35	00	5000	100	00	30000	600	00

2½p   £0·025

No.	£	p	No.	£	p	No.	£	p	No.	£	p
1/16	0	00	34	0	85	72*	1	80	110	2	75
1/8	0	00½	35	0	87½	73	1	82½	111	2	77½
1/4	0	00½	36*	0	90	74	1	85	112	2	80
1/2	0	01½	37	0	92½	75	1	87½	113	2	82½
3/4	0	02	38	0	95	76	1	90	114	2	85
1½	0	04	39	0	97½	77	1	92½	115	2	87½
2	0	05	**40**	1	00	78	1	95	116	2	90
3	0	07½	41	1	02½	79	1	97½	117	2	92½
4	0	10	42	1	05	**80**	2	00	118	2	95
5	0	12½	43	1	07½	81	2	02½	119	2	97½
6	0	15	44	1	10	82	2	05	120*	3	00
7	0	17½	45	1	12½	83	2	07½	128	3	20
8	0	20	46	1	15	84*	2	10	130	3	25
9	0	22½	47	1	17½	85	2	12½	140	3	50
10	0	25	48*	1	20	86	2	15	144*	3	60
11	0	27½	49	1	22½	87	2	17½	150	3	75
12*	0	30	**50**	1	25	88	2	20	156	3	90
13	0	32½	51	1	27½	89	2	22½	168	4	20
14	0	35	52	1	30	**90**	2	25	196	4	90
15	0	37½	53	1	32½	91	2	27½	200	5	00
16	0	40	54	1	35	92	2	30	220	5	50
17	0	42½	55	1	37½	93	2	32½	224	5	60
18	0	45	56	1	40	94	2	35	256	6	40
19	0	47½	57	1	42½	95	2	37½	280	7	00
20	0	50	58	1	45	96*	2	40	300	7	50
21	0	52½	59	1	47½	97	2	42½	365	9	12½
22	0	55	**60***	1	50	98	2	45	400	10	00
23	0	57½	61	1	52½	99	2	47½	480	12	00
24*	0	60	62	1	55	**100**	2	50	500	12	50
25	0	62½	63	1	57½	101	2	52½	516	12	90
26	0	65	64	1	60	102	2	55	560	14	00
27	0	67½	65	1	62½	103	2	57½	600	15	00
28	0	70	66	1	65	104	2	60	625	15	62½
29	0	72½	67	1	67½	105	2	62½	640	16	00
30	0	75	68	1	70	106	2	65	700	17	50
31	0	77½	69	1	72½	107	2	67½	750	18	75
32	0	80	**70**	1	75	108*	2	70	800	20	00
33	0	82½	71	1	77½	109	2	72½	900	22	50

No.	£	p	No.	£	p	No.	£	p
1000	25	00	1760	44	00	6000	150	00
1016	25	40	2000	50	00	7000	175	00
1094	27	35	2240	56	00	7500	187	50
1120	28	00	2500	62	50	10000	250	00
1250	31	25	3000	75	00	15000	375	00
1500	37	50	4000	100	00	20000	500	00
1750	43	75	5000	125	00	30000	750	00

No.	£	p	No.	£	p	No.	£	p	No.	£	p
$\frac{1}{16}$	0	00	34	1	02	72*	2	16	110	3	30
$\frac{1}{8}$	0	00½	35	1	05	73	2	19	111	3	33
$\frac{1}{4}$	0	01	36*	1	08	74	2	22	112	3	36
$\frac{1}{2}$	0	01½	37	1	11	75	2	25	113	3	39
$\frac{3}{4}$	0	02½	38	1	14	76	2	28	114	3	42
1½	0	04½	39	1	17	77	2	31	115	3	45
2	0	06	40	1	20	78	2	34	116	3	48
3	0	09	41	1	23	79	2	37	117	3	51
4	0	12	42	1	26	80	2	40	118	3	54
5	0	15	43	1	29	81	2	43	119	3	57
6	0	18	44	1	32	82	2	46	120*	3	60
7	0	21	45	1	35	83	2	49	128	3	84
8	0	24	46	1	38	84*	2	52	130	3	90
9	0	27	47	1	41	85	2	55	140	4	20
10	0	30	48*	1	44	86	2	58	144*	4	32
11	0	33	49	1	47	87	2	61	150	4	50
12*	0	36	50	1	50	88	2	64	156	4	68
13	0	39	51	1	53	89	2	67	168	5	04
14	0	42	52	1	56	90	2	70	196	5	88
15	0	45	53	1	59	91	2	73	200	6	00
16	0	48	54	1	62	92	2	76	220	6	60
17	0	51	55	1	65	93	2	79	224	6	72
18	0	54	56	1	68	94	2	82	256	7	68
19	0	57	57	1	71	95	2	85	280	8	40
20	0	60	58	1	74	96*	2	88	300	9	00
21	0	63	59	1	77	97	2	91	365	10	95
22	0	66	60*	1	80	98	2	94	400	12	00
23	0	69	61	1	83	99	2	97	480	14	40
24*	0	72	62	1	86	100	3	00	500	15	00
25	0	75	63	1	89	101	3	03	516	15	48
26	0	78	64	1	92	102	3	06	560	16	80
27	0	81	65	1	95	103	3	09	600	18	00
28	0	84	66	1	98	104	3	12	625	18	75
29	0	87	67	2	01	105	3	15	640	19	20
30	0	90	68	2	04	106	3	18	700	21	00
31	0	93	69	2	07	107	3	21	750	22	50
32	0	96	70	2	10	108*	3	24	800	24	00
33	0	99	71	2	13	109	3	27	900	27	00

No.	£	p	No.	£	p	No.	£	p
1000	30	00	1760	52	80	6000	180	00
1016	30	48	2000	60	00	7000	210	00
1094	32	82	2240	67	20	7500	225	00
1120	33	60	2500	75	00	10000	300	00
1250	37	50	3000	90	00	15000	450	00
1500	45	00	4000	120	00	20000	600	00
1750	52	50	5000	150	00	30000	900	00

$3\frac{1}{2}$p   £0·035

No.	£	p	No.	£	p	No.	£	p	No.	£	p
$\frac{1}{16}$	0	00	34	1	19	72*	2	52	110	3	85
$\frac{1}{8}$	0	00½	35	1	22½	73	2	55½	111	3	88½
$\frac{1}{4}$	0	01	36*	1	26	74	2	59	112	3	92
$\frac{1}{2}$	0	02	37	1	29½	75	2	62½	113	3	95½
$\frac{3}{4}$	0	02½	38	1	33	76	2	66	114	3	99
1½	0	05½	39	1	36½	77	2	69½	115	4	02½
2	0	07	40	1	40	78	2	73	116	4	06
3	0	10½	41	1	43½	79	2	76½	117	4	09½
4	0	14	42	1	47	80	2	80	118	4	13
5	0	17½	43	1	50½	81	2	83½	119	4	16½
6	0	21	44	1	54	82	2	87	120*	4	20
7	0	24½	45	1	57½	83	2	90½	128	4	48
8	0	28	46	1	61	84*	2	94	130	4	55
9	0	31½	47	1	64½	85	2	97½	140	4	90
10	0	35	48*	1	68	86	3	01	144*	5	04
11	0	38½	49	1	71½	87	3	04½	150	5	25
12*	0	42	50	1	75	88	3	08	156	5	46
13	0	45½	51	1	78½	89	3	11½	168	5	88
14	0	49	52	1	82	90	3	15	196	6	86
15	0	52½	53	1	85½	91	3	18½	200	7	00
16	0	56	54	1	89	92	3	22	220	7	70
17	0	59½	55	1	92½	93	3	25½	224	7	84
18	0	63	56	1	96	94	3	29	256	8	96
19	0	66½	57	1	99½	95	3	32½	280	9	80
20	0	70	58	2	03	96*	3	36	300	10	50
21	0	73½	59	2	06½	97	3	39½	365	12	77½
22	0	77	60*	2	10	98	3	43	400	14	00
23	0	80½	61	2	13½	99	3	46½	480	16	80
24*	0	84	62	2	17	100	3	50	500	17	50
25	0	87½	63	2	20½	101	3	53½	516	18	06
26	0	91	64	2	24	102	3	57	560	19	60
27	0	94½	65	2	27½	103	3	60½	600	21	00
28	0	98	66	2	31	104	3	64	625	21	87½
29	1	01½	67	2	34½	105	3	67½	640	22	40
30	1	05	68	2	38	106	3	71	700	24	50
31	1	08½	69	2	41½	107	3	74½	750	26	25
32	1	12	70	2	45	108*	3	78	800	28	00
33	1	15½	71	2	48½	109	3	81½	900	31	50

No.	£	p	No.	£	p	No.	£	p
1000	35	00	1760	61	60	6000	210	00
1016	35	56	2000	70	00	7000	245	00
1094	38	29	2240	78	40	7500	262	50
1120	39	20	2500	87	50	10000	350	00
1250	43	75	3000	105	00	15000	525	00
1500	52	50	4000	140	00	20000	700	00
1750	61	25	5000	175	00	30000	1050	00

No.	£	p	No.	£	p	No.	£	p	No.	£	p
1/16	0	00½	34	1	36	72*	2	88	110	4	40
1/8	0	00½	35	1	40	73	2	92	111	4	44
1/4	0	01	36*	1	44	74	2	96	112	4	48
1/2	0	02	37	1	48	75	3	00	113	4	52
3/4	0	03	38	1	52	76	3	04	114	4	56
1½	0	06	39	1	56	77	3	08	115	4	60
2	0	08	40	1	60	78	3	12	116	4	64
3	0	12	41	1	64	79	3	16	117	4	68
4	0	16	42	1	68	80	3	20	118	4	72
5	0	20	43	1	72	81	3	24	119	4	76
6	0	24	44	1	76	82	3	28	120*	4	80
7	0	28	45	1	80	83	3	32	128	5	12
8	0	32	46	1	84	84*	3	36	130	5	20
9	0	36	47	1	88	85	3	40	140	5	60
10	0	40	48*	1	92	86	3	44	144*	5	76
11	0	44	49	1	96	87	3	48	150	6	00
12*	0	48	50	2	00	88	3	52	156	6	24
13	0	52	51	2	04	89	3	56	168	6	72
14	0	56	52	2	08	90	3	60	196	7	84
15	0	60	53	2	12	91	3	64	200	8	00
16	0	64	54	2	16	92	3	68	220	8	80
17	0	68	55	2	20	93	3	72	224	8	96
18	0	72	56	2	24	94	3	76	256	10	24
19	0	76	57	2	28	95	3	80	280	11	20
20	0	80	58	2	32	96*	3	84	300	12	00
21	0	84	59	2	36	97	3	88	365	14	60
22	0	88	60*	2	40	98	3	92	400	16	00
23	0	92	61	2	44	99	3	96	480	19	20
24*	0	96	62	2	48	100	4	00	500	20	00
25	1	00	63	2	52	101	4	04	516	20	64
26	1	04	64	2	56	102	4	08	560	22	40
27	1	08	65	2	60	103	4	12	600	24	00
28	1	12	66	2	64	104	4	16	625	25	00
29	1	16	67	2	68	105	4	20	640	25	60
30	1	20	68	2	72	106	4	24	700	28	00
31	1	24	69	2	76	107	4	28	750	30	00
32	1	28	70	2	80	108*	4	32	800	32	00
33	1	32	71	2	84	109	4	36	900	36	00

No.	£	p	No.	£	p	No.	£	p
1000	40	00	1760	70	40	6000	240	00
1016	40	64	2000	80	00	7000	280	00
1094	43	76	2240	89	60	7500	300	00
1120	44	80	2500	100	00	10000	400	00
1250	50	00	3000	120	00	15000	600	00
1500	60	00	4000	160	00	20000	800	00
1750	70	00	5000	200	00	30000	1200	00

4½p   £0·045

No.	£	p	No.	£	p	No.	£	p	No.	£	p
1/16	0	00½	34	1	53	72*	3	24	110	4	95
1/8	0	00½	35	1	57½	73	3	28½	111	4	99½
1/4	0	01	36*	1	62	74	3	33	112	5	04
1/2	0	02½	37	1	66½	75	3	37½	113	5	08½
3/4	0	03½	38	1	71	76	3	42	114	5	13
1½	0	07	39	1	75½	77	3	46½	115	5	17½
2	0	09	40	1	80	78	3	51	116	5	22
3	0	13½	41	1	84½	79	3	55½	117	5	26½
4	0	18	42	1	89	80	3	60	118	5	31
5	0	22½	43	1	93½	81	3	64½	119	5	35½
6	0	27	44	1	98	82	3	69	120*	5	40
7	0	31½	45	2	02½	83	3	73½	128	5	76
8	0	36	46	2	07	84*	3	78	130	5	85
9	0	40½	47	2	11½	85	3	82½	140	6	30
10	0	45	48*	2	16	86	3	87	144*	6	48
11	0	49½	49	2	20½	87	3	91½	150	6	75
12*	0	54	50	2	25	88	3	96	156	7	02
13	0	58½	51	2	29½	89	4	00½	168	7	56
14	0	63	52	2	34	90	4	05	196	8	82
15	0	67½	53	2	38½	91	4	09½	200	9	00
16	0	72	54	2	43	92	4	14	220	9	90
17	0	76½	55	2	47½	93	4	18½	224	10	08
18	0	81	56	2	52	94	4	23	256	11	52
19	0	85½	57	2	56½	95	4	27½	280	12	60
20	0	90	58	2	61	96*	4	32	300	13	50
21	0	94½	59	2	65½	97	4	36½	365	16	42½
22	0	99	60*	2	70	98	4	41	400	18	00
23	1	03½	61	2	74½	99	4	45½	480	21	60
24*	1	08	62	2	79	100	4	50	500	22	50
25	1	12½	63	2	83½	101	4	54½	516	23	22
26	1	17	64	2	88	102	4	59	560	25	20
27	1	21½	65	2	92½	103	4	63½	600	27	00
28	1	26	66	2	97	104	4	68	625	28	12½
29	1	30½	67	3	01½	105	4	72½	640	28	80
30	1	35	68	3	06	106	4	77	700	31	50
31	1	39½	69	3	10½	107	4	81½	750	33	75
32	1	44	70	3	15	108*	4	86	800	36	00
33	1	48½	71	3	19½	109	4	90½	900	40	50

No.	£	p	No.	£	p	No.	£	p
1000	45	00	1760	79	20	6000	270	00
1016	45	72	2000	90	00	7000	315	00
1094	49	23	2240	100	80	7500	337	50
1120	50	40	2500	112	50	10000	450	00
1250	56	25	3000	135	00	15000	675	00
1500	67	50	4000	180	00	20000	900	00
1750	78	75	5000	225	00	30000	1350	00

No.	£	p	No.	£	p	No.	£	p	No.	£	p
1/16	0	00½	34	1	70	72*	3	60	110	5	50
1/8	0	00½	35	1	75	73	3	65	111	5	55
1/4	0	01½	36*	1	80	74	3	70	112	5	60
1/2	0	02½	37	1	85	75	3	75	113	5	65
3/4	0	04	38	1	90	76	3	80	114	5	70
1½	0	07½	39	1	95	77	3	85	115	5	75
2	0	10	**40**	2	00	78	3	90	116	5	80
3	0	15	41	2	05	79	3	95	117	5	85
4	0	20	42	2	10	**80**	4	00	118	5	90
5	0	25	43	2	15	81	4	05	119	5	95
6	0	30	44	2	20	82	4	10	120*	6	00
7	0	35	45	2	25	83	4	15	128	6	40
8	0	40	46	2	30	84*	4	20	130	6	50
9	0	45	47	2	35	85	4	25	140	7	00
10	0	50	48*	2	40	86	4	30	144*	7	20
11	0	55	49	2	45	87	4	35	150	7	50
12*	0	60	**50**	2	50	88	4	40	156	7	80
13	0	65	51	2	55	89	4	45	168	8	40
14	0	70	52	2	60	**90**	4	50	196	9	80
15	0	75	53	2	65	91	4	55	200	10	00
16	0	80	54	2	70	92	4	60	220	11	00
17	0	85	55	2	75	93	4	65	224	11	20
18	0	90	56	2	80	94	4	70	256	12	80
19	0	95	57	2	85	95	4	75	280	14	00
20	1	00	58	2	90	96*	4	80	300	15	00
21	1	05	59	2	95	97	4	85	365	18	25
22	1	10	**60***	3	00	98	4	90	400	20	00
23	1	15	61	3	05	99	4	95	480	24	00
24*	1	20	62	3	10	**100**	5	00	500	25	00
25	1	25	63	3	15	101	5	05	516	25	80
26	1	30	64	3	20	102	5	10	560	28	00
27	1	35	65	3	25	103	5	15	600	30	00
28	1	40	66	3	30	104	5	20	625	31	25
29	1	45	67	3	35	105	5	25	640	32	00
30	1	50	68	3	40	106	5	30	700	35	00
31	1	55	69	3	45	107	5	35	750	37	50
32	1	60	**70**	3	50	108*	5	40	800	40	00
33	1	65	71	3	55	109	5	45	900	45	00

No.	£	p	No.	£	p	No.	£	p
1000	50	00	1760	88	00	6000	300	00
1016	50	80	2000	100	00	7000	350	00
1094	54	70	2240	112	00	7500	375	00
1120	56	00	2500	125	00	10000	500	00
1250	62	50	3000	150	00	15000	750	00
1500	75	00	4000	200	00	20000	1000	00
1750	87	50	5000	250	00	30000	1500	00

No.	£	p	No.	£	p	No.	£	p	No.	£	p
1/16	0	00½	34	1	87	72*	3	96	110	6	05
1/8	0	00½	35	1	92½	73	4	01½	111	6	10½
¼	0	01½	36*	1	98	74	4	07	112	6	16
½	0	03	37	2	03½	75	4	12½	113	6	21½
¾	0	04	38	2	09	76	4	18	114	6	27
1½	0	08½	39	2	14½	77	4	23½	115	6	32½
2	0	11	**40**	2	20	78	4	29	116	6	38
3	0	16½	41	2	25½	79	4	34½	117	6	43½
4	0	22	42	2	31	**80**	4	40	118	6	49
5	0	27½	43	2	36½	81	4	45½	119	6	54½
6	0	33	44	2	42	82	4	51	120*	6	60
7	0	38½	45	2	47½	83	4	56½	128	7	04
8	0	44	46	2	53	84*	4	62	130	7	15
9	0	49½	47	2	58½	85	4	67½	140	7	70
10	0	55	48*	2	64	86	4	73	144*	7	92
11	0	60½	49	2	69½	87	4	78½	150	8	25
12*	0	66	**50**	2	75	88	4	84	156	8	58
13	0	71½	51	2	80½	89	4	89½	168	9	24
14	0	77	52	2	86	**90**	4	95	196	10	78
15	0	82½	53	2	91½	91	5	00½	200	11	00
16	0	88	54	2	97	92	5	06	220	12	10
17	0	93½	55	3	02½	93	5	11½	224	12	32
18	0	99	56	3	08	94	5	17	256	14	08
19	1	04½	57	3	13½	95	5	22½	280	15	40
20	1	10	58	3	19	96*	5	28	300	16	50
21	1	15½	59	3	24½	97	5	33½	365	20	07½
22	1	21	**60***	3	30	98	5	39	400	22	00
23	1	26½	61	3	35½	99	5	44½	480	26	40
24*	1	32	62	3	41	**100**	5	50	500	27	50
25	1	37½	63	3	46½	101	5	55½	516	28	38
26	1	43	64	3	52	102	5	61	560	30	80
27	1	48½	65	3	57½	103	5	66½	600	33	00
28	1	54	66	3	63	104	5	72	625	34	37½
29	1	59½	67	3	68½	105	5	77½	640	35	20
30	1	65	68	3	74	106	5	83	700	38	50
31	1	70½	69	3	79½	107	5	88½	750	41	25
32	1	76	**70**	3	85	108*	5	94	800	44	00
33	1	81½	71	3	90½	109	5	99½	900	49	50

No.	£	p	No.	£	p	No.	£	p
1000	55	00	1760	96	80	6000	330	00
1016	55	88	2000	110	00	7000	385	00
1094	60	17	2240	123	20	7500	412	50
1120	61	60	2500	137	50	10000	550	00
1250	68	75	3000	165	00	15000	825	00
1500	82	50	4000	220	00	20000	1100	00
1750	96	25	5000	275	00	30000	1650	00

No.	£	p	No.	£	p	No.	£	p	No.	£	p
$\frac{1}{16}$	0	00½	34	2	04	72*	4	32	110	6	60
$\frac{1}{8}$	0	01	35	2	10	73	4	38	111	6	66
$\frac{1}{4}$	0	01½	36*	2	16	74	4	44	112	6	72
$\frac{1}{2}$	0	03	37	2	22	75	4	50	113	6	78
$\frac{3}{4}$	0	04½	38	2	28	76	4	56	114	6	84
1½	0	09	39	2	34	77	4	62	115	6	90
2	0	12	40	2	40	78	4	68	116	6	96
3	0	18	41	2	46	79	4	74	117	7	02
4	0	24	42	2	52	80	4	80	118	7	08
5	0	30	43	2	58	81	4	86	119	7	14
6	0	36	44	2	64	82	4	92	120*	7	20
7	0	42	45	2	70	83	4	98	128	7	68
8	0	48	46	2	76	84*	5	04	130	7	80
9	0	54	47	2	82	85	5	10	140	8	40
10	0	60	48*	2	88	86	5	16	144*	8	64
11	0	66	49	2	94	87	5	22	150	9	00
12*	0	72	50	3	00	88	5	28	156	9	36
13	0	78	51	3	06	89	5	34	168	10	08
14	0	84	52	3	12	90	5	40	196	11	76
15	0	90	53	3	18	91	5	46	200	12	00
16	0	96	54	3	24	92	5	52	220	13	20
17	1	02	55	3	30	93	5	58	224	13	44
18	1	08	56	3	36	94	5	64	256	15	36
19	1	14	57	3	42	95	5	70	280	16	80
20	1	20	58	3	48	96*	5	76	300	18	00
21	1	26	59	3	54	97	5	82	365	21	90
22	1	32	60*	3	60	98	5	88	400	24	00
23	1	38	61	3	66	99	5	94	480	28	80
24*	1	44	62	3	72	100	6	00	500	30	00
25	1	50	63	3	78	101	6	06	516	30	96
26	1	56	64	3	84	102	6	12	560	33	60
27	1	62	65	3	90	103	6	18	600	36	00
28	1	68	66	3	96	104	6	24	625	37	50
29	1	74	67	4	02	105	6	30	640	38	40
30	1	80	68	4	08	106	6	36	700	42	00
31	1	86	69	4	14	107	6	42	750	45	00
32	1	92	70	4	20	108*	6	48	800	48	00
33	1	98	71	4	26	109	6	54	900	54	00

No.	£	p	No.	£	p	No.	£	p
1000	60	00	1760	105	60	6000	360	00
1016	60	96	2000	120	00	7000	420	00
1094	65	64	2240	134	40	7500	450	00
1120	67	20	2500	150	00	10000	600	00
1250	75	00	3000	180	00	15000	900	00
1500	90	00	4000	240	00	20000	1200	00
1750	105	00	5000	300	00	30000	1800	00

6½p   £0·065

No.	£	p	No.	£	p	No.	£	p	No.	£	p
1/16	0	00½	34	2	21	72*	4	68	110	7	15
1/8	0	01	35	2	27½	73	4	74½	111	7	21½
1/4	0	01½	36*	2	34	74	4	81	112	7	28
1/2	0	03½	37	2	40½	75	4	87½	113	7	34½
3/4	0	05	38	2	47	76	4	94	114	7	41
1½	0	10	39	2	53½	77	5	00½	115	7	47½
2	0	13	40	2	60	78	5	07	116	7	54
3	0	19½	41	2	66½	79	5	13½	117	7	60½
4	0	26	42	2	73	80	5	20	118	7	67
5	0	32½	43	2	79½	81	5	26½	119	7	73½
6	0	39	44	2	86	82	5	33	120*	7	80
7	0	45½	45	2	92½	83	5	39½	128	8	32
8	0	52	46	2	99	84*	5	46	130	8	45
9	0	58½	47	3	05½	85	5	52½	140	9	10
10	0	65	48*	3	12	86	5	59	144*	9	36
11	0	71½	49	3	18½	87	5	65½	150	9	75
12*	0	78	50	3	25	88	5	72	156	10	14
13	0	84½	51	3	31½	89	5	78½	168	10	92
14	0	91	52	3	38	90	5	85	196	12	74
15	0	97½	53	3	44½	91	5	91½	200	13	00
16	1	04	54	3	51	92	5	98	220	14	30
17	1	10½	55	3	57½	93	6	04½	224	14	56
18	1	17	56	3	64	94	6	11	256	16	64
19	1	23½	57	3	70½	95	6	17½	280	18	20
20	1	30	58	3	77	96*	6	24	300	19	50
21	1	36½	59	3	83½	97	6	30½	365	23	72½
22	1	43	60*	3	90	98	6	37	400	26	00
23	1	49½	61	3	96½	99	6	43½	480	31	20
24*	1	56	62	4	03	100	6	50	500	32	50
25	1	62½	63	4	09½	101	6	56½	516	33	54
26	1	69	64	4	16	102	6	63	560	36	40
27	1	75½	65	4	22½	103	6	69½	600	39	00
28	1	82	66	4	29	104	6	76	625	40	62½
29	1	88½	67	4	35½	105	6	82½	640	41	60
30	1	95	68	4	42	106	6	89	700	45	50
31	2	01½	69	4	48½	107	6	95½	750	48	75
32	2	08	70	4	55	108*	7	02	800	52	00
33	2	14½	71	4	61½	109	7	08½	900	58	50

No.	£	p	No.	£	p	No.	£	p
1000	65	00	1760	114	40	6000	390	00
1016	66	04	2000	130	00	7000	455	00
1094	71	11	2240	145	60	7500	487	50
1120	72	80	2500	162	50	10000	650	00
1250	81	25	3000	195	00	15000	975	00
1500	97	50	4000	260	00	20000	1300	00
1750	113	75	5000	325	00	30000	1950	00

No.	£	p	No.	£	p	No.	£	p	No.	£	p
$\frac{1}{16}$	0	00½	34	2	38	72*	5	04	110	7	70
$\frac{1}{8}$	0	01	35	2	45	73	5	11	111	7	77
$\frac{1}{4}$	0	02	36*	2	52	74	5	18	112	7	84
$\frac{1}{2}$	0	03½	37	2	59	75	5	25	113	7	91
$\frac{3}{4}$	0	05½	38	2	66	76	5	32	114	7	98
1½	0	10½	39	2	73	77	5	39	115	8	05
2	0	14	**40**	2	80	78	5	46	116	8	12
3	0	21	41	2	87	79	5	53	117	8	19
4	0	28	42	2	94	**80**	5	60	118	8	26
5	0	35	43	3	01	81	5	67	119	8	33
6	0	42	44	3	08	82	5	74	120*	8	40
7	0	49	45	3	15	83	5	81	128	8	96
8	0	56	46	3	22	84*	5	88	130	9	10
9	0	63	47	3	29	85	5	95	140	9	80
10	0	70	48*	3	36	86	6	02	144*	10	08
11	0	77	49	3	43	87	6	09	150	10	50
12*	0	84	**50**	3	50	88	6	16	156	10	92
13	0	91	51	3	57	89	6	23	168	11	76
14	0	98	52	3	64	**90**	6	30	196	13	72
15	1	05	53	3	71	91	6	37	200	14	00
16	1	12	54	3	78	92	6	44	220	15	40
17	1	19	55	3	85	93	6	51	224	15	68
18	1	26	56	3	92	94	6	58	256	17	92
19	1	33	57	3	99	95	6	65	280	19	60
20	1	40	58	4	06	96*	6	72	300	21	00
21	1	47	59	4	13	97	6	79	365	25	55
22	1	54	60*	4	20	98	6	86	400	28	00
23	1	61	61	4	27	99	6	93	480	33	60
24*	1	68	62	4	34	**100**	7	00	500	35	00
25	1	75	63	4	41	101	7	07	516	36	12
26	1	82	64	4	48	102	7	14	560	39	20
27	1	89	65	4	55	103	7	21	600	42	00
28	1	96	66	4	62	104	7	28	625	43	75
29	2	03	67	4	69	105	7	35	640	44	80
30	2	10	68	4	76	106	7	42	700	49	00
31	2	17	69	4	83	107	7	49	750	52	50
32	2	24	**70**	4	90	108*	7	56	800	56	00
33	2	31	71	4	97	109	7	63	900	63	00

No.	£	p	No.	£	p	No.	£	p
1000	70	00	1760	123	20	6000	420	00
1016	71	12	2000	140	00	7000	490	00
1094	76	58	2240	156	80	7500	525	00
1120	78	40	2500	175	00	10000	700	00
1250	87	50	3000	210	00	15000	1050	00
1500	105	00	4000	280	00	20000	1400	00
1750	122	50	5000	350	00	30000	2100	00

7½p £0·075

No.	£	p	No.	£	p	No.	£	p	No.	£	p
1/16	0	00½	34	2	55	72*	5	40	110	8	25
1/8	0	01	35	2	62½	73	5	47½	111	8	32½
1/4	0	02	36*	2	70	74	5	55	112	8	40
1/2	0	04	37	2	77½	75	5	62½	113	8	47½
3/4	0	05½	38	2	85	76	5	70	114	8	55
1½	0	11½	39	2	92½	77	5	77½	115	8	62½
2	0	15	40	3	00	78	5	85	116	8	70
3	0	22½	41	3	07½	79	5	92½	117	8	77½
4	0	30	42	3	15	80	6	00	118	8	85
5	0	37½	43	3	22½	81	6	07½	119	8	92½
6	0	45	44	3	30	82	6	15	120*	9	00
7	0	52½	45	3	37½	83	6	22½	128	9	60
8	0	60	46	3	45	84*	6	30	130	9	75
9	0	67½	47	3	52½	85	6	37½	140	10	50
10	0	75	48*	3	60	86	6	45	144*	10	80
11	0	82½	49	3	67½	87	6	52½	150	11	25
12*	0	90	50	3	75	88	6	60	156	11	70
13	0	97½	51	3	82½	89	6	67½	168	12	60
14	1	05	52	3	90	90	6	75	196	14	70
15	1	12½	53	3	97½	91	6	82½	200	15	00
16	1	20	54	4	05	92	6	90	220	16	50
17	1	27½	55	4	12½	93	6	97½	224	16	80
18	1	35	56	4	20	94	7	05	256	19	20
19	1	42½	57	4	27½	95	7	12½	280	21	00
20	1	50	58	4	35	96*	7	20	300	22	50
21	1	57½	59	4	42½	97	7	27½	365	27	37½
22	1	65	60*	4	50	98	7	35	400	30	00
23	1	72½	61	4	57½	99	7	42½	480	36	00
24*	1	80	62	4	65	100	7	50	500	37	50
25	1	87½	63	4	72½	101	7	57½	516	38	70
26	1	95	64	4	80	102	7	65	560	42	00
27	2	02½	65	4	87½	103	7	72½	600	45	00
28	2	10	66	4	95	104	7	80	625	46	87½
29	2	17½	67	5	02½	105	7	87½	640	48	00
30	2	25	68	5	10	106	7	95	700	52	50
31	2	32½	69	5	17½	107	8	02½	750	56	25
32	2	40	70	5	25	108*	8	10	800	60	00
33	2	47½	71	5	32½	109	8	17½	900	67	50

No.	£	p	No.	£	p	No.	£	p
1000	75	00	1760	132	00	6000	450	00
1016	76	20	2000	150	00	7000	525	00
1094	82	05	2240	168	00	7500	562	50
1120	84	00	2500	187	50	10000	750	00
1250	93	75	3000	225	00	15000	1125	00
1500	112	50	4000	300	00	20000	1500	00
1750	131	25	5000	375	00	30000	2250	00

No.	£	p	No.	£	p	No.	£	p	No.	£	p
$\frac{1}{16}$	0	00½	34	2	72	72*	5	76	110	8	80
$\frac{1}{8}$	0	01	35	2	80	73	5	84	111	8	88
$\frac{1}{4}$	0	02	36*	2	88	74	5	92	112	8	96
$\frac{1}{2}$	0	04	37	2	96	75	6	00	113	9	04
$\frac{3}{4}$	0	06	38	3	04	76	6	08	114	9	12
1½	0	12	39	3	12	77	6	16	115	9	20
2	0	16	40	3	20	78	6	24	116	9	28
3	0	24	41	3	28	79	6	32	117	9	36
4	0	32	42	3	36	80	6	40	118	9	44
5	0	40	43	3	44	81	6	48	119	9	52
6	0	48	44	3	52	82	6	56	120*	9	60
7	0	56	45	3	60	83	6	64	128	10	24
8	0	64	46	3	68	84*	6	72	130	10	40
9	0	72	47	3	76	85	6	80	140	11	20
10	0	80	48*	3	84	86	6	88	144*	11	52
11	0	88	49	3	92	87	6	96	150	12	00
12*	0	96	50	4	00	88	7	04	156	12	48
13	1	04	51	4	08	89	7	12	168	13	44
14	1	12	52	4	16	90	7	20	196	15	68
15	1	20	53	4	24	91	7	28	200	16	00
16	1	28	54	4	32	92	7	36	220	17	60
17	1	36	55	4	40	93	7	44	224	17	92
18	1	44	56	4	48	94	7	52	256	20	48
19	1	52	57	4	56	95	7	60	280	22	40
20	1	60	58	4	64	96*	7	68	300	24	00
21	1	68	59	4	72	97	7	76	365	29	20
22	1	76	60*	4	80	98	7	84	400	32	00
23	1	84	61	4	88	99	7	92	480	38	40
24*	1	92	62	4	96	100	8	00	500	40	00
25	2	00	63	5	04	101	8	08	516	41	28
26	2	08	64	5	12	102	8	16	560	44	80
27	2	16	65	5	20	103	8	24	600	48	00
28	2	24	66	5	28	104	8	32	625	50	00
29	2	32	67	5	36	105	8	40	640	51	20
30	2	40	68	5	44	106	8	48	700	56	00
31	2	48	69	5	52	107	8	56	750	60	00
32	2	56	70	5	60	108*	8	64	800	64	00
33	2	64	71	5	68	109	8	72	900	72	00

No.	£	p	No.	£	p	No.	£	p
1000	80	00	1760	140	80	6000	480	00
1016	81	28	2000	160	00	7000	560	00
1094	87	52	2240	179	20	7500	600	00
1120	89	60	2500	200	00	10000	800	00
1250	100	00	3000	240	00	15000	1200	00
1500	120	00	4000	320	00	20000	1600	00
1750	140	00	5000	400	00	30000	2400	00

8½p　　　　　　　　　　　　　　　　£0·085

No.	£	p	No.	£	p	No.	£	p	No.	£	p	No.	£	p
1/16	0	00½	34	2	89	72*	6	12	110	9	35	1000	85	00
1/8	0	01	35	2	97½	73	6	20½	111	9	43½			
1/4	0	02	36*	3	06	74	6	29	112	9	52			
1/2	0	04½	37	3	14½	75	6	37½	113	9	60½			
3/4	0	06½	38	3	23	76	6	46	114	9	69			
1½	0	13	39	3	31½	77	6	54½	115	9	77½			
2	0	17	40	3	40	78	6	63	116	9	86			
3	0	25½	41	3	48½	79	6	71½	117	9	94½			
4	0	34	42	3	57	80	6	80	118	10	03			
5	0	42½	43	3	65½	81	6	88½	119	10	11½			
6	0	51	44	3	74	82	6	97	120*	10	20			
7	0	59½	45	3	82½	83	7	05½	128	10	88			
8	0	68	46	3	91	84*	7	14	130	11	05			
9	0	76½	47	3	99½	85	7	22½	140	11	90			
10	0	85	48*	4	08	86	7	31	144*	12	24			
11	0	93½	49	4	16½	87	7	39½	150	12	75			
12*	1	02	50	4	25	88	7	48	156	13	26			
13	1	10½	51	4	33½	89	7	56½	168	14	28			
14	1	19	52	4	42	90	7	65	196	16	66			
15	1	27½	53	4	50½	91	7	73½	200	17	00			
16	1	36	54	4	59	92	7	82	220	18	70			
17	1	44½	55	4	67½	93	7	90½	224	19	04			
18	1	53	56	4	76	94	7	99	256	21	76			
19	1	61½	57	4	84½	95	8	07½	280	23	80			
20	1	70	58	4	93	96*	8	16	300	25	50			
21	1	78½	59	5	01½	97	8	24½	365	31	02½			
22	1	87	60*	5	10	98	8	33	400	34	00			
23	1	95½	61	5	18½	99	8	41½	480	40	80			
24*	2	04	62	5	27	100	8	50	500	42	50			
25	2	12½	63	5	35½	101	8	58½	516	43	86			
26	2	21	64	5	44	102	8	67	560	47	60			
27	2	29½	65	5	52½	103	8	75½	600	51	00			
28	2	38	66	5	61	104	8	84	625	53	12½			
29	2	46½	67	5	69½	105	8	92½	640	54	40			
30	2	55	68	5	78	106	9	01	700	59	50			
31	2	63½	69	5	86½	107	9	09½	750	63	75			
32	2	72	70	5	95	108*	9	18	800	68	00			
33	2	80½	71	6	03½	109	9	26½	900	76	50			

No.	£	p	No.	£	p	No.	£	p
1000	85	00	1760	149	60	6000	510	00
1016	86	36	2000	170	00	7000	595	00
1094	92	99	2240	190	40	7500	637	50
1120	95	20	2500	212	50	10000	850	00
1250	106	25	3000	255	00	15000	1275	00
1500	127	50	4000	340	00	20000	1700	00
1750	148	75	5000	425	00	30000	2550	00

No.	£	p	No.	£	p	No.	£	p	No.	£	p
1/16	0	00½	34	3	06	72*	6	48	110	9	90
1/8	0	01	35	3	15	73	6	57	111	9	99
1/4	0	02½	36*	3	24	74	6	66	112	10	08
1/2	0	04½	37	3	33	75	6	75	113	10	17
3/4	0	07	38	3	42	76	6	84	114	10	26
1½	0	13½	39	3	51	77	6	93	115	10	35
2	0	18	40	3	60	78	7	02	116	10	44
3	0	27	41	3	69	79	7	11	117	10	53
4	0	36	42	3	78	80	7	20	118	10	62
5	0	45	43	3	87	81	7	29	119	10	71
6	0	54	44	3	96	82	7	38	120*	10	80
7	0	63	45	4	05	83	7	47	128	11	52
8	0	72	46	4	14	84*	7	56	130	11	70
9	0	81	47	4	23	85	7	65	140	12	60
10	0	90	48*	4	32	86	7	74	144*	12	96
11	0	99	49	4	41	87	7	83	150	13	50
12*	1	08	50	4	50	88	7	92	156	14	04
13	1	17	51	4	59	89	8	01	168	15	12
14	1	26	52	4	68	90	8	10	196	17	64
15	1	35	53	4	77	91	8	19	200	18	00
16	1	44	54	4	86	92	8	28	220	19	80
17	1	53	55	4	95	93	8	37	224	20	16
18	1	62	56	5	04	94	8	46	256	23	04
19	1	71	57	5	13	95	8	55	280	25	20
20	1	80	58	5	22	96*	8	64	300	27	00
21	1	89	59	5	31	97	8	73	365	32	85
22	1	98	60*	5	40	98	8	82	400	36	00
23	2	07	61	5	49	99	8	91	480	43	20
24*	2	16	62	5	58	100	9	00	500	45	00
25	2	25	63	5	67	101	9	09	516	46	44
26	2	34	64	5	76	102	9	18	560	50	40
27	2	43	65	5	85	103	9	27	600	54	00
28	2	52	66	5	94	104	9	36	625	56	25
29	2	61	67	6	03	105	9	45	640	57	60
30	2	70	68	6	12	106	9	54	700	63	00
31	2	79	69	6	21	107	9	63	750	67	50
32	2	88	70	6	30	108*	9	72	800	72	00
33	2	97	71	6	39	109	9	81	900	81	00

No.	£	p	No.	£	p	No.	£	p
1000	90	00	1760	158	40	6000	540	00
1016	91	44	2000	180	00	7000	630	00
1094	98	46	2240	201	60	7500	675	00
1120	100	80	2500	225	00	10000	900	00
1250	112	50	3000	270	00	15000	1350	00
1500	135	00	4000	360	00	20000	1800	00
1750	157	50	5000	450	00	30000	2700	00

No.	£	p	No.	£	p	No.	£	p	No.	£	p
1/16	0	00½	34	3	23	72*	6	84	110	10	45
1/8	0	01	35	3	32½	73	6	93½	111	10	54½
1/4	0	02½	36*	3	42	74	7	03	112	10	64
1/2	0	05	37	3	51½	75	7	12½	113	10	73½
3/4	0	07	38	3	61	76	7	22	114	10	83
1½	0	14½	39	3	70½	77	7	31½	115	10	92½
2	0	19	40	3	80	78	7	41	116	11	02
3	0	28½	41	3	89½	79	7	50½	117	11	11½
4	0	38	42	3	99	80	7	60	118	11	21
5	0	47½	43	4	08½	81	7	69½	119	11	30½
6	0	57	44	4	18	82	7	79	120*	11	40
7	0	66½	45	4	27½	83	7	88½	128	12	16
8	0	76	46	4	37	84*	7	98	130	12	35
9	0	85½	47	4	46½	85	8	07½	140	13	30
10	0	95	48*	4	56	86	8	17	144*	13	68
11	1	04½	49	4	65½	87	8	26½	150	14	25
12*	1	14	50	4	75	88	8	36	156	14	82
13	1	23½	51	4	84½	89	8	45½	168	15	96
14	1	33	52	4	94	90	8	55	196	18	62
15	1	42½	53	5	03½	91	8	64½	200	19	00
16	1	52	54	5	13	92	8	74	220	20	90
17	1	61½	55	5	22½	93	8	83½	224	21	28
18	1	71	56	5	32	94	8	93	256	24	32
19	1	80½	57	5	41½	95	9	02½	280	26	60
20	1	90	58	5	51	96*	9	12	300	28	50
21	1	99½	59	5	60½	97	9	21½	365	34	67½
22	2	09	60*	5	70	98	9	31	400	38	00
23	2	18½	61	5	79½	99	9	40½	480	45	60
24*	2	28	62	5	89	100	9	50	500	47	50
25	2	37½	63	5	98½	101	9	59½	516	49	02
26	2	47	64	6	08	102	9	69	560	53	20
27	2	56½	65	6	17½	103	9	78½	600	57	00
28	2	66	66	6	27	104	9	88	625	59	37½
29	2	75½	67	6	36½	105	9	97½	640	60	80
30	2	85	68	6	46	106	10	07	700	66	50
31	2	94½	69	6	55½	107	10	16½	750	71	25
32	3	04	70	6	65	108*	10	26	800	76	00
33	3	13½	71	6	74½	109	10	35½	900	85	50

No.	£	p	No.	£	p	No.	£	p
1000	95	00	1760	167	20	6000	570	00
1016	96	52	2000	190	00	7000	665	00
1094	103	93	2240	212	80	7500	712	50
1120	106	40	2500	237	50	10000	950	00
1250	118	75	3000	285	00	15000	1425	00
1500	142	50	4000	380	00	20000	1900	00
1750	166	25	5000	475	00	30000	2850	00

No.	£	p	No.	£	p	No.	£	p	No.	£	p
1/16	0	00½	34	3	40	72*	7	20	110	11	00
1/8	0	01½	35	3	50	73	7	30	111	11	10
1/4	0	02½	36*	3	60	74	7	40	112	11	20
1/2	0	05	37	3	70	75	7	50	113	11	30
3/4	0	07½	38	3	80	76	7	60	114	11	40
1½	0	15	39	3	90	77	7	70	115	11	50
2	0	20	40	4	00	78	7	80	116	11	60
3	0	30	41	4	10	79	7	90	117	11	70
4	0	40	42	4	20	80	8	00	118	11	80
5	0	50	43	4	30	81	8	10	119	11	90
6	0	60	44	4	40	82	8	20	120*	12	00
7	0	70	45	4	50	83	8	30	128	12	80
8	0	80	46	4	60	84*	8	40	130	13	00
9	0	90	47	4	70	85	8	50	140	14	00
10	1	00	48*	4	80	86	8	60	144*	14	40
11	1	10	49	4	90	87	8	70	150	15	00
12*	1	20	50	5	00	88	8	80	156	15	60
13	1	30	51	5	10	89	8	90	168	16	80
14	1	40	52	5	20	90	9	00	196	19	60
15	1	50	53	5	30	91	9	10	200	20	00
16	1	60	54	5	40	92	9	20	220	22	00
17	1	70	55	5	50	93	9	30	224	22	40
18	1	80	56	5	60	94	9	40	256	25	60
19	1	90	57	5	70	95	9	50	280	28	00
20	2	00	58	5	80	96*	9	60	300	30	00
21	2	10	59	5	90	97	9	70	365	36	50
22	2	20	60*	6	00	98	9	80	400	40	00
23	2	30	61	6	10	99	9	90	480	48	00
24*	2	40	62	6	20	100	10	00	500	50	00
25	2	50	63	6	30	101	10	10	516	51	60
26	2	60	64	6	40	102	10	20	560	56	00
27	2	70	65	6	50	103	10	30	600	60	00
28	2	80	66	6	60	104	10	40	625	62	50
29	2	90	67	6	70	105	10	50	640	64	00
30	3	00	68	6	80	106	10	60	700	70	00
31	3	10	69	6	90	107	10	70	750	75	00
32	3	20	70	7	00	108*	10	80	800	80	00
33	3	30	71	7	10	109	10	90	900	90	00

No.	£	p	No.	£	p	No.	£	p
1000	100	00	1760	176	00	6000	600	00
1016	101	60	2000	200	00	7000	700	00
1094	109	40	2240	224	00	7500	750	00
1120	112	00	2500	250	00	10000	1000	00
1250	125	00	3000	300	00	15000	1500	00
1500	150	00	4000	400	00	20000	2000	00
1750	175	00	5000	500	00	30000	3000	00

10½p £0·105

No.	£	p	No.	£	p	No.	£	p	No.	£	p
1/16	0	00½	34	3	57	72*	7	56	110	11	55
1/8	0	01½	35	3	67½	73	7	66½	111	11	65½
1/4	0	02½	36*	3	78	74	7	77	112	11	76
1/2	0	05½	37	3	88½	75	7	87½	113	11	86½
3/4	0	08	38	3	99	76	7	98	114	11	97
1½	0	16	39	4	09½	77	8	08½	115	12	07½
2	0	21	40	4	20	78	8	19	116	12	18
3	0	31½	41	4	30½	79	8	29½	117	12	28½
4	0	42	42	4	41	80	8	40	118	12	39
5	0	52½	43	4	51½	81	8	50½	119	12	49½
6	0	63	44	4	62	82	8	61	120*	12	60
7	0	73½	45	4	72½	83	8	71½	128	13	44
8	0	84	46	4	83	84*	8	82	130	13	65
9	0	94½	47	4	93½	85	8	92½	140	14	70
10	1	05	48*	5	04	86	9	03	144*	15	12
11	1	15½	49	5	14½	87	9	13½	150	15	75
12*	1	26	50	5	25	88	9	24	156	16	38
13	1	36½	51	5	35½	89	9	34½	168	17	64
14	1	47	52	5	46	90	9	45	196	20	58
15	1	57½	53	5	56½	91	9	55½	200	21	00
16	1	68	54	5	67	92	9	66	220	23	10
17	1	78½	55	5	77½	93	9	76½	224	23	52
18	1	89	56	5	88	94	9	87	256	26	88
19	1	99½	57	5	98½	95	9	97½	280	29	40
20	2	10	58	6	09	96*	10	08	300	31	50
21	2	20½	59	6	19½	97	10	18½	365	38	32½
22	2	31	60*	6	30	98	10	29	400	42	00
23	2	41½	61	6	40½	99	10	39½	480	50	40
24*	2	52	62	6	51	100	10	50	500	52	50
25	2	62½	63	6	61½	101	10	60½	516	54	18
26	2	73	64	6	72	102	10	71	560	58	80
27	2	83½	65	6	82½	103	10	81½	600	63	00
28	2	94	66	6	93	104	10	92	625	65	62½
29	3	04½	67	7	03½	105	11	02½	640	67	20
30	3	15	68	7	14	106	11	13	700	73	50
31	3	25½	69	7	24½	107	11	23½	750	78	75
32	3	36	70	7	35	108*	11	34	800	84	00
33	3	46½	71	7	45½	109	11	44½	900	94	50

No.	£	p	No.	£	p	No.	£	p
1000	105	00	1760	184	80	6000	630	00
1016	106	68	2000	210	00	7000	735	00
1094	114	87	2240	235	20	7500	787	50
1120	117	60	2500	262	50	10000	1050	00
1250	131	25	3000	315	00	15000	1575	00
1500	157	50	4000	420	00	20000	2100	00
1750	183	75	5000	525	00	30000	3150	00

No.	£	p	No.	£	p	No.	£	p	No.	£	p
1/16	0	00½	34	3	74	72*	7	92	110	12	10
1/8	0	01½	35	3	85	73	8	03	111	12	21
1/4	0	03	36*	3	96	74	8	14	112	12	32
1/2	0	05½	37	4	07	75	8	25	113	12	43
3/4	0	08½	38	4	18	76	8	36	114	12	54
1½	0	16½	39	4	29	77	8	47	115	12	65
2	0	22	40	4	40	78	8	58	116	12	76
3	0	33	41	4	51	79	8	69	117	12	87
4	0	44	42	4	62	80	8	80	118	12	98
5	0	55	43	4	73	81	8	91	119	13	09
6	0	66	44	4	84	82	9	02	120*	13	20
7	0	77	45	4	95	83	9	13	128	14	08
8	0	88	46	5	06	84*	9	24	130	14	30
9	0	99	47	5	17	85	9	35	140	15	40
10	1	10	48*	5	28	86	9	46	144*	15	84
11	1	21	49	5	39	87	9	57	150	16	50
12*	1	32	50	5	50	88	9	68	156	17	16
13	1	43	51	5	61	89	9	79	168	18	48
14	1	54	52	5	72	90	9	90	196	21	56
15	1	65	53	5	83	91	10	01	200	22	00
16	1	76	54	5	94	92	10	12	220	24	20
17	1	87	55	6	05	93	10	23	224	24	64
18	1	98	56	6	16	94	10	34	256	28	16
19	2	09	57	6	27	95	10	45	280	30	80
20	2	20	58	6	38	96*	10	56	300	33	00
21	2	31	59	6	49	97	10	67	365	40	15
22	2	42	60*	6	60	98	10	78	400	44	00
23	2	53	61	6	71	99	10	89	480	52	80
24*	2	64	62	6	82	100	11	00	500	55	00
25	2	75	63	6	93	101	11	11	516	56	76
26	2	86	64	7	04	102	11	22	560	61	60
27	2	97	65	7	15	103	11	33	600	66	00
28	3	08	66	7	26	104	11	44	625	68	75
29	3	19	67	7	37	105	11	55	640	70	40
30	3	30	68	7	48	106	11	66	700	77	00
31	3	41	69	7	59	107	11	77	750	82	50
32	3	52	70	7	70	108*	11	88	800	88	00
33	3	63	71	7	81	109	11	99	900	99	00

No.	£	p	No.	£	p	No.	£	p
1000	110	00	1760	193	60	6000	660	00
1016	111	76	2000	220	00	7000	770	00
1094	120	34	2240	246	40	7500	825	00
1120	123	20	2500	275	00	10000	1100	00
1250	137	50	3000	330	00	15000	1650	00
1500	165	00	4000	440	00	20000	2200	00
1750	192	50	5000	550	00	30000	3300	00

11½p　　　　　　£0·115

No.	£	p	No.	£	p	No.	£	p	No.	£	p
1/16	0	00½	34	3	91	72*	8	28	110	12	65
1/8	0	01½	35	4	02½	73	8	39½	111	12	76½
1/4	0	03	36*	4	14	74	8	51	112	12	88
1/2	0	06	37	4	25½	75	8	62½	113	12	99½
3/4	0	08½	38	4	37	76	8	74	114	13	11
1½	0	17½	39	4	48½	77	8	85½	115	13	22½
2	0	23	40	4	60	78	8	97	116	13	34
3	0	34½	41	4	71½	79	9	08½	117	13	45½
4	0	46	42	4	83	80	9	20	118	13	57
5	0	57½	43	4	94½	81	9	31½	119	13	68½
6	0	69	44	5	06	82	9	43	120*	13	80
7	0	80½	45	5	17½	83	9	54½	128	14	72
8	0	92	46	5	29	84*	9	66	130	14	95
9	1	03½	47	5	40½	85	9	77½	140	16	10
10	1	15	48*	5	52	86	9	89	144*	16	56
11	1	26½	49	5	63½	87	10	00½	150	17	25
12*	1	38	50	5	75	88	10	12	156	17	94
13	1	49½	51	5	86½	89	10	23½	168	19	32
14	1	61	52	5	98	90	10	35	196	22	54
15	1	72½	53	6	09½	91	10	46½	200	23	00
16	1	84	54	6	21	92	10	58	220	25	30
17	1	95½	55	6	32½	93	10	69½	224	25	76
18	2	07	56	6	44	94	10	81	256	29	44
19	2	18½	57	6	55½	95	10	92½	280	32	20
20	2	30	58	6	67	96*	11	04	300	34	50
21	2	41½	59	6	78½	97	11	15½	365	41	97½
22	2	53	60*	6	90	98	11	27	400	46	00
23	2	64½	61	7	01½	99	11	38½	480	55	20
24*	2	76	62	7	13	100	11	50	500	57	50
25	2	87½	63	7	24½	101	11	61½	516	59	34
26	2	99	64	7	36	102	11	73	560	64	40
27	3	10½	65	7	47½	103	11	84½	600	69	00
28	3	22	66	7	59	104	11	96	625	71	87½
29	3	33½	67	7	70½	105	12	07½	640	73	60
30	3	45	68	7	82	106	12	19	700	80	50
31	3	56½	69	7	93½	107	12	30½	750	86	25
32	3	68	70	8	05	108*	12	42	800	92	00
33	3	79½	71	8	16½	109	12	53½	900	103	50

No.	£	p	No.	£	p	No.	£	p
1000	115	00	1760	202	40	6000	690	00
1016	116	84	2000	230	00	7000	805	00
1094	125	81	2240	257	60	7500	862	50
1120	128	80	2500	287	50	10000	1150	00
1250	143	75	3000	345	00	15000	1725	00
1500	172	50	4000	460	00	20000	2300	00
1750	201	25	5000	575	00	30000	3450	00

No.	£	p	No.	£	p	No.	£	p	No.	£	p
1/16	0	01	34	4	08	72*	8	64	110	13	20
1/8	0	01½	35	4	20	73	8	76	111	13	32
1/4	0	03	36*	4	32	74	8	88	112	13	44
1/2	0	06	37	4	44	75	9	00	113	13	56
3/4	0	09	38	4	56	76	9	12	114	13	68
1½	0	18	39	4	68	77	9	24	115	13	80
2	0	24	40	4	80	78	9	36	116	13	92
3	0	36	41	4	92	79	9	48	117	14	04
4	0	48	42	5	04	80	9	60	118	14	16
5	0	60	43	5	16	81	9	72	119	14	28
6	0	72	44	5	28	82	9	84	120*	14	40
7	0	84	45	5	40	83	9	96	128	15	36
8	0	96	46	5	52	84*	10	08	130	15	60
9	1	08	47	5	64	85	10	20	140	16	80
10	1	20	48*	5	76	86	10	32	144*	17	28
11	1	32	49	5	88	87	10	44	150	18	00
12*	1	44	50	6	00	88	10	56	156	18	72
13	1	56	51	6	12	89	10	68	168	20	16
14	1	68	52	6	24	90	10	80	196	23	52
15	1	80	53	6	36	91	10	92	200	24	00
16	1	92	54	6	48	92	11	04	220	26	40
17	2	04	55	6	60	93	11	16	224	26	88
18	2	16	56	6	72	94	11	28	256	30	72
19	2	28	57	6	84	95	11	40	280	33	60
20	2	40	58	6	96	96*	11	52	300	36	00
21	2	52	59	7	08	97	11	64	365	43	80
22	2	64	60*	7	20	98	11	76	400	48	00
23	2	76	61	7	32	99	11	88	480	57	60
24*	2	88	62	7	44	100	12	00	500	60	00
25	3	00	63	7	56	101	12	12	516	61	92
26	3	12	64	7	68	102	12	24	560	67	20
27	3	24	65	7	80	103	12	36	600	72	00
28	3	36	66	7	92	104	12	48	625	75	00
29	3	48	67	8	04	105	12	60	640	76	80
30	3	60	68	8	16	106	12	72	700	84	00
31	3	72	69	8	28	107	12	84	750	90	00
32	3	84	70	8	40	108*	12	96	800	96	00
33	3	96	71	8	52	109	13	08	900	108	00

No.	£	p	No.	£	p	No.	£	p
1000	120	00	1760	211	20	6000	720	00
1016	121	92	2000	240	00	7000	840	00
1094	131	28	2240	268	80	7500	900	00
1120	134	40	2500	300	00	10000	1200	00
1250	150	00	3000	360	00	15000	1800	00
1500	180	00	4000	480	00	20000	2400	00
1750	210	00	5000	600	00	30000	3600	00

No.	£	p	No.	£	p	No.	£	p	No.	£	p
1/16	0	01	34	4	25	72*	9	00	110	13	75
1/8	0	01½	35	4	37½	73	9	12½	111	13	87½
1/4	0	03	36*	4	50	74	9	25	112	14	00
1/2	0	06½	37	4	62½	75	9	37½	113	14	12½
3/4	0	09½	38	4	75	76	9	50	114	14	25
1½	0	19	39	4	87½	77	9	62½	115	14	37½
2	0	25	40	5	00	78	9	75	116	14	50
3	0	37½	41	5	12½	79	9	87½	117	14	62½
4	0	50	42	5	25	80	10	00	118	14	75
5	0	62½	43	5	37½	81	10	12½	119	14	87½
6	0	75	44	5	50	82	10	25	120*	15	00
7	0	87½	45	5	62½	83	10	37½	128	16	00
8	1	00	46	5	75	84*	10	50	130	16	25
9	1	12½	47	5	87½	85	10	62½	140	17	50
10	1	25	48*	6	00	86	10	75	144*	18	00
11	1	37½	49	6	12½	87	10	87½	150	18	75
12*	1	50	50	6	25	88	11	00	156	19	50
13	1	62½	51	6	37½	89	11	12½	168	21	00
14	1	75	52	6	50	90	11	25	196	24	50
15	1	87½	53	6	62½	91	11	37½	200	25	00
16	2	00	54	6	75	92	11	50	220	27	50
17	2	12½	55	6	87½	93	11	62½	224	28	00
18	2	25	56	7	00	94	11	75	256	32	00
19	2	37½	57	7	12½	95	11	87½	280	35	00
20	2	50	58	7	25	96*	12	00	300	37	50
21	2	62½	59	7	37½	97	12	12½	365	45	62½
22	2	75	60*	7	50	98	12	25	400	50	00
23	2	87½	61	7	62½	99	12	37½	480	60	00
24*	3	00	62	7	75	100	12	50	500	62	50
25	3	12½	63	7	87½	101	12	62½	516	64	50
26	3	25	64	8	00	102	12	75	560	70	00
27	3	37½	65	8	12½	103	12	87½	600	75	00
28	3	50	66	8	25	104	13	00	625	78	12½
29	3	62½	67	8	37½	105	13	12½	640	80	00
30	3	75	68	8	50	106	13	25	700	87	50
31	3	87½	69	8	62½	107	13	37½	750	93	75
32	4	00	70	8	75	108*	13	50	800	100	00
33	4	12½	71	8	87½	109	13	62½	900	112	50

No.	£	p	No.	£	p	No.	£	p
1000	125	00	1760	220	00	6000	750	00
1016	127	00	2000	250	00	7000	875	00
1094	136	75	2240	280	00	7500	937	50
1120	140	00	2500	312	50	10000	1250	00
1250	156	25	3000	375	00	15000	1875	00
1500	187	50	4000	500	00	20000	2500	00
1750	218	75	5000	625	00	30000	3750	00

No.	£	p	No.	£	p	No.	£	p	No.	£	p
$\frac{1}{16}$	0	01	34	4	42	72*	9	36	110	14	30
$\frac{1}{8}$	0	01½	35	4	55	73	9	49	111	14	43
$\frac{1}{4}$	0	03½	36*	4	68	74	9	62	112	14	56
$\frac{1}{2}$	0	06½	37	4	81	75	9	75	113	14	69
$\frac{3}{4}$	0	10	38	4	94	76	9	88	114	14	82
1½	0	19½	39	5	07	77	10	01	115	14	95
2	0	26	40	5	20	78	10	14	116	15	08
3	0	39	41	5	33	79	10	27	117	15	21
4	0	52	42	5	46	80	10	40	118	15	34
5	0	65	43	5	59	81	10	53	119	15	47
6	0	78	44	5	72	82	10	66	120*	15	60
7	0	91	45	5	85	83	10	79	128	16	64
8	1	04	46	5	98	84*	10	92	130	16	90
9	1	17	47	6	11	85	11	05	140	18	20
10	1	30	48*	6	24	86	11	18	144*	18	72
11	1	43	49	6	37	87	11	31	150	19	50
12*	1	56	50	6	50	88	11	44	156	20	28
13	1	69	51	6	63	89	11	57	168	21	84
14	1	82	52	6	76	90	11	70	196	25	48
15	1	95	53	6	89	91	11	83	200	26	00
16	2	08	54	7	02	92	11	96	220	28	60
17	2	21	55	7	15	93	12	09	224	29	12
18	2	34	56	7	28	94	12	22	256	33	28
19	2	47	57	7	41	95	12	35	280	36	40
20	2	60	58	7	54	96*	12	48	300	39	00
21	2	73	59	7	67	97	12	61	365	47	45
22	2	86	60*	7	80	98	12	74	400	52	00
23	2	99	61	7	93	99	12	87	480	62	40
24*	3	12	62	8	06	100	13	00	500	65	00
25	3	25	63	8	19	101	13	13	516	67	08
26	3	38	64	8	32	102	13	26	560	72	80
27	3	51	65	8	45	103	13	39	600	78	00
28	3	64	66	8	58	104	13	52	625	81	25
29	3	77	67	8	71	105	13	65	640	83	20
30	3	90	68	8	84	106	13	78	700	91	00
31	4	03	69	8	97	107	13	91	750	97	50
32	4	16	70	9	10	108*	14	04	800	104	00
33	4	29	71	9	23	109	14	17	900	117	00

No.	£	p	No.	£	p	No.	£	p
1000	130	00	1760	228	80	6000	780	00
1016	132	08	2000	260	00	7000	910	00
1094	142	22	2240	291	20	7500	975	00
1120	145	60	2500	325	00	10000	1300	00
1250	162	50	3000	390	00	15000	1950	00
1500	195	00	4000	520	00	20000	2600	00
1750	227	50	5000	650	00	30000	3900	00

13½p £0·135

No.	£	p	No.	£	p	No.	£	p	No.	£	p
1/16	0	01	34	4	59	72*	9	72	110	14	85
1/8	0	01½	35	4	72½	73	9	85½	111	14	98½
1/4	0	03½	36*	4	86	74	9	99	112	15	12
1/2	0	07	37	4	99½	75	10	12½	113	15	25½
3/4	0	10	38	5	13	76	10	26	114	15	39
1½	0	20½	39	5	26½	77	10	39½	115	15	52½
2	0	27	40	5	40	78	10	53	116	15	66
3	0	40½	41	5	53½	79	10	66½	117	15	79½
4	0	54	42	5	67	80	10	80	118	15	93
5	0	67½	43	5	80½	81	10	93½	119	16	06½
6	0	81	44	5	94	82	11	07	120*	16	20
7	0	94½	45	6	07½	83	11	20½	128	17	28
8	1	08	46	6	21	84*	11	34	130	17	55
9	1	21½	47	6	34½	85	11	47½	140	18	90
10	1	35	48*	6	48	86	11	61	144*	19	44
11	1	48½	49	6	61½	87	11	74½	150	20	25
12*	1	62	50	6	75	88	11	88	156	21	06
13	1	75½	51	6	88½	89	12	01½	168	22	68
14	1	89	52	7	02	90	12	15	196	26	46
15	2	02½	53	7	15½	91	12	28½	200	27	00
16	2	16	54	7	29	92	12	42	220	29	70
17	2	29½	55	7	42½	93	12	55½	224	30	24
18	2	43	56	7	56	94	12	69	256	34	56
19	2	56½	57	7	69½	95	12	82½	280	37	80
20	2	70	58	7	83	96*	12	96	300	40	50
21	2	83½	59	7	96½	97	13	09½	365	49	27½
22	2	97	60*	8	10	98	13	23	400	54	00
23	3	10½	61	8	23½	99	13	36½	480	64	80
24*	3	24	62	8	37	100	13	50	500	67	50
25	3	37½	63	8	50½	101	13	63½	516	69	66
26	3	51	64	8	64	102	13	77	560	75	60
27	3	64½	65	8	77½	103	13	90½	600	81	00
28	3	78	66	8	91	104	14	04	625	84	37½
29	3	91½	67	9	04½	105	14	17½	640	86	40
30	4	05	68	9	18	106	14	31	700	94	50
31	4	18½	69	9	31½	107	14	44½	750	101	25
32	4	32	70	9	45	108*	14	58	800	108	00
33	4	45½	71	9	58½	109	14	71½	900	121	50

No.	£	p	No.	£	p	No.	£	p
1000	135	00	1760	237	60	6000	810	00
1016	137	16	2000	270	00	7000	945	00
1094	147	69	2240	302	40	7500	1012	50
1120	151	20	2500	337	50	10000	1350	00
1250	168	75	3000	405	00	15000	2025	00
1500	202	50	4000	540	00	20000	2700	00
1750	236	25	5000	675	00	30000	4050	00

No.	£	p	No.	£	p	No.	£	p	No.	£	p
$\frac{1}{16}$	0	01	34	4	76	72*	10	08	110	15	40
$\frac{1}{8}$	0	02	35	4	90	73	10	22	111	15	54
$\frac{1}{4}$	0	03½	36*	5	04	74	10	36	112	15	68
$\frac{1}{2}$	0	07	37	5	18	75	10	50	113	15	82
$\frac{3}{4}$	0	10½	38	5	32	76	10	64	114	15	96
1½	0	21	39	5	46	77	10	78	115	16	10
2	0	28	40	5	60	78	10	92	116	16	24
3	0	42	41	5	74	79	11	06	117	16	38
4	0	56	42	5	88	80	11	20	118	16	52
5	0	70	43	6	02	81	11	34	119	16	66
6	0	84	44	6	16	82	11	48	120*	16	80
7	0	98	45	6	30	83	11	62	128	17	92
8	1	12	46	6	44	84*	11	76	130	18	20
9	1	26	47	6	58	85	11	90	140	19	60
10	1	40	48*	6	72	86	12	04	144*	20	16
11	1	54	49	6	86	87	12	18	150	21	00
12*	1	68	50	7	00	88	12	32	156	21	84
13	1	82	51	7	14	89	12	46	168	23	52
14	1	96	52	7	28	90	12	60	196	27	44
15	2	10	53	7	42	91	12	74	200	28	00
16	2	24	54	7	56	92	12	88	220	30	80
17	2	38	55	7	70	93	13	02	224	31	36
18	2	52	56	7	84	94	13	16	256	35	84
19	2	66	57	7	98	95	13	30	280	39	20
20	2	80	58	8	12	96*	13	44	300	42	00
21	2	94	59	8	26	97	13	58	365	51	10
22	3	08	60*	8	40	98	13	72	400	56	00
23	3	22	61	8	54	99	13	86	480	67	20
24*	3	36	62	8	68	100	14	00	500	70	00
25	3	50	63	8	82	101	14	14	516	72	24
26	3	64	64	8	96	102	14	28	560	78	40
27	3	78	65	9	10	103	14	42	600	84	00
28	3	92	66	9	24	104	14	56	625	87	50
29	4	06	67	9	38	105	14	70	640	89	60
30	4	20	68	9	52	106	14	84	700	98	00
31	4	34	69	9	66	107	14	98	750	105	00
32	4	48	70	9	80	108*	15	12	800	112	00
33	4	62	71	9	94	109	15	26	900	126	00

No.	£	p	No.	£	p	No.	£	p
1000	140	00	1760	246	40	6000	840	00
1016	142	24	2000	280	00	7000	980	00
1094	153	16	2240	313	60	7500	1050	00
1120	156	80	2500	350	00	10000	1400	00
1250	175	00	3000	420	00	15000	2100	00
1500	210	00	4000	560	00	20000	2800	00
1750	245	00	5000	700	00	30000	4200	00

14½p £0·145

No.	£	p	No.	£	p	No.	£	p	No.	£	p
1/16	0	01	34	4	93	72*	10	44	110	15	95
1/8	0	02	35	5	07½	73	10	58½	111	16	09½
1/4	0	03½	36*	5	22	74	10	73	112	16	24
1/2	0	07½	37	5	36½	75	10	87½	113	16	38½
3/4	0	11	38	5	51	76	11	02	114	16	53
1½	0	22	39	5	65½	77	11	16½	115	16	67½
2	0	29	40	5	80	78	11	31	116	16	82
3	0	43½	41	5	94½	79	11	45½	117	16	96½
4	0	58	42	6	09	80	11	60	118	17	11
5	0	72½	43	6	23½	81	11	74½	119	17	25½
6	0	87	44	6	38	82	11	89	120*	17	40
7	1	01½	45	6	52½	83	12	03½	128	18	56
8	1	16	46	6	67	84*	12	18	130	18	85
9	1	30½	47	6	81½	85	12	32½	140	20	30
10	1	45	48*	6	96	86	12	47	144*	20	88
11	1	59½	49	7	10½	87	12	61½	150	21	75
12*	1	74	50	7	25	88	12	76	156	22	62
13	1	88½	51	7	39½	89	12	90½	168	24	36
14	2	03	52	7	54	90	13	05	196	28	42
15	2	17½	53	7	68½	91	13	19½	200	29	00
16	2	32	54	7	83	92	13	34	220	31	90
17	2	46½	55	7	97½	93	13	48½	224	32	48
18	2	61	56	8	12	94	13	63	256	37	12
19	2	75½	57	8	26½	95	13	77½	280	40	60
20	2	90	58	8	41	96*	13	92	300	43	50
21	3	04½	59	8	55½	97	14	06½	365	52	92½
22	3	19	60*	8	70	98	14	21	400	58	00
23	3	33½	61	8	84½	99	14	35½	480	69	60
24*	3	48	62	8	99	100	14	50	500	72	50
25	3	62½	63	9	13½	101	14	64½	516	74	82
26	3	77	64	9	28	102	14	79	560	81	20
27	3	91½	65	9	42½	103	14	93½	600	87	00
28	4	06	66	9	57	104	15	08	625	90	62½
29	4	20½	67	9	71½	105	15	22½	640	92	80
30	4	35	68	9	86	106	15	37	700	101	50
31	4	49½	69	10	00½	107	15	51½	750	108	75
32	4	64	70	10	15	108*	15	66	800	116	00
33	4	78½	71	10	29½	109	15	80½	900	130	50

No.	£	p	No.	£	p	No.	£	p
1000	145	00	1760	255	20	6000	870	00
1016	147	32	2000	290	00	7000	1015	00
1094	158	63	2240	324	80	7500	1087	50
1120	162	40	2500	362	50	10000	1450	00
1250	181	25	3000	435	00	15000	2175	00
1500	217	50	4000	580	00	20000	2900	00
1750	253	75	5000	725	00	30000	4350	00

No.	£	p	No.	£	p	No.	£	p	No.	£	p
1/16	0	01	34	5	10	72*	10	80	110	16	50
1/8	0	02	35	5	25	73	10	95	111	16	65
1/4	0	04	36*	5	40	74	11	10	112	16	80
1/2	0	07½	37	5	55	75	11	25	113	16	95
3/4	0	11½	38	5	70	76	11	40	114	17	10
1½	0	22½	39	5	85	77	11	55	115	17	25
2	0	30	40	6	00	78	11	70	116	17	40
3	0	45	41	6	15	79	11	85	117	17	55
4	0	60	42	6	30	80	12	00	118	17	70
5	0	75	43	6	45	81	12	15	119	17	85
6	0	90	44	6	60	82	12	30	120*	18	00
7	1	05	45	6	75	83	12	45	128	19	20
8	1	20	46	6	90	84*	12	60	130	19	50
9	1	35	47	7	05	85	12	75	140	21	00
10	1	50	48*	7	20	86	12	90	144*	21	60
11	1	65	49	7	35	87	13	05	150	22	50
12*	1	80	50	7	50	88	13	20	156	23	40
13	1	95	51	7	65	89	13	35	168	25	20
14	2	10	52	7	80	90	13	50	196	29	40
15	2	25	53	7	95	91	13	65	200	30	00
16	2	40	54	8	10	92	13	80	220	33	00
17	2	55	55	8	25	93	13	95	224	33	60
18	2	70	56	8	40	94	14	10	256	38	40
19	2	85	57	8	55	95	14	25	280	42	00
20	3	00	58	8	70	96*	14	40	300	45	00
21	3	15	59	8	85	97	14	55	365	54	75
22	3	30	60*	9	00	98	14	70	400	60	00
23	3	45	61	9	15	99	14	85	480	72	00
24*	3	60	62	9	30	100	15	00	500	75	00
25	3	75	63	9	45	101	15	15	516	77	40
26	3	90	64	9	60	102	15	30	560	84	00
27	4	05	65	9	75	103	15	45	600	90	00
28	4	20	66	9	90	104	15	60	625	93	75
29	4	35	67	10	05	105	15	75	640	96	00
30	4	50	68	10	20	106	15	90	700	105	00
31	4	65	69	10	35	107	16	05	750	112	50
32	4	80	70	10	50	108*	16	20	800	120	00
33	4	95	71	10	65	109	16	35	900	135	00

No.	£	p	No.	£	p	No.	£	p
1000	150	00	1760	264	00	6000	900	00
1016	152	40	2000	300	00	7000	1050	00
1094	164	10	2240	336	00	7500	1125	00
1120	168	00	2500	375	00	10000	1500	00
1250	187	50	3000	450	00	15000	2250	00
1500	225	00	4000	600	00	20000	3000	00
1750	262	50	5000	750	00	30000	4500	00

15½p £0·155

No.	£	p	No.	£	p	No.	£	p	No.	£	p
1/16	0	01	34	5	27	72*	11	16	110	17	05
1/8	0	02	35	5	42½	73	11	31½	111	17	20½
1/4	0	04	36*	5	58	74	11	47	112	17	36
1/2	0	08	37	5	73½	75	11	62½	113	17	51½
3/4	0	11½	38	5	89	76	11	78	114	17	67
1½	0	23½	39	6	04½	77	11	93½	115	17	82½
2	0	31	40	6	20	78	12	09	116	17	98
3	0	46½	41	6	35½	79	12	24½	117	18	13½
4	0	62	42	6	51	80	12	40	118	18	29
5	0	77½	43	6	66½	81	12	55½	119	18	44½
6	0	93	44	6	82	82	12	71	120*	18	60
7	1	08½	45	6	97½	83	12	86½	128	19	84
8	1	24	46	7	13	84*	13	02	130	20	15
9	1	39½	47	7	28½	85	13	17½	140	21	70
10	1	55	48*	7	44	86	13	33	144*	22	32
11	1	70½	49	7	59½	87	13	48½	150	23	25
12*	1	86	50	7	75	88	13	64	156	24	18
13	2	01½	51	7	90½	89	13	79½	168	26	04
14	2	17	52	8	06	90	13	95	196	30	38
15	2	32½	53	8	21½	91	14	10½	200	31	00
16	2	48	54	8	37	92	14	26	220	34	10
17	2	63½	55	8	52½	93	14	41½	224	34	72
18	2	79	56	8	68	94	14	57	256	39	68
19	2	94½	57	8	83½	95	14	72½	280	43	40
20	3	10	58	8	99	96*	14	88	300	46	50
21	3	25½	59	9	14½	97	15	03½	365	56	57½
22	3	41	60*	9	30	98	15	19	400	62	00
23	3	56½	61	9	45½	99	15	34½	480	74	40
24*	3	72	62	9	61	100	15	50	500	77	50
25	3	87½	63	9	76½	101	15	65½	516	79	98
26	4	03	64	9	92	102	15	81	560	86	80
27	4	18½	65	10	07½	103	15	96½	600	93	00
28	4	34	66	10	23	104	16	12	625	96	87½
29	4	49½	67	10	38½	105	16	27½	640	99	20
30	4	65	68	10	54	106	16	43	700	108	50
31	4	80½	69	10	69½	107	16	58½	750	116	25
32	4	96	70	10	85	108*	16	74	800	124	00
33	5	11½	71	11	00½	109	16	89½	900	139	50

No.	£	p	No.	£	p	No.	£	p
1000	155	00	1760	272	80	6000	930	00
1016	157	48	2000	310	00	7000	1085	00
1094	169	57	2240	347	20	7500	1162	50
1120	173	60	2500	387	50	10000	1550	00
1250	193	75	3000	465	00	15000	2325	00
1500	232	50	4000	620	00	20000	3100	00
1750	271	25	5000	775	00	30000	4650	00

No.	£	p	No.	£	p	No.	£	p	No.	£	p
1/16	0	01	34	5	44	72*	11	52	110	17	60
1/8	0	02	35	5	60	73	11	68	111	17	76
1/4	0	04	36*	5	76	74	11	84	112	17	92
1/2	0	08	37	5	92	75	12	00	113	18	08
3/4	0	12	38	6	08	76	12	16	114	18	24
1½	0	24	39	6	24	77	12	32	115	18	40
2	0	32	40	6	40	78	12	48	116	18	56
3	0	48	41	6	56	79	12	64	117	18	72
4	0	64	42	6	72	80	12	80	118	18	88
5	0	80	43	6	88	81	12	96	119	19	04
6	0	96	44	7	04	82	13	12	120*	19	20
7	1	12	45	7	20	83	13	28	128	20	48
8	1	28	46	7	36	84*	13	44	130	20	80
9	1	44	47	7	52	85	13	60	140	22	40
10	1	60	48*	7	68	86	13	76	144*	23	04
11	1	76	49	7	84	87	13	92	150	24	00
12*	1	92	50	8	00	88	14	08	156	24	96
13	2	08	51	8	16	89	14	24	168	26	88
14	2	24	52	8	32	90	14	40	196	31	36
15	2	40	53	8	48	91	14	56	200	32	00
16	2	56	54	8	64	92	14	72	220	35	20
17	2	72	55	8	80	93	14	88	224	35	84
18	2	88	56	8	96	94	15	04	256	40	96
19	3	04	57	9	12	95	15	20	280	44	80
20	3	20	58	9	28	96*	15	36	300	48	00
21	3	36	59	9	44	97	15	52	365	58	40
22	3	52	60*	9	60	98	15	68	400	64	00
23	3	68	61	9	76	99	15	84	480	76	80
24*	3	84	62	9	92	100	16	00	500	80	00
25	4	00	63	10	08	101	16	16	516	82	56
26	4	16	64	10	24	102	16	32	560	89	60
27	4	32	65	10	40	103	16	48	600	96	00
28	4	48	66	10	56	104	16	64	625	100	00
29	4	64	67	10	72	105	16	80	640	102	40
30	4	80	68	10	88	106	16	96	700	112	00
31	4	96	69	11	04	107	17	12	750	120	00
32	5	12	70	11	20	108*	17	28	800	128	00
33	5	28	71	11	36	109	17	44	900	144	00

No.	£	p	No.	£	p	No.	£	p
1000	160	00	1760	281	60	6000	960	00
1016	162	56	2000	320	00	7000	1120	00
1094	175	04	2240	358	40	7500	1200	00
1120	179	20	2500	400	00	10000	1600	00
1250	200	00	3000	480	00	15000	2400	00
1500	240	00	4000	640	00	20000	3200	00
1750	280	00	5000	800	00	30000	4800	00

16½p   £0·165

No.	£	p	No.	£	p	No.	£	p	No.	£	p
1/16	0	01	34	5	61	72*	11	88	110	18	15
1/8	0	02	35	5	77½	73	12	04½	111	18	31½
1/4	0	04	36*	5	94	74	12	21	112	18	48
1/2	0	08½	37	6	10½	75	12	37½	113	18	64½
1/2	0	12½	38	6	27	76	12	54	114	18	81
3/4	0	12½	38	6	27	76	12	54	114	18	81
1½	0	25	39	6	43½	77	12	70½	115	18	97½
2	0	33	40	6	60	78	12	87	116	19	14
3	0	49½	41	6	76½	79	13	03½	117	19	30½
4	0	66	42	6	93	80	13	20	118	19	47
5	0	82½	43	7	09½	81	13	36½	119	19	63½
6	0	99	44	7	26	82	13	53	120*	19	80
7	1	15½	45	7	42½	83	13	69½	128	21	12
8	1	32	46	7	59	84*	13	86	130	21	45
9	1	48½	47	7	75½	85	14	02½	140	23	10
10	1	65	48*	7	92	86	14	19	144*	23	76
11	1	81½	49	8	08½	87	14	35½	150	24	75
12*	1	98	50	8	25	88	14	52	156	25	74
13	2	14½	51	8	41½	89	14	68½	168	27	72
14	2	31	52	8	58	90	14	85	196	32	34
15	2	47½	53	8	74½	91	15	01½	200	33	00
16	2	64	54	8	91	92	15	18	220	36	30
17	2	80½	55	9	07½	93	15	34½	224	36	96
18	2	97	56	9	24	94	15	51	256	42	24
19	3	13½	57	9	40½	95	15	67½	280	46	20
20	3	30	58	9	57	96*	15	84	300	49	50
21	3	46½	59	9	73½	97	16	00½	365	60	22½
22	3	63	60*	9	90	98	16	17	400	66	00
23	3	79½	61	10	06½	99	16	33½	480	79	20
24*	3	96	62	10	23	100	16	50	500	82	50
25	4	12½	63	10	39½	101	16	66½	516	85	14
26	4	29	64	10	56	102	16	83	560	92	40
27	4	45½	65	10	72½	103	16	99½	600	99	00
28	4	62	66	10	89	104	17	16	625	103	12½
29	4	78½	67	11	05½	105	17	32½	640	105	60
30	4	95	68	11	22	106	17	49	700	115	50
31	5	11½	69	11	38½	107	17	65½	750	123	75
32	5	28	70	11	55	108*	17	82	800	132	00
33	5	44½	71	11	71½	109	17	98½	900	148	50

No.	£	p	No.	£	p	No.	£	p
1000	165	00	1760	290	40	6000	990	00
1016	167	64	2000	330	00	7000	1155	00
1094	180	51	2240	369	60	7500	1237	50
1120	184	80	2500	412	50	10000	1650	00
1250	206	25	3000	495	00	15000	2475	00
1500	247	50	4000	660	00	20000	3300	00
1750	288	75	5000	825	00	30000	4950	00

17p £0·17

No.	£	p	No.	£	p	No.	£	p	No.	£	p
$\frac{1}{16}$	0	01	34	5	78	72*	12	24	110	18	70
$\frac{1}{8}$	0	02	35	5	95	73	12	41	111	18	87
$\frac{1}{4}$	0	04½	36*	6	12	74	12	58	112	19	04
$\frac{1}{2}$	0	08½	37	6	29	75	12	75	113	19	21
$\frac{3}{4}$	0	13	38	6	46	76	12	92	114	19	38
1½	0	25½	39	6	63	77	13	09	115	19	55
2	0	34	40	6	80	78	13	26	116	19	72
3	0	51	41	6	97	79	13	43	117	19	89
4	0	68	42	7	14	80	13	60	118	20	06
5	0	85	43	7	31	81	13	77	119	20	23
6	1	02	44	7	48	82	13	94	120*	20	40
7	1	19	45	7	65	83	14	11	128	21	76
8	1	36	46	7	82	84*	14	28	130	22	10
9	1	53	47	7	99	85	14	45	140	23	80
10	1	70	48*	8	16	86	14	62	144*	24	48
11	1	87	49	8	33	87	14	79	150	25	50
12*	2	04	50	8	50	88	14	96	156	26	52
13	2	21	51	8	67	89	15	13	168	28	56
14	2	38	52	8	84	90	15	30	196	33	32
15	2	55	53	9	01	91	15	47	200	34	00
16	2	72	54	9	18	92	15	64	220	37	40
17	2	89	55	9	35	93	15	81	224	38	08
18	3	06	56	9	52	94	15	98	256	43	52
19	3	23	57	9	69	95	16	15	280	47	60
20	3	40	58	9	86	96*	16	32	300	51	00
21	3	57	59	10	03	97	16	49	365	62	05
22	3	74	60*	10	20	98	16	66	400	68	00
23	3	91	61	10	37	99	16	83	480	81	60
24*	4	08	62	10	54	100	17	00	500	85	00
25	4	25	63	10	71	101	17	17	516	87	72
26	4	42	64	10	88	102	17	34	560	95	20
27	4	59	65	11	05	103	17	51	600	102	00
28	4	76	66	11	22	104	17	68	625	106	25
29	4	93	67	11	39	105	17	85	640	108	80
30	5	10	68	11	56	106	18	02	700	119	00
31	5	27	69	11	73	107	18	19	750	127	50
32	5	44	70	11	90	108*	18	36	800	136	00
33	5	61	71	12	07	109	18	53	900	153	00

No.	£	p	No.	£	p	No.	£	p
1000	170	00	1760	299	20	6000	1020	00
1016	172	72	2000	340	00	7000	1190	00
1094	185	98	2240	380	80	7500	1275	00
1120	190	40	2500	425	00	10000	1700	00
1250	212	50	3000	510	00	15000	2550	00
1500	255	00	4000	680	00	20000	3400	00
1750	297	50	5000	850	00	30000	5100	00

No.	£	p	No.	£	p	No.	£	p	No.	£	p
1/16	0	01	34	5	95	72*	12	60	110	19	25
1/8	0	02	35	6	12½	73	12	77½	111	19	42½
1/4	0	04½	36*	6	30	74	12	95	112	19	60
1/2	0	09	37	6	47½	75	13	12½	113	19	77½
3/4	0	13	38	6	65	76	13	30	114	19	95
1½	0	26½	39	6	82½	77	13	47½	115	20	12½
2	0	35	40	7	00	78	13	65	116	20	30
3	0	52½	41	7	17½	79	13	82½	117	20	47½
4	0	70	42	7	35	80	14	00	118	20	65
5	0	87½	43	7	52½	81	14	17½	119	20	82½
6	1	05	44	7	70	82	14	35	120*	21	00
7	1	22½	45	7	87½	83	14	52½	128	22	40
8	1	40	46	8	05	84*	14	70	130	22	75
9	1	57½	47	8	22½	85	14	87½	140	24	50
10	1	75	48*	8	40	86	15	05	144*	25	20
11	1	92½	49	8	57½	87	15	22½	150	26	25
12*	2	10	50	8	75	88	15	40	156	27	30
13	2	27½	51	8	92½	89	15	57½	168	29	40
14	2	45	52	9	10	90	15	75	196	34	30
15	2	62½	53	9	27½	91	15	92½	200	35	00
16	2	80	54	9	45	92	16	10	220	38	50
17	2	97½	55	9	62½	93	16	27½	224	39	20
18	3	15	56	9	80	94	16	45	256	44	80
19	3	32½	57	9	97½	95	16	62½	280	49	00
20	3	50	58	10	15	96*	16	80	300	52	50
21	3	67½	59	10	32½	97	16	97½	365	63	87½
22	3	85	60*	10	50	98	17	15	400	70	00
23	4	02½	61	10	67½	99	17	32½	480	84	00
24*	4	20	62	10	85	100	17	50	500	87	50
25	4	37½	63	11	02½	101	17	67½	516	90	30
26	4	55	64	11	20	102	17	85	560	98	00
27	4	72½	65	11	37½	103	18	02½	600	105	00
28	4	90	66	11	55	104	18	20	625	109	37½
29	5	07½	67	11	72½	105	18	37½	640	112	00
30	5	25	68	11	90	106	18	55	700	122	50
31	5	42½	69	12	07½	107	18	72½	750	131	25
32	5	60	70	12	25	108*	18	90	800	140	00
33	5	77½	71	12	42½	109	19	07½	900	157	50

No.	£	p	No.	£	p	No.	£	p
1000	175	00	1760	308	00	6000	1050	00
1016	177	80	2000	350	00	7000	1225	00
1094	191	45	2240	392	00	7500	1312	50
1120	196	00	2500	437	50	10000	1750	00
1250	218	75	3000	525	00	15000	2625	00
1500	262	50	4000	700	00	20000	3500	00
1750	306	25	5000	875	00	30000	5250	00

No.	£	p	No.	£	p	No.	£	p	No.	£	p
$\frac{1}{16}$	0	01	34	6	12	72*	12	96	110	19	80
$\frac{1}{8}$	0	02½	35	6	30	73	13	14	111	19	98
$\frac{1}{4}$	0	04½	36*	6	48	74	13	32	112	20	16
$\frac{1}{2}$	0	09	37	6	66	75	13	50	113	20	34
$\frac{3}{4}$	0	13½	38	6	84	76	13	68	114	20	52
1½	0	27	39	7	02	77	13	86	115	20	70
2	0	36	40	7	20	78	14	04	116	20	88
3	0	54	41	7	38	79	14	22	117	21	06
4	0	72	42	7	56	80	14	40	118	21	24
5	0	90	43	7	74	81	14	58	119	21	42
6	1	08	44	7	92	82	14	76	120*	21	60
7	1	26	45	8	10	83	14	94	128	23	04
8	1	44	46	8	28	84*	15	12	130	23	40
9	1	62	47	8	46	85	15	30	140	25	20
10	1	80	48*	8	64	86	15	48	144*	25	92
11	1	98	49	8	82	87	15	66	150	27	00
12*	2	16	50	9	00	88	15	84	156	28	08
13	2	34	51	9	18	89	16	02	168	30	24
14	2	52	52	9	36	90	16	20	196	35	28
15	2	70	53	9	54	91	16	38	200	36	00
16	2	88	54	9	72	92	16	56	220	39	60
17	3	06	55	9	90	93	16	74	224	40	32
18	3	24	56	10	08	94	16	92	256	46	08
19	3	42	57	10	26	95	17	10	280	50	40
20	3	60	58	10	44	96*	17	28	300	54	00
21	3	78	59	10	62	97	17	46	365	65	70
22	3	96	60*	10	80	98	17	64	400	72	00
23	4	14	61	10	98	99	17	82	480	86	40
24*	4	32	62	11	16	100	18	00	500	90	00
25	4	50	63	11	34	101	18	18	516	92	88
26	4	68	64	11	52	102	18	36	560	100	80
27	4	86	65	11	70	103	18	54	600	108	00
28	5	04	66	11	88	104	18	72	625	112	50
29	5	22	67	12	06	105	18	90	640	115	20
30	5	40	68	12	24	106	19	08	700	126	00
31	5	58	69	12	42	107	19	26	750	135	00
32	5	76	70	12	60	108*	19	44	800	144	00
33	5	94	71	12	78	109	19	62	900	162	00

No.	£	p	No.	£	p	No.	£	p
1000	180	00	1760	316	80	6000	1080	00
1016	182	88	2000	360	00	7000	1260	00
1094	196	92	2240	403	20	7500	1350	00
1120	201	60	2500	450	00	10000	1800	00
1250	225	00	3000	540	00	15000	2700	00
1500	270	00	4000	720	00	20000	3600	00
1750	315	00	5000	900	00	30000	5400	00

18½p   £0·185

No.	£	p	No.	£	p	No.	£	p	No.	£	p
1/16	0	01	34	6	29	72*	13	32	110	20	35
1/8	0	02½	35	6	47½	73	13	50½	111	20	53½
1/4	0	04½	36*	6	66	74	13	69	112	20	72
1/2	0	09½	37	6	84½	75	13	87½	113	20	90½
3/4	0	14	38	7	03	76	14	06	114	21	09
1½	0	28	39	7	21½	77	14	24½	115	21	27½
2	0	37	40	7	40	78	14	43	116	21	46
3	0	55½	41	7	58½	79	14	61½	117	21	64½
4	0	74	42	7	77	80	14	80	118	21	83
5	0	92½	43	7	95½	81	14	98½	119	22	01½
6	1	11	44	8	14	82	15	17	120*	22	20
7	1	29½	45	8	32½	83	15	35½	128	23	68
8	1	48	46	8	51	84*	15	54	130	24	05
9	1	66½	47	8	69½	85	15	72½	140	25	90
10	1	85	48*	8	88	86	15	91	144*	26	64
11	2	03½	49	9	06½	87	16	09½	150	27	75
12*	2	22	50	9	25	88	16	28	156	28	86
13	2	40½	51	9	43½	89	16	46½	168	31	08
14	2	59	52	9	62	90	16	65	196	36	26
15	2	77½	53	9	80½	91	16	83½	200	37	00
16	2	96	54	9	99	92	17	02	220	40	70
17	3	14½	55	10	17½	93	17	20½	224	41	44
18	3	33	56	10	36	94	17	39	256	47	36
19	3	51½	57	10	54½	95	17	57½	280	51	80
20	3	70	58	10	73	96*	17	76	300	55	50
21	3	88½	59	10	91½	97	17	94½	365	67	52½
22	4	07	60*	11	10	98	18	13	400	74	00
23	4	25½	61	11	28½	99	18	31½	480	88	80
24*	4	44	62	11	47	100	18	50	500	92	50
25	4	62½	63	11	65½	101	18	68½	516	95	46
26	4	81	64	11	84	102	18	87	560	103	60
27	4	99½	65	12	02½	103	19	05½	600	111	00
28	5	18	66	12	21	104	19	24	625	115	62½
29	5	36½	67	12	39½	105	19	42½	640	118	40
30	5	55	68	12	58	106	19	61	700	129	50
31	5	73½	69	12	76½	107	19	79½	750	138	75
32	5	92	70	12	95	108*	19	98	800	148	00
33	6	10½	71	13	13½	109	20	16½	900	166	50

No.	£	p	No.	£	p	No.	£	p
1000	185	00	1760	325	60	6000	1110	00
1016	187	96	2000	370	00	7000	1295	00
1094	202	39	2240	414	40	7500	1387	50
1120	207	20	2500	462	50	10000	1850	00
1250	231	25	3000	555	00	15000	2775	00
1500	277	50	4000	740	00	20000	3700	00
1750	323	75	5000	925	00	30000	5550	00

No.	£	p	No.	£	p	No.	£	p	No.	£	p
1/16	0	01	34	6	46	72*	13	68	110	20	90
1/8	0	02½	35	6	65	73	13	87	111	21	09
1/4	0	05	36*	6	84	74	14	06	112	21	28
1/2	0	09½	37	7	03	75	14	25	113	21	47
3/4	0	14½	38	7	22	76	14	44	114	21	66
1½	0	28½	39	7	41	77	14	63	115	21	85
2	0	38	40	7	60	78	14	82	116	22	04
3	0	57	41	7	79	79	15	01	117	22	23
4	0	76	42	7	98	80	15	20	118	22	42
5	0	95	43	8	17	81	15	39	119	22	61
6	1	14	44	8	36	82	15	58	120*	22	80
7	1	33	45	8	55	83	15	77	128	24	32
8	1	52	46	8	74	84*	15	96	130	24	70
9	1	71	47	8	93	85	16	15	140	26	60
10	1	90	48*	9	12	86	16	34	144*	27	36
11	2	09	49	9	31	87	16	53	150	28	50
12*	2	28	50	9	50	88	16	72	156	29	64
13	2	47	51	9	69	89	16	91	168	31	92
14	2	66	52	9	88	90	17	10	196	37	24
15	2	85	53	10	07	91	17	29	200	38	00
16	3	04	54	10	26	92	17	48	220	41	80
17	3	23	55	10	45	93	17	67	224	42	56
18	3	42	56	10	64	94	17	86	256	48	64
19	3	61	57	10	83	95	18	05	280	53	20
20	3	80	58	11	02	96*	18	24	300	57	00
21	3	99	59	11	21	97	18	43	365	69	35
22	4	18	60*	11	40	98	18	62	400	76	00
23	4	37	61	11	59	99	18	81	480	91	20
24*	4	56	62	11	78	100	19	00	500	95	00
25	4	75	63	11	97	101	19	19	516	98	04
26	4	94	64	12	16	102	19	38	560	106	40
27	5	13	65	12	35	103	19	57	600	114	00
28	5	32	66	12	54	104	19	76	625	118	75
29	5	51	67	12	73	105	19	95	640	121	60
30	5	70	68	12	92	106	20	14	700	133	00
31	5	89	69	13	11	107	20	33	750	142	50
32	6	08	70	13	30	108*	20	52	800	152	00
33	6	27	71	13	49	109	20	71	900	171	00

No.	£	p	No.	£	p	No.	£	p
1000	190	00	1760	334	40	6000	1140	00
1016	193	04	2000	380	00	7000	1330	00
1094	207	86	2240	425	60	7500	1425	00
1120	212	80	2500	475	00	10000	1900	00
1250	237	50	3000	570	00	15000	2850	00
1500	285	00	4000	760	00	20000	3800	00
1750	332	50	5000	950	00	30000	5700	00

19½p £0·195

No.	£	p	No.	£	p	No.	£	p	No.	£	p
1/16	0	01	34	6	63	72*	14	04	110	21	45
1/8	0	02½	35	6	82½	73	14	23½	111	21	64½
1/4	0	05	36*	7	02	74	14	43	112	21	84
1/2	0	10	37	7	21½	75	14	62½	113	22	03½
3/4	0	14½	38	7	41	76	14	82	114	22	23
1½	0	29½	39	7	60½	77	15	01½	115	22	42½
2	0	39	40	7	80	78	15	21	116	22	62
3	0	58½	41	7	99½	79	15	40½	117	22	81½
4	0	78	42	8	19	80	15	60	118	23	01
5	0	97½	43	8	38½	81	15	79½	119	23	20½
6	1	17	44	8	58	82	15	99	120*	23	40
7	1	36½	45	8	77½	83	16	18½	128	24	96
8	1	56	46	8	97	84*	16	38	130	25	35
9	1	75½	47	9	16½	85	16	57½	140	27	30
10	1	95	48*	9	36	86	16	77	144*	28	08
11	2	14½	49	9	55½	87	16	96½	150	29	25
12*	2	34	50	9	75	88	17	16	156	30	42
13	2	53½	51	9	94½	89	17	35½	168	32	76
14	2	73	52	10	14	90	17	55	196	38	22
15	2	92½	53	10	33½	91	17	74½	200	39	00
16	3	12	54	10	53	92	17	94	220	42	90
17	3	31½	55	10	72½	93	18	13½	224	43	68
18	3	51	56	10	92	94	18	33	256	49	92
19	3	70½	57	11	11½	95	18	52½	280	54	60
20	3	90	58	11	31	96*	18	72	300	58	50
21	4	09½	59	11	50½	97	18	91½	365	71	17½
22	4	29	60*	11	70	98	19	11	400	78	00
23	4	48½	61	11	89½	99	19	30½	480	93	60
24*	4	68	62	12	09	100	19	50	500	97	50
25	4	87½	63	12	28½	101	19	69½	516	100	62
26	5	07	64	12	48	102	19	89	560	109	20
27	5	26½	65	12	67½	103	20	08½	600	117	00
28	5	46	66	12	87	104	20	28	625	121	87½
29	5	65½	67	13	06½	105	20	47½	640	124	80
30	5	85	68	13	26	106	20	67	700	136	50
31	6	04½	69	13	45½	107	20	86½	750	146	25
32	6	24	70	13	65	108*	21	06	800	156	00
33	6	43½	71	13	84½	109	21	25½	900	175	50

No.	£	p	No.	£	p	No.	£	p
1000	195	00	1760	343	20	6000	1170	00
1016	198	12	2000	390	00	7000	1365	00
1094	213	33	2240	436	80	7500	1462	50
1120	218	40	2500	487	50	10000	1950	00
1250	243	75	3000	585	00	15000	2925	00
1500	292	50	4000	780	00	20000	3900	00
1750	341	25	5000	975	00	30000	5850	00

No.	£	p	No.	£	p	No.	£	p	No.	£	p
$\frac{1}{16}$	0	01½	34	6	80	72*	14	40	110	22	00
$\frac{1}{8}$	0	02½	35	7	00	73	14	60	111	22	20
$\frac{1}{4}$	0	05	36*	7	20	74	14	80	112	22	40
$\frac{1}{2}$	0	10	37	7	40	75	15	00	113	22	60
$\frac{3}{4}$	0	15	38	7	60	76	15	20	114	22	80
1½	0	30	39	7	80	77	15	40	115	23	00
2	0	40	**40**	8	00	78	15	60	116	23	20
3	0	60	41	8	20	79	15	80	117	23	40
4	0	80	42	8	40	**80**	16	00	118	23	60
5	1	00	43	8	60	81	16	20	119	23	80
6	1	20	44	8	80	82	16	40	120*	24	00
7	1	40	45	9	00	83	16	60	128	25	60
8	1	60	46	9	20	84*	16	80	130	26	00
9	1	80	47	9	40	85	17	00	140	28	00
10	2	00	48*	9	60	86	17	20	144*	28	80
11	2	20	49	9	80	87	17	40	150	30	00
12*	2	40	**50**	10	00	88	17	60	156	31	20
13	2	60	51	10	20	89	17	80	168	33	60
14	2	80	52	10	40	**90**	18	00	196	39	20
15	3	00	53	10	60	91	18	20	200	40	00
16	3	20	54	10	80	92	18	40	220	44	00
17	3	40	55	11	00	93	18	60	224	44	80
18	3	60	56	11	20	94	18	80	256	51	20
19	3	80	57	11	40	95	19	00	280	56	00
20	4	00	58	11	60	96*	19	20	300	60	00
21	4	20	59	11	80	97	19	40	365	73	00
22	4	40	**60***	12	00	98	19	60	400	80	00
23	4	60	61	12	20	99	19	80	480	96	00
24*	4	80	62	12	40	**100**	20	00	500	100	00
25	5	00	63	12	60	101	20	20	516	103	20
26	5	20	64	12	80	102	20	40	560	112	00
27	5	40	65	13	00	103	20	60	600	120	00
28	5	60	66	13	20	104	20	80	625	125	00
29	5	80	67	13	40	105	21	00	640	128	00
30	6	00	68	13	60	106	21	20	700	140	00
31	6	20	69	13	80	107	21	40	750	150	00
32	6	40	**70**	14	00	108*	21	60	800	160	00
33	6	60	71	14	20	109	21	80	900	180	00

No.	£	p	No.	£	p	No.	£	p
1000	200	00	1760	352	00	6000	1200	00
1016	203	20	2000	400	00	7000	1400	00
1094	218	80	2240	448	00	7500	1500	00
1120	224	00	2500	500	00	10000	2000	00
1250	250	00	3000	600	00	15000	3000	00
1500	300	00	4000	800	00	20000	4000	00
1750	350	00	5000	1000	00	30000	6000	00

No.	£	p	No.	£	p	No.	£	p	No.	£	p
1/16	0	01½	34	7	14	72*	15	12	110	23	10
1/8	0	02½	35	7	35	73	15	33	111	23	31
1/4	0	05½	36*	7	56	74	15	54	112	23	52
1/2	0	10½	37	7	77	75	15	75	113	23	73
3/4	0	16	38	7	98	76	15	96	114	23	94
1½	0	31½	39	8	19	77	16	17	115	24	15
2	0	42	40	8	40	78	16	38	116	24	36
3	0	63	41	8	61	79	16	59	117	24	57
4	0	84	42	8	82	80	16	80	118	24	78
5	1	05	43	9	03	81	17	01	119	24	99
6	1	26	44	9	24	82	17	22	120*	25	20
7	1	47	45	9	45	83	17	43	128	26	88
8	1	68	46	9	66	84*	17	64	130	27	30
9	1	89	47	9	87	85	17	85	140	29	40
10	2	10	48*	10	08	86	18	06	144*	30	24
11	2	31	49	10	29	87	18	27	150	31	50
12*	2	52	50	10	50	88	18	48	156	32	76
13	2	73	51	10	71	89	18	69	168	35	28
14	2	94	52	10	92	90	18	90	196	41	16
15	3	15	53	11	13	91	19	11	200	42	00
16	3	36	54	11	34	92	19	32	220	46	20
17	3	57	55	11	55	93	19	53	224	47	04
18	3	78	56	11	76	94	19	74	256	53	76
19	3	99	57	11	97	95	19	95	280	58	80
20	4	20	58	12	18	96*	20	16	300	63	00
21	4	41	59	12	39	97	20	37	365	76	65
22	4	62	60*	12	60	98	20	58	400	84	00
23	4	83	61	12	81	99	20	79	480	100	80
24*	5	04	62	13	02	100	21	00	500	105	00
25	5	25	63	13	23	101	21	21	516	108	36
26	5	46	64	13	44	102	21	42	560	117	60
27	5	67	65	13	65	103	21	63	600	126	00
28	5	88	66	13	86	104	21	84	625	131	25
29	6	09	67	14	07	105	22	05	640	134	40
30	6	30	68	14	28	106	22	26	700	147	00
31	6	51	69	14	49	107	22	47	750	157	50
32	6	72	70	14	70	108*	22	68	800	168	00
33	6	93	71	14	91	109	22	89	900	189	00

No.	£	p	No.	£	p	No.	£	p
1000	210	00	1760	369	60	6000	1260	00
1016	213	36	2000	420	00	7000	1470	00
1094	229	74	2240	470	40	7500	1575	00
1120	235	20	2500	525	00	10000	2100	00
1250	262	50	3000	630	00	15000	3150	00
1500	315	00	4000	840	00	20000	4200	00
1750	367	50	5000	1050	00	30000	6300	00

No.	£	p	No.	£	p	No.	£	p	No.	£	p
$\frac{1}{16}$	0	01½	34	7	48	72*	15	84	110	24	20
$\frac{1}{8}$	0	03	35	7	70	73	16	06	111	24	42
$\frac{1}{4}$	0	05½	36*	7	92	74	16	28	112	24	64
$\frac{1}{2}$	0	11	37	8	14	75	16	50	113	24	86
$\frac{3}{4}$	0	16½	38	8	36	76	16	72	114	25	08
1½	0	33	39	8	58	77	16	94	115	25	30
2	0	44	40	8	80	78	17	16	116	25	52
3	0	66	41	9	02	79	17	38	117	25	74
4	0	88	42	9	24	80	17	60	118	25	96
5	1	10	43	9	46	81	17	82	119	26	18
6	1	32	44	9	68	82	18	04	120*	26	40
7	1	54	45	9	90	83	18	26	128	28	16
8	1	76	46	10	12	84*	18	48	130	28	60
9	1	98	47	10	34	85	18	70	140	30	80
10	2	20	48*	10	56	86	18	92	144*	31	68
11	2	42	49	10	78	87	19	14	150	33	00
12*	2	64	50	11	00	88	19	36	156	34	32
13	2	86	51	11	22	89	19	58	168	36	96
14	3	08	52	11	44	90	19	80	196	43	12
15	3	30	53	11	66	91	20	02	200	44	00
16	3	52	54	11	88	92	20	24	220	48	40
17	3	74	55	12	10	93	20	46	224	49	28
18	3	96	56	12	32	94	20	68	256	56	32
19	4	18	57	12	54	95	20	90	280	61	60
20	4	40	58	12	76	96*	21	12	300	66	00
21	4	62	59	12	98	97	21	34	365	80	30
22	4	84	60*	13	20	98	21	56	400	88	00
23	5	06	61	13	42	99	21	78	480	105	60
24*	5	28	62	13	64	100	22	00	500	110	00
25	5	50	63	13	86	101	22	22	516	113	52
26	5	72	64	14	08	102	22	44	560	123	20
27	5	94	65	14	30	103	22	66	600	132	00
28	6	16	66	14	52	104	22	88	625	137	50
29	6	38	67	14	74	105	23	10	640	140	80
30	6	60	68	14	96	106	23	32	700	154	00
31	6	82	69	15	18	107	23	54	750	165	00
32	7	04	70	15	40	108*	23	76	800	176	00
33	7	26	71	15	62	109	23	98	900	198	00

No.	£	p	No.	£	p	No.	£	p
1000	220	00	1760	387	20	6000	1320	00
1016	223	52	2000	440	00	7000	1540	00
1094	240	68	2240	492	80	7500	1650	00
1120	246	40	2500	550	00	10000	2200	00
1250	275	00	3000	660	00	15000	3300	00
1500	330	00	4000	880	00	20000	4400	00
1750	385	00	5000	1100	00	30000	6600	00

No.	£	p	No.	£	p	No.	£	p	No.	£	p
1/16	0	01½	34	7	65	72*	16	20	110	24	75
⅛	0	03	35	7	87½	73	16	42½	111	24	97½
¼	0	05½	36*	8	10	74	16	65	112	25	20
½	0	11½	37	8	32½	75	16	87½	113	25	42½
¾	0	17	38	8	55	76	17	10	114	25	65
1½	0	34	39	8	77½	77	17	32½	115	25	87½
2	0	45	**40**	9	00	78	17	55	116	26	10
3	0	67½	41	9	22½	79	17	77½	117	26	32½
4	0	90	42	9	45	**80**	18	00	118	26	55
5	1	12½	43	9	67½	81	18	22½	119	26	77½
6	1	35	44	9	90	82	18	45	120*	27	00
7	1	57½	45	10	12½	83	18	67½	128	28	80
8	1	80	46	10	35	84*	18	90	130	29	25
9	2	02½	47	10	57½	85	19	12½	140	31	50
10	2	25	48*	10	80	86	19	35	144*	32	40
11	2	47½	49	11	02½	87	19	57½	150	33	75
12*	2	70	**50**	11	25	88	19	80	156	35	10
13	2	92½	51	11	47½	89	20	02½	168	37	80
14	3	15	52	11	70	**90**	20	25	196	44	10
15	3	37½	53	11	92½	91	20	47½	200	45	00
16	3	60	54	12	15	92	20	70	220	49	50
17	3	82½	55	12	37½	93	20	92½	224	50	40
18	4	05	56	12	60	94	21	15	256	57	60
19	4	27½	57	12	82½	95	21	37½	280	63	00
20	4	50	58	13	05	96*	21	60	300	67	50
21	4	72½	59	13	27½	97	21	82½	365	82	12½
22	4	95	**60***	13	50	98	22	05	400	90	00
23	5	17½	61	13	72½	99	22	27½	480	108	00
24*	5	40	62	13	95	**100**	22	50	500	112	50
25	5	62½	63	14	17½	101	22	72½	516	116	10
26	5	85	64	14	40	102	22	95	560	126	00
27	6	07½	65	14	62½	103	23	17½	600	135	00
28	6	30	66	14	85	104	23	40	625	140	62½
29	6	52½	67	15	07½	105	23	62½	640	144	00
30	6	75	68	15	30	106	23	85	700	157	50
31	6	97½	69	15	52½	107	24	07½	750	168	75
32	7	20	**70**	15	75	108*	24	30	800	180	00
33	7	42½	71	15	97½	109	24	52½	900	202	50

No.	£	p	No.	£	p	No.	£	p
1000	225	00	1760	396	00	6000	1350	00
1016	228	60	2000	450	00	7000	1575	00
1094	246	15	2240	504	00	7500	1687	50
1120	252	00	2500	562	50	10000	2250	00
1250	281	25	3000	675	00	15000	3375	00
1500	337	50	4000	900	00	20000	4500	00
1750	393	75	5000	1125	00	30000	6750	00

No.	£	p	No.	£	p	No.	£	p	No.	£	p
1/16	0	01½	34	7	82	72*	16	56	110	25	30
1/8	0	03	35	8	05	73	16	79	111	25	53
1/4	0	06	36*	8	28	74	17	02	112	25	76
1/2	0	11½	37	8	51	75	17	25	113	25	99
3/4	0	17½	38	8	74	76	17	48	114	26	22
1½	0	34½	39	8	97	77	17	71	115	26	45
2	0	46	40	9	20	78	17	94	116	26	68
3	0	69	41	9	43	79	18	17	117	26	91
4	0	92	42	9	66	80	18	40	118	27	14
5	1	15	43	9	89	81	18	63	119	27	37
6	1	38	44	10	12	82	18	86	120*	27	60
7	1	61	45	10	35	83	19	09	128	29	44
8	1	84	46	10	58	84*	19	32	130	29	90
9	2	07	47	10	81	85	19	55	140	32	20
10	2	30	48*	11	04	86	19	78	144*	33	12
11	2	53	49	11	27	87	20	01	150	34	50
12*	2	76	50	11	50	88	20	24	156	35	88
13	2	99	51	11	73	89	20	47	168	38	64
14	3	22	52	11	96	90	20	70	196	45	08
15	3	45	53	12	19	91	20	93	200	46	00
16	3	68	54	12	42	92	21	16	220	50	60
17	3	91	55	12	65	93	21	39	224	51	52
18	4	14	56	12	88	94	21	62	256	58	88
19	4	37	57	13	11	95	21	85	280	64	40
20	4	60	58	13	34	96*	22	08	300	69	00
21	4	83	59	13	57	97	22	31	365	83	95
22	5	06	60*	13	80	98	22	54	400	92	00
23	5	29	61	14	03	99	22	77	480	110	40
24*	5	52	62	14	26	100	23	00	500	115	00
25	5	75	63	14	49	101	23	23	516	118	68
26	5	98	64	14	72	102	23	46	560	128	80
27	6	21	65	14	95	103	23	69	600	138	00
28	6	44	66	15	18	104	23	92	625	143	75
29	6	67	67	15	41	105	24	15	640	147	20
30	6	90	68	15	64	106	24	38	700	161	00
31	7	13	69	15	87	107	24	61	750	172	50
32	7	36	70	16	10	108*	24	84	800	184	00
33	7	59	71	16	33	109	25	07	900	207	00

No.	£	p	No.	£	p	No.	£	p
1000	230	00	1760	404	80	6000	1380	00
1016	233	68	2000	460	00	7000	1610	00
1094	251	62	2240	515	20	7500	1725	00
1120	257	60	2500	575	00	10000	2300	00
1250	287	50	3000	690	00	15000	3450	00
1500	345	00	4000	920	00	20000	4600	00
1750	402	50	5000	1150	00	30000	6900	00

No.	£	p	No.	£	p	No.	£	p	No.	£	p
$\frac{1}{16}$	0	01$\frac{1}{2}$	34	8	16	72*	17	28	110	26	40
$\frac{1}{8}$	0	03	35	8	40	73	17	52	111	26	64
$\frac{1}{4}$	0	06	36*	8	64	74	17	76	112	26	88
$\frac{1}{2}$	0	12	37	8	88	75	18	00	113	27	12
$\frac{3}{4}$	0	18	38	9	12	76	18	24	114	27	36
1$\frac{1}{2}$	0	36	39	9	36	77	18	48	115	27	60
2	0	48	40	9	60	78	18	72	116	27	84
3	0	72	41	9	84	79	18	96	117	28	08
4	0	96	42	10	08	80	19	20	118	28	32
5	1	20	43	10	32	81	19	44	119	28	56
6	1	44	44	10	56	82	19	68	120*	28	80
7	1	68	45	10	80	83	19	92	128	30	72
8	1	92	46	11	04	84*	20	16	130	31	20
9	2	16	47	11	28	85	20	40	140	33	60
10	2	40	48*	11	52	86	20	64	144*	34	56
11	2	64	49	11	76	87	20	88	150	36	00
12*	2	88	50	12	00	88	21	12	156	37	44
13	3	12	51	12	24	89	21	36	168	40	32
14	3	36	52	12	48	90	21	60	196	47	04
15	3	60	53	12	72	91	21	84	200	48	00
16	3	84	54	12	96	92	22	08	220	52	80
17	4	08	55	13	20	93	22	32	224	53	76
18	4	32	56	13	44	94	22	56	256	61	44
19	4	56	57	13	68	95	22	80	280	67	20
20	4	80	58	13	92	96*	23	04	300	72	00
21	5	04	59	14	16	97	23	28	365	87	60
22	5	28	60*	14	40	98	23	52	400	96	00
23	5	52	61	14	64	99	23	76	480	115	20
24*	5	76	62	14	88	100	24	00	500	120	00
25	6	00	63	15	12	101	24	24	516	123	84
26	6	24	64	15	36	102	24	48	560	134	40
27	6	48	65	15	60	103	24	72	600	144	00
28	6	72	66	15	84	104	24	96	625	150	00
29	6	96	67	16	08	105	25	20	640	153	60
30	7	20	68	16	32	106	25	44	700	168	00
31	7	44	69	16	56	107	25	68	750	180	00
32	7	68	70	16	80	108*	25	92	800	192	00
33	7	92	71	17	04	109	26	16	900	216	00

No.	£	p	No.	£	p	No.	£	p
1000	240	00	1760	422	40	6000	1440	00
1016	243	84	2000	480	00	7000	1680	00
1094	262	56	2240	537	60	7500	1800	00
1120	268	80	2500	600	00	10000	2400	00
1250	300	00	3000	720	00	15000	3600	00
1500	360	00	4000	960	00	20000	4800	00
1750	420	00	5000	1200	00	30000	7200	00

No.	£	p	No.	£	p	No.	£	p	No.	£	p
$\frac{1}{16}$	0	01½	34	8	50	72*	18	00	110	27	50
$\frac{1}{8}$	0	03	35	8	75	73	18	25	111	27	75
$\frac{1}{4}$	0	06½	36*	9	00	74	18	50	112	28	00
$\frac{1}{2}$	0	12½	37	9	25	75	18	75	113	28	25
$\frac{3}{4}$	0	19	38	9	50	76	19	00	114	28	50
1½	0	37½	39	9	75	77	19	25	115	28	75
2	0	50	**40**	10	00	78	19	50	116	29	00
3	0	75	41	10	25	79	19	75	117	29	25
4	1	00	42	10	50	**80**	20	00	118	29	50
5	1	25	43	10	75	81	20	25	119	29	75
6	1	50	44	11	00	82	20	50	120*	30	00
7	1	75	45	11	25	83	20	75	128	32	00
8	2	00	46	11	50	84*	21	00	130	32	50
9	2	25	47	11	75	85	21	25	140	35	00
10	2	50	48*	12	00	86	21	50	144*	36	00
11	2	75	49	12	25	87	21	75	150	37	50
12*	3	00	**50**	12	50	88	22	00	156	39	00
13	3	25	51	12	75	89	22	25	168	42	00
14	3	50	52	13	00	**90**	22	50	196	49	00
15	3	75	53	13	25	91	22	75	200	50	00
16	4	00	54	13	50	92	23	00	220	55	00
17	4	25	55	13	75	93	23	25	224	56	00
18	4	50	56	14	00	94	23	50	256	64	00
19	4	75	57	14	25	95	23	75	280	70	00
20	5	00	58	14	50	96*	24	00	300	75	00
21	5	25	59	14	75	97	24	25	365	91	25
22	5	50	**60***	15	00	98	24	50	400	100	00
23	5	75	61	15	25	99	24	75	480	120	00
24*	6	00	62	15	50	**100**	25	00	500	125	00
25	6	25	63	15	75	101	25	25	516	129	00
26	6	50	64	16	00	102	25	50	560	140	00
27	6	75	65	16	25	103	25	75	600	150	00
28	7	00	66	16	50	104	26	00	625	156	25
29	7	25	67	16	75	105	26	25	640	160	00
30	7	50	68	17	00	106	26	50	700	175	00
31	7	75	69	17	25	107	26	75	750	187	50
32	8	00	**70**	17	50	108*	27	00	800	200	00
33	8	25	71	17	75	109	27	25	900	225	00

No.	£	p	No.	£	p	No.	£	p
1000	250	00	1760	440	00	6000	1500	00
1016	254	00	2000	500	00	7000	1750	00
1094	273	50	2240	560	00	7500	1875	00
1120	280	00	2500	625	00	10000	2500	00
1250	312	50	3000	750	00	15000	3750	00
1500	375	00	4000	1000	00	20000	5000	00
1750	437	50	5000	1250	00	30000	7500	00

26p £0·26

No.	£	p	No.	£	p	No.	£	p	No.	£	p
$\frac{1}{16}$	0	01½	34	8	84	72*	18	72	110	28	60
$\frac{1}{8}$	0	03½	35	9	10	73	18	98	111	28	86
$\frac{1}{4}$	0	06½	36*	9	36	74	19	24	112	29	12
$\frac{1}{2}$	0	13	37	9	62	75	19	50	113	29	38
$\frac{3}{4}$	0	19½	38	9	88	76	19	76	114	29	64
1½	0	39	39	10	14	77	20	02	115	29	90
2	0	52	40	10	40	78	20	28	116	30	16
3	0	78	41	10	66	79	20	54	117	30	42
4	1	04	42	10	92	80	20	80	118	30	68
5	1	30	43	11	18	81	21	06	119	30	94
6	1	56	44	11	44	82	21	32	120*	31	20
7	1	82	45	11	70	83	21	58	128	33	28
8	2	08	46	11	96	84*	21	84	130	33	80
9	2	34	47	12	22	85	22	10	140	36	40
10	2	60	48*	12	48	86	22	36	144*	37	44
11	2	86	49	12	74	87	22	62	150	39	00
12*	3	12	50	13	00	88	22	88	156	40	56
13	3	38	51	13	26	89	23	14	168	43	68
14	3	64	52	13	52	90	23	40	196	50	96
15	3	90	53	13	78	91	23	66	200	52	00
16	4	16	54	14	04	92	23	92	220	57	20
17	4	42	55	14	30	93	24	18	224	58	24
18	4	68	56	14	56	94	24	44	256	66	56
19	4	94	57	14	82	95	24	70	280	72	80
20	5	20	58	15	08	96*	24	96	300	78	00
21	5	46	59	15	34	97	25	22	365	94	90
22	5	72	60*	15	60	98	25	48	400	104	00
23	5	98	61	15	86	99	25	74	480	124	80
24*	6	24	62	16	12	100	26	00	500	130	00
25	6	50	63	16	38	101	26	26	516	134	16
26	6	76	64	16	64	102	26	52	560	145	60
27	7	02	65	16	90	103	26	78	600	156	00
28	7	28	66	17	16	104	27	04	625	162	50
29	7	54	67	17	42	105	27	30	640	166	40
30	7	80	68	17	68	106	27	56	700	182	00
31	8	06	69	17	94	107	27	82	750	195	00
32	8	32	70	18	20	108*	28	08	800	208	00
33	8	58	71	18	46	109	28	34	900	234	00

No.	£	p	No.	£	p	No.	£	p
1000	260	00	1760	457	60	6000	1560	00
1016	264	16	2000	520	00	7000	1820	00
1094	284	44	2240	582	40	7500	1950	00
1120	291	20	2500	650	00	10000	2600	00
1250	325	00	3000	780	00	15000	3900	00
1500	390	00	4000	1040	00	20000	5200	00
1750	455	00	5000	1300	00	30000	7800	00

No.	£	p	No.	£	p	No.	£	p	No.	£	p
1/16	0	01½	34	9	18	72*	19	44	110	29	70
⅛	0	03½	35	9	45	73	19	71	111	29	97
¼	0	07	36*	9	72	74	19	98	112	30	24
½	0	13½	37	9	99	75	20	25	113	30	51
¾	0	20½	38	10	26	76	20	52	114	30	78
1½	0	40½	39	10	53	77	20	79	115	31	05
2	0	54	40	10	80	78	21	06	116	31	32
3	0	81	41	11	07	79	21	33	117	31	59
4	1	08	42	11	34	80	21	60	118	31	86
5	1	35	43	11	61	81	21	87	119	32	13
6	1	62	44	11	88	82	22	14	120*	32	40
7	1	89	45	12	15	83	22	41	128	34	56
8	2	16	46	12	42	84*	22	68	130	35	10
9	2	43	47	12	69	85	22	95	140	37	80
10	2	70	48*	12	96	86	23	22	144*	38	88
11	2	97	49	13	23	87	23	49	150	40	50
12*	3	24	50	13	50	88	23	76	156	42	12
13	3	51	51	13	77	89	24	03	168	45	36
14	3	78	52	14	04	90	24	30	196	52	92
15	4	05	53	14	31	91	24	57	200	54	00
16	4	32	54	14	58	92	24	84	220	59	40
17	4	59	55	14	85	93	25	11	224	60	48
18	4	86	56	15	12	94	25	38	256	69	12
19	5	13	57	15	39	95	25	65	280	75	60
20	5	40	58	15	66	96*	25	92	300	81	00
21	5	67	59	15	93	97	26	19	365	98	55
22	5	94	60*	16	20	98	26	46	400	108	00
23	6	21	61	16	47	99	26	73	480	129	60
24*	6	48	62	16	74	100	27	00	500	135	00
25	6	75	63	17	01	101	27	27	516	139	32
26	7	02	64	17	28	102	27	54	560	151	20
27	7	29	65	17	55	103	27	81	600	162	00
28	7	56	66	17	82	104	28	08	625	168	75
29	7	83	67	18	09	105	28	35	640	172	80
30	8	10	68	18	36	106	28	62	700	189	00
31	8	37	69	18	63	107	28	89	750	202	50
32	8	64	70	18	90	108*	29	16	800	216	00
33	8	91	71	19	17	109	29	43	900	243	00

No.	£	p	No.	£	p	No.	£	p
1000	270	00	1760	475	20	6000	1620	00
1016	274	32	2000	540	00	7000	1890	00
1094	295	38	2240	604	80	7500	2025	00
1120	302	40	2500	675	00	10000	2700	00
1250	337	50	3000	810	00	15000	4050	00
1500	405	00	4000	1080	00	20000	5400	00
1750	472	50	5000	1350	00	30000	8100	00

No.	£	p	No.	£	p	No.	£	p	No.	£	p
1/16	0	01½	34	9	35	72*	19	80	110	30	25
1/8	0	03½	35	9	62½	73	20	07½	111	30	52½
1/4	0	07	36*	9	90	74	20	35	112	30	80
1/2	0	14	37	10	17½	75	20	62½	113	31	07½
3/4	0	20½	38	10	45	76	20	90	114	31	35
1½	0	41½	39	10	72½	77	21	17½	115	31	62½
2	0	55	40	11	00	78	21	45	116	31	90
3	0	82½	41	11	27½	79	21	72½	117	32	17½
4	1	10	42	11	55	80	22	00	118	32	45
5	1	37½	43	11	82½	81	22	27½	119	32	72½
6	1	65	44	12	10	82	22	55	120*	33	00
7	1	92½	45	12	37½	83	22	82½	128	35	20
8	2	20	46	12	65	84*	23	10	130	35	75
9	2	47½	47	12	92½	85	23	37½	140	38	50
10	2	75	48*	13	20	86	23	65	144*	39	60
11	3	02½	49	13	47½	87	23	92½	150	41	25
12*	3	30	50	13	75	88	24	20	156	42	90
13	3	57½	51	14	02½	89	24	47½	168	46	20
14	3	85	52	14	30	90	24	75	196	53	90
15	4	12½	53	14	57½	91	25	02½	200	55	00
16	4	40	54	14	85	92	25	30	220	60	50
17	4	67½	55	15	12½	93	25	57½	224	61	60
18	4	95	56	15	40	94	25	85	256	70	40
19	5	22½	57	15	67½	95	26	12½	280	77	00
20	5	50	58	15	95	96*	26	40	300	82	50
21	5	77½	59	16	22½	97	26	67½	365	100	37½
22	6	05	60*	16	50	98	26	95	400	110	00
23	6	32½	61	16	77½	99	27	22½	480	132	00
24*	6	60	62	17	05	100	27	50	500	137	50
25	6	87½	63	17	32½	101	27	77½	516	141	90
26	7	15	64	17	60	102	28	05	560	154	00
27	7	42½	65	17	87½	103	28	32½	600	165	00
28	7	70	66	18	15	104	28	60	625	171	87½
29	7	97½	67	18	42½	105	28	87½	640	176	00
30	8	25	68	18	70	106	29	15	700	192	50
31	8	52½	69	18	97½	107	29	42½	750	206	25
32	8	80	70	19	25	108*	29	70	800	220	00
33	9	07½	71	19	52½	109	29	97½	900	247	50

No.	£	p	No.	£	p	No.	£	p
1000	275	00	1760	484	00	6000	1650	00
1016	279	40	2000	550	00	7000	1925	00
1094	300	85	2240	616	00	7500	2062	50
1120	308	00	2500	687	50	10000	2750	00
1250	343	75	3000	825	00	15000	4125	00
1500	412	50	4000	1100	00	20000	5500	00
1750	481	25	5000	1375	00	30000	8250	00

No.	£	p	No.	£	p	No.	£	p	No.	£	p
1/16	0	02	34	9	52	72*	20	16	110	30	80
1/8	0	03½	35	9	80	73	20	44	111	31	08
1/4	0	07	36*	10	08	74	20	72	112	31	36
1/2	0	14	37	10	36	75	21	00	113	31	64
3/4	0	21	38	10	64	76	21	28	114	31	92
1½	0	42	39	10	92	77	21	56	115	32	20
2	0	56	40	11	20	78	21	84	116	32	48
3	0	84	41	11	48	79	22	12	117	32	76
4	1	12	42	11	76	80	22	40	118	33	04
5	1	40	43	12	04	81	22	68	119	33	32
6	1	68	44	12	32	82	22	96	120*	33	60
7	1	96	45	12	60	83	23	24	128	35	84
8	2	24	46	12	88	84*	23	52	130	36	40
9	2	52	47	13	16	85	23	80	140	39	20
10	2	80	48*	13	44	86	24	08	144*	40	32
11	3	08	49	13	72	87	24	36	150	42	00
12*	3	36	50	14	00	88	24	64	156	43	68
13	3	64	51	14	28	89	24	92	168	47	04
14	3	92	52	14	56	90	25	20	196	54	88
15	4	20	53	14	84	91	25	48	200	56	00
16	4	48	54	15	12	92	25	76	220	61	60
17	4	76	55	15	40	93	26	04	224	62	72
18	5	04	56	15	68	94	26	32	256	71	68
19	5	32	57	15	96	95	26	60	280	78	40
20	5	60	58	16	24	96*	26	88	300	84	00
21	5	88	59	16	52	97	27	16	365	102	20
22	6	16	60*	16	80	98	27	44	400	112	00
23	6	44	61	17	08	99	27	72	480	134	40
24*	6	72	62	17	36	100	28	00	500	140	00
25	7	00	63	17	64	101	28	28	516	144	48
26	7	28	64	17	92	102	28	56	560	156	80
27	7	56	65	18	20	103	28	84	600	168	00
28	7	84	66	18	48	104	29	12	625	175	00
29	8	12	67	18	76	105	29	40	640	179	20
30	8	40	68	19	04	106	29	68	700	196	00
31	8	68	69	19	32	107	29	96	750	210	00
32	8	96	70	19	60	108*	30	24	800	224	00
33	9	24	71	19	88	109	30	52	900	252	00

No.	£	p	No.	£	p	No.	£	p
1000	280	00	1760	492	80	6000	1680	00
1016	284	48	2000	560	00	7000	1960	00
1094	306	32	2240	627	20	7500	2100	00
1120	313	60	2500	700	00	10000	2800	00
1250	350	00	3000	840	00	15000	4200	00
1500	420	00	4000	1120	00	20000	5600	00
1750	490	00	5000	1400	00	30000	8400	00

No.	£	p	No.	£	p	No.	£	p	No.	£	p
1/16	0	02	34	9	86	72*	20	88	110	31	90
1/8	0	03½	35	10	15	73	21	17	111	32	19
1/4	0	07½	36*	10	44	74	21	46	112	32	48
1/2	0	14½	37	10	73	75	21	75	113	32	77
3/4	0	22	38	11	02	76	22	04	114	33	06
1½	0	43½	39	11	31	77	22	33	115	33	35
2	0	58	40	11	60	78	22	62	116	33	64
3	0	87	41	11	89	79	22	91	117	33	93
4	1	16	42	12	18	80	23	20	118	34	22
5	1	45	43	12	47	81	23	49	119	34	51
6	1	74	44	12	76	82	23	78	120*	34	80
7	2	03	45	13	05	83	24	07	128	37	12
8	2	32	46	13	34	84*	24	36	130	37	70
9	2	61	47	13	63	85	24	65	140	40	60
10	2	90	48*	13	92	86	24	94	144*	41	76
11	3	19	49	14	21	87	25	23	150	43	50
12*	3	48	50	14	50	88	25	52	156	45	24
13	3	77	51	14	79	89	25	81	168	48	72
14	4	06	52	15	08	90	26	10	196	56	84
15	4	35	53	15	37	91	26	39	200	58	00
16	4	64	54	15	66	92	26	68	220	63	80
17	4	93	55	15	95	93	26	97	224	64	96
18	5	22	56	16	24	94	27	26	256	74	24
19	5	51	57	16	53	95	27	55	280	81	20
20	5	80	58	16	82	96*	27	84	300	87	00
21	6	09	59	17	11	97	28	13	365	105	85
22	6	38	60*	17	40	98	28	42	400	116	00
23	6	67	61	17	69	99	28	71	480	139	20
24*	6	96	62	17	98	100	29	00	500	145	00
25	7	25	63	18	27	101	29	29	516	149	64
26	7	54	64	18	56	102	29	58	560	162	40
27	7	83	65	18	85	103	29	87	600	174	00
28	8	12	66	19	14	104	30	16	625	181	25
29	8	41	67	19	43	105	30	45	640	185	60
30	8	70	68	19	72	106	30	74	700	203	00
31	8	99	69	20	01	107	31	03	750	217	50
32	9	28	70	20	30	108*	31	32	800	232	00
33	9	57	71	20	59	109	31	61	900	261	00

No.	£	p	No.	£	p	No.	£	p
1000	290	00	1760	510	40	6000	1740	00
1016	294	64	2000	580	00	7000	2030	00
1094	317	26	2240	649	60	7500	2175	00
1120	324	80	2500	725	00	10000	2900	00
1250	362	50	3000	870	00	15000	4350	00
1500	435	00	4000	1160	00	20000	5800	00
1750	507	50	5000	1450	00	30000	8700	00

30p £0·30

No.	£	p	No.	£	p	No.	£	p	No.	£	p
1/16	0	02	34	10	20	72*	21	60	110	33	00
1/8	0	04	35	10	50	73	21	90	111	33	30
1/4	0	07½	36*	10	80	74	22	20	112	33	60
1/2	0	15	37	11	10	75	22	50	113	33	90
3/4	0	22½	38	11	40	76	22	80	114	34	20
1½	0	45	39	11	70	77	23	10	115	34	50
2	0	60	40	12	00	78	23	40	116	34	80
3	0	90	41	12	30	79	23	70	117	35	10
4	1	20	42	12	60	80	24	00	118	35	40
5	1	50	43	12	90	81	24	30	119	35	70
6	1	80	44	13	20	82	24	60	120*	36	00
7	2	10	45	13	50	83	24	90	128	38	40
8	2	40	46	13	80	84*	25	20	130	39	00
9	2	70	47	14	10	85	25	50	140	42	00
10	3	00	48*	14	40	86	25	80	144*	43	20
11	3	30	49	14	70	87	26	10	150	45	00
12*	3	60	50	15	00	88	26	40	156	46	80
13	3	90	51	15	30	89	26	70	168	50	40
14	4	20	52	15	60	90	27	00	196	58	80
15	4	50	53	15	90	91	27	30	200	60	00
16	4	80	54	16	20	92	27	60	220	66	00
17	5	10	55	16	50	93	27	90	224	67	20
18	5	40	56	16	80	94	28	20	256	76	80
19	5	70	57	17	10	95	28	50	280	84	00
20	6	00	58	17	40	96*	28	80	300	90	00
21	6	30	59	17	70	97	29	10	365	109	50
22	6	60	60*	18	00	98	29	40	400	120	00
23	6	90	61	18	30	99	29	70	480	144	00
24*	7	20	62	18	60	100	30	00	500	150	00
25	7	50	63	18	90	101	30	30	516	154	80
26	7	80	64	19	20	102	30	60	560	168	00
27	8	10	65	19	50	103	30	90	600	180	00
28	8	40	66	19	80	104	31	20	625	187	50
29	8	70	67	20	10	105	31	50	640	192	00
30	9	00	68	20	40	106	31	80	700	210	00
31	9	30	69	20	70	107	32	10	750	225	00
32	9	60	70	21	00	108*	32	40	800	240	00
33	9	90	71	21	30	109	32	70	900	270	00

No.	£	p	No.	£	p	No.	£	p
1000	300	00	1760	528	00	6000	1800	00
1016	304	80	2000	600	00	7000	2100	00
1094	328	20	2240	672	00	7500	2250	00
1120	336	00	2500	750	00	10000	3000	00
1250	375	00	3000	900	00	15000	4500	00
1500	450	00	4000	1200	00	20000	6000	00
1750	525	00	5000	1500	00	30000	9000	00

31p   £0·31

No.	£	p	No.	£	p	No.	£	p	No.	£	p
1/16	0	02	34	10	54	72*	22	32	110	34	10
1/8	0	04	35	10	85	73	22	63	111	34	41
1/4	0	08	36*	11	16	74	22	94	112	34	72
1/2	0	15½	37	11	47	75	23	25	113	35	03
3/4	0	23½	38	11	78	76	23	56	114	35	34
1½	0	46½	39	12	09	77	23	87	115	35	65
2	0	62	40	12	40	78	24	18	116	35	96
3	0	93	41	12	71	79	24	49	117	36	27
4	1	24	42	13	02	80	24	80	118	36	58
5	1	55	43	13	33	81	25	11	119	36	89
6	1	86	44	13	64	82	25	42	120*	37	20
7	2	17	45	13	95	83	25	73	128	39	68
8	2	48	46	14	26	84*	26	04	130	40	30
9	2	79	47	14	57	85	26	35	140	43	40
10	3	10	48*	14	88	86	26	66	144*	44	64
11	3	41	49	15	19	87	26	97	150	46	50
12*	3	72	50	15	50	88	27	28	156	48	36
13	4	03	51	15	81	89	27	59	168	52	08
14	4	34	52	16	12	90	27	90	196	60	76
15	4	65	53	16	43	91	28	21	200	62	00
16	4	96	54	16	74	92	28	52	220	68	20
17	5	27	55	17	05	93	28	83	224	69	44
18	5	58	56	17	36	94	29	14	256	79	36
19	5	89	57	17	67	95	29	45	280	86	80
20	6	20	58	17	98	96*	29	76	300	93	00
21	6	51	59	18	29	97	30	07	365	113	15
22	6	82	60*	18	60	98	30	38	400	124	00
23	7	13	61	18	91	99	30	69	480	148	80
24*	7	44	62	19	22	100	31	00	500	155	00
25	7	75	63	19	53	101	31	31	516	159	96
26	8	06	64	19	84	102	31	62	560	173	60
27	8	37	65	20	15	103	31	93	600	186	00
28	8	68	66	20	46	104	32	24	625	193	75
29	8	99	67	20	77	105	32	55	640	198	40
30	9	30	68	21	08	106	32	86	700	217	00
31	9	61	69	21	39	107	33	17	750	232	50
32	9	92	70	21	70	108*	33	48	800	248	00
33	10	23	71	22	01	109	33	79	900	279	00

No.	£	p	No.	£	p	No.	£	p
1000	310	00	1760	545	60	6000	1860	00
1016	314	96	2000	620	00	7000	2170	00
1094	339	14	2240	694	40	7500	2325	00
1120	347	20	2500	775	00	10000	3100	00
1250	387	50	3000	930	00	15000	4650	00
1500	465	00	4000	1240	00	20000	6200	00
1750	542	50	5000	1550	00	30000	9300	00

No.	£	p	No.	£	p	No.	£	p	No.	£	p
1/16	0	02	34	10	88	72*	23	04	110	35	20
1/8	0	04	35	11	20	73	23	36	111	35	52
1/4	0	08	36*	11	52	74	23	68	112	35	84
1/2	0	16	37	11	84	75	24	00	113	36	16
3/4	0	24	38	12	16	76	24	32	114	36	48
1½	0	48	39	12	48	77	24	64	115	36	80
2	0	64	**40**	12	80	78	24	96	116	37	12
3	0	96	41	13	12	79	25	28	117	37	44
4	1	28	42	13	44	**80**	25	60	118	37	76
5	1	60	43	13	76	81	25	92	119	38	08
6	1	92	44	14	08	82	26	24	120*	38	40
7	2	24	45	14	40	83	26	56	128	40	96
8	2	56	46	14	72	84*	26	88	130	41	60
9	2	88	47	15	04	85	27	20	140	44	80
10	3	20	48*	15	36	86	27	52	144*	46	08
11	3	52	49	15	68	87	27	84	150	48	00
12*	3	84	**50**	16	00	88	28	16	156	49	92
13	4	16	51	16	32	89	28	48	168	53	76
14	4	48	52	16	64	**90**	28	80	196	62	72
15	4	80	53	16	96	91	29	12	200	64	00
16	5	12	54	17	28	92	29	44	220	70	40
17	5	44	55	17	60	93	29	76	224	71	68
18	5	76	56	17	92	94	30	08	256	81	92
19	6	08	57	18	24	95	30	40	280	89	60
20	6	40	58	18	56	96*	30	72	300	96	00
21	6	72	59	18	88	97	31	04	365	116	80
22	7	04	**60***	19	20	98	31	36	400	128	00
23	7	36	61	19	52	99	31	68	480	153	60
24*	7	68	62	19	84	**100**	32	00	500	160	00
25	8	00	63	20	16	101	32	32	516	165	12
26	8	32	64	20	48	102	32	64	560	179	20
27	8	64	65	20	80	103	32	96	600	192	00
28	8	96	66	21	12	104	33	28	625	200	00
29	9	28	67	21	44	105	33	60	640	204	80
30	9	60	68	21	76	106	33	92	700	224	00
31	9	92	69	22	08	107	34	24	750	240	00
32	10	24	**70**	22	40	108*	34	56	800	256	00
33	10	56	71	22	72	109	34	88	900	288	00

No.	£	p	No.	£	p	No.	£	p
1000	320	00	1760	563	20	6000	1920	00
1016	325	12	2000	640	00	7000	2240	00
1094	350	08	2240	716	80	7500	2400	00
1120	358	40	2500	800	00	10000	3200	00
1250	400	00	3000	960	00	15000	4800	00
1500	480	00	4000	1280	00	20000	6400	00
1750	560	00	5000	1600	00	30000	9600	00

No.	£	p	No.	£	p	No.	£	p	No.	£	p
1/16	0	02	34	11	05	72*	23	40	110	35	75
1/8	0	04	35	11	37½	73	23	72½	111	36	07½
1/4	0	08	36*	11	70	74	24	05	112	36	40
1/2	0	16½	37	12	02½	75	24	37½	113	36	72½
3/4	0	24½	38	12	35	76	24	70	114	37	05
1½	0	49	39	12	67½	77	25	02½	115	37	37½
2	0	65	40	13	00	78	25	35	116	37	70
3	0	97½	41	13	32½	79	25	67½	117	38	02½
4	1	30	42	13	65	80	26	00	118	38	35
5	1	62½	43	13	97½	81	26	32½	119	38	67½
6	1	95	44	14	30	82	26	65	120*	39	00
7	2	27½	45	14	62½	83	26	97½	128	41	60
8	2	60	46	14	95	84*	27	30	130	42	25
9	2	92½	47	15	27½	85	27	62½	140	45	50
10	3	25	48*	15	60	86	27	95	144*	46	80
11	3	57½	49	15	92½	87	28	27½	150	48	75
12*	3	90	50	16	25	88	28	60	156	50	70
13	4	22½	51	16	57½	89	28	92½	168	54	60
14	4	55	52	16	90	90	29	25	196	63	70
15	4	87½	53	17	22½	91	29	57½	200	65	00
16	5	20	54	17	55	92	29	90	220	71	50
17	5	52½	55	17	87½	93	30	22½	224	72	80
18	5	85	56	18	20	94	30	55	256	83	20
19	6	17½	57	18	52½	95	30	87½	280	91	00
20	6	50	58	18	85	96*	31	20	300	97	50
21	6	82½	59	19	17½	97	31	52½	365	118	62½
22	7	15	60*	19	50	98	31	85	400	130	00
23	7	47½	61	19	82½	99	32	17½	480	156	00
24*	7	80	62	20	15	100	32	50	500	162	50
25	8	12½	63	20	47½	101	32	82½	516	167	70
26	8	45	64	20	80	102	33	15	560	182	00
27	8	77½	65	21	12½	103	33	47½	600	195	00
28	9	10	66	21	45	104	33	80	625	203	12½
29	9	42½	67	21	77½	105	34	12½	640	208	00
30	9	75	68	22	10	106	34	45	700	227	50
31	10	07½	69	22	42½	107	34	77½	750	243	75
32	10	40	70	22	75	108*	35	10	800	260	00
33	10	72½	71	23	07½	109	35	42½	900	292	50

No.	£	p	No.	£	p	No.	£	p
1000	325	00	1760	572	00	6000	1950	00
1016	330	20	2000	650	00	7000	2275	00
1094	355	55	2240	728	00	7500	2437	50
1120	364	00	2500	812	50	10000	3250	00
1250	406	25	3000	975	00	15000	4875	00
1500	487	50	4000	1300	00	20000	6500	00
1750	568	75	5000	1625	00	30000	9750	00

33p   £0·33

No.	£	p	No.	£	p	No.	£	p	No.	£	p
1/16	0	02	34	11	22	72*	23	76	110	36	30
1/8	0	04	35	11	55	73	24	09	111	36	63
1/4	0	08½	36*	11	88	74	24	42	112	36	96
1/2	0	16½	37	12	21	75	24	75	113	37	29
3/4	0	25	38	12	54	76	25	08	114	37	62
1½	0	49½	39	12	87	77	25	41	115	37	95
2	0	66	40	13	20	78	25	74	116	38	28
3	0	99	41	13	53	79	26	07	117	38	61
4	1	32	42	13	86	80	26	40	118	38	94
5	1	65	43	14	19	81	26	73	119	39	27
6	1	98	44	14	52	82	27	06	120*	39	60
7	2	31	45	14	85	83	27	39	128	42	24
8	2	64	46	15	18	84*	27	72	130	42	90
9	2	97	47	15	51	85	28	05	140	46	20
10	3	30	48*	15	84	86	28	38	144*	47	52
11	3	63	49	16	17	87	28	71	150	49	50
12*	3	96	50	16	50	88	29	04	156	51	48
13	4	29	51	16	83	89	29	37	168	55	44
14	4	62	52	17	16	90	29	70	196	64	68
15	4	95	53	17	49	91	30	03	200	66	00
16	5	28	54	17	82	92	30	36	220	72	60
17	5	61	55	18	15	93	30	69	224	73	92
18	5	94	56	18	48	94	31	02	256	84	48
19	6	27	57	18	81	95	31	35	280	92	40
20	6	60	58	19	14	96*	31	68	300	99	00
21	6	93	59	19	47	97	32	01	365	120	45
22	7	26	60*	19	80	98	32	34	400	132	00
23	7	59	61	20	13	99	32	67	480	158	40
24*	7	92	62	20	46	100	33	00	500	165	00
25	8	25	63	20	79	101	33	33	516	170	28
26	8	58	64	21	12	102	33	66	560	184	80
27	8	91	65	21	45	103	33	99	600	198	00
28	9	24	66	21	78	104	34	32	625	206	25
29	9	57	67	22	11	105	34	65	640	211	20
30	9	90	68	22	44	106	34	98	700	231	00
31	10	23	69	22	77	107	35	31	750	247	50
32	10	56	70	23	10	108*	35	64	800	264	00
33	10	89	71	23	43	109	35	97	900	297	00

No.	£	p	No.	£	p	No.	£	p
1000	330	00	1760	580	80	6000	1980	00
1016	335	28	2000	660	00	7000	2310	00
1094	361	02	2240	739	20	7500	2475	00
1120	369	60	2500	825	00	10000	3300	00
1250	412	50	3000	990	00	15000	4950	00
1500	495	00	4000	1320	00	20000	6600	00
1750	577	50	5000	1650	00	30000	9900	00

34p   £0·34

No.	£	p	No.	£	p	No.	£	p	No.	£	p
$\frac{1}{16}$	0	02	34	11	56	72*	24	48	110	37	40
$\frac{1}{8}$	0	04½	35	11	90	73	24	82	111	37	74
$\frac{3}{16}$	0	06½	36*	12	24	74	25	16	112	38	08
$\frac{1}{4}$	0	08½	37	12	58	75	25	50	113	38	42
$\frac{1}{2}$	0	17	38	12	92	76	25	84	114	38	76
$\frac{3}{4}$	0	25½	39	13	26	77	26	18	115	39	10
1½	0	51	40	13	60	78	26	52	116	39	44
2	0	68	41	13	94	79	26	86	117	39	78
3	1	02	42	14	28	80	27	20	118	40	12
4	1	36	43	14	62	81	27	54	119	40	46
5	1	70	44	14	96	82	27	88	120*	40	80
6	2	04	45	15	30	83	28	22	128	43	52
7	2	38	46	15	64	84*	28	56	130	44	20
8	2	72	47	15	98	85	28	90	140	47	60
9	3	06	48*	16	32	86	29	24	144*	48	96
10	3	40	49	16	66	87	29	58	150	51	00
11	3	74	50	17	00	88	29	92	156	53	04
12*	4	08	51	17	34	89	30	26	168	57	12
13	4	42	52	17	68	90	30	60	196	66	64
14	4	76	53	18	02	91	30	94	200	68	00
15	5	10	54	18	36	92	31	28	220	74	80
16	5	44	55	18	70	93	31	62	224	76	16
17	5	78	56	19	04	94	31	96	256	87	04
18	6	12	57	19	38	95	32	30	280	95	20
19	6	46	58	19	72	96*	32	64	300	102	00
20	6	80	59	20	06	97	32	98	365	124	10
21	7	14	60*	20	40	98	33	32	400	136	00
22	7	48	61	20	74	99	33	66	480	163	20
23	7	82	62	21	08	100	34	00	500	170	00
24*	8	16	63	21	42	101	34	34	516	175	44
25	8	50	64	21	76	102	34	68	560	190	40
26	8	84	65	22	10	103	35	02	600	204	00
27	9	18	66	22	44	104	35	36	625	212	50
28	9	52	67	22	78	105	35	70	640	217	60
29	9	86	68	23	12	106	36	04	700	238	00
30	10	20	69	23	46	107	36	38	750	255	00
31	10	54	70	23	80	108*	36	72	800	272	00
32	10	88	71	24	14	109	37	06	900	306	00
33	11	22									

No.	£	p	No.	£	p	No.	£	p
1000	340	00	1760	598	40	6000	2040	00
1016	345	44	2000	680	00	7000	2380	00
1094	371	96	2240	761	60	7500	2550	00
1120	380	80	2500	850	00	10000	3400	00
1250	425	00	3000	1020	00	15000	5100	00
1500	510	00	4000	1360	00	20000	6800	00
1750	595	00	5000	1700	00	30000	10200	00

No.	£	p	No.	£	p	No.	£	p	No.	£	p
$\frac{1}{16}$	0	02	34	11	90	72*	25	20	110	38	50
$\frac{1}{8}$	0	04½	35	12	25	73	25	55	111	38	85
$\frac{1}{4}$	0	09	36*	12	60	74	25	90	112	39	20
$\frac{1}{2}$	0	17½	37	12	95	75	26	25	113	39	55
$\frac{3}{4}$	0	26½	38	13	30	76	26	60	114	39	90
1½	0	52½	39	13	65	77	26	95	115	40	25
2	0	70	40	14	00	78	27	30	116	40	60
3	1	05	41	14	35	79	27	65	117	40	95
4	1	40	42	14	70	80	28	00	118	41	30
5	1	75	43	15	05	81	28	35	119	41	65
6	2	10	44	15	40	82	28	70	120*	42	00
7	2	45	45	15	75	83	29	05	128	44	80
8	2	80	46	16	10	84*	29	40	130	45	50
9	3	15	47	16	45	85	29	75	140	49	00
10	3	50	48*	16	80	86	30	10	144*	50	40
11	3	85	49	17	15	87	30	45	150	52	50
12*	4	20	50	17	50	88	30	80	156	54	60
13	4	55	51	17	85	89	31	15	168	58	80
14	4	90	52	18	20	90	31	50	196	68	60
15	5	25	53	18	55	91	31	85	200	70	00
16	5	60	54	18	90	92	32	20	220	77	00
17	5	95	55	19	25	93	32	55	224	78	40
18	6	30	56	19	60	94	32	90	256	89	60
19	6	65	57	19	95	95	33	25	280	98	00
20	7	00	58	20	30	96*	33	60	300	105	00
21	7	35	59	20	65	97	33	95	365	127	75
22	7	70	60*	21	00	98	34	30	400	140	00
23	8	05	61	21	35	99	34	65	480	168	00
24*	8	40	62	21	70	100	35	00	500	175	00
25	8	75	63	22	05	101	35	35	516	180	60
26	9	10	64	22	40	102	35	70	560	196	00
27	9	45	65	22	75	103	36	05	600	210	00
28	9	80	66	23	10	104	36	40	625	218	75
29	10	15	67	23	45	105	36	75	640	224	00
30	10	50	68	23	80	106	37	10	700	245	00
31	10	85	69	24	15	107	37	45	750	262	50
32	11	20	70	24	50	108*	37	80	800	280	00
33	11	55	71	24	85	109	38	15	900	315	00

No.	£	p	No.	£	p	No.	£	p
1000	350	00	1760	616	00	6000	2100	00
1016	355	60	2000	700	00	7000	2450	00
1094	382	90	2240	784	00	7500	2625	00
1120	392	00	2500	875	00	10000	3500	00
1250	437	50	3000	1050	00	15000	5250	00
1500	525	00	4000	1400	00	20000	7000	00
1750	612	50	5000	1750	00	30000	10500	00

36p
£0·36

No.	£	p	No.	£	p	No.	£	p	No.	£	p
1/16	0	02½	34	12	24	72*	25	92	110	39	60
1/8	0	04½	35	12	60	73	26	28	111	39	96
1/4	0	09	36*	12	96	74	26	64	112	40	32
1/2	0	18	37	13	32	75	27	00	113	40	68
3/4	0	27	38	13	68	76	27	36	114	41	04
1½	0	54	39	14	04	77	27	72	115	41	40
2	0	72	40	14	40	78	28	08	116	41	76
3	1	08	41	14	76	79	28	44	117	42	12
4	1	44	42	15	12	80	28	80	118	42	48
5	1	80	43	15	48	81	29	16	119	42	84
6	2	16	44	15	84	82	29	52	120*	43	20
7	2	52	45	16	20	83	29	88	128	46	08
8	2	88	46	16	56	84*	30	24	130	46	80
9	3	24	47	16	92	85	30	60	140	50	40
10	3	60	48*	17	28	86	30	96	144*	51	84
11	3	96	49	17	64	87	31	32	150	54	00
12*	4	32	50	18	00	88	31	68	156	56	16
13	4	68	51	18	36	89	32	04	168	60	48
14	5	04	52	18	72	90	32	40	196	70	56
15	5	40	53	19	08	91	32	76	200	72	00
16	5	76	54	19	44	92	33	12	220	79	20
17	6	12	55	19	80	93	33	48	224	80	64
18	6	48	56	20	16	94	33	84	256	92	16
19	6	84	57	20	52	95	34	20	280	100	80
20	7	20	58	20	88	96*	34	56	300	108	00
21	7	56	59	21	24	97	34	92	365	131	40
22	7	92	60*	21	60	98	35	28	400	144	00
23	8	28	61	21	96	99	35	64	480	172	80
24*	8	64	62	22	32	100	36	00	500	180	00
25	9	00	63	22	68	101	36	36	516	185	76
26	9	36	64	23	04	102	36	72	560	201	60
27	9	72	65	23	40	103	37	08	600	216	00
28	10	08	66	23	76	104	37	44	625	225	00
29	10	44	67	24	12	105	37	80	640	230	40
30	10	80	68	24	48	106	38	16	700	252	00
31	11	16	69	24	84	107	38	52	750	270	00
32	11	52	70	25	20	108*	38	88	800	288	00
33	11	88	71	25	56	109	39	24	900	324	00

No.	£	p	No.	£	p	No.	£	p
1000	360	00	1760	633	60	6000	2160	00
1016	365	76	2000	720	00	7000	2520	00
1094	393	84	2240	806	40	7500	2700	00
1120	403	20	2500	900	00	10000	3600	00
1250	450	00	3000	1080	00	15000	5400	00
1500	540	00	4000	1440	00	20000	7200	00
1750	630	00	5000	1800	00	30000	10800	00

No.	£	p	No.	£	p	No.	£	p	No.	£	p
1/16	0	02½	34	12	58	72*	26	64	110	40	70
1/8	0	04½	35	12	95	73	27	01	111	41	07
1/4	0	09½	36*	13	32	74	27	38	112	41	44
1/2	0	18½	37	13	69	75	27	75	113	41	81
3/4	0	28	38	14	06	76	28	12	114	42	18
1½	0	55½	39	14	43	77	28	49	115	42	55
2	0	74	40	14	80	78	28	86	116	42	92
3	1	11	41	15	17	79	29	23	117	43	29
4	1	48	42	15	54	80	29	60	118	43	66
5	1	85	43	15	91	81	29	97	119	44	03
6	2	22	44	16	28	82	30	34	120*	44	40
7	2	59	45	16	65	83	30	71	128	47	36
8	2	96	46	17	02	84*	31	08	130	48	10
9	3	33	47	17	39	85	31	45	140	51	80
10	3	70	48*	17	76	86	31	82	144*	53	28
11	4	07	49	18	13	87	32	19	150	55	50
12*	4	44	50	18	50	88	32	56	156	57	72
13	4	81	51	18	87	89	32	93	168	62	16
14	5	18	52	19	24	90	33	30	196	72	52
15	5	55	53	19	61	91	33	67	200	74	00
16	5	92	54	19	98	92	34	04	220	81	40
17	6	29	55	20	35	93	34	41	224	82	88
18	6	66	56	20	72	94	34	78	256	94	72
19	7	03	57	21	09	95	35	15	280	103	60
20	7	40	58	21	46	96*	35	52	300	111	00
21	7	77	59	21	83	97	35	89	365	135	05
22	8	14	60*	22	20	98	36	26	400	148	00
23	8	51	61	22	57	99	36	63	480	177	60
24*	8	88	62	22	94	100	37	00	500	185	00
25	9	25	63	23	31	101	37	37	516	190	92
26	9	62	64	23	68	102	37	74	560	207	20
27	9	99	65	24	05	103	38	11	600	222	00
28	10	36	66	24	42	104	38	48	625	231	25
29	10	73	67	24	79	105	38	85	640	236	80
30	11	10	68	25	16	106	39	22	700	259	00
31	11	47	69	25	53	107	39	59	750	277	50
32	11	84	70	25	90	108*	39	96	800	296	00
33	12	21	71	26	27	109	40	33	900	333	00

No.	£	p	No.	£	p	No.	£	p
1000	370	00	1760	651	20	6000	2220	00
1016	375	92	2000	740	00	7000	2590	00
1094	404	78	2240	828	80	7500	2775	00
1120	414	40	2500	925	00	10000	3700	00
1250	462	50	3000	1110	00	15000	5550	00
1500	555	00	4000	1480	00	20000	7400	00
1750	647	50	5000	1850	00	30000	11100	00

37½p £0·375

No.	£	p	No.	£	p	No.	£	p	No.	£	p
1/16	0	02½	34	12	75	72*	27	00	110	41	25
1/8	0	04½	35	13	12½	73	27	37½	111	41	62½
1/4	0	09½	36*	13	50	74	27	75	112	42	00
1/2	0	19	37	13	87½	75	28	12½	113	42	37½
3/4	0	28	38	14	25	76	28	50	114	42	75
1½	0	56½	39	14	62½	77	28	87½	115	43	12½
2	0	75	**40**	15	00	78	29	25	116	43	50
3	1	12½	41	15	37½	79	29	62½	117	43	87½
4	1	50	42	15	75	**80**	30	00	118	44	25
5	1	87½	43	16	12½	81	30	37½	119	44	62½
6	2	25	44	16	50	82	30	75	120*	45	00
7	2	62½	45	16	87½	83	31	12½	128	48	00
8	3	00	46	17	25	84*	31	50	130	48	75
9	3	37½	47	17	62½	85	31	87½	140	52	50
10	3	75	48*	18	00	86	32	25	144*	54	00
11	4	12½	49	18	37½	87	32	62½	150	56	25
12*	4	50	**50**	18	75	88	33	00	156	58	50
13	4	87½	51	19	12½	89	33	37½	168	63	00
14	5	25	52	19	50	**90**	33	75	196	73	50
15	5	62½	53	19	87½	91	34	12½	200	75	00
16	6	00	54	20	25	92	34	50	220	82	50
17	6	37½	55	20	62½	93	34	87½	224	84	00
18	6	75	56	21	00	94	35	25	256	96	00
19	7	12½	57	21	37½	95	35	62½	280	105	00
20	7	50	58	21	75	96*	36	00	300	112	50
21	7	87½	59	22	12½	97	36	37½	365	136	87½
22	8	25	**60***	22	50	98	36	75	400	150	00
23	8	62½	61	22	87½	99	37	12½	480	180	00
24*	9	00	62	23	25	**100**	37	50	500	187	50
25	9	37½	63	23	62½	101	37	87½	516	193	50
26	9	75	64	24	00	102	38	25	560	210	00
27	10	12½	65	24	37½	103	38	62½	600	225	00
28	10	50	66	24	75	104	39	00	625	234	37½
29	10	87½	67	25	12½	105	39	37½	640	240	00
30	11	25	68	25	50	106	39	75	700	262	50
31	11	62½	69	25	87½	107	40	12½	750	281	25
32	12	00	**70**	26	25	108*	40	50	800	300	00
33	12	37½	71	26	62½	109	40	87½	900	337	50

No.	£	p	No.	£	p	No.	£	p
1000	375	00	1760	660	00	6000	2250	00
1016	381	00	2000	750	00	7000	2625	00
1094	410	25	2240	840	00	7500	2812	50
1120	420	00	2500	937	50	10000	3750	00
1250	468	75	3000	1125	00	15000	5625	00
1500	562	50	4000	1500	00	20000	7500	00
1750	656	25	5000	1875	00	30000	11250	00

No.	£	p	No.	£	p	No.	£	p	No.	£	p
$\frac{1}{16}$	0	02½	34	12	92	72*	27	36	110	41	80
$\frac{1}{8}$	0	05	35	13	30	73	27	74	111	42	18
$\frac{1}{4}$	0	09½	36*	13	68	74	28	12	112	42	56
$\frac{1}{2}$	0	19	37	14	06	75	28	50	113	42	94
$\frac{3}{4}$	0	28½	38	14	44	76	28	88	114	43	32
1½	0	57	39	14	82	77	29	26	115	43	70
2	0	76	40	15	20	78	29	64	116	44	08
3	1	14	41	15	58	79	30	02	117	44	46
4	1	52	42	15	96	80	30	40	118	44	84
5	1	90	43	16	34	81	30	78	119	45	22
6	2	28	44	16	72	82	31	16	120*	45	60
7	2	66	45	17	10	83	31	54	128	48	64
8	3	04	46	17	48	84*	31	92	130	49	40
9	3	42	47	17	86	85	32	30	140	53	20
10	3	80	48*	18	24	86	32	68	144*	54	72
11	4	18	49	18	62	87	33	06	150	57	00
12*	4	56	50	19	00	88	33	44	156	59	28
13	4	94	51	19	38	89	33	82	168	63	84
14	5	32	52	19	76	90	34	20	196	74	48
15	5	70	53	20	14	91	34	58	200	76	00
16	6	08	54	20	52	92	34	96	220	83	60
17	6	46	55	20	90	93	35	34	224	85	12
18	6	84	56	21	28	94	35	72	256	97	28
19	7	22	57	21	66	95	36	10	280	106	40
20	7	60	58	22	04	96*	36	48	300	114	00
21	7	98	59	22	42	97	36	86	365	138	70
22	8	36	60*	22	80	98	37	24	400	152	00
23	8	74	61	23	18	99	37	62	480	182	40
24*	9	12	62	23	56	100	38	00	500	190	00
25	9	50	63	23	94	101	38	38	516	196	08
26	9	88	64	24	32	102	38	76	560	212	80
27	10	26	65	24	70	103	39	14	600	228	00
28	10	64	66	25	08	104	39	52	625	237	50
29	11	02	67	25	46	105	39	90	640	243	20
30	11	40	68	25	84	106	40	28	700	266	00
31	11	78	69	26	22	107	40	66	750	285	00
32	12	16	70	26	60	108*	41	04	800	304	00
33	12	54	71	26	98	109	41	42	900	342	00

No.	£	p	No.	£	p	No.	£	p
1000	380	00	1760	668	80	6000	2280	00
1016	386	08	2000	760	00	7000	2660	00
1094	415	72	2240	851	20	7500	2850	00
1120	425	60	2500	950	00	10000	3800	00
1250	475	00	3000	1140	00	15000	5700	00
1500	570	00	4000	1520	00	20000	7600	00
1750	665	00	5000	1900	00	30000	11400	00

No.	£	p	No.	£	p	No.	£	p	No.	£	p
1/16	0	02½	34	13	26	72*	28	08	110	42	90
1/8	0	05	35	13	65	73	28	47	111	43	29
1/4	0	10	36*	14	04	74	28	86	112	43	68
1/2	0	19½	37	14	43	75	29	25	113	44	07
3/4	0	29½	38	14	82	76	29	64	114	44	46
1½	0	58½	39	15	21	77	30	03	115	44	85
2	0	78	40	15	60	78	30	42	116	45	24
3	1	17	41	15	99	79	30	81	117	45	63
4	1	56	42	16	38	80	31	20	118	46	02
5	1	95	43	16	77	81	31	59	119	46	41
6	2	34	44	17	16	82	31	98	120*	46	80
7	2	73	45	17	55	83	32	37	128	49	92
8	3	12	46	17	94	84*	32	76	130	50	70
9	3	51	47	18	33	85	33	15	140	54	60
10	3	90	48*	18	72	86	33	54	144*	56	16
11	4	29	49	19	11	87	33	93	150	58	50
12*	4	68	50	19	50	88	34	32	156	60	84
13	5	07	51	19	89	89	34	71	168	65	52
14	5	46	52	20	28	90	35	10	196	76	44
15	5	85	53	20	67	91	35	49	200	78	00
16	6	24	54	21	06	92	35	88	220	85	80
17	6	63	55	21	45	93	36	27	224	87	36
18	7	02	56	21	84	94	36	66	256	99	84
19	7	41	57	22	23	95	37	05	280	109	20
20	7	80	58	22	62	96*	37	44	300	117	00
21	8	19	59	23	01	97	37	83	365	142	35
22	8	58	60*	23	40	98	38	22	400	156	00
23	8	97	61	23	79	99	38	61	480	187	20
24*	9	36	62	24	18	100	39	00	500	195	00
25	9	75	63	24	57	101	39	39	516	201	24
26	10	14	64	24	96	102	39	78	560	218	40
27	10	53	65	25	35	103	40	17	600	234	00
28	10	92	66	25	74	104	40	56	625	243	75
29	11	31	67	26	13	105	40	95	640	249	60
30	11	70	68	26	52	106	41	34	700	273	00
31	12	09	69	26	91	107	41	73	750	292	50
32	12	48	70	27	30	108*	42	12	800	312	00
33	12	87	71	27	69	109	42	51	900	351	00

No.	£	p	No.	£	p	No.	£	p
1000	390	00	1760	686	40	6000	2340	00
1016	396	24	2000	780	00	7000	2730	00
1094	426	66	2240	873	60	7500	2925	00
1120	436	80	2500	975	00	10000	3900	00
1250	487	50	3000	1170	00	15000	5850	00
1500	585	00	4000	1560	00	20000	7800	00
1750	682	50	5000	1950	00	30000	11700	00

No.	£	p	No.	£	p	No.	£	p	No.	£	p
$\frac{1}{16}$	0	02½	34	13	60	72*	28	80	110	44	00
$\frac{1}{8}$	0	05	35	14	00	73	29	20	111	44	40
$\frac{1}{4}$	0	10	36*	14	40	74	29	60	112	44	80
$\frac{1}{2}$	0	20	37	14	80	75	30	00	113	45	20
$\frac{3}{4}$	0	30	38	15	20	76	30	40	114	45	60
1½	0	60	39	15	60	77	30	80	115	46	00
2	0	80	40	16	00	78	31	20	116	46	40
3	1	20	41	16	40	79	31	60	117	46	80
4	1	60	42	16	80	80	32	00	118	47	20
5	2	00	43	17	20	81	32	40	119	47	60
6	2	40	44	17	60	82	32	80	120*	48	00
7	2	80	45	18	00	83	33	20	128	51	20
8	3	20	46	18	40	84*	33	60	130	52	00
9	3	60	47	18	80	85	34	00	140	56	00
10	4	00	48*	19	20	86	34	40	144*	57	60
11	4	40	49	19	60	87	34	80	150	60	00
12*	4	80	50	20	00	88	35	20	156	62	40
13	5	20	51	20	40	89	35	60	168	67	20
14	5	60	52	20	80	90	36	00	196	78	40
15	6	00	53	21	20	91	36	40	200	80	00
16	6	40	54	21	60	92	36	80	220	88	00
17	6	80	55	22	00	93	37	20	224	89	60
18	7	20	56	22	40	94	37	60	256	102	40
19	7	60	57	22	80	95	38	00	280	112	00
20	8	00	58	23	20	96*	38	40	300	120	00
21	8	40	59	23	60	97	38	80	365	146	00
22	8	80	60*	24	00	98	39	20	400	160	00
23	9	20	61	24	40	99	39	60	480	192	00
24*	9	60	62	24	80	100	40	00	500	200	00
25	10	00	63	25	20	101	40	40	516	206	40
26	10	40	64	25	60	102	40	80	560	224	00
27	10	80	65	26	00	103	41	20	600	240	00
28	11	20	66	26	40	104	41	60	625	250	00
29	11	60	67	26	80	105	42	00	640	256	00
30	12	00	68	27	20	106	42	40	700	280	00
31	12	40	69	27	60	107	42	80	750	300	00
32	12	80	70	28	00	108*	43	20	800	320	00
33	13	20	71	28	40	109	43	60	900	360	00

No.	£	p	No.	£	p	No.	£	p
1000	400	00	1760	704	00	6000	2400	00
1016	406	40	2000	800	00	7000	2800	00
1094	437	60	2240	896	00	7500	3000	00
1120	448	00	2500	1000	00	10000	4000	00
1250	500	00	3000	1200	00	15000	6000	00
1500	600	00	4000	1600	00	20000	8000	00
1750	700	00	5000	2000	00	30000	12000	00

No.	£	p	No.	£	p	No.	£	p	No.	£	p
$\frac{1}{16}$	0	02½	34	13	94	72*	29	52	110	45	10
$\frac{1}{8}$	0	05	35	14	35	73	29	93	111	45	51
$\frac{1}{4}$	0	10½	36*	14	76	74	30	34	112	45	92
$\frac{1}{2}$	0	20½	37	15	17	75	30	75	113	46	33
$\frac{3}{4}$	0	31	38	15	58	76	31	16	114	46	74
$1\frac{1}{2}$	0	61½	39	15	99	77	31	57	115	47	15
2	0	82	**40**	16	40	78	31	98	116	47	56
3	1	23	41	16	81	79	32	39	117	47	97
4	1	64	42	17	22	**80**	32	80	118	48	38
5	2	05	43	17	63	81	33	21	119	48	79
6	2	46	44	18	04	82	33	62	120*	49	20
7	2	87	45	18	45	83	34	03	128	52	48
8	3	28	46	18	86	84*	34	44	130	53	30
9	3	69	47	19	27	85	34	85	140	57	40
10	4	10	48*	19	68	86	35	26	144*	59	04
11	4	51	49	20	09	87	35	67	150	61	50
12*	4	92	**50**	20	50	88	36	08	156	63	96
13	5	33	51	20	91	89	36	49	168	68	88
14	5	74	52	21	32	**90**	36	90	196	80	36
15	6	15	53	21	73	91	37	31	200	82	00
16	6	56	54	22	14	92	37	72	220	90	20
17	6	97	55	22	55	93	38	13	224	91	84
18	7	38	56	22	96	94	38	54	256	104	96
19	7	79	57	23	37	95	38	95	280	114	80
20	8	20	58	23	78	96*	39	36	300	123	00
21	8	61	59	24	19	97	39	77	365	149	65
22	9	02	**60***	24	60	98	40	18	400	164	00
23	9	43	61	25	01	99	40	59	480	196	80
24*	9	84	62	25	42	**100**	41	00	500	205	00
25	10	25	63	25	83	101	41	41	516	211	56
26	10	66	64	26	24	102	41	82	560	229	60
27	11	07	65	26	65	103	42	23	600	246	00
28	11	48	66	27	06	104	42	64	625	256	25
29	11	89	67	27	47	105	43	05	640	262	40
30	12	30	68	27	88	106	43	46	700	287	00
31	12	71	69	28	29	107	43	87	750	307	50
32	13	12	**70**	28	70	108*	44	28	800	328	00
33	13	53	71	29	11	109	44	69	900	369	00

No.	£	p	No.	£	p	No.	£	p
1000	410	00	1760	721	60	6000	2460	00
1016	416	56	2000	820	00	7000	2870	00
1094	448	54	2240	918	40	7500	3075	00
1120	459	20	2500	1025	00	10000	4100	00
1250	512	50	3000	1230	00	15000	6150	00
1500	615	00	4000	1640	00	20000	8200	00
1750	717	50	5000	2050	00	30000	12300	00

No.	£	p	No.	£	p	No.	£	p	No.	£	p
1/16	0	02½	34	14	28	72*	30	24	110	46	20
1/8	0	05½	35	14	70	73	30	66	111	46	62
1/4	0	10½	36*	15	12	74	31	08	112	47	04
1/2	0	21	37	15	54	75	31	50	113	47	46
3/4	0	31½	38	15	96	76	31	92	114	47	88
1½	0	63	39	16	38	77	32	34	115	48	30
2	0	84	**40**	16	80	78	32	76	116	48	72
3	1	26	41	17	22	79	33	18	117	49	14
4	1	68	42	17	64	**80**	33	60	118	49	56
5	2	10	43	18	06	81	34	02	119	49	98
6	2	52	44	18	48	82	34	44	120*	50	40
7	2	94	45	18	90	83	34	86	128	53	76
8	3	36	46	19	32	84*	35	28	130	54	60
9	3	78	47	19	74	85	35	70	140	58	80
10	4	20	48*	20	16	86	36	12	144*	60	48
11	4	62	49	20	58	87	36	54	150	63	00
12*	5	04	**50**	21	00	88	36	96	156	65	52
13	5	46	51	21	42	89	37	38	168	70	56
14	5	88	52	21	84	**90**	37	80	196	82	32
15	6	30	53	22	26	91	38	22	200	84	00
16	6	72	54	22	68	92	38	64	220	92	40
17	7	14	55	23	10	93	39	06	224	94	08
18	7	56	56	23	52	94	39	48	256	107	52
19	7	98	57	23	94	95	39	90	280	117	60
20	8	40	58	24	36	96*	40	32	300	126	00
21	8	82	59	24	78	97	40	74	365	153	30
22	9	24	60*	25	20	98	41	16	400	168	00
23	9	66	61	25	62	99	41	58	480	201	60
24*	10	08	62	26	04	**100**	42	00	500	210	00
25	10	50	63	26	46	101	42	42	516	216	72
26	10	92	64	26	88	102	42	84	560	235	20
27	11	34	65	27	30	103	43	26	600	252	00
28	11	76	66	27	72	104	43	68	625	262	50
29	12	18	67	28	14	105	44	10	640	268	80
30	12	60	68	28	56	106	44	52	700	294	00
31	13	02	69	28	98	107	44	94	750	315	00
32	13	44	**70**	29	40	108*	45	36	800	336	00
33	13	86	71	29	82	109	45	78	900	378	00

No.	£	p	No.	£	p	No.	£	p
1000	420	00	1760	739	20	6000	2520	00
1016	426	72	2000	840	00	7000	2940	00
1094	459	48	2240	940	80	7500	3150	00
1120	470	40	2500	1050	00	10000	4200	00
1250	525	00	3000	1260	00	15000	6300	00
1500	630	00	4000	1680	00	20000	8400	00
1750	735	00	5000	2100	00	30000	12600	00

No.	£	p	No.	£	p	No.	£	p	No.	£	p
1/16	0	02½	34	14	45	72*	30	60	110	46	75
⅛	0	05½	35	14	87½	73	31	02½	111	47	17½
¼	0	10½	36*	15	30	74	31	45	112	47	60
½	0	21½	37	15	72½	75	31	87½	113	48	02½
¾	0	32	38	16	15	76	32	30	114	48	45
1½	0	64	39	16	57½	77	32	72½	115	48	87½
2	0	85	**40**	17	00	78	33	15	116	49	30
3	1	27½	41	17	42½	79	33	57½	117	49	72½
4	1	70	42	17	85	**80**	34	00	118	50	15
5	2	12½	43	18	27½	81	34	42½	119	50	57½
6	2	55	44	18	70	82	34	85	120*	51	00
7	2	97½	45	19	12½	83	35	27½	128	54	40
8	3	40	46	19	55	84*	35	70	130	55	25
9	3	82½	47	19	97½	85	36	12½	140	59	50
10	4	25	48*	20	40	86	36	55	144*	61	20
11	4	67½	49	20	82½	87	36	97½	150	63	75
12*	5	10	**50**	21	25	88	37	40	156	66	30
13	5	52½	51	21	67½	89	37	82½	168	71	40
14	5	95	52	22	10	**90**	38	25	196	83	30
15	6	37½	53	22	52½	91	38	67½	200	85	00
16	6	80	54	22	95	92	39	10	220	93	50
17	7	22½	55	23	37½	93	39	52½	224	95	20
18	7	65	56	23	80	94	39	95	256	108	80
19	8	07½	57	24	22½	95	40	37½	280	119	00
20	8	50	58	24	65	96*	40	80	300	127	50
21	8	92½	59	25	07½	97	41	22½	365	155	12½
22	9	35	60*	25	50	98	41	65	400	170	00
23	9	77½	61	25	92½	99	42	07½	480	204	00
24*	10	20	62	26	35	**100**	42	50	500	212	50
25	10	62½	63	26	77½	101	42	92½	516	219	30
26	11	05	64	27	20	102	43	35	560	238	00
27	11	47½	65	27	62½	103	43	77½	600	255	00
28	11	90	66	28	05	104	44	20	625	265	62½
29	12	32½	67	28	47½	105	44	62½	640	272	00
30	12	75	68	28	90	106	45	05	700	297	50
31	13	17½	69	29	32½	107	45	47½	750	318	75
32	13	60	**70**	29	75	108*	45	90	800	340	00
33	14	02½	71	30	17½	109	46	32½	900	382	50

No.	£	p	No.	£	p	No.	£	p
1000	425	00	1760	748	00	6000	2550	00
1016	431	80	2000	850	00	7000	2975	00
1094	464	95	2240	952	00	7500	3187	50
1120	476	00	2500	1062	50	10000	4250	00
1250	531	25	3000	1275	00	15000	6375	00
1500	637	50	4000	1700	00	20000	8500	00
1750	743	75	5000	2125	00	30000	12750	00

No.	£	p	No.	£	p	No.	£	p	No.	£	p
1/16	0	02½	34	14	62	72*	30	96	110	47	30
1/8	0	05½	35	15	05	73	31	39	111	47	73
1/4	0	11	36*	15	48	74	31	82	112	48	16
1/2	0	21½	37	15	91	75	32	25	113	48	59
3/4	0	32½	38	16	34	76	32	68	114	49	02
1½	0	64½	39	16	77	77	33	11	115	49	45
2	0	86	40	17	20	78	33	54	116	49	88
3	1	29	41	17	63	79	33	97	117	50	31
4	1	72	42	18	06	80	34	40	118	50	74
5	2	15	43	18	49	81	34	83	119	51	17
6	2	58	44	18	92	82	35	26	120*	51	60
7	3	01	45	19	35	83	35	69	128	55	04
8	3	44	46	19	78	84*	36	12	130	55	90
9	3	87	47	20	21	85	36	55	140	60	20
10	4	30	48*	20	64	86	36	98	144*	61	92
11	4	73	49	21	07	87	37	41	150	64	50
12*	5	16	50	21	50	88	37	84	156	67	08
13	5	59	51	21	93	89	38	27	168	72	24
14	6	02	52	22	36	90	38	70	196	84	28
15	6	45	53	22	79	91	39	13	200	86	00
16	6	88	54	23	22	92	39	56	220	94	60
17	7	31	55	23	65	93	39	99	224	96	32
18	7	74	56	24	08	94	40	42	256	110	08
19	8	17	57	24	51	95	40	85	280	120	40
20	8	60	58	24	94	96*	41	28	300	129	00
21	9	03	59	25	37	97	41	71	365	156	95
22	9	46	60*	25	80	98	42	14	400	172	00
23	9	89	61	26	23	99	42	57	480	206	40
24*	10	32	62	26	66	100	43	00	500	215	00
25	10	75	63	27	09	101	43	43	516	221	88
26	11	18	64	27	52	102	43	86	560	240	80
27	11	61	65	27	95	103	44	29	600	258	00
28	12	04	66	28	38	104	44	72	625	268	75
29	12	47	67	28	81	105	45	15	640	275	20
30	12	90	68	29	24	106	45	58	700	301	00
31	13	33	69	29	67	107	46	01	750	322	50
32	13	76	70	30	10	108*	46	44	800	344	00
33	14	19	71	30	53	109	46	87	900	387	00

No.	£	p	No.	£	p	No.	£	p
1000	430	00	1760	756	80	6000	2580	00
1016	436	88	2000	860	00	7000	3010	00
1094	470	42	2240	963	20	7500	3225	00
1120	481	60	2500	1075	00	10000	4300	00
1250	537	50	3000	1290	00	15000	6450	00
1500	645	00	4000	1720	00	20000	8600	00
1750	752	50	5000	2150	00	30000	12900	00

No.	£	p	No.	£	p	No.	£	p	No.	£	p
1/16	0	03	34	14	96	72*	31	68	110	48	40
1/8	0	05½	35	15	40	73	32	12	111	48	84
1/4	0	11	36*	15	84	74	32	56	112	49	28
1/2	0	22	37	16	28	75	33	00	113	49	72
3/4	0	33	38	16	72	76	33	44	114	50	16
1½	0	66	39	17	16	77	33	88	115	50	60
2	0	88	40	17	60	78	34	32	116	51	04
3	1	32	41	18	04	79	34	76	117	51	48
4	1	76	42	18	48	80	35	20	118	51	92
5	2	20	43	18	92	81	35	64	119	52	36
6	2	64	44	19	36	82	36	08	120*	52	80
7	3	08	45	19	80	83	36	52	128	56	32
8	3	52	46	20	24	84*	36	96	130	57	20
9	3	96	47	20	68	85	37	40	140	61	60
10	4	40	48*	21	12	86	37	84	144*	63	36
11	4	84	49	21	56	87	38	28	150	66	00
12*	5	28	50	22	00	88	38	72	156	68	64
13	5	72	51	22	44	89	39	16	168	73	92
14	6	16	52	22	88	90	39	60	196	86	24
15	6	60	53	23	32	91	40	04	200	88	00
16	7	04	54	23	76	92	40	48	220	96	80
17	7	48	55	24	20	93	40	92	224	98	56
18	7	92	56	24	64	94	41	36	256	112	64
19	8	36	57	25	08	95	41	80	280	123	20
20	8	80	58	25	52	96*	42	24	300	132	00
21	9	24	59	25	96	97	42	68	365	160	60
22	9	68	60*	26	40	98	43	12	400	176	00
23	10	12	61	26	84	99	43	56	480	211	20
24*	10	56	62	27	28	100	44	00	500	220	00
25	11	00	63	27	72	101	44	44	516	227	04
26	11	44	64	28	16	102	44	88	560	246	40
27	11	88	65	28	60	103	45	32	600	264	00
28	12	32	66	29	04	104	45	76	625	275	00
29	12	76	67	29	48	105	46	20	640	281	60
30	13	20	68	29	92	106	46	64	700	308	00
31	13	64	69	30	36	107	47	08	750	330	00
32	14	08	70	30	80	108*	47	52	800	352	00
33	14	52	71	31	24	109	47	96	900	396	00

No.	£	p	No.	£	p	No.	£	p
1000	440	00	1760	774	40	6000	2640	00
1016	447	04	2000	880	00	7000	3080	00
1094	481	36	2240	985	60	7500	3300	00
1120	492	80	2500	1100	00	10000	4400	00
1250	550	00	3000	1320	00	15000	6600	00
1500	660	00	4000	1760	00	20000	8800	00
1750	770	00	5000	2200	00	30000	13200	00

No.	£	p	No.	£	p	No.	£	p	No.	£	p
$\frac{1}{16}$	0	03	34	15	30	72*	32	40	110	49	50
$\frac{1}{8}$	0	05½	35	15	75	73	32	85	111	49	95
$\frac{1}{4}$	0	11½	36*	16	20	74	33	30	112	50	40
$\frac{1}{2}$	0	22½	37	16	65	75	33	75	113	50	85
$\frac{3}{4}$	0	34	38	17	10	76	34	20	114	51	30
1½	0	67½	39	17	55	77	34	65	115	51	75
2	0	90	40	18	00	78	35	10	116	52	20
3	1	35	41	18	45	79	35	55	117	52	65
4	1	80	42	18	90	80	36	00	118	53	10
5	2	25	43	19	35	81	36	45	119	53	55
6	2	70	44	19	80	82	36	90	120*	54	00
7	3	15	45	20	25	83	37	35	128	57	60
8	3	60	46	20	70	84*	37	80	130	58	50
9	4	05	47	21	15	85	38	25	140	63	00
10	4	50	48*	21	60	86	38	70	144*	64	80
11	4	95	49	22	05	87	39	15	150	67	50
12*	5	40	50	22	50	88	39	60	156	70	20
13	5	85	51	22	95	89	40	05	168	75	60
14	6	30	52	23	40	90	40	50	196	88	20
15	6	75	53	23	85	91	40	95	200	90	00
16	7	20	54	24	30	92	41	40	220	99	00
17	7	65	55	24	75	93	41	85	224	100	80
18	8	10	56	25	20	94	42	30	256	115	20
19	8	55	57	25	65	95	42	75	280	126	00
20	9	00	58	26	10	96*	43	20	300	135	00
21	9	45	59	26	55	97	43	65	365	164	25
22	9	90	60*	27	00	98	44	10	400	180	00
23	10	35	61	27	45	99	44	55	480	216	00
24*	10	80	62	27	90	100	45	00	500	225	00
25	11	25	63	28	35	101	45	45	516	232	20
26	11	70	64	28	80	102	45	90	560	252	00
27	12	15	65	29	25	103	46	35	600	270	00
28	12	60	66	29	70	104	46	80	625	281	25
29	13	05	67	30	15	105	47	25	640	288	00
30	13	50	68	30	60	106	47	70	700	315	00
31	13	95	69	31	05	107	48	15	750	337	50
32	14	40	70	31	50	108*	48	60	800	360	00
33	14	85	71	31	95	109	49	05	900	405	00

No.	£	p	No.	£	p	No.	£	p
1000	450	00	1760	792	00	6000	2700	00
1016	457	20	2000	900	00	7000	3150	00
1094	492	30	2240	1008	00	7500	3375	00
1120	504	00	2500	1125	00	10000	4500	00
1250	562	50	3000	1350	00	15000	6750	00
1500	675	00	4000	1800	00	20000	9000	00
1750	787	50	5000	2250	00	30000	13500	00

No.	£	p	No.	£	p	No.	£	p	No.	£	p
1/16	0	03	34	15	64	72*	33	12	110	50	60
1/8	0	06	35	16	10	73	33	58	111	51	06
1/4	0	11½	36*	16	56	74	34	04	112	51	52
1/2	0	23	37	17	02	75	34	50	113	51	98
3/4	0	34½	38	17	48	76	34	96	114	52	44
1½	0	69	39	17	94	77	35	42	115	52	90
2	0	92	40	18	40	78	35	88	116	53	36
3	1	38	41	18	86	79	36	34	117	53	82
4	1	84	42	19	32	80	36	80	118	54	28
5	2	30	43	19	78	81	37	26	119	54	74
6	2	76	44	20	24	82	37	72	120*	55	20
7	3	22	45	20	70	83	38	18	128	58	88
8	3	68	46	21	16	84*	38	64	130	59	80
9	4	14	47	21	62	85	39	10	140	64	40
10	4	60	48*	22	08	86	39	56	144*	66	24
11	5	06	49	22	54	87	40	02	150	69	00
12*	5	52	50	23	00	88	40	48	156	71	76
13	5	98	51	23	46	89	40	94	168	77	28
14	6	44	52	23	92	90	41	40	196	90	16
15	6	90	53	24	38	91	41	86	200	92	00
16	7	36	54	24	84	92	42	32	220	101	20
17	7	82	55	25	30	93	42	78	224	103	04
18	8	28	56	25	76	94	43	24	256	117	76
19	8	74	57	26	22	95	43	70	280	128	80
20	9	20	58	26	68	96*	44	16	300	138	00
21	9	66	59	27	14	97	44	62	365	167	90
22	10	12	60*	27	60	98	45	08	400	184	00
23	10	58	61	28	06	99	45	54	480	220	80
24*	11	04	62	28	52	100	46	00	500	230	00
25	11	50	63	28	98	101	46	46	516	237	36
26	11	96	64	29	44	102	46	92	560	257	60
27	12	42	65	29	90	103	47	38	600	276	00
28	12	88	66	30	36	104	47	84	625	287	50
29	13	34	67	30	82	105	48	30	640	294	40
30	13	80	68	31	28	106	48	76	700	322	00
31	14	26	69	31	74	107	49	22	750	345	00
32	14	72	70	32	20	108*	49	68	800	368	00
33	15	18	71	32	66	109	50	14	900	414	00

No.	£	p	No.	£	p	No.	£	p
1000	460	00	1760	809	60	6000	2760	00
1016	467	36	2000	920	00	7000	3220	00
1094	503	24	2240	1030	40	7500	3450	00
1120	515	20	2500	1150	00	10000	4600	00
1250	575	00	3000	1380	00	15000	6900	00
1500	690	00	4000	1840	00	20000	9200	00
1750	805	00	5000	2300	00	30000	13800	00

No.	£	p	No.	£	p	No.	£	p	No.	£	p
1/16	0	03	34	15	98	72*	33	84	110	51	70
1/8	0	06	35	16	45	73	34	31	111	52	17
1/8	0	06	36*	16	92	74	34	78	112	52	64
1/4	0	12	37	17	39	75	35	25	113	53	11
1/2	0	23½	38	17	86	76	35	72	114	53	58
3/4	0	35½	39	18	33	77	36	19	115	54	05
1½	0	70½	40	18	80	78	36	66	116	54	52
2	0	94	41	19	27	79	37	13	117	54	99
3	1	41	42	19	74	80	37	60	118	55	46
4	1	88	43	20	21	81	38	07	119	55	93
5	2	35	44	20	68	82	38	54	120*	56	40
6	2	82	45	21	15	83	39	01	128	60	16
7	3	29	46	21	62	84*	39	48	130	61	10
8	3	76	47	22	09	85	39	95	140	65	80
9	4	23	48*	22	56	86	40	42	144*	67	68
10	4	70	49	23	03	87	40	89	150	70	50
11	5	17	50	23	50	88	41	36	156	73	32
12*	5	64	51	23	97	89	41	83	168	78	96
13	6	11	52	24	44	90	42	30	196	92	12
14	6	58	53	24	91	91	42	77	200	94	00
15	7	05	54	25	38	92	43	24	220	103	40
16	7	52	55	25	85	93	43	71	224	105	28
17	7	99	56	26	32	94	44	18	256	120	32
18	8	46	57	26	79	95	44	65	280	131	60
19	8	93	58	27	26	96*	45	12	300	141	00
20	9	40	59	27	73	97	45	59	365	171	55
21	9	87	60*	28	20	98	46	06	400	188	00
22	10	34	61	28	67	99	46	53	480	225	60
23	10	81	62	29	14	100	47	00	500	235	00
24*	11	28	63	29	61	101	47	47	516	242	52
25	11	75	64	30	08	102	47	94	560	263	20
26	12	22	65	30	55	103	48	41	600	282	00
27	12	69	66	31	02	104	48	88	625	293	75
28	13	16	67	31	49	105	49	35	640	300	80
29	13	63	68	31	96	106	49	82	700	329	00
30	14	10	69	32	43	107	50	29	750	352	50
31	14	57	70	32	90	108*	50	76	800	376	00
32	15	04	71	33	37	109	51	23	900	423	00
33	15	51									

No.	£	p	No.	£	p	No.	£	p
1000	470	00	1760	827	20	6000	2820	00
1016	477	52	2000	940	00	7000	3290	00
1094	514	18	2240	1052	80	7500	3525	00
1120	526	40	2500	1175	00	10000	4700	00
1250	587	50	3000	1410	00	15000	7050	00
1500	705	00	4000	1880	00	20000	9400	00
1750	822	50	5000	2350	00	30000	14100	00

47½p   £0·475

No.	£	p	No.	£	p	No.	£	p	No.	£	p
1/16	0	03	34	16	15	72*	34	20	110	52	25
1/8	0	06	35	16	62½	73	34	67½	111	52	72½
1/4	0	12	36*	17	10	74	35	15	112	53	20
1/2	0	24	37	17	57½	75	35	62½	113	53	67½
3/4	0	35½	38	18	05	76	36	10	114	54	15
1½	0	71½	39	18	52½	77	36	57½	115	54	62½
2	0	95	40	19	00	78	37	05	116	55	10
3	1	42½	41	19	47½	79	37	52½	117	55	57½
4	1	90	42	19	95	80	38	00	118	56	05
5	2	37½	43	20	42½	81	38	47½	119	56	52½
6	2	85	44	20	90	82	38	95	120*	57	00
7	3	32½	45	21	37½	83	39	42½	128	60	80
8	3	80	46	21	85	84*	39	90	130	61	75
9	4	27½	47	22	32½	85	40	37½	140	66	50
10	4	75	48*	22	80	86	40	85	144*	68	40
11	5	22½	49	23	27½	87	41	32½	150	71	25
12*	5	70	50	23	75	88	41	80	156	74	10
13	6	17½	51	24	22½	89	42	27½	168	79	80
14	6	65	52	24	70	90	42	75	196	93	10
15	7	12½	53	25	17½	91	43	22½	200	95	00
16	7	60	54	25	65	92	43	70	220	104	50
17	8	07½	55	26	12½	93	44	17½	224	106	40
18	8	55	56	26	60	94	44	65	256	121	60
19	9	02½	57	27	07½	95	45	12½	280	133	00
20	9	50	58	27	55	96*	45	60	300	142	50
21	9	97½	59	28	02½	97	46	07½	365	173	37½
22	10	45	60*	28	50	98	46	55	400	190	00
23	10	92½	61	28	97½	99	47	02½	480	228	00
24*	11	40	62	29	45	100	47	50	500	237	50
25	11	87½	63	29	92½	101	47	97½	516	245	10
26	12	35	64	30	40	102	48	45	560	266	00
27	12	82½	65	30	87½	103	48	92½	600	285	00
28	13	30	66	31	35	104	49	40	625	296	87½
29	13	77½	67	31	82½	105	49	87½	640	304	00
30	14	25	68	32	30	106	50	35	700	332	50
31	14	72½	69	32	77½	107	50	82½	750	356	25
32	15	20	70	33	25	108*	51	30	800	380	00
33	15	67½	71	33	72½	109	51	77½	900	427	50

No.	£	p	No.	£	p	No.	£	p
1000	475	00	1760	836	00	6000	2850	00
1016	482	60	2000	950	00	7000	3325	00
1094	519	65	2240	1064	00	7500	3562	50
1120	532	00	2500	1187	50	10000	4750	00
1250	593	75	3000	1425	00	15000	7125	00
1500	712	50	4000	1900	00	20000	9500	00
1750	831	25	5000	2375	00	30000	14250	00

No.	£	p	No.	£	p	No.	£	p	No.	£	p
1/16	0	03	34	16	32	72*	34	56	110	52	80
1/8	0	06	35	16	80	73	35	04	111	53	28
1/4	0	12	36*	17	28	74	35	52	112	53	76
1/2	0	24	37	17	76	75	36	00	113	54	24
3/4	0	36	38	18	24	76	36	48	114	54	72
1½	0	72	39	18	72	77	36	96	115	55	20
2	0	96	40	19	20	78	37	44	116	55	68
3	1	44	41	19	68	79	37	92	117	56	16
4	1	92	42	20	16	80	38	40	118	56	64
5	2	40	43	20	64	81	38	88	119	57	12
6	2	88	44	21	12	82	39	36	120*	57	60
7	3	36	45	21	60	83	39	84	128	61	44
8	3	84	46	22	08	84*	40	32	130	62	40
9	4	32	47	22	56	85	40	80	140	67	20
10	4	80	48*	23	04	86	41	28	144*	69	12
11	5	28	49	23	52	87	41	76	150	72	00
12*	5	76	50	24	00	88	42	24	156	74	88
13	6	24	51	24	48	89	42	72	168	80	64
14	6	72	52	24	96	90	43	20	196	94	08
15	7	20	53	25	44	91	43	68	200	96	00
16	7	68	54	25	92	92	44	16	220	105	60
17	8	16	55	26	40	93	44	64	224	107	52
18	8	64	56	26	88	94	45	12	256	122	88
19	9	12	57	27	36	95	45	60	280	134	40
20	9	60	58	27	84	96*	46	08	300	144	00
21	10	08	59	28	32	97	46	56	365	175	20
22	10	56	60*	28	80	98	47	04	400	192	00
23	11	04	61	29	28	99	47	52	480	230	40
24*	11	52	62	29	76	100	48	00	500	240	00
25	12	00	63	30	24	101	48	48	516	247	68
26	12	48	64	30	72	102	48	96	560	268	80
27	12	96	65	31	20	103	49	44	600	288	00
28	13	44	66	31	68	104	49	92	625	300	00
29	13	92	67	32	16	105	50	40	640	307	20
30	14	40	68	32	64	106	50	88	700	336	00
31	14	88	69	33	12	107	51	36	750	360	00
32	15	36	70	33	60	108*	51	84	800	384	00
33	15	84	71	34	08	109	52	32	900	432	00

No.	£	p	No.	£	p	No.	£	p
1000	480	00	1760	844	80	6000	2880	00
1016	487	68	2000	960	00	7000	3360	00
1094	525	12	2240	1075	20	7500	3600	00
1120	537	60	2500	1200	00	10000	4800	00
1250	600	00	3000	1440	00	15000	7200	00
1500	720	00	4000	1920	00	20000	9600	00
1750	840	00	5000	2400	00	30000	14400	00

No.	£	p	No.	£	p	No.	£	p	No.	£	p
1/16	0	03	34	16	66	72*	35	28	110	53	90
1/8	0	06	35	17	15	73	35	77	111	54	39
1/4	0	12½	36*	17	64	74	36	26	112	54	88
1/2	0	24½	37	18	13	75	36	75	113	55	37
3/4	0	37	38	18	62	76	37	24	114	55	86
1½	0	73½	39	19	11	77	37	73	115	56	35
2	0	98	40	19	60	78	38	22	116	56	84
3	1	47	41	20	09	79	38	71	117	57	33
4	1	96	42	20	58	80	39	20	118	57	82
5	2	45	43	21	07	81	39	69	119	58	31
6	2	94	44	21	56	82	40	18	120*	58	80
7	3	43	45	22	05	83	40	67	128	62	72
8	3	92	46	22	54	84*	41	16	130	63	70
9	4	41	47	23	03	85	41	65	140	68	60
10	4	90	48*	23	52	86	42	14	144*	70	56
11	5	39	49	24	01	87	42	63	150	73	50
12*	5	88	50	24	50	88	43	12	156	76	44
13	6	37	51	24	99	89	43	61	168	82	32
14	6	86	52	25	48	90	44	10	196	96	04
15	7	35	53	25	97	91	44	59	200	98	00
16	7	84	54	26	46	92	45	08	220	107	80
17	8	33	55	26	95	93	45	57	224	109	76
18	8	82	56	27	44	94	46	06	256	125	44
19	9	31	57	27	93	95	46	55	280	137	20
20	9	80	58	28	42	96*	47	04	300	147	00
21	10	29	59	28	91	97	47	53	365	178	85
22	10	78	60*	29	40	98	48	02	400	196	00
23	11	27	61	29	89	99	48	51	480	235	20
24*	11	76	62	30	38	100	49	00	500	245	00
25	12	25	63	30	87	101	49	49	516	252	84
26	12	74	64	31	36	102	49	98	560	274	40
27	13	23	65	31	85	103	50	47	600	294	00
28	13	72	66	32	34	104	50	96	625	306	25
29	14	21	67	32	83	105	51	45	640	313	60
30	14	70	68	33	32	106	51	94	700	343	00
31	15	19	69	33	81	107	52	43	750	367	50
32	15	68	70	34	30	108*	52	92	800	392	00
33	16	17	71	34	79	109	53	41	900	441	00

No.	£	p	No.	£	p	No.	£	p
1000	490	00	1760	862	40	6000	2940	00
1016	497	84	2000	980	00	7000	3430	00
1094	536	06	2240	1097	60	7500	3675	00
1120	548	80	2500	1225	00	10000	4900	00
1250	612	50	3000	1470	00	15000	7350	00
1500	735	00	4000	1960	00	20000	9800	00
1750	857	50	5000	2450	00	30000	14700	00

No.	£	p	No.	£	p	No.	£	p	No.	£	p
$\frac{1}{16}$	0	03	34	17	00	72*	36	00	110	55	00
$\frac{1}{8}$	0	06½	35	17	50	73	36	50	111	55	50
$\frac{1}{4}$	0	12½	36*	18	00	74	37	00	112	56	00
$\frac{1}{2}$	0	25	37	18	50	75	37	50	113	56	50
$\frac{3}{4}$	0	37½	38	19	00	76	38	00	114	57	00
1½	0	75	39	19	50	77	38	50	115	57	50
2	1	00	40	20	00	78	39	00	116	58	00
3	1	50	41	20	50	79	39	50	117	58	50
4	2	00	42	21	00	80	40	00	118	59	00
5	2	50	43	21	50	81	40	50	119	59	50
6	3	00	44	22	00	82	41	00	120*	60	00
7	3	50	45	22	50	83	41	50	128	64	00
8	4	00	46	23	00	84*	42	00	130	65	00
9	4	50	47	23	50	85	42	50	140	70	00
10	5	00	48*	24	00	86	43	00	144*	72	00
11	5	50	49	24	50	87	43	50	150	75	00
12*	6	00	50	25	00	88	44	00	156	78	00
13	6	50	51	25	50	89	44	50	168	84	00
14	7	00	52	26	00	90	45	00	196	98	00
15	7	50	53	26	50	91	45	50	200	100	00
16	8	00	54	27	00	92	46	00	220	110	00
17	8	50	55	27	50	93	46	50	224	112	00
18	9	00	56	28	00	94	47	00	256	128	00
19	9	50	57	28	50	95	47	50	280	140	00
20	10	00	58	29	00	96*	48	00	300	150	00
21	10	50	59	29	50	97	48	50	365	182	50
22	11	00	60*	30	00	98	49	00	400	200	00
23	11	50	61	30	50	99	49	50	480	240	00
24*	12	00	62	31	00	100	50	00	500	250	00
25	12	50	63	31	50	101	50	50	516	258	00
26	13	00	64	32	00	102	51	00	560	280	00
27	13	50	65	32	50	103	51	50	600	300	00
28	14	00	66	33	00	104	52	00	625	312	50
29	14	50	67	33	50	105	52	50	640	320	00
30	15	00	68	34	00	106	53	00	700	350	00
31	15	50	69	34	50	107	53	50	750	375	00
32	16	00	70	35	00	108*	54	00	800	400	00
33	16	50	71	35	50	109	54	50	900	450	00

No.	£	p	No.	£	p	No.	£	p
1000	500	00	1760	880	00	6000	3000	00
1016	508	00	2000	1000	00	7000	3500	00
1094	547	00	2240	1120	00	7500	3750	00
1120	560	00	2500	1250	00	10000	5000	00
1250	625	00	3000	1500	00	15000	7500	00
1500	750	00	4000	2000	00	20000	10000	00
1750	875	00	5000	2500	00	30000	15000	00

51p £0·51

No.	£	p	No.	£	p	No.	£	p	No.	£	p
1/16	0	03	34	17	34	72*	36	72	110	56	10
1/8	0	06½	35	17	85	73	37	23	111	56	61
1/4	0	13	36*	18	36	74	37	74	112	57	12
1/2	0	25½	37	18	87	75	38	25	113	57	63
3/4	0	38½	38	19	38	76	38	76	114	58	14
1½	0	76½	39	19	89	77	39	27	115	58	65
2	1	02	40	20	40	78	39	78	116	59	16
3	1	53	41	20	91	79	40	29	117	59	67
4	2	04	42	21	42	80	40	80	118	60	18
5	2	55	43	21	93	81	41	31	119	60	69
6	3	06	44	22	44	82	41	82	120*	61	20
7	3	57	45	22	95	83	42	33	128	65	28
8	4	08	46	23	46	84*	42	84	130	66	30
9	4	59	47	23	97	85	43	35	140	71	40
10	5	10	48*	24	48	86	43	86	144*	73	44
11	5	61	49	24	99	87	44	37	150	76	50
12*	6	12	50	25	50	88	44	88	156	79	56
13	6	63	51	26	01	89	45	39	168	85	68
14	7	14	52	26	52	90	45	90	196	99	96
15	7	65	53	27	03	91	46	41	200	102	00
16	8	16	54	27	54	92	46	92	220	112	20
17	8	67	55	28	05	93	47	43	224	114	24
18	9	18	56	28	56	94	47	94	256	130	56
19	9	69	57	29	07	95	48	45	280	142	80
20	10	20	58	29	58	96*	48	96	300	153	00
21	10	71	59	30	09	97	49	47	365	186	15
22	11	22	60*	30	60	98	49	98	400	204	00
23	11	73	61	31	11	99	50	49	480	244	80
24*	12	24	62	31	62	100	51	00	500	255	00
25	12	75	63	32	13	101	51	51	516	263	16
26	13	26	64	32	64	102	52	02	560	285	60
27	13	77	65	33	15	103	52	53	600	306	00
28	14	28	66	33	66	104	53	04	625	318	75
29	14	79	67	34	17	105	53	55	640	326	40
30	15	30	68	34	68	106	54	06	700	357	00
31	15	81	69	35	19	107	54	57	750	382	50
32	16	32	70	35	70	108*	55	08	800	408	00
33	16	83	71	36	21	109	55	59	900	459	00

No.	£	p	No.	£	p	No.	£	p
1000	510	00	1760	897	60	6000	3060	00
1016	518	16	2000	1020	00	7000	3570	00
1094	557	94	2240	1142	40	7500	3825	00
1120	571	20	2500	1275	00	10000	5100	00
1250	637	50	3000	1530	00	15000	7650	00
1500	765	00	4000	2040	00	20000	10200	00
1750	892	50	5000	2550	00	30000	15300	00

No.	£	p	No.	£	p	No.	£	p	No.	£	p
1/16	0	03½	34	17	68	72*	37	44	110	57	20
1/8	0	06½	35	18	20	73	37	96	111	57	72
1/4	0	13	36*	18	72	74	38	48	112	58	24
1/2	0	26	37	19	24	75	39	00	113	58	76
3/4	0	39	38	19	76	76	39	52	114	59	28
1½	0	78	39	20	28	77	40	04	115	59	80
2	1	04	40	20	80	78	40	56	116	60	32
3	1	56	41	21	32	79	41	08	117	60	84
4	2	08	42	21	84	80	41	60	118	61	36
5	2	60	43	22	36	81	42	12	119	61	88
6	3	12	44	22	88	82	42	64	120*	62	40
7	3	64	45	23	40	83	43	16	128	66	56
8	4	16	46	23	92	84*	43	68	130	67	60
9	4	68	47	24	44	85	44	20	140	72	80
10	5	20	48*	24	96	86	44	72	144*	74	88
11	5	72	49	25	48	87	45	24	150	78	00
12*	6	24	50	26	00	88	45	76	156	81	12
13	6	76	51	26	52	89	46	28	168	87	36
14	7	28	52	27	04	90	46	80	196	101	92
15	7	80	53	27	56	91	47	32	200	104	00
16	8	32	54	28	08	92	47	84	220	114	40
17	8	84	55	28	60	93	48	36	224	116	48
18	9	36	56	29	12	94	48	88	256	133	12
19	9	88	57	29	64	95	49	40	280	145	60
20	10	40	58	30	16	96*	49	92	300	156	00
21	10	92	59	30	68	97	50	44	365	189	80
22	11	44	60*	31	20	98	50	96	400	208	00
23	11	96	61	31	72	99	51	48	480	249	60
24*	12	48	62	32	24	100	52	00	500	260	00
25	13	00	63	32	76	101	52	52	516	268	32
26	13	52	64	33	28	102	53	04	560	291	20
27	14	04	65	33	80	103	53	56	600	312	00
28	14	56	66	34	32	104	54	08	625	325	00
29	15	08	67	34	84	105	54	60	640	332	80
30	15	60	68	35	36	106	55	12	700	364	00
31	16	12	69	35	88	107	55	64	750	390	00
32	16	64	70	36	40	108*	56	16	800	416	00
33	17	16	71	36	92	109	56	68	900	468	00

No.	£	p	No.	£	p	No.	£	p
1000	520	00	1760	915	20	6000	3120	00
1016	528	32	2000	1040	00	7000	3640	00
1094	568	88	2240	1164	80	7500	3900	00
1120	582	40	2500	1300	00	10000	5200	00
1250	650	00	3000	1560	00	15000	7800	00
1500	780	00	4000	2080	00	20000	10400	00
1750	910	00	5000	2600	00	30000	15600	00

No.	£	p	No.	£	p	No.	£	p	No.	£	p
1/16	0	03½	34	17	85	72*	37	80	110	57	75
1/8	0	06½	35	18	37½	73	38	32½	111	58	27½
1/4	0	13	36*	18	90	74	38	85	112	58	80
1/2	0	26½	37	19	42½	75	39	37½	113	59	32½
3/4	0	39½	38	19	95	76	39	90	114	59	85
1½	0	79	39	20	47½	77	40	42½	115	60	37½
2	1	05	40	21	00	78	40	95	116	60	90
3	1	57½	41	21	52½	79	41	47½	117	61	42½
4	2	10	42	22	05	80	42	00	118	61	95
5	2	62½	43	22	57½	81	42	52½	119	62	47½
6	3	15	44	23	10	82	43	05	120*	63	00
7	3	67½	45	23	62½	83	43	57½	128	67	20
8	4	20	46	24	15	84*	44	10	130	68	25
9	4	72½	47	24	67½	85	44	62½	140	73	50
10	5	25	48*	25	20	86	45	15	144*	75	60
11	5	77½	49	25	72½	87	45	67½	150	78	75
12*	6	30	50	26	25	88	46	20	156	81	90
13	6	82½	51	26	77½	89	46	72½	168	88	20
14	7	35	52	27	30	90	47	25	196	102	90
15	7	87½	53	27	82½	91	47	77½	200	105	00
16	8	40	54	28	35	92	48	30	220	115	50
17	8	92½	55	28	87½	93	48	82½	224	117	60
18	9	45	56	29	40	94	49	35	256	134	40
19	9	97½	57	29	92½	95	49	87½	280	147	00
20	10	50	58	30	45	96*	50	40	300	157	50
21	11	02½	59	30	97½	97	50	92½	365	191	62½
22	11	55	60*	31	50	98	51	45	400	210	00
23	12	07½	61	32	02½	99	51	97½	480	252	00
24*	12	60	62	32	55	100	52	50	500	262	50
25	13	12½	63	33	07½	101	53	02½	516	270	90
26	13	65	64	33	60	102	53	55	560	294	00
27	14	17½	65	34	12½	103	54	07½	600	315	00
28	14	70	66	34	65	104	54	60	625	328	12½
29	15	22½	67	35	17½	105	55	12½	640	336	00
30	15	75	68	35	70	106	55	65	700	367	50
31	16	27½	69	36	22½	107	56	17½	750	393	75
32	16	80	70	36	75	108*	56	70	800	420	00
33	17	32½	71	37	27½	109	57	22½	900	472	50

No.	£	p	No.	£	p	No.	£	p
1000	525	00	1760	924	00	6000	3150	00
1016	533	40	2000	1050	00	7000	3675	00
1094	574	35	2240	1176	00	7500	3937	50
1120	588	00	2500	1312	50	10000	5250	00
1250	656	25	3000	1575	00	15000	7875	00
1500	787	50	4000	2100	00	20000	10500	00
1750	918	75	5000	2625	00	30000	15750	00

No.	£	p	No.	£	p	No.	£	p	No.	£	p
1/16	0	03½	34	18	02	72*	38	16	110	58	30
1/8	0	06½	35	18	55	73	38	69	111	58	83
1/4	0	13½	36*	19	08	74	39	22	112	59	36
1/2	0	26½	37	19	61	75	39	75	113	59	89
3/4	0	40	38	20	14	76	40	28	114	60	42
1½	0	79½	39	20	67	77	40	81	115	60	95
2	1	06	40	21	20	78	41	34	116	61	48
3	1	59	41	21	73	79	41	87	117	62	01
4	2	12	42	22	26	80	42	40	118	62	54
5	2	65	43	22	79	81	42	93	119	63	07
6	3	18	44	23	32	82	43	46	120*	63	60
7	3	71	45	23	85	83	43	99	128	67	84
8	4	24	46	24	38	84*	44	52	130	68	90
9	4	77	47	24	91	85	45	05	140	74	20
10	5	30	48*	25	44	86	45	58	144*	76	32
11	5	83	49	25	97	87	46	11	150	79	50
12*	6	36	50	26	50	88	46	64	156	82	68
13	6	89	51	27	03	89	47	17	168	89	04
14	7	42	52	27	56	90	47	70	196	103	88
15	7	95	53	28	09	91	48	23	200	106	00
16	8	48	54	28	62	92	48	76	220	116	60
17	9	01	55	29	15	93	49	29	224	118	72
18	9	54	56	29	68	94	49	82	256	135	68
19	10	07	57	30	21	95	50	35	280	148	40
20	10	60	58	30	74	96*	50	88	300	159	00
21	11	13	59	31	27	97	51	41	365	193	45
22	11	66	60*	31	80	98	51	94	400	212	00
23	12	19	61	32	33	99	52	47	480	254	40
24*	12	72	62	32	86	100	53	00	500	265	00
25	13	25	63	33	39	101	53	53	516	273	48
26	13	78	64	33	92	102	54	06	560	296	80
27	14	31	65	34	45	103	54	59	600	318	00
28	14	84	66	34	98	104	55	12	625	331	25
29	15	37	67	35	51	105	55	65	640	339	20
30	15	90	68	36	04	106	56	18	700	371	00
31	16	43	69	36	57	107	56	71	750	397	50
32	16	96	70	37	10	108*	57	24	800	424	00
33	17	49	71	37	63	109	57	77	900	477	00

No.	£	p	No.	£	p	No.	£	p
1000	530	00	1760	932	80	6000	3180	00
1016	538	48	2000	1060	00	7000	3710	00
1094	579	82	2240	1187	20	7500	3975	00
1120	593	60	2500	1325	00	10000	5300	00
1250	662	50	3000	1590	00	15000	7950	00
1500	795	00	4000	2120	00	20000	10600	00
1750	927	50	5000	2650	00	30000	15900	00

54p   £0·54

No.	£	p	No.	£	p	No.	£	p	No.	£	p
1/16	0	03½	34	18	36	72*	38	88	110	59	40
1/8	0	07	35	18	90	73	39	42	111	59	94
1/4	0	13½	36*	19	44	74	39	96	112	60	48
1/2	0	27	37	19	98	75	40	50	113	61	02
3/4	0	40½	38	20	52	76	41	04	114	61	56
1½	0	81	39	21	06	77	41	58	115	62	10
2	1	08	**40**	21	60	78	42	12	116	62	64
3	1	62	41	22	14	79	42	66	117	63	18
4	2	16	42	22	68	**80**	43	20	118	63	72
5	2	70	43	23	22	81	43	74	119	64	26
6	3	24	44	23	76	82	44	28	120*	64	80
7	3	78	45	24	30	83	44	82	128	69	12
8	4	32	46	24	84	84*	45	36	130	70	20
9	4	86	47	25	38	85	45	90	140	75	60
10	5	40	48*	25	92	86	46	44	144*	77	76
11	5	94	49	26	46	87	46	98	150	81	00
12*	6	48	**50**	27	00	88	47	52	156	84	24
13	7	02	51	27	54	89	48	06	168	90	72
14	7	56	52	28	08	**90**	48	60	196	105	84
15	8	10	53	28	62	91	49	14	200	108	00
16	8	64	54	29	16	92	49	68	220	118	80
17	9	18	55	29	70	93	50	22	224	120	96
18	9	72	56	30	24	94	50	76	256	138	24
19	10	26	57	30	78	95	51	30	280	151	20
20	10	80	58	31	32	96*	51	84	300	162	00
21	11	34	59	31	86	97	52	38	365	197	10
22	11	88	**60***	32	40	98	52	92	400	216	00
23	12	42	61	32	94	99	53	46	480	259	20
24*	12	96	62	33	48	**100**	54	00	500	270	00
25	13	50	63	34	02	101	54	54	516	278	64
26	14	04	64	34	56	102	55	08	560	302	40
27	14	58	65	35	10	103	55	62	600	324	00
28	15	12	66	35	64	104	56	16	625	337	50
29	15	66	67	36	18	105	56	70	640	345	60
30	16	20	68	36	72	106	57	24	700	378	00
31	16	74	69	37	26	107	57	78	750	405	00
32	17	28	**70**	37	80	108*	58	32	800	432	00
33	17	82	71	38	34	109	58	86	900	486	00

No.	£	p	No.	£	p	No.	£	p
1000	540	00	1760	950	40	6000	3240	00
1016	548	64	2000	1080	00	7000	3780	00
1094	590	76	2240	1209	60	7500	4050	00
1120	604	80	2500	1350	00	10000	5400	00
1250	675	00	3000	1620	00	15000	8100	00
1500	810	00	4000	2160	00	20000	10800	00
1750	945	00	5000	2700	00	30000	16200	00

No.	£	p	No.	£	p	No.	£	p	No.	£	p
$\frac{1}{16}$	0	03½	34	18	70	72*	39	60	110	60	50
$\frac{1}{8}$	0	07	35	19	25	73	40	15	111	61	05
$\frac{1}{4}$	0	14	36*	19	80	74	40	70	112	61	60
$\frac{1}{2}$	0	27½	37	20	35	75	41	25	113	62	15
$\frac{3}{4}$	0	41½	38	20	90	76	41	80	114	62	70
1½	0	82½	39	21	45	77	42	35	115	63	25
2	1	10	**40**	22	00	78	42	90	116	63	80
3	1	65	41	22	55	79	43	45	117	64	35
4	2	20	42	23	10	**80**	44	00	118	64	90
5	2	75	43	23	65	81	44	55	119	65	45
6	3	30	44	24	20	82	45	10	120*	66	00
7	3	85	45	24	75	83	45	65	128	70	40
8	4	40	46	25	30	84*	46	20	130	71	50
9	4	95	47	25	85	85	46	75	140	77	00
10	5	50	48*	26	40	86	47	30	144*	79	20
11	6	05	49	26	95	87	47	85	150	82	50
12*	6	60	**50**	27	50	88	48	40	156	85	80
13	7	15	51	28	05	89	48	95	168	92	40
14	7	70	52	28	60	**90**	49	50	196	107	80
15	8	25	53	29	15	91	50	05	200	110	00
16	8	80	54	29	70	92	50	60	220	121	00
17	9	35	55	30	25	93	51	15	224	123	20
18	9	90	56	30	80	94	51	70	256	140	80
19	10	45	57	31	35	95	52	25	280	154	00
20	11	00	58	31	90	96*	52	80	300	165	00
21	11	55	59	32	45	97	53	35	365	200	75
22	12	10	**60***	33	00	98	53	90	400	220	00
23	12	65	61	33	55	99	54	45	480	264	00
24*	13	20	62	34	10	**100**	55	00	500	275	00
25	13	75	63	34	65	101	55	55	516	283	80
26	14	30	64	35	20	102	56	10	560	308	00
27	14	85	65	35	75	103	56	65	600	330	00
28	15	40	66	36	30	104	57	20	625	343	75
29	15	95	67	36	85	105	57	75	640	352	00
30	16	50	68	37	40	106	58	30	700	385	00
31	17	05	69	37	95	107	58	85	750	412	50
32	17	60	**70**	38	50	108*	59	40	800	440	00
33	18	15	71	39	05	109	59	95	900	495	00

No.	£	p	No.	£	p	No.	£	p
1000	550	00	1760	968	00	6000	3300	00
1016	558	80	2000	1100	00	7000	3850	00
1094	601	70	2240	1232	00	7500	4125	00
1120	616	00	2500	1375	00	10000	5500	00
1250	687	50	3000	1650	00	15000	8250	00
1500	825	00	4000	2200	00	20000	11000	00
1750	962	50	5000	2750	00	30000	16500	00

No.	£	p	No.	£	p	No.	£	p	No.	£	p
$\frac{1}{16}$	0	03½	34	19	04	72*	40	32	110	61	60
$\frac{1}{8}$	0	07	35	19	60	73	40	88	111	62	16
$\frac{1}{4}$	0	14	36*	20	16	74	41	44	112	62	72
$\frac{1}{2}$	0	28	37	20	72	75	42	00	113	63	28
$\frac{3}{4}$	0	42	38	21	28	76	42	56	114	63	84
1½	0	84	39	21	84	77	43	12	115	64	40
2	1	12	**40**	22	40	78	43	68	116	64	96
3	1	68	41	22	96	79	44	24	117	65	52
4	2	24	42	23	52	**80**	44	80	118	66	08
5	2	80	43	24	08	81	45	36	119	66	64
6	3	36	44	24	64	82	45	92	120*	67	20
7	3	92	45	25	20	83	46	48	128	71	68
8	4	48	46	25	76	84*	47	04	130	72	80
9	5	04	47	26	32	85	47	60	140	78	40
10	5	60	48*	26	88	86	48	16	144*	80	64
11	6	16	49	27	44	87	48	72	150	84	00
12*	6	72	**50**	28	00	88	49	28	156	87	36
13	7	28	51	28	56	89	49	84	168	94	08
14	7	84	52	29	12	**90**	50	40	196	109	76
15	8	40	53	29	68	91	50	96	200	112	00
16	8	96	54	30	24	92	51	52	220	123	20
17	9	52	55	30	80	93	52	08	224	125	44
18	10	08	56	31	36	94	52	64	256	143	36
19	10	64	57	31	92	95	53	20	280	156	80
20	11	20	58	32	48	96*	53	76	300	168	00
21	11	76	59	33	04	97	54	32	365	204	40
22	12	32	60*	33	60	98	54	88	400	224	00
23	12	88	61	34	16	99	55	44	480	268	80
24*	13	44	62	34	72	**100**	56	00	500	280	00
25	14	00	63	35	28	101	56	56	516	288	96
26	14	56	64	35	84	102	57	12	560	313	60
27	15	12	65	36	40	103	57	68	600	336	00
28	15	68	66	36	96	104	58	24	625	350	00
29	16	24	67	37	52	105	58	80	640	358	40
30	16	80	68	38	08	106	59	36	700	392	00
31	17	36	69	38	64	107	59	92	750	420	00
32	17	92	**70**	39	20	108*	60	48	800	448	00
33	18	48	71	39	76	109	61	04	900	504	00

No.	£	p	No.	£	p	No.	£	p
1000	560	00	1760	985	60	6000	3360	00
1016	568	96	2000	1120	00	7000	3920	00
1094	612	64	2240	1254	40	7500	4200	00
1120	627	20	2500	1400	00	10000	5600	00
1250	700	00	3000	1680	00	15000	8400	00
1500	840	00	4000	2240	00	20000	11200	00
1750	980	00	5000	2800	00	30000	16800	00

No.	£	p	No.	£	p	No.	£	p	No.	£	p
1/16	0	03½	34	19	38	72*	41	04	110	62	70
1/8	0	07	35	19	95	73	41	61	111	63	27
1/4	0	14½	36*	20	52	74	42	18	112	63	84
1/2	0	28½	37	21	09	75	42	75	113	64	41
3/4	0	43	38	21	66	76	43	32	114	64	98
1½	0	85½	39	22	23	77	43	89	115	65	55
2	1	14	40	22	80	78	44	46	116	66	12
3	1	71	41	23	37	79	45	03	117	66	69
4	2	28	42	23	94	80	45	60	118	67	26
5	2	85	43	24	51	81	46	17	119	67	83
6	3	42	44	25	08	82	46	74	120*	68	40
7	3	99	45	25	65	83	47	31	128	72	96
8	4	56	46	26	22	84*	47	88	130	74	10
9	5	13	47	26	79	85	48	45	140	79	80
10	5	70	48*	27	36	86	49	02	144*	82	08
11	6	27	49	27	93	87	49	59	150	85	50
12*	6	84	50	28	50	88	50	16	156	88	92
13	7	41	51	29	07	89	50	73	168	95	76
14	7	98	52	29	64	90	51	30	196	111	72
15	8	55	53	30	21	91	51	87	200	114	00
16	9	12	54	30	78	92	52	44	220	125	40
17	9	69	55	31	35	93	53	01	224	127	68
18	10	26	56	31	92	94	53	58	256	145	92
19	10	83	57	32	49	95	54	15	280	159	60
20	11	40	58	33	06	96*	54	72	300	171	00
21	11	97	59	33	63	97	55	29	365	208	05
22	12	54	60*	34	20	98	55	86	400	228	00
23	13	11	61	34	77	99	56	43	480	273	60
24*	13	68	62	35	34	100	57	00	500	285	00
25	14	25	63	35	91	101	57	57	516	294	12
26	14	82	64	36	48	102	58	14	560	319	20
27	15	39	65	37	05	103	58	71	600	342	00
28	15	96	66	37	62	104	59	28	625	356	25
29	16	53	67	38	19	105	59	85	640	364	80
30	17	10	68	38	76	106	60	42	700	399	00
31	17	67	69	39	33	107	60	99	750	427	50
32	18	24	70	39	90	108*	61	56	800	456	00
33	18	81	71	40	47	109	62	13	900	513	00

No.	£	p	No.	£	p	No.	£	p
1000	570	00	1760	1003	20	6000	3420	00
1016	579	12	2000	1140	00	7000	3990	00
1094	623	58	2240	1276	80	7500	4275	00
1120	638	40	2500	1425	00	10000	5700	00
1250	712	50	3000	1710	00	15000	8550	00
1500	855	00	4000	2280	00	20000	11400	00
1750	997	50	5000	2850	00	30000	17100	00

57½p   £0·575

No.	£	p	No.	£	p	No.	£	p	No.	£	p
1/16	0	03½	34	19	55	72*	41	40	110	63	25
1/8	0	07	35	20	12½	73	41	97½	111	63	82½
1/4	0	14½	36*	20	70	74	42	55	112	64	40
1/2	0	29	37	21	27½	75	43	12½	113	64	97½
3/4	0	43	38	21	85	76	43	70	114	65	55
1½	0	86½	39	22	42½	77	44	27½	115	66	12½
2	1	15	40	23	00	78	44	85	116	66	70
3	1	72½	41	23	57½	79	45	42½	117	67	27½
4	2	30	42	24	15	80	46	00	118	67	85
5	2	87½	43	24	72½	81	46	57½	119	68	42½
6	3	45	44	25	30	82	47	15	120*	69	00
7	4	02½	45	25	87½	83	47	72½	128	73	60
8	4	60	46	26	45	84*	48	30	130	74	75
9	5	17½	47	27	02½	85	48	87½	140	80	50
10	5	75	48*	27	60	86	49	45	144*	82	80
11	6	32½	49	28	17½	87	50	02½	150	86	25
12*	6	90	50	28	75	88	50	60	156	89	70
13	7	47½	51	29	32½	89	51	17½	168	96	60
14	8	05	52	29	90	90	51	75	196	112	70
15	8	62½	53	30	47½	91	52	32½	200	115	00
16	9	20	54	31	05	92	52	90	220	126	50
17	9	77½	55	31	62½	93	53	47½	224	128	80
18	10	35	56	32	20	94	54	05	256	147	20
19	10	92½	57	32	77½	95	54	62½	280	161	00
20	11	50	58	33	35	96*	55	20	300	172	50
21	12	07½	59	33	92½	97	55	77½	365	209	87½
22	12	65	60*	34	50	98	56	35	400	230	00
23	13	22½	61	35	07½	99	56	92½	480	276	00
24*	13	80	62	35	65	100	57	50	500	287	50
25	14	37½	63	36	22½	101	58	07½	516	296	70
26	14	95	64	36	80	102	58	65	560	322	00
27	15	52½	65	37	37½	103	59	22½	600	345	00
28	16	10	66	37	95	104	59	80	625	359	37½
29	16	67½	67	38	52½	105	60	37½	640	368	00
30	17	25	68	39	10	106	60	95	700	402	50
31	17	82½	69	39	67½	107	61	52½	750	431	25
32	18	40	70	40	25	108*	62	10	800	460	00
33	18	97½	71	40	82½	109	62	67½	900	517	50

No.	£	p	No.	£	p	No.	£	p
1000	575	00	1760	1012	00	6000	3450	00
1016	584	20	2000	1150	00	7000	4025	00
1094	629	05	2240	1288	00	7500	4312	50
1120	644	00	2500	1437	50	10000	5750	00
1250	718	75	3000	1725	00	15000	8625	00
1500	862	50	4000	2300	00	20000	11500	00
1750	1006	25	5000	2875	00	30000	17250	00

No.	£	p	No.	£	p	No.	£	p	No.	£	p
$\frac{1}{16}$	0	03½	34	19	72	72*	41	76	110	63	80
$\frac{1}{8}$	0	07½	35	20	30	73	42	34	111	64	38
$\frac{1}{4}$	0	14½	36*	20	88	74	42	92	112	64	96
$\frac{1}{2}$	0	29	37	21	46	75	43	50	113	65	54
$\frac{3}{4}$	0	43½	38	22	04	76	44	08	114	66	12
$1\frac{1}{2}$	0	87	39	22	62	77	44	66	115	66	70
2	1	16	**40**	23	20	78	45	24	116	67	28
3	1	74	41	23	78	79	45	82	117	67	86
4	2	32	42	24	36	**80**	46	40	118	68	44
5	2	90	43	24	94	81	46	98	119	69	02
6	3	48	44	25	52	82	47	56	120*	69	60
7	4	06	45	26	10	83	48	14	128	74	24
8	4	64	46	26	68	84*	48	72	130	75	40
9	5	22	47	27	26	85	49	30	140	81	20
10	5	80	48*	27	84	86	49	88	144*	83	52
11	6	38	49	28	42	87	50	46	150	87	00
12*	6	96	**50**	29	00	88	51	04	156	90	48
13	7	54	51	29	58	89	51	62	168	97	44
14	8	12	52	30	16	**90**	52	20	196	113	68
15	8	70	53	30	74	91	52	78	200	116	00
16	9	28	54	31	32	92	53	36	220	127	60
17	9	86	55	31	90	93	53	94	224	129	92
18	10	44	56	32	48	94	54	52	256	148	48
19	11	02	57	33	06	95	55	10	280	162	40
20	11	60	58	33	64	96*	55	68	300	174	00
21	12	18	59	34	22	97	56	26	365	211	70
22	12	76	**60***	34	80	98	56	84	400	232	00
23	13	34	61	35	38	99	57	42	480	278	40
24*	13	92	62	35	96	**100**	58	00	500	290	00
25	14	50	63	36	54	101	58	58	516	299	28
26	15	08	64	37	12	102	59	16	560	324	80
27	15	66	65	37	70	103	59	74	600	348	00
28	16	24	66	38	28	104	60	32	625	362	50
29	16	82	67	38	86	105	60	90	640	371	20
30	17	40	68	39	44	106	61	48	700	406	00
31	17	98	69	40	02	107	62	06	750	435	00
32	18	56	**70**	40	60	108*	62	64	800	464	00
33	19	14	71	41	18	109	63	22	900	522	00

No.	£	p	No.	£	p	No.	£	p
1000	580	00	1760	1020	80	6000	3480	00
1016	589	28	2000	1160	00	7000	4060	00
1094	634	52	2240	1299	20	7500	4350	00
1120	649	60	2500	1450	00	10000	5800	00
1250	725	00	3000	1740	00	15000	8700	00
1500	870	00	4000	2320	00	20000	11600	00
1750	1015	00	5000	2900	00	30000	17400	00

No.	£	p	No.	£	p	No.	£	p	No.	£	p
1/16	0	03½	34	20	06	72*	42	48	110	64	90
1/8	0	07½	35	20	65	73	43	07	111	65	49
1/4	0	15	36*	21	24	74	43	66	112	66	08
1/2	0	29½	37	21	83	75	44	25	113	66	67
3/4	0	44½	38	22	42	76	44	84	114	67	26
1½	0	88½	39	23	01	77	45	43	115	67	85
2	1	18	40	23	60	78	46	02	116	68	44
3	1	77	41	24	19	79	46	61	117	69	03
4	2	36	42	24	78	80	47	20	118	69	62
5	2	95	43	25	37	81	47	79	119	70	21
6	3	54	44	25	96	82	48	38	120*	70	80
7	4	13	45	26	55	83	48	97	128	75	52
8	4	72	46	27	14	84*	49	56	130	76	70
9	5	31	47	27	73	85	50	15	140	82	60
10	5	90	48*	28	32	86	50	74	144*	84	96
11	6	49	49	28	91	87	51	33	150	88	50
12*	7	08	50	29	50	88	51	92	156	92	04
13	7	67	51	30	09	89	52	51	168	99	12
14	8	26	52	30	68	90	53	10	196	115	64
15	8	85	53	31	27	91	53	69	200	118	00
16	9	44	54	31	86	92	54	28	220	129	80
17	10	03	55	32	45	93	54	87	224	132	16
18	10	62	56	33	04	94	55	46	256	151	04
19	11	21	57	33	63	95	56	05	280	165	20
20	11	80	58	34	22	96*	56	64	300	177	00
21	12	39	59	34	81	97	57	23	365	215	35
22	12	98	60*	35	40	98	57	82	400	236	00
23	13	57	61	35	99	99	58	41	480	283	20
24*	14	16	62	36	58	100	59	00	500	295	00
25	14	75	63	37	17	101	59	59	516	304	44
26	15	34	64	37	76	102	60	18	560	330	40
27	15	93	65	38	35	103	60	77	600	354	00
28	16	52	66	38	94	104	61	36	625	368	75
29	17	11	67	39	53	105	61	95	640	377	60
30	17	70	68	40	12	106	62	54	700	413	00
31	18	29	69	40	71	107	63	13	750	442	50
32	18	88	70	41	30	108*	63	72	800	472	00
33	19	47	71	41	89	109	64	31	900	531	00

No.	£	p	No.	£	p	No.	£	p
1000	590	00	1760	1038	40	6000	3540	00
1016	599	44	2000	1180	00	7000	4130	00
1094	645	46	2240	1321	60	7500	4425	00
1120	660	80	2500	1475	00	10000	5900	00
1250	737	50	3000	1770	00	15000	8850	00
1500	885	00	4000	2360	00	20000	11800	00
1750	1032	50	5000	2950	00	30000	17700	00

No.	£	p	No.	£	p	No.	£	p	No.	£	p
1/16	0	04	34	20	40	72*	43	20	110	66	00
1/8	0	07½	35	21	00	73	43	80	111	66	60
1/4	0	15	36*	21	60	74	44	40	112	67	20
1/2	0	30	37	22	20	75	45	00	113	67	80
3/4	0	45	38	22	80	76	45	60	114	68	40
1½	0	90	39	23	40	77	46	20	115	69	00
2	1	20	40	24	00	78	46	80	116	69	60
3	1	80	41	24	60	79	47	40	117	70	20
4	2	40	42	25	20	80	48	00	118	70	80
5	3	00	43	25	80	81	48	60	119	71	40
6	3	60	44	26	40	82	49	20	120*	72	00
7	4	20	45	27	00	83	49	80	128	76	80
8	4	80	46	27	60	84*	50	40	130	78	00
9	5	40	47	28	20	85	51	00	140	84	00
10	6	00	48*	28	80	86	51	60	144*	86	40
11	6	60	49	29	40	87	52	20	150	90	00
12*	7	20	50	30	00	88	52	80	156	93	60
13	7	80	51	30	60	89	53	40	168	100	80
14	8	40	52	31	20	90	54	00	196	117	60
15	9	00	53	31	80	91	54	60	200	120	00
16	9	60	54	32	40	92	55	20	220	132	00
17	10	20	55	33	00	93	55	80	224	134	40
18	10	80	56	33	60	94	56	40	256	153	60
19	11	40	57	34	20	95	57	00	280	168	00
20	12	00	58	34	80	96*	57	60	300	180	00
21	12	60	59	35	40	97	58	20	365	219	00
22	13	20	60*	36	00	98	58	80	400	240	00
23	13	80	61	36	60	99	59	40	480	288	00
24*	14	40	62	37	20	100	60	00	500	300	00
25	15	00	63	37	80	101	60	60	516	309	60
26	15	60	64	38	40	102	61	20	560	336	00
27	16	20	65	39	00	103	61	80	600	360	00
28	16	80	66	39	60	104	62	40	625	375	00
29	17	40	67	40	20	105	63	00	640	384	00
30	18	00	68	40	80	106	63	60	700	420	00
31	18	60	69	41	40	107	64	20	750	450	00
32	19	20	70	42	00	108*	64	80	800	480	00
33	19	80	71	42	60	109	65	40	900	540	00

No.	£	p	No.	£	p	No.	£	p
1000	600	00	1760	1056	00	6000	3600	00
1016	609	60	2000	1200	00	7000	4200	00
1094	656	40	2240	1344	00	7500	4500	00
1120	672	00	2500	1500	00	10000	6000	00
1250	750	00	3000	1800	00	15000	9000	00
1500	900	00	4000	2400	00	20000	12000	00
1750	1050	00	5000	3000	00	30000	18000	00

No.	£	p	No.	£	p	No.	£	p	No.	£	p
$\frac{1}{16}$	0	04	34	20	74	72*	43	92	110	67	10
$\frac{1}{8}$	0	07½	35	21	35	73	44	53	111	67	71
$\frac{1}{4}$	0	15½	36*	21	96	74	45	14	112	68	32
$\frac{1}{2}$	0	30½	37	22	57	75	45	75	113	68	93
$\frac{3}{4}$	0	46	38	23	18	76	46	36	114	69	54
1½	0	91½	39	23	79	77	46	97	115	70	15
2	1	22	40	24	40	78	47	58	116	70	76
3	1	83	41	25	01	79	48	19	117	71	37
4	2	44	42	25	62	80	48	80	118	71	98
5	3	05	43	26	23	81	49	41	119	72	59
6	3	66	44	26	84	82	50	02	120*	73	20
7	4	27	45	27	45	83	50	63	128	78	08
8	4	88	46	28	06	84*	51	24	130	79	30
9	5	49	47	28	67	85	51	85	140	85	40
10	6	10	48*	29	28	86	52	46	144*	87	84
11	6	71	49	29	89	87	53	07	150	91	50
12*	7	32	50	30	50	88	53	68	156	95	16
13	7	93	51	31	11	89	54	29	168	102	48
14	8	54	52	31	72	90	54	90	196	119	56
15	9	15	53	32	33	91	55	51	200	122	00
16	9	76	54	32	94	92	56	12	220	134	20
17	10	37	55	33	55	93	56	73	224	136	64
18	10	98	56	34	16	94	57	34	256	156	16
19	11	59	57	34	77	95	57	95	280	170	80
20	12	20	58	35	38	96*	58	56	300	183	00
21	12	81	59	35	99	97	59	17	365	222	65
22	13	42	60*	36	60	98	59	78	400	244	00
23	14	03	61	37	21	99	60	39	480	292	80
24*	14	64	62	37	82	100	61	00	500	305	00
25	15	25	63	38	43	101	61	61	516	314	76
26	15	86	64	39	04	102	62	22	560	341	60
27	16	47	65	39	65	103	62	83	600	366	00
28	17	08	66	40	26	104	63	44	625	381	25
29	17	69	67	40	87	105	64	05	640	390	40
30	18	30	68	41	48	106	64	66	700	427	00
31	18	91	69	42	09	107	65	27	750	457	50
32	19	52	70	42	70	108*	65	88	800	488	00
33	20	13	71	43	31	109	66	49	900	549	00

No.	£	p	No.	£	p	No.	£	p
1000	610	00	1760	1073	60	6000	3660	00
1016	619	76	2000	1220	00	7000	4270	00
1094	667	34	2240	1366	40	7500	4575	00
1120	683	20	2500	1525	00	10000	6100	00
1250	762	50	3000	1830	00	15000	9150	00
1500	915	00	4000	2440	00	20000	12200	00
1750	1067	50	5000	3050	00	30000	18300	00

No.	£	p	No.	£	p	No.	£	p	No.	£	p
$\frac{1}{16}$	0	04	34	21	08	72*	44	64	110	68	20
$\frac{1}{8}$	0	08	35	21	70	73	45	26	111	68	82
$\frac{1}{4}$	0	15½	36*	22	32	74	45	88	112	69	44
$\frac{1}{2}$	0	31	37	22	94	75	46	50	113	70	06
$\frac{3}{4}$	0	46½	38	23	56	76	47	12	114	70	68
1½	0	93	39	24	18	77	47	74	115	71	30
2	1	24	40	24	80	78	48	36	116	71	92
3	1	86	41	25	42	79	48	98	117	72	54
4	2	48	42	26	04	80	49	60	118	73	16
5	3	10	43	26	66	81	50	22	119	73	78
6	3	72	44	27	28	82	50	84	120*	74	40
7	4	34	45	27	90	83	51	46	128	79	36
8	4	96	46	28	52	84*	52	08	130	80	60
9	5	58	47	29	14	85	52	70	140	86	80
10	6	20	48*	29	76	86	53	32	144*	89	28
11	6	82	49	30	38	87	53	94	150	93	00
12*	7	44	50	31	00	88	54	56	156	96	72
13	8	06	51	31	62	89	55	18	168	104	16
14	8	68	52	32	24	90	55	80	196	121	52
15	9	30	53	32	86	91	56	42	200	124	00
16	9	92	54	33	48	92	57	04	220	136	40
17	10	54	55	34	10	93	57	66	224	138	88
18	11	16	56	34	72	94	58	28	256	158	72
19	11	78	57	35	34	95	58	90	280	173	60
20	12	40	58	35	96	96*	59	52	300	186	00
21	13	02	59	36	58	97	60	14	365	226	30
22	13	64	60*	37	20	98	60	76	400	248	00
23	14	26	61	37	82	99	61	38	480	297	60
24*	14	88	62	38	44	100	62	00	500	310	00
25	15	50	63	39	06	101	62	62	516	319	92
26	16	12	64	39	68	102	63	24	560	347	20
27	16	74	65	40	30	103	63	86	600	372	00
28	17	36	66	40	92	104	64	48	625	387	50
29	17	98	67	41	54	105	65	10	640	396	80
30	18	60	68	42	16	106	65	72	700	434	00
31	19	22	69	42	78	107	66	34	750	465	00
32	19	84	70	43	40	108*	66	96	800	496	00
33	20	46	71	44	02	109	67	58	900	558	00

No.	£	p	No.	£	p	No.	£	p
1000	620	00	1760	1091	20	6000	3720	00
1016	629	92	2000	1240	00	7000	4340	00
1094	678	28	2240	1388	80	7500	4650	00
1120	694	40	2500	1550	00	10000	6200	00
1250	775	00	3000	1860	00	15000	9300	00
1500	930	00	4000	2480	00	20000	12400	00
1750	1085	00	5000	3100	00	30000	18600	00

62½p   £0·625

No.	£	p	No.	£	p	No.	£	p	No.	£	p
1/16	0	04	34	21	25	72*	45	00	110	68	75
1/8	0	08	35	21	87½	73	45	62½	111	69	37½
1/4	0	15½	36*	22	50	74	46	25	112	70	00
1/2	0	31½	37	23	12½	75	46	87½	113	70	62½
3/4	0	47	38	23	75	76	47	50	114	71	25
1½	0	94	39	24	37½	77	48	12½	115	71	87½
2	1	25	40	25	00	78	48	75	116	72	50
3	1	87½	41	25	62½	79	49	37½	117	73	12½
4	2	50	42	26	25	80	50	00	118	73	75
5	3	12½	43	26	87½	81	50	62½	119	74	37½
6	3	75	44	27	50	82	51	25	120*	75	00
7	4	37½	45	28	12½	83	51	87½	128	80	00
8	5	00	46	28	75	84*	52	50	130	81	25
9	5	62½	47	29	37½	85	53	12½	140	87	50
10	6	25	48*	30	00	86	53	75	144*	90	00
11	6	87½	49	30	62½	87	54	37½	150	93	75
12*	7	50	50	31	25	88	55	00	156	97	50
13	8	12½	51	31	87½	89	55	62½	168	105	00
14	8	75	52	32	50	90	56	25	196	122	50
15	9	37½	53	33	12½	91	56	87½	200	125	00
16	10	00	54	33	75	92	57	50	220	137	50
17	10	62½	55	34	37½	93	58	12½	224	140	00
18	11	25	56	35	00	94	58	75	256	160	00
19	11	87½	57	35	62½	95	59	37½	280	175	00
20	12	50	58	36	25	96*	60	00	300	187	50
21	13	12½	59	36	87½	97	60	62½	365	228	12½
22	13	75	60*	37	50	98	61	25	400	250	00
23	14	37½	61	38	12½	99	61	87½	480	300	00
24*	15	00	62	38	75	100	62	50	500	312	50
25	15	62½	63	39	37½	101	63	12½	516	322	50
26	16	25	64	40	00	102	63	75	560	350	00
27	16	87½	65	40	62½	103	64	37½	600	375	00
28	17	50	66	41	25	104	65	00	625	390	62½
29	18	12½	67	41	87½	105	65	62½	640	400	00
30	18	75	68	42	50	106	66	25	700	437	50
31	19	37½	69	43	12½	107	66	87½	750	468	75
32	20	00	70	43	75	108*	67	50	800	500	00
33	20	62½	71	44	37½	109	68	12½	900	562	50

No.	£	p	No.	£	p	No.	£	p
1000	625	00	1760	1100	00	6000	3750	00
1016	635	00	2000	1250	00	7000	4375	00
1094	683	75	2240	1400	00	7500	4687	50
1120	700	00	2500	1562	50	10000	6250	00
1250	781	25	3000	1875	00	15000	9375	00
1500	937	50	4000	2500	00	20000	12500	00
1750	1093	75	5000	3125	00	30000	18750	00

No.	£	p	No.	£	p	No.	£	p	No.	£	p
$\frac{1}{16}$	0	04	34	21	42	72*	45	36	110	69	30
$\frac{1}{8}$	0	08	35	22	05	73	45	99	111	69	93
$\frac{1}{4}$	0	16	36*	22	68	74	46	62	112	70	56
$\frac{1}{2}$	0	31½	37	23	31	75	47	25	113	71	19
$\frac{3}{4}$	0	47½	38	23	94	76	47	88	114	71	82
1½	0	94½	39	24	57	77	48	51	115	72	45
2	1	26	**40**	25	20	78	49	14	116	73	08
3	1	89	41	25	83	79	49	77	117	73	71
4	2	52	42	26	46	**80**	50	40	118	74	34
5	3	15	43	27	09	81	51	03	119	74	97
6	3	78	44	27	72	82	51	66	120*	75	60
7	4	41	45	28	35	83	52	29	128	80	64
8	5	04	46	28	98	84*	52	92	130	81	90
9	5	67	47	29	61	85	53	55	140	88	20
10	6	30	48*	30	24	86	54	18	144*	90	72
11	6	93	49	30	87	87	54	81	150	94	50
12*	7	56	**50**	31	50	88	55	44	156	98	28
13	8	19	51	32	13	89	56	07	168	105	84
14	8	82	52	32	76	**90**	56	70	196	123	48
15	9	45	53	33	39	91	57	33	200	126	00
16	10	08	54	34	02	92	57	96	220	138	60
17	10	71	55	34	65	93	58	59	224	141	12
18	11	34	56	35	28	94	59	22	256	161	28
19	11	97	57	35	91	95	59	85	280	176	40
20	12	60	58	36	54	96*	60	48	300	189	00
21	13	23	59	37	17	97	61	11	365	229	95
22	13	86	60*	37	80	98	61	74	400	252	00
23	14	49	61	38	43	99	62	37	480	302	40
24*	15	12	62	39	06	**100**	63	00	500	315	00
25	15	75	63	39	69	101	63	63	516	325	08
26	16	38	64	40	32	102	64	26	560	352	80
27	17	01	65	40	95	103	64	89	600	378	00
28	17	64	66	41	58	104	65	52	625	393	75
29	18	27	67	42	21	105	66	15	640	403	20
30	18	90	68	42	84	106	66	78	700	441	00
31	19	53	69	43	47	107	67	41	750	472	50
32	20	16	**70**	44	10	108*	68	04	800	504	00
33	20	79	71	44	73	109	68	67	900	567	00

No.	£	p	No.	£	p	No.	£	p
1000	630	00	1760	1108	80	6000	3780	00
1016	640	08	2000	1260	00	7000	4410	00
1094	689	22	2240	1411	20	7500	4725	00
1120	705	60	2500	1575	00	10000	6300	00
1250	787	50	3000	1890	00	15000	9450	00
1500	945	00	4000	2520	00	20000	12600	00
1750	1102	50	5000	3150	00	30000	18900	00

No.	£	p	No.	£	p	No.	£	p	No.	£	p
1/16	0	04	34	21	76	72*	46	08	110	70	40
1/8	0	08	35	22	40	73	46	72	111	71	04
1/4	0	16	36*	23	04	74	47	36	112	71	68
1/2	0	32	37	23	68	75	48	00	113	72	32
3/4	0	48	38	24	32	76	48	64	114	72	96
1½	0	96	39	24	96	77	49	28	115	73	60
2	1	28	40	25	60	78	49	92	116	74	24
3	1	92	41	26	24	79	50	56	117	74	88
4	2	56	42	26	88	80	51	20	118	75	52
5	3	20	43	27	52	81	51	84	119	76	16
6	3	84	44	28	16	82	52	48	120*	76	80
7	4	48	45	28	80	83	53	12	128	81	92
8	5	12	46	29	44	84*	53	76	130	83	20
9	5	76	47	30	08	85	54	40	140	89	60
10	6	40	48*	30	72	86	55	04	144*	92	16
11	7	04	49	31	36	87	55	68	150	96	00
12*	7	68	50	32	00	88	56	32	156	99	84
13	8	32	51	32	64	89	56	96	168	107	52
14	8	96	52	33	28	90	57	60	196	125	44
15	9	60	53	33	92	91	58	24	200	128	00
16	10	24	54	34	56	92	58	88	220	140	80
17	10	88	55	35	20	93	59	52	224	143	36
18	11	52	56	35	84	94	60	16	256	163	84
19	12	16	57	36	48	95	60	80	280	179	20
20	12	80	58	37	12	96*	61	44	300	192	00
21	13	44	59	37	76	97	62	08	365	233	60
22	14	08	60*	38	40	98	62	72	400	256	00
23	14	72	61	39	04	99	63	36	480	307	20
24*	15	36	62	39	68	100	64	00	500	320	00
25	16	00	63	40	32	101	64	64	516	330	24
26	16	64	64	40	96	102	65	28	560	358	40
27	17	28	65	41	60	103	65	92	600	384	00
28	17	92	66	42	24	104	66	56	625	400	00
29	18	56	67	42	88	105	67	20	640	409	60
30	19	20	68	43	52	106	67	84	700	448	00
31	19	84	69	44	16	107	68	48	750	480	00
32	20	48	70	44	80	108*	69	12	800	512	00
33	21	12	71	45	44	109	69	76	900	576	00

No.	£	p	No.	£	p	No.	£	p
1000	640	00	1760	1126	40	6000	3840	00
1016	650	24	2000	1280	00	7000	4480	00
1094	700	16	2240	1433	60	7500	4800	00
1120	716	80	2500	1600	00	10000	6400	00
1250	800	00	3000	1920	00	15000	9600	00
1500	960	00	4000	2560	00	20000	12800	00
1750	1120	00	5000	3200	00	30000	19200	00

65p   £0·65

No.	£	p	No.	£	p	No.	£	p	No.	£	p
1/16	0	04	34	22	10	72*	46	80	110	71	50
1/8	0	08	35	22	75	73	47	45	111	72	15
1/4	0	16½	36*	23	40	74	48	10	112	72	80
1/2	0	32½	37	24	05	75	48	75	113	73	45
3/4	0	49	38	24	70	76	49	40	114	74	10
1½	0	97½	39	25	35	77	50	05	115	74	75
2	1	30	40	26	00	78	50	70	116	75	40
3	1	95	41	26	65	79	51	35	117	76	05
4	2	60	42	27	30	80	52	00	118	76	70
5	3	25	43	27	95	81	52	65	119	77	35
6	3	90	44	28	60	82	53	30	120*	78	00
7	4	55	45	29	25	83	53	95	128	83	20
8	5	20	46	29	90	84*	54	60	130	84	50
9	5	85	47	30	55	85	55	25	140	91	00
10	6	50	48*	31	20	86	55	90	144*	93	60
11	7	15	49	31	85	87	56	55	150	97	50
12*	7	80	50	32	50	88	57	20	156	101	40
13	8	45	51	33	15	89	57	85	168	109	20
14	9	10	52	33	80	90	58	50	196	127	40
15	9	75	53	34	45	91	59	15	200	130	00
16	10	40	54	35	10	92	59	80	220	143	00
17	11	05	55	35	75	93	60	45	224	145	60
18	11	70	56	36	40	94	61	10	256	166	40
19	12	35	57	37	05	95	61	75	280	182	00
20	13	00	58	37	70	96*	62	40	300	195	00
21	13	65	59	38	35	97	63	05	365	237	25
22	14	30	60*	39	00	98	63	70	400	260	00
23	14	95	61	39	65	99	64	35	480	312	00
24*	15	60	62	40	30	100	65	00	500	325	00
25	16	25	63	40	95	101	65	65	516	335	40
26	16	90	64	41	60	102	66	30	560	364	00
27	17	55	65	42	25	103	66	95	600	390	00
28	18	20	66	42	90	104	67	60	625	406	25
29	18	85	67	43	55	105	68	25	640	416	00
30	19	50	68	44	20	106	68	90	700	455	00
31	20	15	69	44	85	107	69	55	750	487	50
32	20	80	70	45	50	108*	70	20	800	520	00
33	21	45	71	46	15	109	70	85	900	585	00

No.	£	p	No.	£	p	No.	£	p
1000	650	00	1760	1144	00	6000	3900	00
1016	660	40	2000	1300	00	7000	4550	00
1094	711	10	2240	1456	00	7500	4875	00
1120	728	00	2500	1625	00	10000	6500	00
1250	812	50	3000	1950	00	15000	9750	00
1500	975	00	4000	2600	00	20000	13000	00
1750	1137	50	5000	3250	00	30000	19500	00

No.	£	p	No.	£	p	No.	£	p	No.	£	p
$\frac{1}{16}$	0	04	34	22	44	72*	47	52	110	72	60
$\frac{1}{8}$	0	08½	35	23	10	73	48	18	111	73	26
$\frac{1}{4}$	0	16½	36*	23	76	74	48	84	112	73	92
$\frac{1}{2}$	0	33	37	24	42	75	49	50	113	74	58
$\frac{3}{4}$	0	49½	38	25	08	76	50	16	114	75	24
1½	0	99	39	25	74	77	50	82	115	75	90
2	1	32	**40**	26	40	78	51	48	116	76	56
3	1	98	41	27	06	79	52	14	117	77	22
4	2	64	42	27	72	**80**	52	80	118	77	88
5	3	30	43	28	38	81	53	46	119	78	54
6	3	96	44	29	04	82	54	12	120*	79	20
7	4	62	45	29	70	83	54	78	128	84	48
8	5	28	46	30	36	84*	55	44	130	85	80
9	5	94	47	31	02	85	56	10	140	92	40
10	6	60	48*	31	68	86	56	76	144*	95	04
11	7	26	49	32	34	87	57	42	150	99	00
12*	7	92	**50**	33	00	88	58	08	156	102	96
13	8	58	51	33	66	89	58	74	168	110	88
14	9	24	52	34	32	**90**	59	40	196	129	36
15	9	90	53	34	98	91	60	06	200	132	00
16	10	56	54	35	64	92	60	72	220	145	20
17	11	22	55	36	30	93	61	38	224	147	84
18	11	88	56	36	96	94	62	04	256	168	96
19	12	54	57	37	62	95	62	70	280	184	80
20	13	20	58	38	28	96*	63	36	300	198	00
21	13	86	59	38	94	97	64	02	365	240	90
22	14	52	**60***	39	60	98	64	68	400	264	00
23	15	18	61	40	26	99	65	34	480	316	80
24*	15	84	62	40	92	**100**	66	00	500	330	00
25	16	50	63	41	58	101	66	66	516	340	56
26	17	16	64	42	24	102	67	32	560	369	60
27	17	82	65	42	90	103	67	98	600	396	00
28	18	48	66	43	56	104	68	64	625	412	50
29	19	14	67	44	22	105	69	30	640	422	40
30	19	80	68	44	88	106	69	96	700	462	00
31	20	46	69	45	54	107	70	62	750	495	00
32	21	12	**70**	46	20	108*	71	28	800	528	00
33	21	78	71	46	86	109	71	94	900	594	00

No.	£	p	No.	£	p	No.	£	p
1000	660	00	1760	1161	60	6000	3960	00
1016	670	56	2000	1320	00	7000	4620	00
1094	722	04	2240	1478	40	7500	4950	00
1120	739	20	2500	1650	00	10000	6600	00
1250	825	00	3000	1980	00	15000	9900	00
1500	990	00	4000	2640	00	20000	13200	00
1750	1155	00	5000	3300	00	30000	19800	00

No.	£	p	No.	£	p	No.	£	p	No.	£	p
1/16	0	04	34	22	78	72*	48	24	110	73	70
1/8	0	08½	35	23	45	73	48	91	111	74	37
1/4	0	17	36*	24	12	74	49	58	112	75	04
1/2	0	33½	37	24	79	75	50	25	113	75	71
3/4	0	50½	38	25	46	76	50	92	114	76	38
1½	1	00½	39	26	13	77	51	59	115	77	05
2	1	34	40	26	80	78	52	26	116	77	72
3	2	01	41	27	47	79	52	93	117	78	39
4	2	68	42	28	14	80	53	60	118	79	06
5	3	35	43	28	81	81	54	27	119	79	73
6	4	02	44	29	48	82	54	94	120*	80	40
7	4	69	45	30	15	83	55	61	128	85	76
8	5	36	46	30	82	84*	56	28	130	87	10
9	6	03	47	31	49	85	56	95	140	93	80
10	6	70	48*	32	16	86	57	62	144*	96	48
11	7	37	49	32	83	87	58	29	150	100	50
12*	8	04	50	33	50	88	58	96	156	104	52
13	8	71	51	34	17	89	59	63	168	112	56
14	9	38	52	34	84	90	60	30	196	131	32
15	10	05	53	35	51	91	60	97	200	134	00
16	10	72	54	36	18	92	61	64	220	147	40
17	11	39	55	36	85	93	62	31	224	150	08
18	12	06	56	37	52	94	62	98	256	171	52
19	12	73	57	38	19	95	63	65	280	187	60
20	13	40	58	38	86	96*	64	32	300	201	00
21	14	07	59	39	53	97	64	99	365	244	55
22	14	74	60*	40	20	98	65	66	400	268	00
23	15	41	61	40	87	99	66	33	480	321	60
24*	16	08	62	41	54	100	67	00	500	335	00
25	16	75	63	42	21	101	67	67	516	345	72
26	17	42	64	42	88	102	68	34	560	375	20
27	18	09	65	43	55	103	69	01	600	402	00
28	18	76	66	44	22	104	69	68	625	418	75
29	19	43	67	44	89	105	70	35	640	428	80
30	20	10	68	45	56	106	71	02	700	469	00
31	20	77	69	46	23	107	71	69	750	502	50
32	21	44	70	46	90	108*	72	36	800	536	00
33	22	11	71	47	57	109	73	03	900	603	00

No.	£	p	No.	£	p	No.	£	p
1000	670	00	1760	1179	20	6000	4020	00
1016	680	72	2000	1340	00	7000	4690	00
1094	732	98	2240	1500	80	7500	5025	00
1120	750	40	2500	1675	00	10000	6700	00
1250	837	50	3000	2010	00	15000	10050	00
1500	1005	00	4000	2680	00	20000	13400	00
1750	1172	50	5000	3350	00	30000	20100	00

67½p £0·675

No.	£	p	No.	£	p	No.	£	p	No.	£	p
1/16	0	04	34	22	95	72*	48	60	110	74	25
1/8	0	08½	35	23	62½	73	49	27½	111	74	92½
1/4	0	17	36*	24	30	74	49	95	112	75	60
1/2	0	34	37	24	97½	75	50	62½	113	76	27½
3/4	0	50½	38	25	65	76	51	30	114	76	95
1½	1	01½	39	26	32½	77	51	97½	115	77	62½
2	1	35	40	27	00	78	52	65	116	78	30
3	2	02½	41	27	67½	79	53	32½	117	78	97½
4	2	70	42	28	35	80	54	00	118	79	65
5	3	37½	43	29	02½	81	54	67½	119	80	32½
6	4	05	44	29	70	82	55	35	120*	81	00
7	4	72½	45	30	37½	83	56	02½	128	86	40
8	5	40	46	31	05	84*	56	70	130	87	75
9	6	07½	47	31	72½	85	57	37½	140	94	50
10	6	75	48*	32	40	86	58	05	144*	97	20
11	7	42½	49	33	07½	87	58	72½	150	101	25
12*	8	10	50	33	75	88	59	40	156	105	30
13	8	77½	51	34	42½	89	60	07½	168	113	40
14	9	45	52	35	10	90	60	75	196	132	30
15	10	12½	53	35	77½	91	61	42½	200	135	00
16	10	80	54	36	45	92	62	10	220	148	50
17	11	47½	55	37	12½	93	62	77½	224	151	20
18	12	15	56	37	80	94	63	45	256	172	80
19	12	82½	57	38	47½	95	64	12½	280	189	00
20	13	50	58	39	15	96*	64	80	300	202	50
21	14	17½	59	39	82½	97	65	47½	365	246	37½
22	14	85	60*	40	50	98	66	15	400	270	00
23	15	52½	61	41	17½	99	66	82½	480	324	00
24*	16	20	62	41	85	100	67	50	500	337	50
25	16	87½	63	42	52½	101	68	17½	516	348	30
26	17	55	64	43	20	102	68	85	560	378	00
27	18	22½	65	43	87½	103	69	52½	600	405	00
28	18	90	66	44	55	104	70	20	625	421	87½
29	19	57½	67	45	22½	105	70	87½	640	432	00
30	20	25	68	45	90	106	71	55	700	472	50
31	20	92½	69	46	57½	107	72	22½	750	506	25
32	21	60	70	47	25	108*	72	90	800	540	00
33	22	27½	71	47	92½	109	73	57½	900	607	50

No.	£	p	No.	£	p	No.	£	p
1000	675	00	1760	1188	00	6000	4050	00
1016	685	80	2000	1350	00	7000	4725	00
1094	738	45	2240	1512	00	7500	5062	50
1120	756	00	2500	1687	50	10000	6750	00
1250	843	75	3000	2025	00	15000	10125	00
1500	1012	50	4000	2700	00	20000	13500	00
1750	1181	25	5000	3375	00	30000	20250	00

No.	£	p	No.	£	p	No.	£	p	No.	£	p
1/16	0	04½	34	23	12	72*	48	96	110	74	80
1/8	0	08½	35	23	80	73	49	64	111	75	48
1/4	0	17	36*	24	48	74	50	32	112	76	16
1/2	0	34	37	25	16	75	51	00	113	76	84
3/4	0	51	38	25	84	76	51	68	114	77	52
1½	1	02	39	26	52	77	52	36	115	78	20
2	1	36	**40**	27	20	78	53	04	116	78	88
3	2	04	41	27	88	79	53	72	117	79	56
4	2	72	42	28	56	**80**	54	40	118	80	24
5	3	40	43	29	24	81	55	08	119	80	92
6	4	08	44	29	92	82	55	76	120*	81	60
7	4	76	45	30	60	83	56	44	128	87	04
8	5	44	46	31	28	84*	57	12	130	88	40
9	6	12	47	31	96	85	57	80	140	95	20
10	6	80	48*	32	64	86	58	48	144*	97	92
11	7	48	49	33	32	87	59	16	150	102	00
12*	8	16	**50**	34	00	88	59	84	156	106	08
13	8	84	51	34	68	89	60	52	168	114	24
14	9	52	52	35	36	**90**	61	20	196	133	28
15	10	20	53	36	04	91	61	88	200	136	00
16	10	88	54	36	72	92	62	56	220	149	60
17	11	56	55	37	40	93	63	24	224	152	32
18	12	24	56	38	08	94	63	92	256	174	08
19	12	92	57	38	76	95	64	60	280	190	40
20	13	60	58	39	44	96*	65	28	300	204	00
21	14	28	59	40	12	97	65	96	365	248	20
22	14	96	**60***	40	80	98	66	64	400	272	00
23	15	64	61	41	48	99	67	32	480	326	40
24*	16	32	62	42	16	**100**	68	00	500	340	00
25	17	00	63	42	84	101	68	68	516	350	88
26	17	68	64	43	52	102	69	36	560	380	80
27	18	36	65	44	20	103	70	04	600	408	00
28	19	04	66	44	88	104	70	72	625	425	00
29	19	72	67	45	56	105	71	40	640	435	20
30	20	40	68	46	24	106	72	08	700	476	00
31	21	08	69	46	92	107	72	76	750	510	00
32	21	76	**70**	47	60	108*	73	44	800	544	00
33	22	44	71	48	28	109	74	12	900	612	00

No.	£	p	No.	£	p	No.	£	p
1000	680	00	1760	1196	80	6000	4080	00
1016	690	88	2000	1360	00	7000	4760	00
1094	743	92	2240	1523	20	7500	5100	00
1120	761	60	2500	1700	00	10000	6800	00
1250	850	00	3000	2040	00	15000	10200	00
1500	1020	00	4000	2720	00	20000	13600	00
1750	1190	00	5000	3400	00	30000	20400	00

No.	£	p	No.	£	p	No.	£	p	No.	£	p
1/16	0	04½	34	23	46	72*	49	68	110	75	90
1/8	0	08½	35	24	15	73	50	37	111	76	59
1/4	0	17½	36*	24	84	74	51	06	112	77	28
1/2	0	34½	37	25	53	75	51	75	113	77	97
3/4	0	52	38	26	22	76	52	44	114	78	66
1½	1	03½	39	26	91	77	53	13	115	79	35
2	1	38	40	27	60	78	53	82	116	80	04
3	2	07	41	28	29	79	54	51	117	80	73
4	2	76	42	28	98	80	55	20	118	81	42
5	3	45	43	29	67	81	55	89	119	82	11
6	4	14	44	30	36	82	56	58	120*	82	80
7	4	83	45	31	05	83	57	27	128	88	32
8	5	52	46	31	74	84*	57	96	130	89	70
9	6	21	47	32	43	85	58	65	140	96	60
10	6	90	48*	33	12	86	59	34	144*	99	36
11	7	59	49	33	81	87	60	03	150	103	50
12*	8	28	50	34	50	88	60	72	156	107	64
13	8	97	51	35	19	89	61	41	168	115	92
14	9	66	52	35	88	90	62	10	196	135	24
15	10	35	53	36	57	91	62	79	200	138	00
16	11	04	54	37	26	92	63	48	220	151	80
17	11	73	55	37	95	93	64	17	224	154	56
18	12	42	56	38	64	94	64	86	256	176	64
19	13	11	57	39	33	95	65	55	280	193	20
20	13	80	58	40	02	96*	66	24	300	207	00
21	14	49	59	40	71	97	66	93	365	251	85
22	15	18	60*	41	40	98	67	62	400	276	00
23	15	87	61	42	09	99	68	31	480	331	20
24*	16	56	62	42	78	100	69	00	500	345	00
25	17	25	63	43	47	101	69	69	516	356	04
26	17	94	64	44	16	102	70	38	560	386	40
27	18	63	65	44	85	103	71	07	600	414	00
28	19	32	66	45	54	104	71	76	625	431	25
29	20	01	67	46	23	105	72	45	640	441	60
30	20	70	68	46	92	106	73	14	700	483	00
31	21	39	69	47	61	107	73	83	750	517	50
32	22	08	70	48	30	108*	74	52	800	552	00
33	22	77	71	48	99	109	75	21	900	621	00

No.	£	p	No.	£	p	No.	£	p
1000	690	00	1760	1214	40	6000	4140	00
1016	701	04	2000	1380	00	7000	4830	00
1094	754	86	2240	1545	60	7500	5175	00
1120	772	80	2500	1725	00	10000	6900	00
1250	862	50	3000	2070	00	15000	10350	00
1500	1035	00	4000	2760	00	20000	13800	00
1750	1207	50	5000	3450	00	30000	20700	00

70p £0·70

No.	£	p	No.	£	p	No.	£	p	No.	£	p
$\frac{1}{16}$	0	04½	34	23	80	72*	50	40	110	77	00
$\frac{1}{8}$	0	09	35	24	50	73	51	10	111	77	70
$\frac{1}{4}$	0	17½	36*	25	20	74	51	80	112	78	40
$\frac{1}{2}$	0	35	37	25	90	75	52	50	113	79	10
$\frac{3}{4}$	0	52½	38	26	60	76	53	20	114	79	80
1½	1	05	39	27	30	77	53	90	115	80	50
2	1	40	**40**	28	00	78	54	60	116	81	20
3	2	10	41	28	70	79	55	30	117	81	90
4	2	80	42	29	40	**80**	56	00	118	82	60
5	3	50	43	30	10	81	56	70	119	83	30
6	4	20	44	30	80	82	57	40	120*	84	00
7	4	90	45	31	50	83	58	10	128	89	60
8	5	60	46	32	20	84*	58	80	130	91	00
9	6	30	47	32	90	85	59	50	140	98	00
10	7	00	48*	33	60	86	60	20	144*	100	80
11	7	70	49	34	30	87	60	90	150	105	00
12*	8	40	**50**	35	00	88	61	60	156	109	20
13	9	10	51	35	70	89	62	30	168	117	60
14	9	80	52	36	40	**90**	63	00	196	137	20
15	10	50	53	37	10	91	63	70	200	140	00
16	11	20	54	37	80	92	64	40	220	154	00
17	11	90	55	38	50	93	65	10	224	156	80
18	12	60	56	39	20	94	65	80	256	179	20
19	13	30	57	39	90	95	66	50	280	196	00
20	14	00	58	40	60	96*	67	20	300	210	00
21	14	70	59	41	30	97	67	90	365	255	50
22	15	40	**60***	42	00	98	68	60	400	280	00
23	16	10	61	42	70	99	69	30	480	336	00
24*	16	80	62	43	40	**100**	70	00	500	350	00
25	17	50	63	44	10	101	70	70	516	361	20
26	18	20	64	44	80	102	71	40	560	392	00
27	18	90	65	45	50	103	72	10	600	420	00
28	19	60	66	46	20	104	72	80	625	437	50
29	20	30	67	46	90	105	73	50	640	448	00
30	21	00	68	47	60	106	74	20	700	490	00
31	21	70	69	48	30	107	74	90	750	525	00
32	22	40	**70**	49	00	108*	75	60	800	560	00
33	23	10	71	49	70	109	76	30	900	630	00

No.	£	p	No.	£	p	No.	£	p
1000	700	00	1760	1232	00	6000	4200	00
1016	711	20	2000	1400	00	7000	4900	00
1094	765	80	2240	1568	00	7500	5250	00
1120	784	00	2500	1750	00	10000	7000	00
1250	875	00	3000	2100	00	15000	10500	00
1500	1050	00	4000	2800	00	20000	14000	00
1750	1225	00	5000	3500	00	30000	21000	00

No.	£	p	No.	£	p	No.	£	p	No.	£	p
$\frac{1}{16}$	0	04½	34	24	14	72*	51	12	110	78	10
$\frac{1}{8}$	0	09	35	24	85	73	51	83	111	78	81
$\frac{1}{4}$	0	18	36*	25	56	74	52	54	112	79	52
$\frac{1}{2}$	0	35½	37	26	27	75	53	25	113	80	23
$\frac{3}{4}$	0	53½	38	26	98	76	53	96	114	80	94
1½	1	06½	39	27	69	77	54	67	115	81	65
2	1	42	**40**	28	40	78	55	38	116	82	36
3	2	13	41	29	11	79	56	09	117	83	07
4	2	84	42	29	82	**80**	56	80	118	83	78
5	3	55	43	30	53	81	57	51	119	84	49
6	4	26	44	31	24	82	58	22	120*	85	20
7	4	97	45	31	95	83	58	93	128	90	88
8	5	68	46	32	66	84*	59	64	130	92	30
9	6	39	47	33	37	85	60	35	140	99	40
10	7	10	48*	34	08	86	61	06	144*	102	24
11	7	81	49	34	79	87	61	77	150	106	50
12*	8	52	**50**	35	50	88	62	48	156	110	76
13	9	23	51	36	21	89	63	19	168	119	28
14	9	94	52	36	92	**90**	63	90	196	139	16
15	10	65	53	37	63	91	64	61	200	142	00
16	11	36	54	38	34	92	65	32	220	156	20
17	12	07	55	39	05	93	66	03	224	159	04
18	12	78	56	39	76	94	66	74	256	181	76
19	13	49	57	40	47	95	67	45	280	198	80
20	14	20	58	41	18	96*	68	16	300	213	00
21	14	91	59	41	89	97	68	87	365	259	15
22	15	62	**60***	42	60	98	69	58	400	284	00
23	16	33	61	43	31	99	70	29	480	340	80
24*	17	04	62	44	02	**100**	71	00	500	355	00
25	17	75	63	44	73	101	71	71	516	366	36
26	18	46	64	45	44	102	72	42	560	397	60
27	19	17	65	46	15	103	73	13	600	426	00
28	19	88	66	46	86	104	73	84	625	443	75
29	20	59	67	47	57	105	74	55	640	454	40
30	21	30	68	48	28	106	75	26	700	497	00
31	22	01	69	48	99	107	75	97	750	532	50
32	22	72	**70**	49	70	108*	76	68	800	568	00
33	23	43	71	50	41	109	77	39	900	639	00

No.	£	p	No.	£	p	No.	£	p
1000	710	00	1760	1249	60	6000	4260	00
1016	721	36	2000	1420	00	7000	4970	00
1094	776	74	2240	1590	40	7500	5325	00
1120	795	20	2500	1775	00	10000	7100	00
1250	887	50	3000	2130	00	15000	10650	00
1500	1065	00	4000	2840	00	20000	14200	00
1750	1242	50	5000	3550	00	30000	21300	00

No.	£	p	No.	£	p	No.	£	p	No.	£	p
1/16	0	04½	34	24	48	72*	51	84	110	79	20
1/8	0	09	35	25	20	73	52	56	111	79	92
1/4	0	18	36*	25	92	74	53	28	112	80	64
1/2	0	36	37	26	64	75	54	00	113	81	36
3/4	0	54	38	27	36	76	54	72	114	82	08
1½	1	08	39	28	08	77	55	44	115	82	80
2	1	44	40	28	80	78	56	16	116	83	52
3	2	16	41	29	52	79	56	88	117	84	24
4	2	88	42	30	24	80	57	60	118	84	96
5	3	60	43	30	96	81	58	32	119	85	68
6	4	32	44	31	68	82	59	04	120*	86	40
7	5	04	45	32	40	83	59	76	128	92	16
8	5	76	46	33	12	84*	60	48	130	93	60
9	6	48	47	33	84	85	61	20	140	100	80
10	7	20	48*	34	56	86	61	92	144*	103	68
11	7	92	49	35	28	87	62	64	150	108	00
12*	8	64	50	36	00	88	63	36	156	112	32
13	9	36	51	36	72	89	64	08	168	120	96
14	10	08	52	37	44	90	64	80	196	141	12
15	10	80	53	38	16	91	65	52	200	144	00
16	11	52	54	38	88	92	66	24	220	158	40
17	12	24	55	39	60	93	66	96	224	161	28
18	12	96	56	40	32	94	67	68	256	184	32
19	13	68	57	41	04	95	68	40	280	201	60
20	14	40	58	41	76	96*	69	12	300	216	00
21	15	12	59	42	48	97	69	84	365	262	80
22	15	84	60*	43	20	98	70	56	400	288	00
23	16	56	61	43	92	99	71	28	480	345	60
24*	17	28	62	44	64	100	72	00	500	360	00
25	18	00	63	45	36	101	72	72	516	371	52
26	18	72	64	46	08	102	73	44	560	403	20
27	19	44	65	46	80	103	74	16	600	432	00
28	20	16	66	47	52	104	74	88	625	450	00
29	20	88	67	48	24	105	75	60	640	460	80
30	21	60	68	48	96	106	76	32	700	504	00
31	22	32	69	49	68	107	77	04	750	540	00
32	23	04	70	50	40	108*	77	76	800	576	00
33	23	76	71	51	12	109	78	48	900	648	00

No.	£	p	No.	£	p	No.	£	p
1000	720	00	1760	1267	20	6000	4320	00
1016	731	52	2000	1440	00	7000	5040	00
1094	787	68	2240	1612	80	7500	5400	00
1120	806	40	2500	1800	00	10000	7200	00
1250	900	00	3000	2160	00	15000	10800	00
1500	1080	00	4000	2880	00	20000	14400	00
1750	1260	00	5000	3600	00	30000	21600	00

No.	£	p	No.	£	p	No.	£	p	No.	£	p
1/16	0	04½	34	24	65	72*	52	20	110	79	75
1/8	0	09	35	25	37½	73	52	92½	111	80	47½
1/4	0	18	36*	26	10	74	53	65	112	81	20
1/2	0	36½	37	26	82½	75	54	37½	113	81	92½
3/4	0	54½	38	27	55	76	55	10	114	82	65
1½	1	09	39	28	27½	77	55	82½	115	83	37½
2	1	45	40	29	00	78	56	55	116	84	10
3	2	17½	41	29	72½	79	57	27½	117	84	82½
4	2	90	42	30	45	80	58	00	118	85	55
5	3	62½	43	31	17½	81	58	72½	119	86	27½
6	4	35	44	31	90	82	59	45	120*	87	00
7	5	07½	45	32	62½	83	60	17½	128	92	80
8	5	80	46	33	35	84*	60	90	130	94	25
9	6	52½	47	34	07½	85	61	62½	140	101	50
10	7	25	48*	34	80	86	62	35	144*	104	40
11	7	97½	49	35	52½	87	63	07½	150	108	75
12*	8	70	50	36	25	88	63	80	156	113	10
13	9	42½	51	36	97½	89	64	52½	168	121	80
14	10	15	52	37	70	90	65	25	196	142	10
15	10	87½	53	38	42½	91	65	97½	200	145	00
16	11	60	54	39	15	92	66	70	220	159	50
17	12	32½	55	39	87½	93	67	42½	224	162	40
18	13	05	56	40	60	94	68	15	256	185	60
19	13	77½	57	41	32½	95	68	87½	280	203	00
20	14	50	58	42	05	96*	69	60	300	217	50
21	15	22½	59	42	77½	97	70	32½	365	264	62½
22	15	95	60*	43	50	98	71	05	400	290	00
23	16	67½	61	44	22½	99	71	77½	480	348	00
24*	17	40	62	44	95	100	72	50	500	362	50
25	18	12½	63	45	67½	101	73	22½	516	374	10
26	18	85	64	46	40	102	73	95	560	406	00
27	19	57½	65	47	12½	103	74	67½	600	435	00
28	20	30	66	47	85	104	75	40	625	453	12½
29	21	02½	67	48	57½	105	76	12½	640	464	00
30	21	75	68	49	30	106	76	85	700	507	50
31	22	47½	69	50	02½	107	77	57½	750	543	75
32	23	20	70	50	75	108*	78	30	800	580	00
33	23	92½	71	51	47½	109	79	02½	900	652	50

No.	£	p	No.	£	p	No.	£	p
1000	725	00	1760	1276	00	6000	4350	00
1016	736	60	2000	1450	00	7000	5075	00
1094	793	15	2240	1624	00	7500	5437	50
1120	812	00	2500	1812	50	10000	7250	00
1250	906	25	3000	2175	00	15000	10875	00
1500	1087	50	4000	2900	00	20000	14500	00
1750	1268	75	5000	3625	00	30000	21750	00

73p   £0·73

No.	£	p	No.	£	p	No.	£	p	No.	£	p
$\frac{1}{16}$	0	04½	34	24	82	72*	52	56	110	80	30
$\frac{1}{8}$	0	09	35	25	55	73	53	29	111	81	03
$\frac{1}{4}$	0	18½	36*	26	28	74	54	02	112	81	76
$\frac{1}{2}$	0	36½	37	27	01	75	54	75	113	82	49
$\frac{3}{4}$	0	55	38	27	74	76	55	48	114	83	22
1½	1	09½	39	28	47	77	56	21	115	83	95
2	1	46	40	29	20	78	56	94	116	84	68
3	2	19	41	29	93	79	57	67	117	85	41
4	2	92	42	30	66	80	58	40	118	86	14
5	3	65	43	31	39	81	59	13	119	86	87
6	4	38	44	32	12	82	59	86	120*	87	60
7	5	11	45	32	85	83	60	59	128	93	44
8	5	84	46	33	58	84*	61	32	130	94	90
9	6	57	47	34	31	85	62	05	140	102	20
10	7	30	48*	35	04	86	62	78	144*	105	12
11	8	03	49	35	77	87	63	51	150	109	50
12*	8	76	50	36	50	88	64	24	156	113	88
13	9	49	51	37	23	89	64	97	168	122	64
14	10	22	52	37	96	90	65	70	196	143	08
15	10	95	53	38	69	91	66	43	200	146	00
16	11	68	54	39	42	92	67	16	220	160	60
17	12	41	55	40	15	93	67	89	224	163	52
18	13	14	56	40	88	94	68	62	256	186	88
19	13	87	57	41	61	95	69	35	280	204	40
20	14	60	58	42	34	96*	70	08	300	219	00
21	15	33	59	43	07	97	70	81	365	266	45
22	16	06	60*	43	80	98	71	54	400	292	00
23	16	79	61	44	53	99	72	27	480	350	40
24*	17	52	62	45	26	100	73	00	500	365	00
25	18	25	63	45	99	101	73	73	516	376	68
26	18	98	64	46	72	102	74	46	560	408	80
27	19	71	65	47	45	103	75	19	600	438	00
28	20	44	66	48	18	104	75	92	625	456	25
29	21	17	67	48	91	105	76	65	640	467	20
30	21	90	68	49	64	106	77	38	700	511	00
31	22	63	69	50	37	107	78	11	750	547	50
32	23	36	70	51	10	108*	78	84	800	584	00
33	24	09	71	51	83	109	79	57	900	657	00

No.	£	p	No.	£	p	No.	£	p
1000	730	00	1760	1284	80	6000	4380	00
1016	741	68	2000	1460	00	7000	5110	00
1094	798	62	2240	1635	20	7500	5475	00
1120	817	60	2500	1825	00	10000	7300	00
1250	912	50	3000	2190	00	15000	10950	00
1500	1095	00	4000	2920	00	20000	14600	00
1750	1277	50	5000	3650	00	30000	21900	00

No.	£	p	No.	£	p	No.	£	p	No.	£	p
1/16	0	04½	34	25	16	72*	53	28	110	81	40
1/8	0	09½	35	25	90	73	54	02	111	82	14
1/4	0	18½	36*	26	64	74	54	76	112	82	88
1/2	0	37	37	27	38	75	55	50	113	83	62
3/4	0	55½	38	28	12	76	56	24	114	84	36
1½	1	11	39	28	86	77	56	98	115	85	10
2	1	48	40	29	60	78	57	72	116	85	84
3	2	22	41	30	34	79	58	46	117	86	58
4	2	96	42	31	08	80	59	20	118	87	32
5	3	70	43	31	82	81	59	94	119	88	06
6	4	44	44	32	56	82	60	68	120*	88	80
7	5	18	45	33	30	83	61	42	128	94	72
8	5	92	46	34	04	84*	62	16	130	96	20
9	6	66	47	34	78	85	62	90	140	103	60
10	7	40	48*	35	52	86	63	64	144*	106	56
11	8	14	49	36	26	87	64	38	150	111	00
12*	8	88	50	37	00	88	65	12	156	115	44
13	9	62	51	37	74	89	65	86	168	124	32
14	10	36	52	38	48	90	66	60	196	145	04
15	11	10	53	39	22	91	67	34	200	148	00
16	11	84	54	39	96	92	68	08	220	162	80
17	12	58	55	40	70	93	68	82	224	165	76
18	13	32	56	41	44	94	69	56	256	189	44
19	14	06	57	42	18	95	70	30	280	207	20
20	14	80	58	42	92	96*	71	04	300	222	00
21	15	54	59	43	66	97	71	78	365	270	10
22	16	28	60*	44	40	98	72	52	400	296	00
23	17	02	61	45	14	99	73	26	480	355	20
24*	17	76	62	45	88	100	74	00	500	370	00
25	18	50	63	46	62	101	74	74	516	381	84
26	19	24	64	47	36	102	75	48	560	414	40
27	19	98	65	48	10	103	76	22	600	444	00
28	20	72	66	48	84	104	76	96	625	462	50
29	21	46	67	49	58	105	77	70	640	473	60
30	22	20	68	50	32	106	78	44	700	518	00
31	22	94	69	51	06	107	79	18	750	555	00
32	23	68	70	51	80	108*	79	92	800	592	00
33	24	42	71	52	54	109	80	66	900	666	00

No.	£	p	No.	£	p	No.	£	p
1000	740	00	1760	1302	40	6000	4440	00
1016	751	84	2000	1480	00	7000	5180	00
1094	809	56	2240	1657	60	7500	5550	00
1120	828	80	2500	1850	00	10000	7400	00
1250	925	00	3000	2220	00	15000	11100	00
1500	1110	00	4000	2960	00	20000	14800	00
1750	1295	00	5000	3700	00	30000	22200	00

No.	£	p	No.	£	p	No.	£	p	No.	£	p
$\frac{1}{16}$	0	04½	34	25	50	72*	54	00	110	82	50
$\frac{1}{8}$	0	09½	35	26	25	73	54	75	111	83	25
$\frac{1}{4}$	0	19	36*	27	00	74	55	50	112	84	00
$\frac{1}{2}$	0	37½	37	27	75	75	56	25	113	84	75
$\frac{3}{4}$	0	56½	38	28	50	76	57	00	114	85	50
$1\frac{1}{2}$	1	12½	39	29	25	77	57	75	115	86	25
2	1	50	40	30	00	78	58	50	116	87	00
3	2	25	41	30	75	79	59	25	117	87	75
4	3	00	42	31	50	80	60	00	118	88	50
5	3	75	43	32	25	81	60	75	119	89	25
6	4	50	44	33	00	82	61	50	120*	90	00
7	5	25	45	33	75	83	62	25	128	96	00
8	6	00	46	34	50	84*	63	00	130	97	50
9	6	75	47	35	25	85	63	75	140	105	00
10	7	50	48*	36	00	86	64	50	144*	108	00
11	8	25	49	36	75	87	65	25	150	112	50
12*	9	00	50	37	50	88	66	00	156	117	00
13	9	75	51	38	25	89	66	75	168	126	00
14	10	50	52	39	00	90	67	50	196	147	00
15	11	25	53	39	75	91	68	25	200	150	00
16	12	00	54	40	50	92	69	00	220	165	00
17	12	75	55	41	25	93	69	75	224	168	00
18	13	50	56	42	00	94	70	50	256	192	00
19	14	25	57	42	75	95	71	25	280	210	00
20	15	00	58	43	50	96*	72	00	300	225	00
21	15	75	59	44	25	97	72	75	365	273	75
22	16	50	60*	45	00	98	73	50	400	300	00
23	17	25	61	45	75	99	74	25	480	360	00
24*	18	00	62	46	50	100	75	00	500	375	00
25	18	75	63	47	25	101	75	75	516	387	00
26	19	50	64	48	00	102	76	50	560	420	00
27	20	25	65	48	75	103	77	25	600	450	00
28	21	00	66	49	50	104	78	00	625	468	75
29	21	75	67	50	25	105	78	75	640	480	00
30	22	50	68	51	00	106	79	50	700	525	00
31	23	25	69	51	75	107	80	25	750	562	50
32	24	00	70	52	50	108*	81	00	800	600	00
33	24	75	71	53	25	109	81	75	900	675	00

No.	£	p	No.	£	p	No.	£	p
1000	750	00	1760	1320	00	6000	4500	00
1016	762	00	2000	1500	00	7000	5250	00
1094	820	50	2240	1680	00	7500	5625	00
1120	840	00	2500	1875	00	10000	7500	00
1250	937	50	3000	2250	00	15000	11250	00
1500	1125	00	4000	3000	00	20000	15000	00
1750	1312	50	5000	3750	00	30000	22500	00

No.	£	p	No.	£	p	No.	£	p	No.	£	p
$\frac{1}{16}$	0	05	34	25	84	72*	54	72	110	83	60
$\frac{1}{8}$	0	09½	35	26	60	73	55	48	111	84	36
$\frac{1}{4}$	0	19	36*	27	36	74	56	24	112	85	12
$\frac{1}{2}$	0	38	37	28	12	75	57	00	113	85	88
$\frac{3}{4}$	0	57	38	28	88	76	57	76	114	86	64
1½	1	14	39	29	64	77	58	52	115	87	40
2	1	52	40	30	40	78	59	28	116	88	16
3	2	28	41	31	16	79	60	04	117	88	92
4	3	04	42	31	92	80	60	80	118	89	68
5	3	80	43	32	68	81	61	56	119	90	44
6	4	56	44	33	44	82	62	32	120*	91	20
7	5	32	45	34	20	83	63	08	128	97	28
8	6	08	46	34	96	84*	63	84	130	98	80
9	6	84	47	35	72	85	64	60	140	106	40
10	7	60	48*	36	48	86	65	36	144*	109	44
11	8	36	49	37	24	87	66	12	150	114	00
12*	9	12	50	38	00	88	66	88	156	118	56
13	9	88	51	38	76	89	67	64	168	127	68
14	10	64	52	39	52	90	68	40	196	148	96
15	11	40	53	40	28	91	69	16	200	152	00
16	12	16	54	41	04	92	69	92	220	167	20
17	12	92	55	41	80	93	70	68	224	170	24
18	13	68	56	42	56	94	71	44	256	194	56
19	14	44	57	43	32	95	72	20	280	212	80
20	15	20	58	44	08	96*	72	96	300	228	00
21	15	96	59	44	84	97	73	72	365	277	40
22	16	72	60*	45	60	98	74	48	400	304	00
23	17	48	61	46	36	99	75	24	480	364	80
24*	18	24	62	47	12	100	76	00	500	380	00
25	19	00	63	47	88	101	76	76	516	392	16
26	19	76	64	48	64	102	77	52	560	425	60
27	20	52	65	49	40	103	78	28	600	456	00
28	21	28	66	50	16	104	79	04	625	475	00
29	22	04	67	50	92	105	79	80	640	486	40
30	22	80	68	51	68	106	80	56	700	532	00
31	23	56	69	52	44	107	81	32	750	570	00
32	24	32	70	53	20	108*	82	08	800	608	00
33	25	08	71	53	96	109	82	84	900	684	00

No.	£	p	No.	£	p	No.	£	p
1000	760	00	1760	1337	60	6000	4560	00
1016	772	16	2000	1520	00	7000	5320	00
1094	831	44	2240	1702	40	7500	5700	00
1120	851	20	2500	1900	00	10000	7600	00
1250	950	00	3000	2280	00	15000	11400	00
1500	1140	00	4000	3040	00	20000	15200	00
1750	1330	00	5000	3800	00	30000	22800	00

No.	£	p	No.	£	p	No.	£	p	No.	£	p
1/16	0	05	34	26	18	72*	55	44	110	84	70
1/8	0	09½	35	26	95	73	56	21	111	85	47
1/4	0	19½	36*	27	72	74	56	98	112	86	24
1/2	0	38½	37	28	49	75	57	75	113	87	01
3/4	0	58	38	29	26	76	58	52	114	87	78
1½	1	15½	39	30	03	77	59	29	115	88	55
2	1	54	40	30	80	78	60	06	116	89	32
3	2	31	41	31	57	79	60	83	117	90	09
4	3	08	42	32	34	80	61	60	118	90	86
5	3	85	43	33	11	81	62	37	119	91	63
6	4	62	44	33	88	82	63	14	120*	92	40
7	5	39	45	34	65	83	63	91	128	98	56
8	6	16	46	35	42	84*	64	68	130	100	10
9	6	93	47	36	19	85	65	45	140	107	80
10	7	70	48*	36	96	86	66	22	144*	110	88
11	8	47	49	37	73	87	66	99	150	115	50
12*	9	24	50	38	50	88	67	76	156	120	12
13	10	01	51	39	27	89	68	53	168	129	36
14	10	78	52	40	04	90	69	30	196	150	92
15	11	55	53	40	81	91	70	07	200	154	00
16	12	32	54	41	58	92	70	84	220	169	40
17	13	09	55	42	35	93	71	61	224	172	48
18	13	86	56	43	12	94	72	38	256	197	12
19	14	63	57	43	89	95	73	15	280	215	60
20	15	40	58	44	66	96*	73	92	300	231	00
21	16	17	59	45	43	97	74	69	365	281	05
22	16	94	60*	46	20	98	75	46	400	308	00
23	17	71	61	46	97	99	76	23	480	369	60
24*	18	48	62	47	74	100	77	00	500	385	00
25	19	25	63	48	51	101	77	77	516	397	32
26	20	02	64	49	28	102	78	54	560	431	20
27	20	79	65	50	05	103	79	31	600	462	00
28	21	56	66	50	82	104	80	08	625	481	25
29	22	33	67	51	59	105	80	85	640	492	80
30	23	10	68	52	36	106	81	62	700	539	00
31	23	87	69	53	13	107	82	39	750	577	50
32	24	64	70	53	90	108*	83	16	800	616	00
33	25	41	71	54	67	109	83	93	900	693	00

No.	£	p	No.	£	p	No.	£	p
1000	770	00	1760	1355	20	6000	4620	00
1016	782	32	2000	1540	00	7000	5390	00
1094	842	38	2240	1724	80	7500	5775	00
1120	862	40	2500	1925	00	10000	7700	00
1250	962	50	3000	2310	00	15000	11550	00
1500	1155	00	4000	3080	00	20000	15400	00
1750	1347	50	5000	3850	00	30000	23100	00

No.	£	p	No.	£	p	No.	£	p	No.	£	p
1/16	0	05	34	26	35	72*	55	80	110	85	25
1/8	0	09½	35	27	12½	73	56	57½	111	86	02½
1/4	0	19½	36*	27	90	74	57	35	112	86	80
1/2	0	39	37	28	67½	75	58	12½	113	87	57½
3/4	0	58	38	29	45	76	58	90	114	88	35
1½	1	16½	39	30	22½	77	59	67½	115	89	12½
2	1	55	40	31	00	78	60	45	116	89	90
3	2	32½	41	31	77½	79	61	22½	117	90	67½
4	3	10	42	32	55	80	62	00	118	91	45
5	3	87½	43	33	32½	81	62	77½	119	92	22½
6	4	65	44	34	10	82	63	55	120*	93	00
7	5	42½	45	34	87½	83	64	32½	128	99	20
8	6	20	46	35	65	84*	65	10	130	100	75
9	6	97½	47	36	42½	85	65	87½	140	108	50
10	7	75	48*	37	20	86	66	65	144*	111	60
11	8	52½	49	37	97½	87	67	42½	150	116	25
12*	9	30	50	38	75	88	68	20	156	120	90
13	10	07½	51	39	52½	89	68	97½	168	130	20
14	10	85	52	40	30	90	69	75	196	151	90
15	11	62½	53	41	07½	91	70	52½	200	155	00
16	12	40	54	41	85	92	71	30	220	170	50
17	13	17½	55	42	62½	93	72	07½	224	173	60
18	13	95	56	43	40	94	72	85	256	198	40
19	14	72½	57	44	17½	95	73	62½	280	217	00
20	15	50	58	44	95	96*	74	40	300	232	50
21	16	27½	59	45	72½	97	75	17½	365	282	87½
22	17	05	60*	46	50	98	75	95	400	310	00
23	17	82½	61	47	27½	99	76	72½	480	372	00
24*	18	60	62	48	05	100	77	50	500	387	50
25	19	37½	63	48	82½	101	78	27½	516	399	90
26	20	15	64	49	60	102	79	05	560	434	00
27	20	92½	65	50	37½	103	79	82½	600	465	00
28	21	70	66	51	15	104	80	60	625	484	37½
29	22	47½	67	51	92½	105	81	37½	640	496	00
30	23	25	68	52	70	106	82	15	700	542	50
31	24	02½	69	53	47½	107	82	92½	750	581	25
32	24	80	70	54	25	108*	83	70	800	620	00
33	25	57½	71	55	02½	109	84	47½	900	697	50

No.	£	p	No.	£	p	No.	£	p
1000	775	00	1760	1364	00	6000	4650	00
1016	787	40	2000	1550	00	7000	5425	00
1094	847	85	2240	1736	00	7500	5812	50
1120	868	00	2500	1937	50	10000	7750	00
1250	968	75	3000	2325	00	15000	11625	00
1500	1162	50	4000	3100	00	20000	15500	00
1750	1356	25	5000	3875	00	30000	23250	00

No.	£	p	No.	£	p	No.	£	p	No.	£	p
1/16	0	05	34	26	52	72*	56	16	110	85	80
1/8	0	10	35	27	30	73	56	94	111	86	58
1/4	0	19½	36*	28	08	74	57	72	112	87	36
1/2	0	39	37	28	86	75	58	50	113	88	14
3/4	0	58½	38	29	64	76	59	28	114	88	92
1½	1	17	39	30	42	77	60	06	115	89	70
2	1	56	40	31	20	78	60	84	116	90	48
3	2	34	41	31	98	79	61	62	117	91	26
4	3	12	42	32	76	80	62	40	118	92	04
5	3	90	43	33	54	81	63	18	119	92	82
6	4	68	44	34	32	82	63	96	120*	93	60
7	5	46	45	35	10	83	64	74	128	99	84
8	6	24	46	35	88	84*	65	52	130	101	40
9	7	02	47	36	66	85	66	30	140	109	20
10	7	80	48*	37	44	86	67	08	144*	112	32
11	8	58	49	38	22	87	67	86	150	117	00
12*	9	36	50	39	00	88	68	64	156	121	68
13	10	14	51	39	78	89	69	42	168	131	04
14	10	92	52	40	56	90	70	20	196	152	88
15	11	70	53	41	34	91	70	98	200	156	00
16	12	48	54	42	12	92	71	76	220	171	60
17	13	26	55	42	90	93	72	54	224	174	72
18	14	04	56	43	68	94	73	32	256	199	68
19	14	82	57	44	46	95	74	10	280	218	40
20	15	60	58	45	24	96*	74	88	300	234	00
21	16	38	59	46	02	97	75	66	365	284	70
22	17	16	60*	46	80	98	76	44	400	312	00
23	17	94	61	47	58	99	77	22	480	374	40
24*	18	72	62	48	36	100	78	00	500	390	00
25	19	50	63	49	14	101	78	78	516	402	48
26	20	28	64	49	92	102	79	56	560	436	80
27	21	06	65	50	70	103	80	34	600	468	00
28	21	84	66	51	48	104	81	12	625	487	50
29	22	62	67	52	26	105	81	90	640	499	20
30	23	40	68	53	04	106	82	68	700	546	00
31	24	18	69	53	82	107	83	46	750	585	00
32	24	96	70	54	60	108*	84	24	800	624	00
33	25	74	71	55	38	109	85	02	900	702	00

No.	£	p	No.	£	p	No.	£	p
1000	780	00	1760	1372	80	6000	4680	00
1016	792	48	2000	1560	00	7000	5460	00
1094	853	32	2240	1747	20	7500	5850	00
1120	873	60	2500	1950	00	10000	7800	00
1250	975	00	3000	2340	00	15000	11700	00
1500	1170	00	4000	3120	00	20000	15600	00
1750	1365	00	5000	3900	00	30000	23400	00

No.	£	p	No.	£	p	No.	£	p	No.	£	p
1/16	0	05	34	26	86	72*	56	88	110	86	90
1/8	0	10	35	27	65	73	57	67	111	87	69
1/4	0	20	36*	28	44	74	58	46	112	88	48
1/2	0	39½	37	29	23	75	59	25	113	89	27
3/4	0	59½	38	30	02	76	60	04	114	90	06
1½	1	18½	39	30	81	77	60	83	115	90	85
2	1	58	40	31	60	78	61	62	116	91	64
3	2	37	41	32	39	79	62	41	117	92	43
4	3	16	42	33	18	80	63	20	118	93	22
5	3	95	43	33	97	81	63	99	119	94	01
6	4	74	44	34	76	82	64	78	120*	94	80
7	5	53	45	35	55	83	65	57	128	101	12
8	6	32	46	36	34	84*	66	36	130	102	70
9	7	11	47	37	13	85	67	15	140	110	60
10	7	90	48*	37	92	86	67	94	144*	113	76
11	8	69	49	38	71	87	68	73	150	118	50
12*	9	48	50	39	50	88	69	52	156	123	24
13	10	27	51	40	29	89	70	31	168	132	72
14	11	06	52	41	08	90	71	10	196	154	84
15	11	85	53	41	87	91	71	89	200	158	00
16	12	64	54	42	66	92	72	68	220	173	80
17	13	43	55	43	45	93	73	47	224	176	96
18	14	22	56	44	24	94	74	26	256	202	24
19	15	01	57	45	03	95	75	05	280	221	20
20	15	80	58	45	82	96*	75	84	300	237	00
21	16	59	59	46	61	97	76	63	365	288	35
22	17	38	60*	47	40	98	77	42	400	316	00
23	18	17	61	48	19	99	78	21	480	379	20
24*	18	96	62	48	98	100	79	00	500	395	00
25	19	75	63	49	77	101	79	79	516	407	64
26	20	54	64	50	56	102	80	58	560	442	40
27	21	33	65	51	35	103	81	37	600	474	00
28	22	12	66	52	14	104	82	16	625	493	75
29	22	91	67	52	93	105	82	95	640	505	60
30	23	70	68	53	72	106	83	74	700	553	00
31	24	49	69	54	51	107	84	53	750	592	50
32	25	28	70	55	30	108*	85	32	800	632	00
33	26	07	71	56	09	109	86	11	900	711	00

No.	£	p	No.	£	p	No.	£	p
1000	790	00	1760	1390	40	6000	4740	00
1016	802	64	2000	1580	00	7000	5530	00
1094	864	26	2240	1769	60	7500	5925	00
1120	884	80	2500	1975	00	10000	7900	00
1250	987	50	3000	2370	00	15000	11850	00
1500	1185	00	4000	3160	00	20000	15800	00
1750	1382	50	5000	3950	00	30000	23700	00

No.	£	p	No.	£	p	No.	£	p	No.	£	p
1/16	0	05	34	27	20	72*	57	60	110	88	00
1/8	0	10	35	28	00	73	58	40	111	88	80
1/4	0	20	36*	28	80	74	59	20	112	89	60
1/2	0	40	37	29	60	75	60	00	113	90	40
3/4	0	60	38	30	40	76	60	80	114	91	20
1½	1	20	39	31	20	77	61	60	115	92	00
2	1	60	40	32	00	78	62	40	116	92	80
3	2	40	41	32	80	79	63	20	117	93	60
4	3	20	42	33	60	80	64	00	118	94	40
5	4	00	43	34	40	81	64	80	119	95	20
6	4	80	44	35	20	82	65	60	120*	96	00
7	5	60	45	36	00	83	66	40	128	102	40
8	6	40	46	36	80	84*	67	20	130	104	00
9	7	20	47	37	60	85	68	00	140	112	00
10	8	00	48*	38	40	86	68	80	144*	115	20
11	8	80	49	39	20	87	69	60	150	120	00
12*	9	60	50	40	00	88	70	40	156	124	80
13	10	40	51	40	80	89	71	20	168	134	40
14	11	20	52	41	60	90	72	00	196	156	80
15	12	00	53	42	40	91	72	80	200	160	00
16	12	80	54	43	20	92	73	60	220	176	00
17	13	60	55	44	00	93	74	40	224	179	20
18	14	40	56	44	80	94	75	20	256	204	80
19	15	20	57	45	60	95	76	00	280	224	00
20	16	00	58	46	40	96*	76	80	300	240	00
21	16	80	59	47	20	97	77	60	365	292	00
22	17	60	60*	48	00	98	78	40	400	320	00
23	18	40	61	48	80	99	79	20	480	384	00
24*	19	20	62	49	60	100	80	00	500	400	00
25	20	00	63	50	40	101	80	80	516	412	80
26	20	80	64	51	20	102	81	60	560	448	00
27	21	60	65	52	00	103	82	40	600	480	00
28	22	40	66	52	80	104	83	20	625	500	00
29	23	20	67	53	60	105	84	00	640	512	00
30	24	00	68	54	40	106	84	80	700	560	00
31	24	80	69	55	20	107	85	60	750	600	00
32	25	60	70	56	00	108*	86	40	800	640	00
33	26	40	71	56	80	109	87	20	900	720	00

No.	£	p	No.	£	p	No.	£	p
1000	800	00	1760	1408	00	6000	4800	00
1016	812	80	2000	1600	00	7000	5600	00
1094	875	20	2240	1792	00	7500	6000	00
1120	896	00	2500	2000	00	10000	8000	00
1250	1000	00	3000	2400	00	15000	12000	00
1500	1200	00	4000	3200	00	20000	16000	00
1750	1400	00	5000	4000	00	30000	24000	00

81p   £0·81

No.	£	p	No.	£	p	No.	£	p	No.	£	p
$\frac{1}{16}$	0	05	34	27	54	72*	58	32	110	89	10
$\frac{1}{8}$	0	10	35	28	35	73	59	13	111	89	91
$\frac{1}{4}$	0	20½	36*	29	16	74	59	94	112	90	72
$\frac{1}{2}$	0	40½	37	29	97	75	60	75	113	91	53
$\frac{3}{4}$	0	61	38	30	78	76	61	56	114	92	34
1½	1	21½	39	31	59	77	62	37	115	93	15
2	1	62	**40**	32	40	78	63	18	116	93	96
3	2	43	41	33	21	79	63	99	117	94	77
4	3	24	42	34	02	**80**	64	80	118	95	58
5	4	05	43	34	83	81	65	61	119	96	39
6	4	86	44	35	64	82	66	42	120*	97	20
7	5	67	45	36	45	83	67	23	128	103	68
8	6	48	46	37	26	84*	68	04	130	105	30
9	7	29	47	38	07	85	68	85	140	113	40
10	8	10	48*	38	88	86	69	66	144*	116	64
11	8	91	49	39	69	87	70	47	150	121	50
12*	9	72	**50**	40	50	88	71	28	156	126	36
13	10	53	51	41	31	89	72	09	168	136	08
14	11	34	52	42	12	**90**	72	90	196	158	76
15	12	15	53	42	93	91	73	71	200	162	00
16	12	96	54	43	74	92	74	52	220	178	20
17	13	77	55	44	55	93	75	33	224	181	44
18	14	58	56	45	36	94	76	14	256	207	36
19	15	39	57	46	17	95	76	95	280	226	80
20	16	20	58	46	98	96*	77	76	300	243	00
21	17	01	59	47	79	97	78	57	365	295	65
22	17	82	**60***	48	60	98	79	38	400	324	00
23	18	63	61	49	41	99	80	19	480	388	80
24*	19	44	62	50	22	**100**	81	00	500	405	00
25	20	25	63	51	03	101	81	81	516	417	96
26	21	06	64	51	84	102	82	62	560	453	60
27	21	87	65	52	65	103	83	43	600	486	00
28	22	68	66	53	46	104	84	24	625	506	25
29	23	49	67	54	27	105	85	05	640	518	40
30	24	30	68	55	08	106	85	86	700	567	00
31	25	11	69	55	89	107	86	67	750	607	50
32	25	92	**70**	56	70	108*	87	48	800	648	00
33	26	73	71	57	51	109	88	29	900	729	00

No.	£	p	No.	£	p	No.	£	p
1000	810	00	1760	1425	60	6000	4860	00
1016	822	96	2000	1620	00	7000	5670	00
1094	886	14	2240	1814	40	7500	6075	00
1120	907	20	2500	2025	00	10000	8100	00
1250	1012	50	3000	2430	00	15000	12150	00
1500	1215	00	4000	3240	00	20000	16200	00
1750	1417	50	5000	4050	00	30000	24300	00

No.	£	p	No.	£	p	No.	£	p	No.	£	p
$\frac{1}{16}$	0	05	34	27	88	72*	59	04	110	90	20
$\frac{1}{8}$	0	10½	35	28	70	73	59	86	111	91	02
$\frac{1}{4}$	0	20½	36*	29	52	74	60	68	112	91	84
$\frac{1}{2}$	0	41	37	30	34	75	61	50	113	92	66
$\frac{3}{4}$	0	61½	38	31	16	76	62	32	114	93	48
1½	1	23	39	31	98	77	63	14	115	94	30
2	1	64	40	32	80	78	63	96	116	95	12
3	2	46	41	33	62	79	64	78	117	95	94
4	3	28	42	34	44	80	65	60	118	96	76
5	4	10	43	35	26	81	66	42	119	97	58
6	4	92	44	36	08	82	67	24	120*	98	40
7	5	74	45	36	90	83	68	06	128	104	96
8	6	56	46	37	72	84*	68	88	130	106	60
9	7	38	47	38	54	85	69	70	140	114	80
10	8	20	48*	39	36	86	70	52	144*	118	08
11	9	02	49	40	18	87	71	34	150	123	00
12*	9	84	50	41	00	88	72	16	156	127	92
13	10	66	51	41	82	89	72	98	168	137	76
14	11	48	52	42	64	90	73	80	196	160	72
15	12	30	53	43	46	91	74	62	200	164	00
16	13	12	54	44	28	92	75	44	220	180	40
17	13	94	55	45	10	93	76	26	224	183	68
18	14	76	56	45	92	94	77	08	256	209	92
19	15	58	57	46	74	95	77	90	280	229	60
20	16	40	58	47	56	96*	78	72	300	246	00
21	17	22	59	48	38	97	79	54	365	299	30
22	18	04	60*	49	20	98	80	36	400	328	00
23	18	86	61	50	02	99	81	18	480	393	60
24*	19	68	62	50	84	100	82	00	500	410	00
25	20	50	63	51	66	101	82	82	516	423	12
26	21	32	64	52	48	102	83	64	560	459	20
27	22	14	65	53	30	103	84	46	600	492	00
28	22	96	66	54	12	104	85	28	625	512	50
29	23	78	67	54	94	105	86	10	640	524	80
30	24	60	68	55	76	106	86	92	700	574	00
31	25	42	69	56	58	107	87	74	750	615	00
32	26	24	70	57	40	108*	88	56	800	656	00
33	27	06	71	58	22	109	89	38	900	738	00

No.	£	p	No.	£	p	No.	£	p
1000	820	00	1760	1443	20	6000	4920	00
1016	833	12	2000	1640	00	7000	5740	00
1094	897	08	2240	1836	80	7500	6150	00
1120	918	40	2500	2050	00	10000	8200	00
1250	1025	00	3000	2460	00	15000	12300	00
1500	1230	00	4000	3280	00	20000	16400	00
1750	1435	00	5000	4100	00	30000	24600	00

82½p £0·825

No.	£	p	No.	£	p	No.	£	p	No.	£	p
1/16	0	05	34	28	05	72*	59	40	110	90	75
1/8	0	10½	35	28	87½	73	60	22½	111	91	57½
1/4	0	20½	36*	29	70	74	61	05	112	92	40
1/2	0	41½	37	30	52½	75	61	87½	113	93	22½
3/4	0	62	38	31	35	76	62	70	114	94	05
1½	1	24	39	32	17½	77	63	52½	115	94	87½
2	1	65	40	33	00	78	64	35	116	95	70
3	2	47½	41	33	82½	79	65	17½	117	96	52½
4	3	30	42	34	65	80	66	00	118	97	35
5	4	12½	43	35	47½	81	66	82½	119	98	17½
6	4	95	44	36	30	82	67	65	120*	99	00
7	5	77½	45	37	12½	83	68	47½	128	105	60
8	6	60	46	37	95	84*	69	30	130	107	25
9	7	42½	47	38	77½	85	70	12½	140	115	50
10	8	25	48*	39	60	86	70	95	144*	118	80
11	9	07½	49	40	42½	87	71	77½	150	123	75
12*	9	90	50	41	25	88	72	60	156	128	70
13	10	72½	51	42	07½	89	73	42½	168	138	60
14	11	55	52	42	90	90	74	25	196	161	70
15	12	37½	53	43	72½	91	75	07½	200	165	00
16	13	20	54	44	55	92	75	90	220	181	50
17	14	02½	55	45	37½	93	76	72½	224	184	80
18	14	85	56	46	20	94	77	55	256	211	20
19	15	67½	57	47	02½	95	78	37½	280	231	00
20	16	50	58	47	85	96*	79	20	300	247	50
21	17	32½	59	48	67½	97	80	02½	365	301	12½
22	18	15	60*	49	50	98	80	85	400	330	00
23	18	97½	61	50	32½	99	81	67½	480	396	00
24*	19	80	62	51	15	100	82	50	500	412	50
25	20	62½	63	51	97½	101	83	32½	516	425	70
26	21	45	64	52	80	102	84	15	560	462	00
27	22	27½	65	53	62½	103	84	97½	600	495	00
28	23	10	66	54	45	104	85	80	625	515	62½
29	23	92½	67	55	27½	105	86	62½	640	528	00
30	24	75	68	56	10	106	87	45	700	577	50
31	25	57½	69	56	92½	107	88	27½	750	618	75
32	26	40	70	57	75	108*	89	10	800	660	00
33	27	22½	71	58	57½	109	89	92½	900	742	50

No.	£	p	No.	£	p	No.	£	p
1000	825	00	1760	1452	00	6000	4950	00
1016	838	20	2000	1650	00	7000	5775	00
1094	902	55	2240	1848	00	7500	6187	50
1120	924	00	2500	2062	50	10000	8250	00
1250	1031	25	3000	2475	00	15000	12375	00
1500	1237	50	4000	3300	00	20000	16500	00
1750	1443	75	5000	4125	00	30000	24750	00

No.	£	p	No.	£	p	No.	£	p	No.	£	p
1/16	0	05	34	28	22	72*	59	76	110	91	30
1/8	0	10½	35	29	05	73	60	59	111	92	13
1/4	0	21	36*	29	88	74	61	42	112	92	96
1/2	0	41½	37	30	71	75	62	25	113	93	79
3/4	0	62½	38	31	54	76	63	08	114	94	62
1½	1	24½	39	32	37	77	63	91	115	95	45
2	1	66	**40**	33	20	78	64	74	116	96	28
3	2	49	41	34	03	79	65	57	117	97	11
4	3	32	42	34	86	**80**	66	40	118	97	94
5	4	15	43	35	69	81	67	23	119	98	77
6	4	98	44	36	52	82	68	06	120*	99	60
7	5	81	45	37	35	83	68	89	128	106	24
8	6	64	46	38	18	84*	69	72	130	107	90
9	7	47	47	39	01	85	70	55	140	116	20
10	8	30	48*	39	84	86	71	38	144*	119	52
11	9	13	49	40	67	87	72	21	150	124	50
12*	9	96	**50**	41	50	88	73	04	156	129	48
13	10	79	51	42	33	89	73	87	168	139	44
14	11	62	52	43	16	**90**	74	70	196	162	68
15	12	45	53	43	99	91	75	53	200	166	00
16	13	28	54	44	82	92	76	36	220	182	60
17	14	11	55	45	65	93	77	19	224	185	92
18	14	94	56	46	48	94	78	02	256	212	48
19	15	77	57	47	31	95	78	85	280	232	40
20	16	60	58	48	14	96*	79	68	300	249	00
21	17	43	59	48	97	97	80	51	365	302	95
22	18	26	**60***	49	80	98	81	34	400	332	00
23	19	09	61	50	63	99	82	17	480	398	40
24*	19	92	62	51	46	**100**	83	00	500	415	00
25	20	75	63	52	29	101	83	83	516	428	28
26	21	58	64	53	12	102	84	66	560	464	80
27	22	41	65	53	95	103	85	49	600	498	00
28	23	24	66	54	78	104	86	32	625	518	75
29	24	07	67	55	61	105	87	15	640	531	20
30	24	90	68	56	44	106	87	98	700	581	00
31	25	73	69	57	27	107	88	81	750	622	50
32	26	56	**70**	58	10	108*	89	64	800	664	00
33	27	39	71	58	93	109	90	47	900	747	00

No.	£	p	No.	£	p	No.	£	p
1000	830	00	1760	1460	80	6000	4980	00
1016	843	28	2000	1660	00	7000	5810	00
1094	908	02	2240	1859	20	7500	6225	00
1120	929	60	2500	2075	00	10000	8300	00
1250	1037	50	3000	2490	00	15000	12450	00
1500	1245	00	4000	3320	00	20000	16600	00
1750	1452	50	5000	4150	00	30000	24900	00

No.	£	p	No.	£	p	No.	£	p	No.	£	p
1/16	0	05½	34	28	56	72*	60	48	110	92	40
1/8	0	10½	35	29	40	73	61	32	111	93	24
1/4	0	21	36*	30	24	74	62	16	112	94	08
1/2	0	42	37	31	08	75	63	00	113	94	92
3/4	0	63	38	31	92	76	63	84	114	95	76
1½	1	26	39	32	76	77	64	68	115	96	60
2	1	68	40	33	60	78	65	52	116	97	44
3	2	52	41	34	44	79	66	36	117	98	28
4	3	36	42	35	28	80	67	20	118	99	12
5	4	20	43	36	12	81	68	04	119	99	96
6	5	04	44	36	96	82	68	88	120*	100	80
7	5	88	45	37	80	83	69	72	128	107	52
8	6	72	46	38	64	84*	70	56	130	109	20
9	7	56	47	39	48	85	71	40	140	117	60
10	8	40	48*	40	32	86	72	24	144*	120	96
11	9	24	49	41	16	87	73	08	150	126	00
12*	10	08	50	42	00	88	73	92	156	131	04
13	10	92	51	42	84	89	74	76	168	141	12
14	11	76	52	43	68	90	75	60	196	164	64
15	12	60	53	44	52	91	76	44	200	168	00
16	13	44	54	45	36	92	77	28	220	184	80
17	14	28	55	46	20	93	78	12	224	188	16
18	15	12	56	47	04	94	78	96	256	215	04
19	15	96	57	47	88	95	79	80	280	235	20
20	16	80	58	48	72	96*	80	64	300	252	00
21	17	64	59	49	56	97	81	48	365	306	60
22	18	48	60*	50	40	98	82	32	400	336	00
23	19	32	61	51	24	99	83	16	480	403	20
24*	20	16	62	52	08	100	84	00	500	420	00
25	21	00	63	52	92	101	84	84	516	433	44
26	21	84	64	53	76	102	85	68	560	470	40
27	22	68	65	54	60	103	86	52	600	504	00
28	23	52	66	55	44	104	87	36	625	525	00
29	24	36	67	56	28	105	88	20	640	537	60
30	25	20	68	57	12	106	89	04	700	588	00
31	26	04	69	57	96	107	89	88	750	630	00
32	26	88	70	58	80	108*	90	72	800	672	00
33	27	72	71	59	64	109	91	56	900	756	00

No.	£	p	No.	£	p	No.	£	p
1000	840	00	1760	1478	40	6000	5040	00
1016	853	44	2000	1680	00	7000	5880	00
1094	918	96	2240	1881	60	7500	6300	00
1120	940	80	2500	2100	00	10000	8400	00
1250	1050	00	3000	2520	00	15000	12600	00
1500	1260	00	4000	3360	00	20000	16800	00
1750	1470	00	5000	4200	00	30000	25200	00

85p £0·85

No.	£	p	No.	£	p	No.	£	p	No.	£	p
$\frac{1}{16}$	0	05½	34	28	90	72*	61	20	110	93	50
$\frac{1}{8}$	0	10½	35	29	75	73	62	05	111	94	35
$\frac{1}{4}$	0	21½	36*	30	60	74	62	90	112	95	20
$\frac{1}{2}$	0	42½	37	31	45	75	63	75	113	96	05
$\frac{3}{4}$	0	64	38	32	30	76	64	60	114	96	90
$1\frac{1}{2}$	1	27½	39	33	15	77	65	45	115	97	75
2	1	70	**40**	34	00	78	66	30	116	98	60
3	2	55	41	34	85	79	67	15	117	99	45
4	3	40	42	35	70	**80**	68	00	118	100	30
5	4	25	43	36	55	81	68	85	119	101	15
6	5	10	44	37	40	82	69	70	120*	102	00
7	5	95	45	38	25	83	70	55	128	108	80
8	6	80	46	39	10	84*	71	40	130	110	50
9	7	65	47	39	95	85	72	25	140	119	00
10	8	50	48*	40	80	86	73	10	144*	122	40
11	9	35	49	41	65	87	73	95	150	127	50
12*	10	20	**50**	42	50	88	74	80	156	132	60
13	11	05	51	43	35	89	75	65	168	142	80
14	11	90	52	44	20	**90**	76	50	196	166	60
15	12	75	53	45	05	91	77	35	200	170	00
16	13	60	54	45	90	92	78	20	220	187	00
17	14	45	55	46	75	93	79	05	224	190	40
18	15	30	56	47	60	94	79	90	256	217	60
19	16	15	57	48	45	95	80	75	280	238	00
20	17	00	58	49	30	96*	81	60	300	255	00
21	17	85	59	50	15	97	82	45	365	310	25
22	18	70	60*	51	00	98	83	30	400	340	00
23	19	55	61	51	85	99	84	15	480	408	00
24*	20	40	62	52	70	**100**	85	00	500	425	00
25	21	25	63	53	55	101	85	85	516	438	60
26	22	10	64	54	40	102	86	70	560	476	00
27	22	95	65	55	25	103	87	55	600	510	00
28	23	80	66	56	10	104	88	40	625	531	25
29	24	65	67	56	95	105	89	25	640	544	00
30	25	50	68	57	80	106	90	10	700	595	00
31	26	35	69	58	65	107	90	95	750	637	50
32	27	20	**70**	59	50	108*	91	80	800	680	00
33	28	05	71	60	35	109	92	65	900	765	00

No.	£	p	No.	£	p	No.	£	p
1000	850	00	1760	1496	00	6000	5100	00
1016	863	60	2000	1700	00	7000	5950	00
1094	929	90	2240	1904	00	7500	6375	00
1120	952	00	2500	2125	00	10000	8500	00
1250	1062	50	3000	2550	00	15000	12750	00
1500	1275	00	4000	3400	00	20000	17000	00
1750	1487	50	5000	4250	00	30000	25500	00

No.	£	p	No.	£	p	No.	£	p	No.	£	p
$\frac{1}{16}$	0	05½	34	29	24	72*	61	92	110	94	60
$\frac{1}{8}$	0	11	35	30	10	73	62	78	111	95	46
$\frac{1}{4}$	0	21½	36*	30	96	74	63	64	112	96	32
$\frac{1}{2}$	0	43	37	31	82	75	64	50	113	97	18
$\frac{3}{4}$	0	64½	38	32	68	76	65	36	114	98	04
1½	1	29	39	33	54	77	66	22	115	98	90
2	1	72	40	34	40	78	67	08	116	99	76
3	2	58	41	35	26	79	67	94	117	100	62
4	3	44	42	36	12	80	68	80	118	101	48
5	4	30	43	36	98	81	69	66	119	102	34
6	5	16	44	37	84	82	70	52	120*	103	20
7	6	02	45	38	70	83	71	38	128	110	08
8	6	88	46	39	56	84*	72	24	130	111	80
9	7	74	47	40	42	85	73	10	140	120	40
10	8	60	48*	41	28	86	73	96	144*	123	84
11	9	46	49	42	14	87	74	82	150	129	00
12*	10	32	50	43	00	88	75	68	156	134	16
13	11	18	51	43	86	89	76	54	168	144	48
14	12	04	52	44	72	90	77	40	196	168	56
15	12	90	53	45	58	91	78	26	200	172	00
16	13	76	54	46	44	92	79	12	220	189	20
17	14	62	55	47	30	93	79	98	224	192	64
18	15	48	56	48	16	94	80	84	256	220	16
19	16	34	57	49	02	95	81	70	280	240	80
20	17	20	58	49	88	96*	82	56	300	258	00
21	18	06	59	50	74	97	83	42	365	313	90
22	18	92	60*	51	60	98	84	28	400	344	00
23	19	78	61	52	46	99	85	14	480	412	80
24*	20	64	62	53	32	100	86	00	500	430	00
25	21	50	63	54	18	101	86	86	516	443	76
26	22	36	64	55	04	102	87	72	560	481	60
27	23	22	65	55	90	103	88	58	600	516	00
28	24	08	66	56	76	104	89	44	625	537	50
29	24	94	67	57	62	105	90	30	640	550	40
30	25	80	68	58	48	106	91	16	700	602	00
31	26	66	69	59	34	107	92	02	750	645	00
32	27	52	70	60	20	108*	92	88	800	688	00
33	28	38	71	61	06	109	93	74	900	774	00

No.	£	p	No.	£	p	No.	£	p
1000	860	00	1760	1513	60	6000	5160	00
1016	873	76	2000	1720	00	7000	6020	00
1094	940	84	2240	1926	40	7500	6450	00
1120	963	20	2500	2150	00	10000	8600	00
1250	1075	00	3000	2580	00	15000	12900	00
1500	1290	00	4000	3440	00	20000	17200	00
1750	1505	00	5000	4300	00	30000	25800	00

No.	£	p	No.	£	p	No.	£	p	No.	£	p
$\frac{1}{16}$	0	05½	34	29	58	72*	62	64	110	95	70
$\frac{1}{8}$	0	11	35	30	45	73	63	51	111	96	57
$\frac{1}{4}$	0	22	36*	31	32	74	64	38	112	97	44
$\frac{1}{2}$	0	43½	37	32	19	75	65	25	113	98	31
$\frac{3}{4}$	0	65½	38	33	06	76	66	12	114	99	18
1½	1	30½	39	33	93	77	66	99	115	100	05
2	1	74	**40**	34	80	78	67	86	116	100	92
3	2	61	41	35	67	79	68	73	117	101	79
4	3	48	42	36	54	**80**	69	60	118	102	66
5	4	35	43	37	41	81	70	47	119	103	53
6	5	22	44	38	28	82	71	34	120*	104	40
7	6	09	45	39	15	83	72	21	128	111	36
8	6	96	46	40	02	84*	73	08	130	113	10
9	7	83	47	40	89	85	73	95	140	121	80
10	8	70	48*	41	76	86	74	82	144*	125	28
11	9	57	49	42	63	87	75	69	150	130	50
12*	10	44	**50**	43	50	88	76	56	156	135	72
13	11	31	51	44	37	89	77	43	168	146	16
14	12	18	52	45	24	**90**	78	30	196	170	52
15	13	05	53	46	11	91	79	17	200	174	00
16	13	92	54	46	98	92	80	04	220	191	40
17	14	79	55	47	85	93	80	91	224	194	88
18	15	66	56	48	72	94	81	78	256	222	72
19	16	53	57	49	59	95	82	65	280	243	60
20	17	40	58	50	46	96*	83	52	300	261	00
21	18	27	59	51	33	97	84	39	365	317	55
22	19	14	**60***	52	20	98	85	26	400	348	00
23	20	01	61	53	07	99	86	13	480	417	60
24*	20	88	62	53	94	**100**	87	00	500	435	00
25	21	75	63	54	81	101	87	87	516	448	92
26	22	62	64	55	68	102	88	74	560	487	20
27	23	49	65	56	55	103	89	61	600	522	00
28	24	36	66	57	42	104	90	48	625	543	75
29	25	23	67	58	29	105	91	35	640	556	80
30	26	10	68	59	16	106	92	22	700	609	00
31	26	97	69	60	03	107	93	09	750	652	50
32	27	84	**70**	60	90	108*	93	96	800	696	00
33	28	71	71	61	77	109	94	83	900	783	00

No.	£	p	No.	£	p	No.	£	p
1000	870	00	1760	1531	20	6000	5220	00
1016	883	92	2000	1740	00	7000	6090	00
1094	951	78	2240	1948	80	7500	6525	00
1120	974	40	2500	2175	00	10000	8700	00
1250	1087	50	3000	2610	00	15000	13050	00
1500	1305	00	4000	3480	00	20000	17400	00
1750	1522	50	5000	4350	00	30000	26100	00

87½p £0·875

No.	£	p	No.	£	p	No.	£	p	No.	£	p
1/16	0	05½	34	29	75	72*	63	00	110	96	25
1/8	0	11	35	30	62½	73	63	87½	111	97	12½
1/4	0	22	36*	31	50	74	64	75	112	98	00
1/2	0	44	37	32	37½	75	65	62½	113	98	87½
3/4	0	65½	38	33	25	76	66	50	114	99	75
1½	1	31½	39	34	12½	77	67	37½	115	100	62½
2	1	75	40	35	00	78	68	25	116	101	50
3	2	62½	41	35	87½	79	69	12½	117	102	37½
4	3	50	42	36	75	80	70	00	118	103	25
5	4	37½	43	37	62½	81	70	87½	119	104	12½
6	5	25	44	38	50	82	71	75	120*	105	00
7	6	12½	45	39	37½	83	72	62½	128	112	00
8	7	00	46	40	25	84*	73	50	130	113	75
9	7	87½	47	41	12½	85	74	37½	140	122	50
10	8	75	48*	42	00	86	75	25	144*	126	00
11	9	62½	49	42	87½	87	76	12½	150	131	25
12*	10	50	50	43	75	88	77	00	156	136	50
13	11	37½	51	44	62½	89	77	87½	168	147	00
14	12	25	52	45	50	90	78	75	196	171	50
15	13	12½	53	46	37½	91	79	62½	200	175	00
16	14	00	54	47	25	92	80	50	220	192	50
17	14	87½	55	48	12½	93	81	37½	224	196	00
18	15	75	56	49	00	94	82	25	256	224	00
19	16	62½	57	49	87½	95	83	12½	280	245	00
20	17	50	58	50	75	96*	84	00	300	262	50
21	18	37½	59	51	62½	97	84	87½	365	319	37½
22	19	25	60*	52	50	98	85	75	400	350	00
23	20	12½	61	53	37½	99	86	62½	480	420	00
24*	21	00	62	54	25	100	87	50	500	437	50
25	21	87½	63	55	12½	101	88	37½	516	451	50
26	22	75	64	56	00	102	89	25	560	490	00
27	23	62½	65	56	87½	103	90	12½	600	525	00
28	24	50	66	57	75	104	91	00	625	546	87½
29	25	37½	67	58	62½	105	91	87½	640	560	00
30	26	25	68	59	50	106	92	75	700	612	50
31	27	12½	69	60	37½	107	93	62½	750	656	25
32	28	00	70	61	25	108*	94	50	800	700	00
33	28	87½	71	62	12½	109	95	37½	900	787	50

No.	£	p	No.	£	p	No.	£	p
1000	875	00	1760	1540	00	6000	5250	00
1016	889	00	2000	1750	00	7000	6125	00
1094	957	25	2240	1960	00	7500	6562	50
1120	980	00	2500	2187	50	10000	8750	00
1250	1093	75	3000	2625	00	15000	13125	00
1500	1312	50	4000	3500	00	20000	17500	00
1750	1531	25	5000	4375	00	30000	26250	00

No.	£	p	No.	£	p	No.	£	p	No.	£	p
1/16	0	05½	34	29	92	72*	63	36	110	96	80
1/8	0	11	35	30	80	73	64	24	111	97	68
1/4	0	22	36*	31	68	74	65	12	112	98	56
1/2	0	44	37	32	56	75	66	00	113	99	44
3/4	0	66	38	33	44	76	66	88	114	100	32
1½	1	32	39	34	32	77	67	76	115	101	20
2	1	76	40	35	20	78	68	64	116	102	08
3	2	64	41	36	08	79	69	52	117	102	96
4	3	52	42	36	96	80	70	40	118	103	84
5	4	40	43	37	84	81	71	28	119	104	72
6	5	28	44	38	72	82	72	16	120*	105	60
7	6	16	45	39	60	83	73	04	128	112	64
8	7	04	46	40	48	84*	73	92	130	114	40
9	7	92	47	41	36	85	74	80	140	123	20
10	8	80	48*	42	24	86	75	68	144*	126	72
11	9	68	49	43	12	87	76	56	150	132	00
12*	10	56	50	44	00	88	77	44	156	137	28
13	11	44	51	44	88	89	78	32	168	147	84
14	12	32	52	45	76	90	79	20	196	172	48
15	13	20	53	46	64	91	80	08	200	176	00
16	14	08	54	47	52	92	80	96	220	193	60
17	14	96	55	48	40	93	81	84	224	197	12
18	15	84	56	49	28	94	82	72	256	225	28
19	16	72	57	50	16	95	83	60	280	246	40
20	17	60	58	51	04	96*	84	48	300	264	00
21	18	48	59	51	92	97	85	36	365	321	20
22	19	36	60*	52	80	98	86	24	400	352	00
23	20	24	61	53	68	99	87	12	480	422	40
24*	21	12	62	54	56	100	88	00	500	440	00
25	22	00	63	55	44	101	88	88	516	454	08
26	22	88	64	56	32	102	89	76	560	492	80
27	23	76	65	57	20	103	90	64	600	528	00
28	24	64	66	58	08	104	91	52	625	550	00
29	25	52	67	58	96	105	92	40	640	563	20
30	26	40	68	59	84	106	93	28	700	616	00
31	27	28	69	60	72	107	94	16	750	660	00
32	28	16	70	61	60	108*	95	04	800	704	00
33	29	04	71	62	48	109	95	92	900	792	00

No.	£	p	No.	£	p	No.	£	p
1000	880	00	1760	1548	80	6000	5280	00
1016	894	08	2000	1760	00	7000	6160	00
1094	962	72	2240	1971	20	7500	6600	00
1120	985	60	2500	2200	00	10000	8800	00
1250	1100	00	3000	2640	00	15000	13200	00
1500	1320	00	4000	3520	00	20000	17600	00
1750	1540	00	5000	4400	00	30000	26400	00

No.	£	p	No.	£	p	No.	£	p	No.	£	p
1/16	0	05½	34	30	26	72*	64	08	110	97	90
1/8	0	11	35	31	15	73	64	97	111	98	79
1/4	0	22½	36*	32	04	74	65	86	112	99	68
1/2	0	44½	37	32	93	75	66	75	113	100	57
3/4	0	67	38	33	82	76	67	64	114	101	46
1½	1	33½	39	34	71	77	68	53	115	102	35
2	1	78	40	35	60	78	69	42	116	103	24
3	2	67	41	36	49	79	70	31	117	104	13
4	3	56	42	37	38	80	71	20	118	105	02
5	4	45	43	38	27	81	72	09	119	105	91
6	5	34	44	39	16	82	72	98	120*	106	80
7	6	23	45	40	05	83	73	87	128	113	92
8	7	12	46	40	94	84*	74	76	130	115	70
9	8	01	47	41	83	85	75	65	140	124	60
10	8	90	48*	42	72	86	76	54	144*	128	16
11	9	79	49	43	61	87	77	43	150	133	50
12*	10	68	50	44	50	88	78	32	156	138	84
13	11	57	51	45	39	89	79	21	168	149	52
14	12	46	52	46	28	90	80	10	196	174	44
15	13	35	53	47	17	91	80	99	200	178	00
16	14	24	54	48	06	92	81	88	220	195	80
17	15	13	55	48	95	93	82	77	224	199	36
18	16	02	56	49	84	94	83	66	256	227	84
19	16	91	57	50	73	95	84	55	280	249	20
20	17	80	58	51	62	96*	85	44	300	267	00
21	18	69	59	52	51	97	86	33	365	324	85
22	19	58	60*	53	40	98	87	22	400	356	00
23	20	47	61	54	29	99	88	11	480	427	20
24*	21	36	62	55	18	100	89	00	500	445	00
25	22	25	63	56	07	101	89	89	516	459	24
26	23	14	64	56	96	102	90	78	560	498	40
27	24	03	65	57	85	103	91	67	600	534	00
28	24	92	66	58	74	104	92	56	625	556	25
29	25	81	67	59	63	105	93	45	640	569	60
30	26	70	68	60	52	106	94	34	700	623	00
31	27	59	69	61	41	107	95	23	750	667	50
32	28	48	70	62	30	108*	96	12	800	712	00
33	29	37	71	63	19	109	97	01	900	801	00

No.	£	p	No.	£	p	No.	£	p
1000	890	00	1760	1566	40	6000	5340	00
1016	904	24	2000	1780	00	7000	6230	00
1094	973	66	2240	1993	60	7500	6675	00
1120	996	80	2500	2225	00	10000	8900	00
1250	1112	50	3000	2670	00	15000	13350	00
1500	1335	00	4000	3560	00	20000	17800	00
1750	1557	50	5000	4450	00	30000	26700	00

No.	£	p	No.	£	p	No.	£	p	No.	£	p
1/16	0	05½	34	30	60	72*	64	80	110	99	00
1/8	0	11½	35	31	50	73	65	70	111	99	90
1/4	0	22½	36*	32	40	74	66	60	112	100	80
1/2	0	45	37	33	30	75	67	50	113	101	70
3/4	0	67½	38	34	20	76	68	40	114	102	60
1½	1	35	39	35	10	77	69	30	115	103	50
2	1	80	40	36	00	78	70	20	116	104	40
3	2	70	41	36	90	79	71	10	117	105	30
4	3	60	42	37	80	80	72	00	118	106	20
5	4	50	43	38	70	81	72	90	119	107	10
6	5	40	44	39	60	82	73	80	120*	108	00
7	6	30	45	40	50	83	74	70	128	115	20
8	7	20	46	41	40	84*	75	60	130	117	00
9	8	10	47	42	30	85	76	50	140	126	00
10	9	00	48*	43	20	86	77	40	144*	129	60
11	9	90	49	44	10	87	78	30	150	135	00
12*	10	80	50	45	00	88	79	20	156	140	40
13	11	70	51	45	90	89	80	10	168	151	20
14	12	60	52	46	80	90	81	00	196	176	40
15	13	50	53	47	70	91	81	90	200	180	00
16	14	40	54	48	60	92	82	80	220	198	00
17	15	30	55	49	50	93	83	70	224	201	60
18	16	20	56	50	40	94	84	60	256	230	40
19	17	10	57	51	30	95	85	50	280	252	00
20	18	00	58	52	20	96*	86	40	300	270	00
21	18	90	59	53	10	97	87	30	365	328	50
22	19	80	60*	54	00	98	88	20	400	360	00
23	20	70	61	54	90	99	89	10	480	432	00
24*	21	60	62	55	80	100	90	00	500	450	00
25	22	50	63	56	70	101	90	90	516	464	40
26	23	40	64	57	60	102	91	80	560	504	00
27	24	30	65	58	50	103	92	70	600	540	00
28	25	20	66	59	40	104	93	60	625	562	50
29	26	10	67	60	30	105	94	50	640	576	00
30	27	00	68	61	20	106	95	40	700	630	00
31	27	90	69	62	10	107	96	30	750	675	00
32	28	80	70	63	00	108*	97	20	800	720	00
33	29	70	71	63	90	109	98	10	900	810	00

No.	£	p	No.	£	p	No.	£	p
1000	900	00	1760	1584	00	6000	5400	00
1016	914	40	2000	1800	00	7000	6300	00
1094	984	60	2240	2016	00	7500	6750	00
1120	1008	00	2500	2250	00	10000	9000	00
1250	1125	00	3000	2700	00	15000	13500	00
1500	1350	00	4000	3600	00	20000	18000	00
1750	1575	00	5000	4500	00	30000	27000	00

No.	£	p	No.	£	p	No.	£	p	No.	£	p
1/16	0	05½	34	30	94	72*	65	52	110	100	10
1/8	0	11½	35	31	85	73	66	43	111	101	01
1/4	0	23	36*	32	76	74	67	34	112	101	92
1/2	0	45½	37	33	67	75	68	25	113	102	83
3/4	0	68½	38	34	58	76	69	16	114	103	74
1½	1	36½	39	35	49	77	70	07	115	104	65
2	1	82	40	36	40	78	70	98	116	105	56
3	2	73	41	37	31	79	71	89	117	106	47
4	3	64	42	38	22	80	72	80	118	107	38
5	4	55	43	39	13	81	73	71	119	108	29
6	5	46	44	40	04	82	74	62	120*	109	20
7	6	37	45	40	95	83	75	53	128	116	48
8	7	28	46	41	86	84*	76	44	130	118	30
9	8	19	47	42	77	85	77	35	140	127	40
10	9	10	48*	43	68	86	78	26	144*	131	04
11	10	01	49	44	59	87	79	17	150	136	50
12*	10	92	50	45	50	88	80	08	156	141	96
13	11	83	51	46	41	89	80	99	168	152	88
14	12	74	52	47	32	90	81	90	196	178	36
15	13	65	53	48	23	91	82	81	200	182	00
16	14	56	54	49	14	92	83	72	220	200	20
17	15	47	55	50	05	93	84	63	224	203	84
18	16	38	56	50	96	94	85	54	256	232	96
19	17	29	57	51	87	95	86	45	280	254	80
20	18	20	58	52	78	96*	87	36	300	273	00
21	19	11	59	53	69	97	88	27	365	332	15
22	20	02	60*	54	60	98	89	18	400	364	00
23	20	93	61	55	51	99	90	09	480	436	80
24*	21	84	62	56	42	100	91	00	500	455	00
25	22	75	63	57	33	101	91	91	516	469	56
26	23	66	64	58	24	102	92	82	560	509	60
27	24	57	65	59	15	103	93	73	600	546	00
28	25	48	66	60	06	104	94	64	625	568	75
29	26	39	67	60	97	105	95	55	640	582	40
30	27	30	68	61	88	106	96	46	700	637	00
31	28	21	69	62	79	107	97	37	750	682	50
32	29	12	70	63	70	108*	98	28	800	728	00
33	30	03	71	64	61	109	99	19	900	819	00

No.	£	p	No.	£	p	No.	£	p
1000	910	00	1760	1601	60	6000	5460	00
1016	924	56	2000	1820	00	7000	6370	00
1094	995	54	2240	2038	40	7500	6825	00
1120	1019	20	2500	2275	00	10000	9100	00
1250	1137	50	3000	2730	00	15000	13650	00
1500	1365	00	4000	3640	00	20000	18200	00
1750	1592	50	5000	4550	00	30000	27300	00

No.	£	p	No.	£	p	No.	£	p	No.	£	p
1/16	0	06	34	31	28	72*	66	24	110	101	20
1/8	0	11½	35	32	20	73	67	16	111	102	12
1/4	0	23	36*	33	12	74	68	08	112	103	04
1/2	0	46	37	34	04	75	69	00	113	103	96
3/4	0	69	38	34	96	76	69	92	114	104	88
1½	1	38	39	35	88	77	70	84	115	105	80
2	1	84	**40**	36	80	78	71	76	116	106	72
3	2	76	41	37	72	79	72	68	117	107	64
4	3	68	42	38	64	**80**	73	60	118	108	56
5	4	60	43	39	56	81	74	52	119	109	48
6	5	52	44	40	48	82	75	44	**120***	110	40
7	6	44	45	41	40	83	76	36	128	117	76
8	7	36	46	42	32	84*	77	28	130	119	60
9	8	28	47	43	24	85	78	20	140	128	80
10	9	20	48*	44	16	86	79	12	144*	132	48
11	10	12	49	45	08	87	80	04	150	138	00
12*	11	04	**50**	46	00	88	80	96	156	143	52
13	11	96	51	46	92	89	81	88	168	154	56
14	12	88	52	47	84	**90**	82	80	196	180	32
15	13	80	53	48	76	91	83	72	200	184	00
16	14	72	54	49	68	92	84	64	220	202	40
17	15	64	55	50	60	93	85	56	224	206	08
18	16	56	56	51	52	94	86	48	256	235	52
19	17	48	57	52	44	95	87	40	280	257	60
20	18	40	58	53	36	96*	88	32	300	276	00
21	19	32	59	54	28	97	89	24	365	335	80
22	20	24	**60***	55	20	98	90	16	400	368	00
23	21	16	61	56	12	99	91	08	480	441	60
24*	22	08	62	57	04	**100**	92	00	500	460	00
25	23	00	63	57	96	101	92	92	516	474	72
26	23	92	64	58	88	102	93	84	560	515	20
27	24	84	65	59	80	103	94	76	600	552	00
28	25	76	66	60	72	104	95	68	625	575	00
29	26	68	67	61	64	105	96	60	640	588	80
30	27	60	68	62	56	106	97	52	700	644	00
31	28	52	69	63	48	107	98	44	750	690	00
32	29	44	**70**	64	40	108*	99	36	800	736	00
33	30	36	71	65	32	109	100	28	900	828	00

No.	£	p	No.	£	p	No.	£	p
1000	920	00	1760	1619	20	6000	5520	00
1016	934	72	2000	1840	00	7000	6440	00
1094	1006	48	2240	2060	80	7500	6900	00
1120	1030	40	2500	2300	00	10000	9200	00
1250	1150	00	3000	2760	00	15000	13800	00
1500	1380	00	4000	3680	00	20000	18400	00
1750	1610	00	5000	4600	00	30000	27600	00

92½p   £0·925

No.	£	p	No.	£	p	No.	£	p	No.	£	p
1/16	0	06	34	31	45	72*	66	60	110	101	75
1/8	0	11½	35	32	37½	73	67	52½	111	102	67½
1/4	0	23	36*	33	30	74	68	45	112	103	60
1/2	0	46½	37	34	22½	75	69	37½	113	104	52½
3/4	0	69½	38	35	15	76	70	30	114	105	45
1½	1	39	39	36	07½	77	71	22½	115	106	37½
2	1	85	40	37	00	78	72	15	116	107	30
3	2	77½	41	37	92½	79	73	07½	117	108	22½
4	3	70	42	38	85	80	74	00	118	109	15
5	4	62½	43	39	77½	81	74	92½	119	110	07½
6	5	55	44	40	70	82	75	85	120*	111	00
7	6	47½	45	41	62½	83	76	77½	128	118	40
8	7	40	46	42	55	84*	77	70	130	120	25
9	8	32½	47	43	47½	85	78	62½	140	129	50
10	9	25	48*	44	40	86	79	55	144*	133	20
11	10	17½	49	45	32½	87	80	47½	150	138	75
12*	11	10	50	46	25	88	81	40	156	144	30
13	12	02½	51	47	17½	89	82	32½	168	155	40
14	12	95	52	48	10	90	83	25	196	181	30
15	13	87½	53	49	02½	91	84	17½	200	185	00
16	14	80	54	49	95	92	85	10	220	203	50
17	15	72½	55	50	87½	93	86	02½	224	207	20
18	16	65	56	51	80	94	86	95	256	236	80
19	17	57½	57	52	72½	95	87	87½	280	259	00
20	18	50	58	53	65	96*	88	80	300	277	50
21	19	42½	59	54	57½	97	89	72½	365	337	62½
22	20	35	60*	55	50	98	90	65	400	370	00
23	21	27½	61	56	42½	99	91	57½	480	444	00
24*	22	20	62	57	35	100	92	50	500	462	50
25	23	12½	63	58	27½	101	93	42½	516	477	30
26	24	05	64	59	20	102	94	35	560	518	00
27	24	97½	65	60	12½	103	95	27½	600	555	00
28	25	90	66	61	05	104	96	20	625	578	12½
29	26	82½	67	61	97½	105	97	12½	640	592	00
30	27	75	68	62	90	106	98	05	700	647	50
31	28	67½	69	63	82½	107	98	97½	750	693	75
32	29	60	70	64	75	108*	99	90	800	740	00
33	30	52½	71	65	67½	109	100	82½	900	832	50

No.	£	p	No.	£	p	No.	£	p
1000	925	00	1760	1628	00	6000	5550	00
1016	939	80	2000	1850	00	7000	6475	00
1094	1011	95	2240	2072	00	7500	6937	50
1120	1036	00	2500	2312	50	10000	9250	00
1250	1156	25	3000	2775	00	15000	13875	00
1500	1387	50	4000	3700	00	20000	18500	00
1750	1618	75	5000	4625	00	30000	27750	00

No.	£	p	No.	£	p	No.	£	p	No.	£	p
1/16	0	06	34	31	62	72*	66	96	110	102	30
1/8	0	11½	35	32	55	73	67	89	111	103	23
1/4	0	23½	36*	33	48	74	68	82	112	104	16
1/2	0	46½	37	34	41	75	69	75	113	105	09
3/4	0	70	38	35	34	76	70	68	114	106	02
1½	1	39½	39	36	27	77	71	61	115	106	95
2	1	86	40	37	20	78	72	54	116	107	88
3	2	79	41	38	13	79	73	47	117	108	81
4	3	72	42	39	06	80	74	40	118	109	74
5	4	65	43	39	99	81	75	33	119	110	67
6	5	58	44	40	92	82	76	26	120*	111	60
7	6	51	45	41	85	83	77	19	128	119	04
8	7	44	46	42	78	84*	78	12	130	120	90
9	8	37	47	43	71	85	79	05	140	130	20
10	9	30	48*	44	64	86	79	98	144*	133	92
11	10	23	49	45	57	87	80	91	150	139	50
12*	11	16	50	46	50	88	81	84	156	145	08
13	12	09	51	47	43	89	82	77	168	156	24
14	13	02	52	48	36	90	83	70	196	182	28
15	13	95	53	49	29	91	84	63	200	186	00
16	14	88	54	50	22	92	85	56	220	204	60
17	15	81	55	51	15	93	86	49	224	208	32
18	16	74	56	52	08	94	87	42	256	238	08
19	17	67	57	53	01	95	88	35	280	260	40
20	18	60	58	53	94	96*	89	28	300	279	00
21	19	53	59	54	87	97	90	21	365	339	45
22	20	46	60*	55	80	98	91	14	400	372	00
23	21	39	61	56	73	99	92	07	480	446	40
24*	22	32	62	57	66	100	93	00	500	465	00
25	23	25	63	58	59	101	93	93	516	479	88
26	24	18	64	59	52	102	94	86	560	520	80
27	25	11	65	60	45	103	95	79	600	558	00
28	26	04	66	61	38	104	96	72	625	581	25
29	26	97	67	62	31	105	97	65	640	595	20
30	27	90	68	63	24	106	98	58	700	651	00
31	28	83	69	64	17	107	99	51	750	697	50
32	29	76	70	65	10	108*	100	44	800	744	00
33	30	69	71	66	03	109	101	37	900	837	00

No.	£	p	No.	£	p	No.	£	p
1000	930	00	1760	1636	80	6000	5580	00
1016	944	88	2000	1860	00	7000	6510	00
1094	1017	42	2240	2083	20	7500	6975	00
1120	1041	60	2500	2325	00	10000	9300	00
1250	1162	50	3000	2790	00	15000	13950	00
1500	1395	00	4000	3720	00	20000	18600	00
1750	1627	50	5000	4650	00	30000	27900	00

No.	£	p	No.	£	p	No.	£	p	No.	£	p
1/16	0	06	34	31	96	72*	67	68	110	103	40
1/8	0	12	35	32	90	73	68	62	111	104	34
1/4	0	23½	36*	33	84	74	69	56	112	105	28
1/2	0	47	37	34	78	75	70	50	113	106	22
3/4	0	70½	38	35	72	76	71	44	114	107	16
1½	1	41	39	36	66	77	72	38	115	108	10
2	1	88	**40**	37	60	78	73	32	116	109	04
3	2	82	41	38	54	79	74	26	117	109	98
4	3	76	42	39	48	**80**	75	20	118	110	92
5	4	70	43	40	42	81	76	14	119	111	86
6	5	64	44	41	36	82	77	08	120*	112	80
7	6	58	45	42	30	83	78	02	128	120	32
8	7	52	46	43	24	84*	78	96	130	122	20
9	8	46	47	44	18	85	79	90	140	131	60
10	9	40	48*	45	12	86	80	84	144*	135	36
11	10	34	49	46	06	87	81	78	150	141	00
12*	11	28	**50**	47	00	88	82	72	156	146	64
13	12	22	51	47	94	89	83	66	168	157	92
14	13	16	52	48	88	**90**	84	60	196	184	24
15	14	10	53	49	82	91	85	54	200	188	00
16	15	04	54	50	76	92	86	48	220	206	80
17	15	98	55	51	70	93	87	42	224	210	56
18	16	92	56	52	64	94	88	36	256	240	64
19	17	86	57	53	58	95	89	30	280	263	20
20	18	80	58	54	52	96*	90	24	300	282	00
21	19	74	59	55	46	97	91	18	365	343	10
22	20	68	**60***	56	40	98	92	12	400	376	00
23	21	62	61	57	34	99	93	06	480	451	20
24*	22	56	62	58	28	**100**	94	00	500	470	00
25	23	50	63	59	22	101	94	94	516	485	04
26	24	44	64	60	16	102	95	88	560	526	40
27	25	38	65	61	10	103	96	82	600	564	00
28	26	32	66	62	04	104	97	76	625	587	50
29	27	26	67	62	98	105	98	70	640	601	60
30	28	20	68	63	92	106	99	64	700	658	00
31	29	14	69	64	86	107	100	58	750	705	00
32	30	08	**70**	65	80	108*	101	52	800	752	00
33	31	02	71	66	74	109	102	46	900	846	00

No.	£	p	No.	£	p	No.	£	p
1000	940	00	1760	1654	40	6000	5640	00
1016	955	04	2000	1880	00	7000	6580	00
1094	1028	36	2240	2105	60	7500	7050	00
1120	1052	80	2500	2350	00	10000	9400	00
1250	1175	00	3000	2820	00	15000	14100	00
1500	1410	00	4000	3760	00	20000	18800	00
1750	1645	00	5000	4700	00	30000	28200	00

No.	£	p	No.	£	p	No.	£	p	No.	£	p
$\frac{1}{16}$	0	06	34	32	30	72*	68	40	110	104	50
$\frac{1}{8}$	0	12	35	33	25	73	69	35	111	105	45
$\frac{1}{4}$	0	24	36*	34	20	74	70	30	112	106	40
$\frac{1}{2}$	0	47½	37	35	15	75	71	25	113	107	35
$\frac{3}{4}$	0	71½	38	36	10	76	72	20	114	108	30
1½	1	42½	39	37	05	77	73	15	115	109	25
2	1	90	40	38	00	78	74	10	116	110	20
3	2	85	41	38	95	79	75	05	117	111	15
4	3	80	42	39	90	80	76	00	118	112	10
5	4	75	43	40	85	81	76	95	119	113	05
6	5	70	44	41	80	82	77	90	120*	114	00
7	6	65	45	42	75	83	78	85	128	121	60
8	7	60	46	43	70	84*	79	80	130	123	50
9	8	55	47	44	65	85	80	75	140	133	00
10	9	50	48*	45	60	86	81	70	144*	136	80
11	10	45	49	46	55	87	82	65	150	142	50
12*	11	40	50	47	50	88	83	60	156	148	20
13	12	35	51	48	45	89	84	55	168	159	60
14	13	30	52	49	40	90	85	50	196	186	20
15	14	25	53	50	35	91	86	45	200	190	00
16	15	20	54	51	30	92	87	40	220	209	00
17	16	15	55	52	25	93	88	35	224	212	80
18	17	10	56	53	20	94	89	30	256	243	20
19	18	05	57	54	15	95	90	25	280	266	00
20	19	00	58	55	10	96*	91	20	300	285	00
21	19	95	59	56	05	97	92	15	365	346	75
22	20	90	60*	57	00	98	93	10	400	380	00
23	21	85	61	57	95	99	94	05	480	456	00
24*	22	80	62	58	90	100	95	00	500	475	00
25	23	75	63	59	85	101	95	95	516	490	20
26	24	70	64	60	80	102	96	90	560	532	00
27	25	65	65	61	75	103	97	85	600	570	00
28	26	60	66	62	70	104	98	80	625	593	75
29	27	55	67	63	65	105	99	75	640	608	00
30	28	50	68	64	60	106	100	70	700	665	00
31	29	45	69	65	55	107	101	65	750	712	50
32	30	40	70	66	50	108*	102	60	800	760	00
33	31	35	71	67	45	109	103	55	900	855	00

No.	£	p	No.	£	p	No.	£	p
1000	950	00	1760	1672	00	6000	5700	00
1016	965	20	2000	1900	00	7000	6650	00
1094	1039	30	2240	2128	00	7500	7125	00
1120	1064	00	2500	2375	00	10000	9500	00
1250	1187	50	3000	2850	00	15000	14250	00
1500	1425	00	4000	3800	00	20000	19000	00
1750	1662	50	5000	4750	00	30000	28500	00

96p

£0·96

No.	£	p	No.	£	p	No.	£	p	No.	£	p
1/16	0	06	34	32	64	72*	69	12	110	105	60
1/8	0	12	35	33	60	73	70	08	111	106	56
1/4	0	24	36*	34	56	74	71	04	112	107	52
1/2	0	48	37	35	52	75	72	00	113	108	48
3/4	0	72	38	36	48	76	72	96	114	109	44
1½	1	44	39	37	44	77	73	92	115	110	40
2	1	92	40	38	40	78	74	88	116	111	36
3	2	88	41	39	36	79	75	84	117	112	32
4	3	84	42	40	32	80	76	80	118	113	28
5	4	80	43	41	28	81	77	76	119	114	24
6	5	76	44	42	24	82	78	72	120*	115	20
7	6	72	45	43	20	83	79	68	128	122	88
8	7	68	46	44	16	84*	80	64	130	124	80
9	8	64	47	45	12	85	81	60	140	134	40
10	9	60	48*	46	08	86	82	56	144*	138	24
11	10	56	49	47	04	87	83	52	150	144	00
12*	11	52	50	48	00	88	84	48	156	149	76
13	12	48	51	48	96	89	85	44	168	161	28
14	13	44	52	49	92	90	86	40	196	188	16
15	14	40	53	50	88	91	87	36	200	192	00
16	15	36	54	51	84	92	88	32	220	211	20
17	16	32	55	52	80	93	89	28	224	215	04
18	17	28	56	53	76	94	90	24	256	245	76
19	18	24	57	54	72	95	91	20	280	268	80
20	19	20	58	55	68	96*	92	16	300	288	00
21	20	16	59	56	64	97	93	12	365	350	40
22	21	12	60*	57	60	98	94	08	400	384	00
23	22	08	61	58	56	99	95	04	480	460	80
24*	23	04	62	59	52	100	96	00	500	480	00
25	24	00	63	60	48	101	96	96	516	495	36
26	24	96	64	61	44	102	97	92	560	537	60
27	25	92	65	62	40	103	98	88	600	576	00
28	26	88	66	63	36	104	99	84	625	600	00
29	27	84	67	64	32	105	100	80	640	614	40
30	28	80	68	65	28	106	101	76	700	672	00
31	29	76	69	66	24	107	102	72	750	720	00
32	30	72	70	67	20	108*	103	68	800	768	00
33	31	68	71	68	16	109	104	64	900	864	00

No.	£	p	No.	£	p	No.	£	p
1000	960	00	1760	1689	60	6000	5760	00
1016	975	36	2000	1920	00	7000	6720	00
1094	1050	24	2240	2150	40	7500	7200	00
1120	1075	20	2500	2400	00	10000	9600	00
1250	1200	00	3000	2880	00	15000	14400	00
1500	1440	00	4000	3840	00	20000	19200	00
1750	1680	00	5000	4800	00	30000	28800	00

No.	£	p	No.	£	p	No.	£	p	No.	£	p
$\frac{1}{16}$	0	06	34	32	98	72*	69	84	110	106	70
$\frac{1}{8}$	0	12	35	33	95	73	70	81	111	107	67
$\frac{1}{4}$	0	24¼	36*	34	92	74	71	78	112	108	64
$\frac{1}{2}$	0	48½	37	35	89	75	72	75	113	109	61
$\frac{3}{4}$	0	73	38	36	86	76	73	72	114	110	58
1½	1	45½	39	37	83	77	74	69	115	111	55
2	1	94	40	38	80	78	75	66	116	112	52
3	2	91	41	39	77	79	76	63	117	113	49
4	3	88	42	40	74	80	77	60	118	114	46
5	4	85	43	41	71	81	78	57	119	115	43
6	5	82	44	42	68	82	79	54	120*	116	40
7	6	79	45	43	65	83	80	51	128	124	16
8	7	76	46	44	62	84*	81	48	130	126	10
9	8	73	47	45	59	85	82	45	140	135	80
10	9	70	48*	46	56	86	83	42	144*	139	68
11	10	67	49	47	53	87	84	39	150	145	50
12*	11	64	50	48	50	88	85	36	156	151	32
13	12	61	51	49	47	89	86	33	168	162	96
14	13	58	52	50	44	90	87	30	196	190	12
15	14	55	53	51	41	91	88	27	200	194	00
16	15	52	54	52	38	92	89	24	220	213	40
17	16	49	55	53	35	93	90	21	224	217	28
18	17	46	56	54	32	94	91	18	256	248	32
19	18	43	57	55	29	95	92	15	280	271	60
20	19	40	58	56	26	96*	93	12	300	291	00
21	20	37	59	57	23	97	94	09	365	354	05
22	21	34	60*	58	20	98	95	06	400	388	00
23	22	31	61	59	17	99	96	03	480	465	60
24*	23	28	62	60	14	100	97	00	500	485	00
25	24	25	63	61	11	101	97	97	516	500	52
26	25	22	64	62	08	102	98	94	560	543	20
27	26	19	65	63	05	103	99	91	600	582	00
28	27	16	66	64	02	104	100	88	625	606	25
29	28	13	67	64	99	105	101	85	640	620	80
30	29	10	68	65	96	106	102	82	700	679	00
31	30	07	69	66	93	107	103	79	750	727	50
32	31	04	70	67	90	108*	104	76	800	776	00
33	32	01	71	68	87	109	105	73	900	873	00

No.	£	p	No.	£	p	No.	£	p
1000	970	00	1760	1707	20	6000	5820	00
1016	985	52	2000	1940	00	7000	6790	00
1094	1061	18	2240	2172	80	7500	7275	00
1120	1086	40	2500	2425	00	10000	9700	00
1250	1212	50	3000	2910	00	15000	14550	00
1500	1455	00	4000	3880	00	20000	19400	00
1750	1697	50	5000	4850	00	30000	29100	00

No.	£	p	No.	£	p	No.	£	p	No.	£	p
1/16	0	06	34	33	15	72*	70	20	110	107	25
1/8	0	12	35	34	12½	73	71	17½	111	108	22½
1/4	0	24½	36*	35	10	74	72	15	112	109	20
1/2	0	49	37	36	07½	75	73	12½	113	110	17½
3/4	0	73	38	37	05	76	74	10	114	111	15
1½	1	46½	39	38	02½	77	75	07½	115	112	12½
2	1	95	40	39	00	78	76	05	116	113	10
3	2	92½	41	39	97½	79	77	02½	117	114	07½
4	3	90	42	40	95	80	78	00	118	115	05
5	4	87½	43	41	92½	81	78	97½	119	116	02½
6	5	85	44	42	90	82	79	95	120*	117	00
7	6	82½	45	43	87½	83	80	92½	128	124	80
8	7	80	46	44	85	84*	81	90	130	126	75
9	8	77½	47	45	82½	85	82	87½	140	136	50
10	9	75	48*	46	80	86	83	85	144*	140	40
11	10	72½	49	47	77½	87	84	82½	150	146	25
12*	11	70	50	48	75	88	85	80	156	152	10
13	12	67½	51	49	72½	89	86	77½	168	163	80
14	13	65	52	50	70	90	87	75	196	191	10
15	14	62½	53	51	67½	91	88	72½	200	195	00
16	15	60	54	52	65	92	89	70	220	214	50
17	16	57½	55	53	62½	93	90	67½	224	218	40
18	17	55	56	54	60	94	91	65	256	249	60
19	18	52½	57	55	57½	95	92	62½	280	273	00
20	19	50	58	56	55	96*	93	60	300	292	50
21	20	47½	59	57	52½	97	94	57½	365	355	87½
22	21	45	60*	58	50	98	95	55	400	390	00
23	22	42½	61	59	47½	99	96	52½	480	468	00
24*	23	40	62	60	45	100	97	50	500	487	50
25	24	37½	63	61	42½	101	98	47½	516	503	10
26	25	35	64	62	40	102	99	45	560	546	00
27	26	32½	65	63	37½	103	100	42½	600	585	00
28	27	30	66	64	35	104	101	40	625	609	37½
29	28	27½	67	65	32½	105	102	37½	640	624	00
30	29	25	68	66	30	106	103	35	700	682	50
31	30	22½	69	67	27½	107	104	32½	750	731	25
32	31	20	70	68	25	108*	105	30	800	780	00
33	32	17½	71	69	22½	109	106	27½	900	877	50

No.	£	p	No.	£	p	No.	£	p
1000	975	00	1760	1716	00	6000	5850	00
1016	990	60	2000	1950	00	7000	6825	00
1094	1066	65	2240	2184	00	7500	7312	50
1120	1092	00	2500	2437	50	10000	9750	00
1250	1218	75	3000	2925	00	15000	14625	00
1500	1462	50	4000	3900	00	20000	19500	00
1750	1706	25	5000	4875	00	30000	29250	00

98p   £0·98

No.	£	p	No.	£	p	No.	£	p	No.	£	p
1/16	0	06	34	33	32	72*	70	56	110	107	80
1/8	0	12½	35	34	30	73	71	54	111	108	78
1/4	0	24½	36*	35	28	74	72	52	112	109	76
1/2	0	49	37	36	26	75	73	50	113	110	74
3/4	0	73½	38	37	24	76	74	48	114	111	72
1½	1	47	39	38	22	77	75	46	115	112	70
2	1	96	40	39	20	78	76	44	116	113	68
3	2	94	41	40	18	79	77	42	117	114	66
4	3	92	42	41	16	80	78	40	118	115	64
5	4	90	43	42	14	81	79	38	119	116	62
6	5	88	44	43	12	82	80	36	120*	117	60
7	6	86	45	44	10	83	81	34	128	125	44
8	7	84	46	45	08	84*	82	32	130	127	40
9	8	82	47	46	06	85	83	30	140	137	20
10	9	80	48*	47	04	86	84	28	144*	141	12
11	10	78	49	48	02	87	85	26	150	147	00
12*	11	76	50	49	00	88	86	24	156	152	88
13	12	74	51	49	98	89	87	22	168	164	64
14	13	72	52	50	96	90	88	20	196	192	08
15	14	70	53	51	94	91	89	18	200	196	00
16	15	68	54	52	92	92	90	16	220	215	60
17	16	66	55	53	90	93	91	14	224	219	52
18	17	64	56	54	88	94	92	12	256	250	88
19	18	62	57	55	86	95	93	10	280	274	40
20	19	60	58	56	84	96*	94	08	300	294	00
21	20	58	59	57	82	97	95	06	365	357	70
22	21	56	60*	58	80	98	96	04	400	392	00
23	22	54	61	59	78	99	97	02	480	470	40
24*	23	52	62	60	76	100	98	00	500	490	00
25	24	50	63	61	74	101	98	98	516	505	68
26	25	48	64	62	72	102	99	96	560	548	80
27	26	46	65	63	70	103	100	94	600	588	00
28	27	44	66	64	68	104	101	92	625	612	50
29	28	42	67	65	66	105	102	90	640	627	20
30	29	40	68	66	64	106	103	88	700	686	00
31	30	38	69	67	62	107	104	86	750	735	00
32	31	36	70	68	60	108*	105	84	800	784	00
33	32	34	71	69	58	109	106	82	900	882	00

No.	£	p	No.	£	p	No.	£	p
1000	980	00	1760	1724	80	6000	5880	00
1016	995	68	2000	1960	00	7000	6860	00
1094	1072	12	2240	2195	20	7500	7350	00
1120	1097	60	2500	2450	00	10000	9800	00
1250	1225	00	3000	2940	00	15000	14700	00
1500	1470	00	4000	3920	00	20000	19600	00
1750	1715	00	5000	4900	00	30000	29400	00

No.	£	p	No.	£	p	No.	£	p	No.	£	p
1/16	0	06	34	33	66	72*	71	28	110	108	90
1/8	0	12½	35	34	65	73	72	27	111	109	89
1/4	0	25	36*	35	64	74	73	26	112	110	88
1/2	0	49½	37	36	63	75	74	25	113	111	87
3/4	0	74½	38	37	62	76	75	24	114	112	86
1½	1	48½	39	38	61	77	76	23	115	113	85
2	1	98	40	39	60	78	77	22	116	114	84
3	2	97	41	40	59	79	78	21	117	115	83
4	3	96	42	41	58	80	79	20	118	116	82
5	4	95	43	42	57	81	80	19	119	117	81
6	5	94	44	43	56	82	81	18	120*	118	80
7	6	93	45	44	55	83	82	17	128	126	72
8	7	92	46	45	54	84*	83	16	130	128	70
9	8	91	47	46	53	85	84	15	140	138	60
10	9	90	48*	47	52	86	85	14	144*	142	56
11	10	89	49	48	51	87	86	13	150	148	50
12*	11	88	50	49	50	88	87	12	156	154	44
13	12	87	51	50	49	89	88	11	168	166	32
14	13	86	52	51	48	90	89	10	196	194	04
15	14	85	53	52	47	91	90	09	200	198	00
16	15	84	54	53	46	92	91	08	220	217	80
17	16	83	55	54	45	93	92	07	224	221	76
18	17	82	56	55	44	94	93	06	256	253	44
19	18	81	57	56	43	95	94	05	280	277	20
20	19	80	58	57	42	96*	95	04	300	297	00
21	20	79	59	58	41	97	96	03	365	361	35
22	21	78	60*	59	40	98	97	02	400	396	00
23	22	77	61	60	39	99	98	01	480	475	20
24*	23	76	62	61	38	100	99	00	500	495	00
25	24	75	63	62	37	101	99	99	516	510	84
26	25	74	64	63	36	102	100	98	560	554	40
27	26	73	65	64	35	103	101	97	600	594	00
28	27	72	66	65	34	104	102	96	625	618	75
29	28	71	67	66	33	105	103	95	640	633	60
30	29	70	68	67	32	106	104	94	700	693	00
31	30	69	69	68	31	107	105	93	750	742	50
32	31	68	70	69	30	108*	106	92	800	792	00
33	32	67	71	70	29	109	107	91	900	891	00

No.	£	p	No.	£	p	No.	£	p
1000	990	00	1760	1742	40	6000	5940	00
1016	1005	84	2000	1980	00	7000	6930	00
1094	1083	06	2240	2217	60	7500	7425	00
1120	1108	80	2500	2475	00	10000	9900	00
1250	1237	50	3000	2970	00	15000	14850	00
1500	1485	00	4000	3960	00	20000	19800	00
1750	1732	50	5000	4950	00	30000	29700	00

No.	£	p	No.	£	p	No.	£	p	No.	£	p
$\frac{1}{16}$	0	06½	34	34	00	72*	72	00	110	110	00
$\frac{1}{8}$	0	12½	35	35	00	73	73	00	111	111	00
$\frac{1}{4}$	0	25	36*	36	00	74	74	00	112	112	00
$\frac{1}{2}$	0	50	37	37	00	75	75	00	113	113	00
$\frac{3}{4}$	0	75	38	38	00	76	76	00	114	114	00
$1\frac{1}{2}$	1	50	39	39	00	77	77	00	115	115	00
2	2	00	**40**	40	00	78	78	00	116	116	00
3	3	00	41	41	00	79	79	00	117	117	00
4	4	00	42	42	00	80	80	00	118	118	00
5	5	00	43	43	00	81	81	00	119	119	00
6	6	00	44	44	00	82	82	00	120*	120	00
7	7	00	45	45	00	83	83	00	128	128	00
8	8	00	46	46	00	84*	84	00	130	130	00
9	9	00	47	47	00	85	85	00	140	140	00
10	10	00	48*	48	00	86	86	00	144*	144	00
11	11	00	49	49	00	87	87	00	150	150	00
12*	12	00	**50**	50	00	88	88	00	156	156	00
13	13	00	51	51	00	89	89	00	168	168	00
14	14	00	52	52	00	**90**	90	00	196	196	00
15	15	00	53	53	00	91	91	00	200	200	00
16	16	00	54	54	00	92	92	00	220	220	00
17	17	00	55	55	00	93	93	00	224	224	00
18	18	00	56	56	00	94	94	00	256	256	00
19	19	00	57	57	00	95	95	00	280	280	00
20	20	00	58	58	00	96*	96	00	300	300	00
21	21	00	59	59	00	97	97	00	365	365	00
22	22	00	**60***	60	00	98	98	00	400	400	00
23	23	00	61	61	00	99	99	00	480	480	00
24*	24	00	62	62	00	**100**	100	00	500	500	00
25	25	00	63	63	00	101	101	00	516	516	00
26	26	00	64	64	00	102	102	00	560	560	00
27	27	00	65	65	00	103	103	00	600	600	00
28	28	00	66	66	00	104	104	00	625	625	00
29	29	00	67	67	00	105	105	00	640	640	00
30	30	00	68	68	00	106	106	00	700	700	00
31	31	00	69	69	00	107	107	00	750	750	00
32	32	00	**70**	70	00	108*	108	00	800	800	00
33	33	00	71	71	00	109	109	00	900	900	00

No.	£	p	No.	£	p	No.	£	p
1000	1000	00	1760	1760	00	6000	6000	00
1016	1016	00	2000	2000	00	7000	7000	00
1094	1094	00	2240	2240	00	7500	7500	00
1120	1120	00	2500	2500	00	10000	10000	00
1250	1250	00	3000	3000	00	15000	15000	00
1500	1500	00	4000	4000	00	20000	20000	00
1750	1750	00	5000	5000	00	30000	30000	00

Section 2

DECIMAL CURRENCY DISCOUNT AND COMMISSION RECKONER

p	£	p	£	p	£	£	£
$\frac{1}{2}$	0·0000	33	0·0008	67	0·0017	1	0·0025
1	0·0000	34	0·0009	$67\frac{1}{2}$	0·0017	2	0·0050
2	0·0001	35	0·0009	68	0·0017	3	0·0075
$2\frac{1}{2}$	0·0001	36	0·0009	69	0·0017	4	0·0100
3	0·0001	37	0·0009	70	0·0018	5	0·0125
4	0·0001	$37\frac{1}{2}$	0·0009	71	0·0018	6	0·0150
5	0·0001	38	0·0010	72	0·0018	7	0·0175
6	0·0002	39	0·0010	$72\frac{1}{2}$	0·0018	8	0·0200
7	0·0002	40	0·0010	73	0·0018	9	0·0225
$7\frac{1}{2}$	0·0002	41	0·0010	74	0·0019	10	0·0250
8	0·0002	42	0·0011	75	0·0019	11	0·0275
9	0·0002	$42\frac{1}{2}$	0·0011	76	0·0019	12	0·0300
10	0·0003	43	0·0011	77	0·0019	13	0·0325
11	0·0003	44	0·0011	$77\frac{1}{2}$	0·0019	14	0·0350
12	0·0003	45	0·0011	78	0·0020	15	0·0375
$12\frac{1}{2}$	0·0003	46	0·0012	79	0·0020	16	0·0400
13	0·0003	47	0·0012	80	0·0020	17	0·0425
14	0·0004	$47\frac{1}{2}$	0·0012	81	0·0020	18	0·0450
15	0·0004	48	0·0012	82	0·0021	19	0·0475
16	0·0004	49	0·0012	$82\frac{1}{2}$	0·0021	20	0·0500
17	0·0004	50	0·0013	83	0·0021	25	0·0625
$17\frac{1}{2}$	0·0004	51	0·0013	84	0·0021	30	0·0750
18	0·0005	52	0·0013	85	0·0021	35	0·0875
19	0·0005	$52\frac{1}{2}$	0·0013	86	0·0022	40	0·1000
20	0·0005	53	0·0013	87	0·0022	45	0·1125
21	0·0005	54	0·0014	$87\frac{1}{2}$	0·0022	50	0·1250
22	0·0006	55	0·0014	88	0·0022	55	0·1375
$22\frac{1}{2}$	0·0006	56	0·0014	89	0·0022	60	0·1500
23	0·0006	57	0·0014	90	0·0023	65	0·1625
24	0·0006	$57\frac{1}{2}$	0·0014	91	0·0023	70	0·1750
25	0·0006	58	0·0015	92	0·0023	75	0·1875
26	0·0007	59	0·0015	$92\frac{1}{2}$	0·0023	80	0·2000
27	0·0007	60	0·0015	93	0·0023	85	0·2125
$27\frac{1}{2}$	0·0007	61	0·0015	94	0·0024	90	0·2250
28	0·0007	62	0·0016	95	0·0024	95	0·2375
29	0·0007	$62\frac{1}{2}$	0·0016	96	0·0024	100	0·2500
30	0·0008	63	0·0016	97	0·0024	110	0·2750
31	0·0008	64	0·0016	$97\frac{1}{2}$	0·0024	120	0·3000
32	0·0008	65	0·0016	98	0·0025	130	0·3250
$32\frac{1}{2}$	0·0008	66	0·0017	99	0·0025	140	0·3500

£	£	£	£	£	£	£	£
150	0·3750	300	0·7500	450	1·1250	700	1·7500
200	0·5000	350	0·8750	500	1·2500	800	2·0000
250	0·6250	400	1·0000	600	1·5000	1000	2·5000

p	£	p	£	p	£	£	£
$\frac{1}{2}$	0·0000	33	0·0012	67	0·0025	1	0·0038
1	0·0000	34	0·0013	$67\frac{1}{2}$	0·0025	2	0·0075
2	0·0001	35	0·0013	68	0·0026	3	0·0113
$2\frac{1}{2}$	0·0001	36	0·0014	69	0·0026	4	0·0150
3	0·0001	37	0·0014	70	0·0026	5	0·0188
4	0·0002	$37\frac{1}{2}$	0·0014	71	0·0027	6	0·0225
5	0·0002	38	0·0014	72	0·0027	7	0·0263
6	0·0002	39	0·0015	$72\frac{1}{2}$	0·0027	8	0·0300
7	0·0003	40	0·0015	73	0·0027	9	0·0338
$7\frac{1}{2}$	0·0003	41	0·0015	74	0·0028	10	0·0375
8	0·0003	42	0·0016	75	0·0028	11	0·0413
9	0·0003	$42\frac{1}{2}$	0·0016	76	0·0029	12	0·0450
10	0·0004	43	0·0016	77	0·0029	13	0·0488
11	0·0004	44	0·0017	$77\frac{1}{2}$	0·0029	14	0·0525
12	0·0005	45	0·0017	78	0·0029	15	0·0563
$12\frac{1}{2}$	0·0005	46	0·0017	79	0·0030	16	0·0600
13	0·0005	47	0·0018	80	0·0030	17	0·0638
14	0·0005	$47\frac{1}{2}$	0·0018	81	0·0030	18	0·0675
15	0·0006	48	0·0018	82	0·0031	19	0·0713
16	0·0006	49	0·0018	$82\frac{1}{2}$	0·0031	20	0·0750
17	0·0006	50	0·0019	83	0·0031	25	0·0938
$17\frac{1}{2}$	0·0007	51	0·0019	84	0·0032	30	0·1125
18	0·0007	52	0·0020	85	0·0032	35	0·1313
19	0·0007	$52\frac{1}{2}$	0·0020	86	0·0032	40	0·1500
20	0·0008	53	0·0020	87	0·0033	45	0·1688
21	0·0008	54	0·0020	$87\frac{1}{2}$	0·0033	50	0·1875
22	0·0008	55	0·0021	88	0·0033	55	0·2063
$22\frac{1}{2}$	0·0008	56	0·0021	89	0·0033	60	0·2250
23	0·0009	57	0·0021	90	0·0034	65	0·2438
24	0·0009	$57\frac{1}{2}$	0·0022	91	0·0034	70	0·2625
25	0·0009	58	0·0022	92	0·0035	75	0·2813
26	0·0010	59	0·0022	$92\frac{1}{2}$	0·0035	80	0·3000
27	0·0010	60	0·0023	93	0·0035	85	0·3188
$27\frac{1}{2}$	0·0010	61	0·0023	94	0·0035	90	0·3375
28	0·0011	62	0·0023	95	0·0036	95	0·3563
29	0·0011	$62\frac{1}{2}$	0·0023	96	0·0036	100	0·3750
30	0·0011	63	0·0024	97	0·0036	110	0·4125
31	0·0012	64	0·0024	$97\frac{1}{2}$	0·0037	120	0·4500
32	0·0012	65	0·0024	98	0·0037	130	0·4875
$32\frac{1}{2}$	0·0012	66	0·0025	99	0·0037	140	0·5250

£	£	£	£	£	£	£	£
150	0·5625	300	1·1250	450	1·6875	700	2·6250
200	0·7500	350	1·3125	500	1·8750	800	3·0000
250	0·9375	400	1·5000	600	2·2500	1000	3·7500

p	£	p	£	p	£	£	£
$\frac{1}{2}$	0·0000	33	0·0017	67	0·0034	1	0·0050
1	0·0001	34	0·0017	$67\frac{1}{2}$	0·0034	2	0·0100
2	0·0001	35	0·0018	68	0·0034	3	0·0150
$2\frac{1}{2}$	0·0001	36	0·0018	69	0·0035	4	0·0200
3	0·0002	37	0·0019	70	0·0035	5	0·0250
4	0·0002	$37\frac{1}{2}$	0·0019	71	0·0036	6	0·0300
5	0·0003	38	0·0019	72	0·0036	7	0·0350
6	0·0003	39	0·0020	$72\frac{1}{2}$	0·0036	8	0·0400
7	0·0004	40	0·0020	73	0·0037	9	0·0450
$7\frac{1}{2}$	0·0004	41	0·0021	74	0·0037	10	0·0500
8	0·0004	42	0·0021	75	0·0038	11	0·0550
9	0·0005	$42\frac{1}{2}$	0·0021	76	0·0038	12	0·0600
10	0·0005	43	0·0022	77	0·0039	13	0·0650
11	0·0006	44	0·0022	$77\frac{1}{2}$	0·0039	14	0·0700
12	0·0006	45	0·0023	78	0·0039	15	0·0750
$12\frac{1}{2}$	0·0006	46	0·0023	79	0·0040	16	0·0800
13	0·0007	47	0·0024	80	0·0040	17	0·0850
14	0·0007	$47\frac{1}{2}$	0·0024	81	0·0041	18	0·0900
15	0·0008	48	0·0024	82	0·0041	19	0·0950
16	0·0008	49	0·0025	$82\frac{1}{2}$	0·0041	20	0·1000
17	0·0009	50	0·0025	83	0·0042	25	0·1250
$17\frac{1}{2}$	0·0009	51	0·0026	84	0·0042	30	0·1500
18	0·0009	52	0·0026	85	0·0043	35	0·1750
19	0·0010	$52\frac{1}{2}$	0·0026	86	0·0043	40	0·2000
20	0·0010	53	0·0027	87	0·0044	45	0·2250
21	0·0011	54	0·0027	$87\frac{1}{2}$	0·0044	50	0·2500
22	0·0011	55	0·0028	88	0·0044	55	0·2750
$22\frac{1}{2}$	0·0011	56	0·0028	89	0·0045	60	0·3000
23	0·0012	57	0·0029	90	0·0045	65	0·3250
24	0·0012	$57\frac{1}{2}$	0·0029	91	0·0046	70	0·3500
25	0·0013	58	0·0029	92	0·0046	75	0·3750
26	0·0013	59	0·0030	$92\frac{1}{2}$	0·0046	80	0·4000
27	0·0014	60	0·0030	93	0·0047	85	0·4250
$27\frac{1}{2}$	0·0014	61	0·0031	94	0·0047	90	0·4500
28	0·0014	62	0·0031	95	0·0048	95	0·4750
29	0·0015	$62\frac{1}{2}$	0·0031	96	0·0048	100	0·5000
30	0·0015	63	0·0032	97	0·0049	110	0·5500
31	0·0016	64	0·0032	$97\frac{1}{2}$	0·0049	120	0·6000
32	0·0016	65	0·0033	98	0·0049	130	0·6500
$32\frac{1}{2}$	0·0016	66	0·0033	99	0·0050	140	0·7000

£	£	£	£	£	£	£	£
150	0·7500	300	1·5000	450	2·2500	700	3·5000
200	1·0000	350	1·7500	500	2·5000	800	4·0000
250	1·2500	400	2·0000	600	3·0000	1000	5·0000

Per Cent

p	£	p	£	p	£	£	£
½	0·0000	33	0·0021	67	0·0042	1	0·0063
1	0·0001	34	0·0021	67½	0·0042	2	0·0125
2	0·0001	35	0·0022	68	0·0043	3	0·0188
2½	0·0002	36	0·0023	69	0·0043	4	0·0250
3	0·0002	37	0·0023	70	0·0044	5	0·0313
4	0·0003	37½	0·0023	71	0·0044	6	0·0375
5	0·0003	38	0·0024	72	0·0045	7	0·0438
6	0·0004	39	0·0024	72½	0·0045	8	0·0500
7	0·0004	40	0·0025	73	0·0046	9	0·0563
7½	0·0005	41	0·0026	74	0·0046	10	0·0625
8	0·0005	42	0·0026	75	0·0047	11	0·0688
9	0·0006	42½	0·0027	76	0·0048	12	0·0750
10	0·0006	43	0·0027	77	0·0048	13	0·0813
11	0·0007	44	0·0028	77½	0·0048	14	0·0875
12	0·0008	45	0·0028	78	0·0049	15	0·0938
12½	0·0008	46	0·0029	79	0·0049	16	0·1000
13	0·0008	47	0·0029	80	0·0050	17	0·1063
14	0·0009	47½	0·0030	81	0·0051	18	0·1125
15	0·0009	48	0·0030	82	0·0051	19	0·1188
16	0·0010	49	0·0031	82½	0·0052	20	0·1250
17	0·0011	50	0·0031	83	0·0052	25	0·1563
17½	0·0011	51	0·0032	84	0·0053	30	0·1875
18	0·0011	52	0·0033	85	0·0053	35	0·2188
19	0·0012	52½	0·0033	86	0·0054	40	0·2500
20	0·0013	53	0·0033	87	0·0054	45	0·2813
21	0·0013	54	0·0034	87½	0·0055	50	0·3125
22	0·0014	55	0·0034	88	0·0055	55	0·3438
22½	0·0014	56	0·0035	89	0·0056	60	0·3750
23	0·0014	57	0·0036	90	0·0056	65	0·4063
24	0·0015	57½	0·0036	91	0·0057	70	0·4375
25	0·0016	58	0·0036	92	0·0058	75	0·4688
26	0·0016	59	0·0037	92½	0·0058	80	0·5000
27	0·0017	60	0·0038	93	0·0058	85	0·5313
27½	0·0017	61	0·0038	94	0·0059	90	0·5625
28	0·0018	62	0·0039	95	0·0059	95	0·5938
29	0·0018	62½	0·0039	96	0·0060	100	0·6250
30	0·0019	63	0·0039	97	0·0061	110	0·6875
31	0·0019	64	0·0040	97½	0·0061	120	0·7500
32	0·0020	65	0·0041	98	0·0061	130	0·8125
32½	0·0020	66	0·0041	99	0·0062	140	0·8750

£	£	£	£	£	£	£	£
150	0·9375	300	1·8750	450	2·8125	700	4·3750
200	1·2500	350	2·1875	500	3·1250	800	5·0000
250	1·5625	400	2·5000	600	3·7500	1000	6·2500

p	£	p	£	p	£	£	£
½ ..	0·0000	33 ..	0·0025	67 ..	0·0050	1 ..	0·0075
1 ..	0·0001	34 ..	0·0026	67½ ..	0·0051	2 ..	0·0150
2 ..	0·0002	35 ..	0·0026	68 ..	0·0051	3 ..	0·0225
2½ ..	0·0002	36 ..	0·0027	69 ..	0·0052	4 ..	0·0300
3 ..	0·0002	37 ..	0·0028	70 ..	0·0053	5 ..	0·0375
4 ..	0·0003	37½ ..	0·0028	71 ..	0·0053	6 ..	0·0450
5 ..	0·0004	38 ..	0·0029	72 ..	0·0054	7 ..	0·0525
6 ..	0·0005	39 ..	0·0029	72½ ..	0·0054	8 ..	0·0600
7 ..	0·0005	40 ..	0·0030	73 ..	0·0055	9 ..	0·0675
7½ ..	0·0006	41 ..	0·0031	74 ..	0·0056	10 ..	0·0750
8 ..	0·0006	42 ..	0·0032	75 ..	0·0056	11 ..	0·0825
9 ..	0·0007	42½ ..	0·0032	76 ..	0·0057	12 ..	0·0900
10 ..	0·0008	43 ..	0·0032	77 ..	0·0058	13 ..	0·0975
11 ..	0·0008	44 ..	0·0033	77½ ..	0·0058	14 ..	0·1050
12 ..	0·0009	45 ..	0·0034	78 ..	0·0059	15 ..	0·1125
12½ ..	0·0009	46 ..	0·0035	79 ..	0·0059	16 ..	0·1200
13 ..	0·0010	47 ..	0·0035	80 ..	0·0060	17 ..	0·1275
14 ..	0·0011	47½ ..	0·0036	81 ..	0·0061	18 ..	0·1350
15 ..	0·0011	48 ..	0·0036	82 ..	0·0062	19 ..	0·1425
16 ..	0·0012	49 ..	0·0037	82½ ..	0·0062	20 ..	0·1500
17 ..	0·0013	50 ..	0·0038	83 ..	0·0062	25 ..	0·1875
17½ ..	0·0013	51 ..	0·0038	84 ..	0·0063	30 ..	0·2250
18 ..	0·0014	52 ..	0·0039	85 ..	0·0064	35 ..	0·2625
19 ..	0·0014	52½ ..	0·0039	86 ..	0·0065	40 ..	0·3000
20 ..	0·0015	53 ..	0·0040	87 ..	0·0065	45 ..	0·3375
21 ..	0·0016	54 ..	0·0041	87½ ..	0·0066	50 ..	0·3750
22 ..	0·0017	55 ..	0·0041	88 ..	0·0066	55 ..	0·4125
22½ ..	0·0017	56 ..	0·0042	89 ..	0·0067	60 ..	0·4500
23 ..	0·0017	57 ..	0·0043	90 ..	0·0068	65 ..	0·4875
24 ..	0·0018	57½ ..	0·0043	91 ..	0·0068	70 ..	0·5250
25 ..	0·0019	58 ..	0·0044	92 ..	0·0069	75 ..	0·5625
26 ..	0·0020	59 ..	0·0044	92½ ..	0·0069	80 ..	0·6000
27 ..	0·0020	60 ..	0·0045	93 ..	0·0070	85 ..	0·6375
27½ ..	0·0021	61 ..	0·0046	94 ..	0·0071	90 ..	0·6750
28 ..	0·0021	62 ..	0·0047	95 ..	0·0071	95 ..	0·7125
29 ..	0·0022	62½ ..	0·0047	96 ..	0·0072	100 ..	0·7500
30 ..	0·0023	63 ..	0·0047	97 ..	0·0073	110 ..	0·8250
31 ..	0·0023	64 ..	0·0048	97½ ..	0·0073	120 ..	0·9000
32 ..	0·0024	65 ..	0·0049	98 ..	0·0074	130 ..	0·9750
32½ ..	0·0024	66 ..	0·0050	99 ..	0·0074	140 ..	1·0500

£	£	£	£	£	£	£	£
150 ..	1·1250	300 ..	2·2500	450 ..	3·3750	700 ..	5·2500
200 ..	1·5000	350 ..	2·6250	500 ..	3·7500	800 ..	6·0000
250 ..	1·8750	400 ..	3·0000	600 ..	4·5000	1000 ..	7·5000

p	£	p	£	p	£	£	£
$\frac{1}{2}$	0·0000	33	0·0029	67	0·0059	1	0·0088
1	0·0001	34	0·0030	$67\frac{1}{2}$	0·0059	2	0·0175
2	0·0002	35	0·0031	68	0·0060	3	0·0263
$2\frac{1}{2}$	0·0002	36	0·0032	69	0·0060	4	0·0350
3	0·0003	37	0·0032	70	0·0061	5	0·0438
4	0·0004	$37\frac{1}{2}$	0·0033	71	0·0062	6	0·0525
5	0·0004	38	0·0033	72	0·0063	7	0·0613
6	0·0005	39	0·0034	$72\frac{1}{2}$	0·0063	8	0·0700
7	0·0006	40	0·0035	73	0·0064	9	0·0788
$7\frac{1}{2}$	0·0007	41	0·0036	74	0·0065	10	0·0875
8	0·0007	42	0·0037	75	0·0066	11	0·0963
9	0·0008	$42\frac{1}{2}$	0·0037	76	0·0067	12	0·1050
10	0·0009	43	0·0038	77	0·0067	13	0·1138
11	0·0010	44	0·0039	$77\frac{1}{2}$	0·0068	14	0·1225
12	0·0011	45	0·0039	78	0·0068	15	0·1313
$12\frac{1}{2}$	0·0011	46	0·0040	79	0·0069	16	0·1400
13	0·0011	47	0·0041	80	0·0070	17	0·1488
14	0·0012	$47\frac{1}{2}$	0·0042	81	0·0071	18	0·1575
15	0·0013	48	0·0042	82	0·0072	19	0·1663
16	0·0014	49	0·0043	$82\frac{1}{2}$	0·0072	20	0·1750
17	0·0015	50	0·0044	83	0·0073	25	0·2188
$17\frac{1}{2}$	0·0015	51	0·0045	84	0·0074	30	0·2625
18	0·0016	52	0·0046	85	0·0074	35	0·3063
19	0·0017	$52\frac{1}{2}$	0·0046	86	0·0075	40	0·3500
20	0·0018	53	0·0046	87	0·0076	45	0·3938
21	0·0018	54	0·0047	$87\frac{1}{2}$	0·0077	50	0·4375
22	0·0019	55	0·0048	88	0·0077	55	0·4813
$22\frac{1}{2}$	0·0020	56	0·0049	89	0·0078	60	0·5250
23	0·0020	57	0·0050	90	0·0079	65	0·5688
24	0·0021	$57\frac{1}{2}$	0·0050	91	0·0080	70	0·6125
25	0·0022	58	0·0051	92	0·0081	75	0·6563
26	0·0023	59	0·0052	$92\frac{1}{2}$	0·0081	80	0·7000
27	0·0024	60	0·0053	93	0·0081	85	0·7438
$27\frac{1}{2}$	0·0024	61	0·0053	94	0·0082	90	0·7875
28	0·0025	62	0·0054	95	0·0083	95	0·8313
29	0·0025	$62\frac{1}{2}$	0·0055	96	0·0084	100	0·8750
30	0·0026	63	0·0055	97	0·0085	110	0·9625
31	0·0027	64	0·0056	$97\frac{1}{2}$	0·0085	120	1·0500
32	0·0028	65	0·0057	98	0·0086	130	1·1375
$32\frac{1}{2}$	0·0028	66	0·0058	99	0·0087	140	1·2250

£	£	£	£	£	£	£	£
150	1·3125	300	2·6250	450	3·9375	700	6·1250
200	1·7500	350	3·0625	500	4·3750	800	7·0000
250	2·1875	400	3·5000	600	5·2500	1000	8·7500

p	£	p	£	p	£	£	£
$\frac{1}{2}$	0·0001	33	0·0033	67	0·0067	1	0·0100
1	0·0001	34	0·0034	$67\frac{1}{2}$	0·0068	2	0·0200
2	0·0002	35	0·0035	68	0·0068	3	0·0300
$2\frac{1}{2}$	0·0003	36	0·0036	69	0·0069	4	0·0400
3	0·0003	37	0·0037	70	0·0070	5	0·0500
4	0·0004	$37\frac{1}{2}$	0·0038	71	0·0071	6	0·0600
5	0·0005	38	0·0038	72	0·0072	7	0·0700
6	0·0006	39	0·0039	$72\frac{1}{2}$	0·0073	8	0·0800
7	0·0007	40	0·0040	73	0·0073	9	0·0900
$7\frac{1}{2}$	0·0008	41	0·0041	74	0·0074	10	0·1000
8	0·0008	42	0·0042	75	0·0075	11	0·1100
9	0·0009	$42\frac{1}{2}$	0·0043	76	0·0076	12	0·1200
10	0·0010	43	0·0043	77	0·0077	13	0·1300
11	0·0011	44	0·0044	$77\frac{1}{2}$	0·0078	14	0·1400
12	0·0012	45	0·0045	78	0·0078	15	0·1500
$12\frac{1}{2}$	0·0013	46	0·0046	79	0·0079	16	0·1600
13	0·0013	47	0·0047	80	0·0080	17	0·1700
14	0·0014	$47\frac{1}{2}$	0·0048	81	0·0081	18	0·1800
15	0·0015	48	0·0048	82	0·0082	19	0·1900
16	0·0016	49	0·0049	$82\frac{1}{2}$	0·0083	20	0·2000
17	0·0017	50	0·0050	83	0·0083	25	0·2500
$17\frac{1}{2}$	0·0018	51	0·0051	84	0·0084	30	0·3000
18	0·0018	52	0·0052	85	0·0085	35	0·3500
19	0·0019	$52\frac{1}{2}$	0·0053	86	0·0086	40	0·4000
20	0·0020	53	0·0053	87	0·0087	45	0·4500
21	0·0021	54	0·0054	$87\frac{1}{2}$	0·0088	50	0·5000
22	0·0022	55	0·0055	88	0·0088	55	0·5500
$22\frac{1}{2}$	0·0023	56	0·0056	89	0·0089	60	0·6000
23	0·0023	57	0·0057	90	0·0090	65	0·6500
24	0·0024	$57\frac{1}{2}$	0·0058	91	0·0091	70	0·7000
25	0·0025	58	0·0058	92	0·0092	75	0·7500
26	0·0026	59	0·0059	$92\frac{1}{2}$	0·0093	80	0·8000
27	0·0027	60	0·0060	93	0·0093	85	0·8500
$27\frac{1}{2}$	0·0028	61	0·0061	94	0·0094	90	0·9000
28	0·0028	62	0·0062	95	0·0095	95	0·9500
29	0·0029	$62\frac{1}{2}$	0·0063	96	0·0096	100	1·0000
30	0·0030	63	0·0063	97	0·0097	110	1·1000
31	0·0031	64	0·0064	$97\frac{1}{2}$	0·0098	120	1·2000
32	0·0032	65	0·0065	98	0·0098	130	1·3000
$32\frac{1}{2}$	0·0033	66	0·0066	99	0·0099	140	1·4000

£	£	£	£	£	£	£	£
150	1·5000	300	3·0000	450	4·5000	700	7·0000
200	2·0000	350	3·5000	500	5·0000	800	8·0000
250	2·5000	400	4·0000	600	6·0000	1000	10·0000

p	£	p	£	p	£	£	£
$\frac{1}{2}$	0·0001	33	0·0041	67	0·0084	1	0·0125
1	0·0001	34	0·0043	$67\frac{1}{2}$	0·0084	2	0·0250
2	0·0003	35	0·0044	68	0·0085	3	0·0375
$2\frac{1}{2}$	0·0003	36	0·0045	69	0·0086	4	0·0500
3	0·0004	37	0·0046	70	0·0088	5	0·0625
4	0·0005	$37\frac{1}{2}$	0·0047	71	0·0089	6	0·0750
5	0·0006	38	0·0048	72	0·0090	7	0·0875
6	0·0008	39	0·0049	$72\frac{1}{2}$	0·0091	8	0·1000
7	0·0009	40	0·0050	73	0·0091	9	0·1125
$7\frac{1}{2}$	0·0009	41	0·0051	74	0·0093	10	0·1250
8	0·0010	42	0·0053	75	0·0094	11	0·1375
9	0·0011	$42\frac{1}{2}$	0·0053	76	0·0095	12	0·1500
10	0·0013	43	0·0054	77	0·0096	13	0·1625
11	0·0014	44	0·0055	$77\frac{1}{2}$	0·0097	14	0·1750
12	0·0015	45	0·0056	78	0·0098	15	0·1875
$12\frac{1}{2}$	0·0016	46	0·0058	79	0·0099	16	0·2000
13	0·0016	47	0·0059	80	0·0100	17	0·2125
14	0·0018	$47\frac{1}{2}$	0·0059	81	0·0101	18	0·2250
15	0·0019	48	0·0060	82	0·0103	19	0·2375
16	0·0020	49	0·0061	$82\frac{1}{2}$	0·0103	20	0·2500
17	0·0021	50	0·0063	83	0·0104	25	0·3125
$17\frac{1}{2}$	0·0022	51	0·0064	84	0·0105	30	0·3750
18	0·0023	52	0·0065	85	0·0106	35	0·4375
19	0·0024	$52\frac{1}{2}$	0·0066	86	0·0108	40	0·5000
20	0·0025	53	0·0066	87	0·0109	45	0·5625
21	0·0026	54	0·0068	$87\frac{1}{2}$	0·0109	50	0·6250
22	0·0028	55	0·0069	88	0·0110	55	0·6875
$22\frac{1}{2}$	0·0028	56	0·0070	89	0·0111	60	0·7500
23	0·0029	57	0·0071	90	0·0113	65	0·8125
24	0·0030	$57\frac{1}{2}$	0·0072	91	0·0114	70	0·8750
25	0·0031	58	0·0073	92	0·0115	75	0·9375
26	0·0033	59	0·0074	$92\frac{1}{2}$	0·0116	80	1·0000
27	0·0034	60	0·0075	93	0·0116	85	1·0625
$27\frac{1}{2}$	0·0034	61	0·0076	94	0·0118	90	1·1250
28	0·0035	62	0·0078	95	0·0119	95	1·1875
29	0·0036	$62\frac{1}{2}$	0·0078	96	0·0120	100	1·2500
30	0·0038	63	0·0079	97	0·0121	110	1·3750
31	0·0039	64	0·0080	$97\frac{1}{2}$	0·0122	120	1·5000
32	0·0040	65	0·0081	98	0·0123	130	1·6250
$32\frac{1}{2}$	0·0041	66	0·0083	99	0·0124	140	1·7500

£	£	£	£	£	£	£	£
150	1·8750	300	3·7500	450	5·6250	700	8·7500
200	2·5000	350	4·3750	500	6·2500	800	10·0000
250	3·1250	400	5·0000	600	7·5000	1000	12·5000

p	£	p	£	p	£	£	£
½	0·0001	33	0·0044	67	0·0089	1	0·0133
1	0·0001	34	0·0045	67½	0·0090	2	0·0267
2	0·0003	35	0·0047	68	0·0091	3	0·0400
2½	0·0003	36	0·0048	69	0·0092	4	0·0533
3	0·0004	37	0·0049	70	0·0093	5	0·0667
4	0·0005	37½	0·0050	71	0·0095	6	0·0800
5	0·0007	38	0·0051	72	0·0096	7	0·0933
6	0·0008	39	0·0052	72½	0·0097	8	0·1067
7	0·0009	40	0·0053	73	0·0097	9	0·1200
7½	0·0010	41	0·0055	74	0·0099	10	0·1333
8	0·0011	42	0·0056	75	0·0100	11	0·1467
9	0·0012	42½	0·0057	76	0·0101	12	0·1600
10	0·0013	43	0·0057	77	0·0103	13	0·1733
11	0·0015	44	0·0059	77½	0·0103	14	0·1867
12	0·0016	45	0·0060	78	0·0104	15	0·2000
12½	0·0017	46	0·0061	79	0·0105	16	0·2133
13	0·0017	47	0·0063	80	0·0107	17	0·2267
14	0·0019	47½	0·0063	81	0·0108	18	0·2400
15	0·0020	48	0·0064	82	0·0109	19	0·2533
16	0·0021	49	0·0065	82½	0·0110	20	0·2667
17	0·0023	50	0·0067	83	0·0111	25	0·3333
17½	0·0023	51	0·0068	84	0·0112	30	0·4000
18	0·0024	52	0·0069	85	0·0113	35	0·4667
19	0·0025	52½	0·0070	86	0·0115	40	0·5333
20	0·0027	53	0·0071	87	0·0116	45	0·6000
21	0·0028	54	0·0072	87½	0·0117	50	0·6667
22	0·0029	55	0·0073	88	0·0117	55	0·7333
22½	0·0030	56	0·0075	89	0·0119	60	0·8000
23	0·0031	57	0·0076	90	0·0120	65	0·8667
24	0·0032	57½	0·0077	91	0·0121	70	0·9333
25	0·0033	58	0·0077	92	0·0123	75	1·0000
26	0·0035	59	0·0079	92½	0·0123	80	1·0667
27	0·0036	60	0·0080	93	0·0124	85	1·1333
27½	0·0037	61	0·0081	94	0·0125	90	1·2000
28	0·0037	62	0·0083	95	0·0127	95	1·2667
29	0·0039	62½	0·0083	96	0·0128	100	1·3333
30	0·0040	63	0·0084	97	0·0129	110	1·4667
31	0·0041	64	0·0085	97½	0·0130	120	1·6000
32	0·0043	65	0·0087	98	0·0131	130	1·7333
32½	0·0043	66	0·0088	99	0·0132	140	1·8667

£	£	£	£	£	£	£	£
150	2·0000	300	4·0000	450	6·0000	700	9·3333
200	2·6667	350	4·6667	500	6·6667	800	10·6667
250	3·3333	400	5·3333	600	8·0000	1000	13·3333

p	£	p	£	p	£	£	£
$\frac{1}{2}$ ..	0·0001	33 ..	0·0050	67 ..	0·0101	1 ..	0·0150
1 ..	0·0002	34 ..	0·0051	$67\frac{1}{2}$ ..	0·0101	2 ..	0·0300
2 ..	0·0003	35 ..	0·0053	68 ..	0·0102	3 ..	0·0450
$2\frac{1}{2}$ ..	0·0004	36 ..	0·0054	69 ..	0·0104	4 ..	0·0600
3 ..	0·0005	37 ..	0·0056	70 ..	0·0105	5 ..	0·0750
4 ..	0·0006	$37\frac{1}{2}$ ..	0·0056	71 ..	0·0107	6 ..	0·0900
5 ..	0·0008	38 ..	0·0057	72 ..	0·0108	7 ..	0·1050
6 ..	0·0009	39 ..	0·0059	$72\frac{1}{2}$ ..	0·0109	8 ..	0·1200
7 ..	0·0011	40 ..	0·0060	73 ..	0·0110	9 ..	0·1350
$7\frac{1}{2}$ ..	0·0011	41 ..	0·0062	74 ..	0·0111	10 ..	0·1500
8 ..	0·0012	42 ..	0·0063	75 ..	0·0113	11 ..	0·1650
9 ..	0·0014	$42\frac{1}{2}$ ..	0·0064	76 ..	0·0114	12 ..	0·1800
10 ..	0·0015	43 ..	0·0065	77 ..	0·0116	13 ..	0·1950
11 ..	0·0017	44 ..	0·0066	$77\frac{1}{2}$ ..	0·0116	14 ..	0·2100
12 ..	0·0018	45 ..	0·0068	78 ..	0·0117	15 ..	0·2250
$12\frac{1}{2}$ ..	0·0019	46 ..	0·0069	79 ..	0·0119	16 ..	0·2400
13 ..	0·0020	47 ..	0·0071	80 ..	0·0120	17 ..	0·2550
14 ..	0·0021	$47\frac{1}{2}$ ..	0·0071	81 ..	0·0122	18 ..	0·2700
15 ..	0·0023	48 ..	0·0072	82 ..	0·0123	19 ..	0·2850
16 ..	0·0024	49 ..	0·0074	$82\frac{1}{2}$ ..	0·0124	20 ..	0·3000
17 ..	0·0026	50 ..	0·0075	83 ..	0·0125	25 ..	0·3750
$17\frac{1}{2}$ ..	0·0026	51 ..	0·0077	84 ..	0·0126	30 ..	0·4500
18 ..	0·0027	52 ..	0·0078	85 ..	0·0128	35 ..	0·5250
19 ..	0·0029	$52\frac{1}{2}$ ..	0·0079	86 ..	0·0129	40 ..	0·6000
20 ..	0·0030	53 ..	0·0080	87 ..	0·0131	45 ..	0·6750
21 ..	0·0032	54 ..	0·0081	$87\frac{1}{2}$ ..	0·0131	50 ..	0·7500
22 ..	0·0033	55 ..	0·0083	88 ..	0·0132	55 ..	0·8250
$22\frac{1}{2}$ ..	0·0034	56 ..	0·0084	89 ..	0·0134	60 ..	0·9000
23 ..	0·0035	57 ..	0·0086	90 ..	0·0135	65 ..	0·9750
24 ..	0·0036	$57\frac{1}{2}$ ..	0·0086	91 ..	0·0137	70 ..	1·0500
25 ..	0·0038	58 ..	0·0087	92 ..	0·0138	75 ..	1·1250
26 ..	0·0039	59 ..	0·0089	$92\frac{1}{2}$ ..	0·0139	80 ..	1·2000
27 ..	0·0041	60 ..	0·0090	93 ..	0·0140	85 ..	1·2750
$27\frac{1}{2}$ ..	0·0041	61 ..	0·0092	94 ..	0·0141	90 ..	1·3500
28 ..	0·0042	62 ..	0·0093	95 ..	0·0143	95 ..	1·4250
29 ..	0·0044	$62\frac{1}{2}$ ..	0·0094	96 ..	0·0144	100 ..	1·5000
30 ..	0·0045	63 ..	0·0095	97 ..	0·0146	110 ..	1·6500
31 ..	0·0047	64 ..	0·0096	$97\frac{1}{2}$ ..	0·0146	120 ..	1·8000
32 ..	0·0048	65 ..	0·0098	98 ..	0·0147	130 ..	1·9500
$32\frac{1}{2}$ ..	0·0049	66 ..	0·0099	99 ..	0·0149	140 ..	2·1000

£	£	£	£	£	£	£	£
150 ..	2·2500	300 ..	4·5000	450 ..	6·7500	700 ..	10·5000
200 ..	3·0000	350 ..	5·2500	500 ..	7·5000	800 ..	12·0000
250 ..	3·7500	400 ..	6·0000	600 ..	9·0000	1000 ..	15·0000

p	£	p	£	p	£	£	£
$\frac{1}{2}$ ..	0·0001	33 ..	0·0055	67 ..	0·0112	1 ..	0·0167
1 ..	0·0002	34 ..	0·0057	$67\frac{1}{2}$ ..	0·0113	2 ..	0·0333
2 ..	0·0003	35 ..	0·0058	68 ..	0·0113	3 ..	0·0500
$2\frac{1}{2}$ ..	0·0004	36 ..	0·0060	69 ..	0·0115	4 ..	0·0667
3 ..	0·0005	37 ..	0·0062	70 ..	0·0117	5 ..	0·0833
4 ..	0·0007	$37\frac{1}{2}$ ..	0·0063	71 ..	0·0118	6 ..	0·1000
5 ..	0·0008	38 ..	0·0063	72 ..	0·0120	7 ..	0·1167
6 ..	0·0010	39 ..	0·0065	$72\frac{1}{2}$ ..	0·0121	8 ..	0·1333
7 ..	0·0012	40 ..	0·0067	73 ..	0·0122	9 ..	0·1500
$7\frac{1}{2}$ ..	0·0013	41 ..	0·0068	74 ..	0·0123	10 ..	0·1667
8 ..	0·0013	42 ..	0·0070	75 ..	0·0125	11 ..	0·1833
9 ..	0·0015	$42\frac{1}{2}$ ..	0·0071	76 ..	0·0127	12 ..	0·2000
10 ..	0·0017	43 ..	0·0072	77 ..	0·0128	13 ..	0·2167
11 ..	0·0018	44 ..	0·0073	$77\frac{1}{2}$ ..	0·0129	14 ..	0·2333
12 ..	0·0020	45 ..	0·0075	78 ..	0·0130	15 ..	0·2500
$12\frac{1}{2}$ ..	0·0021	46 ..	0·0077	79 ..	0·0132	16 ..	0·2667
13 ..	0·0022	47 ..	0·0078	80 ..	0·0133	17 ..	0·2833
14 ..	0·0023	$47\frac{1}{2}$ ..	0·0079	81 ..	0·0135	18 ..	0·3000
15 ..	0·0025	48 ..	0·0080	82 ..	0·0137	19 ..	0·3167
16 ..	0·0027	49 ..	0·0082	$82\frac{1}{2}$ ..	0·0138	20 ..	0·3333
17 ..	0·0028	50 ..	0·0083	83 ..	0·0138	25 ..	0·4167
$17\frac{1}{2}$ ..	0·0029	51 ..	0·0085	84 ..	0·0140	30 ..	0·5000
18 ..	0·0030	52 ..	0·0087	85 ..	0·0142	35 ..	0·5833
19 ..	0·0032	$52\frac{1}{2}$ ..	0·0088	86 ..	0·0143	40 ..	0·6667
20 ..	0·0033	53 ..	0·0088	87 ..	0·0145	45 ..	0·7500
21 ..	0·0035	54 ..	0·0090	$87\frac{1}{2}$ ..	0·0146	50 ..	0·8333
22 ..	0·0037	55 ..	0·0092	88 ..	0·0147	55 ..	0·9167
$22\frac{1}{2}$ ..	0·0038	56 ..	0·0093	89 ..	0·0148	60 ..	1·0000
23 ..	0·0038	57 ..	0·0095	90 ..	0·0150	65 ..	1·0833
24 ..	0·0040	$57\frac{1}{2}$ ..	0·0096	91 ..	0·0152	70 ..	1·1667
25 ..	0·0042	58 ..	0·0097	92 ..	0·0153	75 ..	1·2500
26 ..	0·0043	59 ..	0·0098	$92\frac{1}{2}$ ..	0·0154	80 ..	1·3333
27 ..	0·0045	60 ..	0·0100	93 ..	0·0155	85 ..	1·4167
$27\frac{1}{2}$ ..	0·0046	61 ..	0·0102	94 ..	0·0157	90 ..	1·5000
28 ..	0·0047	62 ..	0·0103	95 ..	0·0158	95 ..	1·5833
29 ..	0·0048	$62\frac{1}{2}$ ..	0·0104	96 ..	0·0160	100 ..	1·6667
30 ..	0·0050	63 ..	0·0105	97 ..	0·0162	110 ..	1·8333
31 ..	0·0052	64 ..	0·0107	$97\frac{1}{2}$ ..	0·0163	120 ..	2·0000
32 ..	0·0053	65 ..	0·0108	98 ..	0·0163	130 ..	2·1667
$32\frac{1}{2}$ ..	0·0054	66 ..	0·0110	99 ..	0·0165	140 ..	2·3333

£	£	£	£	£	£	£	£
150 ..	2·5000	300 ..	5·0000	450 ..	7·5000	700 ..	11·6667
200 ..	3·3333	350 ..	5·8333	500 ..	8·3333	800 ..	13·3333
250 ..	4·1667	400 ..	6·6667	600 ..	10·0000	1000 ..	16·6667

p	£	p	£	p	£	£	£
½	0·0001	33	0·0058	67	0·0117	1	0·0175
1	0·0002	34	0·0060	67½	0·0118	2	0·0350
2	0·0004	35	0·0061	68	0·0119	3	0·0525
2½	0·0004	36	0·0063	69	0·0121	4	0·0700
3	0·0005	37	0·0065	70	0·0123	5	0·0875
4	0·0007	37½	0·0066	71	0·0124	6	0·1050
5	0·0009	38	0·0067	72	0·0126	7	0·1225
6	0·0011	39	0·0068	72½	0·0127	8	0·1400
7	0·0012	40	0·0070	73	0·0128	9	0·1575
7½	0·0013	41	0·0072	74	0·0130	10	0·1750
8	0·0014	42	0·0074	75	0·0131	11	0·1925
9	0·0016	42½	0·0074	76	0·0133	12	0·2100
10	0·0018	43	0·0075	77	0·0135	13	0·2275
11	0·0019	44	0·0077	77½	0·0136	14	0·2450
12	0·0021	45	0·0079	78	0·0137	15	0·2625
12½	0·0022	46	0·0081	79	0·0138	16	0·2800
13	0·0023	47	0·0082	80	0·0140	17	0·2975
14	0·0025	47½	0·0083	81	0·0142	18	0·3150
15	0·0026	48	0·0084	82	0·0144	19	0·3325
16	0·0028	49	0·0086	82½	0·0144	20	0·3500
17	0·0030	50	0·0088	83	0·0145	25	0·4375
17½	0·0031	51	0·0089	84	0·0147	30	0·5250
18	0·0032	52	0·0091	85	0·0149	35	0·6125
19	0·0033	52½	0·0092	86	0·0151	40	0·7000
20	0·0035	53	0·0093	87	0·0152	45	0·7875
21	0·0037	54	0·0095	87½	0·0153	50	0·8750
22	0·0039	55	0·0096	88	0·0154	55	0·9625
22½	0·0039	56	0·0098	89	0·0156	60	1·0500
23	0·0040	57	0·0100	90	0·0158	65	1·1375
24	0·0042	57½	0·0101	91	0·0159	70	1·2250
25	0·0044	58	0·0102	92	0·0161	75	1·3125
26	0·0046	59	0·0103	92½	0·0162	80	1·4000
27	0·0047	60	0·0105	93	0·0163	85	1·4875
27½	0·0048	61	0·0107	94	0·0165	90	1·5750
28	0·0049	62	0·0109	95	0·0166	95	1·6625
29	0·0051	62½	0·0109	96	0·0168	100	1·7500
30	0·0053	63	0·0110	97	0·0170	110	1·9250
31	0·0054	64	0·0112	97½	0·0171	120	2·1000
32	0·0056	65	0·0114	98	0·0172	130	2·2750
32½	0·0057	66	0·0116	99	0·0173	140	2·4500

£	£	£	£	£	£	£	£
150	2·6250	300	5·2500	450	7·8750	700	12·2500
200	3·5000	350	6·1250	500	8·7500	800	14·0000
250	4·3750	400	7·0000	600	10·5000	1000	17·5000

p	£	p	£	p	£	£	£
$\frac{1}{2}$	0·0001	33	0·0066	67	0·0134	1	0·0200
1	0·0002	34	0·0068	$67\frac{1}{2}$	0·0135	2	0·0400
2	0·0004	35	0·0070	68	0·0136	3	0·0600
$2\frac{1}{2}$	0·0005	36	0·0072	69	0·0138	4	0·0800
3	0·0006	37	0·0074	70	0·0140	5	0·1000
4	0·0008	$37\frac{1}{2}$	0·0075	71	0·0142	6	0·1200
5	0·0010	38	0·0076	72	0·0144	7	0·1400
6	0·0012	39	0·0078	$72\frac{1}{2}$	0·0145	8	0·1600
7	0·0014	40	0·0080	73	0·0146	9	0·1800
$7\frac{1}{2}$	0·0015	41	0·0082	74	0·0148	10	0·2000
8	0·0016	42	0·0084	75	0·0150	11	0·2200
9	0·0018	$42\frac{1}{2}$	0·0085	76	0·0152	12	0·2400
10	0·0020	43	0·0086	77	0·0154	13	0·2600
11	0·0022	44	0·0088	$77\frac{1}{2}$	0·0155	14	0·2800
12	0·0024	45	0·0090	78	0·0156	15	0·3000
$12\frac{1}{2}$	0·0025	46	0·0092	79	0·0158	16	0·3200
13	0·0026	47	0·0094	80	0·0160	17	0·3400
14	0·0028	$47\frac{1}{2}$	0·0095	81	0·0162	18	0·3600
15	0·0030	48	0·0096	82	0·0164	19	0·3800
16	0·0032	49	0·0098	$82\frac{1}{2}$	0·0165	20	0·4000
17	0·0034	50	0·0100	83	0·0166	25	0·5000
$17\frac{1}{2}$	0·0035	51	0·0102	84	0·0168	30	0·6000
18	0·0036	52	0·0104	85	0·0170	35	0·7000
19	0·0038	$52\frac{1}{2}$	0·0105	86	0·0172	40	0·8000
20	0·0040	53	0·0106	87	0·0174	45	0·9000
21	0·0042	54	0·0108	$87\frac{1}{2}$	0·0175	50	1·0000
22	0·0044	55	0·0110	88	0·0176	55	1·1000
$22\frac{1}{2}$	0·0045	56	0·0112	89	0·0178	60	1·2000
23	0·0046	57	0·0114	90	0·0180	65	1·3000
24	0·0048	$57\frac{1}{2}$	0·0115	91	0·0182	70	1·4000
25	0·0050	58	0·0116	92	0·0184	75	1·5000
26	0·0052	59	0·0118	$92\frac{1}{2}$	0·0185	80	1·6000
27	0·0054	60	0·0120	93	0·0186	85	1·7000
$27\frac{1}{2}$	0·0055	61	0·0122	94	0·0188	90	1·8000
28	0·0056	62	0·0124	95	0·0190	95	1·9000
29	0·0058	$62\frac{1}{2}$	0·0125	96	0·0192	100	2·0000
30	0·0060	63	0·0126	97	0·0194	110	2·2000
31	0·0062	64	0·0128	$97\frac{1}{2}$	0·0195	120	2·4000
32	0·0064	65	0·0130	98	0·0196	130	2·6000
$32\frac{1}{2}$	0·0065	66	0·0132	99	0·0198	140	2·8000

£	£	£	£	£	£	£	£
150	3·0000	300	6·0000	450	9·0000	700	14·0000
200	4·0000	350	7·0000	500	10·0000	800	16·0000
250	5·0000	400	8·0000	600	12·0000	1000	20·0000

p	£	p	£	p	£	£	£
½	0·0001	33	0·0074	67	0·0151	1	0·0225
1	0·0002	34	0·0077	67½	0·0152	2	0·0450
2	0·0005	35	0·0079	68	0·0153	3	0·0675
2½	0·0006	36	0·0081	69	0·0155	4	0·0900
3	0·0007	37	0·0083	70	0·0158	5	0·1125
4	0·0009	37½	0·0084	71	0·0160	6	0·1350
5	0·0011	38	0·0086	72	0·0162	7	0·1575
6	0·0014	39	0·0088	72½	0·0163	8	0·1800
7	0·0016	40	0·0099	73	0·0164	9	0·2025
7½	0·0017	41	0·0092	74	0·0167	10	0·2250
8	0·0018	42	0·0095	75	0·0169	11	0·2475
9	0·0020	42½	0·0096	76	0·0171	12	0·2700
10	0·0023	43	0·0097	77	0·0173	13	0·2925
11	0·0025	44	0·0099	77½	0·0174	14	0·3150
12	0·0027	45	0·0101	78	0·0176	15	0·3375
12½	0·0028	46	0·0104	79	0·0178	16	0·3600
13	0·0029	47	0·0106	80	0·0180	17	0·3825
14	0·0032	47½	0·0107	81	0·0182	18	0·4050
15	0·0034	48	0·0108	82	0·0185	19	0·4275
16	0·0036	49	0·0110	82½	0·0186	20	0·4500
17	0·0038	50	0·0113	83	0·0187	25	0·5625
17½	0·0039	51	0·0115	84	0·0189	30	0·6750
18	0·0041	52	0·0117	85	0·0191	35	0·7875
19	0·0043	52½	0·0118	86	0·0194	40	0·9000
20	0·0045	53	0·0119	87	0·0196	45	1·0125
21	0·0047	54	0·0122	87½	0·0197	50	1·1250
22	0·0050	55	0·0124	88	0·0198	55	1·2375
22½	0·0051	56	0·0126	89	0·0200	60	1·3500
23	0·0052	57	0·0128	90	0·0203	65	1·4625
24	0·0054	57½	0·0129	91	0·0205	70	1·5750
25	0·0056	58	0·0131	92	0·0207	75	1·6875
26	0·0059	59	0·0133	92½	0·0208	80	1·8000
27	0·0061	60	0·0135	93	0·0209	85	1·9125
27½	0·0062	61	0·0137	94	0·0212	90	2·0250
28	0·0063	62	0·0140	95	0·0214	95	2·1375
29	0·0065	62½	0·0141	96	0·0216	100	2·2500
30	0·0068	63	0·0142	97	0·0218	110	2·4750
31	0·0070	64	0·0144	97½	0·0219	120	2·7000
32	0·0072	65	0·0146	98	0·0221	130	2·9250
32½	0·0073	66	0·0149	99	0·0223	140	3·1500

£	£	£	£	£	£	£	£
150	3·3750	300	6·7500	450	10·1250	700	15·7500
200	4·5000	350	7·8750	500	11·2500	800	18·0000
250	5·6250	400	9·0000	600	13·5000	1000	22·5000

p	£	p	£	p	£	£	£
$\frac{1}{2}$ ..	0·0001	33 ..	0·0083	67 ..	0·0168	1 ..	0·0250
1 ..	0·0003	34 ..	0·0085	$67\frac{1}{2}$ ..	0·0169	2 ..	0·0500
2 ..	0·0005	35 ..	0·0088	68 ..	0·0170	3 ..	0·0750
$2\frac{1}{2}$ ..	0·0006	36 ..	0·0090	69 ..	0·0173	4 ..	0·1000
3 ..	0·0008	37 ..	0·0093	70 ..	0·0175	5 ..	0·1250
4 ..	0·0010	$37\frac{1}{2}$ ..	0·0094	71 ..	0·0178	6 ..	0·1500
5 ..	0·0013	38 ..	0·0095	72 ..	0·0180	7 ..	0·1750
6 ..	0·0015	39 ..	0·0098	$72\frac{1}{2}$ ..	0·0181	8 ..	0·2000
7 ..	0·0018	40 ..	0·0100	73 ..	0·0183	9 ..	0·2250
$7\frac{1}{2}$ ..	0·0019	41 ..	0·0103	74 ..	0·0185	10 ..	0·2500
8 ..	0·0020	42 ..	0·0105	75 ..	0·0188	11 ..	0·2750
9 ..	0·0023	$42\frac{1}{2}$ ..	0·0106	76 ..	0·0190	12 ..	0·3000
10 ..	0·0025	43 ..	0·0108	77 ..	0·0193	13 ..	0·3250
11 ..	0·0028	44 ..	0·0110	$77\frac{1}{2}$ ..	0·0194	14 ..	0·3500
12 ..	0·0030	45 ..	0·0113	78 ..	0·0195	15 ..	0·3750
$12\frac{1}{2}$ ..	0·0031	46 ..	0·0115	79 ..	0·0198	16 ..	0·4000
13 ..	0·0033	47 ..	0·0118	80 ..	0·0200	17 ..	0·4250
14 ..	0·0035	$47\frac{1}{2}$ ..	0·0119	81 ..	0·0203	18 ..	0·4500
15 ..	0·0038	48 ..	0·0120	82 ..	0·0205	19 ..	0·4750
16 ..	0·0040	49 ..	0·0123	$82\frac{1}{2}$ ..	0·0206	20 ..	0·5000
17 ..	0·0043	50 ..	0·0125	83 ..	0·0208	25 ..	0·6250
$17\frac{1}{2}$ ..	0·0044	51 ..	0·0128	84 ..	0·0210	30 ..	0·7500
18 ..	0·0045	52 ..	0·0130	85 ..	0·0213	35 ..	0·8750
19 ..	0·0048	$52\frac{1}{2}$ ..	0·0131	86 ..	0·0215	40 ..	1·0000
20 ..	0·0050	53 ..	0·0133	87 ..	0·0218	45 ..	1·1250
21 ..	0·0053	54 ..	0·0135	$87\frac{1}{2}$ ..	0·0219	50 ..	1·2500
22 ..	0·0055	55 ..	0·0138	88 ..	0·0220	55 ..	1·3750
$22\frac{1}{2}$ ..	0·0056	56 ..	0·0140	89 ..	0·0223	60 ..	1·5000
23 ..	0·0058	57 ..	0·0143	90 ..	0·0225	65 ..	1·6250
24 ..	0·0060	$57\frac{1}{2}$ ..	0·0144	91 ..	0·0228	70 ..	1·7500
25 ..	0·0063	58 ..	0·0145	92 ..	0·0230	75 ..	1·8750
26 ..	0·0065	59 ..	0·0148	$92\frac{1}{2}$ ..	0·0231	80 ..	2·0000
27 ..	0·0068	60 ..	0·0150	93 ..	0·0233	85 ..	2·1250
$27\frac{1}{2}$ ..	0·0069	61 ..	0·0153	94 ..	0·0235	90 ..	2·2500
28 ..	0·0070	62 ..	0·0155	95 ..	0·0238	95 ..	2·3750
29 ..	0·0073	$62\frac{1}{2}$ ..	0·0156	96 ..	0·0240	100 ..	2·5000
30 ..	0·0075	63 ..	0·0158	97 ..	0·0243	110 ..	2·7500
31 ..	0·0078	64 ..	0·0160	$97\frac{1}{2}$ ..	0·0244	120 ..	3·0000
32 ..	0·0080	65 ..	0·0163	98 ..	0·0245	130 ..	3·2500
$32\frac{1}{2}$ ..	0·0081	66 ..	0·0165	99 ..	0·0248	140 ..	3·5000

£	£	£	£	£	£	£	£
150 ..	3·7500	300 ..	7·5000	450 ..	11·2500	700 ..	17·5000
200 ..	5·0000	350 ..	8·7500	500 ..	12·5000	800 ..	20·0000
250 ..	6·2500	400 ..	10·0000	600 ..	15·0000	1000 ..	25·0000

p	£	p	£	p	£	£	£
$\frac{1}{2}$	0·0001	33	0·0091	67	0·0184	1	0·0275
1	0·0003	34	0·0094	$67\frac{1}{2}$	0·0186	2	0·0550
2	0·0006	35	0·0096	68	0·0187	3	0·0825
$2\frac{1}{2}$	0·0007	36	0·0099	69	0·0190	4	0·1100
3	0·0008	37	0·0102	70	0·0193	5	0·1375
4	0·0011	$37\frac{1}{2}$	0·0103	71	0·0195	6	0·1650
5	0·0014	38	0·0105	72	0·0198	7	0·1925
6	0·0017	39	0·0107	$72\frac{1}{2}$	0·0199	8	0·2200
7	0·0019	40	0·0110	73	0·0201	9	0·2475
$7\frac{1}{2}$	0·0021	41	0·0113	74	0·0204	10	0·2750
8	0·0022	42	0·0116	75	0·0206	11	0·3025
9	0·0025	$42\frac{1}{2}$	0·0117	76	0·0209	12	0·3300
10	0·0028	43	0·0118	77	0·0212	13	0·3575
11	0·0030	44	0·0121	$77\frac{1}{2}$	0·0213	14	0·3850
12	0·0033	45	0·0124	78	0·0215	15	0·4125
$12\frac{1}{2}$	0·0034	46	0·0127	79	0·0217	16	0·4400
13	0·0036	47	0·0129	80	0·0220	17	0·4675
14	0·0039	$47\frac{1}{2}$	0·0131	81	0·0223	18	0·4950
15	0·0041	48	0·0132	82	0·0226	19	0·5225
16	0·0044	49	0·0135	$82\frac{1}{2}$	0·0227	20	0·5500
17	0·0047	50	0·0138	83	0·0228	25	0·6875
$17\frac{1}{2}$	0·0048	51	0·0140	84	0·0231	30	0·8250
18	0·0050	52	0·0143	85	0·0234	35	0·9625
19	0·0052	$52\frac{1}{2}$	0·0144	86	0·0237	40	1·1000
20	0·0055	53	0·0146	87	0·0239	45	1·2375
21	0·0058	54	0·0149	$87\frac{1}{2}$	0·0241	50	1·3750
22	0·0061	55	0·0151	88	0·0242	55	1·5125
$22\frac{1}{2}$	0·0062	56	0·0154	89	0·0245	60	1·6500
23	0·0063	57	0·0157	90	0·0248	65	1·7875
24	0·0066	$57\frac{1}{2}$	0·0158	91	0·0250	70	1·9250
25	0·0069	58	0·0160	92	0·0253	75	2·0625
26	0·0072	59	0·0162	$92\frac{1}{2}$	0·0254	80	2·2000
27	0·0074	60	0·0165	93	0·0256	85	2·3375
$27\frac{1}{2}$	0·0076	61	0·0168	94	0·0259	90	2·4750
28	0·0077	62	0·0171	95	0·0261	95	2·6125
29	0·0080	$62\frac{1}{2}$	0·0172	96	0·0264	100	2·7500
30	0·0083	63	0·0173	97	0·0267	110	3·0250
31	0·0085	64	0·0176	$97\frac{1}{2}$	0·0268	120	3·3000
32	0·0088	65	0·0179	98	0·0270	130	3·5750
$32\frac{1}{2}$	0·0089	66	0·0182	99	0·0272	140	3·8500

£	£	£	£	£	£	£	£
150	4·1250	300	8·2500	450	12·3750	700	19·2500
200	5·5000	350	9·6250	500	13·7500	800	22·0000
250	6·8750	400	11·0000	600	16·5000	1000	27·5000

p	£	p	£	p	£	£	£
½	0·0002	33	0·0099	67	0·0201	1	0·0300
1	0·0003	34	0·0102	67½	0·0203	2	0·0600
2	0·0006	35	0·0105	68	0·0204	3	0·0900
2½	0·0008	36	0·0108	69	0·0207	4	0·1200
3	0·0009	37	0·0111	70	0·0210	5	0·1500
4	0·0012	37½	0·0113	71	0·0213	6	0·1800
5	0·0015	38	0·0114	72	0·0216	7	0·2100
6	0·0018	39	0·0117	72½	0·0218	8	0·2400
7	0·0021	40	0·0120	73	0·0219	9	0·2700
7½	0·0023	41	0·0123	74	0·0222	10	0·3000
8	0·0024	42	0·0126	75	0·0225	11	0·3300
9	0·0027	42½	0·0128	76	0·0228	12	0·3600
10	0·0030	43	0·0129	77	0·0231	13	0·3900
11	0·0033	44	0·0132	77½	0·0233	14	0·4200
12	0·0036	45	0·0135	78	0·0234	15	0·4500
12½	0·0038	46	0·0138	79	0·0237	16	0·4800
13	0·0039	47	0·0141	80	0·0240	17	0·5100
14	0·0042	47½	0·0143	81	0·0243	18	0·5400
15	0·0045	48	0·0144	82	0·0246	19	0·5700
16	0·0048	49	0·0147	82½	0·0248	20	0·6000
17	0·0051	50	0·0150	83	0·0249	25	0·7500
17½	0·0053	51	0·0153	84	0·0252	30	0·9000
18	0·0054	52	0·0156	85	0·0255	35	1·0500
19	0·0057	52½	0·0158	86	0·0258	40	1·2000
20	0·0060	53	0·0159	87	0·0261	45	1·3500
21	0·0063	54	0·0162	87½	0·0263	50	1·5000
22	0·0066	55	0·0165	88	0·0264	55	1·6500
22½	0·0068	56	0·0168	89	0·0267	60	1·8000
23	0·0069	57	0·0171	90	0·0270	65	1·9500
24	0·0072	57½	0·0173	91	0·0273	70	2·1000
25	0·0075	58	0·0174	92	0·0276	75	2·2500
26	0·0078	59	0·0177	92½	0·0278	80	2·4000
27	0·0081	60	0·0180	93	0·0279	85	2·5500
27½	0·0083	61	0·0183	94	0·0282	90	2·7000
28	0·0084	62	0·0186	95	0·0285	95	2·8500
29	0·0087	62½	0·0188	96	0·0288	100	3·0000
30	0·0090	63	0·0189	97	0·0291	110	3·3000
31	0·0093	64	0·0192	97½	0·0293	120	3·6000
32	0·0096	65	0·0195	98	0·0294	130	3·9000
32½	0·0098	66	0·0198	99	0·0297	140	4·2000

£	£	£	£	£	£	£	£
150	4·5000	300	9·0000	450	13·5000	700	21·0000
200	6·0000	350	10·5000	500	15·0000	800	24·0000
250	7·5000	400	12·0000	600	18·0000	1000	30·0000

p	£	p	£	p	£	£	£
$\frac{1}{2}$ ..	0·0002	33 ..	0·0107	67 ..	0·0218	1 ..	0·0325
1 ..	0·0003	34 ..	0·0111	$67\frac{1}{2}$ ..	0·0219	2 ..	0·0650
2 ..	0·0007	35 ..	0·0114	68 ..	0·0221	3 ..	0·0975
$2\frac{1}{2}$ ..	0·0008	36 ..	0·0117	69 ..	0·0224	4 ..	0·1300
3 ..	0·0010	37 ..	0·0120	70 ..	0·0228	5 ..	0·1625
4 ..	0·0013	$37\frac{1}{2}$ ..	0·0122	71 ..	0·0231	6 ..	0·1950
5 ..	0·0016	38 ..	0·0124	72 ..	0·0234	7 ..	0·2275
6 ..	0·0020	39 ..	0·0127	$72\frac{1}{2}$ ..	0·0236	8 ..	0·2600
7 ..	0·0023	40 ..	0·0130	73 ..	0·0237	9 ..	0·2925
$7\frac{1}{2}$ ..	0·0024	41 ..	0·0133	74 ..	0·0241	10 ..	0·3250
8 ..	0·0026	42 ..	0·0137	75 ..	0·0244	11 ..	0·3575
9 ..	0·0029	$42\frac{1}{2}$ ..	0·0138	76 ..	0·0247	12 ..	0·3900
10 ..	0·0033	43 ..	0·0140	77 ..	0·0250	13 ..	0·4225
11 ..	0·0036	44 ..	0·0143	$77\frac{1}{2}$ ..	0·0252	14 ..	0·4550
12 ..	0·0039	45 ...	0·0146	78 ..	0·0254	15 ..	0·4875
$12\frac{1}{2}$ ..	0·0041	46 ..	0·0150	79 ..	0·0257	16 ..	0·5200
13 ..	0·0042	47 ..	0·0153	80 ..	0·0260	17 ..	0·5525
14 ..	0·0046	$47\frac{1}{2}$ ..	0·0154	81 ..	0·0263	18 ..	0·5850
15 ..	0·0049	48 ..	0·0156	82 ..	0·0267	19 ..	0·6175
16 ..	0·0052	49 ..	0·0159	$82\frac{1}{2}$ ..	0·0268	20 ..	0·6500
17 ..	0·0055	50 ..	0·0163	83 ..	0·0270	25 ..	0·8125
$17\frac{1}{2}$ ..	0·0057	51 ..	0·0166	84 ..	0·0273	30 ..	0·9750
18 ..	0·0059	52 ..	0·0169	85 ..	0·0276	35 ..	1·1375
19 ..	0·0062	$52\frac{1}{2}$ ..	0·0171	86 ..	0·0280	40 ..	1·3000
20 ..	0·0065	53 ..	0·0172	87 ..	0·0283	45 ..	1·4625
21 ..	0·0068	54 ..	0·0176	$87\frac{1}{2}$ ..	0·0284	50 ..	1·6250
22 ..	0·0072	55 ..	0·0179	88 ..	0·0286	55 ..	1·7875
$22\frac{1}{2}$ ..	0·0073	56 ..	0·0182	89 ..	0·0289	60 ..	1·9500
23 ..	0·0075	57 ..	0·0185	90 ..	0·0293	65 ..	2·1125
24 ..	0·0078	$57\frac{1}{2}$ ..	0·0187	91 ..	0·0296	70 ..	2·2750
25 ..	0·0081	58 ..	0·0189	92 ..	0·0299	75 ..	2·4375
26 ..	0·0085	59 ..	0·0192	$92\frac{1}{2}$ ..	0·0301	80 ..	2·6000
27 ..	0·0088	60 ..	0·0195	93 ..	0·0302	85 ..	2·7625
$27\frac{1}{4}$ ..	0·0089	61 ..	0·0198	94 ..	0·0306	90 ..	2·9250
28 ..	0·0091	62 ..	0·0202	95 ..	0·0309	95 ..	3·0875
29 ..	0·0094	$62\frac{1}{2}$ ..	0·0203	96 ..	0·0312	100 ..	3·2500
30 ..	0·0098	63 ..	0·0205	97 ..	0·0315	110 ..	3·5750
31 ..	0·0101	64 ..	0·0208	$97\frac{1}{2}$ ..	0·0317	120 ..	3·9000
32 ..	0·0104	65 ..	0·0211	98 ..	0·0319	130 ..	4·2250
$32\frac{1}{2}$ ..	0·0106	66 ..	0·0215	99 ..	0·0322	140 ..	4·5500

£	£	£	£	£	£	£	£
150 ..	4·8750	300 ..	9·7500	450 ..	14·6250	700 ..	22·7500
200 ..	6·5000	350 ..	11·3750	500 ..	16·2500	800 ..	26·0000
250 ..	8·1250	400 ..	13·0000	600 ..	19·5000	1000 ..	32·5000

p	£	p	£	p	£	£	£
½ ..	0·0002	33 ..	0·0110	67 ..	0·0223	1 ..	0·0333
1 ..	0·0003	34 ..	0·0113	67½ ..	0·0225	2 ..	0·0667
2 ..	0·0007	35 ..	0·0117	68 ..	0·0227	3 ..	0·1000
2½ ..	0·0008	36 ..	0·0120	69 ..	0·0230	4 ..	0·1333
3 ..	0·0010	37 ..	0·0123	70 ..	0·0233	5 ..	0·1667
4 ..	0·0013	37½ ..	0·0125	71 ..	0·0237	6 ..	0·2000
5 ..	0·0017	38 ..	0·0127	72 ..	0·0240	7 ..	0·2333
6 ..	0·0020	39 ..	0·0130	72½ ..	0·0242	8 ..	0·2667
7 ..	0·0023	40 ..	0·0133	73 ..	0·0243	9 ..	0·3000
7½ ..	0·0025	41 ..	0·0137	74 ..	0·0247	10 ..	0·3333
8 ..	0·0027	42 ..	0·0140	75 ..	0·0250	11 ..	0·3667
9 ..	0·0030	42½ ..	0·0142	76 ..	0·0253	12 ..	0·4000
10 ..	0·0033	43 ..	0·0143	77 ..	0·0257	13 ..	0·4333
11 ..	0·0037	44 ..	0·0147	77½ ..	0·0258	14 ..	0·4667
12 ..	0·0040	45 ..	0·0150	78 ..	0·0260	15 ..	0·5000
12½ ..	0·0042	46 ..	0·0153	79 ..	0·0263	16 ..	0·5333
13 ..	0·0043	47 ..	0·0157	80 ..	0·0267	17 ..	0·5667
14 ..	0·0047	47½ ..	0·0158	81 ..	0·0270	18 ..	0·6000
15 ..	0·0050	48 ..	0·0160	82 ..	0·0273	19 ..	0·6333
16 ..	0·0053	49 ..	0·0163	82½ ..	0·0275	20 ..	0·6667
17 ..	0·0057	50 ..	0·0167	83 ..	0·0277	25 ..	0·8333
17½ ..	0·0058	51 ..	0·0170	84 ..	0·0280	30 ..	1·0000
18 ..	0·0060	52 ..	0·0173	85 ..	0·0283	35 ..	1·1667
19 ..	0·0063	52½ ..	0·0175	86 ..	0·0287	40 ..	1·3333
20 ..	0·0067	53 ..	0·0177	87 ..	0·0290	45 ..	1·5000
21 ..	0·0070	54 ..	0·0180	87½ ..	0·0292	50 ..	1·6667
22 ..	0·0073	55 ..	0·0183	88 ..	0·0293	55 ..	1·8333
22½ ..	0·0075	56 ..	0·0187	89 ..	0·0297	60 ..	2·0000
23 ..	0·0077	57 ..	0·0190	90 ..	0·0300	65 ..	2·1667
24 ..	0·0080	57½ ..	0·0192	91 ..	0·0303	70 ..	2·3333
25 ..	0·0083	58 ..	0·0193	92 ..	0·0307	75 ..	2·5000
26 ..	0·0087	59 ..	0·0197	92½ ..	0·0308	80 ..	2·6667
27 ..	0·0090	60 ..	0·0200	93 ..	0·0310	85 ..	2·8333
27½ ..	0·0092	61 ..	0·0203	94 ..	0·0313	90 ..	3·0000
28 ..	0·0093	62 ..	0·0207	95 ..	0·0317	95 ..	3·1667
29 ..	0·0097	62½ ..	0·0268	96 ..	0·0320	100 ..	3·3333
30 ..	0·0100	63 ..	0·0210	97 ..	0·0323	110 ..	3·6667
31 ..	0·0103	64 ..	0·0213	97½ ..	0·0325	120 ..	4·0000
32 ..	0·0107	65 ..	0·0217	98 ..	0·0327	130 ..	4·3333
32½ ..	0·0108	66 ..	0·0220	99 ..	0·0330	140 ..	4·6667

£	£	£	£	£	£	£	£
150 ..	5·0000	300 ..	10·0000	450 ..	15·0000	700 ..	23·3333
200 ..	6·6667	350 ..	11·6667	500 ..	16·6667	800 ..	26·6667
250 ..	8·3333	400 ..	13·3333	600 ..	20·0000	1000 ..	33·3333

p	£	p	£	p	£	£	£
$\frac{1}{2}$ ..	0·0002	33 ..	0·0116	67 ..	0·0235	1 ..	0·0350
1 ..	0·0004	34 ..	0·0119	$67\frac{1}{2}$ ..	0·0236	2 ..	0·0700
2 ..	0·0007	35 ..	0·0123	68 ..	0·0238	3 ..	0·1050
$2\frac{1}{2}$ ..	0·0009	36 ..	0·0126	69 ..	0·0242	4 ..	0·1400
3 ..	0·0011	37 ..	0·0130	70 ..	0·0245	5 ..	0·1750
4 ..	0·0014	$37\frac{1}{2}$ ..	0·0131	71 ..	0·0249	6 ..	0·2100
5 ..	0·0018	38 ..	0·0133	72 ..	0·0252	7 ..	0·2450
6 ..	0·0021	39 ..	0·0137	$72\frac{1}{2}$ ..	0·0254	8 ..	0·2800
7 ..	0·0025	40 ..	0·0140	73 ..	0·0256	9 ..	0·3150
$7\frac{1}{2}$ ..	0·0026	41 ..	0·0144	74 ..	0·0259	10 ..	0·3500
8 ..	0·0028	42 ..	0·0147	75 ..	0·0263	11 ..	0·3850
9 ..	0·0032	$42\frac{1}{2}$ ..	0·0149	76 ..	0·0266	12 ..	0·4200
10 ..	0·0035	43 ..	0·0151	77 ..	0·0270	13 ..	0·4550
11 ..	0·0039	44 ..	0·0154	$77\frac{1}{2}$ ..	0·0271	14 ..	0·4900
12 ..	0·0042	45 ..	0·0158	78 ..	0·0273	15 ..	0·5250
$12\frac{1}{2}$ ..	0·0044	46 ..	0·0161	79 ..	0·0277	16 ..	0·5600
13 ..	0·0046	47 ..	0·0165	80 ..	0·0280	17 ..	0·5950
14 ..	0·0049	$47\frac{1}{2}$ ..	0·0166	81 ..	0·0284	18 ..	0·6300
15 ..	0·0053	48 ..	0·0168	82 ..	0·0287	19 ..	0·6650
16 ..	0·0056	49 ..	0·0172	$82\frac{1}{2}$ ..	0·0289	20 ..	0·7000
17 ..	0·0060	50 ..	0·0175	83 ..	0·0291	25 ..	0·8750
$17\frac{1}{2}$ ..	0·0061	51 ..	0·0179	84 ..	0·0294	30 ..	1·0500
18 ..	0·0063	52 ..	0·0182	85 ..	0·0298	35 ..	1·2250
19 ..	0·0067	$52\frac{1}{2}$ ..	0·0184	86 ..	0·0301	40 ..	1·4000
20 ..	0·0070	53 ..	0·0186	87 ..	0·0305	45 ..	1·5750
21 ..	0·0074	54 ..	0·0189	$87\frac{1}{2}$ ..	0·0306	50 ..	1·7500
22 ..	0·0077	55 ..	0·0193	88 ..	0·0308	55 ..	1·9250
$22\frac{1}{2}$ ..	0·0079	56 ..	0·0196	89 ..	0·0312	60 ..	2·1000
23 ..	0·0081	57 ..	0·0200	90 ..	0·0315	65 ..	2·2750
24 ..	0·0084	$57\frac{1}{2}$ ..	0·0201	91 ..	0·0319	70 ..	2·4500
25 ..	0·0088	58 ..	0·0203	92 ..	0·0322	75 ..	2·6250
26 ..	0·0091	59 ..	0·0207	$92\frac{1}{2}$ ..	0·0324	80 ..	2·8000
27 ..	0·0095	60 ..	0·0210	93 ..	0·0326	85 ..	2·9750
$27\frac{1}{2}$ ..	0·0096	61 ..	0·0214	94 ..	0·0329	90 ..	3·1500
28 ..	0·0098	62 ..	0·0217	95 ..	0·0333	95 ..	3·3250
29 ..	0·0102	$62\frac{1}{2}$ ..	0·0219	96 ..	0·0336	100 ..	3·5000
30 ..	0·0105	63 ..	0·0221	97 ..	0·0340	110 ..	3·8500
31 ..	0·0109	64 ..	0·0224	$97\frac{1}{2}$ ..	0·0341	120 ..	4·2000
32 ..	0·0112	65 ..	0·0228	98 ..	0·0343	130 ..	4·5500
$32\frac{1}{2}$ ..	0·0114	66 ..	0·0231	99 ..	0·0347	140 ..	4·9000

£	£	£	£	£	£	£	£
150 ..	5·2500	300 ..	10·5000	450 ..	15·7500	700 ..	24·5000
200 ..	7·0000	350 ..	12·2500	500 ..	17·5000	800 ..	28·0000
250 ..	8·7500	400 ..	14·0000	600 ..	21·0000	1000 ..	35·0000

p	£	p	£	p	£	£	£
$\frac{1}{2}$ ..	0·0002	33 ..	0·0124	67 ..	0·0251	1 ..	0·0375
1 ..	0·0004	34 ..	0·0128	$67\frac{1}{2}$ ..	0·0253	2 ..	0·0750
2 ..	0·0008	35 ..	0·0131	68 ..	0·0255	3 ..	0·1125
$2\frac{1}{2}$ ..	0·0009	36 ..	0·0135	69 ..	0·0259	4 ..	0·1500
3 ..	0·0011	37 ..	0·0139	70 ..	0·0263	5 ..	0·1875
4 ..	0·0015	$37\frac{1}{2}$ ..	0·0141	71 ..	0·0266	6 ..	0·2250
5 ..	0·0019	38 ..	0·0143	72 ..	0·0270	7 ..	0·2625
6 ..	0·0023	39 ..	0·0146	$72\frac{1}{2}$ ..	0·0272	8 ..	0·3000
7 ..	0·0026	40 ..	0·0150	73 ..	0·0274	9 ..	0·3375
$7\frac{1}{2}$ ..	0·0028	41 ..	0·0154	74 ..	0·0278	10 ..	0·3750
8 ..	0·0030	42 ..	0·0158	75 ..	0·0281	11 ..	0·4125
9 ..	0·0034	$42\frac{1}{2}$ ..	0·0159	76 ..	0·0285	12 ..	0·4500
10 ..	0·0038	43 ..	0·0161	77 ..	0·0289	13 ..	0·4875
11 ..	0·0041	44 ..	0·0165	$77\frac{1}{2}$ ..	0·0291	14 ..	0·5250
12 ..	0·0045	45 ..	0·0169	78 ..	0·0293	15 ..	0·5625
$12\frac{1}{2}$ ..	0·0047	46 ..	0·0173	79 ..	0·0296	16 ..	0·6000
13 ..	0·0049	47 ..	0·0176	80 ..,	0·0300	17 ..	0·6375
14 ..	0·0053	$47\frac{1}{2}$ ..	0·0178	81 ..	0·0304	18 ..	0·6750
15 ..	0·0056	48 ..,	0·0180	82 ..,	0·0308	19 ..	0·7125
16 ..	0·0060	49 ..	0·0184	$82\frac{1}{2}$ ..	0·0309	20 ..	0·7500
17 ..	0·0064	50 ..	0·0188	83 ..	0·0311	25 ..	0·9375
$17\frac{1}{2}$ ..	0·0066	51 ..	0·0191	84 ..	0·0315	30 ..	1·1250
18 ..	0·0068	52 ..	0·0195	85 ..	0·0319	35 ..	1·3125
19 ..	0·0071	$52\frac{1}{2}$ ..	0·0197	86 ..	0·0323	40 ..	1·5000
20 ..	0·0075	53 ..	0·0199	87 ..	0·0326	45 ..	1·6875
21 ..	0·0079	54 ..	0·0203	$87\frac{1}{2}$ ..	0·0328	50 ..	1·8750
22 ..	0·0083	55 ..	0·0206	88 ..	0·0330	55 ..	2·0625
$22\frac{1}{2}$ ..	0·0084	56 ..	0·0210	89 ..	0·0334	60 ..	2·2500
23 ..	0·0086	57 ..	0·0214	90 ..	0·0338	65 ..	2·4375
24 ..	0·0090	$57\frac{1}{2}$ ..	0·0216	91 ..	0·0341	70 ..	2·6250
25 ..	0·0094	58 ..	0·0218	92 ..	0·0345	75 ..	2·8125
26 ..	0·0098	59 ..	0·0221	$92\frac{1}{2}$ ..	0·0347	80 ..	3·0000
27 ..	0·0101	60 ..	0·0225	93 ..	0·0349	85 ..	3·1875
$27\frac{1}{2}$ ..	0·0103	61 ..	0·0229	94 ..	0·0353	90 ..	3·3750
28 ..	0·0105	62 ..	0·0233	95 ..	0·0356	95 ..	3·5625
29 ..	0·0109	$62\frac{1}{2}$ ..	0·0234	96 ..	0·0360	100 ..	3·7500
30 ..	0·0113	63 ..	0·0236	97 ..	0·0364	110 ..	4·1250
31 ..	0·0116	64 ..	0·0240	$97\frac{1}{2}$ ..	0·0366	120 ..	4·5000
32 ..	0·0120	65 ..	0·0244	98 ..	0·0368	130 ..	4·8750
$32\frac{1}{2}$ ..	0·0122	66 ..	0·0248	99 ..	0·0371	140 ..	5·2500

£	£	£	£	£	£	£	£
150 ..	5·6250	300 ..	11·2500	450 ..	16·8750	700 ..	26·2500
200 ..	7·5000	350 ..	13·1250	500 ..	18·7500	800 ..	30·0000
250 ..	9·3750	400 ..	15·0000	600 ..	22·5000	1000 ..	37·5000

p	£	p	£	p	£	£	£
½	0·0002	33	0·0132	67	0·0268	1	0·0400
1	0·0004	34	0·0136	67½	0·0270	2	0·0800
2	0·0008	35	0·0140	68	0·0272	3	0·1200
2½	0·0010	36	0·0144	69	0·0276	4	0·1600
3	0·0012	37	0·0148	70	0·0280	5	0·2000
4	0·0016	37½	0·0150	71	0·0284	6	0·2400
5	0·0020	38	0·0152	72	0·0288	7	0·2800
6	0·0024	39	0·0156	72½	0·0290	8	0·3200
7	0·0028	40	0·0160	73	0·0292	9	0·3600
7½	0·0030	41	0·0164	74	0·0296	10	0·4000
8	0·0032	42	0·0168	75	0·0300	11	0·4400
9	0·0036	42½	0·0170	76	0·0304	12	0·4800
10	0·0040	43	0·0172	77	0·0308	13	0·5200
11	0·0044	44	0·0176	77½	0·0310	14	0·5600
12	0·0048	45	0·0180	78	0·0312	15	0·6000
12½	0·0050	46	0·0184	79	0·0316	16	0·6400
13	0·0052	47	0·0188	80	0·0320	17	0·6800
14	0·0056	47½	0·0190	81	0·0324	18	0·7200
15	0·0060	48	0·0192	82	0·0328	19	0·7600
16	0·0064	49	0·0196	82½	0·0330	20	0·8000
17	0·0068	50	0·0200	83	0·0332	25	1·0000
17½	0·0070	51	0·0204	84	0·0336	30	1·2000
18	0·0072	52	0·0208	85	0·0340	35	1·4000
19	0·0076	52½	0·0210	86	0·0344	40	1·6000
20	0·0080	53	0·0212	87	0·0348	45	1·8000
21	0·0084	54	0·0216	87½	0·0350	50	2·0000
22	0·0088	55	0·0220	88	0·0352	55	2·2000
22½	0·0090	56	0·0224	89	0·0356	60	2·4000
23	0·0092	57	0·0228	90	0·0360	65	2·6000
24	0·0096	57½	0·0230	91	0·0364	70	2·8000
25	0·0100	58	0·0232	92	0·0368	75	3·0000
26	0·0104	59	0·0236	92½	0·0370	80	3·2000
27	0·0108	60	0·0240	93	0·0372	85	3·4000
27½	0·0110	61	0·0244	94	0·0376	90	3·6000
28	0·0112	62	0·0248	95	0·0380	95	3·8000
29	0·0116	62½	0·0250	96	0·0384	100	4·0000
30	0·0120	63	0·0252	97	0·0388	110	4·4000
31	0·0124	64	0·0256	97½	0·0390	120	4·8000
32	0·0128	65	0·0260	98	0·0392	130	5·2000
32½	0·0130	66	0·0264	99	0·0396	140	5·6000

£	£	£	£	£	£	£	£
150	6·0000	300	12·0000	450	18·0000	700	28·0000
200	8·0000	350	14·0000	500	20·0000	800	32·0000
250	10·0000	400	16·0000	600	24·0000	1000	40·0000

p	£	p	£	p	£	£	£
$\frac{1}{2}$	0·0002	33	0·0140	67	0·0285	1	0·0425
1	0·0004	34	0·0145	$67\frac{1}{2}$	0·0287	2	0·0850
2	0·0009	35	0·0149	68	0·0289	3	0·1275
$2\frac{1}{2}$	0·0011	36	0·0153	69	0·0293	4	0·1700
3	0·0013	37	0·0157	70	0·0298	5	0·2125
4	0·0017	$37\frac{1}{2}$	0·0159	71	0·0302	6	0·2550
5	0·0021	38	0·0162	72	0·0306	7	0·2975
6	0·0026	39	0·0166	$72\frac{1}{2}$	0·0308	8	0·3400
7	0·0030	40	0·0170	73	0·0310	9	0·3825
$7\frac{1}{2}$	0·0032	41	0·0174	74	0·0315	10	0·4250
8	0·0034	42	0·0179	75	0·0319	11	0·4675
9	0·0038	$42\frac{1}{2}$	0·0181	76	0·0323	12	0·5100
10	0·0043	43	0·0183	77	0·0327	13	0·5525
11	0·0047	44	0·0187	$77\frac{1}{2}$	0·0329	14	0·5950
12	0·0051	45	0·0191	78	0·0332	15	0·6375
$12\frac{1}{2}$	0·0053	46	0·0196	79	0·0336	16	0·6800
13	0·0055	47	0·0200	80	0·0340	17	0·7225
14	0·0060	$47\frac{1}{2}$	0·0202	81	0·0344	18	0·7650
15	0·0064	48	0·0204	82	0·0349	19	0·8075
16	0·0068	49	0·0208	$82\frac{1}{2}$	0·0351	20	0·8500
17	0·0072	50	0·0213	83	0·0353	25	1·0625
$17\frac{1}{2}$	0·0074	51	0·0217	84	0·0357	30	1·2750
18	0·0077	52	0·0221	85	0·0361	35	1·4875
19	0·0081	$52\frac{1}{2}$	0·0223	86	0·0366	40	1·7000
20	0·0085	53	0·0225	87	0·0370	45	1·9125
21	0·0089	54	0·0230	$87\frac{1}{2}$	0·0372	50	2·1250
22	0·0094	55	0·0234	88	0·0374	55	2·3375
$22\frac{1}{2}$	0·0096	56	0·0238	89	0·0378	60	2·5500
23	0·0098	57	0·0242	90	0·0383	65	2·7625
24	0·0102	$57\frac{1}{2}$	0·0244	91	0·0387	70	2·9750
25	0·0106	58	0·0247	92	0·0391	75	3·1875
26	0·0111	59	0·0251	$92\frac{1}{2}$	0·0393	80	3·4000
27	0·0115	60	0·0255	93	0·0395	85	3·6125
$27\frac{1}{2}$	0·0117	61	0·0259	94	0·0400	90	3·8250
28	0·0119	62	0·0264	95	0·0404	95	4·0375
29	0·0123	$62\frac{1}{2}$	0·0266	96	0·0408	100	4·2500
30	0·0128	63	0·0268	97	0·0412	110	4·6750
31	0·0132	64	0·0272	$97\frac{1}{2}$	0·0414	120	5·1000
32	0·0136	65	0·0276	98	0·0417	130	5·5250
$32\frac{1}{2}$	0·0138	66	0·0281	99	0·0421	140	5·9500

£	£	£	£	£	£	£	£
150	6·3750	300	12·7500	450	19·1250	700	29·7500
200	8·5000	350	14·8750	500	21·2500	800	34·0000
250	10·6250	400	17·0000	600	25·5000	1000	42·5000

p	£	p	£	p	£	£	£
$\frac{1}{2}$ ..	0·0002	33 ..	0·0149	67 ..	0·0302	1 ..	0·0450
1 ..	0·0005	34 ..	0·0153	$67\frac{1}{2}$ ..	0·0304	2 ..	0·0900
2 ..	0·0009	35 ..	0·0158	68 ..	0·0306	3 ..	0·1350
$2\frac{1}{2}$ ..	0·0011	36 ..	0·0162	69 ..	0·0311	4 ..	0·1800
3 ..	0·0014	37 ..	0·0167	70 ..	0·0315	5 ..	0·2250
4 ..	0·0018	$37\frac{1}{2}$ ..	0·0169	71 ..	0·0320	6 ..	0·2700
5 ..	0·0023	38 ..	0·0171	72 ..	0·0324	7 ..	0·3150
6 ..	0·0027	39 ..	0·0176	$72\frac{1}{2}$ ..	0·0326	8 ..	0·3600
7 ..	0·0032	40 ..	0·0180	73 ..	0·0329	9 ..	0·4050
$7\frac{1}{2}$ ..	0·0034	41 ..	0·0185	74 ..	0·0333	10 ..	0·4500
8 ..	0·0036	42 ..	0·0189	75 ..	0·0338	11 ..	0·4950
9 ..	0·0041	$42\frac{1}{2}$ ..	0·0191	76 ..	0·0342	12 ..	0·5400
10 ..	0·0045	43 ..	0·0194	77 ..	0·0347	13 ..	0·5850
11 ..	0·0050	44 ..	0·0198	$77\frac{1}{2}$ ..	0·0349	14 ..	0·6300
12 ..	0·0054	45 ..	0·0203	78 ..	0·0351	15 ..	0·6750
$12\frac{1}{2}$ ..	0·0056	46 ..	0·0207	79 ..	0·0356	16 ..	0·7200
13 ..	0·0059	47 ..	0·0212	80 ..	0·0360	17 ..	0·7650
14 ..	0·0063	$47\frac{1}{2}$ ..	0·0214	81 ..	0·0365	18 ..	0·8100
15 ..	0·0068	48 ..	0·0216	82 ..	0·0369	19 ..	0·8550
16 ..	0·0072	49 ..	0·0221	$82\frac{1}{2}$ ..	0·0371	20 ..	0·9000
17 ..	0·0077	50 ..	0·0225	83 ..	0·0374	25 ..	1·1250
$17\frac{1}{2}$ ..	0·0079	51 ..	0·0230	84 ..	0·0378	30 ..	1·3500
18 ..	0·0081	52 ..	0·0234	85 ..	0·0383	35 ..	1·5750
19 ..	0·0086	$52\frac{1}{2}$ ..	0·0236	86 ..	0·0387	40 ..	1·8000
20 ..	0·0090	53 ..	0·0239	87 ..	0·0392	45 ..	2·0250
21 ..	0·0095	54 ..	0·0243	$87\frac{1}{2}$ ..	0·0394	50 ..	2·2500
22 ..	0·0099	55 ..	0·0248	88 ..	0·0396	55 ..	2·4750
$22\frac{1}{2}$ ..	0·0101	56 ..	0·0252	89 ..	0·0401	60 ..	2·7000
23 ..	0·0104	57 ..	0·0257	90 ..	0·0405	65 ..	2·9250
24 ..	0·0108	$57\frac{1}{2}$ ..	0·0259	91 ..	0·0410	70 ..	3·1500
25 ..	0·0113	58 ..	0·0261	92 ..	0·0414	75 ..	3·3750
26 ..	0·0117	59 ..	0·0266	$92\frac{1}{2}$ ..	0·0416	80 ..	3·6000
27 ..	0·0122	60 ..	0·0270	93 ..	0·0419	85 ..	3·8250
$27\frac{1}{2}$ ..	0·0124	61 ..	0·0275	94 ..	0·0423	90 ..	4·0500
28 ..	0·0126	62 ..	0·0279	95 ..	0·0428	95 ..	4·2750
29 ..	0·0131	$62\frac{1}{2}$ ..	0·0281	96 ..	0·0432	100 ..	4·5000
30 ..	0·0135	63 ..	0·0284	97 ..	0·0437	110 ..	4·9500
31 ..	0·0140	64 ..	0·0288	$97\frac{1}{2}$ ..	0·0439	120 ..	5·4000
32 ..	0·0144	65 ..	0·0293	98 ..	0·0441	130 ..	5·8500
$32\frac{1}{2}$ ..	0·0146	66 ..	0·0297	99 ..	0·0446	140 ..	6·3000

£	£	£	£	£	£	£	£
150 ..	6·7500	300 ..	13·5000	450 ..	20·2500	700 ..	31·5000
200 ..	9·0000	350 ..	15·7500	500 ..	22·5000	800 ..	36·0000
250 ..	11·2500	400 ..	18·0000	600 ..	27·0000	1000 ..	45·0000

p	£	p	£	p	£		£		£
$\frac{1}{2}$	0·0002	33	0·0157	67	0·0318	1		0·0475
1	0·0005	34	0·0162	$67\frac{1}{2}$	0·0321	2		0·0950
2	0·0010	35	0·0166	68	0·0323	3		0·1425
$2\frac{1}{2}$	0·0012	36	0·0171	69	0·0328	4		0·1900
3	0·0014	37	0·0176	70	0·0333	5		0·2375
4	0·0019	$37\frac{1}{2}$	0·0178	71	0·0337	6		0·2850
5	0·0024	38	0·0181	72	0·0342	7		0·3325
6	0·0029	39	0·0185	$72\frac{1}{2}$	0·0344	8		0·3800
7	0·0033	40	0·0190	73	0·0347	9		0·4275
$7\frac{1}{2}$	0·0036	41	0·0195	74	0·0352	10		0·4750
8	0·0038	42	0·0200	75	0·0356	11		0·5225
9	0·0043	$42\frac{1}{2}$	0·0202	76	0·0361	12		0·5700
10	0·0048	43	0·0204	77	0·0366	13		0·6175
11	0·0052	44	0·0209	$77\frac{1}{2}$	0·0368	14		0·6650
12	0·0057	45	0·0214	78	0·0371	15		0·7125
$12\frac{1}{2}$	0·0059	46	0·0219	79	0·0375	16		0·7600
13	0·0062	47	0·0223	80	0·0380	17		0·8075
14	0·0067	$47\frac{1}{2}$	0·0226	81	0·0385	18		0·8550
15	0·0071	48	0·0228	82	0·0390	19		0·9025
16	0·0076	49	0·0233	$82\frac{1}{2}$	0·0392	20		0·9500
17	0·0081	50	0·0238	83	0·0394	25		1·1875
$17\frac{1}{2}$	0·0083	51	0·0242	84	0·0399	30		1·4250
18	0·0086	52	0·0247	85	0·0404	35		1·6625
19	0·0090	$52\frac{1}{2}$	0·0249	86	0·0409	40		1·9000
20	0·0095	53	0·0252	87	0·0413	45		2·1375
21	0·0100	54	0·0257	$87\frac{1}{2}$	0·0416	50		2·3750
22	0·0105	55	0·0261	88	0·0418	55		2·6125
$22\frac{1}{2}$	0·0107	56	0·0266	89	0·0423	60		2·8500
23	0·0109	57	0·0271	90	0·0428	65		3·0875
24	0·0114	$57\frac{1}{2}$	0·0273	91	0·0432	70		3·3250
25	0·0119	58	0·0276	92	0·0437	75		3·5625
26	0·0124	59	0·0280	$92\frac{1}{2}$	0·0439	80		3·8000
27	0·0128	60	0·0285	93	0·0442	85		4·0375
$27\frac{1}{2}$	0·0131	61	0·0290	94	0·0447	90		4·2750
28	0·0133	62	0·0295	95	0·0451	95		4·5125
29	0·0138	$62\frac{1}{2}$	0·0297	96	0·0456	100		4·7500
30	0·0143	63	0·0299	97	0·0461	110		5·2250
31	0·0147	64	0·0304	$97\frac{1}{2}$	0·0463	120		5·7000
32	0·0152	65	0·0309	98	0·0466	130		6·1750
$32\frac{1}{2}$	0·0154	66	0·0314	99	0·0470	140		6·6500

£	£	£	£	£	£	£	£
150	7·1250	300	14·2500	450	21·3750	700	33·2500
200	9·5000	350	16·6250	500	23·7500	800	38·0000
250	11·8750	400	19·0000	600	28·5000	1000	47·5000

p	£	p	£	p	£	£	£
½ ..	0·0003	33 ..	0·0165	67 ..	0·0335	1 ..	0·0500
1 ..	0·0005	34 ..	0·0170	67½ ..	0·0338	2 ..	0·1000
2 ..	0·0010	35 ..	0·0175	68 ..	0·0340	3 ..	0·1500
2½ ..	0·0013	36 ..	0·0180	69 ..	0·0345	4 ..	0·2000
3 ..	0·0015	37 ..	0·0185	70 ..	0·0350	5 ..	0·2500
4 ..	0·0020	37½ ..	0·0188	71 ..	0·0355	6 ..	0·3000
5 ..	0·0025	38 ..	0·0190	72 ..	0·0360	7 ..	0·3500
6 ..	0·0030	39 ..	0·0195	72½ ..	0·0363	8 ..	0·4000
7 ..	0·0035	40 ..	0·0200	73 ..	0·0365	9 ..	0·4500
7½ ..	0·0038	41 ..	0·0205	74 ..	0·0370	10 ..	0·5000
8 ..	0·0040	42 ..	0·0210	75 ..	0·0375	11 ..	0·5500
9 ..	0·0045	42½ ..	0·0213	76 ..	0·0380	12 ..	0·6000
10 ..	0·0050	43 ..	0·0215	77 ..	0·0385	13 ..	0·6500
11 ..	0·0055	44 ..	0·0220	77½ ..	0·0388	14 ..	0·7000
12 ..	0·0060	45 ..	0·0225	78 ..	0·0390	15 ..	0·7500
12½ ..	0·0063	46 ..	0·0230	79 ..	0·0395	16 ..	0·8000
13 ..	0·0065	47 ..	0·0235	80 ..	0·0400	17 ..	0·8500
14 ..	0·0070	47½ ..	0·0238	81 ..	0·0405	18 ..	0·9000
15 ..	0·0075	48 ..	0·0240	82 ..	0·0410	19 ..	0·9500
16 ..	0·0080	49 ..	0·0245	82½ ..	0·0413	20 ..	1·0000
17 ..	0·0085	50 ..	0·0250	83 ..	0·0415	25 ..	1·2500
17½ ..	0·0088	51 ..	0·0255	84 ..	0·0420	30 ..	1·5000
18 ..	0·0090	52 ..	0·0260	85 ..	0·0425	35 ..	1·7500
19 ..	0·0095	52½ ..	0·0263	86 ..	0·0430	40 ..	2·0000
20 ..	0·0100	53 ..	0·0265	87 ..	0·0435	45 ..	2·2500
21 ..	0·0105	54 ..	0·0270	87½ ..	0·0438	50 ..	2·5000
22 ..	0·0110	55 ..	0·0275	88 ..	0·0440	55 ..	2·7500
22½ ..	0·0113	56 ..	0·0280	89 ..	0·0445	60 ..	3·0000
23 ..	0·0115	57 ..	0·0285	90 ..	0·0450	65 ..	3·2500
24 ..	0·0120	57½ ..	0·0288	91 ..	0·0455	70 ..	3·5000
25 ..	0·0125	58 ..	0·0290	92 ..	0·0460	75 ..	3·7500
26 ..	0·0130	59 ..	0·0295	92½ ..	0·0463	80 ..	4·0000
27 ..	0·0135	60 ..	0·0300	93 ..	0·0465	85 ..	4·2500
27½ ..	0·0138	61 ..	0·0305	94 ..	0·0470	90 ..	4·5000
28 ..	0·0140	62 ..	0·0310	95 ..	0·0475	95 ..	4·7500
29 ..	0·0145	62½ ..	0·0313	96 ..	0·0480	100 ..	5·0000
30 ..	0·0150	63 ..	0·0315	97 ..	0·0485	110 ..	5·5000
31 ..	0·0155	64 ..	0·0320	97½ ..	0·0488	120 ..	6·0000
32 ..	0·0160	65 ..	0·0325	98 ..	0·0490	130 ..	6·5000
32½ ..	0·0163	66 ..	0·0330	99 ..	0·0495	140 ..	7·0000

£	£	£	£	£	£	£	£
150 ..	7·5000	300 ..	15·0000	450 ..	22·5000	700 ..	35·0000
200 ..	10·0000	350 ..	17·5000	500 ..	25·0000	800 ..	40·0000
250 ..	12·5000	400 ..	20·0000	600 ..	30·0000	1000 ..	50·0000

p	£	p	£	p	£	£	£
$\frac{1}{2}$	0·0003	33	0·0173	67	0·0352	1	0·0525
1	0·0005	34	0·0179	$67\frac{1}{2}$	0·0354	2	0·1050
2	0·0011	35	0·0184	68	0·0357	3	0·1575
$2\frac{1}{2}$	0·0013	36	0·0189	69	0·0362	4	0·2100
3	0·0016	37	0·0194	70	0·0368	5	0·2625
4	0·0021	$37\frac{1}{2}$	0·0197	71	0·0373	6	0·3150
5	0·0026	38	0·0200	72	0·0378	7	0·3675
6	0·0032	39	0·0205	$72\frac{1}{2}$	0·0381	8	0·4200
7	0·0037	40	0·0210	73	0·0383	9	0·4725
$7\frac{1}{2}$	0·0039	41	0·0215	74	0·0389	10	0·5250
8	0·0042	42	0·0221	75	0·0394	11	0·5775
9	0·0047	$42\frac{1}{2}$	0·0223	76	0·0399	12	0·6300
10	0·0053	43	0·0226	77	0·0404	13	0·6825
11	0·0058	44	0·0231	$77\frac{1}{2}$	0·0407	14	0·7350
12	0·0063	45	0·0236	78	0·0410	15	0·7875
$12\frac{1}{2}$	0·0066	46	0·0242	79	0·0415	16	0·8400
13	0·0068	47	0·0247	80	0·0420	17	0·8925
14	0·0074	$47\frac{1}{2}$	0·0249	81	0·0425	18	0·9450
15	0·0079	48	0·0252	82	0·0431	19	0·9975
16	0·0084	49	0·0257	$82\frac{1}{2}$	0·0433	20	1·0500
17	0·0089	50	0·0263	83	0·0436	25	1·3125
$17\frac{1}{2}$	0·0092	51	0·0268	84	0·0441	30	1·5750
18	0·0095	52	0·0273	85	0·0446	35	1·8375
19	0·0100	$52\frac{1}{2}$	0·0276	86	0·0452	40	2·1000
20	0·0105	53	0·0278	87	0·0457	45	2·3625
21	0·0110	54	0·0284	$87\frac{1}{2}$	0·0459	50	2·6250
22	0·0116	55	0·0289	88	0·0462	55	2·8875
$22\frac{1}{2}$	0·0118	56	0·0294	89	0·0467	60	3·1500
23	0·0121	57	0·0299	90	0·0473	65	3·4125
24	0·0126	$57\frac{1}{2}$	0·0302	91	0·0478	70	3·6750
25	0·0131	58	0·0305	92	0·0483	75	3·9375
26	0·0137	59	0·0310	$92\frac{1}{2}$	0·0486	80	4·2000
27	0·0142	60	0·0315	93	0·0488	85	4·4625
$27\frac{1}{2}$	0·0144	61	0·0320	94	0·0494	90	4·7250
28	0·0147	62	0·0326	95	0·0499	95	4·9875
29	0·0152	$62\frac{1}{2}$	0·0328	96	0·0504	100	5·2500
30	0·0158	63	0·0331	97	0·0509	110	5·7750
31	0·0163	64	0·0336	$97\frac{1}{2}$	0·0512	120	6·3000
32	0·0168	65	0·0341	98	0·0515	130	6·8250
$32\frac{1}{2}$	0·0171	66	0·0347	99	0·0520	140	7·3500

£	£	£	£	£	£	£	£
150	7·8750	300	15·7500	450	23·6250	700	36·7500
200	10·5000	350	18·3750	500	26·2500	800	42·0000
250	13·1250	400	21·0000	600	31·5000	1000	52·5000

p	£	p	£	p	£	£	£
$\frac{1}{2}$	0·0003	33	0·0182	67	0·0369	1	0·0550
1	0·0006	34	0·0187	$67\frac{1}{2}$	0·0371	2	0·1100
2	0·0011	35	0·0193	68	0·0374	3	0·1650
$2\frac{1}{2}$	0·0014	36	0·0198	69	0·0380	4	0·2200
3	0·0017	37	0·0204	70	0·0385	5	0·2750
4	0·0022	$37\frac{1}{2}$	0·0206	71	0·0391	6	0·3300
5	0·0028	38	0·0209	72	0·0396	7	0·3850
6	0·0033	39	0·0215	$72\frac{1}{2}$	0·0399	8	0·4400
7	0·0039	40	0·0220	73	0·0402	9	0·4950
$7\frac{1}{2}$	0·0041	41	0·0226	74	0·0407	10	0·5500
8	0·0044	42	0·0231	75	0·0413	11	0·6050
9	0·0050	$42\frac{1}{2}$	0·0234	76	0·0418	12	0·6600
10	0·0055	43	0·0237	77	0·0424	13	0·7150
11	0·0061	44	0·0242	$77\frac{1}{2}$	0·0426	14	0·7700
12	0·0066	45	0·0248	78	0·0429	15	0·8250
$12\frac{1}{2}$	0·0069	46	0·0253	79	0·0435	16	0·8800
13	0·0072	47	0·0259	80	0·0440	17	0·9350
14	0·0077	$47\frac{1}{2}$	0·0261	81	0·0446	18	0·9900
15	0·0083	48	0·0264	82	0·0451	19	1·0450
16	0·0088	49	0·0270	$82\frac{1}{2}$	0·0454	20	1·1000
17	0·0094	50	0·0275	83	0·0457	25	1·3750
$17\frac{1}{2}$	0·0096	51	0·0281	84	0·0462	30	1·6500
18	0·0099	52	0·0286	85	0·0468	35	1·9250
19	0·0105	$52\frac{1}{2}$	0·0289	86	0·0473	40	2·2000
20	0·0110	53	0·0292	87	0·0479	45	2·4750
21	0·0116	54	0·0297	$87\frac{1}{2}$	0·0481	50	2·7500
22	0·0121	55	0·0303	88	0·0484	55	3·0250
$22\frac{1}{2}$	0·0124	56	0·0308	89	0·0490	60	3·3000
23	0·0127	57	0·0314	90	0·0495	65	3·5750
24	0·0132	$57\frac{1}{2}$	0·0316	91	0·0501	70	3·8500
25	0·0138	58	0·0319	92	0·0506	75	4·1250
26	0·0143	59	0·0325	$92\frac{1}{2}$	0·0509	80	4·4000
27	0·0149	60	0·0330	93	0·0512	85	4·6750
$27\frac{1}{2}$	0·0151	61	0·0336	94	0·0517	90	4·9500
28	0·0154	62	0·0341	95	0·0523	95	5·2250
29	0·0160	$62\frac{1}{2}$	0·0344	96	0·0528	100	5·5000
30	0·0165	63	0·0347	97	0·0534	110	6·0500
31	0·0171	64	0·0352	$97\frac{1}{2}$	0·0536	120	6·6000
32	0·0176	65	0·0358	98	0·0539	130	7·1500
$32\frac{1}{2}$	0·0179	66	0·0363	99	0·0545	140	7·7000

£	£	£	£	£	£	£	£
150	8·2500	300	16·5000	450	24·7500	700	38·5000
200	11·0000	350	19·2500	500	27·5000	800	44·0000
250	13·7500	400	22·0000	600	33·0000	1000	55·0000

p	£	p	£	p	£	£	£
½	0·0003	33	0·0190	67	0·0385	1	0·0575
1	0·0006	34	0·0196	67½	0·0388	2	0·1150
2	0·0012	35	0·0201	68	0·0391	3	0·1725
2½	0·0014	36	0·0207	69	0·0397	4	0·2300
3	0·0017	37	0·0213	70	0·0403	5	0·2875
4	0·0023	37½	0·0216	71	0·0408	6	0·3450
5	0·0029	38	0·0219	72	0·0414	7	0·4025
6	0·0035	39	0·0224	72½	0·0417	8	0·4600
7	0·0040	40	0·0230	73	0·0420	9	0·5175
7½	0·0043	41	0·0236	74	0·0426	10	0·5750
8	0·0046	42	0·0242	75	0·0431	11	0·6325
9	0·0052	42½	0·0244	76	0·0437	12	0·6900
10	0·0058	43	0·0247	77	0·0443	13	0·7475
11	0·0063	44	0·0253	77½	0·0446	14	0·8050
12	0·0069	45	0·0259	78	0·0449	15	0·8625
12½	0·0072	46	0·0265	79	0·0454	16	0·9200
13	0·0075	47	0·0270	80	0·0460	17	0·9775
14	0·0081	47½	0·0273	81	0·0466	18	1·0350
15	0·0086	48	0·0276	82	0·0472	19	1·0925
16	0·0092	49	0·0282	82½	0·0474	20	1·1500
17	0·0098	50	0·0288	83	0·0477	25	1·4375
17½	0·0101	51	0·0293	84	0·0483	30	1·7250
18	0·0104	52	0·0299	85	0·0489	35	2·0125
19	0·0109	52½	0·0302	86	0·0495	40	2·3000
20	0·0115	53	0·0305	87	0·0500	45	2·5875
21	0·0121	54	0·0311	87½	0·0503	50	2·8750
22	0·0127	55	0·0316	88	0·0506	55	3·1625
22½	0·0129	56	0·0322	89	0·0512	60	3·4500
23	0·0132	57	0·0328	90	0·0518	65	3·7375
24	0·0138	57½	0·0331	91	0·0523	70	4·0250
25	0·0144	58	0·0334	92	0·0529	75	4·3125
26	0·0150	59	0·0339	92½	0·0532	80	4·6000
27	0·0155	60	0·0345	93	0·0535	85	4·8875
27½	0·0158	61	0·0351	94	0·0541	90	5·1750
28	0·0161	62	0·0357	95	0·0546	95	5·4625
29	0·0167	62½	0·0359	96	0·0552	100	5·7500
30	0·0173	63	0·0362	97	0·0558	110	6·3250
31	0·0178	64	0·0368	97½	0·0561	120	6·9000
32	0·0184	65	0·0374	98	0·0564	130	7·4750
32½	0·0187	66	0·0380	99	0·0569	140	8·0500

£	£	£	£	£	£	£	£
150	8·6250	300	17·2500	450	25·8750	700	40·2500
200	11·5000	350	20·1250	500	28·7500	800	46·0000
250	14·3750	400	23·0000	600	34·5000	1000	57·5000

p	£	p	£	p	£	£	£
½	0·0003	33	0·0198	67	0·0402	1	0·0600
1	0·0006	34	0·0204	67½	0·0405	2	0·1200
2	0·0012	35	0·0210	68	0·0408	3	0·1800
2½	0·0015	36	0·0216	69	0·0414	4	0·2400
3	0·0018	37	0·0222	70	0·0420	5	0·3000
4	0·0024	37½	0·0225	71	0·0426	6	0·3600
5	0·0030	38	0·0228	72	0·0432	7	0·4200
6	0·0036	39	0·0234	72½	0·0435	8	0·4800
7	0·0042	40	0·0240	73	0·0438	9	0·5400
7½	0·0045	41	0·0246	74	0·0444	10	0·6000
8	0·0048	42	0·0252	75	0·0450	11	0·6600
9	0·0054	42½	0·0255	76	0·0456	12	0·7200
10	0·0060	43	0·0258	77	0·0462	13	0·7800
11	0·0066	44	0·0264	77½	0·0465	14	0·8400
12	0·0072	45	0·0270	78	0·0468	15	0·9000
12½	0·0075	46	0·0276	79	0·0474	16	0·9600
13	0·0078	47	0·0282	80	0·0480	17	1·0200
14	0·0084	47½	0·0285	81	0·0486	18	1·0800
15	0·0090	48	0·0288	82	0·0492	19	1·1400
16	0·0096	49	0·0294	82½	0·0495	20	1·2000
17	0·0102	50	0·0300	83	0·0498	25	1·5000
17½	0·0105	51	0·0306	84	0·0504	30	1·8000
18	0·0108	52	0·0312	85	0·0510	35	2·1000
19	0·0114	52½	0·0315	86	0·0516	40	2·4000
20	0·0120	53	0·0318	87	0·0522	45	2·7000
21	0·0126	54	0·0324	87½	0·0525	50	3·0000
22	0·0132	55	0·0330	88	0·0528	55	3·3000
22½	0·0135	56	0·0336	89	0·0534	60	3·6000
23	0·0138	57	0·0342	90	0·0540	65	3·9000
24	0·0144	57½	0·0345	91	0·0546	70	4·2000
25	0·0150	58	0·0348	92	0·0552	75	4·5000
26	0·0156	59	0·0354	92½	0·0555	80	4·8000
27	0·0162	60	0·0360	93	0·0558	85	5·1000
27½	0·0165	61	0·0366	94	0·0564	90	5·4000
28	0·0168	62	0·0372	95	0·0570	95	5·7000
29	0·0174	62½	0·0375	96	0·0576	100	6·0000
30	0·0180	63	0·0378	97	0·0582	110	6·6000
31	0·0186	64	0·0384	97½	0·0585	120	7·2000
32	0·0192	65	0·0390	98	0·0588	130	7·8000
32½	0·0195	66	0·0396	99	0·0594	140	8·4000

£	£	£	£	£	£	£	£
150	9·0000	300	18·0000	450	27·0000	700	42·0000
200	12·0000	350	21·0000	500	30·0000	800	48·0000
250	15·0000	400	24·0000	600	36·0000	1000	60·0000

p	£	p	£	p	£	£	£
½ ..	0·0003	33 ..	0·0206	67 ..	0·0419	1 ..	0·0625
1 ..	0·0006	34 ..	0·0213	67½ ..	0·0422	2 ..	0·1250
2 ..	0·0013	35 ..	0·0219	68 ..	0·0425	3 ..	0·1875
2½ ..	0·0016	36 ..	0·0225	69 ..	0·0431	4 ..	0·2500
3 ..	0·0019	37 ..	0·0231	70 ..	0·0438	5 ..	0·3125
4 ..	0·0025	37½ ..	0·0234	71 ..	0·0444	6 ..	0·3750
5 ..	0·0031	38 ..	0·0238	72 ..	0·0450	7 ..	0·4375
6 ..	0·0038	39 ..	0·0244	72½ ..	0·0453	8 ..	0·5000
7 ..	0·0044	40 ..	0·0250	73 ..	0·0456	9 ..	0·5625
7½ ..	0·0047	41 ..	0·0256	74 ..	0·0463	10 ..	0·6250
8 ..	0·0050	42 ..	0·0263	75 ..	0·0469	11 ..	0·6875
9 ..	0·0056	42½ ..	0·0266	76 ..	0·0475	12 ..	0·7500
10 ..	0·0063	43 ..	0·0269	77 ..	0·0481	13 ..	0·8125
11 ..	0·0069	44 ..	0·0275	77½ ..	0·0484	14 ..	0·8750
12 ..	0·0075	45 ..	0·0281	78 ..	0·0488	15 ..	0·9375
12½ ..	0·0078	46 ..	0·0288	79 ..	0·0494	16 ..	1·0000
13 ..	0·0081	47 ..	0·0294	80 ..	0·0500	17 ..	1·0625
14 ..	0·0088	47½ ..	0·0297	81 ..	0·0506	18 ..	1·1250
15 ..	0·0094	48 ..	0·0300	82 ..	0·0513	19 ..	1·1875
16 ..	0·0100	49 ..	0·0306	82½ ..	0·0516	20 ..	1·2500
17 ..	0·0106	50 ..	0·0313	83 ..	0·0519	25 ..	1·5625
17½ ..	0·0109	51 ..	0·0319	84 ..	0·0525	30 ..	1·8750
18 ..	0·0113	52 ..	0·0325	85 ..	0·0531	35 ..	2·1875
19 ..	0·0119	52½ ..	0·0328	86 ..	0·0538	40 ..	2·5000
20 ..	0·0125	53 ..	0·0331	87 ..	0·0544	45 ..	2·8125
21 ..	0·0131	54 ..	0·0338	87½ ..	0·0547	50 ..	3·1250
22 ..	0·0138	55 ..	0·0344	88 ..	0·0550	55 ..	3·4375
22½ ..	0·0141	56 ..	0·0350	89 ..	0·0556	60 ..	3·7500
23 ..	0·0144	57 ..	0·0356	90 ..	0·0563	65 ..	4·0625
24 ..	0·0150	57½ ..	0·0359	91 ..	0·0569	70 ..	4·3750
25 ..	0·0156	58 ..	0·0363	92 ..	0·0575	75 ..	4·6875
26 ..	0·0163	59 ..	0·0369	92½ ..	0·0578	80 ..	5·0000
27 ..	0·0169	60 ..	0·0375	93 ..	0·0581	85 ..	5·3125
27½ ..	0·0172	61 ..	0·0381	94 ..	0·0588	90 ..	5·6250
28 ..	0·0175	62 ..	0·0388	95 ..	0·0594	95 ..	5·9375
29 ..	0·0181	62½ ..	0·0391	96 ..	0·0600	100 ..	6·2500
30 ..	0·0188	63 ..	0·0394	97 ..	0·0606	110 ..	6·8750
31 ..	0·0194	64 ..	0·0400	97½ ..	0·0609	120 ..	7·5000
32 ..	0·0200	65 ..	0·0406	98 ..	0·0613	130 ..	8·1250
32½ ..	0·0203	66 ..	0·0413	99 ..	0·0619	140 ..	8·7500

£	£	£	£	£	£	£	£
150 ..	9·3750	300 ..	18·7500	450 ..	28·1250	700 ..	43·7500
200 ..	12·5000	350 ..	21·8750	500 ..	31·2500	800 ..	50·0000
250 ..	15·6250	400 ..	25·0000	600 ..	37·5000	1000 ..	62·5000

p	£	p	£	p	£	£	£
$\frac{1}{2}$	0·0003	33	0·0215	67	0·0436	1	0·0650
1	0·0007	34	0·0221	$67\frac{1}{2}$	0·0439	2	0·1300
2	0·0013	35	0·0228	68	0·0442	3	0·1950
$2\frac{1}{2}$	0·0016	36	0·0234	69	0·0449	4	0·2600
3	0·0020	37	0·0241	70	0·0455	5	0·3250
4	0·0026	$37\frac{1}{2}$	0·0244	71	0·0462	6	0·3900
5	0·0033	38	0·0247	72	0·0468	7	0·4550
6	0·0039	39	0·0254	$72\frac{1}{2}$	0·0471	8	0·5200
7	0·0046	40	0·0260	73	0·0475	9	0·5850
$7\frac{1}{2}$	0·0049	41	0·0267	74	0·0481	10	0·6500
8	0·0052	42	0·0273	75	0·0488	11	0·7150
9	0·0059	$42\frac{1}{2}$	0·0276	76	0·0494	12	0·7800
10	0·0065	43	0·0280	77	0·0501	13	0·8450
11	0·0072	44	0·0286	$77\frac{1}{2}$	0·0504	14	0·9100
12	0·0078	45	0·0293	78	0·0507	15	0·9750
$12\frac{1}{2}$	0·0081	46	0·0299	79	0·0514	16	1·0400
13	0·0085	47	0·0306	80	0·0520	17	1·1050
14	0·0091	$47\frac{1}{2}$	0·0309	81	0·0527	18	1·1700
15	0·0098	48	0·0312	82	0·0533	19	1·2350
16	0·0104	49	0·0319	$82\frac{1}{2}$	0·0536	20	1·3000
17	0·0111	50	0·0325	83	0·0540	25	1·6250
$17\frac{1}{2}$	0·0114	51	0·0332	84	0·0546	30	1·9500
18	0·0117	52	0·0338	85	0·0553	35	2·2750
19	0·0124	$52\frac{1}{2}$	0·0341	86	0·0559	40	2·6000
20	0·0130	53	0·0345	87	0·0566	45	2·9250
21	0·0137	54	0·0351	$87\frac{1}{2}$	0·0569	50	3·2500
22	0·0143	55	0·0358	88	0·0572	55	3·5750
$22\frac{1}{2}$	0·0146	56	0·0364	89	0·0579	60	3·9000
23	0·0150	57	0·0371	90	0·0585	65	4·2250
24	0·0156	$57\frac{1}{2}$	0·0374	91	0·0592	70	4·5500
25	0·0163	58	0·0377	92	0·0598	75	4·8750
26	0·0169	59	0·0384	$92\frac{1}{2}$	0·0601	80	5·2000
27	0·0176	60	0·0390	93	0·0605	85	5·5250
$27\frac{1}{2}$	0·0179	61	0·0397	94	0·0611	90	5·8500
28	0·0182	62	0·0403	95	0·0618	95	6·1750
29	0·0189	$62\frac{1}{2}$	0·0406	96	0·0624	100	6·5000
30	0·0195	63	0·0410	97	0·0631	110	7·1500
31	0·0202	64	0·0416	$97\frac{1}{2}$	0·0634	120	7·8000
32	0·0208	65	0·0423	98	0·0637	130	8·4500
$32\frac{1}{2}$	0·0211	66	0·0429	99	0·0644	140	9·1000

£	£	£	£	£	£	£	£
150	9·7500	300	19·5000	450	29·2500	700	45·5000
200	13·0000	350	22·7500	500	32·5000	800	52·0000
250	16·2500	400	26·0000	600	39·0000	1000	65·0000

p	£	p	£	p	£	£	£
$\frac{1}{2}$ ..	0·0003	33 ..	0·0220	67 ..	0·0447	1 ..	0·0667
1 ..	0·0007	34 ..	0·0227	$67\frac{1}{2}$ ..	0·0450	2 ..	0·1333
2 ..	0·0013	35 ..	0·0233	68 ..	0·0453	3 ..	0·2000
$2\frac{1}{2}$ ..	0·0017	36 ..	0·0240	69 ..	0·0460	4 ..	0·2667
3 ..	0·0020	37 ..	0·0247	70 ..	0·0467	5 ..	0·3333
4 ..	0·0027	$37\frac{1}{2}$ ..	0·0250	71 ..	0·0473	6 ..	0·4000
5 ..	0·0033	38 ..	0·0253	72 ..	0·0480	7 ..	0·4667
6 ..	0·0040	39 ..	0·0260	$72\frac{1}{2}$ ..	0·0483	8 ..	0·5333
7 ..	0·0047	40 ..	0·0267	73 ..	0·0487	9 ..	0·6000
$7\frac{1}{2}$ ..	0·0050	41 ..	0·0273	74 ..	0·0493	10 ..	0·6667
8 ..	0·0053	42 ..	0·0280	75 ..	0·0500	11 ..	0·7333
9 ..	0·0060	$42\frac{1}{2}$ ..	0·0283	76 ..	0·0507	12 ..	0·8000
10 ..	0·0067	43 ..	0·0287	77 ..	0·0513	13 ..	0·8667
11 ..	0·0073	44 ..	0·0293	$77\frac{1}{2}$ ..	0·0517	14 ..	0·9333
12 ..	0·0080	45 ..	0·0300	78 ..	0·0520	15 ..	1·0000
$12\frac{1}{2}$ ..	0·0083	46 ..	0·0307	79 ..	0·0527	16 ..	1·0667
13 ..	0·0087	47 ..	0·0313	80 ..	0·0533	17 ..	1·1333
14 ..	0·0093	$47\frac{1}{2}$ ..	0·0317	81 ..	0·0540	18 ..	1·2000
15 ..	0·0100	48 ..	0·0320	82 ..	0·0547	19 ..	1·2667
16 ..	0·0107	49 ..	0·0327	$82\frac{1}{2}$ ..	0·0550	20 ..	1·3333
17 ..	0·0113	50 ..	0·0333	83 ..	0·0553	25 ..	1·6667
$17\frac{1}{2}$ ..	0·0117	51 ..	0·0340	84 ..	0·0560	30 ..	2·0000
18 ..	0·0120	52 ..	0·0347	85 ..	0·0567	35 ..	2·3333
19 ..	0·0127	$52\frac{1}{2}$ ..	0·0350	86 ..	0·0573	40 ..	2·6667
20 ..	0·0133	53 ..	0·0353	87 ..	0·0580	45 ..	3·0000
21 ..	0·0140	54 ..	0·0360	$87\frac{1}{2}$ ..	0·0583	50 ..	3·3333
22 ..	0·0147	55 ..	0·0367	88 ..	0·0537	55 ..	3·6667
$22\frac{1}{2}$ ..	0·0150	56 ..	0·0373	89 ..	0·0593	60 ..	4·0000
23 ..	0·0153	57 ..	0·0380	90 ..	0·0600	65 ..	4·3333
24 ..	0·0160	$57\frac{1}{2}$ ..	0·0383	91 ..	0·0607	70 ..	4·6667
25 ..	0·0167	58 ..	0·0387	92 ..	0·0613	75 ..	5·0000
26 ..	0·0173	59 ..	0·0393	$92\frac{1}{2}$ ..	0·0617	80 ..	5·3333
27 ..	0·0180	60 ..	0·0400	93 ..	0·0620	85 ..	5·6667
$27\frac{1}{2}$ ..	0·0183	61 ..	0·0407	94 ..	0·0627	90 ..	6·0000
28 ..	0·0187	62 ..	0·0413	95 ..	0·0633	95 ..	6·3333
29 ..	0·0193	$62\frac{1}{2}$ ..	0·0417	96 ..	0·0640	100 ..	6·6667
30 ..	0·0200	63 ..	0·0420	97 ..	0·0647	110 ..	7·3333
31 ..	0·0207	64 ..	0·0427	$97\frac{1}{2}$ ..	0·0650	120 ..	8·0000
32 ..	0·0213	65 ..	0·0433	98 ..	0·0653	130 ..	8·6667
$32\frac{1}{2}$ ..	0·0217	66 ..	0·0440	99 ..	0·0660	140 ..	9·3333

£	£	£	£	£	£	£	£
150 ..	10·0000	300 ..	20·0000	450 ..	30·0000	700 ..	46·6667
200 ..	13·3333	350 ..	23·3333	500 ..	33·3333	800 ..	53·3333
250 ..	16·6667	400 ..	26·6667	600 ..	40·0000	1000 ..	66·6667

p	£	p	£	p	£	£	£
$\frac{1}{2}$	0·0003	33	0·0223	67	0·0452	1	0·0675
1	0·0007	34	0·0230	$67\frac{1}{2}$	0·0456	2	0·1350
2	0·0014	35	0·0236	68	0·0459	3	0·2025
$2\frac{1}{2}$	0·0017	36	0·0243	69	0·0466	4	0·2700
3	0·0020	37	0·0250	70	0·0473	5	0·3375
4	0·0027	$37\frac{1}{2}$	0·0253	71	0·0479	6	0·4050
5	0·0034	38	0·0257	72	0·0486	7	0·4725
6	0·0041	39	0·0263	$72\frac{1}{2}$	0·0489	8	0·5400
7	0·0047	40	0·0270	73	0·0493	9	0·6075
$7\frac{1}{2}$	0·0051	41	0·0277	74	0·0500	10	0·6750
8	0·0054	42	0·0284	75	0·0506	11	0·7425
9	0·0061	$42\frac{1}{2}$	0·0287	76	0·0513	12	0·8100
10	0·0068	43	0·0290	77	0·0520	13	0·8775
11	0·0074	44	0·0297	$77\frac{1}{2}$	0·0523	14	0·9450
12	0·0081	45	0·0304	78	0·0527	15	1·0125
$12\frac{1}{2}$	0·0084	46	0·0311	79	0·0533	16	1·0800
13	0·0088	47	0·0317	80	0·0540	17	1·1475
14	0·0095	$47\frac{1}{2}$	0·0321	81	0·0547	18	1·2150
15	0·0101	48	0·0324	82	0·0554	19	1·2825
16	0·0108	49	0·0331	$82\frac{1}{2}$	0·0557	20	1·3500
17	0·0115	50	0·0338	83	0·0560	25	1·6875
$17\frac{1}{2}$	0·0118	51	0·0344	84	0·0567	30	2·0250
18	0·0122	52	0·0351	85	0·0574	35	2·3625
19	0·0128	$52\frac{1}{2}$	0·0354	86	0·0581	40	2·7000
20	0·0135	53	0·0358	87	0·0587	45	3·0375
21	0·0142	54	0·0365	$87\frac{1}{2}$	0·0591	50	3·3750
22	0·0149	55	0·0371	88	0·0594	55	3·7125
$22\frac{1}{2}$	0·0152	56	0·0378	89	0·0601	60	4·0500
23	0·0155	57	0·0385	90	0·0608	65	4·3875
24	0·0162	$57\frac{1}{2}$	0·0388	91	0·0614	70	4·7250
25	0·0169	58	0·0392	92	0·0621	75	5·0625
26	0·0176	59	0·0398	$92\frac{1}{2}$	0·0624	80	5·4000
27	0·0182	60	0·0405	93	0·0628	85	5·7375
$27\frac{1}{2}$	0·0186	61	0·0412	94	0·0635	90	6·0750
28	0·0189	62	0·0419	95	0·0641	95	6·4125
29	0·0196	$62\frac{1}{2}$	0·0422	96	0·0648	100	6·7500
30	0·0203	63	0·0425	97	0·0655	110	7·4250
31	0·0209	64	0·0432	$97\frac{1}{2}$	0·0658	120	8·1000
32	0·0216	65	0·0439	98	0·0662	130	8·7750
$32\frac{1}{2}$	0·0219	66	0·0446	99	0·0668	140	9·4500

£	£	£	£	£	£	£	£
150	10·1250	300	20·2500	450	30·3750	700	47·2500
200	13·5000	350	23·6250	500	33·7500	800	54·0000
250	16·8750	400	27·0000	600	40·5000	1000	67·5000

Per Cent

p	£	p	£	p	£	£	£
$\frac{1}{2}$ ..	0·0004	33 ..	0·0231	67 ..	0·0469	1 ..	0·0700
1 ..	0·0007	34 ..	0·0238	$67\frac{1}{2}$ ..	0·0473	2 ..	0·1400
2 ..	0·0014	35 ..	0·0245	68 ..	0·0476	3 ..	0·2100
$2\frac{1}{2}$ ..	0·0018	36 ..	0·0252	69 ..	0·0483	4 ..	0·2800
3 ..	0·0021	37 ..	0·0259	70 ..	0·0490	5 ..	0·3500
4 ..	0·0028	$37\frac{1}{2}$ ..	0·0263	71 ..	0·0497	6 ..	0·4200
5 ..	0·0035	38 ..	0·0266	72 ..	0·0504	7 ..	0·4900
6 ..	0·0042	39 ..	0·0273	$72\frac{1}{2}$ ..	0·0508	8 ..	0·5600
7 ..	0·0049	40 ..	0·0280	73 ..	0·0511	9 ..	0·6300
$7\frac{1}{2}$ ..	0·0053	41 ..	0·0287	74 ..	0·0518	10 ..	0·7000
8 ..	0·0056	42 ..	0·0294	75 ..	0·0525	11 ..	0·7700
9 ..	0·0063	$42\frac{1}{2}$ ..	0·0298	76 ..	0·0532	12 ..	0·8400
10 ..	0·0070	43 ..	0·0301	77 ..	0·0539	13 ..	0·9100
11 ..	0·0077	44 ..	0·0308	$77\frac{1}{2}$ ..	0·0543	14 ..	0·9800
12 ..	0·0084	45 ..	0·0315	78 ..	0·0546	15 ..	1·0500
$12\frac{1}{2}$ ..	0·0088	46 ..	0·0322	79 ..	0·0553	16 ..	1·1200
13 ..	0·0091	47 ..	0·0329	80 ..	0·0560	17 ..	1·1900
14 ..	0·0098	$47\frac{1}{2}$ ..	0·0333	81 ..	0·0567	18 ..	1·2600
15 ..	0·0105	48 ..	0·0336	82 ..	0·0574	19 ..	1·3300
16 ..	0·0112	49 ..	0·0343	$82\frac{1}{2}$ ..	0·0578	20 ..	1·4000
17 ..	0·0119	50 ..	0·0350	83 ..	0·0581	25 ..	1·7500
$17\frac{1}{2}$ ..	0·0123	51 ..	0·0357	84 ..	0·0588	30 ..	2·1000
18 ..	0·0126	52 ..	0·0364	85 ..	0·0595	35 ..	2·4500
19 ..	0·0133	$52\frac{1}{2}$ ..	0·0368	86 ..	0·0602	40 ..	2·8000
20 ..	0·0140	53 ..	0·0371	87 ..	0·0609	45 ..	3·1500
21 ..	0·0147	54 ..	0·0378	$87\frac{1}{2}$ ..	0·0613	50 ..	3·5000
22 ..	0·0154	55 ..	0·0385	88 ..	0·0616	55 ..	3·8500
$22\frac{1}{2}$ ..	0·0158	56 ..	0·0392	89 ..	0·0623	60 ..	4·2000
23 ..	0·0161	57 ..	0·0399	90 ..	0·0630	65 ..	4·5500
24 ..	0·0168	$57\frac{1}{2}$ ..	0·0403	91 ..	0·0637	70 ..	4·9000
25 ..	0·0175	58 ..	0·0406	92 ..	0·0644	75 ..	5·2500
26 ..	0·0182	59 ..	0·0413	$92\frac{1}{2}$ ..	0·0648	80 ..	5·6000
27 ..	0·0189	60 ..	0·0420	93 ..	0·0651	85 ..	5·9500
$27\frac{1}{2}$ ..	0·0193	61 ..	0·0427	94 ..	0·0658	90 ..	6·3000
28 ..	0·0196	62 ..	0·0434	95 ..	0·0665	95 ..	6·6500
29 ..	0·0203	$62\frac{1}{2}$ ..	0·0438	96 ..	0·0672	100 ..	7·0000
30 ..	0·0210	63 ..	0·0441	97 ..	0·0679	110 ..	7·7000
31 ..	0·0217	64 ..	0·0448	$97\frac{1}{2}$ ..	0·0683	120 ..	8·4000
32 ..	0·0224	65 ..	0·0455	98 ..	0·0686	130 ..	9·1000
$32\frac{1}{2}$ ..	0·0228	66 ..	0·0462	99 ..	0·0693	140 ..	9·8000

£	£	£	£	£	£	£	£
150 ..	10·5000	300 ..	21·0000	450 ..	31·5000	700 ..	49·0000
200 ..	14·0000	350 ..	24·5000	500 ..	35·0000	800 ..	56·0000
250 ..	17·5000	400 ..	28·0000	600 ..	42·0000	1000 ..	70·0000

p	£	p	£	p	£	£	£
$\frac{1}{2}$	0·0004	33	0·0239	67	0·0486	1	0·0725
1	0·0007	34	0·0247	$67\frac{1}{2}$	0·0489	2	0·1450
2	0·0015	35	0·0254	68	0·0493	3	0·2175
$2\frac{1}{2}$	0·0018	36	0·0261	69	0·0500	4	0·2900
3	0·0022	37	0·0268	70	0·0508	5	0·3625
4	0·0029	$37\frac{1}{2}$	0·0272	71	0·0515	6	0·4350
5	0·0036	38	0·0276	72	0·0522	7	0·5075
6	0·0044	39	0·0283	$72\frac{1}{2}$	0·0526	8	0·5800
7	0·0051	40	0·0290	73	0·0529	9	0·6525
$7\frac{1}{2}$	0·0054	41	0·0297	74	0·0537	10	0·7250
8	0·0058	42	0·0305	75	0·0544	11	0·7975
9	0·0065	$42\frac{1}{2}$	0·0308	76	0·0551	12	0·8700
10	0·0073	43	0·0312	77	0·0558	13	0·9425
11	0·0080	44	0·0319	$77\frac{1}{2}$	0·0562	14	1·0150
12	0·0087	45	0·0326	78	0·0566	15	1·0875
$12\frac{1}{2}$	0·0091	46	0·0334	79	0·0573	16	1·1600
13	0·0094	47	0·0341	80	0·0580	17	1·2325
14	0·0102	$47\frac{1}{2}$	0·0344	81	0·0587	18	1·3050
15	0·0109	48	0·0348	82	0·0595	19	1·3775
16	0·0116	49	0·0355	$82\frac{1}{2}$	0·0598	20	1·4500
17	0·0123	50	0·0363	83	0·0602	25	1·8125
$17\frac{1}{2}$	0·0127	51	0·0370	84	0·0609	30	2·1750
18	0·0131	52	0·0377	85	0·0616	35	2·5375
19	0·0138	$52\frac{1}{2}$	0·0381	86	0·0624	40	2·9000
20	0·0145	53	0·0384	87	0·0631	45	3·2625
21	0·0152	54	0·0392	$87\frac{1}{2}$	0·0634	50	3·6250
22	0·0160	55	0·0399	88	0·0638	55	3·9875
$22\frac{1}{2}$	0·0163	56	0·0406	89	0·0645	60	4·3500
23	0·0167	57	0·0413	90	0·0653	65	4·7125
24	0·0174	$57\frac{1}{2}$	0·0417	91	0·0660	70	5·0750
25	0·0181	58	0·0421	92	0·0667	75	5·4375
26	0·0189	59	0·0428	$92\frac{1}{2}$	0·0671	80	5·8000
27	0·0196	60	0·0435	93	0·0674	85	6·1625
$27\frac{1}{2}$	0·0199	61	0·0442	94	0·0682	90	6·5250
28	0·0203	62	0·0450	95	0·0689	95	6·8875
29	0·0210	$62\frac{1}{2}$	0·0453	96	0·0696	100	7·2500
30	0·0218	63	0·0457	97	0·0703	110	7·9750
31	0·0225	64	0·0464	$97\frac{1}{2}$	0·0707	120	8·7000
32	0·0232	65	0·0471	98	0·0711	130	9·4250
$32\frac{1}{2}$	0·0236	66	0·0479	99	0·0718	140	10·1500

£	£	£	£	£	£	£	£
150	10·8750	300	21·7500	450	32·6250	700	50·7500
200	14·5000	350	25·3750	500	36·2500	800	58·0000
250	18·1250	400	29·0000	600	43·5000	1000	72·5000

p	£	p	£	p	£	£	£
$\frac{1}{2}$	0·0004	33	0·0248	67	0·0503	1	0·0750
1	0·0008	34	0·0255	$67\frac{1}{2}$	0·0506	2	0·1500
2	0·0015	35	0·0263	68	0·0510	3	0·2250
$2\frac{1}{2}$	0·0019	36	0·0270	69	0·0518	4	0·3000
3	0·0023	37	0·0278	70	0·0525	5	0·3750
4	0·0030	$37\frac{1}{2}$	0·0281	71	0·0533	6	0·4500
5	0·0038	38	0·0285	72	0·0540	7	0·5250
6	0·0045	39	0·0293	$72\frac{1}{2}$	0·0544	8	0·6000
7	0·0053	40	0·0300	73	0·0548	9	0·6750
$7\frac{1}{2}$	0·0056	41	0·0308	74	0·0555	10	0·7500
8	0·0060	42	0·0315	75	0·0563	11	0·8250
9	0·0068	$42\frac{1}{2}$	0·0319	76	0·0570	12	0·9000
10	0·0075	43	0·0323	77	0·0578	13	0·9750
11	0·0083	44	0·0330	$77\frac{1}{2}$	0·0581	14	1·0500
12	0·0090	45	0·0338	78	0·0585	15	1·1250
$12\frac{1}{2}$	0·0094	46	0·0345	79	0·0593	16	1·2000
13	0·0098	47	0·0353	80	0·0600	17	1·2750
14	0·0105	$47\frac{1}{2}$	0·0356	81	0·0608	18	1·3500
15	0·0113	48	0·0360	82	0·0615	19	1·4250
16	0·0120	49	0·0368	$82\frac{1}{2}$	0·0619	20	1·5000
17	0·0128	50	0·0375	83	0·0623	25	1·8750
$17\frac{1}{2}$	0·0131	51	0·0383	84	0·0630	30	2·2500
18	0·0135	52	0·0390	85	0·0638	35	2·6250
19	0·0143	$52\frac{1}{2}$	0·0394	86	0·0645	40	3·0000
20	0·0150	53	0·0398	87	0·0653	45	3·3750
21	0·0158	54	0·0405	$87\frac{1}{2}$	0·0656	50	3·7500
22	0·0165	55	0·0413	88	0·0660	55	4·1250
$22\frac{1}{2}$	0·0169	56	0·0420	89	0·0668	60	4·5000
23	0·0173	57	0·0428	90	0·0675	65	4·8750
24	0·0180	$57\frac{1}{2}$	0·0431	91	0·0683	70	5·2500
25	0·0188	58	0·0435	92	0·0690	75	5·6250
26	0·0195	59	0·0443	$92\frac{1}{2}$	0·0694	80	6·0000
27	0·0203	60	0·0450	93	0·0698	85	6·3750
$27\frac{1}{2}$	0·0206	61	0·0458	94	0·0705	90	6·7500
28	0·0210	62	0·0465	95	0·0713	95	7·1250
29	0·0218	$62\frac{1}{2}$	0·0469	96	0·0720	100	7·5000
30	0·0225	63	0·0473	97	0·0728	110	8·2500
31	0·0233	64	0·0480	$97\frac{1}{2}$	0·0731	120	9·0000
32	0·0240	65	0·0488	98	0·0735	130	9·7500
$32\frac{1}{2}$	0·0244	66	0·0495	99	0·0743	140	10·5000

£	£	£	£	£	£	£	£
150	11·2500	300	22·5000	450	33·7500	700	52·5000
200	15·0000	350	26·2500	500	37·5000	800	60·0000
250	18·7500	400	30·0000	600	45·0000	1000	75·0000

p	£	p	£	p	£	£	£
$\frac{1}{2}$	0·0004	33	0·0256	67	0·0519	1	0·0775
1	0·0008	34	0·0264	$67\frac{1}{2}$	0·0523	2	0·1550
2	0·0016	35	0·0271	68	0·0527	3	0·2325
$2\frac{1}{2}$	0·0019	36	0·0279	69	0·0535	4	0·3100
3	0·0023	37	0·0287	70	0·0543	5	0·3875
4	0·0031	$37\frac{1}{2}$	0·0291	71	0·0550	6	0·4650
5	0·0039	38	0·0295	72	0·0558	7	0·5425
6	0·0047	39	0·0302	$72\frac{1}{2}$	0·0562	8	0·6200
7	0·0054	40	0·0310	73	0·0566	9	0·6975
$7\frac{1}{2}$	0·0058	41	0·0318	74	0·0574	10	0·7750
8	0·0062	42	0·0326	75	0·0581	11	0·8525
9	0·0070	$42\frac{1}{2}$	0·0329	76	0·0589	12	0·9300
10	0·0078	43	0·0333	77	0·0597	13	1·0075
11	0·0085	44	0·0341	$77\frac{1}{2}$	0·0601	14	1·0850
12	0·0093	45	0·0349	78	0·0605	15	1·1625
$12\frac{1}{2}$	0·0097	46	0·0357	79	0·0612	16	1·2400
13	0·0101	47	0·0364	80	0·0620	17	1·3175
14	0·0109	$47\frac{1}{2}$	0·0368	81	0·0628	18	1·3950
15	0·0116	48	0·0372	82	0·0636	19	1·4725
16	0·0124	49	0·0380	$82\frac{1}{2}$	0·0639	20	1·5500
17	0·0132	50	0·0388	83	0·0643	25	1·9375
$17\frac{1}{2}$	0·0136	51	0·0395	84	0·0651	30	2·3250
18	0·0140	52	0·0403	85	0·0659	35	2·7125
19	0·0147	$52\frac{1}{2}$	0·0407	86	0·0667	40	3·1000
20	0·0155	53	0·0411	87	0·0674	45	3·4875
21	0·0163	54	0·0419	$87\frac{1}{2}$	0·0678	50	3·8750
22	0·0171	55	0·0426	88	0·0682	55	4·2625
$22\frac{1}{2}$	0·0174	56	0·0434	89	0·0690	60	4·6500
23	0·0178	57	0·0442	90	0·0698	65	5·0375
24	0·0186	$57\frac{1}{2}$	0·0446	91	0·0705	70	5·4250
25	0·0194	58	0·0450	92	0·0713	75	5·8125
26	0·0202	59	0·0457	$92\frac{1}{2}$	0·0717	80	6·2000
27	0·0209	60	0·0465	93	0·0721	85	6·5875
$27\frac{1}{2}$	0·0213	61	0·0473	94	0·0729	90	6·9750
28	0·0217	62	0·0481	95	0·0736	95	7·3625
29	0·0225	$62\frac{1}{2}$	0·0484	96	0·0744	100	7·7500
30	0·0233	63	0·0488	97	0·0752	110	8·5250
31	0·0240	64	0·0496	$97\frac{1}{2}$	0·0756	120	9·3000
32	0·0248	65	0·0504	98	0·0760	130	10·0750
$32\frac{1}{2}$	0·0252	66	0·0512	99	0·0767	140	10·8500

£	£	£	£	£	£	£	£
150	11·6250	300	23·2500	450	34·8750	700	54·2500
200	15·5000	350	27·1250	500	38·7500	800	62·0000
250	19·3750	400	31·0000	600	46·5000	1000	77·5000

p	£	p	£	p	£	£	£
½	0·0004	33	0·0264	67	0·0536	1	0·0800
1	0·0008	34	0·0272	67½	0·0540	2	0·1600
2	0·0016	35	0·0280	68	0·0544	3	0·2400
2½	0·0020	36	0·0288	69	0·0552	4	0·3200
3	0·0024	37	0·0296	70	0·0560	5	0·4000
4	0·0032	37½	0·0300	71	0·0568	6	0·4800
5	0·0040	38	0·0304	72	0·0576	7	0·5600
6	0·0048	39	0·0312	72½	0·0580	8	0·6400
7	0·0056	40	0·0320	73	0·0584	9	0·7200
7½	0·0060	41	0·0328	74	0·0592	10	0·8000
8	0·0064	42	0·0336	75	0·0600	11	0·8800
9	0·0072	42½	0·0340	76	0·0608	12	0·9600
10	0·0080	43	0·0344	77	0·0616	13	1·0400
11	0·0088	44	0·0352	77½	0·0620	14	1·1200
12	0·0096	45	0·0360	78	0·0624	15	1·2000
12½	0·0100	46	0·0368	79	0·0632	16	1·2800
13	0·0104	47	0·0376	80	0·0640	17	1·3600
14	0·0112	47½	0·0380	81	0·0648	18	1·4400
15	0·0120	48	0·0384	82	0·0656	19	1·5200
16	0·0128	49	0·0392	82½	0·0660	20	1·6000
17	0·0136	50	0·0400	83	0·0664	25	2·0000
17½	0·0140	51	0·0408	84	0·0672	30	2·4000
18	0·0144	52	0·0416	85	0·0680	35	2·8000
19	0·0152	52½	0·0420	86	0·0688	40	3·2000
20	0·0160	53	0·0424	87	0·0696	45	3·6000
21	0·0168	54	0·0432	87½	0·0700	50	4·0000
22	0·0176	55	0·0440	88	0·0704	55	4·4000
22½	0·0180	56	0·0448	89	0·0712	60	4·8000
23	0·0184	57	0·0456	90	0·0720	65	5·2000
24	0·0192	57½	0·0460	91	0·0728	70	5·6000
25	0·0200	58	0·0464	92	0·0736	75	6·0000
26	0·0208	59	0·0472	92½	0·0740	80	6·4000
27	0·0216	60	0·0480	93	0·0744	85	6·8000
27½	0·0220	61	0·0488	94	0·0752	90	7·2000
28	0·0224	62	0·0496	95	0·0760	95	7·6000
29	0·0232	62½	0·0500	96	0·0768	100	8·0000
30	0·0240	63	0·0504	97	0·0776	110	8·8000
31	0·0248	64	0·0512	97½	0·0780	120	9·6000
32	0·0256	65	0·0520	98	0·0784	130	10·4000
32½	0·0260	66	0·0528	99	0·0792	140	11·2000

£	£	£	£	£	£	£	£
150	12·0000	300	24·0000	450	36·0000	700	56·0000
200	16·0000	350	28·0000	500	40·0000	800	64·0000
250	20·0000	400	32·0000	600	48·0000	1000	80·0000

p	£	p	£	p	£	£	£
½	0·0004	33	0·0272	67	0·0553	1	0·0825
1	0·0008	34	0·0281	67½	0·0557	2	0·1650
2	0·0017	35	0·0289	68	0·0561	3	0·2475
2½	0·0021	36	0·0297	69	0·0569	4	0·3300
3	0·0025	37	0·0305	70	0·0578	5	0·4125
4	0·0033	37½	0·0309	71	0·0586	6	0·4950
5	0·0041	38	0·0314	72	0·0594	7	0·5775
6	0·0050	39	0·0322	72½	0·0598	8	0·6600
7	0·0058	40	0·0330	73	0·0602	9	0·7425
7½	0·0062	41	0·0338	74	0·0611	10	0·8250
8	0·0066	42	0·0347	75	0·0619	11	0·9075
9	0·0074	42½	0·0351	76	0·0627	12	0·9900
10	0·0083	43	0·0355	77	0·0635	13	1·0725
11	0·0091	44	0·0363	77½	0·0639	14	1·1550
12	0·0099	45	0·0371	78	0·0644	15	1·2375
12½	0·0103	46	0·0380	79	0·0652	16	1·3200
13	0·0107	47	0·0388	80	0·0660	17	1·4025
14	0·0116	47½	0·0392	81	0·0668	18	1·4850
15	0·0124	48	0·0396	82	0·0677	19	1·5675
16	0·0132	49	0·0404	82½	0·0681	20	1·6500
17	0·0140	50	0·0413	83	0·0685	25	2·0625
17½	0·0144	51	0·0421	84	0·0693	30	2·4750
18	0·0149	52	0·0429	85	0·0701	35	2·8875
19	0·0157	52½	0·0433	86	0·0710	40	3·3000
20	0·0165	53	0·0437	87	0·0718	45	3·7125
21	0·0173	54	0·0446	87½	0·0722	50	4·1250
22	0·0182	55	0·0454	88	0·0726	55	4·5375
22½	0·0186	56	0·0462	89	0·0734	60	4·9500
23	0·0190	57	0·0470	90	0·0743	65	5·3625
24	0·0198	57½	0·0474	91	0·0751	70	5·7750
25	0·0206	58	0·0479	92	0·0759	75	6·1875
26	0·0215	59	0·0487	92½	0·0763	80	6·6000
27	0·0223	60	0·0495	93	0·0767	85	7·0125
27½	0·0227	61	0·0503	94	0·0776	90	7·4250
28	0·0231	62	0·0512	95	0·0784	95	7·8375
29	0·0239	62½	0·0516	96	0·0792	100	8·2500
30	0·0248	63	0·0520	97	0·0800	110	9·0750
31	0·0256	64	0·0528	97½	0·0804	120	9·9000
32	0·0264	65	0·0536	98	0·0809	130	10·7250
32½	0·0268	66	0·0545	99	0·0817	140	11·5500

£	£	£	£	£	£	£	£
150	12·3750	300	24·7500	450	37·1250	700	57·7500
200	16·5000	350	28·8750	500	41·2500	800	66·0000
250	20·6250	400	33·0000	600	49·5000	1000	82·5000

p	£	p	£	p	£	£	£
$\frac{1}{2}$	0·0004	33	0·0281	67	0·0570	1	0·0850
1	0·0009	34	0·0289	$67\frac{1}{2}$	0·0574	2	0·1700
2	0·0017	35	0·0298	68	0·0578	3	0·2550
$2\frac{1}{2}$	0·0021	36	0·0306	69	0·0587	4	0·3400
3	0·0026	37	0·0315	70	0·0595	5	0·4250
4	0·0034	$37\frac{1}{2}$	0·0319	71	0·0604	6	0·5100
5	0·0043	38	0·0323	72	0·0612	7	0·5950
6	0·0051	39	0·0332	$72\frac{1}{2}$	0·0616	8	0·6800
7	0·0060	40	0·0340	73	0·0621	9	0·7650
$7\frac{1}{2}$	0·0064	41	0·0349	74	0·0629	10	0·8500
8	0·0068	42	0·0357	75	0·0638	11	0·9350
9	0·0077	$42\frac{1}{2}$	0·0361	76	0·0646	12	1·0200
10	0·0085	43	0·0366	77	0·0655	13	1·1050
11	0·0094	44	0·0374	$77\frac{1}{2}$	0·0659	14	1·1900
12	0·0102	45	0·0383	78	0·0663	15	1·2750
$12\frac{1}{2}$	0·0106	46	0·0391	79	0·0672	16	1·3600
13	0·0111	47	0·0400	80	0·0680	17	1·4450
14	0·0119	$47\frac{1}{2}$	0·0404	81	0·0689	18	1·5300
15	0·0128	48	0·0408	82	0·0697	19	1·6150
16	0·0136	49	0·0417	$82\frac{1}{2}$	0·0701	20	1·7000
17	0·0145	50	0·0425	83	0·0706	25	2·1250
$17\frac{1}{2}$	0·0149	51	0·0434	84	0·0714	30	2·5500
18	0·0153	52	0·0442	85	0·0723	35	2·9750
19	0·0162	$52\frac{1}{2}$	0·0446	86	0·0731	40	3·4000
20	0·0170	53	0·0451	87	0·0740	45	3·8250
21	0·0179	54	0·0459	$87\frac{1}{2}$	0·0744	50	4·2500
22	0·0187	55	0·0468	88	0·0748	55	4·6750
$22\frac{1}{2}$	0·0191	56	0·0476	89	0·0757	60	5·1000
23	0·0196	57	0·0485	90	0·0765	65	5·5250
24	0·0204	$57\frac{1}{2}$	0·0489	91	0·0774	70	5·9500
25	0·0213	58	0·0493	92	0·0782	75	6·3750
26	0·0221	59	0·0502	$92\frac{1}{2}$	0·0786	80	6·8000
27	0·0230	60	0·0510	93	0·0791	85	7·2250
$27\frac{1}{2}$	0·0234	61	0·0519	94	0·0799	90	7·6500
28	0·0238	62	0·0527	95	0·0808	95	8·0750
29	0·0247	$62\frac{1}{2}$	0·0531	96	0·0816	100	8·5000
30	0·0255	63	0·0536	97	0·0825	110	9·3500
31	0·0264	64	0·0544	$97\frac{1}{2}$	0·0829	120	10·2000
32	0·0272	65	0·0553	98	0·0833	130	11·0500
$32\frac{1}{2}$	0·0276	66	0·0561	99	0·0842	140	11·9000

£	£	£	£	£	£	£	£
150	12·7500	300	25·5000	450	38·2500	700	59·5000
200	17·0000	350	29·7500	500	42·5000	800	68·0000
250	21·2500	400	34·0000	600	51·0000	1000	85·0000

p	£	p	£	p	£	£	£
$\frac{1}{2}$	0·0004	33	0·0289	67	0·0586	1	0·0875
1	0·0009	34	0·0298	$67\frac{1}{2}$	0·0591	2	0·1750
2	0·0018	35	0·0306	68	0·0595	3	0·2625
$2\frac{1}{2}$	0·0022	36	0·0315	69	0·0604	4	0·3500
3	0·0026	37	0·0324	70	0·0613	5	0·4375
4	0·0035	$37\frac{1}{2}$	0·0328	71	0·0621	6	0·5250
5	0·0044	38	0·0333	72	0·0630	7	0·6125
6	0·0053	39	0·0341	$72\frac{1}{2}$	0·0634	8	0·7000
7	0·0061	40	0·0350	73	0·0639	9	0·7875
$7\frac{1}{2}$	0·0066	41	0·0359	74	0·0648	10	0·8750
8	0·0070	42	0·0368	75	0·0656	11	0·9625
9	0·0079	$42\frac{1}{2}$	0·0372	76	0·0665	12	1·0500
10	0·0088	43	0·0376	77	0·0674	13	1·1375
11	0·0096	44	0·0385	$77\frac{1}{2}$	0·0678	14	1·2250
12	0·0105	45	0·0394	78	0·0683	15	1·3125
$12\frac{1}{2}$	0·0109	46	0·0403	79	0·0691	16	1·4000
13	0·0114	47	0·0411	80	0·0700	17	1·4875
14	0·0123	$47\frac{1}{2}$	0·0416	81	0·0709	18	1·5750
15	0·0131	48	0·0420	82	0·0718	19	1·6625
16	0·0140	49	0·0429	$82\frac{1}{2}$	0·0722	20	1·7500
17	0·0149	50	0·0438	83	0·0726	25	2·1875
$17\frac{1}{2}$	0·0153	51	0·0446	84	0·0735	30	2·6250
18	0·0158	52	0·0455	85	0·0744	35	3·0625
19	0·0166	$52\frac{1}{2}$	0·0459	86	0·0753	40	3·5000
20	0·0175	53	0·0464	87	0·0761	45	3·9375
21	0·0184	54	0·0473	$87\frac{1}{2}$	0·0766	50	4·3750
22	0·0193	55	0·0481	88	0·0770	55	4·8125
$22\frac{1}{2}$	0·0197	56	0·0490	89	0·0779	60	5·2500
23	0·0201	57	0·0499	90	0·0788	65	5·6875
24	0·0210	$57\frac{1}{2}$	0·0503	91	0·0796	70	6·1250
25	0·0219	58	0·0508	92	0·0805	75	6·5625
26	0·0228	59	0·0516	$92\frac{1}{2}$	0·0809	80	7·0000
27	0·0236	60	0·0525	93	0·0814	85	7·4375
$27\frac{1}{2}$	0·0241	61	0·0534	94	0·0823	90	7·8750
28	0·0245	62	0·0543	95	0·0831	95	8·3125
29	0·0254	$62\frac{1}{2}$	0·0547	96	0·0840	100	8·7500
30	0·0263	63	0·0551	97	0·0849	110	9·6250
31	0·0271	64	0·0560	$97\frac{1}{2}$	0·0853	120	10·5000
32	0·0280	65	0·0569	98	0·0858	130	11·3750
$32\frac{1}{2}$	0·0284	66	0·0578	99	0·0866	140	12·2500

£	£	£	£	£	£	£	£
150	13·1250	300	26·2500	450	39·3750	700	61·2500
200	17·5000	350	30·6250	500	43·7500	800	70·0000
250	21·8750	400	35·0000	600	52·5000	1000	87·5000

p	£	p	£	p	£	£	£
½	.. 0·0005	33	.. 0·0297	67	.. 0·0603	1	.. 0·0900
1	.. 0·0009	34	.. 0·0306	67½	.. 0·0608	2	.. 0·1800
2	.. 0·0018	35	.. 0·0315	68	.. 0·0612	3	.. 0·2700
2½	.. 0·0023	36	.. 0·0324	69	.. 0·0621	4	.. 0·3600
3	.. 0·0027	37	.. 0·0333	70	.. 0·0630	5	.. 0·4500
4	.. 0·0036	37½	.. 0·0338	71	.. 0·0639	6	.. 0·5400
5	.. 0·0045	38	.. 0·0342	72	.. 0·0648	7	.. 0·6300
6	.. 0·0054	39	.. 0·0351	72½	.. 0·0653	8	.. 0·7200
7	.. 0·0063	40	.. 0·0360	73	.. 0·0657	9	.. 0·8100
7½	.. 0·0068	41	.. 0·0369	74	.. 0·0666	10	.. 0·9000
8	.. 0·0072	42	.. 0·0378	75	.. 0·0675	11	.. 0·9900
9	.. 0·0081	42½	.. 0·0383	76	.. 0·0684	12	.. 1·0800
10	.. 0·0090	43	.. 0·0387	77	.. 0·0693	13	.. 1·1700
11	.. 0·0099	44	.. 0·0396	77½	.. 0·0698	14	.. 1·2600
12	.. 0·0108	45	.. 0·0405	78	.. 0·0702	15	.. 1·3500
12½	.. 0·0113	46	.. 0·0414	79	.. 0·0711	16	.. 1·4400
13	.. 0·0117	47	.. 0·0423	80	.. 0·0720	17	.. 1·5300
14	.. 0·0126	47½	.. 0·0428	81	.. 0·0729	18	.. 1·6200
15	.. 0·0135	48	.. 0·0432	82	.. 0·0738	19	.. 1·7100
16	.. 0·0144	49	.. 0·0441	82½	.. 0·0743	20	.. 1·8000
17	.. 0·0153	50	.. 0·0450	83	.. 0·0747	25	.. 2·2500
17½	.. 0·0158	51	.. 0·0459	84	.. 0·0756	30	.. 2·7000
18	.. 0·0162	52	.. 0·0468	85	.. 0·0765	35	.. 3·1500
19	.. 0·0171	52½	.. 0·0473	86	.. 0·0774	40	.. 3·6000
20	.. 0·0180	53	.. 0·0477	87	.. 0·0783	45	.. 4·0500
21	.. 0·0189	54	.. 0·0486	87½	.. 0·0788	50	.. 4·5000
22	.. 0·0198	55	.. 0·0495	88	.. 0·0792	55	.. 4·9500
22½	.. 0·0203	56	.. 0·0504	89	.. 0·0801	60	.. 5·4000
23	.. 0·0207	57	.. 0·0513	90	.. 0·0810	65	.. 5·8500
24	.. 0·0216	57½	.. 0·0518	91	.. 0·0819	70	.. 6·3000
25	.. 0·0225	58	.. 0·0522	92	.. 0·0828	75	.. 6·7500
26	.. 0·0234	59	.. 0·0531	92½	.. 0·0833	80	.. 7·2000
27	.. 0·0243	60	.. 0·0540	93	.. 0·0837	85	.. 7·6500
27½	.. 0·0248	61	.. 0·0549	94	.. 0·0846	90	.. 8·1000
28	.. 0·0252	62	.. 0·0558	95	.. 0·0855	95	.. 8·5500
29	.. 0·0261	62½	.. 0·0563	96	.. 0·0864	100	.. 9·0000
30	.. 0·0270	63	.. 0·0567	97	.. 0·0873	110	.. 9·9000
31	.. 0·0279	64	.. 0·0576	97½	.. 0·0878	120	.. 10·8000
32	.. 0·0288	65	.. 0·0585	98	.. 0·0882	130	.. 11·7000
32½	.. 0·0293	66	.. 0·0594	99	.. 0·0891	140	.. 12·6000

£	£	£	£	£	£	£	£
150	.. 13·5000	300	.. 27·0000	450	.. 40·5000	700	.. 63·0000
200	.. 18·0000	350	.. 31·5000	500	.. 45·0000	800	.. 72·0000
250	.. 22·5000	400	.. 36·0000	600	.. 54·0000	1000	.. 90·0000

p	£	p	£	p	£	£	£
$\frac{1}{2}$	0·0005	33	0·0305	67	0·0620	1	0·0925
1	0·0009	34	0·0315	$67\frac{1}{2}$	0·0624	2	0·1850
2	0·0019	35	0·0324	68	0·0629	3	0·2775
$2\frac{1}{2}$	0·0023	36	0·0333	69	0·0638	4	0·3700
3	0·0028	37	0·0342	70	0·0648	5	0·4625
4	0·0037	$37\frac{1}{2}$	0·0347	71	0·0657	6	0·5550
5	0·0046	38	0·0352	72	0·0666	7	0·6475
6	0·0056	39	0·0361	$72\frac{1}{2}$	0·0671	8	0·7400
7	0·0065	40	0·0370	73	0·0675	9	0·8325
$7\frac{1}{2}$	0·0069	41	0·0379	74	0·0685	10	0·9250
8	0·0074	42	0·0389	75	0·0694	11	1·0175
9	0·0083	$42\frac{1}{2}$	0·0393	76	0·0703	12	1·1100
10	0·0093	43	0·0398	77	0·0712	13	1·2025
11	0·0102	44	0·0407	$77\frac{1}{2}$	0·0717	14	1·2950
12	0·0111	45	0·0416	78	0·0722	15	1·3875
$12\frac{1}{2}$	0·0116	46	0·0426	79	0·0731	16	1·4800
13	0·0120	47	0·0435	80	0·0740	17	1·5725
14	0·0130	$47\frac{1}{2}$	0·0439	81	0·0749	18	1·6650
15	0·0139	48	0·0444	82	0·0759	19	1·7575
16	0·0148	49	0·0453	$82\frac{1}{2}$	0·0763	20	1·8500
17	0·0157	50	0·0463	83	0·0768	25	2·3125
$17\frac{1}{2}$	0·0162	51	0·0472	84	0·0777	30	2·7750
18	0·0167	52	0·0481	85	0·0786	35	3·2375
19	0·0176	$52\frac{1}{2}$	0·0486	86	0·0796	40	3·7000
20	0·0185	53	0·0490	87	0·0805	45	4·1625
21	0·0194	54	0·0500	$87\frac{1}{2}$	0·0809	50	4·6250
22	0·0204	55	0·0509	88	0·0814	55	5·0875
$22\frac{1}{2}$	0·0208	56	0·0518	89	0·0823	60	5·5500
23	0·0213	57	0·0527	90	0·0833	65	6·0125
24	0·0222	$57\frac{1}{2}$	0·0532	91	0·0842	70	6·4750
25	0·0231	58	0·0537	92	0·0851	75	6·9375
26	0·0241	59	0·0546	$92\frac{1}{2}$	0·0856	80	7·4000
27	0·0250	60	0·0555	93	0·0860	85	7·8625
$27\frac{1}{2}$	0·0254	61	0·0564	94	0·0870	90	8·3250
28	0·0259	62	0·0574	95	0·0879	95	8·7875
29	0·0268	$62\frac{1}{2}$	0·0578	96	0·0888	100	9·2500
30	0·0278	63	0·0583	97	0·0897	110	10·1750
31	0·0287	64	0·0592	$97\frac{1}{2}$	0·0902	120	11·1000
32	0·0296	65	0·0601	98	0·0907	130	12·0250
$32\frac{1}{2}$	0·0301	66	0·0611	99	0·0916	140	12·9500

£	£	£	£	£	£	£	£
150	13·8750	300	27·7500	450	41·6250	700	64·7500
200	18·5000	350	32·3750	500	46·2500	800	74·0000
250	23·1250	400	37·0000	600	55·5000	1000	92·5000

p	£	p	£	p	£	£	£
$\frac{1}{2}$	0·0005	33	0·0314	67	0·0637	1	0·0950
1	0·0010	34	0·0323	$67\frac{1}{2}$	0·0641	2	0·1900
2	0·0019	35	0·0333	68	0·0646	3	0·2850
$2\frac{1}{2}$	0·0024	36	0·0342	69	0·0656	4	0·3800
3	0·0029	37	0·0352	70	0·0665	5	0·4750
4	0·0038	$37\frac{1}{2}$	0·0356	71	0·0675	6	0·5700
5	0·0048	38	0·0361	72	0·0684	7	0·6650
6	0·0057	39	0·0371	$72\frac{1}{2}$	0·0689	8	0·7600
7	0·0067	40	0·0380	73	0·0694	9	0·8550
$7\frac{1}{2}$	0·0071	41	0·0390	74	0·0703	10	0·9500
8	0·0076	42	0·0399	75	0·0713	11	1·0450
9	0·0086	$42\frac{1}{2}$	0·0404	76	0·0722	12	1·1400
10	0·0095	43	0·0409	77	0·0732	13	1·2350
11	0·0105	44	0·0418	$77\frac{1}{2}$	0·0736	14	1·3300
12	0·0114	45	0·0428	78	0·0741	15	1·4250
$12\frac{1}{2}$	0·0119	46	0·0437	79	0·0751	16	1·5200
13	0·0124	47	0·0447	80	0·0760	17	1·6150
14	0·0133	$47\frac{1}{2}$	0·0451	81	0·0770	18	1·7100
15	0·0143	48	0·0456	82	0·0779	19	1·8050
16	0·0152	49	0·0466	$82\frac{1}{2}$	0·0784	20	1·9000
17	0·0162	50	0·0475	83	0·0789	25	2·3750
$17\frac{1}{2}$	0·0166	51	0·0485	84	0·0798	30	2·8500
18	0·0171	52	0·0494	85	0·0808	35	3·3250
19	0·0181	$52\frac{1}{2}$	0·0499	86	0·0817	40	3·8000
20	0·0190	53	0·0504	87	0·0827	45	4·2750
21	0·0200	54	0·0513	$87\frac{1}{2}$	0·0831	50	4·7500
22	0·0209	55	0·0523	88	0·0836	55	5·2250
$22\frac{1}{2}$	0·0214	56	0·0532	89	0·0846	60	5·7000
23	0·0219	57	0·0542	90	0·0855	65	6·1750
24	0·0228	$57\frac{1}{2}$	0·0546	91	0·0865	70	6·6500
25	0·0238	58	0·0551	92	0·0874	75	7·1250
26	0·0247	59	0·0561	$92\frac{1}{2}$	0·0879	80	7·6000
27	0·0257	60	0·0570	93	0·0884	85	8·0750
$27\frac{1}{2}$	0·0261	61	0·0580	94	0·0893	90	8·5500
28	0·0266	62	0·0589	95	0·0903	95	9·0250
29	0·0276	$62\frac{1}{2}$	0·0594	96	0·0912	100	9·5000
30	0·0285	63	0·0599	97	0·0922	110	10·4500
31	0·0295	64	0·0608	$97\frac{1}{2}$	0·0926	120	11·4000
32	0·0304	65	0·0618	98	0·0931	130	12·3500
$32\frac{1}{2}$	0·0309	66	0·0627	99	0·0941	140	13·3000

£	£	£	£	£	£	£	£
150	14·2500	300	28·5000	450	42·7500	700	66·5000
200	19·0000	350	33·2500	500	47·5000	800	76·0000
250	23·7500	400	38·0000	600	57·0000	1000	95·0000

p	£	p	£	p	£	£	£
½	0·0005	33	0·0322	67	0·0653	1	0·0975
1	0·0010	34	0·0332	67½	0·0658	2	0·1950
2	0·0020	35	0·0341	68	0·0663	3	0·2925
2½	0·0024	36	0·0351	69	0·0673	4	0·3900
3	0·0029	37	0·0361	70	0·0683	5	0·4875
4	0·0039	37½	0·0366	71	0·0692	6	0·5850
5	0·0049	38	0·0371	72	0·0702	7	0·6825
6	0·0059	39	0·0380	72½	0·0707	8	0·7800
7	0·0068	40	0·0390	73	0·0712	9	0·8775
7½	0·0073	41	0·0400	74	0·0722	10	0·9750
8	0·0078	42	0·0410	75	0·0731	11	1·0725
9	0·0088	42½	0·0414	76	0·0741	12	1·1700
10	0·0098	43	0·0419	77	0·0751	13	1·2675
11	0·0107	44	0·0429	77½	0·0756	14	1·3650
12	0·0117	45	0·0439	78	0·0761	15	1·4625
12½	0·0122	46	0·0449	79	0·0770	16	1·5600
13	0·0127	47	0·0458	80	0·0780	17	1·6575
14	0·0137	47½	0·0463	81	0·0799	18	1·7550
15	0·0146	48	0·0468	82	0·0800	19	1·8525
16	0·0156	49	0·0478	82½	0·0804	20	1·9500
17	0·0166	50	0·0488	83	0·0809	25	2·4375
17½	0·0171	51	0·0497	84	0·0819	30	2·9250
18	0·0176	52	0·0507	85	0·0829	35	3·4125
19	0·0185	52½	0·0512	86	0·0839	40	3·9000
20	0·0195	53	0·0517	87	0·0848	45	4·3875
21	0·0205	54	0·0527	87½	0·0853	50	4·8750
22	0·0215	55	0·0536	88	0·0858	55	5·3625
22½	0·0219	56	0·0546	89	0·0868	60	5·8500
23	0·0224	57	0·0556	90	0·0878	65	6·3375
24	0·0234	57½	0·0561	91	0·0887	70	6·8250
25	0·0244	58	0·0566	92	0·0897	75	7·3125
26	0·0254	59	0·0575	92½	0·0902	80	7·8000
27	0·0263	60	0·0585	93	0·0907	85	8·2875
27½	0·0268	61	0·0595	94	0·0917	90	8·7750
28	0·0273	62	0·0605	95	0·0926	95	9·2625
29	0·0283	62½	0·0609	96	0·0936	100	9·7500
30	0·0293	63	0·0614	97	0·0946	110	10·7250
31	0·0302	64	0·0624	97½	0·0951	120	11·7000
32	0·0312	65	0·0634	98	0·0956	130	12·6750
32½	0·0317	66	0·0644	99	0·0965	140	13·6500

£	£	£	£	£	£	£	£
150	14·6250	300	29·2500	450	43·8750	700	68·2500
200	19·5000	350	34·1250	500	48·7500	800	78·0000
250	24·3750	400	39·0000	600	58·5000	1000	97·5000

p	£	p	£	p	£	£	£
½	0·0005	33	0·0330	67	0·0670	1	0·1000
1	0·0010	34	0·0340	67½	0·0675	2	0·2000
2	0·0020	35	0·0350	68	0·0680	3	0·3000
2½	0·0025	36	0·0360	69	0·0690	4	0·4000
3	0·0030	37	0·0370	70	0·0700	5	0·5000
4	0·0040	37½	0·0375	71	0·0710	6	0·6000
5	0·0050	38	0·0380	72	0·0720	7	0·7000
6	0·0060	39	0·0390	72½	0·0725	8	0·8000
7	0·0070	40	0·0400	73	0·0730	9	0·9000
7½	0·0075	41	0·0410	74	0·0740	10	1·0000
8	0·0080	42	0·0420	75	0·0750	11	1·1000
9	0·0090	42½	0·0425	76	0·0760	12	1·2000
10	0·0100	43	0·0430	77	0·0770	13	1·3000
11	0·0110	44	0·0440	77½	0·0775	14	1·4000
12	0·0120	45	0·0450	78	0·0780	15	1·5000
12½	0·0125	46	0·0460	79	0·0790	16	1·6000
13	0·0130	47	0·0470	80	0·0800	17	1·7000
14	0·0140	47½	0·0475	81	0·0810	18	1·8000
15	0·0150	48	0·0480	82	0·0820	19	1·9000
16	0·0160	49	0·0490	82½	0·0825	20	2·0000
17	0·0170	50	0·0500	83	0·0830	25	2·5000
17½	0·0175	51	0·0510	84	0·0840	30	3·0000
18	0·0180	52	0·0520	85	0·0850	35	3·5000
19	0·0190	52½	0·0525	86	0·0860	40	4·0000
20	0·0200	53	0·0530	87	0·0870	45	4·5000
21	0·0210	54	0·0540	87½	0·0875	50	5·0000
22	0·0220	55	0·0550	88	0·0880	55	5·5000
22½	0·0225	56	0·0560	89	0·0890	60	6·0000
23	0·0230	57	0·0570	90	0·0900	65	6·5000
24	0·0240	57½	0·0575	91	0·0910	70	7·0000
25	0·0250	58	0·0580	92	0·0920	75	7·5000
26	0·0260	59	0·0590	92½	0·0925	80	8·0000
27	0·0270	60	0·0600	93	0·0930	85	8·5000
27½	0·0275	61	0·0610	94	0·0940	90	9·0000
28	0·0280	62	0·0620	95	0·0950	95	9·5000
29	0·0290	62½	0·0625	96	0·0960	100	10·0000
30	0·0300	63	0·0630	97	0·0970	110	11·0000
31	0·0310	64	0·0640	97½	0·0975	120	12·0000
32	0·0320	65	0·0650	98	0·0980	130	13·0000
32½	0·0325	66	0·0660	99	0·0990	140	14·0000

£	£	£	£	£	£	£	£
150	15·0000	300	30·0000	450	45·0000	700	70·0000
200	20·0000	350	35·0000	500	50·0000	800	80·0000
250	25·0000	400	40·0000	600	60·0000	1000	100·0000

p	£	p	£	p	£	£	£
½	0·0005	33	0·0347	67	0·0704	1	0·1050
1	0·0011	34	0·0357	67½	0·0709	2	0·2100
2	0·0021	35	0·0368	68	0·0714	3	0·3150
2½	0·0026	36	0·0378	69	0·0725	4	0·4200
3	0·0032	37	0·0389	70	0·0735	5	0·5250
4	0·0042	37½	0·0394	71	0·0746	6	0·6300
5	0·0053	38	0·0399	72	0·0756	7	0·7350
6	0·0063	39	0·0410	72½	0·0761	8	0·8400
7	0·0074	40	0·0420	73	0·0767	9	0·9450
7½	0·0079	41	0·0431	74	0·0777	10	1·0500
8	0·0084	42	0·0441	75	0·0788	11	1·1550
9	0·0095	42½	0·0446	76	0·0798	12	1·2600
10	0·0105	43	0·0452	77	0·0809	13	1·3650
11	0·0116	44	0·0462	77½	0·0814	14	1·4700
12	0·0126	45	0·0473	78	0·0819	15	1·5750
12½	0·0131	46	0·0483	79	0·0830	16	1·6800
13	0·0137	47	0·0494	80	0·0840	17	1·7850
14	0·0147	47½	0·0499	81	0·0851	18	1·8900
15	0·0158	48	0·0504	82	0·0861	19	1·9950
16	0·0168	49	0·0515	82½	0·0866	20	2·1000
17	0·0179	50	0·0525	83	0·0872	25	2·6250
17½	0·0184	51	0·0536	84	0·0882	30	3·1500
18	0·0189	52	0·0546	85	0·0893	35	3·6750
19	0·0200	52½	0·0551	86	0·0903	40	4·2000
20	0·0210	53	0·0557	87	0·0914	45	4·7250
21	0·0221	54	0·0567	87½	0·0919	50	5·2500
22	0·0231	55	0·0578	88	0·0924	55	5·7750
22½	0·0236	56	0·0588	89	0·0935	60	6·3000
23	0·0242	57	0·0599	90	0·0945	65	6·8250
24	0·0252	57½	0·0604	91	0·0956	70	7·3500
25	0·0263	58	0·0609	92	0·0966	75	7·8750
26	0·0273	59	0·0620	92½	0·0971	80	8·4000
27	0·0284	60	0·0630	93	0·0977	85	8·9250
27½	0·0289	61	0·0641	94	0·0987	90	9·4500
28	0·0294	62	0·0651	95	0·0998	95	9·9750
29	0·0305	62½	0·0656	96	0·1008	100	10·5000
30	0·0315	63	0·0662	97	0·1019	110	11·5500
31	0·0326	64	0·0672	97½	0·1024	120	12·6000
32	0·0336	65	0·0683	98	0·1029	130	13·6500
32½	0·0341	66	0·0693	99	0·1040	140	14·7000

£	£	£	£	£	£	£	£
150	15·7500	300	31·5000	450	47·2500	700	73·5000
200	21·0000	350	36·7500	500	52·5000	800	84·0000
250	26·2500	400	42·0000	600	63·0000	1000	105·0000

p	£	p	£	p	£	£	£
$\frac{1}{2}$ ..	0·0006	33 ..	0·0371	67 ..	0·0754	1 ..	0·1125
1 ..	0·0011	34 ..	0·0383	$67\frac{1}{2}$ ..	0·0759	2 ..	0·2250
2 ..	0·0023	35 ..	0·0394	68 ..	0·0765	3 ..	0·3375
$2\frac{1}{2}$ ..	0·0028	36 ..	0·0405	69 ..	0·0776	4 ..	0·4500
3 ..	0·0034	37 ..	0·0416	70 ..	0·0788	5 ..	0·5625
4 ..	0·0045	$37\frac{1}{2}$ ..	0·0422	71 ..	0·0799	6 ..	0·6750
5 ..	0·0056	38 ..	0·0428	72 ..	0·0810	7 ..	0·7875
6 ..	0·0068	39 ..	0·0439	$72\frac{1}{2}$ ..	0·0816	8 ..	0·9000
7 ..	0·0079	40 ..	0·0450	73 ..	0·0821	9 ..	1·0125
$7\frac{1}{2}$ ..	0·0084	41 ..	0·0461	74 ..	0·0833	10 ..	1·1250
8 ..	0·0090	42 ..	0·0473	75 ..	0·0844	11 ..	1·2375
9 ..	0·0101	$42\frac{1}{2}$ ..	0·0478	76 ..	0·0855	12 ..	1·3500
10 ..	0·0113	43 ..	0·0484	77 ..	0·0866	13 ..	1·4625
11 ..	0·0124	44 ..	0·0495	$77\frac{1}{2}$ ..	0·0872	14 ..	1·5750
12 ..	0·0135	45 ..	0·0506	78 ..	0·0878	15 ..	1·6875
$12\frac{1}{2}$ ..	0·0141	46 ..	0·0518	79 ..	0·0889	16 ..	1·8000
13 ..	0·0146	47 ..	0·0529	80 ..	0·0900	17 ..	1·9125
14 ..	0·0158	$47\frac{1}{2}$ ..	0·0534	81 ..	0·0911	18 ..	2·0250
15 ..	0·0169	48 ..	0·0540	82 ..	0·0923	19 ..	2·1375
16 ..	0·0180	49 ..	0·0551	$82\frac{1}{2}$ ..	0·0928	20 ..	2·2500
17 ..	0·0191	50 ..	0·0563	83 ..	0·0934	25 ..	2·8125
$17\frac{1}{2}$ ..	0·0197	51 ..	0·0574	84 ..	0·0945	30 ..	3·3750
18 ..	0·0203	52 ..	0·0585	85 ..	0·0956	35 ..	3·9375
19 ..	0·0214	$52\frac{1}{2}$ ..	0·0591	86 ..	0·0968	40 ..	4·5000
20 ..	0·0225	53 ..	0·0596	87 ..	0·0979	45 ..	5·0625
21 ..	0·0236	54 ..	0·0608	$87\frac{1}{2}$ ..	0·0984	50 ..	5·6250
22 ..	0·0248	55 ..	0·0619	88 ..	0·0990	55 ..	6·1875
$22\frac{1}{2}$ ..	0·0253	56 ..	0·0630	89 ..	0·1001	60 ..	6·7500
23 ..	0·0259	57 ..	0·0641	90 ..	0·1013	65 ..	7·3125
24 ..	0·0270	$57\frac{1}{2}$ ..	0·0647	91 ..	0·1024	70 ..	7·8750
25 ..	0·0281	58 ..	0·0653	92 ..	0·1035	75 ..	8·4375
26 ..	0·0293	59 ..	0·0664	$92\frac{1}{2}$ ..	0·1041	80 ..	9·0000
27 ..	0·0304	60 ..	0·0675	93 ..	0·1046	85 ..	9·5625
$27\frac{1}{2}$ ..	0·0309	61 ..	0·0686	94 ..	0·1058	90 ..	10·1250
28 ..	0·0315	62 ..	0·0698	95 ..	0·1069	95 ..	10·6875
29 ..	0·0326	$62\frac{1}{2}$ ..	0·0703	96 ..	0·1080	100 ..	11·2500
30 ..	0·0338	63 ..	0·0709	97 ..	0·1091	110 ..	12·3750
31 ..	0·0349	64 ..	0·0720	$97\frac{1}{2}$ ..	0·1097	120 ..	13·5000
32 ..	0·0360	65 ..	0·0731	98 ..	0·1103	130 ..	14·6250
$32\frac{1}{2}$ ..	0·0366	66 ..	0·0743	99 ..	0·1114	140 ..	15·7500

£	£	£	£	£	£	£	£
150 ..	16·8750	300 ..	33·7500	450 ..	50·6250	700 ..	78·7500
200 ..	22·5000	350 ..	39·3750	500 ..	56·2500	800 ..	90·0000
250 ..	28·1250	400 ..	45·0000	600 ..	67·5000	1000 ..	112·5000

p	£	p	£	p	£	£	£
½	0·0006	33	0·0396	67	0·0804	1	0·1200
1	0·0012	34	0·0408	67½	0·0810	2	0·2400
2	0·0024	35	0·0420	68	0·0816	3	0·3600
2½	0·0030	36	0·0432	69	0·0828	4	0·4800
3	0·0036	37	0·0444	70	0·0840	5	0·6000
4	0·0048	37½	0·0450	71	0·0852	6	0·7200
5	0·0060	38	0·0456	72	0·0864	7	0·8400
6	0·0072	39	0·0468	72½	0·0870	8	0·9600
7	0·0084	40	0·0480	73	0·0876	9	1·0800
7½	0·0090	41	0·0492	74	0·0888	10	1·2000
8	0·0096	42	0·0504	75	0·0900	11	1·3200
9	0·0108	42½	0·0510	76	0·0912	12	1·4400
10	0·0120	43	0·0516	77	0·0924	13	1·5600
11	0·0132	44	0·0528	77½	0·0930	14	1·6800
12	0·0144	45	0·0540	78	0·0936	15	1·8000
12½	0·0150	46	0·0552	79	0·0948	16	1·9200
13	0·0156	47	0·0564	80	0·0960	17	2·0400
14	0·0168	47½	0·0570	81	0·0972	18	2·1600
15	0·0180	48	0·0576	82	0·0984	19	2·2800
16	0·0192	49	0·0588	82½	0·0990	20	2·4000
17	0·0204	50	0·0600	83	0·0996	25	3·0000
17½	0·0210	51	0·0612	84	0·1008	30	3·6000
18	0·0216	52	0·0624	85	0·1020	35	4·2000
19	0·0228	52½	0·0630	86	0·1032	40	4·8000
20	0·0240	53	0·0636	87	0·1044	45	5·4000
21	0·0252	54	0·0648	87½	0·1050	50	6·0000
22	0·0264	55	0·0660	88	0·1056	55	6·6000
22½	0·0270	56	0·0672	89	0·1068	60	7·2000
23	0·0276	57	0·0684	90	0·1080	65	7·8000
24	0·0288	57½	0·0690	91	0·1092	70	8·4000
25	0·0300	58	0·0696	92	0·1104	75	9·0000
26	0·0312	59	0·0708	92½	0·1110	80	9·6000
27	0·0324	60	0·0720	93	0·1116	85	10·2000
27½	0·0330	61	0·0732	94	0·1128	90	10·8000
28	0·0336	62	0·0744	95	0·1140	95	11·4000
29	0·0348	62½	0·0750	96	0·1152	100	12·0000
30	0·0360	63	0·0756	97	0·1164	110	13·2000
31	0·0372	64	0·0768	97½	0·1170	120	14·4000
32	0·0384	65	0·0780	98	0·1176	130	15·6000
32½	0·0390	66	0·0792	99	0·1188	140	16·8000

£	£	£	£	£	£	£	£
150	18·0000	300	36·0000	450	54·0000	700	84·0000
200	24·0000	350	42·0000	500	60·0000	800	96·0000
250	30·0000	400	48·0000	600	72·0000	1000	120·0000

p	£	p	£	p	£	£	£
½ ..	0·0006	33 ..	0·0413	.67 ..	0·0838	1 ..	0·1250
1 ..	0·0013	34 ..	0·0425	67½ ..	0·0844	2 ..	0·2500
2 ..	0·0025	35 ..	0·0438	68 ..	0·0850	3 ..	0·3750
2½ ..	0·0031	36 ..	0·0450	69 ..	0·0863	4 ..	0·5000
3 ..	0·0038	37 ..	0·0463	70 ..	0·0875	5 ..	0·6250
4 ..	0·0050	37½ ..	0·0469	71 ..	0·0888	6 ..	0·7500
5 ..	0·0063	38 ..	0·0475	72 ..	0·0900	7 ..	0·8750
6 ..	0·0075	39 ..	0·0488	72½ ..	0·0906	8 ..	1·0000
7 ..	0·0088	40 ..	0·0500	73 ..	0·0913	9 ..	1·1250
7½ ..	0·0094	41 ..	0·0513	74 ..	0·0925	10 ..	1·2500
8 ..	0·0100	42 ..	0·0525	75 ..	0·0938	11 ..	1·3750
9 ..	0·0113	42½ ..	0·0531	76 ..	0·0950	12 ..	1·5000
10 ..	0·0125	43 ..	0·0538	77 ..	0·0963	13 ..	1·6250
11 ..	0·0138	44 ..	0·0550	77½ ..	0·0969	14 ..	1·7500
12 ..	0·0150	45 ..	0·0563	78 ..	0·0975	15 ..	1·8750
12½ ..	0·0156	46 ..	0·0575	79 ..	0·0988	16 ..	2·0000
13 ..	0·0163	47 ..	0·0588	80 ..	0·1000	17 ..	2·1250
14 ..	0·0175	47½ ..	0·0594	81 ..	0·1013	18 ..	2·2500
15 ..	0·0188	48 ..	0·0600	82 ..	0·1025	19 ..	2·3750
16 ..	0·0200	49 ..	0·0613	82½ ..	0·1031	20 ..	2·5000
17 ..	0·0213	50 ..	0·0625	83 ..	0·1038	25 ..	3·1250
17½ ..	0·0219	51 ..	0·0638	84 ..	0·1050	30 ..	3·7500
18 ..	0·0225	52 ..	0·0650	85 ..	0·1063	35 ..	4·3750
19 ..	0·0238	52½ ..	0·0656	86 ..	0·1075	40 ..	5·0000
20 ..	0·0250	53 ..	0·0663	87 ..	0·1088	45 ..	5·6250
21 ..	0·0263	54 ..	0·0675	87½ ..	0·1094	50 ..	6·2500
22 ..	0·0275	55 ..	0·0688	88 ..	0·1100	55 ..	6·8750
22½ ..	0·0281	56 ..	0·0700	89 ..	0·1113	60 ..	7·5000
23 ..	0·0288	57 ..	0·0713	90 ..	0·1125	65 ..	8·1250
24 ..	0·0300	57½ ..	0·0719	91 ..	0·1138	70 ..	8·7500
25 ..	0·0313	58 ..	0·0725	92 ..	0·1150	75 ..	9·3750
26 ..	0·0325	59 ..	0·0738	92½ ..	0·1156	80 ..	10·0000
27 ..	0·0338	60 ..	0·0750	93 ..	0·1163	85 ..	10·6250
27½ ..	0·0344	61 ..	0·0763	94 ..	0·1175	90 ..	11·2500
28 ..	0·0350	62 ..	0·0775	95 ..	0·1188	95 ..	11·8750
29 ..	0·0363	62½ ..	0·0781	96 ..	0·1200	100 ..	12·5000
30 ..	0·0375	63 ..	0·0788	97 ..	0·1213	110 ..	13·7500
31 ..	0·0388	64 ..	0·0800	97½ ..	0·1219	120 ..	15·0000
32 ..	0·0400	65 ..	0·0813	98 ..	0·1225	130 ..	16·2500
32½ ..	0·0406	66 ..	0·0825	99 ..	0·1238	140 ..	17·5000

£	£	£	£	£	£	£	£
150 ..	18·7500	300 ..	37·5000	450 ..	56·2500	700 ..	87·5000
200 ..	25·0000	350 ..	43·7500	500 ..	62·5000	800 ..	100·0000
250 ..	31·2500	400 ..	50·0000	600 ..	75·0000	1000 ..	125·0000

p	£	p	£	p	£	£	£
½	0·0007	33	0·0429	67	0·0871	1	0·1300
1	0·0013	34	0·0442	67½	0·0878	2	0·2600
2	0·0026	35	0·0455	68	0·0884	3	0·3900
2½	0·0033	36	0·0468	69	0·0897	4	0·5200
3	0·0039	37	0·0481	70	0·0910	5	0·6500
4	0·0052	37½	0·0488	71	0·0923	6	0·7800
5	0·0065	38	0·0494	72	0·0936	7	0·9100
6	0·0078	39	0·0507	72½	0·0943	8	1·0400
7	0·0091	40	0·0520	73	0·0949	9	1·1700
7½	0·0098	41	0·0533	74	0·0962	10	1·3000
8	0·0104	42	0·0546	75	0·0975	11	1·4300
9	0·0117	42½	0·0553	76	0·0988	12	1·5600
10	0·0130	43	0·0559	77	0·1001	13	1·6900
11	0·0143	44	0·0572	77½	0·1008	14	1·8200
12	0·0156	45	0·0585	78	0·1014	15	1·9500
12½	0·0163	46	0·0598	79	0·1027	16	2·0800
13	0·0169	47	0·0611	80	0·1040	17	2·2100
14	0·0182	47½	0·0618	81	0·1053	18	2·3400
15	0·0195	48	0·0624	82	0·1066	19	2·4700
16	0·0208	49	0·0637	82½	0·1073	20	2·6000
17	0·0221	50	0·0650	83	0·1079	25	3·2500
17½	0·0228	51	0·0663	84	0·1092	30	3·9000
18	0·0234	52	0·0676	85	0·1105	35	4·5500
19	0·0247	52½	0·0683	86	0·1118	40	5·2000
20	0·0260	53	0·0689	87	0·1131	45	5·8500
21	0·0273	54	0·0702	87½	0·1138	50	6·5000
22	0·0286	55	0·0715	88	0·1144	55	7·1500
22½	0·0293	56	0·0728	89	0·1157	60	7·8000
23	0·0299	57	0·0741	90	0·1170	65	8·4500
24	0·0312	57½	0·0748	91	0·1183	70	9·1000
25	0·0325	58	0·0754	92	0·1196	75	9·7500
26	0·0338	59	0·0767	92½	0·1203	80	10·4000
27	0·0351	60	0·0780	93	0·1209	85	11·0500
27½	0·0358	61	0·0793	94	0·1222	90	11·7000
28	0·0364	62	0·0806	95	0·1235	95	12·3500
29	0·0377	62½	0·0813	96	0·1248	100	13·0000
30	0·0390	63	0·0819	97	0·1261	110	14·3000
31	0·0403	64	0·0832	97½	0·1268	120	15·6000
32	0·0416	65	0·0845	98	0·1274	130	16·9000
32½	0·0423	66	0·0858	99	0·1287	140	18·2000

£	£	£	£	£	£	£	£
150	19·5000	300	39·0000	450	58·5000	700	91·0000
200	26·0000	350	45·5000	500	65·0000	800	104·0000
250	32·5000	400	52·0000	600	78·0000	1000	130·0000

p	£	p	£	p	£	£	£
½	0·0008	33	0·0495	67	0·1005	1	0·1500
1	0·0015	34	0·0510	67½	0·1013	2	0·3000
2	0·0030	35	0·0525	68	0·1020	3	0·4500
2½	0·0038	36	0·0540	69	0·1035	4	0·6000
3	0·0045	37	0·0555	70	0·1050	5	0·7500
4	0·0060	37½	0·0563	71	0·1065	6	0·9000
5	0·0075	38	0·0570	72	0·1080	7	1·0500
6	0·0090	39	0·0585	72½	0·1088	8	1·2000
7	0·0105	40	0·0600	73	0·1095	9	1·3500
7½	0·0113	41	0·0615	74	0·1110	10	1·5000
8	0·0120	42	0·0630	75	0·1125	11	1·6500
9	0·0135	42½	0·0638	76	0·1140	12	1·8000
10	0·0150	43	0·0645	77	0·1155	13	1·9500
11	0·0165	44	0·0660	77½	0·1163	14	2·1000
12	0·0180	45	0·0675	78	0·1170	15	2·2500
12½	0·0188	46	0·0690	79	0·1185	16	2·4000
13	0·0195	47	0·0705	80	0·1200	17	2·5500
14	0·0210	47½	0·0713	81	0·1215	18	2·7000
15	0·0225	48	0·0720	82	0·1230	19	2·8500
16	0·0240	49	0·0735	82½	0·1238	20	3·0000
17	0·0255	50	0·0750	83	0·1245	25	3·7500
17½	0·0263	51	0·0765	84	0·1260	30	4·5000
18	0·0270	52	0·0780	85	0·1275	35	5·2500
19	0·0285	52½	0·0788	86	0·1290	40	6·0000
20	0·0300	53	0·0795	87	0·1305	45	6·7500
21	0·0315	54	0·0810	87½	0·1313	50	7·5000
22	0·0330	55	0·0825	88	0·1320	55	8·2500
22½	0·0338	56	0·0840	89	0·1335	60	9·0000
23	0·0345	57	0·0855	90	0·1350	65	9·7500
24	0·0360	57½	0·0863	91	0·1365	70	10·5000
25	0·0375	58	0·0870	92	0·1380	75	11·2500
26	0·0390	59	0·0885	92½	0·1388	80	12·0000
27	0·0405	60	0·0900	93	0·1395	85	12·7500
27½	0·0413	61	0·0915	94	0·1410	90	13·5000
28	0·0420	62	0·0930	95	0·1425	95	14·2500
29	0·0435	62½	0·0938	96	0·1440	100	15·0000
30	0·0450	63	0·0945	97	0·1455	110	16·5000
31	0·0465	64	0·0960	97½	0·1463	120	18·0000
32	0·0480	65	0·0975	98	0·1470	130	19·5000
32½	0·0488	66	0·0990	99	0·1485	140	21·0000

£	£	£	£	£	£	£	£
150	22·5000	300	45·0000	450	67·5000	700	105·0000
200	30·0000	350	52·5000	500	75·0000	800	120·0000
250	37·5000	400	60·0000	600	90·0000	1000	150·0000

p	£	p	£	p	£	£	£
½	0·0008	33	0·0550	67	0·1117	1	0·1667
1	0·0017	34	0·0567	67½	0·1125	2	0·3333
2	0·0033	35	0·0583	68	0·1133	3	0·5000
2½	0·0042	36	0·0600	69	0·1150	4	0·6667
3	0·0050	37	0·0617	70	0·1167	5	0·8333
4	0·0067	37½	0·0625	71	0·1183	6	1·0000
5	0·0083	38	0·0633	72	0·1200	7	1·1667
6	0·0100	39	0·0650	72½	0·1208	8	1·3333
7	0·0117	40	0·0667	73	0·1217	9	1·5000
7½	0·0125	41	0·0683	74	0·1233	10	1·6667
8	0·0133	42	0·0700	75	0·1250	11	1·8333
9	0·0150	42½	0·0708	76	0·1267	12	2·0000
10	0·0167	43	0·0717	77	0·1283	13	2·1667
11	0·0183	44	0·0733	77½	0·1292	14	2·3333
12	0·0200	45	0·0750	78	0·1300	15	2·5000
12½	0·0208	46	0·0767	79	0·1317	16	2·6667
13	0·0217	47	0·0783	80	0·1333	17	2·8333
14	0·0233	47½	0·0792	81	0·1350	18	3·0000
15	0·0250	48	0·0800	82	0·1367	19	3·1667
16	0·0267	49	0·0817	82½	0·1375	20	3·3333
17	0·0283	50	0·0833	83	0·1383	25	4·1667
17½	0·0292	51	0·0850	84	0·1400	30	5·0000
18	0·0300	52	0·0867	85	0·1417	35	5·8333
19	0·0317	52½	0·0875	86	0·1433	40	6·6667
20	0·0333	53	0·0883	87	0·1450	45	7·5000
21	0·0350	54	0·0900	87½	0·1458	50	8·3333
22	0·0367	55	0·0917	88	0·1467	55	9·1667
22½	0·0375	56	0·0933	89	0·1483	60	10·0000
23	0·0383	57	0·0950	90	0·1500	65	10·8333
24	0·0400	57½	0·0958	91	0·1517	70	11·6667
25	0·0417	58	0·0967	92	0·1533	75	12·5000
26	0·0433	59	0·0983	92½	0·1542	80	13·3333
27	0·0450	60	0·1000	93	0·1550	85	14·1667
27½	0·0458	61	0·1017	94	0·1567	90	15·0000
28	0·0467	62	0·1033	95	0·1583	95	15·8333
29	0·0483	62½	0·1042	96	0·1600	100	16·6667
30	0·0500	63	0·1050	97	0·1617	110	18·3333
31	0·0517	64	0·1067	97½	0·1625	120	20·0000
32	0·0533	65	0·1083	98	0·1633	130	21·6667
32½	0·0542	66	0·1100	99	0·1650	140	23·3333

£	£	£	£	£	£	£	£
150	25·0000	300	50·0000	450	75·0000	700	116·6667
200	33·3333	350	58·3333	500	83·3333	800	133·3333
250	41·6667	400	66·6667	600	100·0000	1000	166·6667

17½   Per Cent   17½

p	£	p	£	p	£	£	£
½	0·0009	33	0·0578	67	0·1173	1	0·1750
1	0·0018	34	0·0595	67½	0·1181	2	0·3500
2	0·0035	35	0·0613	68	0·1190	3	0·5250
2½	0·0044	36	0·0630	69	0·1208	4	0·7000
3	0·0053	37	0·0648	70	0·1225	5	0·8750
4	0·0070	37½	0·0656	71	0·1243	6	1·0500
5	0·0088	38	0·0665	72	0·1260	7	1·2250
6	0·0105	39	0·0683	72½	0·1269	8	1·4000
7	0·0123	40	0·0700	73	0·1278	9	1·5750
7½	0·0131	41	0·0718	74	0·1295	10	1·7500
8	0·0140	42	0·0735	75	0·1313	11	1·9250
9	0·0158	42½	0·0744	76	0·1330	12	2·1000
10	0·0175	43	0·0753	77	0·1348	13	2·2750
11	0·0193	44	0·0770	77½	0·1356	14	2·4500
12	0·0210	45	0·0788	78	0·1365	15	2·6250
12½	0·0219	46	0·0805	79	0·1383	16	2·8000
13	0·0228	47	0·0823	80	0·1400	17	2·9750
14	0·0245	47½	0·0831	81	0·1418	18	3·1500
15	0·0263	48	0·0840	82	0·1435	19	3·3250
16	0·0280	49	0·0858	82½	0·1444	20	3·5000
17	0·0298	50	0·0875	83	0·1453	25	4·3750
17½	0·0306	51	0·0893	84	0·1470	30	5·2500
18	0·0315	52	0·0910	85	0·1488	35	6·1250
19	0·0333	52½	0·0919	86	0·1505	40	7·0000
20	0·0350	53	0·0928	87	0·1523	45	7·8750
21	0·0368	54	0·0945	87½	0·1531	50	8·7500
22	0·0385	55	0·0963	88	0·1540	55	9·6250
22½	0·0394	56	0·0980	89	0·1558	60	10·5000
23	0·0403	57	0·0998	90	0·1575	65	11·3750
24	0·0420	57½	0·1006	91	0·1593	70	12·2500
25	0·0438	58	0·1015	92	0·1610	75	13·1250
26	0·0455	59	0·1033	92½	0·1619	80	14·0000
27	0·0473	60	0·1050	93	0·1628	85	14·8750
27½	0·0481	61	0·1068	94	0·1645	90	15·7500
28	0·0490	62	0·1085	95	0·1663	95	16·6250
29	0·0508	62½	0·1094	96	0·1680	100	17·5000
30	0·0525	63	0·1103	97	0·1698	110	19·2500
31	0·0543	64	0·1120	97½	0·1706	120	21·0000
32	0·0560	65	0·1138	98	0·1715	130	22·7500
32½	0·0569	66	0·1155	99	0·1733	140	24·5000

£	£	£	£	£	£	£	£
150	26·2500	300	52·5000	450	78·7500	700	122·5000
200	35·0000	350	61·2500	500	87·5000	800	140·0000
250	43·7500	400	70·0000	600	105·0000	1000	175·0000

p	£	p	£	p	£	£	£
½ ..	0·0010	33 ..	0·0660	67 ..	0·1340	1 ..	0·2000
1 ..	0·0020	34 ..	0·0680	67½ ..	0·1350	2 ..	0·4000
2 ..	0·0040	35 ..	0·0700	68 ..	0·1360	3 ..	0·6000
2½ ..	0·0050	36 ..	0·0720	69 ..	0·1380	4 ..	0·8000
3 ..	0·0060	37 ..	0·0740	70 ..	0·1400	5 ..	1·0000
4 ..	0·0080	37½ ..	0·0750	71 ..	0·1420	6 ..	1·2000
5 ..	0·0100	38 ..	0·0760	72 ..	0·1440	7 ..	1·4000
6 ..	0·0120	39 ..	0·0780	72½ ..	0·1450	8 ..	1·6000
7 ..	0·0140	40 ..	0·0800	73 ..	0·1460	9 ..	1·8000
7½ ..	0·0150	41 ..	0·0820	74 ..	0·1480	10 ..	2·0000
8 ..	0·0160	42 ..	0·0840	75 ..	0·1500	11 ..	2·2000
9 ..	0·0180	42½ ..	0·0850	76 ..	0·1520	12 ..	2·4000
10 ..	0·0200	43 ..	0·0860	77 ..	0·1540	13 ..	2·6000
11 ..	0·0220	44 ..	0·0880	77½ ..	0·1550	14 ..	2·8000
12 ..	0·0240	45 ..	0·0900	78 ..	0·1560	15 ..	3·0000
12½ ..	0·0250	46 ..	0·0920	79 ..	0·1580	16 ..	3·2000
13 ..	0·0260	47 ..	0·0940	80 ..	0·1600	17 ..	3·4000
14 ..	0·0280	47½ ..	0·0950	81 ..	0·1620	18 ..	3·6000
15 ..	0·0300	48 ..	0·0960	82 ..	0·1640	19 ..	3·8000
16 ..	0·0320	49 ..	0·0980	82½ ..	0·1650	20 ..	4·0000
17 ..	0·0340	50 ..	0·1000	83 ..	0·1660	25 ..	5·0000
17½ ..	0·0350	51 ..	0·1020	84 ..	0·1680	30 ..	6·0000
18 ..	0·0360	52 ..	0·1040	85 ..	0·1700	35 ..	7·0000
19 ..	0·0380	52½ ..	0·1050	86 ..	0·1720	40 ..	8·0000
20 ..	0·0400	53 ..	0·1060	87 ..	0·1740	45 ..	9·0000
21 ..	0·0420	54 ..	0·1080	87½ ..	0·1750	50 ..	10·0000
22 ..	0·0440	55 ..	0·1100	88 ..	0·1760	55 ..	11·0000
22½ ..	0·0450	56 ..	0·1120	89 ..	0·1780	60 ..	12·0000
23 ..	0·0460	57 ..	0·1140	90 ..	0·1800	65 ..	13·0000
24 ..	0·0480	57½ ..	0·1150	91 ..	0·1820	70 ..	14·0000
25 ..	0·0500	58 ..	0·1160	92 ..	0·1840	75 ..	15·0000
26 ..	0·0520	59 ..	0·1180	92½ ..	0·1850	80 ..	16·0000
27 ..	0·0540	60 ..	0·1200	93 ..	0·1860	85 ..	17·0000
27½ ..	0·0550	61 ..	0·1220	94 ..	0·1880	90 ..	18·0000
28 ..	0·0560	62 ..	0·1240	95 ..	0·1900	95 ..	19·0000
29 ..	0·0580	62½ ..	0·1250	96 ..	0·1920	100 ..	20·0000
30 ..	0·0600	63 ..	0·1260	97 ..	0·1940	110 ..	22·0000
31 ..	0·0620	64 ..	0·1280	97½ ..	0·1950	120 ..	24·0000
32 ..	0·0640	65 ..	0·1300	98 ..	0·1960	130 ..	26·0000
32½ ..	0·0650	66 ..	0·1320	99 ..	0·1980	140 ..	28·0000

£	£	£	£	£	£	£	£
150 ..	30·0000	300 ..	60·0000	450 ..	90·0000	700 ..	140·0000
200 ..	40·0000	350 ..	70·0000	500 ..	100·0000	800 ..	160·0000
250 ..	50·0000	400 ..	80·0000	600 ..	120·0000	1000 ..	200·0000

p	£	p	£	p	£	£	£
½ ..	0·0011	33 ..	0·0726	67 ..	0·1474	1 ..	0·2200
1 ..	0·0022	34 ..	0·0748	67½ ..	0·1485	2 ..	0·4400
2 ..	0·0044	35 ..	0·0770	68 ..	0·1496	3 ..	0·6600
2½ ..	0·0055	36 ..	0·0792	69 ..	0·1518	4 ..	0·8800
3 ..	0·0066	37 ..	0·0814	70 ..	0·1540	5 ..	1·1000
4 ..	0·0088	37½ ..	0·0825	71 ..	0·1562	6 ..	1·3200
5 ..	0·0110	38 ..	0·0836	72 ..	0·1584	7 ..	1·5400
6 ..	0·0132	39 ..	0·0858	72½ ..	0·1595	8 ..	1·7600
7 ..	0·0154	40 ..	0·0880	73 ..	0·1606	9 ..	1·9800
7½ ..	0·0165	41 ..	0·0902	74 ..	0·1628	10 ..	2·2000
8 ..	0·0176	42 ..	0·0924	75 ..	0·1650	11 ..	2·4200
9 ..	0·0198	42½ ..	0·0935	76 ..	0·1672	12 ..	2·6400
10 ..	0·0220	43 ..	0·0946	77 ..	0·1694	13 ..	2·8600
11 ..	0·0242	44 ..	0·0968	77½ ..	0·1705	14 ..	3·0800
12 ..	0·0264	45 ..	0·0990	78 ..	0·1716	15 ..	3·3000
12½ ..	0·0275	46 ..	0·1012	79 ..	0·1738	16 ..	3·5200
13 ..	0·0286	47 ..	0·1034	80 ..	0·1760	17 ..	3·7400
14 ..	0·0308	47½ ..	0·1045	81 ..	0·1782	18 ..	3·9600
15 ..	0·0330	48 ..	0·1056	82 ..	0·1804	19 ..	4·1800
16 ..	0·0352	49 ..	0·1078	82½ ..	0·1815	20 ..	4·4000
17 ..	0·0374	50 ..	0·1100	83 ..	0·1826	25 ..	5·5000
17½ ..	0·0385	51 ..	0·1122	84 ..	0·1848	30 ..	6·6000
18 ..	0·0396	52 ..	0·1144	85 ..	0·1870	35 ..	7·7000
19 ..	0·0418	52½ ..	0·1155	86 ..	0·1892	40 ..	8·8000
20 ..	0·0440	53 ..	0·1166	87 ..	0·1914	45 ..	9·9000
21 ..	0·0462	54 ..	0·1188	87½ ..	0·1925	50 ..	11·0000
22 ..	0·0484	55 ..	0·1210	88 ..	0·1936	55 ..	12·1000
22½ ..	0·0495	56 ..	0·1232	89 ..	0·1958	60 ..	13·2000
23 ..	0·0506	57 ..	0·1254	90 ..	0·1980	65 ..	14·3000
24 ..	0·0528	57½ ..	0·1265	91 ..	0·2002	70 ..	15·4000
25 ..	0·0550	58 ..	0·1276	92 ..	0·2024	75 ..	16·5000
26 ..	0·0572	59 ..	0·1298	92½ ..	0·2035	80 ..	17·6000
27 ..	0·0594	60 ..	0·1320	93 ..	0·2046	85 ..	18·7000
27½ ..	0·0605	61 ..	0·1342	94 ..	0·2068	90 ..	19·8000
28 ..	0·0616	62 ..	0·1364	95 ..	0·2090	95 ..	20·9000
29 ..	0·0638	62½ ..	0·1375	96 ..	0·2112	100 ..	22·0000
30 ..	0·0660	63 ..	0·1386	97 ..	0·2134	110 ..	24·2000
31 ..	0·0682	64 ..	0·1408	97½ ..	0·2145	120 ..	26·4000
32 ..	0·0704	65 ..	0·1430	98 ..	0·2156	130 ..	28·6000
32½ ..	0·0715	66 ..	0·1452	99 ..	0·2178	140 ..	30·8000

£	£	£	£	£	£	£	£
150 ..	33·0000	300 ..	66·0000	450..	99·0000	700 ..	154·0000
200 ..	44·0000	350 ..	77·0000	500..	110·0000	800 ..	176·0000
250 ..	55·0000	400 ..	88·0000	600..	132·0000	1000 ..	220·0000

p		£	p		£	p		£	£		£
½	..	0·0011	33	..	0·0743	67	..	0·1508	1	..	0·2250
1	..	0·0023	34	..	0·0765	67½	..	0·1519	2	..	0·4500
2	..	0·0045	35	..	0·0788	68	..	0·1530	3	..	0·6750
2½	..	0·0056	36	..	0·0810	69	..	0·1553	4	..	0·9000
3	..	0·0068	37	..	0·0833	70	..	0·1575	5	..	1·1250
4	..	0·0090	37½	..	0·0844	71	..	0·1598	6	..	1·3500
5	..	0·0113	38	..	0·0855	72	..	0·1620	7	..	1·5750
6	..	0·0135	39	..	0·0878	72½	..	0·1631	8	..	1·8000
7	..	0·0158	40	..	0·0900	73	..	0·1643	9	..	2·0250
7½	..	0·0169	41	..	0·0923	74	..	0·1665	10	..	2·2500
8	..	0·0180	42	..	0·0945	75	..	0·1688	11	..	2·4750
9	..	0·0203	42½	..	0·0956	76	..	0·1710	12	..	2·7000
10	..	0·0225	43	..	0·0968	77	..	0·1733	13	..	2·9250
11	..	0·0248	44	..	0·0990	77½	..	0·1744	14	..	3·1500
12	..	0·0270	45	..	0·1013	78	..	0·1755	15	..	3·3750
12½	..	0·0281	46	..	0·1035	79	..	0·1778	16	..	3·6000
13	..	0·0293	47	..	0·1058	80	..	0·1800	17	..	3·8250
14	..	0·0315	47½	..	0·1069	81	..	0·1823	18	..	4·0500
15	..	0·0338	48	..	0·1080	82	..	0·1845	19	..	4·2750
16	..	0·0360	49	..	0·1103	82½	..	0·1856	20	..	4·5000
17	..	0·0383	50	..	0·1125	83	..	0·1868	25	..	5·6250
17½	..	0·0394	51	..	0·1148	84	..	0·1890	30	..	6·7500
18	..	0·0405	52	..	0·1170	85	..	0·1913	35	..	7·8750
19	..	0·0428	52½	..	0·1181	86	..	0·1935	40	..	9·0000
20	..	0·0450	53	..	0·1193	87	..	0·1958	45	..	10·1250
21	..	0·0473	54	..	0·1215	87½	..	0·1969	50	..	11·2500
22	..	0·0495	55	..	0·1238	88	..	0·1980	55	..	12·3750
22½	..	0·0506	56	..	0·1260	89	..	0·2003	60	..	13·5000
23	..	0·0518	57	..	0·1283	90	..	0·2025	65	..	14·6250
24	..	0·0540	57½	..	0·1294	91	..	0·2048	70	..	15·7500
25	..	0·0563	58	..	0·1305	92	..	0·2070	75	..	16·8750
26	..	0·0585	59	..	0·1328	92½	..	0·2081	80	..	18·0000
27	..	0·0608	60	..	0·1350	93	..	0·2093	85	..	19·1250
27½	..	0·0619	61	..	0·1373	94	..	0·2115	90	..	20·2500
28	..	0·0630	62	..	0·1395	95	..	0·2138	95	..	21·3750
29	..	0·0653	62½	..	0·1406	96	..	0·2160	100	..	22·5000
30	..	0·0675	63	..	0·1418	97	..	0·2183	110	..	24·7500
31	..	0·0698	64	..	0·1440	97½	..	0·2194	120	..	27·0000
32	..	0·0720	65	..	0·1463	98	..	0·2205	130	..	29·2500
32½	..	0·0731	66	..	0·1485	99	..	0·2228	140	..	31·5000

£		£	£		£	£		£	£		£
150	..	33·7500	300	..	67·5000	450	..	101·2500	700	..	157·5000
200	..	45·0000	350	..	78·7500	500	..	112·5000	800	..	180·0000
250	..	56·2500	400	..	90·0000	600	..	135·0000	1000	..	225·0000

p	£	p	£	p	£	£	£
½ ..	0·0012	33 ..	0·0792	67 ..	0·1608	1 ..	0·2400
1 ..	0·0024	34 ..	0·0816	67½ ..	0·1620	2 ..	0·4800
2 ..	0·0048	35 ..	0·0840	68 ..	0·1632	3 ..	0·7200
2½ ..	0·0060	36 ..	0·0864	69 ..	0·1656	4 ..	0·9600
3 ..	0·0072	37 ..	0·0888	70 ..	0·1680	5 ..	1·2000
4 ..	0·0096	37½ ..	0·0900	71 ..	0·1704	6 ..	1·4400
5 ..	0·0120	38 ..	0·0912	72 ..	0·1728	7 ..	1·6800
6 ..	0·0144	39 ..	0·0936	72½ ..	0·1740	8 ..	1·9200
7 ..	0·0168	40 ..	0·0960	73 ..	0·1752	9 ..	2·1600
7½ ..	0·0180	41 ..	0·0984	74 ..	0·1776	10 ..	2·4000
8 ..	0·0192	42 ..	0·1008	75 ..	0·1800	11 ..	2·6400
9 ..	0·0216	42½ ..	0·1020	76 ..	0·1824	12 ..	2·8800
10 ..	0·0240	43 ..	0·1032	77 ..	0·1848	13 ..	3·1200
11 ..	0·0264	44 ..	0·1056	77½ ..	0·1860	14 ..	3·3600
12 ..	0·0288	45 ..	0·1080	78 ..	0·1872	15 ..	3·6000
12½ ..	0·0300	46 ..	0·1104	79 ..	0·1896	16 ..	3·8400
13 ..	0·0312	47 ..	0·1128	80 ..	0·1920	17 ..	4·0800
14 ..	0·0336	47½ ..	0·1140	81 ..	0·1944	18 ..	4·3200
15 ..	0·0360	48 ..	0·1152	82 ..	0·1968	19 ..	4·5600
16 ..	0·0384	49 ..	0·1176	82½ ..	0·1980	20 ..	4·8000
17 ..	0·0408	50 ..	0·1200	83 ..	0·1992	25 ..	6·0000
17½ ..	0·0420	51 ..	0·1224	84 ..	0·2016	30 ..	7·2000
18 ..	0·0432	52 ..	0·1248	85 ..	0·2040	35 ..	8·4000
19 ..	0·0456	52½ ..	0·1260	86 ..	0·2064	40 ..	9·6000
20 ..	0·0480	53 ..	0·1272	87 ..	0·2088	45 ..	10·8000
21 ..	0·0504	54 ..	0·1296	87½ ..	0·2100	50 ..	12·0000
22 ..	0·0528	55 ..	0·1320	88 ..	0·2112	55 ..	13·2000
22½ ..	0·0540	56 ..	0·1344	89 ..	0·2136	60 ..	14·4000
23 ..	0·0552	57 ..	0·1368	90 ..	0·2160	65 ..	15·6000
24 ..	0·0576	57½ ..	0·1380	91 ..	0·2184	70 ..	16·8000
25 ..	0·0600	58 ..	0·1392	92 ..	0·2208	75 ..	18·0000
26 ..	0·0624	59 ..	0·1416	92½ ..	0·2220	80 ..	19·2000
27 ..	0·0648	60 ..	0·1440	93 ..	0·2232	85 ..	20·4000
27½ ..	0·0660	61 ..	0·1464	94 ..	0·2256	90 ..	21·6000
28 ..	0·0672	62 ..	0·1488	95 ..	0·2280	95 ..	22·8000
29 ..	0·0696	62½ ..	0·1500	96 ..	0·2304	100 ..	24·0000
30 ..	0·0720	63 ..	0·1512	97 ..	0·2328	110 ..	26·4000
31 ..	0·0744	64 ..	0·1536	97½ ..	0·2340	120 ..	28·8000
32 ..	0·0768	65 ..	0·1560	98 ..	0·2352	130 ..	31·2000
32½ ..	0·0780	66 ..	0·1584	99 ..	0·2376	140 ..	33·6000

£	£	£	£	£	£	£	£
150 ..	36·0000	300 ..	72·0000	450 ..	108·0000	700 ..	168·0000
200 ..	48·0000	350 ..	84·0000	500 ..	120·0000	800 ..	192·0000
250 ..	60·0000	400 ..	96·0000	600 ..	144·0000	1000 ..	240·0000

p	£	p	£	p	£	£	£
½	0·0013	33	0·0825	67	0·1675	1	0·2500
1	0·0025	34	0·0850	67½	0·1688	2	0·5000
2	0·0050	35	0·0875	68	0·1700	3	0·7500
2½	0·0063	36	0·0900	69	0·1725	4	1·0000
3	0·0075	37	0·0925	70	0·1750	5	1·2500
4	0·0100	37½	0·0938	71	0·1775	6	1·5000
5	0·0125	38	0·0950	72	0·1800	7	1·7500
6	0·0150	39	0·0975	72½	0·1813	8	2·0000
7	0·0175	40	0·1000	73	0·1825	9	2·2500
7½	0·0188	41	0·1025	74	0·1850	10	2·5000
8	0·0200	42	0·1050	75	0·1875	11	2·7500
9	0·0225	42½	0·1063	76	0·1900	12	3·0000
10	0·0250	43	0·1075	77	0·1925	13	3·2500
11	0·0275	44	0·1100	77½	0·1938	14	3·5000
12	0·0300	45	0·1125	78	0·1950	15	3·7500
12½	0·0313	46	0·1150	79	0·1975	16	4·0000
13	0·0325	47	0·1175	80	0·2000	17	4·2500
14	0·0350	47½	0·1188	81	0·2025	18	4·5000
15	0·0375	48	0·1200	82	0·2050	19	4·7500
16	0·0400	49	0·1225	82½	0·2063	20	5·0000
17	0·0425	50	0·1250	83	0·2075	25	6·2500
17½	0·0438	51	0·1275	84	0·2100	30	7·5000
18	0·0450	52	0·1300	85	0·2125	35	8·7500
19	0·0475	52½	0·1313	86	0·2150	40	10·0000
20	0·0500	53	0·1325	87	0·2175	45	11·2500
21	0·0525	54	0·1350	87½	0·2188	50	12·5000
22	0·0550	55	0·1375	88	0·2200	55	13·7500
22½	0·0563	56	0·1400	89	0·2225	60	15·0000
23	0·0575	57	0·1425	90	0·2250	65	16·2500
24	0·0600	57½	0·1438	91	0·2275	70	17·5000
25	0·0625	58	0·1450	92	0·2300	75	18·7500
26	0·0650	59	0·1475	92½	0·2313	80	20·0000
27	0·0675	60	0·1500	93	0·2325	85	21·2500
27½	0·0688	61	0·1525	94	0·2350	90	22·5000
28	0·0700	62	0·1550	95	0·2375	95	23·7500
29	0·0725	62½	0·1563	96	0·2400	100	25·0000
30	0·0750	63	0·1575	97	0·2425	110	27·5000
31	0·0775	64	0·1600	97½	0·2438	120	30·0000
32	0·0800	65	0·1625	98	0·2450	130	32·5000
32½	0·0813	66	0·1650	99	0·2475	140	35·0000

£	£	£	£	£	£	£	£
150	37·5000	300	75·0000	450	112·5000	700	175·0000
200	50·0000	350	87·5000	500	125·0000	800	200·0000
250	62·5000	400	100·0000	600	150·0000	1000	250·0000

p	£	p	£	p	£	£	£
½	0·0013	33	0·0842	67	0·1709	1	0·2550
1	0·0026	34	0·0867	67½	0·1721	2	0·5100
2	0·0051	35	0·0893	68	0·1734	3	0·7650
2½	0·0064	36	0·0918	69	0·1760	4	1·0200
3	0·0077	37	0·0944	70	0·1785	5	1·2750
4	0·0102	37½	0·0956	71	0·1811	6	1·5300
5	0·0128	38	0·0969	72	0·1836	7	1·7850
6	0·0153	39	0·0995	72½	0·1849	8	2·0400
7	0·0179	40	0·1020	73	0·1862	9	2·2950
7½	0·0190	41	0·1046	74	0·1887	10	2·5500
8	0·0204	42	0·1071	75	0·1913	11	2·8050
9	0·0230	42½	0·1084	76	0·1938	12	3·0600
10	0·0256	43	0·1097	77	0·1964	13	3·3150
11	0·0280	44	0·1122	77½	0·1976	14	3·5700
12	0·0306	45	0·1148	78	0·1989	15	3·8250
12½	0·0319	46	0·1173	79	0·2015	16	4·0800
13	0·0332	47	0·1199	80	0·2040	17	4·3350
14	0·0357	47½	0·1211	81	0·2066	18	4·5900
15	0·0383	48	0·1224	82	0·2091	19	4·8450
16	0·0408	49	0·1250	82½	0·2104	20	5·1000
17	0·0433	50	0·1275	83	0·2117	25	6·3750
17½	0·0446	51	0·1301	84	0·2142	30	7·6500
18	0·0459	52	0·1326	85	0·2168	35	8·9250
19	0·0485	52½	0·1339	86	0·2193	40	10·2000
20	0·0510	53	0·1352	87	0·2219	45	11·4750
21	0·0536	54	0·1377	87½	0·2231	50	12·7500
22	0·0561	55	0·1403	88	0·2244	55	14·0250
22½	0·0574	56	0·1428	89	0·2270	60	15·3000
23	0·0587	57	0·1454	90	0·2295	65	16·5750
24	0·0612	57½	0·1466	91	0·2321	70	17·8500
25	0·0640	58	0·1479	92	0·2346	75	19·1250
26	0·0663	59	0·1505	92½	0·2359	80	20·4000
27	0·0689	60	0·1530	93	0·2372	85	21·6750
27½	0·0701	61	0·1556	94	0·2397	90	22·9500
28	0·0714	62	0·1581	95	0·2423	95	24·2250
29	0·0740	62½	0·1594	96	0·2448	100	25·5000
30	0·0765	63	0·1607	97	0·2474	110	28·0500
31	0·0791	64	0·1632	97½	0·2486	120	30·6000
32	0·0816	65	0·1658	98	0·2499	130	33·1500
32½	0·0829	66	0·1683	99	0·2525	140	35·7000

£	£	£	£	£	£	£	£
150	38·2500	300	76·5000	450	114·7500	700	178·5000
200	51·0000	350	89·2500	500	127·5000	800	204·0000
250	63·7500	400	102·0000	600	153·0000	1000	255·0000

p	£	p	£	p	£	£	£
¼	0·0013	33	0·0858	67	0·1742	1	0·2600
1	0·0026	34	0·0884	67½	0·1755	2	0·5200
2	0·0052	35	0·0910	68	0·1768	3	0·7800
2½	0·0065	36	0·0936	69	0·1794	4	1·0400
3	0·0078	37	0·0962	70	0·1820	5	1·3000
4	0·0104	37½	0·0975	71	0·1846	6	1·5600
5	0·0130	38	0·0988	72	0·1872	7	1·8200
6	0·0156	39	0·1014	72½	0·1885	8	2·0800
7	0·0182	40	0·1040	73	0·1898	9	2·3400
7½	0·0195	41	0·1066	74	0·1924	10	2·6000
8	0·0208	42	0·1092	75	0·1950	11	2·8600
9	0·0234	42½	0·1105	76	0·1976	12	3·1200
10	0·0260	43	0·1118	77	0·2002	13	3·3800
11	0·0286	44	0·1144	77½	0·2015	14	3·6400
12	0·0312	45	0·1170	78	0·2028	15	3·9000
12½	0·0325	46	0·1196	79	0·2054	16	4·1600
13	0·0338	47	0·1222	80	0·2080	17	4·4200
14	0·0364	47½	0·1235	81	0·2106	18	4·6800
15	0·0390	48	0·1248	82	0·2132	19	4·9400
16	0·0416	49	0·1274	82½	0·2145	20	5·2000
17	0·0442	50	0·1300	83	0·2158	25	6·5000
17½	0·0455	51	0·1326	84	0·2184	30	7·8000
18	0·0468	52	0·1352	85	0·2210	35	9·1000
19	0·0494	52½	0·1365	86	0·2236	40	10·4000
20	0·0520	53	0·1378	87	0·2262	45	11·7000
21	0·0546	54	0·1404	87½	0·2275	50	13·0000
22	0·0572	55	0·1430	88	0·2288	55	14·3000
22½	0·0585	56	0·1456	89	0·2314	60	15·6000
23	0·0598	57	0·1482	90	0·2340	65	16·9000
24	0·0624	57½	0·1495	91	0·2366	70	18·2000
25	0·0650	58	0·1508	92	0·2392	75	19·5000
26	0·0676	59	0·1534	92½	0·2405	80	20·8000
27	0·0702	60	0·1560	93	0·2418	85	22·1000
27½	0·0715	61	0·1586	94	0·2444	90	23·4000
28	0·0728	62	0·1612	95	0·2470	95	24·7000
29	0·0754	62½	0·1625	96	0·2496	100	26·0000
30	0·0780	63	0·1638	97	0·2522	110	28·6000
31	0·0806	64	0·1664	97½	0·2535	120	31·2000
32	0·0832	65	0·1690	98	0·2548	130	33·8000
32½	0·0845	66	0·1716	99	0·2574	140	36·4000

£	£	£	£	£	£	£	£
150	39·0000	300	78·0000	450	117·0000	700	182·0000
200	52·0000	350	91·0000	500	130·0000	800	208·0000
250	65·0000	400	104·0000	600	156·0000	1000	260·0000

p	£	p	£	p	£	£	£
$\frac{1}{2}$	0·0014	33	0·0891	67	0·1809	1	0·2700
1	0·0027	34	0·0918	$67\frac{1}{2}$	0·1823	2	0·5400
2	0·0054	35	0·0945	68	0·1836	3	0·8100
$2\frac{1}{2}$	0·0068	36	0·0972	69	0·1863	4	1·0800
3	0·0081	37	0·0999	70	0·1890	5	1·3500
4	0·0108	$37\frac{1}{2}$	0·1013	71	0·1917	6	1·6200
5	0·0135	38	0·1026	72	0·1944	7	1·8900
6	0·0162	39	0·1053	$72\frac{1}{2}$	0·1958	8	2·1600
7	0·0189	40	0·1080	73	0·1971	9	2·4300
$7\frac{1}{2}$	0·0203	41	0·1107	74	0·1998	10	2·7000
8	0·0216	42	0·1134	75	0·2025	11	2·9700
9	0·0243	$42\frac{1}{2}$	0·1148	76	0·2052	12	3·2400
10	0·0270	43	0·1161	77	0·2079	13	3·5100
11	0·0297	44	0·1188	$77\frac{1}{2}$	0·2093	14	3·7800
12	0·0324	45	0·1215	78	0·2106	15	4·0500
$12\frac{1}{2}$	0·0338	46	0·1242	79	0·2133	16	4·3200
13	0·0351	47	0·1269	80	0·2160	17	4·5900
14	0·0378	$47\frac{1}{2}$	0·1283	81	0·2187	18	4·8600
15	0·0405	48	0·1296	82	0·2214	19	5·1300
16	0·0432	49	0·1323	$82\frac{1}{2}$	0·2228	20	5·4000
17	0·0459	50	0·1350	83	0·2241	25	6·7500
$17\frac{1}{2}$	0·0473	51	0·1377	84	0·2268	30	8·1000
18	0·0486	52	0·1404	85	0·2295	35	9·4500
19	0·0513	$52\frac{1}{2}$	0·1418	86	0·2322	40	10·8000
20	0·0540	53	0·1431	87	0·2349	45	12·1500
21	0·0567	54	0·1458	$87\frac{1}{2}$	0·2363	50	13·5000
22	0·0594	55	0·1485	88	0·2376	55	14·8500
$22\frac{1}{2}$	0·0608	56	0·1512	89	0·2403	60	16·2000
23	0·0621	57	0·1539	90	0·2430	65	17·5500
24	0·0648	$57\frac{1}{2}$	0·1553	91	0·2457	70	18·9000
25	0·0675	58	0·1566	92	0·2484	75	20·2500
26	0·0702	59	0·1593	$92\frac{1}{2}$	0·2498	80	21·6000
27	0·0729	60	0·1620	93	0·2511	85	22·9500
$27\frac{1}{2}$	0·0743	61	0·1647	94	0·2538	90	24·3000
28	0·0756	62	0·1674	95	0·2565	95	25·6500
29	0·0783	$62\frac{1}{2}$	0·1688	96	0·2592	100	27·0000
30	0·0810	63	0·1701	97	0·2619	110	29·7000
31	0·0837	64	0·1728	$97\frac{1}{2}$	0·2633	120	32·4000
32	0·0864	65	0·1755	98	0·2646	130	35·1000
$32\frac{1}{2}$	0·0878	66	0·1782	99	0·2673	140	37·8000

£	£	£	£	£	£	£	£
150	40·5000	300	81·0000	450	121·5000	700	189·0000
200	54·0000	350	94·5000	500	135·0000	800	216·0000
250	67·5000	400	108·0000	600	162·0000	1000	270·0000

p	£	p	£	p	£	£	£
½	0·0014	33	0·0908	67	0·1843	1	0·2750
1	0·0028	34	0·0935	67½	0·1856	2	0·5500
2	0·0055	35	0·0963	68	0·1870	3	0·8250
2½	0·0069	36	0·0990	69	0·1898	4	1·1000
3	0·0083	37	0·1018	70	0·1925	5	1·3750
4	0·0110	37½	0·1031	71	0·1953	6	1·6500
5	0·0138	38	0·1045	72	0·1980	7	1·9250
6	0·0165	39	0·1073	72½	0·1994	8	2·2000
7	0·0193	40	0·1100	73	0·2008	9	2·4750
7½	0·0206	41	0·1128	74	0·2035	10	2·7500
8	0·0220	42	0·1155	75	0·2063	11	3·0250
9	0·0248	42½	0·1169	76	0·2090	12	3·3000
10	0·0275	43	0·1183	77	0·2118	13	3·5750
11	0·0303	44	0·1210	77½	0·2131	14	3·8500
12	0·0330	45	0·1238	78	0·2145	15	4·1250
12½	0·0344	46	0·1265	79	0·2173	16	4·4000
13	0·0358	47	0·1293	80	0·2200	17	4·6750
14	0·0385	47½	0·1306	81	0·2228	18	4·9500
15	0·0413	48	0·1320	82	0·2255	19	5·2250
16	0·0440	49	0·1348	82½	0·2269	20	5·5000
17	0·0468	50	0·1375	83	0·2283	25	6·8750
17½	0·0481	51	0·1403	84	0·2310	30	8·2500
18	0·0495	52	0·1430	85	0·2338	35	9·6250
19	0·0523	52½	0·1444	86	0·2365	40	11·0000
20	0·0550	53	0·1458	87	0·2393	45	12·3750
21	0·0578	54	0·1485	87½	0·2406	50	13·7500
22	0·0605	55	0·1513	88	0·2420	55	15·1250
22½	0·0619	56	0·1540	89	0·2448	60	16·5000
23	0·0633	57	0·1568	90	0·2475	65	17·8750
24	0·0660	57½	0·1581	91	0·2503	70	19·2500
25	0·0688	58	0·1595	92	0·2530	75	20·6250
26	0·0715	59	0·1623	92½	0·2544	80	22·0000
27	0·0743	60	0·1650	93	0·2558	85	23·3750
27½	0·0756	61	0·1678	94	0·2585	90	24·7500
28	0·0770	62	0·1705	95	0·2613	95	26·1250
29	0·0798	62½	0·1719	96	0·2640	100	27·5000
30	0·0825	63	0·1733	97	0·2668	110	30·2500
31	0·0853	64	0·1760	97½	0·2681	120	33·0000
32	0·0880	65	0·1788	98	0·2695	130	35·7500
32½	0·0894	66	0·1815	99	0·2723	140	38·5000

£	£	£	£	£	£	£	£
150	41·2500	300	82·5000	450	123·7500	700	192·5000
200	55·0000	350	96·2500	500	137·5000	800	220·0000
250	68·7500	400	110·0000	600	165·0000	1000	275·0000

p	£	p	£	p	£	£	£
½	0·0014	33	0·0924	67	0·1876	1	0·2800
1	0·0028	34	0·0952	67½	0·1890	2	0·5600
2	0·0056	35	0·0980	68	0·1904	3	0·8400
2½	0·0070	36	0·1008	69	0·1932	4	1·1200
3	0·0084	37	0·1036	70	0·1960	5	1·4000
4	0·0112	37½	0·1050	71	0·1988	6	1·6800
5	0·0140	38	0·1064	72	0·2016	7	1·9600
6	0·0168	39	0·1092	72½	0·2030	8	2·2400
7	0·0196	40	0·1120	73	0·2044	9	2·5200
7½	0·0210	41	0·1148	74	0·2072	10	2·8000
8	0·0224	42	0·1176	75	0·2100	11	3·0800
9	0·0252	42½	0·1190	76	0·2128	12	3·3600
10	0·0280	43	0·1204	77	0·2156	13	3·6400
11	0·0308	44	0·1232	77½	0·2170	14	3·9200
12	0·0336	45	0·1260	78	0·2184	15	4·2000
12½	0·0350	46	0·1288	79	0·2212	16	4·4800
13	0·0364	47	0·1316	80	0·2240	17	4·7600
14	0·0392	47½	0·1330	81	0·2268	18	5·0400
15	0·0420	48	0·1344	82	0·2296	19	5·3200
16	0·0448	49	0·1372	82½	0·2310	20	5·6000
17	0·0476	50	0·1400	83	0·2324	25	7·0000
17½	0·0490	51	0·1428	84	0·2352	30	8·4000
18	0·0504	52	0·1456	85	0·2380	35	9·8000
19	0·0532	52½	0·1470	86	0·2408	40	11·2000
20	0·0560	53	0·1484	87	0·2436	45	12·6000
21	0·0588	54	0·1512	87½	0·2450	50	14·0000
22	0·0616	55	0·1540	88	0·2464	55	15·4000
22½	0·0630	56	0·1568	89	0·2492	60	16·8000
23	0·0644	57	0·1596	90	0·2520	65	18·2000
24	0·0672	57½	0·1610	91	0·2548	70	19·6000
25	0·0700	58	0·1624	92	0·2576	75	21·0000
26	0·0728	59	0·1652	92½	0·2590	80	22·4000
27	0·0756	60	0·1680	93	0·2604	85	23·8000
27½	0·0770	61	0·1708	94	0·2632	90	25·2000
28	0·0784	62	0·1736	95	0·2660	95	26·6000
29	0·0812	62½	0·1750	96	0·2688	100	28·0000
30	0·0840	63	0·1764	97	0·2716	110	30·8000
31	0·0868	64	0·1792	97½	0·2730	120	33·6000
32	0·0896	65	0·1820	98	0·2744	130	36·4000
32½	0·0910	66	0·1848	99	0·2772	140	39·2000

£	£	£	£	£	£	£	£
150	42·0000	300	84·0000	450	126·0000	700	196·0000
200	56·0000	350	98·0000	500	140·0000	800	224·0000
250	70·0000	400	112·0000	600	168·0000	1000	280·0000

Per Cent

p	£	p	£	p	£	£	£
½	0·0015	33	0·0990	67	0·2010	1	0·3000
1	0·0030	34	0·1020	67½	0·2025	2	0·6000
2	0·0060	35	0·1050	68	0·2040	3	0·9000
2½	0·0075	36	0·1080	69	0·2070	4	1·2000
3	0·0090	37	0·1110	70	0·2100	5	1·5000
4	0·0120	37½	0·1125	71	0·2130	6	1·8000
5	0·0150	38	0·1140	72	0·2160	7	2·1000
6	0·0180	39	0·1170	72½	0·2175	8	2·4000
7	0·0210	40	0·1200	73	0·2190	9	2·7000
7½	0·0225	41	0·1230	74	0·2220	10	3·0000
8	0·0240	42	0·1260	75	0·2250	11	3·3000
9	0·0270	42½	0·1275	76	0·2280	12	3·6000
10	0·0300	43	0·1290	77	0·2310	13	3·9000
11	0·0330	44	0·1320	77½	0·2325	14	4·2000
12	0·0360	45	0·1350	78	0·2340	15	4·5000
12½	0·0375	46	0·1380	79	0·2370	16	4·8000
13	0·0390	47	0·1410	80	0·2400	17	5·1000
14	0·0420	47½	0·1425	81	0·2430	18	5·4000
15	0·0450	48	0·1440	82	0·2460	19	5·7000
16	0·0480	49	0·1470	82½	0·2475	20	6·0000
17	0·0510	50	0·1500	83	0·2490	25	7·5000
17½	0·0525	51	0·1530	84	0·2520	30	9·0000
18	0·0540	52	0·1560	85	0·2550	35	10·5000
19	0·0570	52½	0·1575	86	0·2580	40	12·0000
20	0·0600	53	0·1590	87	0·2610	45	13·5000
21	0·0630	54	0·1620	87½	0·2625	50	15·0000
22	0·0660	55	0·1650	88	0·2640	55	16·5000
22½	0·0675	56	0·1680	89	0·2670	60	18·0000
23	0·0690	57	0·1710	90	0·2700	65	19·5000
24	0·0720	57½	0·1725	91	0·2730	70	21·0000
25	0·0750	58	0·1740	92	0·2760	75	22·5000
26	0·0780	59	0·1770	92½	0·2775	80	24·0000
27	0·0810	60	0·1800	93	0·2790	85	25·5000
27½	0·0825	61	0·1830	94	0·2820	90	27·0000
28	0·0840	62	0·1860	95	0·2850	95	28·5000
29	0·0870	62½	0·1875	96	0·2880	100	30·0000
30	0·0900	63	0·1890	97	0·2910	110	33·0000
31	0·0930	64	0·1920	97½	0·2925	120	36·0000
32	0·0960	65	0·1950	98	0·2940	130	39·0000
32½	0·0975	66	0·1980	99	0·2970	140	42·0000

£	£	£	£	£	£	£	£
150	45·0000	300	90·0000	450	135·0000	700	210·0000
200	60·0000	350	105·0000	500	150·0000	800	240·0000
250	75·0000	400	120·0000	600	180·0000	1000	300·0000

p	£	p	£	p	£	£	£
½	0·0016	33	0·1056	67	0·2144	1	0·3200
1	0·0032	34	0·1088	67½	0·2160	2	0·6400
2	0·0064	35	0·1120	68	0·2176	3	0·9600
2½	0·0080	36	0·1152	69	0·2208	4	1·2800
3	0·0096	37	0·1184	70	0·2240	5	1·6000
4	0·0128	37½	0·1200	71	0·2272	6	1·9200
5	0·0160	38	0·1216	72	0·2304	7	2·2400
6	0·0192	39	0·1248	72½	0·2320	8	2·5600
7	0·0224	40	0·1280	73	0·2336	9	2·8800
7½	0·0240	41	0·1312	74	0·2368	10	3·2000
8	0·0256	42	0·1344	75	0·2400	11	3·5200
9	0·0288	42½	0·1360	76	0·2432	12	3·8400
10	0·0320	43	0·1376	77	0·2464	13	4·1600
11	0·0352	44	0·1408	77½	0·2480	14	4·4800
12	0·0384	45	0·1440	78	0·2496	15	4·8000
12½	0·0400	46	0·1472	79	0·2528	16	5·1200
13	0·0416	47	0·1504	80	0·2560	17	5·4400
14	0·0448	47½	0·1520	81	0·2592	18	5·7600
15	0·0480	48	0·1536	82	0·2624	19	6·0800
16	0·0512	49	0·1568	82½	0·2640	20	6·4000
17	0·0544	50	0·1600	83	0·2656	25	8·0000
17½	0·0560	51	0·1632	84	0·2688	30	9·6000
18	0·0576	52	0·1664	85	0·2720	35	11·2000
19	0·0608	52½	0·1680	86	0·2752	40	12·8000
20	0·0640	53	0·1696	87	0·2784	45	14·4000
21	0·0672	54	0·1728	87½	0·2800	50	16·0000
22	0·0704	55	0·1760	88	0·2816	55	17·6000
22½	0·0720	56	0·1792	89	0·2848	60	19·2000
23	0·0736	57	0·1824	90	0·2880	65	20·8000
24	0·0768	57½	0·1840	91	0·2912	70	22·4000
25	0·0800	58	0·1856	92	0·2944	75	24·0000
26	0·0832	59	0·1888	92½	0·2960	80	25·6000
27	0·0864	60	0·1920	93	0·2976	85	27·2000
27½	0·0880	61	0·1952	94	0·3008	90	28·8000
28	0·0896	62	0·1984	95	0·3040	95	30·4000
29	0·0928	62½	0·2000	96	0·3072	100	32·0000
30	0·0960	63	0·2016	97	0·3104	110	35·2000
31	0·0992	64	0·2048	97½	0·3120	120	38·4000
32	0·1024	65	0·2080	98	0·3136	130	41·6000
32½	0·1040	66	0·2112	99	0·3168	140	44·8000

£	£	£	£	£	£	£	£
150	48·0000	300	96·0000	450	144·0000	700	224·0000
200	64·0000	350	112·0000	500	160·0000	800	256·0000
250	80·0000	400	128·0000	600	192·0000	1000	320·0000

p	£	p	£	p	£	£	£
½	0·0016	33	0·1073	67	0·2178	1	0·3250
1	0·0033	34	0·1105	67½	0·2194	2	0·6500
2	0·0065	35	0·1138	68	0·2210	3	0·9750
2½	0·0081	36	0·1170	69	0·2243	4	1·3000
3	0·0098	37	0·1203	70	0·2275	5	1·6250
4	0·0130	37½	0·1219	71	0·2308	6	1·9500
5	0·0163	38	0·1235	72	0·2340	7	2·2750
6	0·0195	39	0·1268	72½	0·2356	8	2·6000
7	0·0228	40	0·1300	73	0·2373	9	2·9250
7½	0·0244	41	0·1333	74	0·2405	10	3·2500
8	0·0260	42	0·1365	75	0·2438	11	3·5750
9	0·0293	42½	0·1381	76	0·2470	12	3·9000
10	0·0325	43	0·1398	77	0·2503	13	4·2250
11	0·0358	44	0·1430	77½	0·2519	14	4·5500
12	0·0390	45	0·1463	78	0·2535	15	4·8750
12½	0·0406	46	0·1495	79	0·2568	16	5·2000
13	0·0423	47	0·1528	80	0·2600	17	5·5250
14	0·0455	47½	0·1544	81	0·2633	18	5·8500
15	0·0488	48	0·1560	82	0·2665	19	6·1750
16	0·0520	49	0·1593	82½	0·2681	20	6·5000
17	0·0553	50	0·1625	83	0·2698	25	8·1250
17½	0·0569	51	0·1658	84	0·2730	30	9·7500
18	0·0585	52	0·1690	85	0·2763	35	11·3750
19	0·0618	52½	0·1706	86	0·2795	40	13·0000
20	0·0650	53	0·1723	87	0·2828	45	14·6250
21	0·0683	54	0·1755	87½	0·2844	50	16·2500
22	0·0715	55	0·1788	88	0·2860	55	17·8750
22½	0·0731	56	0·1820	89	0·2893	60	19·5000
23	0·0748	57	0·1853	90	0·2925	65	21·1250
24	0·0780	57½	0·1869	91	0·2958	70	22·7500
25	0·0813	58	0·1885	92	0·2990	75	24·3750
26	0·0845	59	0·1918	92½	0·3006	80	26·0000
27	0·0878	60	0·1950	93	0·3023	85	27·6250
27½	0·0894	61	0·1983	94	0·3055	90	29·2500
28	0·0910	62	0·2015	95	0·3088	95	30·8750
29	0·0943	62½	0·2031	96	0·3120	100	32·5000
30	0·0975	63	0·2048	97	0·3153	110	35·7500
31	0·1008	64	0·2080	97½	0·3169	120	39·0000
32	0·1040	65	0·2113	98	0·3185	130	42·2500
32½	0·1056	66	0·2145	99	0·3218	140	45·5000

£	£	£	£	£	£	£	£
150	48·7500	300	97·5000	450	146·2500	700	227·5000
200	65·0000	350	113·7500	500	162·5000	800	260·0000
250	81·2500	400	130·0000	600	195·0000	1000	325·0000

p	£	p	£	p	£	£	£
½	0·0017	33	0·1089	67	0·2211	1	0·3300
1	0·0033	34	0·1122	67½	0·2228	2	0·6600
2	0·0066	35	0·1155	68	0·2244	3	0·9900
2½	0·0083	36	0·1188	69	0·2277	4	1·3200
3	0·0099	37	0·1221	70	0·2310	5	1·6500
4	0·0132	37½	0·1238	71	0·2343	6	1·9800
5	0·0165	38	0·1254	72	0·2376	7	2·3100
6	0·0198	39	0·1287	72½	0·2393	8	2·6400
7	0·0231	40	0·1320	73	0·2409	9	2·9700
7½	0·0248	41	0·1353	74	0·2442	10	3·3000
8	0·0264	42	0·1386	75	0·2475	11	3·6300
9	0·0297	42½	0·1403	76	0·2508	12	3·9600
10	0·0330	43	0·1419	77	0·2541	13	4·2900
11	0·0363	44	0·1452	77½	0·2558	14	4·6200
12	0·0396	45	0·1485	78	0·2574	15	4·9500
12½	0·0413	46	0·1518	79	0·2607	16	5·2800
13	0·0429	47	0·1551	80	0·2640	17	5·6100
14	0·0462	47½	0·1568	81	0·2673	18	5·9400
15	0·0495	48	0·1584	82	0·2706	19	6·2700
16	0·0528	49	0·1617	82½	0·2723	20	6·6000
17	0·0561	50	0·1650	83	0·2739	25	8·2500
17½	0·0578	51	0·1683	84	0·2772	30	9·9000
18	0·0594	52	0·1716	85	0·2805	35	11·5500
19	0·0627	52½	0·1733	86	0·2838	40	13·2000
20	0·0660	53	0·1749	87	0·2871	45	14·8500
21	0·0693	54	0·1782	87½	0·2888	50	16·5000
22	0·0726	55	0·1815	88	0·2904	55	18·1500
22½	0·0743	56	0·1848	89	0·2937	60	19·8000
23	0·0759	57	0·1881	90	0·2970	65	21·4500
24	0·0792	57½	0·1898	91	0·3003	70	23·1000
25	0·0825	58	0·1914	92	0·3036	75	24·7500
26	0·0858	59	0·1947	92½	0·3053	80	26·4000
27	0·0891	60	0·1980	93	0·3069	85	28·0500
27½	0·0908	61	0·2013	94	0·3102	90	29·7000
28	0·0924	62	0·2046	95	0·3135	95	31·3500
29	0·0957	62½	0·2063	96	0·3168	100	33·0000
30	0·0990	63	0·2079	97	0·3201	110	36·3000
31	0·1023	64	0·2112	97½	0·3218	120	39·6000
32	0·1056	65	0·2145	98	0·3234	130	42·9000
32½	0·1073	66	0·2178	99	0·3267	140	46·2000

£	£	£	£	£	£	£	£
150	49·5000	300	99·0000	450	148·5000	700	231·0000
200	66·0000	350	115·5000	500	165·0000	800	264·0000
250	82·5000	400	132·0000	600	198·0000	1000	330·0000

p	£	p	£	p	£	£	£
½	0·0017	33	0·1100	67	0·2233	1	0·3333
1	0·0033	34	0·1133	67½	0·2250	2	0·6667
2	0·0067	35	0·1167	68	0·2267	3	1·0000
2½	0·0083	36	0·1200	69	0·2300	4	1·3333
3	0·0100	37	0·1233	70	0·2333	5	1·6667
4	0·0133	37½	0·1250	71	0·2367	6	2·0000
5	0·0167	38	0·1267	72	0·2400	7	2·3333
6	0·0200	39	0·1300	72½	0·2417	8	2·6667
7	0·0233	40	0·1333	73	0·2433	9	3·0000
7½	0·0250	41	0·1367	74	0·2467	10	3·3333
8	0·0267	42	0·1400	75	0·2500	11	3·6667
9	0·0300	42½	0·1417	76	0·2533	12	4·0000
10	0·0333	43	0·1433	77	0·2567	13	4·3333
11	0·0367	44	0·1467	77½	0·2583	14	4·6667
12	0·0400	45	0·1500	78	0·2600	15	5·0000
12½	0·0417	46	0·1533	79	0·2633	16	5·3333
13	0·0433	47	0·1567	80	0·2667	17	5·6667
14	0·0467	47½	0·1583	81	0·2700	18	6·0000
15	0·0500	48	0·1600	82	0·2733	19	6·3333
16	0·0533	49	0·1633	82½	0·2750	20	6·6667
17	0·0567	50	0·1667	83	0·2767	25	8·3333
17½	0·0583	51	0·1700	84	0·2800	30	10·0000
18	0·0600	52	0·1733	85	0·2833	35	11·6667
19	0·0633	52½	0·1750	86	0·2867	40	13·3333
20	0·0667	53	0·1767	87	0·2900	45	15·0000
21	0·0700	54	0·1800	87½	0·2917	50	16·6667
22	0·0733	55	0·1833	88	0·2933	55	18·3333
22½	0·0750	56	0·1867	89	0·2967	60	20·0000
23	0·0767	57	0·1900	90	0·3000	65	21·6667
24	0·0800	57½	0·1917	91	0·3033	70	23·3333
25	0·0833	58	0·1933	92	0·3067	75	25·0000
26	0·0867	59	0·1967	92½	0·3083	80	26·6667
27	0·0900	60	0·2000	93	0·3100	85	28·3333
27½	0·0917	61	0·2033	94	0·3133	90	30·0000
28	0·0933	62	0·2067	95	0·3167	95	31·6667
29	0·0967	62½	0·2083	96	0·3200	100	33·3333
30	0·1000	63	0·2100	97	0·3233	110	36·6667
31	0·1033	64	0·2133	97½	0·3250	120	40·0000
32	0·1067	65	0·2167	98	0·3267	130	43·3333
32½	0·1083	66	0·2200	99	0·3300	140	46·6667

£	£	£	£	£	£	£	£
150	50·0000	300	100·0000	450	150·0000	700	233·3333
200	66·6667	350	116·6667	500	166·6667	800	266·6667
250	83·3333	400	133·3333	600	200·0000	1000	333·3333

p	£	p	£	p	£	£	£
½	0·0017	33	0·1122	67	0·2278	1	0·3400
1	0·0034	34	0·1156	67½	0·2295	2	0·6800
2	0·0068	35	0·1190	68	0·2312	3	1·0200
2½	0·0085	36	0·1224	69	0·2346	4	1·3600
3	0·0102	37	0·1258	70	0·2380	5	1·7000
4	0·0136	37½	0·1275	71	0·2414	6	2·0400
5	0·0170	38	0·1292	72	0·2448	7	2·3800
6	0·0204	39	0·1326	72½	0·2465	8	2·7200
7	0·0238	40	0·1360	73	0·2482	9	3·0600
7½	0·0255	41	0·1394	74	0·2516	10	3·4000
8	0·0272	42	0·1428	75	0·2550	11	3·7400
9	0·0306	42½	0·1445	76	0·2584	12	4·0800
10	0·0340	43	0·1462	77	0·2618	13	4·4200
11	0·0374	44	0·1496	77½	0·2635	14	4·7600
12	0·0408	45	0·1530	78	0·2652	15	5·1000
12½	0·0425	46	0·1564	79	0·2686	16	5·4400
13	0·0442	47	0·1598	80	0·2720	17	5·7800
14	0·0476	47½	0·1615	81	0·2754	18	6·1200
15	0·0510	48	0·1632	82	0·2788	19	6·4600
16	0·0544	49	0·1666	82½	0·2805	20	6·8000
17	0·0578	50	0·1700	83	0·2822	25	8·5000
17½	0·0595	51	0·1734	84	0·2856	30	10·2000
18	0·0612	52	0·1768	85	0·2890	35	11·9000
19	0·0646	52½	0·1785	86	0·2924	40	13·6000
20	0·0680	53	0·1802	87	0·2958	45	15·3000
21	0·0714	54	0·1836	87½	0·2975	50	17·0000
22	0·0748	55	0·1870	88	0·2992	55	18·7000
22½	0·0765	56	0·1904	89	0·3026	60	20·4000
23	0·0782	57	0·1938	90	0·3060	65	22·1000
24	0·0816	57½	0·1955	91	0·3094	70	23·8000
25	0·0850	58	0·1972	92	0·3128	75	25·5000
26	0·0884	59	0·2006	92½	0·3145	80	27·2000
27	0·0918	60	0·2040	93	0·3162	85	28·9000
27½	0·0935	61	0·2074	94	0·3196	90	30·6000
28	0·0952	62	0·2108	95	0·3230	95	32·3000
29	0·0986	62½	0·2125	96	0·3264	100	34·0000
30	0·1020	63	0·2142	97	0·3298	110	37·4000
31	0·1054	64	0·2176	97½	0·3315	120	40·8000
32	0·1088	65	0·2210	98	0·3332	130	44·2000
32½	0·1105	66	0·2244	99	0·3366	140	47·6000

£	£	£	£	£	£	£	£
150	51·0000	300	102·0000	450	153·0000	700	238·0000
200	68·0000	350	119·0000	500	170·0000	800	272·0000
250	85·0000	400	136·0000	600	204·0000	1000	340·0000

p	£	p	£	p	£	£	£
½	0·0018	33	0·1155	67	0·2345	1	0·3500
1	0·0035	34	0·1190	67½	0·2363	2	0·7000
2	0·0070	35	0·1225	68	0·2380	3	1·0500
2½	0·0088	36	0·1260	69	0·2415	4	1·4000
3	0·0105	37	0·1295	70	0·2450	5	1·7500
4	0·0140	37½	0·1313	71	0·2485	6	2·1000
5	0·0175	38	0·1330	72	0·2520	7	2·4500
6	0·0210	39	0·1365	72½	0·2538	8	2·8000
7	0·0245	40	0·1400	73	0·2555	9	3·1500
7½	0·0263	41	0·1435	74	0·2590	10	3·5000
8	0·0280	42	0·1470	75	0·2625	11	3·8500
9	0·0315	42½	0·1488	76	0·2660	12	4·2000
10	0·0350	43	0·1505	77	0·2695	13	4·5500
11	0·0385	44	0·1540	77½	0·2713	14	4·9000
12	0·0420	45	0·1575	78	0·2730	15	5·2500
12½	0·0438	46	0·1610	79	0·2765	16	5·6000
13	0·0455	47	0·1645	80	0·2800	17	5·9500
14	0·0490	47½	0·1663	81	0·2835	18	6·3000
15	0·0525	48	0·1680	82	0·2870	19	6·6500
16	0·0560	49	0·1715	82½	0·2888	20	7·0000
17	0·0595	50	0·1750	83	0·2905	25	8·7500
17½	0·0613	51	0·1785	84	0·2940	30	10·5000
18	0·0630	52	0·1820	85	0·2975	35	12·2500
19	0·0665	52½	0·1838	86	0·3010	40	14·0000
20	0·0700	53	0·1855	87	0·3045	45	15·7500
21	0·0735	54	0·1890	87½	0·3063	50	17·5000
22	0·0770	55	0·1925	88	0·3080	55	19·2500
22½	0·0788	56	0·1960	89	0·3115	60	21·0000
23	0·0805	57	0·1995	90	0·3150	65	22·7500
24	0·0840	57½	0·2013	91	0·3185	70	24·5000
25	0·0875	58	0·2030	92	0·3220	75	26·2500
26	0·0910	59	0·2065	92½	0·3238	80	28·0000
27	0·0945	60	0·2100	93	0·3255	85	29·7500
27½	0·0963	61	0·2135	94	0·3290	90	31·5000
28	0·0980	62	0·2170	95	0·3325	95	33·2500
29	0·1015	62½	0·2188	96	0·3360	100	35·0000
30	0·1050	63	0·2205	97	0·3395	110	38·5000
31	0·1085	64	0·2240	97½	0·3413	120	42·0000
32	0·1120	65	0·2275	98	0·3430	130	45·5000
32½	0·1138	66	0·2310	99	0·3465	140	49·0000

£	£	£	£	£	£	£	£
150	52·5000	300	105·0000	450	157·5000	700	245·0000
200	70·0000	350	122·5000	500	175·0000	800	280·0000
250	87·5000	400	140·0000	600	210·0000	1000	350·0000

p	£	p	£	p	£	£	£
½	0·0018	33	0·1188	67	0·2412	1	0·3600
1	0·0036	34	0·1224	67½	0·2430	2	0·7200
2	0·0072	35	0·1260	68	0·2448	3	1·0800
2½	0·0090	36	0·1296	69	0·2484	4	1·4400
3	0·0108	37	0·1332	70	0·2520	5	1·8000
4	0·0144	37½	0·1350	71	0·2556	6	2·1600
5	0·0180	38	0·1368	72	0·2592	7	2·5200
6	0·0216	39	0·1404	72½	0·2610	8	2·8800
7	0·0252	40	0·1440	73	0·2628	9	3·2400
7½	0·0270	41	0·1476	74	0·2664	10	3·6000
8	0·0288	42	0·1512	75	0·2700	11	3·9600
9	0·0324	42½	0·1530	76	0·2736	12	4·3200
10	0·0360	43	0·1548	77	0·2772	13	4·6800
11	0·0396	44	0·1584	77½	0·2790	14	5·0400
12	0·0432	45	0·1620	78	0·2808	15	5·4000
12½	0·0450	46	0·1656	79	0·2844	16	5·7600
13	0·0468	47	0·1692	80	0·2880	17	6·1200
14	0·0504	47½	0·1710	81	0·2916	18	6·4800
15	0·0540	48	0·1728	82	0·2952	19	6·8400
16	0·0576	49	0·1764	82½	0·2970	20	7·2000
17	0·0612	50	0·1800	83	0·2988	25	9·0000
17½	0·0630	51	0·1836	84	0·3024	30	10·8000
18	0·0648	52	0·1872	85	0·3060	35	12·6000
19	0·0684	52½	0·1890	86	0·3096	40	14·4000
20	0·0720	53	0·1908	87	0·3132	45	16·2000
21	0·0756	54	0·1944	87½	0·3150	50	18·0000
22	0·0792	55	0·1980	88	0·3168	55	19·8000
22½	0·0810	56	0·2016	89	0·3204	60	21·6000
23	0·0828	57	0·2052	90	0·3240	65	23·4000
24	0·0864	57½	0·2070	91	0·3276	70	25·2000
25	0·0900	58	0·2088	92	0·3312	75	27·0000
26	0·0936	59	0·2124	92½	0·3330	80	28·8000
27	0·0972	60	0·2160	93	0·3348	85	30·6000
27½	0·0990	61	0·2196	94	0·3384	90	32·4000
28	0·1008	62	0·2232	95	0·3420	95	34·2000
29	0·1044	62½	0·2250	96	0·3456	100	36·0000
30	0·1080	63	0·2268	97	0·3492	110	39·6000
31	0·1116	64	0·2304	97½	0·3510	120	43·2000
32	0·1152	65	0·2340	98	0·3528	130	46·8000
32½	0·1170	66	0·2376	99	0·3564	140	50·4000

£	£	£	£	£	£	£	£
150	54·0000	300	108·0000	450	162·0000	700	252·0000
200	72·0000	350	126·0000	500	180·0000	800	288·0000
250	90·0000	400	144·0000	600	216·0000	1000	360·0000

p	£	p	£	p	£	£	£
¼	0·0019	33	0·1221	67	0·2479	1	0·3700
1	0·0037	34	0·1258	67½	0·2498	2	0·7400
2	0·0074	35	0·1295	68	0·2516	3	1·1100
2½	0·0093	36	0·1332	69	0·2553	4	1·4800
3	0·0111	37	0·1369	70	0·2590	5	1·8500
4	0·0148	37½	0·1388	71	0·2627	6	2·2200
5	0·0185	38	0·1406	72	0·2664	7	2·5900
6	0·0222	39	0·1443	72½	0·2683	8	2·9600
7	0·0259	40	0·1480	73	0·2701	9	3·3300
7½	0·0278	41	0·1517	74	0·2738	10	3·7000
8	0·0296	42	0·1554	75	0·2775	11	4·0700
9	0·0333	42½	0·1573	76	0·2812	12	4·4400
10	0·0370	43	0·1591	77	0·2849	13	4·8100
11	0·0407	44	0·1628	77½	0·2868	14	5·1800
12	0·0444	45	0·1665	78	0·2886	15	5·5500
12½	0·0463	46	0·1702	79	0·2923	16	5·9200
13	0·0481	47	0·1739	80	0·2960	17	6·2900
14	0·0518	47½	0·1758	81	0·2997	18	6·6600
15	0·0555	48	0·1776	82	0·3034	19	7·0300
16	0·0592	49	0·1813	82½	0·3053	20	7·4000
17	0·0629	50	0·1850	83	0·3071	25	9·2500
17½	0·0648	51	0·1887	84	0·3108	30	11·1000
18	0·0666	52	0·1924	85	0·3145	35	12·9500
19	0·0703	52½	0·1943	86	0·3182	40	14·8000
20	0·0740	53	0·1961	87	0·3219	45	16·6500
21	0·0777	54	0·1998	87½	0·3238	50	18·5000
22	0·0814	55	0·2035	88	0·3256	55	20·3500
22½	0·0833	56·	0·2072	89	0·3293	60	22·2000
23	0·0851	57	0·2109	90	0·3330	65	24·0500
24	0·0888	57½	0·2128	91	0·3367	70	25·9000
25	0·0925	58	0·2146	92	0·3404	75	27·7500
26	0·0962	59	0·2183	92½	0·3423	80	29·6000
27	0·0999	60	0·2220	93	0·3441	85	31·4500
27½	0·1018	61	0·2257	94	0·3478	90	33·3000
28	0·1036	62	0·2294	95	0·3515	95	35·1500
29	0·1073	62½	0·2313	96	0·3552	100	37·0000
30	0·1110	63	0·2331	97	0·3589	110	40·7000
31	0·1147	64	0·2368	97½	0·3608	120	44·4000
32	0·1184	65	0·2405	98	0·3626	130	48·1000
32½	0·1203	66	0·2442	99	0·3663	140	51·8000

£	£	£	£	£	£	£	£
150	55·5000	300	111·0000	450	166·5000	700	259·0000
200	74·0000	350	129·5000	500	185·0000	800	296·0000
250	92·5000	400	148·0000	600	222·0000	1000	370·0000

p	£	p	£	p	£	£	£
½	0·0019	33	0·1238	67	0·2513	1	0·3750
1	0·0038	34	0·1275	67½	0·2531	2	0·7500
2	0·0075	35	0·1313	68	0·2550	3	1·1250
2½	0·0094	36	0·1350	69	0·2588	4	1·5000
3	0·0113	37	0·1388	70	0·2625	5	1·8750
4	0·0150	37½	0·1406	71	0·2663	6	2·2500
5	0·0188	38	0·1425	72	0·2700	7	2·6250
6	0·0225	39	0·1463	72½	0·2719	8	3·0000
7	0·0263	40	0·1500	73	0·2738	9	3·3750
7½	0·0281	41	0·1538	74	0·2775	10	3·7500
8	0·0300	42	0·1575	75	0·2813	11	4·1250
9	0·0338	42½	0·1594	76	0·2850	12	4·5000
10	0·0375	43	0·1613	77	0·2888	13	4·8750
11	0·0413	44	0·1650	77½	0·2906	14	5·2500
12	0·0450	45	0·1688	78	0·2925	15	5·6250
12½	0·0469	46	0·1725	79	0·2963	16	6·0000
13	0·0488	47	0·1763	80	0·3000	17	6·3750
14	0·0525	47½	0·1781	81	0·3038	18	6·7500
15	0·0563	48	0·1800	82	0·3075	19	7·1250
16	0·0600	49	0·1838	82½	0·3094	20	7·5000
17	0·0638	50	0·1875	83	0·3113	25	9·3750
17½	0·0656	51	0·1913	84	0·3150	30	11·2500
18	0·0675	52	0·1950	85	0·3188	35	13·1250
19	0·0713	52½	0·1969	86	0·3225	40	15·0000
20	0·0750	53	0·1988	87	0·3263	45	16·8750
21	0·0788	54	0·2025	87½	0·3281	50	18·7500
22	0·0825	55	0·2063	88	0·3300	55	20·6250
22½	0·0844	56	0·2100	89	0·3338	60	22·5000
23	0·0863	57	0·2138	90	0·3375	65	24·3750
24	0·0900	57½	0·2156	91	0·3413	70	26·2500
25	0·0938	58	0·2175	92	0·3450	75	28·1250
26	0·0975	59	0·2213	92½	0·3469	80	30·0000
27	0·1013	60	0·2250	93	0·3488	85	31·8750
27½	0·1031	61	0·2288	94	0·3525	90	33·7500
28	0·1050	62	0·2325	95	0·3563	95	35·6250
29	0·1088	62½	0·2344	96	0·3600	100	37·5000
30	0·1125	63	0·2363	97	0·3638	110	41·2500
31	0·1163	64	0·2400	97½	0·3656	120	45·0000
32	0·1200	65	0·2438	98	0·3675	130	48·7500
32½	0·1219	66	0·2475	99	0·3713	140	52·5000

£	£	£	£	£	£	£	£
150	56·2500	300	112·5000	450	168·7500	700	262·5000
200	75·0000	350	131·2500	500	187·5000	800	300·0000
250	93·7500	400	150·0000	600	225·0000	1000	375·0000

p	£	p	£	p	£	£	£
½	0·0019	33	0·1254	67	0·2546	1	0·3800
1	0·0038	34	0·1292	67½	0·2565	2	0·7600
2	0·0076	35	0·1330	68	0·2584	3	1·1400
2½	0·0095	36	0·1368	69	0·2622	4	1·5200
3	0·0114	37	0·1406	70	0·2660	5	1·9000
4	0·0152	37½	0·1425	71	0·2698	6	2·2800
5	0·0190	38	0·1444	72	0·2736	7	2·6600
6	0·0228	39	0·1482	72½	0·2755	8	3·0400
7	0·0266	40	0·1520	73	0·2774	9	3·4200
7½	0·0285	41	0·1558	74	0·2812	10	3·8000
8	0·0304	42	0·1596	75	0·2850	11	4·1800
9	0·0342	42½	0·1615	76	0·2888	12	4·5600
10	0·0380	43	0·1634	77	0·2926	13	4·9400
11	0·0418	44	0·1672	77½	0·2945	14	5·3200
12	0·0456	45	0·1710	78	0·2964	15	5·7000
12½	0·0475	46	0·1748	79	0·3002	16	6·0800
13	0·0494	47	0·1786	80	0·3040	17	6·4600
14	0·0532	47½	0·1805	81	0·3078	18	6·8400
15	0·0570	48	0·1824	82	0·3116	19	7·2200
16	0·0608	49	0·1862	82½	0·3135	20	7·6000
17	0·0646	50	0·1900	83	0·3154	25	9·5000
17½	0·0665	51	0·1938	84	0·3192	30	11·4000
18	0·0684	52	0·1976	85	0·3230	35	13·3000
19	0·0722	52½	0·1995	86	0·3268	40	15·2000
20	0·0760	53	0·2014	87	0·3306	45	17·1000
21	0·0798	54	0·2052	87½	0·3325	50	19·0000
22	0·0836	55	0·2090	88	0·3344	55	20·9000
22½	0·0855	56	0·2128	89	0·3382	60	22·8000
23	0·0874	57	0·2166	90	0·3420	65	24·7000
24	0·0912	57½	0·2185	91	0·3458	70	26·6000
25	0·0950	58	0·2204	92	0·3496	75	28·5000
26	0·0988	59	0·2242	92½	0·3515	80	30·4000
27	0·1026	60	0·2280	93	0·3534	85	32·3000
27½	0·1045	61	0·2318	94	0·3572	90	34·2000
28	0·1064	62	0·2356	95	0·3610	95	36·1000
29	0·1102	62½	0·2375	96	0·3648	100	38·0000
30	0·1140	63	0·2394	97	0·3686	110	41·8000
31	0·1178	64	0·2432	97½	0·3705	120	45·6000
32	0·1216	65	0·2470	98	0·3724	130	49·4000
32½	0·1235	66	0·2508	99	0·3762	140	53·2000

£	£	£	£	£	£	£	£
150	57·0000	300	114·0000	450	171·0000	700	266·0000
200	76·0000	350	133·0000	500	190·0000	800	304·0000
250	95·0000	400	152·0000	600	228·0000	1000	380·0000

p	£	p	£	p	£	£	£
$\frac{1}{2}$	0·0019	33	0·1271	67	0·2580	1	0·3850
1	0·0039	34	0·1309	$67\frac{1}{2}$	0·2599	2	0·7700
2	0·0077	35	0·1348	68	0·2618	3	1·1550
$2\frac{1}{2}$	0·0096	36	0·1386	69	0·2657	4	1·5400
3	0·0116	37	0·1425	70	0·2695	5	1·9250
4	0·0154	$37\frac{1}{2}$	0·1444	71	0·2734	6	2·3100
5	0·0193	38	0·1463	72	0·2772	7	2·6950
6	0·0231	39	0·1502	$72\frac{1}{2}$	0·2791	8	3·0800
7	0·0270	40	0·1540	73	0·2811	9	3·4650
$7\frac{1}{2}$	0·0289	41	0·1579	74	0·2849	10	3·8500
8	0·0308	42	0·1617	75	0·2888	11	4·2350
9	0·0347	$42\frac{1}{2}$	0·1636	76	0·2926	12	4·6200
10	0·0385	43	0·1656	77	0·2965	13	5·0050
11	0·0424	44	0·1694	$77\frac{1}{2}$	0·2984	14	5·3900
12	0·0462	45	0·1733	78	0·3003	15	5·7750
$12\frac{1}{2}$	0·0481	46	0·1771	79	0·3042	16	6·1600
13	0·0501	47	0·1810	80	0·3080	17	6·5450
14	0·0539	$47\frac{1}{2}$	0·1829	81	0·3119	18	6·9300
15	0·0578	48	0·1848	82	0·3157	19	7·3150
16	0·0616	49	0·1887	$82\frac{1}{2}$	0·3176	20	7·7000
17	0·0655	50	0·1925	83	0·3196	25	9·6250
$17\frac{1}{2}$	0·0674	51	0·1964	84	0·3234	30	11·5500
18	0·0693	52	0·2002	85	0·3273	35	13·4750
19	0·0732	$52\frac{1}{2}$	0·2021	86	0·3311	40	15·4000
20	0·0770	53	0·2041	87	0·3350	45	17·3250
21	0·0809	54	0·2079	$87\frac{1}{2}$	0·3369	50	19·2500
22	0·0847	55	0·2118	88	0·3388	55	21·1750
$22\frac{1}{2}$	0·0866	56	0·2156	89	0·3427	60	23·1000
23	0·0886	57	0·2195	90	0·3465	65	25·0250
24	0·0924	$57\frac{1}{2}$	0·2214	91	0·3504	70	26·9500
25	0·0963	58	0·2233	92	0·3542	75	28·8750
26	0·1001	59	0·2272	$92\frac{1}{2}$	0·3561	80	30·8000
27	0·1040	60	0·2310	93	0·3581	85	32·7250
$27\frac{1}{2}$	0·1059	61	0·2349	94	0·3619	90	34·6500
28	0·1078	62	0·2387	95	0·3658	95	36·5750
29	0·1117	$62\frac{1}{2}$	0·2406	96	0·3696	100	38·5000
30	0·1155	63	0·2426	97	0·3735	110	42·3500
31	0·1194	64	0·2464	$97\frac{1}{2}$	0·3754	120	46·2000
32	0·1232	65	0·2503	98	0·3773	130	50·0500
$32\frac{1}{2}$	0·1251	66	0·2541	99	0·3812	140	53·9000

£	£	£	£	£	£	£	£
150	57·7500	300	115·5000	450	173·2500	700	269·5000
200	77·0000	350	134·7500	500	192·5000	800	308·0000
250	96·2500	400	154·0000	600	231·0000	1000	385·0000

p	£	p	£	p	£	£	£
½	.. 0·0020	33	.. 0·1287	67	.. 0·2613	1	.. 0·3900
1	.. 0·0039	34	.. 0·1326	67½	.. 0·2633	2	.. 0·7800
2	.. 0·0078	35	.. 0·1365	68	.. 0·2652	3	.. 1·1700
2½	.. 0·0098	36	.. 0·1404	69	.. 0·2691	4	.. 1·5600
3	.. 0·0117	37	.. 0·1443	70	.. 0·2730	5	.. 1·9500
4	.. 0·0156	37½	.. 0·1463	71	.. 0·2769	6	.. 2·3400
5	.. 0·0195	38	.. 0·1482	72	.. 0·2808	7	.. 2·7300
6	.. 0·0234	39	.. 0·1521	72½	.. 0·2828	8	.. 3·1200
7	.. 0·0273	40	.. 0·1560	73	.. 0·2847	9	.. 3·5100
7½	.. 0·0293	41	.. 0·1599	74	.. 0·2886	10	.. 3·9000
8	.. 0·0312	42	.. 0·1638	75	.. 0·2925	11	.. 4·2900
9	.. 0·0351	42½	.. 0·1658	76	.. 0·2964	12	.. 4·6800
10	.. 0·0390	43	.. 0·1677	77	.. 0·3003	13	.. 5·0700
11	.. 0·0429	44	.. 0·1716	77½	.. 0·3023	14	.. 5·4600
12	.. 0·0468	45	.. 0·1755	78	.. 0·3042	15	.. 5·8500
12½	.. 0·0488	46	.. 0·1794	79	.. 0·3081	16	.. 6·2400
13	.. 0·0507	47	.. 0·1833	80	.. 0·3120	17	.. 6·6300
14	.. 0·0546	47½	.. 0·1853	81	.. 0·3159	18	.. 7·0200
15	.. 0·0585	48	.. 0·1872	82	.. 0·3198	19	.. 7·4100
16	.. 0·0624	49	.. 0·1911	82½	.. 0·3218	20	.. 7·8000
17	.. 0·0663	50	.. 0·1950	83	.. 0·3237	25	.. 9·7500
17½	.. 0·0683	51	.. 0·1989	84	.. 0·3276	30	.. 11·7000
18	.. 0·0702	52	.. 0·2028	85	.. 0·3315	35	.. 13·6500
19	.. 0·0741	52½	.. 0·2048	86	.. 0·3354	40	.. 15·6000
20	.. 0·0780	53	.. 0·2067	87	.. 0·3393	45	.. 17·5500
21	.. 0·0819	54	.. 0·2106	87½	.. 0·3413	50	.. 19·5000
22	.. 0·0858	55	.. 0·2145	88	.. 0·3432	55	.. 21·4500
22½	.. 0·0878	56	.. 0·2184	89	.. 0·3471	60	.. 23·4000
23	.. 0·0897	57	.. 0·2223	90	.. 0·3510	65	.. 25·3500
24	.. 0·0936	57½	.. 0·2243	91	.. 0·3549	70	.. 27·3000
25	.. 0·0975	58	.. 0·2262	92	.. 0·3588	75	.. 29·2500
26	.. 0·1014	59	.. 0·2301	92½	.. 0·3608	80	.. 31·2000
27	.. 0·1053	60	.. 0·2340	93	.. 0·3627	85	.. 33·1500
27½	.. 0·1073	61	.. 0·2379	94	.. 0·3666	90	.. 35·1000
28	.. 0·1092	62	.. 0·2418	95	.. 0·3705	95	.. 37·0500
29	.. 0·1131	62½	.. 0·2438	96	.. 0·3744	100	.. 39·0000
30	.. 0·1170	63	.. 0·2457	97	.. 0·3783	110	.. 42·9000
31	.. 0·1209	64	.. 0·2496	97½	.. 0·3803	120	.. 46·8000
32	.. 0·1248	65	.. 0·2535	98	.. 0·3822	130	.. 50·7000
32½	.. 0·1268	66	.. 0·2574	99	.. 0·3861	140	.. 54·6000

£	£	£	£	£	£	£	£
150	.. 58·5000	300	.. 117·0000	450	.. 175·5000	700	.. 273·0000
200	.. 78·0000	350	.. 136·5000	500	.. 195·0000	800	.. 312·0000
250	.. 97·5000	400	.. 156·0000	600	.. 234·0000	1000	.. 390·0000

p	£	p	£	p	£	£	£
½	0·0020	33	0·1304	67	0·2647	1	0·3950
1	0·0040	34	0·1343	67½	0·2666	2	0·7900
2	0·0079	35	0·1383	68	0·2686	3	1·1850
2½	0·0099	36	0·1422	69	0·2726	4	1·5800
3	0·0119	37	0·1462	70	0·2765	5	1·9750
4	0·0158	37½	0·1481	71	0·2805	6	2·3700
5	0·0198	38	0·1501	72	0·2844	7	2·7650
6	0·0237	39	0·1541	72½	0·2864	8	3·1600
7	0·0277	40	0·1580	73	0·2884	9	3·5550
7½	0·0296	41	0·1620	74	0·2923	10	3·9500
8	0·0316	42	0·1659	75	0·2963	11	4·3450
9	0·0356	42½	0·1679	76	0·3002	12	4·7400
10	0·0395	43	0·1699	77	0·3042	13	5·1350
11	0·0435	44	0·1738	77½	0·3061	14	5·5300
12	0·0474	45	0·1778	78	0·3081	15	5·9250
12½	0·0494	46	0·1817	79	0·3121	16	6·3200
13	0·0514	47	0·1857	80	0·3160	17	6·7150
14	0·0553	47½	0·1876	81	0·3200	18	7·1100
15	0·0593	48	0·1896	82	0·3239	19	7·5050
16	0·0632	49	0·1936	82½	0·3259	20	7·9000
17	0·0672	50	0·1975	83	0·3279	25	9·8750
17½	0·0691	51	0·2015	84	0·3318	30	11·8500
18	0·0711	52	0·2054	85	0·3358	35	13·8250
19	0·0751	52½	0·2074	86	0·3397	40	15·8000
20	0·0790	53	0·2094	87	0·3437	45	17·7750
21	0·0830	54	0·2133	87½	0·3456	50	19·7500
22	0·0869	55	0·2173	88	0·3476	55	21·7250
22½	0·0889	56	0·2212	89	0·3516	60	23·7000
23	0·0909	57	0·2252	90	0·3555	65	25·6750
24	0·0948	57½	0·2271	91	0·3595	70	27·6500
25	0·0988	58	0·2291	92	0·3634	75	29·6250
26	0·1027	59	0·2331	92½	0·3654	80	31·6000
27	0·1067	60	0·2370	93	0·3674	85	33·5750
27½	0·1086	61	0·2410	94	0·3713	90	35·5500
28	0·1106	62	0·2449	95	0·3753	95	37·5250
29	0·1146	62½	0·2469	96	0·3792	100	39·5000
30	0·1185	63	0·2489	97	0·3832	110	43·4500
31	0·1225	64	0·2528	97½	0·3851	120	47·4000
32	0·1264	65	0·2568	98	0·3871	130	51·3500
32½	0·1284	66	0·2607	99	0·3911	140	55·3000

£	£	£	£	£	£	£	£
150	59·2500	300	118·5000	450	177·7500	700	276·5000
200	79·0000	350	138·2500	500	197·5000	800	316·0000
250	98·7500	400	158·0000	600	237·0000	1000	395·0000

p	£	p	£	p	£	£	£
½ ..	0·0020	33 ..	0·1320	67 ..	0·2680	1 ..	0·4000
1 ..	0·0040	34 ..	0·1360	67½ ..	0·2700	2 ..	0·8000
2 ..	0·0080	35 ..	0·1400	68 ..	0·2720	3 ..	1·2000
2½ ..	0·0100	36 ..	0·1440	69 ..	0·2760	4 ..	1·6000
3 ..	0·0120	37 ..	0·1480	70 ..	0·2800	5 ..	2·0000
4 ..	0·0160	37½ ..	0·1500	71 ..	0·2840	6 ..	2·4000
5 ..	0·0200	38 ..	0·1520	72 ..	0·2880	7 ..	2·8000
6 ..	0·0240	39 ..	0·1560	72½ ..	0·2900	8 ..	3·2000
7 ..	0·0280	40 ..	0·1600	73 ..	0·2920	9 ..	3·6000
7½ ..	0·0300	41 ..	0·1640	74 ..	0·2960	10 ..	4·0000
8 ..	0·0320	42 ..	0·1680	75 ..	0·3000	11 ..	4·4000
9 ..	0·0360	42½ ..	0·1700	76 ..	0·3040	12 ..	4·8000
10 ..	0·0400	43 ..	0·1720	77 ..	0·3080	13 ..	5·2000
11 ..	0·0440	44 ..	0·1760	77½ ..	0·3100	14 ..	5·6000
12 ..	0·0480	45 ..	0·1800	78 ..	0·3120	15 ..	6·0000
12½ ..	0·0500	46 ..	0·1840	79 ..	0·3160	16 ..	6·4000
13 ..	0·0520	47 ..	0·1880	80 ..	0·3200	17 ..	6·8000
14 ..	0·0560	47½ ..	0·1900	81 ..	0·3240	18 ..	7·2000
15 ..	0·0600	48 ..	0·1920	82 ..	0·3280	19 ..	7·6000
16 ..	0·0640	49 ..	0·1960	82½ ..	0·3300	20 ..	8·0000
17 ..	0·0680	50 ..	0·2000	83 ..	0·3320	25 ..	10·0000
17½ ..	0·0700	51 ..	0·2040	84 ..	0·3360	30 ..	12·0000
18 ..	0·0720	52 ..	0·2080	85 ..	0·3400	35 ..	14·0000
19 ..	0·0760	52½ ..	0·2100	86 ..	0·3440	40 ..	16·0000
20 ..	0·0800	53 ..	0·2120	87 ..	0·3480	45 ..	18·0000
21 ..	0·0840	54 ..	0·2160	87½ ..	0·3500	50 ..	20·0000
22 ..	0·0880	55 ..	0·2200	88 ..	0·3520	55 ..	22·0000
22½ ..	0·0900	56 ..	0·2240	89 ..	0·3560	60 ..	24·0000
23 ..	0·0920	57 ..	0·2280	90 ..	0·3600	65 ..	26·0000
24 ..	0·0960	57½ ..	0·2300	91 ..	0·3640	70 ..	28·0000
25 ..	0·1000	58 ..	0·2320	92 ..	0·3680	75 ..	30·0000
26 ..	0·1040	59 ..	0·2360	92½ ..	0·3700	80 ..	32·0000
27 ..	0·1080	60 ..	0·2400	93 ..	0·3720	85 ..	34·0000
27½ ..	0·1100	61 ..	0·2440	94 ..	0·3760	90 ..	36·0000
28 ..	0·1120	62 ..	0·2480	95 ..	0·3800	95 ..	38·0000
29 ..	0·1160	62½ ..	0·2500	96 ..	0·3840	100 ..	40·0000
30 ..	0·1200	63 ..	0·2520	97 ..	0·3880	110 ..	44·0000
31 ..	0·1240	64 ..	0·2560	97½ ..	0·3900	120 ..	48·0000
32 ..	0·1280	65 ..	0·2600	98 ..	0·3920	130 ..	52·0000
32½ ..	0·1300	66 ..	0·2640	99 ..	0·3960	140 ..	56·0000

£	£	£	£	£	£	£	£
150 ..	60·0000	300 ..	120·0000	450 ..	180·0000	700 ..	280·0000
200 ..	80·0000	350 ..	140·0000	500 ..	200·0000	800 ..	320·0000
250 ..	100·0000	400 ..	160·0000	600 ..	240·0000	1000 ..	400·0000

Per Cent

p	£	p	£	p	£	£	£
¼	0·0020	33	0·1337	67	0·2714	1	0·4050
1	0·0041	34	0·1377	67½	0·2734	2	0·8100
2	0·0081	35	0·1418	68	0·2754	3	1·2150
2½	0·0101	36	0·1458	69	0·2795	4	1·6200
3	0·0122	37	0·1499	70	0·2835	5	2·0250
4	0·0162	37½	0·1519	71	0·2876	6	2·4300
5	0·0203	38	0·1539	72	0·2916	7	2·8350
6	0·0243	39	0·1580	72½	0·2936	8	3·2400
7	0·0284	40	0·1620	73	0·2957	9	3·6450
7½	0·0304	41	0·1661	74	0·2997	10	4·0500
8	0·0324	42	0·1701	75	0·3038	11	4·4550
9	0·0365	42½	0·1721	76	0·3078	12	4·8600
10	0·0405	43	0·1742	77	0·3119	13	5·2650
11	0·0446	44	0·1782	77½	0·3139	14	5·6700
12	0·0486	45	0·1823	78	0·3159	15	6·0750
12½	0·0506	46	0·1863	79	0·3200	16	6·4800
13	0·0527	47	0·1904	80	0·3240	17	6·8850
14	0·0567	47½	0·1924	81	0·3281	18	7·2900
15	0·0608	48	0·1944	82	0·3321	19	7·6950
16	0·0648	49	0·1985	82½	0·3341	20	8·1000
17	0·0689	50	0·2025	83	0·3362	25	10·1250
17½	0·0709	51	0·2066	84	0·3402	30	12·1500
18	0·0729	52	0·2106	85	0·3443	35	14·1750
19	0·0770	52½	0·2126	86	0·3483	40	16·2000
20	0·0810	53	0·2147	87	0·3524	45	18·2250
21	0·0851	54	0·2187	87½	0·3544	50	20·2500
22	0·0891	55	0·2228	88	0·3564	55	22·2750
22½	0·0911	56	0·2268	89	0·3605	60	24·3000
23	0·0932	57	0·2309	90	0·3645	65	26·3250
24	0·0972	57½	0·2329	91	0·3686	70	28·3500
25	0·1013	58	0·2349	92	0·3726	75	30·3750
26	0·1053	59	0·2390	92½	0·3746	80	32·4000
27	0·1094	60	0·2430	93	0·3767	85	34·4250
27½	0·1114	61	0·2471	94	0·3807	90	36·4500
28	0·1134	62	0·2511	95	0·3848	95	38·4750
29	0·1175	62½	0·2531	96	0·3888	100	40·5000
30	0·1215	63	0·2552	97	0·3929	110	44·5500
31	0·1256	64	0·2592	97½	0·3949	120	48·6000
32	0·1296	65	0·2633	98	0·3969	130	52·6500
32½	0·1316	66	0·2673	99	0·4010	140	56·7000

£	£	£	£	£	£	£	£
150	60·7500	300	121·5000	450	182·2500	700	283·5000
200	81·0000	350	141·7500	500	202·5000	800	324·0000
250	101·2500	400	162·0000	600	243·0000	1000	405·0000

p	£	p	£	p	£	£	£
½	0·0021	33	0·1353	67	0·2747	1	0·4100
1	0·0041	34	0·1394	67½	0·2768	2	0·8200
2	0·0082	35	0·1435	68	0·2788	3	1·2300
2½	0·0103	36	0·1476	69	0·2829	4	1·6400
3	0·0123	37	0·1517	70	0·2870	5	2·0500
4	0·0164	37½	0·1538	71	0·2911	6	2·4600
5	0·0205	38	0·1558	72	0·2952	7	2·8700
6	0·0246	39	0·1599	72½	0·2973	8	3·2800
7	0·0287	40	0·1640	73	0·2993	9	3·6900
7½	0·0308	41	0·1681	74	0·3034	10	4·1000
8	0·0328	42	0·1722	75	0·3075	11	4·5100
9	0·0369	42½	0·1743	76	0·3116	12	4·9200
10	0·0410	43	0·1763	77	0·3157	13	5·3300
11	0·0451	44	0·1804	77½	0·3178	14	5·7400
12	0·0492	45	0·1845	78	0·3198	15	6·1500
12½	0·0513	46	0·1886	79	0·3239	16	6·5600
13	0·0533	47	0·1927	80	0·3280	17	6·9700
14	0·0574	47½	0·1948	81	0·3321	18	7·3800
15	0·0615	48	0·1968	82	0·3362	19	7·7900
16	0·0656	49	0·2009	82½	0·3383	20	8·2000
17	0·0697	50	0·2050	83	0·3403	25	10·2500
17½	0·0718	51	0·2091	84	0·3444	30	12·3000
18	0·0738	52	0·2132	85	0·3485	35	14·3500
19	0·0779	52½	0·2153	86	0·3526	40	16·4000
20	0·0820	53	0·2173	87	0·3567	45	18·4500
21	0·0861	54	0·2214	87½	0·3588	50	20·5000
22	0·0902	55	0·2255	88	0·3608	55	22·5500
22½	0·0923	56	0·2296	89	0·3649	60	24·6000
23	0·0943	57	0·2337	90	0·3690	65	26·6500
24	0·0984	57½	0·2358	91	0·3731	70	28·7000
25	0·1025	58	0·2378	92	0·3772	75	30·7500
26	0·1066	59	0·2419	92½	0·3793	80	32·8000
27	0·1107	60	0·2460	93	0·3813	85	34·8500
27½	0·1128	61	0·2501	94	0·3854	90	36·9000
28	0·1148	62	0·2542	95	0·3895	95	38·9500
29	0·1189	62½	0·2563	96	0·3936	100	41·0000
30	0·1230	63	0·2583	97	0·3977	110	45·1000
31	0·1271	64	0·2624	97½	0·3998	120	49·2000
32	0·1312	65	0·2665	98	0·4018	130	53·3000
32½	0·1333	66	0·2706	99	0·4059	140	57·4000

£	£	£	£	£	£	£	£
150	61·5000	300	123·0000	450	184·5000	700	287·0000
200	82·0000	350	143·5000	500	205·0000	800	328·0000
250	102·5000	400	164·0000	600	246·0000	1000	410·0000

p	£	p	£	p	£	£	£
½ ..	0·0021	33 ..	0·1370	67 ..	0·2781	1 ..	0·4150
1 ..	0·0042	34 ..	0·1411	67½ ..	0·2801	2 ..	0·8300
2 ..	0·0083	35 ..	0·1453	68 ..	0·2822	3 ..	1·2450
2½ ..	0·0104	36 ..	0·1494	69 ..	0·2864	4 ..	1·6600
3 ..	0·0125	37 ..	0·1536	70 ..	0·2905	5 ..	2·0750
4 ..	0·0166	37½ ..	0·1556	71 ..	0·2947	6 ..	2·4900
5 ..	0·0208	38 ..	0·1577	72 ..	0·2988	7 ..	2·9050
6 ..	0·0249	39 ..	0·1619	72½ ..	0·3009	8 ..	3·3200
7 ..	0·0291	40 ..	0·1660	73 ..	0·3030	9 ..	3·7350
7½ ..	0·0311	41 ..	0·1702	74 ..	0·3071	10 ..	4·1500
8 ..	0·0332	42 ..	0·1743	75 ..	0·3113	11 ..	4·5650
9 ..	0·0374	42½ ..	0·1764	76 ..	0·3154	12 ..	4·9800
10 ..	0·0415	43 ..	0·1785	77 ..	0·3196	13 ..	5·3950
11 ..	0·0457	44 ..	0·1826	77½ ..	0·3216	14 ..	5·8100
12 ..	0·0498	45 ..	0·1868	78 ..	0·3237	15 ..	6·2250
12½ ..	0·0519	46 ..	0·1909	79 ..	0·3279	16 ..	6·6400
13 ..	0·0540	47 ..	0·1951	80 ..	0·3320	17 ..	7·0550
14 ..	0·0581	47½ ..	0·1971	81 ..	0·3362	18 ..	7·4700
15 ..	0·0623	48 ..	0·1992	82 ..	0·3403	19 ..	7·8850
16 ..	0·0664	49 ..	0·2034	82½ ..	0·3424	20 ..	8·3000
17 ..	0·0706	59 ..	0·2075	83 ..	0·3445	25 ..	10·3750
17½ ..	0·0726	51 ..	0·2117	84 ..	0·3486	30 ..	12·4500
18 ..	0·0747	52 ..	0·2158	85 ..	0·3528	35 ..	14·5250
19 ..	0·0789	52½ ..	0·2179	86 ..	0·3569	40 ..	16·6000
20 ..	0·0830	53 ..	0·2200	87 ..	0·3611	45 ..	18·6750
21 ..	0·0872	54 ..	0·2241	87½ ..	0·3631	50 ..	20·7500
22 ..	0·0913	55 ..	0·2283	88 ..	0·3652	55 ..	22·8250
22½ ..	0·0934	56 ..	0·2324	89 ..	0·3694	60 ..	24·9000
23 ..	0·0955	57 ..	0·2366	90 ..	0·3735	65 ..	26·9750
24 ..	0·0996	57½ ..	0·2386	91 ..	0·3777	70 ..	29·0500
25 ..	0·1038	58 ..	0·2407	92 ..	0·3818	75 ..	31·1250
26 ..	0·1079	59 ..	0·2449	92½ ..	0·3839	80 ..	33·2000
27 ..	0·1121	60 ..	0·2490	93 ..	0·3860	85 ..	35·2750
27½ ..	0·1141	61 ..	0·2532	94 ..	0·3901	90 ..	37·3500
28 ..	0·1162	62 ..	0·2573	95 ..	0·3943	95 ..	39·4250
29 ..	0·1204	62½ ..	0·2594	96 ..	0·3984	100 ..	41·5000
30 ..	0·1245	63 ..	0·2615	97 ..	0·4026	110 ..	45·6500
31 ..	0·1287	64 ..	0·2656	97½ ..	0·4046	120 ..	49·8000
32 ..	0·1328	65 ..	0·2698	98 ..	0·4067	130 ..	53·9500
32½ ..	0·1349	66 ..	0·2739	99 ..	0·4109	140 ..	58·1000

£	£	£	£	£	£	£	£
150 ..	62·2500	300 ..	124·5000	450 ..	186·7500	700 ..	290·5000
200 ..	83·0000	350 ..	145·2500	500 ..	207·5000	800 ..	332·0000
250 ..	103·7500	400 ..	166·0000	600 ..	249·0000	1000 ..	415·0000

Per Cent

p	£	p	£	p	£	£	£
½ ..	0·0021	33 ..	0·1386	67 ..	0·2814	1 ..	0·4200
1 ..	0·0042	34 ..	0·1428	67½ ..	0·2835	2 ..	0·8400
2 ..	0·0084	35 ..	0·1470	68 ..	0·2856	3 ..	1·2600
2½ ..	0·0105	36 ..	0·1512	69 ..	0·2898	4 ..	1·6800
3 ..	0·0126	37 ..	0·1554	70 ..	0·2940	5 ..	2·1000
4 ..	0·0168	37½ ..	0·1575	71 ..	0·2982	6 ..	2·5200
5 ..	0·0210	38 ..	0·1596	72 ..	0·3024	7 ..	2·9400
6 ..	0·0252	39 ..	0·1638	72½ ..	0·3045	8 ..	3·3600
7 ..	0·0294	40 ..	0·1680	73 ..	0·3066	9 ..	3·7800
7½ ..	0·0315	41 ..	0·1722	74 ..	0·3108	10 ..	4·2000
8 ..	0·0336	42 ..	0·1764	75 ..	0·3150	11 ..	4·6200
9 ..	0·0378	42½ ..	0·1785	76 ..	0·3192	12 ..	5·0400
10 ..	0·0420	43 ..	0·1806	77 ..	0·3234	13 ..	5·4600
11 ..	0·0462	44 ..	0·1848	77½ ..	0·3255	14 ..	5·8800
12 ..	0·0504	45 ..	0·1890	78 ..	0·3276	15 ..	6·3000
12½ ..	0·0525	46 ..	0·1932	79 ..	0·3318	16 ..	6·7200
13 ..	0·0546	47 ..	0·1974	80 ..	0·3360	17 ..	7·1400
14 ..	0·0588	47½ ..	0·1995	81 ..	0·3402	18 ..	7·5600
15 ..	0·0630	48 ..	0·2016	82 ..	0·3444	19 ..	7·9800
16 ..	0·0672	49 ..	0·2058	82½ ..	0·3465	20 ..	8·4000
17 ..	0·0714	50 ..	0·2100	83 ..	0·3486	25 ..	10·5000
17½ ..	0·0735	51 ..	0·2142	84 ..	0·3528	30 ..	12·6000
18 ..	0·0756	52 ..	0·2184	85 ..	0·3570	35 ..	14·7000
19 ..	0·0798	52½ ..	0·2205	86 ..	0·3612	40 ..	16·8000
20 ..	0·0840	53 ..	0·2226	87 ..	0·3654	45 ..	18·9000
21 ..	0·0882	54 ..	0·2268	87½ ..	0·3675	50 ..	21·0000
22 ..	0·0924	55 ..	0·2310	88 ..	0·3696	55 ..	23·1000
22½ ..	0·0945	56 ..	0·2352	89 ..	0·3738	60 ..	25·2000
23 ..	0·0966	57 ..	0·2394	90 ..	0·3780	65 ..	27·3000
24 ..	0·1008	57½ ..	0·2415	91 ..	0·3822	70 ..	29·4000
25 ..	0·1050	58 ..	0·2436	92 ..	0·3864	75 ..	31·5000
26 ..	0·1092	59 ..	0·2478	92½ ..	0·3885	80 ..	33·6000
27 ..	0·1134	60 ..	0·2520	93 ..	0·3906	85 ..	35·7000
27½ ..	0·1155	61 ..	0·2562	94 ..	0·3948	90 ..	37·8000
28 ..	0·1176	62 ..	0·2604	95 ..	0·3990	95 ..	39·9000
29 ..	0·1218	62½ ..	0·2625	96 ..	0·4032	100 ..	42·0000
30 ..	0·1260	63 ..	0·2646	97 ..	0·4074	110 ..	46·2000
31 ..	0·1302	64 ..	0·2688	97½ ..	0·4095	120 ..	50·4000
32 ..	0·1344	65 ..	0·2730	98 ..	0·4116	130 ..	54·6000
32½ ..	0·1365	66 ..	0·2772	99 ..	0·4158	140 ..	58·8000

£	£	£	£	£	£	£	£
150..	63·0000	300..	126·0000	450..	189·0000	700 ..	294·0000
200..	84·0000	350..	147·0000	500..	210·0000	800 ..	336·0000
250..	105·0000	400..	168·0000	600..	252·0000	1000 ..	420·0000

p	£	p	£	p	£	£	£
$\frac{1}{2}$	0·0021	33	0·1403	67	0·2848	1	0·4250
1	0·0043	34	0·1445	$67\frac{1}{2}$	0·2869	2	0·8500
2	0·0085	35	0·1488	68	0·2890	3	1·2750
$2\frac{1}{2}$	0·0106	36	0·1530	69	0·2933	4	1·7000
3	0·0128	37	0·1573	70	0·2975	5	2·1250
4	0·0170	$37\frac{1}{2}$	0·1594	71	0·3018	6	2·5500
5	0·0213	38	0·1615	72	0·3060	7	2·9750
6	0·0255	39	0·1658	$72\frac{1}{2}$	0·3081	8	3·4000
7	0·0298	40	0·1700	73	0·3103	9	3·8250
$7\frac{1}{2}$	0·0319	41	0·1743	74	0·3145	10	4·2500
8	0·0340	42	0·1785	75	0·3188	11	4·6750
9	0·0383	$42\frac{1}{2}$	0·1806	76	0·3230	12	5·1000
10	0·0425	43	0·1828	77	0·3273	13	5·5250
11	0·0468	44	0·1870	$77\frac{1}{2}$	0·3294	14	5·9500
12	0·0510	45	0·1913	78	0·3315	15	6·3750
$12\frac{1}{2}$	0·0531	46	0·1955	79	0·3358	16	6·8000
13	0·0553	47	0·1998	80	0·3400	17	7·2250
14	0·0595	$47\frac{1}{2}$	0·2019	81	0·3443	18	7·6500
15	0·0638	48	0·2040	82	0·3485	19	8·0750
16	0·0680	49	0·2083	$82\frac{1}{2}$	0·3506	20	8·5000
17	0·0723	50	0·2125	83	0·3528	25	10·6250
$17\frac{1}{2}$	0·0744	51	0·2168	84	0·3570	30	12·7500
18	0·0765	52	0·2210	85	0·3613	35	14·8750
19	0·0808	$52\frac{1}{2}$	0·2231	86	0·3655	40	17·0000
20	0·0850	53	0·2253	87	0·3698	45	19·1250
21	0·0893	54	0·2295	$87\frac{1}{2}$	0·3719	50	21·2500
22	0·0935	55	0·2338	88	0·3740	55	23·3750
$22\frac{1}{2}$	0·0956	56	0·2380	89	0·3783	60	25·5000
23	0·0978	57	0·2423	90	0·3825	65	27·6250
24	0·1020	$57\frac{1}{2}$	0·2444	91	0·3868	70	29·7500
25	0·1063	58	0·2465	92	0·3910	75	31·8750
26	0·1105	59	0·2508	$92\frac{1}{2}$	0·3931	80	34·0000
27	0·1148	60	0·2550	93	0·3953	85	36·1250
$27\frac{1}{2}$	0·1169	61	0·2593	94	0·3995	90	38·2500
28	0·1190	62	0·2635	95	0·4038	95	40·3750
29	0·1233	$62\frac{1}{2}$	0·2656	96	0·4080	100	42·5000
30	0·1275	63	0·2678	97	0·4123	110	46·7500
31	0·1318	64	0·2720	$97\frac{1}{2}$	0·4144	120	51·0000
32	0·1360	65	0·2763	98	0·4165	130	55·2500
$32\frac{1}{2}$	0·1381	66	0·2805	99	0·4208	140	59·5000

£	£	£	£	£	£	£	£
150	63·7500	300	127·5000	450	191·2500	700	297·5000
200	85·0000	350	148·7500	500	212·5000	800	340·0000
250	106·2500	400	170·0000	600	255·0000	1000	425·0000

Per Cent

p	£	p	£	p	£	£	£
$\frac{1}{2}$	0·0022	33	0·1419	67	0·2881	1	0·4300
1	0·0043	34	0·1462	$67\frac{1}{2}$	0·2903	2	0·8600
2	0·0086	35	0·1505	68	0·2924	3	1·2900
$2\frac{1}{2}$	0·0108	36	0·1548	69	0·2967	4	1·7200
3	0·0129	37	0·1591	70	0·3010	5	2·1500
4	0·0172	$37\frac{1}{2}$	0·1613	71	0·3053	6	2·5800
5	0·0215	38	0·1634	72	0·3096	7	3·0100
6	0·0258	39	0·1677	$72\frac{1}{2}$	0·3118	8	3·4400
7	0·0301	40	0·1720	73	0·3139	9	3·8700
$7\frac{1}{2}$	0·0323	41	0·1763	74	0·3182	10	4·3000
8	0·0344	42	0·1806	75	0·3225	11	4·7300
9	0·0387	$42\frac{1}{2}$	0·1828	76	0·3268	12	5·1600
10	0·0430	43	0·1849	77	0·3311	13	5·5900
11	0·0473	44	0·1892	$77\frac{1}{2}$	0·3333	14	6·0200
12	0·0516	45	0·1935	78	0·3354	15	6·4500
$12\frac{1}{2}$	0·0538	46	0·1978	79	0·3397	16	6·8800
13	0·0559	47	0·2021	80	0·3440	17	7·3100
14	0·0602	$47\frac{1}{2}$	0·2043	81	0·3483	18	7·7400
15	0·0645	48	0·2064	82	0·3526	19	8·1700
16	0·0688	49	0·2107	$82\frac{1}{2}$	0·3548	20	8·6000
17	0·0731	50	0·2150	83	0·3569	25	10·7500
$17\frac{1}{2}$	0·0753	51	0·2193	84	0·3612	30	12·9000
18	0·0774	52	0·2236	85	0·3655	35	15·0500
19	0·0817	$52\frac{1}{2}$	0·2258	86	0·3698	40	17·2000
20	0·0860	53	0·2279	87	0·3741	45	19·3500
21	0·0903	54	0·2322	$87\frac{1}{2}$	0·3763	50	21·5000
22	0·0946	55	0·2365	88	0·3784	55	23·6500
$22\frac{1}{2}$	0·0968	56	0·2408	89	0·3827	60	25·8000
23	0·0989	57	0·2451	90	0·3870	65	27·9500
24	0·1032	$57\frac{1}{2}$	0·2473	91	0·3913	70	30·1000
25	0·1075	58	0·2494	92	0·3956	75	32·2500
26	0·1118	59	0·2537	$92\frac{1}{2}$	0·3978	80	34·4000
27	0·1161	60	0·2580	93	0·3999	85	36·5500
$27\frac{1}{2}$	0·1183	61	0·2623	94	0·4042	90	38·7000
28	0·1204	62	0·2666	95	0·4085	95	40·8500
29	0·1247	$62\frac{1}{2}$	0·2688	96	0·4128	100	43·0000
30	0·1290	63	0·2709	97	0·4171	110	47·3000
31	0·1333	64	0·2752	$97\frac{1}{2}$	0·4193	120	51·6000
32	0·1376	65	0·2795	98	0·4214	130	55·9000
$32\frac{1}{2}$	0·1398	66	0·2838	99	0·4257	140	60·2000

£	£	£	£	£	£	£	£
150	64·5000	300	129·0000	450	193·5000	700	301·0000
200	86·0000	350	150·5000	500	215·0000	800	344·0000
250	107·5000	400	172·0000	600	258·0000	1000	430·0000

p	£	p	£	p	£	£	£
½	0·0022	33	0·1436	67	0·2915	1	0·4350
1	0·0044	34	0·1479	67½	0·2936	2	0·8700
2	0·0087	35	0·1523	68	0·2958	3	1·3050
2½	0·0109	36	0·1566	69	0·3002	4	1·7400
3	0·0131	37	0·1610	70	0·3045	5	2·1750
4	0·0174	37½	0·1631	71	0·3089	6	2·6100
5	0·0218	38	0·1653	72	0·3132	7	3·0450
6	0·0261	39	0·1697	72½	0·3154	8	3·4800
7	0·0305	40	0·1740	73	0·3176	9	3·9150
7½	0·0326	41	0·1784	74	0·3219	10	4·3500
8	0·0348	42	0·1827	75	0·3263	11	4·7850
9	0·0392	42½	0·1849	76	0·3306	12	5·2200
10	0·0435	43	0·1871	77	0·3350	13	5·6550
11	0·0479	44	0·1914	77½	0·3371	14	6·0900
12	0·0522	45	0·1958	78	0·3393	15	6·5250
12½	0·0544	46	0·2001	79	0·3437	16	6·9600
13	0·0566	47	0·2045	80	0·3480	17	7·3950
14	0·0609	47½	0·2066	81	0·3524	18	7·8300
15	0·0653	48	0·2088	82	0·3567	19	8·2650
16	0·0696	49	0·2132	82½	0·3589	20	8·7000
17	0·0740	50	0·2175	83	0·3611	25	10·8750
17½	0·0761	51	0·2219	84	0·3654	30	13·0500
18	0·0783	52	0·2262	85	0·3698	35	15·2250
19	0·0827	52½	0·2284	86	0·3741	40	17·4000
20	0·0870	53	0·2306	87	0·3785	45	19·5750
21	0·0914	54	0·2349	87½	0·3806	50	21·7500
22	0·0957	55	0·2393	88	0·3828	55	23·9250
22½	0·0979	56	0·2436	89	0·3872	60	26·1000
23	0·1001	57	0·2480	90	0·3915	65	28·2750
24	0·1044	57½	0·2501	91	0·3959	70	30·4500
25	0·1088	58	0·2523	92	0·4002	75	32·6250
26	0·1131	59	0·2567	92½	0·4024	80	34·8000
27	0·1175	60	0·2610	93	0·4046	85	36·9750
27½	0·1196	61	0·2654	94	0·4089	90	39·1500
28	0·1218	62	0·2697	95	0·4133	95	41·3250
29	0·1262	62½	0·2719	96	0·4176	100	43·5000
30	0·1305	63	0·2741	97	0·4220	110	47·8500
31	0·1349	64	0·2784	97½	0·4241	120	52·2000
32	0·1392	65	0·2828	98	0·4263	130	56·5500
32½	0·1414	66	0·2871	99	0·4307	140	60·9000

£	£	£	£	£	£	£	£
150	65·2500	300	130·5000	450	195·7500	700	304·5000
200	87·0000	350	152·2500	500	217·5000	800	348·0000
250	108·7500	400	174·0000	600	261·0000	1000	435·0000

p	£	p	£	p	£	£	£
½	0·0022	33	0·1452	67	0·2948	1	0·4400
1	0·0044	34	0·1496	67½	0·2970	2	0·8800
2	0·0088	35	0·1540	68	0·2992	3	1·3200
2½	0·0110	36	0·1584	69	0·3036	4	1·7600
3	0·0132	37	0·1628	70	0·3080	5	2·2000
4	0·0176	37½	0·1650	71	0·3124	6	2·6400
5	0·0220	38	0·1672	72	0·3168	7	3·0800
6	0·0264	39	0·1716	72½	0·3190	8	3·5200
7	0·0308	40	0·1760	73	0·3212	9	3·9600
7½	0·0330	41	0·1804	74	0·3256	10	4·4000
8	0·0352	42	0·1848	75	0·3300	11	4·8400
9	0·0396	42½	0·1870	76	0·3344	12	5·2800
10	0·0440	43	0·1892	77	0·3388	13	5·7200
11	0·0484	44	0·1936	77½	0·3410	14	6·1600
12	0·0528	45	0·1980	78	0·3432	15	6·6000
12½	0·0550	46	0·2024	79	0·3476	16	7·0400
13	0·0572	47	0·2068	80	0·3520	17	7·4800
14	0·0616	47½	0·2090	81	0·3564	18	7·9200
15	0·0660	48	0·2112	82	0·3608	19	8·3600
16	0·0704	49	0·2156	82½	0·3630	20	8·8000
17	0·0748	50	0·2200	83	0·3652	25	11·0000
17½	0·0770	51	0·2244	84	0·3696	30	13·2000
18	0·0792	52	0·2288	85	0·3740	35	15·4000
19	0·0836	52½	0·2310	86	0·3784	40	17·6000
20	0·0880	53	0·2332	87	0·3828	45	19·8000
21	0·0924	54	0·2376	87½	0·3850	50	22·0000
22	0·0968	55	0·2420	88	0·3872	55	24·2000
22½	0·0990	56	0·2464	89	0·3916	60	26·4000
23	0·1012	57	0·2508	90	0·3960	65	28·6000
24	0·1056	57½	0·2530	91	0·4004	70	30·8000
25	0·1100	58	0·2552	92	0·4048	75	33·0000
26	0·1144	59	0·2596	92½	0·4070	80	35·2000
27	0·1188	60	0·2640	93	0·4092	85	37·4000
27½	0·1210	61	0·2684	94	0·4136	90	39·6000
28	0·1232	62	0·2728	95	0·4180	95	41·8000
29	0·1276	62½	0·2750	96	0·4224	100	44·0000
30	0·1320	63	0·2772	97	0·4268	110	48·4000
31	0·1364	64	0·2816	97½	0·4290	120	52·8000
32	0·1408	65	0·2860	98	0·4312	130	57·2000
32½	0·1430	66	0·2904	99	0·4356	140	61·6000

£	£	£	£	£	£	£	£
150	66·0000	300	132·0000	450	198·0000	700	308·0000
200	88·0000	350	154·0000	500	220·0000	800	352·0000
250	110·0000	400	176·0000	600	264·0000	1000	440·0000

p	£	p	£	p	£	£	£
½	0·0022	33	0·1469	67	0·2982	1	0·4450
1	0·0045	34	0·1513	67½	0·3004	2	0·8900
2	0·0089	35	0·1558	68	0·3026	3	1·3350
2½	0·0111	36	0·1602	69	0·3071	4	1·7800
3	0·0134	37	0·1647	70	0·3115	5	2·2250
4	0·0178	37½	0·1669	71	0·3160	6	2·6700
5	0·0223	38	0·1691	72	0·3204	7	3·1150
6	0·0267	39	0·1736	72½	0·3226	8	3·5600
7	0·0312	40	0·1780	73	0·3249	9	4·0050
7½	0·0334	41	0·1825	74	0·3293	10	4·4500
8	0·0356	42	0·1869	75	0·3338	11	4·8950
9	0·0401	42½	0·1891	76	0·3382	12	5·3400
10	0·0445	43	0·1914	77	0·3427	13	5·7850
11	0·0490	44	0·1958	77½	0·3449	14	6·2300
12	0·0534	45	0·2003	78	0·3471	15	6·6750
12½	0·0556	46	0·2047	79	0·3516	16	7·1200
13	0·0579	47	0·2092	80	0·3560	17	7·5650
14	0·0623	47½	0·2114	81	0·3605	18	8·0100
15	0·0668	48	0·2136	82	0·3649	19	8·4550
16	0·0712	49	0·2181	82½	0·3671	20	8·9000
17	0·0757	50	0·2225	83	0·3694	25	11·1250
17½	0·0779	51	0·2270	84	0·3738	30	13·3500
18	0·0801	52	0·2314	85	0·3783	35	15·5750
19	0·0846	52½	0·2336	86	0·3827	40	17·8000
20	0·0890	53	0·2359	87	0·3872	45	20·0250
21	0·0935	54	0·2403	87½	0·3894	50	22·2500
22	0·0979	55	0·2448	88	0·3916	55	24·4750
22½	0·1001	56	0·2492	89	0·3961	60	26·7000
23	0·1024	57	0·2537	90	0·4005	65	28·9250
24	0·1068	57½	0·2559	91	0·4050	70	31·1500
25	0·1113	58	0·2581	92	0·4094	75	33·3750
26	0·1157	59	0·2626	92½	0·4116	80	35·6000
27	0·1202	60	0·2670	93	0·4139	85	37·8250
27½	0·1224	61	0·2715	94	0·4183	90	40·0500
28	0·1246	62	0·2759	95	0·4228	95	42·2750
29	0·1291	62½	0·2781	96	0·4272	100	44·5000
30	0·1335	63	0·2804	97	0·4317	110	48·9500
31	0·1380	64	0·2848	97½	0·4339	120	53·4000
32	0·1424	65	0·2893	98	0·4361	130	57·8500
32½	0·1446	66	0·2937	99	0·4406	140	62·3000

£	£	£	£	£	£	£	£
150	66·7500	300	133·5000	450	200·2500	700	311·5000
200	89·0000	350	155·7500	500	222·5000	800	356·0000
250	111·2500	400	178·0000	600	267·0000	1000	445·0000

p	£	p	£	p	£	£	£
½ ..	0·0023	33 ..	0·1485	67 ..	0·3015	1 ..	0·4500
1 ..	0·0045	34 ..	0·1530	67½ ..	0·3038	2 ..	0·9000
2 ..	0·0090	35 ..	0·1575	68 ..	0·3060	3 ..	1·3500
2½ ..	0·0113	36 ..	0·1620	69 ..	0·3105	4 ..	1·8000
3 ..	0·0135	37 ..	0·1665	70 ..	0·3150	5 ..	2·2500
4 ..	0·0180	37½ ..	0·1688	71 ..	0·3195	6 ..	2·7000
5 ..	0·0225	38 ..	0·1710	72 ..	0·3240	7 ..	3·1500
6 ..	0·0270	39 ..	0·1755	72½ ..	0·3263	8 ..	3·6000
7 ..	0·0315	40 ..	0·1800	73 ..	0·3285	9 ..	4·0500
7½ ..	0·0338	41 ..	0·1845	74 ..	0·3330	10 ..	4·5000
8 ..	0·0360	42 ..	0·1890	75 ..	0·3375	11 ..	4·9500
9 ..	0·0405	42½ ..	0·1913	76 ..	0·3420	12 ..	5·4000
10 ..	0·0450	43 ..	0·1935	77 ..	0·3465	13 ..	5·8500
11 ..	0·0495	44 ..	0·1980	77½ ..	0·3488	14 ..	6·3000
12 ..	0·0540	45 ..	0·2025	78 ..	0·3510	15 ..	6·7500
12½ ..	0·0563	46 ..	0·2070	79 ..	0·3555	16 ..	7·2000
13 ..	0·0585	47 ..	0·2115	80 ..	0·3600	17 ..	7·6500
14 ..	0·0630	47½ ..	0·2138	81 ..	0·3645	18 ..	8·1000
15 ..	0·0675	48 ..	0·2160	82 ..	0·3690	19 ..	8·5500
16 ..	0·0720	49 ..	0·2205	82½ ..	0·3713	20 ..	9·0000
17 ..	0·0765	50 ..	0·2250	83 ..	0·3735	25 ..	11·2500
17½ ..	0·0788	51 ..	0·2295	84 ..	0·3780	30 ..	13·5000
18 ..	0·0810	52 ..	0·2340	85 ..	0·3825	35 ..	15·7500
19 ..	0·0855	52½ ..	0·2363	86 ..	0·3870	40 ..	18·0000
20 ..	0·0900	53 ..	0·2385	87 ..	0·3915	45 ..	20·2500
21 ..	0·0945	54 ..	0·2430	87½ ..	0·3938	50 ..	22·5000
22 ..	0·0990	55 ..	0·2475	88 ..	0·3960	55 ..	24·7500
22½ ..	0·1013	56 ..	0·2520	89 ..	0·4005	60 ..	27·0000
23 ..	0·1035	57 ..	0·2565	90 ..	0·4050	65 ..	29·5000
24 ..	0·1080	57½ ..	0·2588	91 ..	0·4095	70 ..	31·5000
25 ..	0·1125	58 ..	0·2610	92 ..	0·4140	75 ..	33·7500
26 ..	0·1170	59 ..	0·2655	92½ ..	0·4163	80 ..	36·0000
27 ..	0·1215	60 ..	0·2700	93 ..	0·4185	85 ..	38·2500
27½ ..	0·1238	61 ..	0·2745	94 ..	0·4230	90 ..	40·5000
28 ..	0·1260	62 ..	0·2790	95 ..	0·4275	95 ..	42·7500
29 ..	0·1305	62½ ..	0·2813	96 ..	0·4320	100 ..	45·0000
30 ..	0·1350	63 ..	0·2835	97 ..	0·4365	110 ..	49·5000
31 ..	0·1395	64 ..	0·2880	97½ ..	0·4388	120 ..	54·0000
32 ..	0·1440	65 ..	0·2925	98 ..	0·4410	130 ..	58·5000
32½ ..	0·1463	66 ..	0·2970	99 ..	0·4455	140 ..	63·0000

£	£	£	£	£	£	£	£
150..	67·5000	300..	135·0000	450..	202·5000	700 ..	315·0000
200..	90·0000	350..	157·5000	500..	225·0000	800 ..	360·0000
250..	112·5000	400..	180·0000	600..	270·0000	1000 ..	450·0000

p	£	p	£	p	£	£	£
$\frac{1}{2}$ ..	0·0023	33 ..	0·1502	67 ..	0·3049	1 ..	0·4550
1 ..	0·0046	34 ..	0·1547	$67\frac{1}{2}$ ..	0·3071	2 ..	0·9100
2 ..	0·0091	35 ..	0·1593	68 ..	0·3094	3 ..	1·3650
$2\frac{1}{2}$ ..	0·0114	36 ..	0·1638	69 ..	0·3140	4 ..	1·8200
3 ..	0·0137	37 ..	0·1684	70 ..	0·3185	5 ..	2·2750
4 ..	0·0182	$37\frac{1}{2}$ ..	0·1706	71 ..	0·3231	6 ..	2·7300
5 ..	0·0228	38 ..	0·1729	72 ..	0·3276	7 ..	3·1850
6 ..	0·0273	39 ..	0·1775	$72\frac{1}{2}$ ..	0·3299	8 ..	3·6400
7 ..	0·0319	40 ..	0·1820	73 ..	0·3322	9 ..	4·0950
$7\frac{1}{2}$ ..	0·0341	41 ..	0·1866	74 ..	0·3367	10 ..	4·5500
8 ..	0·0364	42 ..	0·1911	75 ..	0·3413	11 ..	5·0050
9 ..	0·0410	$42\frac{1}{2}$ ..	0·1934	76 ..	0·3458	12 ..	5·4600
10 ..	0·0455	43 ..	0·1957	77 ..	0·3504	13 ..	5·9150
11 ..	0·0501	44 ..	0·2002	$77\frac{1}{2}$ ..	0·3526	14 ..	6·3700
12 ..	0·0546	45 ..	0·2048	78 ..	0·3549	15 ..	6·8250
$12\frac{1}{2}$ ..	0·0569	46 ..	0·2093	79 ..	0·3595	16 ..	7·2800
13 ..	0·0592	47 ..	0·2139	80 ..	0·3640	17 ..	7·7350
14 ..	0·0637	$47\frac{1}{2}$ ..	0·2161	81 ..	0·3686	18 ..	8·1900
15 ..	0·0683	48 ..	0·2184	82 ..	0·3731	19 ..	8·6450
16 ..	0·0728	49 ..	0·2230	$82\frac{1}{2}$ ..	0·3754	20 ..	9·1000
17 ..	0·0774	50 ..	0·2275	83 ..	0·3777	25 ..	11·3750
$17\frac{1}{2}$ ..	0·0796	51 ..	0·2321	84 ..	0·3822	30 ..	13·6500
18 ..	0·0819	52 ..	0·2366	85 ..	0·3868	35 ..	15·9250
19 ..	0·0865	$52\frac{1}{2}$ ..	0·2389	86 ..	0·3913	40 ..	18·2000
20 ..	0·0910	53 ..	0·2412	87 ..	0·3959	45 ..	20·4750
21 ..	0·0956	54 ..	0·2457	$87\frac{1}{2}$ ..	0·3981	50 ..	22·7500
22 ..	0·1001	55 ..	0·2503	88 ..	0·4004	55 ..	25·0250
$22\frac{1}{2}$ ..	0·1024	56 ..	0·2548	89 ..	0·4050	60 ..	27·3000
23 ..	0·1047	57 ..	0·2594	90 ..	0·4095	65 ..	29·5750
24 ..	0·1092	$57\frac{1}{2}$ ..	0·2616	91 ..	0·4141	70 ..	31·8500
25 ..	0·1138	58 ..	0·2639	92 ..	0·4186	75 ..	34·1250
26 ..	0·1183	59 ..	0·2685	$92\frac{1}{2}$ ..	0·4209	80 ..	36·4000
27 ..	0·1229	60 ..	0·2730	93 ..	0·4232	85 ..	38·6750
$27\frac{1}{2}$ ..	0·1251	61 ..	0·2776	94 ..	0·4277	90 ..	40·9500
28 ..	0·1274	62 ..	0·2821	95 ..	0·4323	95 ..	43·2250
29 ..	0·1320	$62\frac{1}{2}$ ..	0·2844	96 ..	0·4368	100 ..	45·5000
30 ..	0·1365	63 ..	0·2867	97 ..	0·4414	110 ..	50·0500
31 ..	0·1411	64 ..	0·2912	$97\frac{1}{2}$ ..	0·4436	120 ..	54·6000
32 ..	0·1456	65 ..	0·2958	98 ..	0·4459	130 ..	59·1500
$32\frac{1}{2}$ ..	0·1479	66 ..	0·3003	99 ..	0·4505	140 ..	63·7000

£	£	£	£	£	£	£	£
150..	68·2500	300..	136·5000	450..	204·7500	700 ..	318·5000
200..	91·0000	350..	159·2500	500..	227·5000	800 ..	364·0000
250..	113·7500	400..	182·0000	600..	273·0000	1000 ..	455·0000

p	£	p	£	p	£	£	£
$\frac{1}{2}$ ..	0·0024	33 ..	0·1568	67 ..	0·3183	1 ..	0·4750
1 ..	0·0048	34 ..	0·1615	$67\frac{1}{2}$ ..	0·3206	2 ..	0·9500
2 ..	0·0095	35 ..	0·1663	68 ..	0·3230	3 ..	1·4250
$2\frac{1}{2}$ ..	0·0119	36 ..	0·1710	69 ..	0·3278	4 ..	1·9000
3 ..	0·0143	37 ..	0·1758	70 ..	0·3325	5 ..	2·3750
4 ..	0·0190	$37\frac{1}{2}$ ..	0·1781	71 ..	0·3373	6 ..	2·8500
5 ..	0·0238	38 ..	0·1805	72 ..	0·3420	7 ..	3·3250
6 ..	0·0285	39 ..	0·1853	$72\frac{1}{2}$ ..	0·3444	8 ..	3·8000
7 ..	0·0333	40 ..	0·1900	73 ..	0·3468	9 ..	4·2750
$7\frac{1}{2}$ ..	0·0356	41 ..	0·1948	74 ..	0·3515	10 ..	4·7500
8 ..	0·0380	42 ..	0·1995	75 ..	0·3563	11 ..	5·2250
9 ..	0·0428	$42\frac{1}{2}$ ..	0·2019	76 ..	0·3610	12 ..	5·7000
10 ..	0·0475	43 ..	0·2043	77 ..	0·3658	13 ..	6·1750
11 ..	0·0523	44 ..	0·2090	$77\frac{1}{2}$ ..	0·3681	14 ..	6·6500
12 ..	0·0570	45 ..	0·2138	78 ..	0·3705	15 ..	7·1250
$12\frac{1}{2}$ ..	0·0594	46 ..	0·2185	79 ..	0·3753	16 ..	7·6000
13 ..	0·0618	47 ..	0·2233	80 ..	0·3800	17 ..	8·0750
14 ..	0·0665	$47\frac{1}{2}$ ..	0·2256	81 ..	0·3848	18 ..	8·5500
15 ..	0·0713	48 ..	0·2280	82 ..	0·3895	19 ..	9·0250
16 ..	0·0760	49 ..	0·2328	$82\frac{1}{2}$ ..	0·3919	20 ..	9·5000
17 ..	0·0808	50 ..	0·2375	83 ..	0·3943	25 ..	11·8750
$17\frac{1}{2}$ ..	0·0831	51 ..	0·2423	84 ..	0·3990	30 ..	14·2500
18 ..	0·0855	52 ..	0·2470	85 ..	0·4038	35 ..	16·6250
19 ..	0·0903	$52\frac{1}{2}$ ..	0·2494	86 ..	0·4085	40 ..	19·0000
20 ..	0·0950	53 ..	0·2518	87 ..	0·4133	45 ..	21·3750
21 ..	0·0998	54 ..	0·2565	$87\frac{1}{2}$ ..	0·4156	50 ..	23·7500
22 ..	0·1045	55 ..	0·2613	88 ..	0·4180	55 ..	26·1250
$22\frac{1}{2}$ ..	0·1069	56 ..	0·2660	89 ..	0·4228	60 ..	28·5000
23 ..	0·1093	57 ..	0·2708	90 ..	0·4275	65 ..	30·8750
24 ..	0·1140	$57\frac{1}{2}$ ..	0·2731	91 ..	0·4323	70 ..	33·2500
25 ..	0·1188	58 ..	0·2755	92 ..	0·4370	75 ..	35·6250
26 ..	0·1235	59 ..	0·2803	$92\frac{1}{2}$ ..	0·4394	80 ..	38·0000
27 ..	0·1283	60 ..	0·2850	93 ..	0·4418	85 ..	40·3750
$27\frac{1}{2}$ ..	0·1306	61 ..	0·2898	94 ..	0·4465	90 ..	42·7500
28 ..	0·1330	62 ..	0·2945	95 ..	0·4513	95 ..	45·1250
29 ..	0·1378	$62\frac{1}{2}$ ..	0·2969	96 ..	0·4560	100 ..	47·5000
30 ..	0·1425	63 ..	0·2993	97 ..	0·4608	110 ..	52·2500
31 ..	0·1473	64 ..	0·3040	$97\frac{1}{2}$ ..	0·4631	120 ..	57·0000
32 ..	0·1520	65 ..	0·3088	98 ..	0·4655	130 ..	61·7500
$32\frac{1}{2}$ ..	0·1544	66 ..	0·3135	99 ..	0·4703	140 ..	66·5000

£	£	£	£	£	£	£	£
150..	71·2500	300..	142·5000	450..	213·7500	700 ..	332·5000
200..	95·0000	350..	166·2500	500..	237·5000	800 ..	380·0000
250..	118·7500	400..	190·0000	600..	285·0000	1000 ..	475·0000

p	£	p	£	p	£	£	£
½	0·0025	33	0·1650	67	0·3350	1	0·5000
1	0·0050	34	0·1700	67½	0·3375	2	1·0000
2	0·0100	35	0·1750	68	0·3400	3	1·5000
2½	0·0125	36	0·1800	69	0·3450	4	2·0000
3	0·0150	37	0·1850	70	0·3500	5	2·5000
4	0·0200	37½	0·1875	71	0·3550	6	3·0000
5	0·0250	38	0·1900	72	0·3600	7	3·5000
6	0·0300	39	0·1950	72½	0·3625	8	4·0000
7	0·0350	40	0·2000	73	0·3650	9	4·5000
7½	0·0375	41	0·2050	74	0·3700	10	5·0000
8	0·0400	42	0·2100	75	0·3750	11	5·5000
9	0·0450	42½	0·2125	76	0·3800	12	6·0000
10	0·0500	43	0·2150	77	0·3850	13	6·5000
11	0·0550	44	0·2200	77½	0·3875	14	7·0000
12	0·0600	45	0·2250	78	0·3900	15	7·5000
12½	0·0625	46	0·2300	79	0·3950	16	8·0000
13	0·0650	47	0·2350	80	0·4000	17	8·5000
14	0·0700	47½	0·2375	81	0·4050	18	9·0000
15	0·0750	48	0·2400	82	0·4100	19	9·5000
16	0·0800	49	0·2450	82½	0·4125	20	10·0000
17	0·0850	50	0·2500	83	0·4150	25	12·5000
17½	0·0875	51	0·2550	84	0·4200	30	15·0000
18	0·0900	52	0·2600	85	0·4250	35	17·5000
19	0·0950	52½	0·2625	86	0·4300	40	20·0000
20	0·1000	53	0·2650	87	0·4350	45	22·5000
21	0·1050	54	0·2700	87½	0·4375	50	25·0000
22	0·1100	55	0·2750	88	0·4400	55	27·5000
22½	0·1125	56	0·2800	89	0·4450	60	30·0000
23	0·1150	57	0·2850	90	0·4500	65	32·5000
24	0·1200	57½	0·2875	91	0·4550	70	35·0000
25	0·1250	58	0·2900	92	0·4600	75	37·5000
26	0·1300	59	0·2950	92½	0·4625	80	40·0000
27	0·1350	60	0·3000	93	0·4650	85	42·5000
27½	0·1375	61	0·3050	94	0·4700	90	45·0000
28	0·1400	62	0·3100	95	0·4750	95	47·5000
29	0·1450	62½	0·3125	96	0·4800	100	50·0000
30	0·1500	63	0·3150	97	0·4850	110	55·0000
31	0·1550	64	0·3200	97½	0·4875	120	60·0000
32	0·1600	65	0·3250	98	0·4900	130	65·0000
32½	0·1625	66	0·3300	99	0·4950	140	70·0000

£	£	£	£	£	£	£	£
150	75·0000	300	150·0000	450	225·0000	700	350·0000
200	100·0000	350	175·0000	500	250·0000	800	400·0000
250	125·0000	400	200·0000	600	300·0000	1000	500·0000

p	£	p	£	p	£	£	£
½	0·0026	33	0·1733	67	0·3518	1	0·5250
1	0·0053	34	0·1785	67½	0·3544	2	1·0500
2	0·0105	35	0·1838	68	0·3570	3	1·5750
2½	0·0131	36	0·1890	69	0·3623	4	2·1000
3	0·0158	37	0·1943	70	0·3675	5	2·6250
4	0·0210	37½	0·1969	71	0·3728	6	3·1500
5	0·0263	38	0·1995	72	0·3780	7	3·6750
6	0·0315	39	0·2048	72½	0·3806	8	4·2000
7	0·0368	40	0·2100	73	0·3833	9	4·7250
7½	0·0394	41	0·2153	74	0·3885	10	5·2500
8	0·0420	42	0·2205	75	0·3938	11	5·7750
9	0·0473	42½	0·2231	76	0·3990	12	6·3000
10	0·0525	43	0·2258	77	0·4043	13	6·8250
11	0·0578	44	0·2310	77½	0·4069	14	7·3500
12	0·0630	45	0·2363	78	0·4095	15	7·8750
12½	0·0656	46	0·2415	79	0·4148	16	8·4000
13	0·0683	47	0·2468	80	0·4200	17	8·9250
14	0·0735	47½	0·2494	81	0·4253	18	9·4500
15	0·0788	48	0·2520	82	0·4305	19	9·9750
16	0·0840	49	0·2573	82½	0·4331	20	10·5000
17	0·0893	50	0·2625	83	0·4358	25	13·1250
17½	0·0919	51	0·2678	84	0·4410	30	15·7500
18	0·0945	52	0·2730	85	0·4463	35	18·3750
19	0·0998	52½	0·2756	86	0·4515	40	21·0000
20	0·1050	53	0·2783	87	0·4568	45	23·6250
21	0·1103	54	0·2835	87½	0·4594	50	26·2500
22	0·1155	55	0·2888	88	0·4620	55	28·8750
22½	0·1181	56	0·2940	89	0·4673	60	31·5000
23	0·1208	57	0·2993	90	0·4725	65	34·1250
24	0·1260	57½	0·3019	91	0·4778	70	36·7500
25	0·1313	58	0·3045	92	0·4830	75	39·3750
26	0·1365	59	0·3098	92½	0·4856	80	42·0000
27	0·1418	60	0·3150	93	0·4883	85	44·6250
27½	0·1444	61	0·3203	94	0·4935	90	47·2500
28	0·1470	62	0·3255	95	0·4988	95	49·8750
29	0·1523	62½	0·3281	96	0·5040	100	52·5000
30	0·1575	63	0·3308	97	0·5093	110	57·7500
31	0·1628	64	0·3360	97½	0·5119	120	63·0000
32	0·1680	65	0·3413	98	0·5145	130	68·2500
32½	0·1706	66	0·3465	99	0·5198	140	73·5000

£	£	£	£	£	£	£	£
150	78·7500	300	157·5000	450	236·2500	700	367·5000
200	105·0000	350	183·7500	500	262·5000	800	420·0000
250	131·2500	400	210·0000	600	315·0000	1000	525·0000

p	£	p	£	p	£	£	£
½	0·0028	33	0·1815	67	0·3685	1	0·5500
1	0·0055	34	0·1870	67½	0·3713	2	1·1000
2	0·0110	35	0·1925	68	0·3740	3	1·6500
2½	0·0138	36	0·1980	69	0·3795	4	2·2000
3	0·0165	37	0·2035	70	0·3850	5	2·7500
4	0·0220	37½	0·2063	71	0·3905	6	3·3000
5	0·0275	38	0·2090	72	0·3960	7	3·8500
6	0·0330	39	0·2145	72½	0·3988	8	4·4000
7	0·0385	40	0·2200	73	0·4015	9	4·9500
7½	0·0413	41	0·2255	74	0·4070	10	5·5000
8	0·0440	42	0·2310	75	0·4125	11	6·0500
9	0·0495	42½	0·2338	76	0·4180	12	6·6000
10	0·0550	43	0·2365	77	0·4235	13	7·1500
11	0·0605	44	0·2420	77½	0·4263	14	7·7000
12	0·0660	45	0·2475	78	0·4290	15	8·2500
12½	0·0688	46	0·2530	79	0·4345	16	8·8000
13	0·0715	47	0·2585	80	0·4400	17	9·3500
14	0·0770	47½	0·2613	81	0·4455	18	9·9000
15	0·0825	48	0·2640	82	0·4510	19	10·4500
16	0·0880	49	0·2695	82½	0·4538	20	11·0000
17	0·0935	50	0·2750	83	0·4565	25	13·7500
17½	0·0963	51	0·2805	84	0·4620	30	16·5000
18	0·0990	52	0·2860	85	0·4675	35	19·2500
19	0·1045	52½	0·2888	86	0·4730	40	22·0000
20	0·1100	53	0·2915	87	0·4785	45	24·7500
21	0·1155	54	0·2970	87½	0·4813	50	27·5000
22	0·1210	55	0·3025	88	0·4840	55	30·2500
22½	0·1238	56	0·3080	89	0·4895	60	33·0000
23	0·1265	57	0·3135	90	0·4950	65	35·7500
24	0·1320	57½	0·3163	91	0·5005	70	38·5000
25	0·1375	58	0·3190	92	0·5060	75	41·2500
26	0·1430	59	0·3245	92½	0·5088	80	44·0000
27	0·1485	60	0·3300	93	0·5115	85	46·7500
27½	0·1513	61	0·3355	94	0·5170	90	49·5000
28	0·1540	62	0·3410	95	0·5225	95	52·2500
29	0·1595	62½	0·3438	96	0·5280	100	55·0000
30	0·1650	63	0·3465	97	0·5335	110	60·5000
31	0·1705	64	0·3520	97½	0·5363	120	66·0000
32	0·1760	65	0·3575	98	0·5390	130	71·5000
32½	0·1788	66	0·3630	99	0·5445	140	77·0000

£	£	£	£	£	£	£	£
150	82·5000	300	165·0000	450	247·5000	700	385·0000
200	110·0000	350	192·5000	500	275·0000	800	440·0000
250	137·5000	400	220·0000	600	330·0000	1000	550·0000

p	£	p	£	p	£	£	£
½	0·0029	33	0·1898	67	0·3853	1	0·5750
1	0·0058	34	0·1955	67½	0·3881	2	1·1500
2	0·0115	35	0·2013	68	0·3910	3	1·7250
2½	0·0144	36	0·2070	69	0·3968	4	2·3000
3	0·0173	37	0·2128	70	0·4025	5	2·8750
4	0·0230	37½	0·2156	71	0·4083	6	3·4500
5	0·0288	38	0·2185	72	0·4140	7	4·0250
6	0·0345	39	0·2243	72½	0·4169	8	4·6000
7	0·0403	40	0·2300	73	0·4198	9	5·1750
7½	0·0431	41	0·2358	74	0·4255	10	5·7500
8	0·0460	42	0·2415	75	0·4313	11	6·3250
9	0·0518	42½	0·2444	76	0·4370	12	6·9000
10	0·0575	43	0·2473	77	0·4428	13	7·4750
11	0·0633	44	0·2530	77½	0·4456	14	8·0500
12	0·0690	45	0·2588	78	0·4485	15	8·6250
12½	0·0719	46	0·2645	79	0·4543	16	9·2000
13	0·0748	47	0·2703	80	0·4600	17	9·7750
14	0·0805	47½	0·2731	81	0·4658	18	10·3500
15	0·0863	48	0·2760	82	0·4715	19	10·9250
16	0·0920	49	0·2818	82½	0·4744	20	11·5000
17	0·0978	50	0·2875	83	0·4773	25	14·3750
17½	0·1006	51	0·2933	84	0·4830	30	17·2500
18	0·1035	52	0·2990	85	0·4888	35	20·1250
19	0·1093	52½	0·3019	86	0·4945	40	23·0000
20	0·1150	53	0·3048	87	0·5003	45	25·8750
21	0·1208	54	0·3105	87½	0·5031	50	28·7500
22	0·1265	55	0·3163	88	0·5060	55	31·6250
22½	0·1294	56	0·3220	89	0·5118	60	34·5000
23	0·1323	57	0·3278	90	0·5175	65	37·3750
24	0·1380	57½	0·3306	91	0·5233	70	40·2500
25	0·1438	58	0·3335	92	0·5290	75	43·1250
26	0·1495	59	0·3393	92½	0·5319	80	46·0000
27	0·1553	60	0·3450	93	0·5348	85	48·8750
27½	0·1581	61	0·3508	94	0·5405	90	51·7500
28	0·1610	62	0·3565	95	0·5463	95	54·6250
29	0·1668	62½	0·3594	96	0·5520	100	57·5000
30	0·1725	63	0·3623	97	0·5578	110	63·2500
31	0·1783	64	0·3680	97½	0·5606	120	69·0000
32	0·1840	65	0·3738	98	0·5635	130	74·7500
32½	0·1869	66	0·3795	99	0·5693	140	80·5000

£	£	£	£	£	£	£	£
150	86·2500	300	172·5000	450	258·7500	700	402·5000
200	115·0000	350	201·2500	500	287·5000	800	460·0000
250	143·7500	400	230·0000	600	345·0000	1000	575·0000

p	£	p	£	p	£	£	£
½	.. 0·0030	33	.. 0·1980	67	.. 0·4020	1	.. 0·6000
1	.. 0·0060	34	.. 0·2040	67½	.. 0·4050	2	.. 1·2000
2	.. 0·0120	35	.. 0·2100	68	.. 0·4080	3	.. 1·8000
2½	.. 0·0150	36	.. 0·2160	69	.. 0·4140	4	.. 2·4000
3	.. 0·0180	37	.. 0·2220	70	.. 0·4200	5	.. 3·0000
4	.. 0·0240	37½	.. 0·2250	71	.. 0·4260	6	.. 3·6000
5	.. 0·0300	38	.. 0·2280	72	.. 0·4320	7	.. 4·2000
6	.. 0·0360	39	.. 0·2340	72½	.. 0·4350	8	.. 4·8000
7	.. 0·0420	40	.. 0·2400	73	.. 0·4380	9	.. 5·4000
7½	.. 0·0450	41	.. 0·2460	74	.. 0·4440	10	.. 6·0000
8	.. 0·0480	42	.. 0·2520	75	.. 0·4500	11	.. 6·6000
9	.. 0·0540	42½	.. 0·2550	76	.. 0·4560	12	.. 7·2000
10	.. 0·0600	43	.. 0·2580	77	.. 0·4620	13	.. 7·8000
11	.. 0·0660	44	.. 0·2640	77½	.. 0·4650	14	.. 8·4000
12	.. 0·0720	45	.. 0·2700	78	.. 0·4680	15	.. 9·0000
12½	.. 0·0750	46	.. 0·2760	79	.. 0·4740	16	.. 9·6000
13	.. 0·0780	47	.. 0·2820	80	.. 0·4800	17	.. 10·2000
14	.. 0·0840	47½	.. 0·2850	81	.. 0·4860	18	.. 10·8000
15	.. 0·0900	48	.. 0·2880	82	.. 0·4920	19	.. 11·4000
16	.. 0·0960	49	.. 0·2940	82½	.. 0·4950	20	.. 12·0000
17	.. 0·1020	50	.. 0·3000	83	.. 0·4980	25	.. 15·0000
17½	.. 0·1050	51	.. 0·3060	84	.. 0·5040	30	.. 18·0000
18	.. 0·1080	52	.. 0·3120	85	.. 0·5100	35	.. 21·0000
19	.. 0·1140	52½	.. 0·3150	86	.. 0·5160	40	.. 24·0000
20	.. 0·1200	53	.. 0·3180	87	.. 0·5220	45	.. 27·0000
21	.. 0·1260	54	.. 0·3240	87½	.. 0·5250	50	.. 30·0000
22	.. 0·1320	55	.. 0·3300	88	.. 0·5280	55	.. 33·0000
22½	.. 0·1350	56	.. 0·3360	89	.. 0·5340	60	.. 36·0000
23	.. 0·1380	57	.. 0·3420	90	.. 0·5400	65	.. 39·0000
24	.. 0·1440	57½	.. 0·3450	91	.. 0·5460	70	.. 42·0000
25	.. 0·1500	58	.. 0·3480	92	.. 0·5520	75	.. 45·0000
26	.. 0·1560	59	.. 0·3540	92½	.. 0·5550	80	.. 48·0000
27	.. 0·1620	60	.. 0·3600	93	.. 0·5580	85	.. 51·0000
27½	.. 0·1650	61	.. 0·3660	94	.. 0·5640	90	.. 54·0000
28	.. 0·1680	62	.. 0·3720	95	.. 0·5700	95	.. 57·0000
29	.. 0·1740	62½	.. 0·3750	96	.. 0·5760	100	.. 60·0000
30	.. 0·1800	63	.. 0·3780	97	.. 0·5820	110	.. 66·0000
31	.. 0·1860	64	.. 0·3840	97½	.. 0·5850	120	.. 72·0000
32	.. 0·1920	65	.. 0·3900	98	.. 0·5880	130	.. 78·0000
32½	.. 0·1950	66	.. 0·3960	99	.. 0·5940	140	.. 84·0000

£	£	£	£	£	£	£	£
150	.. 90·0000	300	.. 180·0000	450	.. 270·0000	700	.. 420·0000
200	.. 120·0000	350	.. 210·0000	500	.. 300·0000	800	.. 480·0000
250	.. 150·0000	400	.. 240·0000	600	.. 360·0000	1000	.. 600·0000

p	£	p	£	p	£	£	£
½	0·0031	33	0·2063	67	0·4188	1	0·6250
1	0·0063	34	0·2125	67½	0·4219	2	1·2500
2	0·0125	35	0·2188	68	0·4250	3	1·8750
2½	0·0156	36	0·2250	69	0·4313	4	2·5000
3	0·0188	37	0·2313	70	0·4375	5	3·1250
4	0·0250	37½	0·2344	71	0·4438	6	3·7500
5	0·0313	38	0·2375	72	0·4500	7	4·3750
6	0·0375	39	0·2438	72½	0·4531	8	5·0000
7	0·0438	40	0·2500	73	0·4563	9	5·6250
7½	0·0469	41	0·2563	74	0·4625	10	6·2500
8	0·0500	42	0·2625	75	0·4688	11	6·8750
9	0·0563	42½	0·2656	76	0·4750	12	7·5000
10	0·0625	43	0·2688	77	0·4813	13	8·1250
11	0·0688	44	0·2750	77½	0·4844	14	8·7500
12	0·0750	45	0·2813	78	0·4875	15	9·3750
12½	0·0781	46	0·2875	79	0·4938	16	10·0000
13	0·0813	47	0·2938	80	0·5000	17	10·6250
14	0·0875	47½	0·2969	81	0·5063	18	11·2500
15	0·0938	48	0·3000	82	0·5125	19	11·8750
16	0·1000	49	0·3063	82½	0·5156	20	12·5000
17	0·1063	50	0·3125	83	0·5188	25	15·6250
17½	0·1094	51	0·3188	84	0·5250	30	18·7500
18	0·1125	52	0·3250	85	0·5313	35	21·8750
19	0·1188	52½	0·3281	86	0·5375	40	25·0000
20	0·1250	53	0·3313	87	0·5438	45	28·1250
21	0·1313	54	0·3375	87½	0·5469	50	31·2500
22	0·1375	55	0·3438	88	0·5500	55	34·3750
22½	0·1406	56	0·3500	89	0·5563	60	37·5000
23	0·1438	57	0·3563	90	0·5625	65	40·6250
24	0·1500	57½	0·3594	91	0·5688	70	43·7500
25	0·1563	58	0·3625	92	0·5750	75	46·8750
26	0·1625	59	0·3688	92½	0·5781	80	50·0000
27	0·1688	60	0·3750	93	0·5813	85	53·1250
27½	0·1719	61	0·3813	94	0·5875	90	56·2500
28	0·1750	62	0·3875	95	0·5938	95	59·3750
29	0·1813	62½	0·3906	96	0·6000	100	62·5000
30	0·1875	63	0·3938	97	0·6063	110	68·7500
31	0·1938	64	0·4000	97½	0·6094	120	75·0000
32	0·2000	65	0·4063	98	0·6125	130	81·2500
32½	0·2031	66	0·4125	99	0·6188	140	87·5000

£	£	£	£	£	£	£	£
150	93·7500	300	187·5000	450	281·2500	700	437·5000
200	125·0000	350	218·7500	500	312·5000	800	500·0000
250	156·2500	400	250·0000	600	375·0000	1000	625·0000

p	£	p	£	p	£	£	£
½ ..	0·0033	33 ..	0·2145	67 ..	0·4355	1 ..	0·6500
1 ..	0·0065	34 ..	0·2210	67½ ..	0·4388	2 ..	1·3000
2 ..	0·0130	35 ..	0·2275	68 ..	0·4420	3 ..	1·9500
2½ ..	0·0163	36 ..	0·2340	69 ..	0·4485	4 ..	2·6000
3 ..	0·0195	37 ..	0·2405	70 ..	0·4550	5 ..	3·2500
4 ..	0·0260	37½ ..	0·2438	71 ..	0·4615	6 ..	3·9000
5 ..	0·0325	38 ..	0·2470	72 ..	0·4680	7 ..	4·5500
6 ..	0·0390	39 ..	0·2535	72½ ..	0·4713	8 ..	5·2000
7 ..	0·0455	40 ..	0·2600	73 ..	0·4745	9 ..	5·8500
7½ ..	0·0488	41 ..	0·2665	74 ..	0·4810	10 ..	6·5000
8 ..	0·0520	42 ..	0·2730	75 ..	0·4875	11 ..	7·1500
9 ..	0·0585	42½ ..	0·2763	76 ..	0·4940	12 ..	7·8000
10 ..	0·0650	43 ..	0·2795	77 ..	0·5005	13 ..	8·4500
11 ..	0·0715	44 ..	0·2860	77½ ..	0·5038	14 ..	9·1000
12 ..	0·0780	45 ..	0·2925	78 ..	0·5070	15 ..	9·7500
12½ ..	0·0813	46 ..	0·2990	79 ..	0·5135	16 ..	10·4000
13 ..	0·0845	47 ..	0·3055	80 ..	0·5200	17 ..	11·0500
14 ..	0·0910	47½ ..	0·3088	81 ..	0·5265	18 ..	11·7000
15 ..	0·0975	48 ..	0·3120	82 ..	0·5330	19 ..	12·3500
16 ..	0·1040	49 ..	0·3185	82½ ..	0·5363	20 ..	13·0000
17 ..	0·1105	50 ..	0·3250	83 ..	0·5395	25 ..	16·2500
17½ ..	0·1138	51 ..	0·3315	84 ..	0·5460	30 ..	19·5000
18 ..	0·1170	52 ..	0·3380	85 ..	0·5525	35 ..	22·7500
19 ..	0·1235	52½ ..	0·3413	86 ..	0·5590	40 ..	26·0000
20 ..	0·1300	53 ..	0·3445	87 ..	0·5655	45 ..	29·2500
21 ..	0·1365	54 ..	0·3510	87½ ..	0·5688	50 ..	32·5000
22 ..	0·1430	55 ..	0·3575	88 ..	0·5720	55 ..	35·7500
22½ ..	0·1463	56 ..	0·3640	89 ..	0·5785	60 ..	39·0000
23 ..	0·1495	57 ..	0·3705	90 ..	0·5850	65 ..	42·2500
24 ..	0·1560	57½ ..	0·3738	91 ..	0·5915	70 ..	45·5000
25 ..	0·1625	58 ..	0·3770	92 ..	0·5980	75 ..	48·7500
26 ..	0·1690	59 ..	0·3835	92½ ..	0·6013	80 ..	52·0000
27 ..	0·1755	60 ..	0·3900	93 ..	0·6045	85 ..	55·2500
27½ ..	0·1788	61 ..	0·3965	94 ..	0·6110	90 ..	58·5000
28 ..	0·1820	62 ..	0·4030	95 ..	0·6175	95 ..	61·7500
29 ..	0·1885	62½ ..	0·4063	96 ..	0·6240	100 ..	65·0000
30 ..	0·1950	63 ..	0·4095	97 ..	0·6305	110 ..	71·5000
31 ..	0·2015	64 ..	0·4160	97½ ..	0·6338	120 ..	78·0000
32 ..	0·2080	65 ..	0·4225	98 ..	0·6370	130 ..	84·5000
32½ ..	0·2113	66 ..	0·4290	99 ..	0·6435	140 ..	91·0000

£	£	£	£	£	£	£	£
150..	97·5000	300..	195·0000	450..	292·5000	700 ..	455·0000
200..	130·0000	350..	227·5000	500..	325·0000	800 ..	520·0000
250..	162·5000	400..	260·0000	600..	390·0000	1000 ..	650·0000

p	£	p	£	p	£	£	£
½	0·0033	33	0·2200	67	0·4467	1	0·6667
1	0·0067	34	0·2267	67½	0·4500	2	1·3333
2	0·0133	35	0·2333	68	0·4533	3	2·0000
2½	0·0167	36	0·2400	69	0·4600	4	2·6667
3	0·0200	37	0·2467	70	0·4667	5	3·3333
4	0·0267	37½	0·2500	71	0·4733	6	4·0000
5	0·0333	38	0·2533	72	0·4800	7	4·6667
6	0·0400	39	0·2600	72½	0·4833	8	5·3333
7	0·0467	40	0·2667	73	0·4867	9	6·0000
7½	0·0500	41	0·2733	74	0·4933	10	6·6667
8	0·0533	42	0·2800	75	0·5000	11	7·3333
9	0·0600	42½	0·2833	76	0·5067	12	8·0000
10	0·0667	43	0·2867	77	0·5133	13	8·6667
11	0·0733	44	0·2933	77½	0·5167	14	9·3333
12	0·0800	45	0·3000	78	0·5200	15	10·0000
12½	0·0833	46	0·3067	79	0·5267	16	10·6667
13	0·0867	47	0·3133	80	0·5333	17	11·3333
14	0·0933	47½	0·3167	81	0·5400	18	12·0000
15	0·1000	48	0·3200	82	0·5467	19	12·6667
16	0·1067	49	0·3267	82½	0·5500	20	13·3333
17	0·1133	50	0·3333	83	0·5533	25	16·6667
17½	0·1167	51	0·3400	84	0·5600	30	20·0000
18	0·1200	52	0·3467	85	0·5667	35	23·3333
19	0·1267	52½	0·3500	86	0·5733	40	26·6667
20	0·1333	53	0·3533	87	0·5800	45	30·0000
21	0·1400	54	0·3600	87½	0·5833	50	33·3333
22	0·1467	55	0·3667	88	0·5867	55	36·6667
22½	0·1500	56	0·3733	89	0·5933	60	40·0000
23	0·1533	57	0·3800	90	0·6000	65	43·3333
24	0·1600	57½	0·3833	91	0·6067	70	46·6667
25	0·1667	58	0·3867	92	0·6133	75	50·0000
26	0·1733	59	0·3933	92½	0·6167	80	53·3333
27	0·1800	60	0·4000	93	0·6200	85	56·6667
27½	0·1833	61	0·4067	94	0·6267	90	60·0000
28	0·1867	62	0·4133	95	0·6333	95	63·3333
29	0·1933	62½	0·4167	96	0·6400	100	66·6667
30	0·2000	63	0·4200	97	0·6467	110	73·3333
31	0·2067	64	0·4267	97½	0·6500	120	80·0000
32	0·2133	65	0·4333	98	0·6533	130	86·6667
32½	0·2167	66	0·4400	99	0·6600	140	93·3333

£	£	£	£	£	£	£	£
150	100·0000	300	200·0000	450	300·0000	700	466·6667
200	133·3333	350	233·3333	500	333·3333	800	533·3333
250	166·6667	400	266·6667	600	400·0000	1000	666·6667

p	£	p	£	p	£	£	£
½	0·0034	33	0·2228	67	0·4523	1	0·6750
1	0·0068	34	0·2295	67½	0·4556	2	1·3500
2	0·0135	35	0·2363	68	0·4590	3	2·0250
2½	0·0169	36	0·2430	69	0·4658	4	2·7000
3	0·0203	37	0·2498	70	0·4725	5	3·3750
4	0·0270	37½	0·2531	71	0·4793	6	4·0500
5	0·0338	38	0·2565	72	0·4860	7	4·7250
6	0·0405	39	0·2633	72½	0·4894	8	5·4000
7	0·0473	40	0·2700	73	0·4928	9	6·0750
7½	0·0506	41	0·2768	74	0·4995	10	6·7500
8	0·0540	42	0·2835	75	0·5063	11	7·4250
9	0·0608	42½	0·2869	76	0·5130	12	8·1000
10	0·0675	43	0·2903	77	0·5198	13	8·7750
11	0·0743	44	0·2970	77½	0·5231	14	9·4500
12	0·0810	45	0·3038	78	0·5265	15	10·1250
12½	0·0844	46	0·3105	79	0·5333	16	10·8000
13	0·0878	47	0·3173	80	0·5400	17	11·4750
14	0·0945	47½	0·3206	81	0·5468	18	12·1500
15	0·1013	48	0·3240	82	0·5535	19	12·8250
16	0·1080	49	0·3308	82½	0·5569	20	13·5000
17	0·1148	50	0·3375	83	0·5603	25	16·8750
17½	0·1181	51	0·3443	84	0·5670	30	20·2500
18	0·1215	52	0·3510	85	0·5738	35	23·6250
19	0·1283	52½	0·3544	86	0·5805	40	27·0000
20	0·1350	53	0·3578	87	0·5873	45	30·3750
21	0·1418	54	0·3645	87½	0·5906	50	33·7500
22	0·1485	55	0·3713	88	0·5940	55	37·1250
22½	0·1519	56	0·3780	89	0·6008	60	40·5000
23	0·1553	57	0·3848	90	0·6075	65	43·8750
24	0·1620	57½	0·3881	91	0·6143	70	47·2500
25	0·1688	58	0·3915	92	0·6210	75	50·6250
26	0·1755	59	0·3983	92½	0·6244	80	54·0000
27	0·1823	60	0·4050	93	0·6278	85	57·3750
27½	0·1856	61	0·4118	94	0·6345	90	60·7500
28	0·1890	62	0·4185	95	0·6413	95	64·1250
29	0·1958	62½	0·4219	96	0·6480	100	67·5000
30	0·2025	63	0·4253	97	0·6548	110	74·2500
31	0·2093	64	0·4320	97½	0·6581	120	81·0000
32	0·2160	65	0·4388	98	0·6615	130	87·7500
32½	0·2194	66	0·4455	99	0·6683	140	94·5000

£	£	£	£	£	£	£	£
150	101·2500	300	202·5000	450	303·7500	700	472·5000
200	135·0000	350	236·2500	500	337·5000	800	540·0000
250	168·7500	400	270·0000	600	405·0000	1000	675·0000

p	£	p	£	p	£	£	£
$\frac{1}{2}$ ..	0·0035	33 ..	0·2310	67 ..	0·4690	1 ..	0·7000
1 ..	0·0070	34 ..	0·2380	$67\frac{1}{2}$ ..	0·4725	2 ..	1·4000
2 ..	0·0140	35 ..	0·2450	68 ..	0·4760	3 ..	2·1000
$2\frac{1}{2}$ ..	0·0175	36 ..	0·2520	69 ..	0·4830	4 ..	2·8000
3 ..	0·0210	37 ..	0·2590	70 ..	0·4900	5 ..	3·5000
4 ..	0·0280	$37\frac{1}{2}$ ..	0·2625	71 ..	0·4970	6 ..	4·2000
5 ..	0·0350	38 ..	0·2660	72 ..	0·5040	7 ..	4·9000
6 ..	0·0420	39 ..	0·2730	$72\frac{1}{2}$ ..	0·5075	8 ..	5·6000
7 ..	0·0490	40 ..	0·2800	73 ..	0·5110	9 ..	6·3000
$7\frac{1}{2}$ ..	0·0525	41 ..	0·2870	74 ..	0·5180	10 ..	7·0000
8 ..	0·0560	42 ..	0·2940	75 ..	0·5250	11 ..	7·7000
9 ..	0·0630	$42\frac{1}{2}$ ..	0·2975	76 ..	0·5320	12 ..	8·4000
10 ..	0·0700	43 ..	0·3010	77 ..	0·5390	13 ..	9·1000
11 ..	0·0770	44 ..	0·3080	$77\frac{1}{2}$ ..	0·5425	14 ..	9·8000
12 ..	0·0840	45 ..	0·3150	78 ..	0·5460	15 ..	10·5000
$12\frac{1}{2}$ ..	0·0875	46 ..	0·3220	79 ..	0·5530	16 ..	11·2000
13 ..	0·0910	47 ..	0·3290	80 ..	0·5600	17 ..	11·9000
14 ..	0·0980	$47\frac{1}{2}$ ..	0·3325	81 ..	0·5670	18 ..	12·6000
15 ..	0·1050	48 ..	0·3360	82 ..	0·5740	19 ..	13·3000
16 ..	0·1120	49 ..	0·3430	$82\frac{1}{2}$ ..	0·5775	20 ..	14·0000
17 ..	0·1190	50 ..	0·3500	83 ..	0·5810	25 ..	17·5000
$17\frac{1}{2}$ ..	0·1225	51 ..	0·3570	84 ..	0·5880	30 ..	21·0000
18 ..	0·1260	52 ..	0·3640	85 ..	0·5950	35 ..	24·5000
19 ..	0·1330	$52\frac{1}{2}$ ..	0·3675	86 ..	0·6020	40 ..	28·0000
20 ..	0·1400	53 ..	0·3710	87 ..	0·6090	45 ..	31·5000
21 ..	0·1470	54 ..	0·3780	$87\frac{1}{2}$ ..	0·6125	50 ..	35·0000
22 ..	0·1540	55 ..	0·3850	88 ..	0·6160	55 ..	38·5000
$22\frac{1}{2}$ ..	0·1575	56 ..	0·3920	89 ..	0·6230	60 ..	42·0000
23 ..	0·1610	57 ..	0·3990	90 ..	0·6300	65 ..	45·5000
24 ..	0·1680	$57\frac{1}{2}$ ..	0·4025	91 ..	0·6370	70 ..	49·0000
25 ..	0·1750	58 ..	0·4060	92 ..	0·6440	75 ..	52·5000
26 ..	0·1820	59 ..	0·4130	$92\frac{1}{2}$ ..	0·6475	80 ..	56·0000
27 ..	0·1890	60 ..	0·4200	93 ..	0·6510	85 ..	59·5000
$27\frac{1}{2}$ ..	0·1925	61 ..	0·4270	94 ..	0·6580	90 ..	63·0000
28 ..	0·1960	62 ..	0·4340	95 ..	0·6650	95 ..	66·5000
29 ..	0·2030	$62\frac{1}{2}$ ..	0·4375	96 ..	0·6720	100 ..	70·0000
30 ..	0·2100	63 ..	0·4410	97 ..	0·6790	110 ..	77·0000
31 ..	0·2170	64 ..	0·4480	$97\frac{1}{2}$ ..	0·6825	120 ..	84·0000
32 ..	0·2240	65 ..	0·4550	98 ..	0·6860	130 ..	91·0000
$32\frac{1}{2}$ ..	0·2275	66 ..	0·4620	99 ..	0·6930	140 ..	98·0000

£	£	£	£	£	£	£	£
150..	105·0000	300..	210·0000	450..	315·0000	700 ..	490·0000
200..	140·0000	350..	245·0000	500..	350·0000	800 ..	560·0000
250..	175·0000	400..	280·0000	600..	420·0000	1000 ..	700·0000

$72\frac{1}{2}$ Per Cent $72\frac{1}{2}$

p	£	p	£	p	£	£	£
$\frac{1}{4}$	0·0036	33	0·2393	67	0·4858	1	0·7250
1	0·0073	34	0·2465	$67\frac{1}{2}$	0·4894	2	1·4500
2	0·0145	35	0·2538	68	0·4930	3	2·1750
$2\frac{1}{2}$	0·0181	36	0·2610	69	0·5003	4	2·9000
3	0·0218	37	0·2683	70	0·5075	5	3·6250
4	0·0290	$37\frac{1}{2}$	0·2719	71	0·5148	6	4·3500
5	0·0363	38	0·2755	72	0·5220	7	5·0750
6	0·0435	39	0·2828	$72\frac{1}{2}$	0·5256	8	5·8000
7	0·0508	40	0·2900	73	0·5293	9	6·5250
$7\frac{1}{2}$	0·0544	41	0·2973	74	0·5365	10	7·2500
8	0·0580	42	0·3045	75	0·5438	11	7·9750
9	0·0653	$42\frac{1}{2}$	0·3081	76	0·5510	12	8·7000
10	0·0725	43	0·3118	77	0·5583	13	9·4250
11	0·0798	44	0·3190	$77\frac{1}{2}$	0·5619	14	10·1500
12	0·0870	45	0·3263	78	0·5655	15	10·8750
$12\frac{1}{2}$	0·0906	46	0·3335	79	0·5728	16	11·6000
13	0·0943	47	0·3408	80	0·5800	17	12·3250
14	0·1015	$47\frac{1}{2}$	0·3444	81	0·5873	18	13·0500
15	0·1088	48	0·3480	82	0·5945	19	13·7750
16	0·1160	49	0·3553	$82\frac{1}{2}$	0·5981	20	14·5000
17	0·1233	50	0·3625	83	0·6018	25	18·1250
$17\frac{1}{2}$	0·1269	51	0·3698	84	0·6090	30	21·7500
18	0·1305	52	0·3770	85	0·6163	35	25·3750
19	0·1378	$52\frac{1}{2}$	0·3806	86	0·6235	40	29·0000
20	0·1450	53	0·3843	87	0·6308	45	32·6250
21	0·1523	54	0·3915	$87\frac{1}{2}$	0·6344	50	36·2500
22	0·1595	55	0·3988	88	0·6380	55	39·8750
$22\frac{1}{2}$	0·1631	56	0·4060	89	0·6453	60	43·5000
23	0·1668	57	0·4133	90	0·6525	65	47·1250
24	0·1740	$57\frac{1}{2}$	0·4169	91	0·6598	70	50·7500
25	0·1813	58	0·4205	92	0·6670	75	54·3750
26	0·1885	59	0·4278	$92\frac{1}{2}$	0·6706	80	58·0000
27	0·1958	60	0·4350	93	0·6743	85	61·6250
$27\frac{1}{2}$	0·1994	61	0·4423	94	0·6815	90	65·2500
28	0·2030	62	0·4495	95	0·6888	95	68·8750
29	0·2103	$62\frac{1}{2}$	0·4531	96	0·6960	100	72·5000
30	0·2175	63	0·4568	97	0·7033	110	79·7500
31	0·2248	64	0·4640	$97\frac{1}{2}$	0·7069	120	87·0000
32	0·2320	65	0·4713	98	0·7105	130	94·2500
$32\frac{1}{2}$	0·2356	66	0·4785	99	0·7178	140	101·5000

£	£	£	£	£	£	£	£
150	108·7500	300	217·5000	450	326·2500	700	507·5000
200	145·0000	350	253·7500	500	362·5000	800	580·0000
250	181·2500	400	290·0000	600	435·0000	1000	725·0000

p	£	p	£	p	£	£	£
½	0·0038	33	0·2475	67	0·5025	1	0·7500
1	0·0075	34	0·2550	67½	0·5063	2	1·5000
2	0·0150	35	0·2625	68	0·5100	3	2·2500
2½	0·0225	36	0·2700	69	0·5175	4	3·0000
3	0·0225	37	0·2775	70	0·5250	5	3·7500
4	0·0300	37½	0·2813	71	0·5325	6	4·5000
5	0·0375	38	0·2850	72	0·5400	7	5·2500
6	0·0450	39	0·2925	72½	0·5438	8	6·0000
7	0·0525	40	0·3000	73	0·5475	9	6·7500
7½	0·0563	41	0·3075	74	0·5550	10	7·5000
8	0·0600	42	0·3150	75	0·5625	11	8·2500
9	0·0675	42½	0·3188	76	0·5700	12	9·0000
10	0·0750	43	0·3225	77	0·5775	13	9·7500
11	0·0825	44	0·3300	77½	0·5813	14	10·5000
12	0·0900	45	0·3375	78	0·5850	15	11·2500
12½	0·0938	46	0·3450	79	0·5925	16	12·0000
13	0·0975	47	0·3525	80	0·6000	17	12·7500
14	0·1050	47½	0·3563	81	0·6075	18	13·5000
15	0·1125	48	0·3600	82	0·6150	19	14·2500
16	0·1200	49	0·3675	82½	0·6188	20	15·0000
17	0·1275	50	0·3750	83	0·6225	25	18·7500
17½	0·1313	51	0·3825	84	0·6300	30	22·5000
18	0·1350	52	0·3900	85	0·6375	35	26·2500
19	0·1425	52½	0·3938	86	0·6450	40	30·0000
20	0·1500	53	0·3975	87	0·6525	45	33·7500
21	0·1575	54	0·4050	87½	0·6563	50	37·5000
22	0·1650	55	0·4125	88	0·6600	55	41·2500
22½	0·1688	56	0·4200	89	0·6675	60	45·0000
23	0·1725	57	0·4275	90	0·6750	65	48·7500
24	0·1800	57½	0·4313	91	0·6825	70	52·5000
25	0·1875	58	0·4350	92	0·6900	75	56·2500
26	0·1950	59	0·4425	92½	0·6938	80	60·0000
27	0·2025	60	0·4500	93	0·6975	85	63·7500
27½	0·2063	61	0·4575	94	0·7050	90	67·5000
28	0·2100	62	0·4650	95	0·7125	95	71·2500
29	0·2175	62½	0·4688	96	0·7200	100	75·0000
30	0·2250	63	0·4725	97	0·7275	110	82·5000
31	0·2325	64	0·4800	97½	0·7313	120	90·0000
32	0·2400	65	0·4875	98	0·7350	130	97·5000
32½	0·2438	66	0·4950	99	0·7425	140	105·0000

£	£	£	£	£	£	£	£
150	112·5000	300	225·0000	450	337·5000	700	525·0000
200	150·0000	350	262·5000	500	375·0000	800	600·0000
250	187·5000	400	300·0000	600	450·0000	1000	750·0000

p	£	p	£	p	£	£	£
½ ..	0·0039	33 ..	0·2558	67 ..	0·5193	1 ..	0·7750
1 ..	0·0078	34 ..	0·2635	67½ ..	0·5231	2 ..	1·5500
2 ..	0·0155	35 ..	0·2713	68 ..	0·5270	3 ..	2·3250
2½ ..	0·0194	36 ..	0·2790	69 ..	0·5348	4 ..	3·1000
3 ..	0·0233	37 ..	0·2868	70 ..	0·5425	5 ..	3·8750
4 ..	0·0310	37½ ..	0·2906	71 ..	0·5503	6 ..	4·6500
5 ..	0·0388	38 ..	0·2945	72 ..	0·5580	7 ..	5·4250
6 ..	0·0465	39 ..	0·3023	72½ ..	0·5619	8 ..	6·2000
7 ..	0·0543	40 ..	0·3100	73 ..	0·5658	9 ..	6·9750
7½ ..	0·0581	41 ..	0·3178	74 ..	0·5735	10 ..	7·7500
8 ..	0·0620	42 ..	0·3255	75 ..	0·5813	11 ..	8·5250
9 ..	0·0698	42½ ..	0·3294	76 ..	0·5890	12 ..	9·3000
10 ..	0·0775	43 ..	0·3333	77 ..	0·5968	13 ..	10·0750
11 ..	0·0853	44 ..	0·3410	77½ ..	0·6006	14 ..	10·8500
12 ..	0·0930	45 ..	0·3488	78 ..	0·6045	15 ..	11·6250
12½ ..	0·0969	46 ..	0·3565	79 ..	0·6123	16 ..	12·4000
13 ..	0·1008	47 ..	0·3643	80 ..	0·6200	17 ..	13·1750
14 ..	0·1085	47½ ..	0·3681	81 ..	0·6278	18 ..	13·9500
15 ..	0·1163	48 ..	0·3720	82 ..	0·6355	19 ..	14·7250
16 ..	0·1240	49 ..	0·3798	82½ ..	0·6394	20 ..	15·5000
17 ..	0·1318	50 ..	0·3875	83 ..	0·6433	25 ..	19·3750
17½ ..	0·1356	51 ..	0·3953	84 ..	0·6510	30 ..	23·2500
18 ..	0·1395	52 ..	0·4030	85 ..	0·6588	35 ..	27·1250
19 ..	0·1473	52½ ..	0·4069	86 ..	0·6665	40 ..	31·0000
20 ..	0·1550	53 ..	0·4108	87 ..	0·6743	45 ..	34·8750
21 ..	0·1628	54 ..	0·4185	87½ ..	0·6781	50 ..	38·7500
22 ..	0·1705	55 ..	0·4263	88 ..	0·6820	55 ..	42·6250
22½ ..	0·1744	56 ..	0·4340	89 ..	0·6898	60 ..	46·5000
23 ..	0·1783	57 ..	0·4418	90 ..	0·6975	65 ..	50·3750
24 ..	0·1860	57½ ..	0·4456	91 ..	0·7053	70 ..	54·2500
25 ..	0·1938	58 ..	0·4495	92 ..	0·7130	75 ..	58·1250
26 ..	0·2015	59 ..	0·4573	92½ ..	0·7169	80 ..	62·0000
27 ..	0·2093	60 ..	0·4650	93 ..	0·7208	85 ..	65·8750
27½ ..	0·2131	61 ..	0·4728	94 ..	0·7285	90 ..	69·7500
28 ..	0·2170	62 ..	0·4805	95 ..	0·7363	95 ..	73·6250
29 ..	0·2248	62½ ..	0·4844	96 ..	0·7440	100 ..	77·5000
30 ..	0·2325	63 ..	0·4883	97 ..	0·7518	110 ..	85·2500
31 ..	0·2403	64 ..	0·4960	97½ ..	0·7556	120 ..	93·0000
32 ..	0·2480	65 ..	0·5038	98 ..	0·7595	130 ..	100·7500
32½ ..	0·2519	66 ..	0·5115	99 ..	0·7673	140 ..	108·5000

£	£	£	£	£	£	£	£
150 ..	116·2500	300 ..	232·5000	450 ..	348·7500	700 ..	542·5000
200 ..	155·0000	350 ..	271·2500	500 ..	387·5000	800 ..	620·0000
250 ..	193·7500	400 ..	310·0000	600 ..	465·0000	1000 ..	775·0000

p	£	p	£	p	£	£	£
½	0·0040	33	0·2640	67	0·5360	1	0·8000
1	0·0080	34	0·2720	67½	0·5400	2	1·6000
2	0·0160	35	0·2800	68	0·5440	3	2·4000
2½	0·0200	36	0·2880	69	0·5520	4	3·2000
3	0·0240	37	0·2960	70	0·5600	5	4·0000
4	0·0320	37½	0·3000	71	0·5680	6	4·8000
5	0·0400	38	0·3040	72	0·5760	7	5·6000
6	0·0480	39	0·3120	72½	0·5800	8	6·4000
7	0·0560	40	0·3200	73	0·5840	9	7·2000
7½	0·0600	41	0·3280	74	0·5920	10	8·0000
8	0·0640	42	0·3360	75	0·6000	11	8·8000
9	0·0720	42½	0·3400	76	0·6080	12	9·6000
10	0·0800	43	0·3440	77	0·6160	13	10·4000
11	0·0880	44	0·3520	77½	0·6200	14	11·2000
12	0·0960	45	0·3600	78	0·6240	15	12·0000
12½	0·1000	46	0·3680	79	0·6320	16	12·8000
13	0·1040	47	0·3760	80	0·6400	17	13·6000
14	0·1120	47½	0·3800	81	0·6480	18	14·4000
15	0·1200	48	0·3840	82	0·6560	19	15·2000
16	0·1280	49	0·3920	82½	0·6600	20	16·0000
17	0·1360	50	0·4000	83	0·6640	25	20·0000
17½	0·1400	51	0·4080	84	0·6720	30	24·0000
18	0·1440	52	0·4160	85	0·6800	35	28·0000
19	0·1520	52½	0·4200	86	0·6880	40	32·0000
20	0·1600	53	0·4240	87	0·6960	45	36·0000
21	0·1680	54	0·4320	87½	0·7000	50	40·0000
22	0·1760	55	0·4400	88	0·7040	55	44·0000
22½	0·1800	56	0·4480	89	0·7120	60	48·0000
23	0·1840	57	0·4560	90	0·7200	65	52·0000
24	0·1920	57½	0·4600	91	0·7280	70	56·0000
25	0·2000	58	0·4640	92	0·7360	75	60·0000
26	0·2080	59	0·4720	92½	0·7400	80	64·0000
27	0·2160	60	0·4800	93	0·7440	85	68·0000
27½	0·2200	61	0·4880	94	0·7520	90	72·0000
28	0·2240	62	0·4960	95	0·7600	95	76·0000
29	0·2320	62½	0·5000	96	0·7680	100	80·0000
30	0·2400	63	0·5040	97	0·7760	110	88·0000
31	0·2480	64	0·5120	97½	0·7800	120	96·0000
32	0·2560	65	0·5200	98	0·7840	130	104·0000
32½	0·2600	66	0·5280	99	0·7920	140	112·0000

£	£	£	£	£	£	£	£
150	120·0000	300	240·0000	450	360·0000	700	560·0000
200	160·0000	350	280·0000	500	400·0000	800	640·0000
250	200·0000	400	320·0000	600	480·0000	1000	800·0000

p	£	p	£	p	£	£	£
½	0·0041	33	0·2723	67	0·5528	1	0·8250
1	0·0083	34	0·2805	67½	0·5569	2	1·6500
2	0·0165	35	0·2888	68	0·5610	3	2·4750
2½	0·0206	36	0·2970	69	0·5693	4	3·3000
3	0·0248	37	0·3053	70	0·5775	5	4·1250
4	0·0330	37½	0·3094	71	0·5858	6	4·9500
5	0·0413	38	0·3135	72	0·5940	7	5·7750
6	0·0495	39	0·3218	72½	0·5981	8	6·6000
7	0·0578	40	0·3300	73	0·6023	9	7·4250
7½	0·0619	41	0·3383	74	0·6105	10	8·2500
8	0·0660	42	0·3465	75	0·6188	11	9·0750
9	0·0743	42½	0·3506	76	0·6270	12	9·9000
10	0·0825	43	0·3548	77	0·6353	13	10·7250
11	0·0908	44	0·3630	77½	0·6394	14	11·5500
12	0·0990	45	0·3713	78	0·6435	15	12·3750
12½	0·1031	46	0·3795	79	0·6518	16	13·2000
13	0·1073	47	0·3878	80	0·6600	17	14·0250
14	0·1155	47½	0·3919	81	0·6683	18	14·8500
15	0·1238	48	0·3960	82	0·6765	19	15·6750
16	0·1320	49	0·4043	82½	0·6806	20	16·5000
17	0·1403	50	0·4125	83	0·6848	25	20·6250
17½	0·1444	51	0·4208	84	0·6930	30	24·7500
18	0·1485	52	0·4290	85	0·7013	35	28·8750
19	0·1568	52½	0·4331	86	0·7095	40	33·0000
20	0·1650	53	0·4373	87	0·7178	45	37·1250
21	0·1733	54	0·4455	87½	0·7219	50	41·2500
22	0·1815	55	0·4538	88	0·7260	55	45·3750
22½	0·1856	56	0·4620	89	0·7343	60	49·5000
23	0·1898	57	0·4703	90	0·7425	65	53·6250
24	0·1980	57½	0·4744	91	0·7508	70	57·7500
25	0·2063	58	0·4785	92	0·7590	75	61·8750
26	0·2145	59	0·4868	92½	0·7631	80	66·0000
27	0·2228	60	0·4950	93	0·7673	85	70·1250
27½	0·2269	61	0·5033	94	0·7755	90	74·2500
28	0·2310	62	0·5115	95	0·7838	95	78·3750
29	0·2393	62½	0·5156	96	0·7920	100	82·5000
30	0·2475	63	0·5198	97	0·8003	110	90·7500
31	0·2558	64	0·5280	97½	0·8044	120	99·0000
32	0·2640	65	0·5363	98	0·8085	130	107·2500
32½	0·2681	66	0·5445	99	0·8168	140	115·5000

£	£	£	£	£	£	£	£
150	123·7500	300	247·5000	450	371·2500	700	577·5000
200	165·0000	350	288·7500	500	412·5000	800	660·0000
250	206·2500	400	330·0000	600	495·0000	1000	825·0000

p		£	p		£	p		£	£		£
½	..	0·0043	33	..	0·2805	67	..	0·5695	1	..	0·8500
1	..	0·0085	34	..	0·2890	67½	..	0·5738	2	..	1·7000
2	..	0·0170	35	..	0·2975	68	..	0·5780	3	..	2·5500
2½	..	0·0213	36	..	0·3060	69	..	0·5865	4	..	3·4000
3	..	0·0255	37	..	0·3145	70	..	0·5950	5	..	4·2500
4	..	0·0340	37½	..	0·3188	71	..	0·6035	6	..	5·1000
5	..	0·0425	38	..	0·3230	72	..	0·6120	7	..	5·9500
6	..	0·0510	39	..	0·3315	72½	..	0·6163	8	..	6·8000
7	..	0·0595	40	..	0·3400	73	..	0·6205	9	..	7·6500
7½	..	0·0638	41	..	0·3485	74	..	0·6290	10	..	8·5000
8	..	0·0680	42	..	0·3570	75	..	0·6375	11	..	9·3500
9	..	0·0765	42½	..	0·3613	76	..	0·6460	12	..	10·2000
10	..	0·0850	43	..	0·3655	77	..	0·6545	13	..	11·0500
11	..	0·0935	44	..	0·3740	77½	..	0·6588	14	..	11·9000
12	..	0·1020	45	..	0·3825	78	..	0·6630	15	..	12·7500
12½	..	0·1063	46	..	0·3910	79	..	0·6715	16	..	13·6000
13	..	0·1105	47	..	0·3995	80	..	0·6800	17	..	14·4500
14	..	0·1190	47½	..	0·4038	81	..	0·6885	18	..	15·3000
15	..	0·1275	48	..	0·4080	82	..	0·6970	19	..	16·1500
16	..	0·1360	49	..	0·4165	82½	..	0·7013	20	..	17·0000
17	..	0·1445	50	..	0·4250	83	..	0·7055	25	..	21·2500
17½	..	0·1488	51	..	0·4335	84	..	0·7140	30	..	25·5000
18	..	0·1530	52	..	0·4420	85	..	0·7225	35	..	29·7500
19	..	0·1615	52½	..	0·4463	86	..	0·7310	40	..	34·0000
20	..	0·1700	53	..	0·4505	87	..	0·7395	45	..	38·2500
21	..	0·1785	54	..	0·4590	87½	..	0·7438	50	..	42·5000
22	..	0·1870	55	..	0·4675	88	..	0·7480	55	..	46·7500
22½	..	0·1913	56	..	0·4760	89	..	0·7565	60	..	51·0000
23	..	0·1955	57	..	0·4845	90	..	0·7650	65	..	55·2500
24	..	0·2040	57½	..	0·4888	91	..	0·7735	70	..	59·5000
25	..	0·2125	58	..	0·4930	92	..	0·7820	75	..	63·7500
26	..	0·2210	59	..	0·5015	92½	..	0·7863	80	..	68·0000
27	..	0·2295	60	..	0·5100	93	..	0·7905	85	..	72·2500
27½	..	0·2338	61	..	0·5185	94	..	0·7990	90	..	76·5000
28	..	0·2380	62	..	0·5270	95	..	0·8075	95	..	80·7500
29	..	0·2465	62½	..	0·5313	96	..	0·8160	100	..	85·0000
30	..	0·2550	63	..	0·5355	97	..	0·8245	110	..	93·5000
31	..	0·2635	64	..	0·5440	97½	..	0·8288	120	..	102·0000
32	..	0·2720	65	..	0·5525	98	..	0·8330	130	..	110·5000
32½	..	0·2763	66	..	0·5610	99	..	0·8415	140	..	119·0000

£		£	£		£	£		£	£		£
150	..	127·5000	300	..	255·0000	450	..	382·5000	700	..	595·0000
200	..	170·0000	350	..	297·5000	500	..	425·0000	800	..	680·0000
250	..	212·5000	400	..	340·0000	600	..	510·0000	1000	..	850·0000

p	£	p	£	p	£	£	£
¼ ..	0·0044	33 ..	0·2888	67 ..	0·5863	1 ..	0·8750
1 ..	0·0088	34 ..	0·2975	67½ ..	0·5906	2 ..	1·7500
2 ..	0·0175	35 ..	0·3063	68 ..	0·5950	3 ..	2·6250
2½ ..	0·0219	36 ..	0·3150	69 ..	0·6038	4 ..	3·5000
3 ..	0·0263	37 ..	0·3238	70 ..	0·6125	5 ..	4·3750
4 ..	0·0350	37½ ..	0·3281	71 ..	0·6213	6 ..	5·2500
5 ..	0·0438	38 ..	0·3325	72 ..	0·6300	7 ..	6·1250
6 ..	0·0525	39 ..	0·3413	72½ ..	0·6344	8 ..	7·0000
7 ..	0·0613	40 ..	0·3500	73 ..	0·6388	9 ..	7·8750
7½ ..	0·0656	41 ..	0·3588	74 ..	0·6475	10 ..	8·7500
8 ..	0·0700	42 ..	0·3675	75 ..	0·6563	11 ..	9·6250
9 ..	0·0788	42½ ..	0·3719	76 ..	0·6650	12 ..	10·5000
10 ..	0·0875	43 ..	0·3763	77 ..	0·6738	13 ..	11·3750
11 ..	0·0963	44 ..	0·3850	77½ ..	0·6781	14 ..	12·2500
12 ..	0·1050	45 ..	0·3938	78 ..	0·6825	15 ..	13·1250
12½ ..	0·1094	46 ..	0·4025	79 ..	0·6913	16 ..	14·0000
13 ..	0·1138	47 ..	0·4113	80 ..	0·7000	17 ..	14·8750
14 ..	0·1225	47½ ..	0·4156	81 ..	0·7088	18 ..	15·7500
15 ..	0·1313	48 ..	0·4200	82 ..	0·7175	19 ..	16·6250
16 ..	0·1400	49 ..	0·4288	82½ ..	0·7219	20 ..	17·5000
17 ..	0·1488	50 ..	0·4375	83 ..	0·7263	25 ..	21·8750
17½ ..	0·1531	51 ..	0·4463	84 ..	0·7350	30 ..	26·2500
18 ..	0·1575	52 ..	0·4550	85 ..	0·7438	35 ..	30·6250
19 ..	0·1663	52½ ..	0·4594	86 ..	0·7525	40 ..	35·0000
20 ..	0·1750	53 ..	0·4638	87 ..	0·7613	45 ..	39·3750
21 ..	0·1838	54 ..	0·4725	87½ ..	0·7656	50 ..	43·7500
22 ..	0·1925	55 ..	0·4813	88 ..	0·7700	55 ..	48·1250
22½ ..	0·1969	56 ..	0·4900	89 ..	0·7788	60 ..	52·5000
23 ..	0·2013	57 ..	0·4988	90 ..	0·7875	65 ..	56·8750
24 ..	0·2100	57½ ..	0·5031	91 ..	0·7963	70 ..	61·2500
25 ..	0·2188	58 ..	0·5075	92 ..	0·8050	75 ..	65·6250
26 ..	0·2275	59 ..	0·5163	92½ ..	0·8094	80 ..	70·0000
27 ..	0·2363	60 ..	0·5250	93 ..	0·8138	85 ..	74·3750
27½ ..	0·2406	61 ..	0·5338	94 ..	0·8225	90 ..	78·7500
28 ..	0·2450	62 ..	0·5425	95 ..	0·8313	95 ..	83·1250
29 ..	0·2538	62½ ..	0·5469	96 ..	0·8400	100 ..	87·5000
30 ..	0·2625	63 ..	0·5513	97 ..	0·8488	110 ..	96·2500
31 ..	0·2713	64 ..	0·5600	97½ ..	0·8531	120 ..	105·0000
32 ..	0·2800	65 ..	0·5688	98 ..	0·8575	130 ..	113·7500
32½ ..	0·2844	66 ..	0·5775	99 ..	0·8663	140 ..	122·5000

£	£	£	£	£	£	£	£
150 ..	131·2500	300 ..	262·5000	450 ..	393·7500	700 ..	612·5000
200 ..	175·0000	350 ..	306·2500	500 ..	437·5000	800 ..	700·0000
250 ..	218·7500	400 ..	350·0000	600 ..	525·0000	1000 ..	875·0000

p	£	p	£	p	£	£	£
½	0·0045	33	0·2970	67	0·6030	1	0·9000
1	0·0090	34	0·3060	67½	0·6075	2	1·8000
2	0·0180	35	0·3150	68	0·6120	3	2·7000
2½	0·0225	36	0·3240	69	0·6210	4	3·6000
3	0·0270	37	0·3330	70	0·6300	5	4·5000
4	0·0360	37½	0·3375	71	0·6390	6	5·4000
5	0·0450	38	0·3420	72	0·6480	7	6·3000
6	0·0540	39	0·3510	72½	0·6525	8	7·2000
7	0·0630	40	0·3600	73	0·6570	9	8·1000
7½	0·0675	41	0·3690	74	0·6660	10	9·0000
8	0·0720	42	0·3780	75	0·6750	11	9·9000
9	0·0810	42½	0·3825	76	0·6840	12	10·8000
10	0·0900	43	0·3870	77	0·6930	13	11·7000
11	0·0990	44	0·3960	77½	0·6975	14	12·6000
12	0·1080	45	0·4050	78	0·7020	15	13·5000
12½	0·1125	46	0·4140	79	0·7110	16	14·4000
13	0·1170	47	0·4230	80	0·7200	17	15·3000
14	0·1260	47½	0·4275	81	0·7290	18	16·2000
15	0·1350	48	0·4320	82	0·7380	19	17·1000
16	0·1440	49	0·4410	82½	0·7425	20	18·0000
17	0·1530	50	0·4500	83	0·7470	25	22·5000
17½	0·1575	51	0·4590	84	0·7560	30	27·0000
18	0·1620	52	0·4680	85	0·7650	35	31·5000
19	0·1710	52½	0·4725	86	0·7740	40	36·0000
20	0·1800	53	0·4770	87	0·7830	45	40·5000
21	0·1890	54	0·4860	87½	0·7875	50	45·0000
22	0·1980	55	0·4950	88	0·7920	55	49·5000
22½	0·2025	56	0·5040	89	0·8010	60	54·0000
23	0·2070	57	0·5130	90	0·8100	65	58·5000
24	0·2160	57½	0·5175	91	0·8190	70	63·0000
25	0·2250	58	0·5220	92	0·8280	75	67·5000
26	0·2340	59	0·5310	92½	0·8325	80	72·0000
27	0·2430	60	0·5400	93	0·8370	85	76·5000
27½	0·2475	61	0·5490	94	0·8460	90	81·0000
28	0·2520	62	0·5580	95	0·8550	95	85·5000
29	0·2610	62½	0·5625	96	0·8640	100	90·0000
30	0·2700	63	0·5670	97	0·8730	110	99·0000
31	0·2790	64	0·5760	97½	0·8775	120	108·0000
32	0·2880	65	0·5850	98	0·8820	130	117·0000
32½	0·2925	66	0·5940	99	0·8910	140	126·0000

£	£	£	£	£	£	£	£
150	135·0000	300	270·0000	450	405·0000	700	630·0000
200	180·0000	350	315·0000	500	450·0000	800	720·0000
250	225·0000	400	360·0000	600	540·0000	1000	900·0000

p	£	p	£	p	£	£	£
½ ..	0·0048	33 ..	0·3135	67 ..	0·6365	1 ..	0·9500
1 ..	0·0095	34 ..	0·3230	67½ ..	0·6413	2 ..	1·9000
2 ..	0·0190	35 ..	0·3325	68 ..	0·6460	3 ...	2·8500
2½ ..	0·0238	36 ..	0·3420	69 ..	0·6555	4 ..	3·8000
3 ..	0·0285	37 ..	0·3515	70 ..	0·6650	5 ..	4·7500
4 ..	0·0380	37½ ..	0·3563	71 ..	0·6745	6 ..	5·7000
5 ..	0·0475	38 ..	0·3610	72 ..	0·6840	7 ..	6·6500
6 ..	0·0570	39 ..	0·3705	72½ ..	0·6888	8 ..	7·6000
7 ..	0·0665	40 ..	0·3800	73 ..	0·6935	9 ..	8·5500
7½ ..	0·0713	41 ..	0·3895	74 ..	0·7030	10 ..	9·5000
8 ..	0·0760	42 ..	0·3990	75 ..	0·7125	11 ..	10·4500
9 ..	0·0855	42½ ..	0·4038	76 ..	0·7220	12 ..	11·4000
10 ..	0·0950	43 ..	0·4085	77 ..	0·7315	13 ..	12·3500
11 ..	0·1045	44 ..	0·4180	77½ ..	0·7363	14 ..	13·3000
12 ..	0·1140	45 ..	0·4275	78 ..	0·7410	15 ..	14·2500
12½ ..	0·1188	46 ..	0·4370	79 ..	0·7505	16 ..	15·2000
13 ..	0·1235	47 ..	0·4465	80 ..	0·7600	17 ..	16·1500
14 ..	0·1330	47½ ..	0·4513	81 ..	0·7695	18 ..	17·1000
15 ..	0·1425	48 ..	0·4560	82 ..	0·7790	19 ..	18·0500
16 ..	0·1520	49 ..	0·4655	82½ ..	0·7838	20 ..	19·0000
17 ..	0·1615	50 ..	0·4750	83 ..	0·7885	25 ..	23·7500
17½ ..	0·1663	51 ..	0·4845	84 ..	0·7980	30 ..	28·5000
18 ..	0·1710	52 ..	0·4940	85 ..	0·8075	35 ..	33·2500
19 ..	0·1805	52½ ..	0·4988	86 ..	0·8170	40 ..	38·0000
20 ..	0·1900	53 ..	0·5035	87 ..	0·8265	45 ..	42·7500
21 ..	0·1995	54 ..	0·5130	87½ ..	0·8313	50 ..	47·5000
22 ..	0·2090	55 ..	0·5225	88 ..	0·8360	55 ..	52·2500
22½ ..	0·2138	56 ..	0·5320	89 ..	0·8455	60 ..	57·0000
23 ..	0·2185	57 ..	0·5415	90 ..	0·8550	65 ..	61·7500
24 ..	0·2280	57½ ..	0·5463	91 ..	0·8645	70 ..	66·5000
25 ..	0·2375	58 ..	0·5510	92 ..	0·8740	75 ..	71·2500
26 ..	0·2470	59 ..	0·5605	92½ ..	0·8788	80 ..	76·0000
27 ..	0·2565	60 ..	0·5700	93 ..	0·8835	85 ..	80·7500
27½ ..	0·2613	61 ..	0·5795	94 ..	0·8930	90 ..	85·5000
28 ..	0·2660	62 ..	0·5890	95 ..	0·9025	95 ..	90·2500
29 ..	0·2755	62½ ..	0·5938	96 ..	0·9120	100 ..	95·0000
30 ..	0·2850	63 ..	0·5985	97 ..	0·9215	110 ..	104·5000
31 ..	0·2945	64 ..	0·6080	97½ ..	0·9263	120 ..	114·0000
32 ..	0·3040	65 ..	0·6175	98 ..	0·9310	130 ..	123·5000
32½ ..	0·3088	66 ..	0·6270	99 ..	0·9405	140 ..	133·0000

£	£	£	£	£	£	£	£
150..	142·5000	300..	285·0000	450..	427·5000	700 ..	665·0000
200..	190·0000	350..	332·5000	500..	475·0000	800 ..	760·0000
250..	237·5000	400..	380·0000	600..	570·0000	1000 ..	950·0000

p	£	p	£	p	£	£	£
¼	0·0049	33	0·3218	67	0·6533	1	0·9750
1	0·0098	34	0·3315	67½	0·6581	2	1·9500
2	0·0195	35	0·3413	68	0·6630	3	2·9250
2½	0·0244	36	0·3510	69	0·6728	4	3·9000
3	0·0293	37	0·3608	70	0·6825	5	4·8750
4	0·0390	37½	0·3656	71	0·6923	6	5·8500
5	0·0488	38	0·3705	72	0·7020	7	6·8250
6	0·0585	39	0·3803	72½	0·7069	8	7·8000
7	0·0683	40	0·3900	73	0·7118	9	8·7750
7½	0·0731	41	0·3998	74	0·7215	10	9·7500
8	0·0780	42	0·4095	75	0·7313	11	10·7250
9	0·0878	42½	0·4144	76	0·7410	12	11·7000
10	0·0975	43	0·4193	77	0·7508	13	12·6750
11	0·1073	44	0·4290	77½	0·7556	14	13·6500
12	0·1170	45	0·4388	78	0·7605	15	14·6250
12½	0·1219	46	0·4485	79	0·7703	16	15·6000
13	0·1268	47	0·4583	80	0·7800	17	16·5750
14	0·1365	47½	0·4631	81	0·7898	18	17·5500
15	0·1463	48	0·4680	82	0·7995	19	18·5250
16	0·1560	49	0·4778	82½	0·8044	20	19·5000
17	0·1658	50	0·4875	83	0·8093	25	24·3750
17½	0·1706	51	0·4973	84	0·8190	30	29·2500
18	0·1755	52	0·5070	85	0·8288	35	34·1250
19	0·1853	52½	0·5119	86	0·8385	40	39·0000
20	0·1950	53	0·5168	87	0·8483	45	43·8750
21	0·2048	54	0·5265	87½	0·8531	50	48·7500
22	0·2145	55	0·5363	88	0·8580	55	53·6250
22½	0·2194	56	0·5460	89	0·8678	60	58·5000
23	0·2243	57	0·5558	90	0·8775	65	63·3750
24	0·2340	57½	0·5606	91	0·8873	70	68·2500
25	0·2438	58	0·5655	92	0·8970	75	73·1250
26	0·2535	59	0·5753	92½	0·9019	80	78·0000
27	0·2633	60	0·5850	93	0·9068	85	82·8750
27½	0·2681	61	0·5948	94	0·9165	90	87·7500
28	0·2730	62	0·6045	95	0·9263	95	92·6250
29	0·2828	62½	0·6094	96	0·9360	100	97·5000
30	0·2925	63	0·6143	97	0·9458	110	107·2500
31	0·3023	64	0·6240	97½	0·9506	120	117·0000
32	0·3120	65	0·6338	98	0·9555	130	126·7500
32½	0·3169	66	0·6435	99	0·9653	140	136·5000

£	£	£	£	£	£	£	£
150	146·2500	300	292·5000	450	438·7500	700	682·5000
200	195·0000	350	341·2500	500	487·5000	800	780·0000
250	243·7500	400	390·0000	600	585·0000	1000	975·0000

Section 3

SUPPLEMENTARY DECIMAL CURRENCY RECKONER FOR OLD PENNY (d) RATES

It seems probable that for some time after the change to decimal currency many rates and item values will continue to be expressed in old pence (d). The following tables have been compiled to meet this situation and cover the lower unit rates which seem likely to be the most troublesome. The values given are an exact extension (to five decimal places) of the **old penny (d)** rate given at the head of each page.

No.	£	No.	£	No.	£	No.	£
1	0·00052	38	0·01979	76	0·03958	114	0·05937
1½	0·00078	39	0·02031	77	0·04010	115	0·05989
2	0·00104	40	0·02083	78	0·04062	116	0·06041
3	0·00156	41	0·02135	79	0.04114	117	0·06093
4	0·00208	42	0·02187	80	0·04167	118	0·06145
5	0·00260	43	0·02239	81	0·04218	119	0·06198
6	0·00312	44	0·02292	82	0·04271	120	0·06250
7	0·00365	45	0·02344	83	0·04323	128	0·06666
8	0·00417	46	0·02396	84	0·04375	130	0·06770
9	0·00469	47	0·02448	85	0·04427	140	0·07291
10	0·00521	48	0·02500	86	0·04479	144	0·07500
11	0·00573	49	0·02552	87	0·04531	150	0·07812
12	0·00625	50	0·02604	88	0·04583	156	0·08124
13	0·00677	51	0·02656	89	0·04635	160	0·08333
14	0·00729	52	0·02708	90	0·04687	168	0·08749
15	0·00781	53	0·02760	91	0·04739	170	0·08854
16	0·00833	54	0·02812	92	0·04791	180	0·09374
17	0·00885	55	0·02864	93	0·04843	190	0·09895
18	0·00937	56	0·02915	94	0·04896	196	0·10208
19	0·00990	57	0·02969	95	0·04948	200	0·10416
20	0·01042	58	0·03021	96	0·05000	220	0·11458
21	0·01094	59	0·03073	97	0·05052	224	0·11666
22	0·01146	60	0·03125	98	0·05104	256	0·13332
23	0·01198	61	0·03177	99	0·05156	280	0·14582
24	0·01250	62	0·03229	100	0·05208	300	0·15624
25	0·01302	63	0·03281	101	0·05260	365	0·19009
26	0·01354	64	0·03333	102	0·05312	400	0·20832
27	0·01406	65	0·03852	103	0·05364	480	0·24998
28	0·01458	66	0·03437	104	0·05416	500	0·26040
29	0·01510	67	0·03489	105	0·05468	516	0·26873
30	0·01562	68	0·03541	106	0·05520	560	0·29165
31	0·01614	69	0·03594	107	0·05573	600	0·31248
32	0·01667	70	0·03646	108	0·05625	625	0·32550
33	0·01719	71	0·03698	109	0·05677	640	0·33331
34	0·01770	72	0·03750	110	0·05729	700	0·36456
35	0·01823	73	0·03802	111	0·05781	750	0·39060
36	0·01875	74	0·03854	112	0·05833	800	0·41664
37	0·01927	75	0·03906	113	0·05885	900	0·46872

No.	£	No.	£	No.	£
1000	0·52080	1760	0·91661	6000	3·12480
1016	0·52913	2000	1·04160	7000	3·64560
1094	0·56976	2240	1·16659	7500	3·90600
1120	0·58330	2500	1·30200	10000	5·20800
1250	0·65100	3000	1·56240	15000	7·81200
1500	0·78120	4000	2·08320	20000	10·41600
1750	0·91140	5000	2·60400	30000	15·62400

No.	£	No.	£	No.	£	No.	£
1	0·00104	38	0·03958	76	0·07917	114	0·11875
1½	0·00156	39	0·04062	77	0·08021	115	0·11979
2	0·00208	40	0·04167	78	0·08125	116	0·12083
3	0·00312	41	0·04271	79	0·08229	117	0·12187
4	0·00417	42	0·04375	80	0·08333	118	0·12292
5	0·00521	43	0·04479	81	0·08437	119	0·12396
6	0·00625	44	0·04583	82	0·08542	120	0·12500
7	0·00729	45	0·04687	83	0·08646	128	0·13333
8	0·00833	46	0·04792	84	0·08750	130	0·13542
9	0·00937	47	0·04896	85	0·08854	140	0·14583
10	0·01042	48	0·05000	86	0·08958	144	0·15000
11	0·01146	49	0·05104	87	0·09062	150	0·15625
12	0·01250	50	0·05208	88	0·09167	156	0·16250
13	0·01354	51	0·05312	89	0·09271	160	0·16667
14	0·01458	52	0·05417	90	0·09375	168	0·17500
15	0·01562	53	0·05521	91	0·09479	170	0·17708
16	0·01667	54	0·05625	92	0·09583	180	0·18750
17	0·01771	55	0·05729	93	0·09687	190	0·19792
18	0·01875	56	0·05833	94	0·09792	196	0·20417
19	0·01979	57	0·05937	95	0·09896	200	0·20833
20	0·02083	58	0·06042	96	0·10000	220	0·22917
21	0·02187	59	0·06146	97	0·10104	224	0·23333
22	0·02292	60	0·06250	98	0·10208	256	0·26667
23	0·02396	61	0·06354	99	0·10312	280	0·29167
24	0·02500	62	0·06458	100	0·10417	300	0·31250
25	0·02604	63	0·06562	101	0·10521	365	0·38020
26	0·02708	64	0·06667	102	0·10625	400	0·41667
27	0·02812	65	0·06771	103	0·10729	480	0·50000
28	0·02916	66	0·06875	104	0·10833	500	0·52083
29	0·03021	67	0·06979	105	0·10937	516	0·53750
30	0·03125	68	0·07083	106	0·11042	560	0·58333
31	0·03229	69	0·07187	107	0·11146	600	0·62500
32	0·03333	70	0·07292	108	0·11250	625	0·65104
33	0·03437	71	0·07396	109	0·11354	640	0·66667
34	0·03542	72	0·07500	110	0·11458	700	0·72917
35	0·03646	73	0·07604	111	0·11562	750	0·78125
36	0·03750	74	0·07708	112	0·11667	800	0·83333
37	0·03854	75	0·07812	113	0·11771	900	0·93750

No.	£	No.	£	No.	£
1000	1·04167	1760	1·83333	6000	6·25000
1016	1·05833	2000	2·08333	7000	7·29167
1094	1·13958	2240	2·33333	7500	7·81250
1120	1·16667	2500	2·60417	10000	10·41666
1250	1·30208	3000	3·12500	15000	15·62500
1500	1·56250	4000	4·16667	20000	20·83333
1750	1·82292	5000	5·20833	30000	31·25000

No.	£	No.	£	No.	£	No.	£
1	0·00156	38	0·05937	76	0·11875	114	0·17812
1½	0·00234	39	0·06094	77	0·12031	115	0·17969
2	0·00312	40	0·06250	78	0·12187	116	0·18125
3	0·00469	41	0·06406	79	0·12344	117	0·18281
4	0·00625	42	0·06562	80	0·12500	118	0·18437
5	0·00781	43	0·06719	81	0·12656	119	0·18594
6	0·00937	44	0·06875	82	0·12812	120	0·18750
7	0·01094	45	0·07031	83	0·12969	128	0·20000
8	0·01250	46	0·07187	84	0·13125	130	0·20312
9	0·01406	47	0·07344	85	0·13281	140	0·21875
10	0·01562	48	0·07500	86	0·13437	144	0·22500
11	0·01719	49	0·07656	87	0·13594	150	0·23437
12	0·01875	50	0·07812	88	0·13750	156	0·24375
13	0·02031	51	0·07969	89	0·13906	160	0·25000
14	0·02187	52	0·08125	90	0·14062	168	0·26250
15	0·02344	53	0·08281	91	0·14219	170	0·26562
16	0·02500	54	0·08437	92	0·14375	180	0·28125
17	0·02656	55	0·08594	93	0·14531	190	0·29687
18	0·02812	56	0·08750	94	0·14687	196	0·30625
19	0·02969	57	0·08906	95	0·14844	200	0·31250
20	0·03125	58	0·09062	96	0·15000	220	0·34375
21	0·03281	59	0·09219	97	0·15156	224	0·35000
22	0·03437	60	0·09375	98	0·15312	256	0·40000
23	0·03594	61	0·09531	99	0·15469	280	0·43750
24	0·03750	62	0·09687	100	0·15625	300	0·46875
25	0·03906	63	0·09844	101	0·15781	365	0·57031
26	0·04062	64	0·10000	102	0·15937	400	0·62500
27	0·04219	65	0·10156	103	0·16094	480	0·75000
28	0·04375	66	0·10312	104	0·16250	500	0·78125
29	0·04531	67	0·10469	105	0·16406	516	0·80625
30	0·04687	68	0·10625	106	0·16562	560	0·87500
31	0·04844	69	0·10781	107	0·16719	600	0·93750
32	0·05000	70	0·10937	108	0·16875	625	0·97656
33	0·05156	71	0·11094	109	0·17031	640	1·00000
34	0·05312	72	0·11250	110	0·17187	700	1·09375
35	0·05469	73	0·11406	111	0·17344	750	1·17187
36	0·05625	74	0·11562	112	0·17500	800	1·25000
37	0·05781	75	0·11719	113	0·17656	900	1·40625

No.	£	No.	£	No.	£
1000	1·56250	1760	2·75000	6000	9·37500
1016	1·58750	2000	3·12500	7000	10·93750
1094	1·70937	2240	3·50000	7500	11·71875
1120	1·75000	2500	3·90625	10000	15·62500
1250	1·95312	3000	4·68750	15000	23·43750
1500	2·34375	4000	6·25000	20000	31·25000
1750	2·73437	5000	7·81250	30000	46·87500

No.	£	No.	£	No.	£	No.	£
1	0·00208	38	0·07917	76	0·15833	114	0·23750
1½	0·00312	39	0·08125	77	0·16042	115	0·23958
2	0·00417	40	0·08333	78	0·16250	116	0·24167
3	0·00625	41	0·08542	79	0·16458	117	0·24375
4	0·00833	42	0·08750	80	0·16667	118	0·24583
5	0·01042	43	0·08958	81	0·16875	119	0·24792
6	0·01250	44	0·09167	82	0·17083	120	0·25000
7	0·01458	45	0·09375	83	0·17292	128	0·26667
8	0·01667	46	0·09583	84	0·17500	130	0·27083
9	0·01875	47	0·09792	85	0·17708	140	0·29167
10	0·02083	48	0·10000	86	0·17917	144	0·30000
11	0·02292	49	0·10208	87	0·18125	150	0·31250
12	0·02500	50	0·10417	88	0·18333	156	0·32500
13	0·02708	51	0·10625	89	0·18542	160	0·33333
14	0·02917	52	0·10833	90	0·18750	168	0·35000
15	0·03125	53	0·11042	91	0·18958	170	0·35417
16	0·03333	54	0·11250	92	0·19167	180	0·37500
17	0·03542	55	0·11458	93	0·19375	190	0·39583
18	0·03750	56	0·11667	94	0·19583	196	0·40833
19	0·03958	57	0·11875	95	0·19792	200	0·41667
20	0·04167	58	0·12083	96	0·20000	220	0·45833
21	0·04375	59	0·12292	97	0·20208	224	0·46667
22	0·04583	60	0·12500	98	0·20417	256	0·53333
23	0·04792	61	0·12708	99	0·20625	280	0·58333
24	0·05000	62	0·12917	100	0·20833	300	0·62500
25	0·05208	63	0·13125	101	0·21042	365	0·76042
26	0·05417	64	0·13333	102	0·21250	400	0·83333
27	0·05625	65	0·13542	103	0·21458	480	1·00000
28	0·05833	66	0·13750	104	0·21667	500	1·04167
29	0·06042	67	0·13958	105	0·21875	516	1·07500
30	0·06250	68	0·14167	106	0·22083	560	1·16667
31	0·06458	69	0·14375	107	0·22292	600	1·25000
32	0·06667	70	0·14583	108	0·22500	625	1·30208
33	0·06875	71	0·14792	109	0·22708	640	1·33333
34	0·07083	72	0·15000	110	0·22916	700	1·45833
35	0·07292	73	0·15208	111	0·23125	750	1·56250
36	0·07500	74	0·15417	112	0·23333	800	1·66667
37	0·07708	75	0·15625	113	0·23542	900	1·87500

No.	£	No.	£	No.	£
1000	2·08333	1760	3·66667	6000	12·50000
1016	2·11667	2000	4·16667	7000	14·58333
1094	2·27917	2240	4·66667	7500	15·62500
1120	2·33333	2500	5·20833	10000	20·83333
1250	2·60417	3000	6·25000	15000	31·25000
1500	3·12500	4000	8·33333	20000	41·66667
1750	3·64583	5000	10·41667	30000	62·50000

No.	£	No.	£	No.	£	No.	£
1	0·00260	38	0·09896	76	0·19792	114	0·29687
1½	0·00391	39	0·10156	77	0·20052	115	0·29948
2	0·00521	40	0·10417	78	0·20312	116	0·30208
3	0·00781	41	0·10677	79	0·20573	117	0·30469
4	0·01042	42	0·10937	80	0·20833	118	0·30729
5	0·01302	43	0·11198	81	0·21094	119	0·30990
6	0·01562	44	0·11458	82	0·21354	120	0·31250
7	0·01823	45	0·11719	83	0·21615	128	0·33333
8	0·02083	46	0·11979	84	0·21875	130	0·33854
9	0·02344	47	0·12240	85	0·22135	140	0·36458
10	0·02604	48	0·12500	86	0·22396	144	0·37500
11	0·02864	49	0·12760	87	0·22656	150	0·39062
12	0·03125	50	0·13021	88	0·22917	156	0·40625
13	0·03385	51	0·13281	89	0·23177	160	0·41667
14	0·03646	52	0·13542	90	0·23437	168	0·43750
15	0·03906	53	0·13802	91	0·23698	170	0·44271
16	0·04167	54	0·14062	92	0·23958	180	0·46875
17	0·04427	55	0·14323	93	0·24219	190	0·49479
18	0·04687	56	0·14583	94	0·24479	196	0·51042
19	0·04948	57	0·14844	95	0·24740	200	0·52083
20	0·05208	58	0·15104	96	0·25000	220	0·57292
21	0·05469	59	0·15364	97	0·25260	224	0·58333
22	0·05729	60	0·15625	98	0·25521	256	0·66667
23	0·05990	61	0·15885	99	0·25781	280	0·72917
24	0·06250	62	0·16146	100	0·26042	300	0·78125
25	0·06510	63	0·16406	101	0·26302	365	0·95052
26	0·06771	64	0·16667	102	0·26562	400	1·04167
27	0·07031	65	0·16927	103	0·26823	480	1·25000
28	0·07292	66	0·17187	104	0·27083	500	1·30208
29	0·07552	67	0·17448	105	0·27344	516	1·34376
30	0·07812	68	0·17708	106	0·27604	560	1·45833
31	0·08073	69	0·17969	107	0·27865	600	1·56250
32	0·08333	70	0·18229	108	0·28125	625	1·62760
33	0·08594	71	0·18490	109	0·28385	640	1·66667
34	0·08854	72	0·18750	110	0·28646	700	1·82292
35	0·09115	73	0·19010	111	0·28906	750	1·95312
36	0·09375	74	0·19271	112	0·29167	800	2·08333
37	0·09635	75	0·19531	113	0·29427	900	2·34375

No.	£	No.	£	No.	£
1000	2·60417	1760	4·58333	6000	15·62500
1016	2·64583	2000	5·20833	7000	18·22917
1094	2·84896	2240	5·83333	7500	19·53125
1120	2·91667	2500	6·51042	10000	26·04167
1250	3·25521	3000	7·81250	15000	39·06250
1500	3·90625	4000	10·41667	20000	52·08333
1750	4·55729	5000	13·02083	30000	78·12500

No.	£	No.	£	No.	£	No.	£
1	0·00312	38	0·11875	76	0·23750	114	0·35625
1½	0·00469	39	0·12187	77	0·24062	115	0·35937
2	0·00625	40	0·12500	78	0·24375	116	0·36250
3	0·00937	41	0·12812	79	0·24687	117	0·36562
4	0·01250	42	0·13125	80	0·25000	118	0·36875
5	0·01562	43	0·13437	81	0·25312	119	0·37187
6	0·01875	44	0·13750	82	0·25625	120	0·37500
7	0·02187	45	0·14062	83	0·25937	128	0·40000
8	0·02500	46	0·14375	84	0·26250	130	0·40625
9	0·02812	47	0·14687	85	0·26562	140	0·43750
10	0·03125	48	0·15000	86	0·26875	144	0·45000
11	0·03437	49	0·15312	87	0·27187	150	0·46875
12	0·03750	50	0·15625	88	0·27500	156	0·48750
13	0·04062	51	0·15937	89	0·27812	160	0·50000
14	0·04375	52	0·16250	90	0·28125	168	0·52500
15	0·04687	53	0·16562	91	0·28437	170	0·53125
16	0·05000	54	0·16875	92	0·28750	180	0·56250
17	0·05312	55	0·17187	93	0·29062	190	0·59375
18	0·05625	56	0·17500	94	0·29375	196	0·61250
19	0·05937	57	0·17812	95	0·29687	200	0·62500
20	0·06250	58	0·18125	96	0·30000	220	0·68750
21	0·06562	59	0·18437	97	0·30312	224	0·70000
22	0·06875	60	0·18750	98	0·30625	256	0·80000
23	0·07187	61	0·19062	99	0·30937	280	0·87500
24	0·07500	62	0·19375	100	0·31250	300	0·93750
25	0·07812	63	0·19687	101	0·31562	365	1·14062
26	0·08125	64	0·20000	102	0·31875	400	1·25000
27	0·08437	65	0·20312	103	0·32187	480	1·50000
28	0·08750	66	0·20625	104	0·32500	500	1·56250
29	0·09062	67	0·20937	105	0·32812	516	1·61250
30	0·09375	68	0·21250	106	0·33125	560	1·75000
31	0·09687	69	0·21562	107	0·33437	600	1·87500
32	0·10000	70	0·21875	108	0·33750	625	1·95312
33	0·10312	71	0·22187	109	0·34062	640	2·00000
34	0·10625	72	0·22500	110	0·34375	700	2·18750
35	0·10937	73	0·22812	111	0·34687	750	2·34375
36	0·11250	74	0·23125	112	0·35000	800	2·50000
37	0·11562	75	0·23437	113	0·35312	900	2·81250

No.	£	No.	£	No.	£
1000	3·12500	1760	5·50000	6000	18·75000
1016	3·17500	2000	6·25000	7000	21·87500
1094	3·41875	2240	7·00000	7500	23·43750
1120	3·50000	2500	7·81250	10000	31·12500
1250	3·90625	3000	9·37500	15000	46·87500
1500	4·68750	4000	12·50000	20000	62·50000
1750	5·46875	5000	15·62500	30000	93·75000

No.	£	No.	£	No.	£	No.	£
1	0·00365	38	0·13854	76	0·27708	114	0·41562
1½	0·00547	39	0·14219	77	0·28073	115	0·41927
2	0·00729	40	0·14583	78	0·28437	116	0·42292
3	0·01094	41	0·14948	79	0·28802	117	0·42656
4	0·01458	42	0·15312	80	0·29167	118	0·43021
5	0·01823	43	0·15677	81	0·29531	119	0·43385
6	0·02187	44	0·16042	82	0·29896	120	0·43750
7	0·02552	45	0·16406	83	0·30260	128	0·46667
8	0·02917	46	0·16771	84	0·30625	130	0·47396
9	0·03281	47	0·17135	85	0·30990	140	0·51042
10	0·03646	48	0·17500	86	0·31354	144	0·52500
11	0·04010	49	0·17865	87	0·31719	150	0·54687
12	0·04375	50	0·18229	88	0·32083	156	0·56875
13	0·04740	51	0·18594	89	0·32448	160	0·58333
14	0·05104	52	0·18958	90	0·32812	168	0·61250
15	0·05469	53	0·19323	91	0·33177	170	0·61980
16	0·05833	54	0·19687	92	0·33542	180	0·65625
17	0·06198	55	0·20052	93	0·33906	190	0·69271
18	0·06562	56	0·20417	94	0·34271	196	0·71458
19	0·06927	57	0·20781	95	0·34635	200	0·72917
20	0·07292	58	0·21146	96	0·35000	220	0·80208
21	0·07656	59	0·21510	97	0·35364	224	0·81667
22	0·08021	60	0·21875	98	0·35730	256	0·93333
23	0·08385	61	0·22240	99	0·36094	280	1·02083
24	0·08750	62	0·22604	100	0·36458	300	1·09375
25	0·09115	63	0·22969	101	0·36823	365	1·33073
26	0·09479	64	0·23333	102	0·37187	400	1·45833
27	0·09844	65	0·23698	103	0·37552	480	1·75000
28	0·10208	66	0·24062	104	0·37917	500	1·82292
29	0·10573	67	0·24427	105	0·38281	516	1·88125
30	0·10937	68	0·24792	106	0·38646	560	2·04167
31	0·11302	69	0·25156	107	0·39010	600	2·18750
32	0·11667	70	0·25521	108	0·39375	625	2·27864
33	0·12031	71	0·25885	109	0·39740	640	2·33333
34	0·12396	72	0·26250	110	0·40104	700	2·55208
35	0·12760	73	0·26615	111	0·40469	750	2·73437
36	0·13125	74	0·26979	112	0·40833	800	2·91667
37	0·13490	75	0·27344	113	0·41198	900	3·28125

No.	£	No.	£	No.	£
1000	3·64583	1760	6·41667	6000	21·87500
1016	3·70417	2000	7·29167	7000	25·52083
1094	3·98854	2240	8·16667	7500	27·34375
1120	4·08333	2500	9·11458	10000	36·45833
1250	4·55729	3000	10·93750	15000	54·68750
1500	5·46875	4000	14·58333	20000	72·91666
1750	6·38021	5000	18·22917	30000	109·37450

No.	£	No.	£	No.	£	No.	£
1	0·00417	38	0·15833	76	0·31667	114	0·47500
1½	0·00625	39	0·16250	77	0·32083	115	0·47917
2	0·00833	40	0·16667	78	0·32500	116	0·48333
3	0·01250	41	0·17083	79	0·32917	117	0·48750
4	0·01667	42	0·17500	80	0·33333	118	0·49167
5	0·02083	43	0·17917	81	0·33750	119	0·49583
6	0·02500	44	0·18333	82	0·34167	120	0·50000
7	0·02917	45	0·18750	83	0·34583	128	0·53333
8	0·03333	46	0·19167	84	0·35000	130	0·54167
9	0·03750	47	0·19583	85	0·35417	140	0·58333
10	0·04167	48	0·20000	86	0·35833	144	0·60000
11	0·04583	49	0·20417	87	0·36250	150	0·62500
12	0·05000	50	0·20833	88	0·36667	156	0·65000
13	0·05417	51	0·21250	89	0·37083	160	0·66667
14	0·05833	52	0·21667	90	0·37500	168	0·70000
15	0·06250	53	0·22083	91	0·37917	170	0·70833
16	0·06667	54	0·22500	92	0·38333	180	0·75000
17	0·07083	55	0·22917	93	0·38750	190	0·79167
18	0·07500	56	0·23333	94	0·39167	196	0·81667
19	0·07917	57	0·23750	95	0·39583	200	0·83333
20	0·08333	58	0·24167	96	0·40000	220	0·91667
21	0·08750	59	0·24583	97	0·40417	224	0·93333
22	0·09167	60	0·25000	98	0·40833	256	1·06666
23	0·09583	61	0·25417	99	0·41250	280	1·16666
24	0·10000	62	0·25833	100	0·41667	300	1·25000
25	0·10417	63	0·26250	101	0·42083	365	1·52083
26	0·10833	64	0·26667	102	0·42500	400	1·66667
27	0·11250	65	0·27083	103	0·42917	480	2·00000
28	0·11667	66	0·27500	104	0·43333	500	2·08333
29	0·12083	67	0·27917	105	0·43750	516	2·15000
30	0·12500	68	0·28333	106	0·44167	560	2·33333
31	0·12917	69	0·28750	107	0·44583	600	2·50000
32	0·13333	70	0·29167	108	0·45000	625	2·60417
33	0·13750	71	0·29583	109	0·45417	640	2·66667
34	0·14167	72	0·30000	110	0·45833	700	2·91667
35	0·14583	73	0·30417	111	0·46250	750	3·12500
36	0·15000	74	0·30833	112	0·46667	800	3·33333
37	0·15417	75	0·31250	113	0·47083	900	3·75000

No.	£	No.	£	No.	£
1000	4·16667	1760	7·33333	6000	25·00000
1016	4·23333	2000	8·33333	7000	29.16667
1094	4·55833	2240	9·33333	7500	31·25000
1120	4·66667	2500	10·41667	10000	41·66667
1250	5·20833	3000	12·50000	15000	62·50000
1500	6·25000	4000	16·66667	20000	83·33333
1750	7·29167	5000	20·83333	30000	125·00000

$1\frac{1}{8}$d OLD PENNY SUPPLEMENTARY TABLE $1\frac{1}{8}$d

No.	£	No.	£	No.	£	No.	£
1	0·00469	38	0·17812	76	0·35625	114	0·53437
1½	0·07031	39	0·18281	77	0·36094	115	0·53906
2	0·00937	40	0·18750	78	0·36562	116	0·54375
3	0·01406	41	0·19219	79	0·37031	117	0·54844
4	0·01875	42	0·19687	80	0·37500	118	0·55312
5	0·02344	43	0·20156	81	0·37969	119	0·55781
6	0·02812	44	0·20625	82	0·38437	120	0·56250
7	0·03281	45	0·21094	83	0·38906	128	0·60000
8	0·03750	46	0·21562	84	0·39375	130	0·60937
9	0·04219	47	0·22031	85	0·39844	140	0·65625
10	0·04687	48	0·22500	86	0·40312	144	0·67500
11	0·05156	49	0·22969	87	0·40781	150	0·70312
12	0·05625	50	0·23437	88	0·41250	156	0·73125
13	0·06094	51	0·23906	89	0·41719	160	0·75000
14	0·06562	52	0·24375	90	0·42187	165	0·77344
15	0·07031	53	0·24844	91	0·42656	170	0·79687
16	0·07500	54	0·25312	92	0·43125	180	0·84375
17	0·07969	55	0·25781	93	0·43594	190	0·89062
18	0·08437	56	0·26250	94	0·44062	196	0·91875
19	0·08906	57	0·26719	95	0·44531	200	0·93750
20	0·09375	58	0·27187	96	0·45000	220	1·03125
21	0·09844	59	0·27656	97	0·45469	224	1·05000
22	0·10312	60	0·28125	98	0·45937	256	1·20000
23	0·10781	61	0·28594	99	0·46406	280	1·31250
24	0·11250	62	0·29062	100	0·46875	300	1·40625
25	0·11719	63	0·29531	101	0·47344	365	1·71094
26	0·12187	64	0·30000	102	0·47812	400	1·87500
27	0·12656	65	0·30469	103	0·48281	480	2·25000
28	0·13125	66	0·30937	104	0·48750	500	2·34375
29	0·13594	67	0·31406	105	0·49219	516	2·41875
30	0·14062	68	0·31875	106	0·49687	560	2·62500
31	0·14531	69	0·32344	107	0·50156	600	2·81250
32	0·15000	70	0·32812	108	0·50625	625	2·92969
33	0·15469	71	0·33281	109	0·51094	640	3·00000
34	0·15937	72	0·33750	110	0·51562	700	3·28125
35	0·16406	73	0·34219	111	0·52031	750	3·51562
36	0·16875	74	0·34688	112	0·52500	800	3·75000
37	0·17344	75	0·35156	113	0·52969	900	4·21875

No.	£	No.	£	No.	£
1000	4·68750	1760	8·25000	6000	28·12500
1016	4·76250	2000	9·37500	7000	32·81250
1094	5·12812	2240	10·50000	7500	35·15625
1120	5·25000	2500	11·71875	10000	46·87500
1250	5·85937	3000	14·06250	15000	70·31250
1500	7·03125	4000	18·75000	20000	93·75000
1750	8·20312	5000	23·43750	30000	140·62500

No.	£	No.	£	No.	£	No.	£
1	0·00521	38	0·19792	76	0·39583	114	0·59375
1½	0·00781	39	0·20312	77	0·40104	115	0·59896
2	0·01042	40	0·20833	78	0·40625	116	0·60417
3	0·01562	41	0·21354	79	0·41146	117	0·60937
4	0·02083	42	0·21875	80	0·41667	118	0·61458
5	0·02604	43	0·22396	81	0·42187	119	0·61979
6	0·03125	44	0·22917	82	0·42708	120	0·62500
7	0·03646	45	0·23437	83	0·43229	128	0·66667
8	0·04167	46	0·23958	84	0·43750	130	0·67708
9	0·04687	47	0·24479	85	0·44271	140	0·72917
10	0·05208	48	0·25000	86	0·44792	144	0·75000
11	0·05729	49	0·25521	87	0·45312	150	0·78125
12	0·06250	50	0·26042	88	0·45833	156	0·81250
13	0·06771	51	0·26562	89	0·46354	160	0·83333
14	0·07292	52	0·27083	90	0·46875	168	0·87500
15	0·07812	53	0·27604	91	0·47396	170	0·88542
16	0·08333	54	0·28125	92	0·47917	180	0·93750
17	0·08854	55	0·28646	93	0·48437	190	1·98958
18	0·09375	56	0·29167	94	0·48958	196	1·02083
19	0·09896	57	0·29687	95	0·49479	200	1·04167
20	0·10417	58	0·30208	96	0·50000	220	1·14583
21	0·10937	59	0·30729	97	0·50521	224	1·16667
22	0·11458	60	0·31250	98	0·51042	256	1·33333
23	0·11979	61	0·31771	99	0·51562	280	1·45833
24	0·12500	62	0·32292	100	0·52083	300	1·56250
25	0·13021	63	0·32812	101	0·52604	365	1·90104
26	0·13542	64	0·33333	102	0·53125	400	2·08333
27	0·14062	65	0·33854	103	0·53646	480	2·50000
28	0·14583	66	0·34375	104	0·54167	500	2·60417
29	0·15104	67	0·34896	105	0·54687	516	2·68750
30	0·15625	68	0·35417	106	0·55208	560	2·91667
31	0·16146	69	0·35937	107	0·55729	600	3·12500
32	0·16667	70	0·36458	108	0·56250	625	3·25521
33	0·17187	71	0·36979	109	0·56771	640	3·33333
34	0·17708	72	0·37500	110	0·57292	700	3·64583
35	0·18229	73	0·38021	111	0·57812	750	3·90625
36	0·18750	74	0·38542	112	0·58333	800	4·16667
37	0·19271	75	0·39062	113	0·58854	900	4·68750

No.	£	No.	£	No.	£
1000	5·20833	1760	9·16667	6000	31·25000
1016	5·29167	2000	10·41667	7000	36·45833
1094	5·69792	2240	11·66667	7500	39·06250
1120	5·83333	2500	13·02083	10000	52·08333
1250	6·51042	3000	15·62500	15000	78·12500
1500	7·81250	4000	20·83333	20000	104·16667
1750	9·11458	5000	26·04167	30000	156·25000

No.	£	No.	£	No.	£	No.	£
1	0·00573	38	0·21771	76	0·43542	114	0·65312
1½	0·00859	39	0·22344	77	0·44115	115	0·65885
2	0·01146	40	0·22917	78	0·44687	116	0·66458
3	0·01719	41	0·23490	79	0·45260	117	0·67031
4	0·02292	42	0·24062	80	0·45833	118	0·67604
5	0·02865	43	0·24635	81	0·46406	119	0·68177
6	0·03437	44	0·25208	82	0·46979	120	0·68750
7	0·04010	45	0·25781	83	0·47552	128	0·73333
8	0·04583	46	0·26354	84	0·48125	130	0·74479
9	0·05156	47	0·26927	85	0·48698	140	0·80208
10	0·05729	48	0·27500	86	0·49271	144	0·82500
11	0·06302	49	0·28073	87	0·49844	150	0·85937
12	0·06875	50	0·28646	88	0·50417	156	0·89375
13	0·07448	51	0·29219	89	0·50990	160	0·91667
14	0·08021	52	0·29792	90	0·51562	168	0·96250
15	0·08594	53	0·30365	91	0·52135	170	0·97396
16	0·09167	54	0·30937	92	0·52708	180	1·03125
17	0·09740	55	0·31510	93	0·53281	190	1·08854
18	0·10312	56	0·32083	94	0·53854	196	1·12292
19	0·10885	57	0·32656	95	0·54427	200	1·14583
20	0·11458	58	0·33229	96	0·55000	220	1·26042
21	0·12031	59	0·33802	97	0·55573	224	1·28333
22	0·12604	60	0·34375	98	0·56146	256	1·46667
23	0·13177	61	0·34948	99	0·56719	280	1·60417
24	0·13750	62	0·35521	100	0·57292	300	1·71875
25	0·14323	63	0·36094	101	0·57865	365	2·09115
26	0·14896	64	0·36667	102	0·58437	400	2·29167
27	0·15469	65	0·37240	103	0·59010	480	2·75000
28	0·16042	66	0·37812	104	0·59583	500	2·86458
29	0·16615	67	0·38385	105	0·60156	516	2·95625
30	0·17187	68	0·38958	106	0·60729	560	3·20833
31	0·17760	69	0·39531	107	0·61302	600	3·43750
32	0·18333	70	0·40104	108	0·61875	625	3·58073
33	0·18906	71	0·40677	109	0·62448	640	3·66667
34	0·19479	72	0·41250	110	0·63021	700	4·01042
35	0·20052	73	0·41823	111	0·63594	750	4·29687
36	0·20625	74	0·42396	112	0·64167	800	4·58333
37	0·21198	75	0·42969	113	0·64740	900	5·15625

No.	£	No.	£	No.	£
1000	5·72917	1760	10·08333	6000	34·37500
1016	5·82083	2000	11·45833	7000	40·10417
1094	6·26771	2240	12·83333	7500	42·96875
1120	6·41667	2500	14·32292	10000	57·29167
1250	7·16146	3000	17·18750	15000	85·93750
1500	8·59375	4000	22·91667	20000	114·58334
1750	10·02604	5000	28·64583	30000	171·87501

No.	£	No.	£	No.	£	No.	£
1	0·00625	38	0·23750	76	0·47500	114	0·71250
1½	0·00937	39	0·24375	77	0·48125	115	0·71875
2	0·01250	40	0·25000	78	0·48750	116	0·72500
3	0·01875	41	0·25625	79	0·49375	117	0·73125
4	0·02500	42	0·26250	80	0·50000	118	0·73750
5	0·03125	43	0·26875	81	0·50625	119	0·74375
6	0·03750	44	0·27500	82	0·51250	120	0·75000
7	0·04375	45	0·28125	83	0·51875	128	0·80000
8	0·05000	46	0·28750	84	0·52500	130	0·81250
9	0·05625	47	0·29375	85	0·53125	140	0·87500
10	0·06250	48	0·30000	86	0·53750	144	0·90000
11	0·06875	49	0·30625	87	0·54375	150	0·93750
12	0·07500	50	0·31250	88	0·55000	156	0·97500
13	0·08125	51	0·31875	89	0·55625	160	1·00000
14	0·08750	52	0·32500	90	0·56250	168	1·05000
15	0·09375	53	0·33125	91	0·56875	170	1·06250
16	0·10000	54	0·33750	92	0·57500	180	1·12500
17	0·10625	55	0·34375	93	0·58125	190	1·18750
18	0·11250	56	0·35000	94	0·58750	196	1·22500
19	0·11875	57	0·35625	95	0·59375	200	1·25000
20	0·12500	58	0·36250	96	0·60000	220	1·37500
21	0·13125	59	0·36875	97	0·60625	224	1·40000
22	0·13750	60	0·37500	98	0·61250	256	1·60000
23	0·14375	61	0·38125	99	0·61875	280	1·75000
24	0·15000	62	0·38750	100	0·62500	300	1·87500
25	0·15625	63	0·39375	101	0·63125	365	2·28125
26	0·16250	64	0·40000	102	0·63750	400	2·50000
27	0·16875	65	0·40625	103	0·64375	480	3·00000
28	0·17500	66	0·41250	104	0·65000	500	3·12500
29	0·18125	67	0·41875	105	0·65625	516	3·22500
30	0·18750	68	0·42500	106	0·66250	560	3·50000
31	0·19375	69	0·43125	107	0·66875	600	3·75000
32	0·20000	70	0·43750	108	0·67500	625	3·90625
33	0·20625	71	0·44375	109	0·68125	640	4·00000
34	0·21250	72	0·45000	110	0·68750	700	4·37500
35	0·21875	73	0·45625	111	0·69375	750	4·68750
36	0·22500	74	0·46250	112	0·70000	800	5·00000
37	0·23125	75	0·46875	113	0·70625	900	5·62500

No.	£	No.	£	No.	£
1000	6·25000	1760	11·00000	6000	37·50000
1016	6·35000	2000	12·50000	7000	43·75000
1094	6·83750	2240	14·00000	7500	46·87500
1120	7·00000	2500	15·62500	10000	62·50000
1250	7·81250	3000	18·75000	15000	93·75000
1500	9·37500	4000	25·00000	20000	125·00000
1750	10·93750	5000	31·25000	30000	187·50000

No.	£	No.	£	No.	£	No.	£
1	0·00677	38	0·25729	76	0·51458	114	0·77187
1½	0·01016	39	0·26406	77	0·52135	115	0·77864
2	0.01354	40	0·27083	78	0·52812	116	0·78542
3	0·02031	41	0·27760	79	0·53490	117	0·79219
4	0·02708	42	0·28437	80	0·54167	118	0·79896
5	0·03385	43	0·29114	81	0·54844	119	0.80573
6	0·04062	44	0·29792	82	0·55521	120	0·81250
7	0·04740	45	0·30469	83	0·56198	128	0·86667
8	0·05417	46	0·31146	84	0·56875	130	0·88021
9	0·06094	47	0·31823	85	0·57552	140	0·94792
10	0·06771	48	0·32500	86	0·58230	144	0·97500
11	0·07448	49	0·33177	87	0·58906	150	1.01562
12	0·08125	50	0·33854	88	0.59583	156	1·05625
13	0·08802	51	0·34531	89	0·60260	160	1·08333
14	0·09479	52	0·35208	90	0·60937	168	1·13750
15	0·10156	53	0·35885	91	0·61614	170	1·15104
16	0·10833	54	0·36562	92	0·62292	180	1·21875
17	0·11510	55	0·37240	93	0·62969	190	1·28646
18	0·12187	56	0·37917	94	0·63646	196	1·32708
19	0·12864	57	0·38594	95	0·64323	200	1·35417
20	0·13542	58	0·39271	96	0·65000	220	1·48958
21	0·14219	59	0·39948	97	0·65677	224	1·51667
22	0·14896	60	0·40625	98	0·66354	256	1·73333
23	0·15573	61	0·41302	99	0·67031	280	1·89583
24	0·16250	62	0·41979	100	0·67708	300	2·03125
25	0·16927	63	0·42656	101	0·68385	365	2·47135
26	0·17604	64	0·43333	102	0·69062	400	2·70833
27	0·18281	65	0·44010	103	0·69740	480	3·25000
28	0·18958	66	0·44687	104	0·70417	500	3·38542
29	0·19635	67	0·45364	105	0·71094	516	3.49375
30	0·20312	68	0·46042	106	0·71771	560	3·79167
31	0·20990	69	0·46719	107	0·72448	600	4·06250
32	0·21667	70	0·47396	108	0·73125	625	4·23177
33	0·22344	71	0·48073	109	0·73802	640	4·33333
34	0·23021	72	0·48750	110	0·74479	700	4·73958
35	0·23698	73	0·49427	111	0·75156	750	5·07812
36	0·24375	74	0·50104	112	0·75833	800	5·41667
37	0·25052	75	0·50781	113	0·76510	900	6·09375

No.	£	No.	£	No.	£
1000	6·77083	1760	11·91667	6000	40·62500
1016	6·87917	2000	13·54167	7000	47·39583
1094	7·40730	2240	15·16667	7500	50·78125
1120	7·58333	2500	16·92708	10000	67·70833
1250	8·46354	3000	20·31250	15000	101·56250
1500	10·15625	4000	27·08333	20000	135·41667
1750	11·84896	5000	33·85417	30000	203·12500

No.	£	No.	£	No.	£	No.	£
1	0·00729	38	0·27708	76	0·55417	114	0·83125
1½	0·01094	39	0·28437	77	0·56146	115	0·83854
2	0·01458	40	0·29167	78	0·56875	116	0·84583
3	0·02187	41	0·29896	79	0·57604	117	0·85312
4	0·02917	42	0·30625	80	0·58333	118	0·86042
5	0·03646	43	0·31354	81	0·59062	119	0·86771
6	0·04375	44	0·32083	82	0·59792	120	0·87500
7	0·05104	45	0·32812	83	0·60521	128	0·93333
8	0·05833	46	0·33542	84	0·61250	130	0·94792
9	0·06562	47	0·34271	85	0·61979	140	1·02083
10	0·07292	48	0·35000	86	0·62708	144	1·05000
11	0·08021	49	0·35729	87	0·63437	150	1·09375
12	0·08750	50	0·36458	88	0·64167	156	1·13750
13	0·09479	51	0·37187	89	0·64896	160	1·16667
14	0·10208	52	0·37917	90	0·65625	168	1·22500
15	0·10937	53	0·38646	91	0·66354	170	1·23958
16	0·11667	54	0·39375	92	0·67083	180	1·31250
17	0·12396	55	0·40104	93	0·67812	190	1·38542
18	0·13125	56	0·40833	94	0·68542	196	1·42917
19	0·13854	57	0·41562	95	0·69271	200	1·45833
20	0·14583	58	0·42292	96	0·70000	220	1·60417
21	0·15312	59	0·43021	97	0·70729	224	1·63333
22	0·16042	60	0·43750	98	0·71458	256	1·86667
23	0·16771	61	0·44479	99	0·72187	280	2·04167
24	0·17500	62	0·45208	100	0·72917	300	2·18750
25	0·18229	63	0·45937	101	0·73646	365	2·66146
26	0·18958	64	0·46667	102	0·74375	400	2·91667
27	0·19687	65	0·47396	103	0·75104	480	3·50000
28	0·20417	66	0·48125	104	0·75833	500	3·64583
29	0·21146	67	0·48854	105	0·76562	516	3·76250
30	0·21875	68	0·49583	106	0·77292	560	4·08333
31	0·22604	69	0·50312	107	0·78021	600	4·37500
32	0·23333	70	0·51042	108	0·78750	625	4·55729
33	0·24062	71	0·51771	109	0·79479	640	4·66667
34	0·24792	72	0·52500	110	0·80208	700	5·10417
35	0·25521	73	0·53229	111	0·80937	750	5·46875
36	0·26250	74	0·53958	112	0·81667	800	5·83333
37	0·26979	75	0·54687	113	0·82396	900	6·56250

No.	£	No.	£	No.	£
1000	7·29167	1760	12·83333	6000	43·75000
1016	7·40833	2000	14·58333	7000	51·04167
1094	7·97708	2240	16·33333	7500	54·68750
1120	8·16667	2500	18·22917	10000	72·91667
1250	10·92146	3000	21·87500	15000	109·37500
1500	10·93750	4000	29·16667	20000	145·83333
1750	12·76042	5000	36·45833	30000	218·75000

No.	£	No.	£	No.	£	No.	£
1	0·00781	38	0·29687	76	0·59375	114	0·89062
1½	0·01172	39	0·30469	77	0·60156	115	0·89844
2	0·01562	40	0·31250	78	0·60937	116	0·90625
3	0·02344	41	0·32031	79	0·61719	117	0·91406
4	0·03125	42	0·32812	80	0·62500	118	0·92187
5	0·03906	43	0·33594	81	0·63281	119	0·92969
6	0·04687	44	0·34375	82	0·64062	120	0·93750
7	0·05469	45	0·35156	83	0·64844	128	1·00000
8	0·06250	46	0·35937	84	0·65625	130	1·01562
9	0·07031	47	0·36719	85	0·66406	140	1·09375
10	0·07812	48	0·37500	86	0·67187	144	1·12500
11	0·08594	49	0·38281	87	0·67969	150	1·17187
12	0·09375	50	0·39062	88	0·68750	156	1·21875
13	0·10156	51	0·39844	89	0·69531	160	1·25000
14	0·10937	52	0·40625	90	0·70312	168	1·31250
15	0·11719	53	0·41406	91	0·71094	170	1·32812
16	0·12500	54	0·42187	92	0·71875	180	1·40625
17	0·13281	55	0·42969	93	0·72656	190	1·48437
18	0·14062	56	0·43750	94	0·73437	196	1·53125
19	0·14844	57	0·44531	95	0·74219	200	1·56250
20	0·15625	58	0·45312	96	0·75000	220	1·71875
21	0·16406	59	0·46094	97	0·75781	224	1·75000
22	0·17187	60	0·46875	98	0·76562	256	2·00000
23	0·17969	61	0·47656	99	0·77344	280	2·18750
24	0·18750	62	0·48437	100	0·78125	300	2·34375
25	0·19531	63	0·49219	101	0·78906	365	2·85156
26	0·20312	64	0·50000	102	0·79687	400	3·12500
27	0·21094	65	0·50781	103	0·80469	480	3·75000
28	0·21875	66	0·51562	104	0·81250	500	3·90625
29	0·22656	67	0·52344	105	0·82031	516	4·03125
30	0·23437	68	0·53125	106	0·82812	560	4·37500
31	0·24219	69	0·53906	107	0·83594	600	4·68750
32	0·25000	70	0·54687	108	0·84375	625	4·88281
33	0·25781	71	0·55469	109	0·85156	640	5·00000
34	0·26562	72	0·56250	110	0·85937	700	5·46875
35	0·27344	73	0·57031	111	0·86719	750	5·85937
36	0·28125	74	0·57812	112	0·87500	800	6·25000
37	0·28906	75	0·58594	113	0·88281	900	7·03125

No.	£	No.	£	No.	£
1000	7·81250	1760	13·75000	6000	46·87500
1016	7·93750	2000	15·62500	7000	54·68750
1094	8·54687	2240	17·50000	7500	58·59375
1120	8·75000	2500	19·53125	10000	78·12500
1250	9·76562	3000	23·43750	15000	117·18750
1500	11·71875	4000	31·25000	20000	156·25000
1750	13·67187	5000	39·06250	30000	234·37500

No.	£	No.	£	No.	£	No.	£
1	0·00833	38	0·31667	76	0·63333	114	0·95000
1½	0·01250	39	0·32500	77	0·64167	115	0·95833
2	0·01667	40	0·33333	78	0·65000	116	0·96667
3	0·02500	41	0·34167	79	0·65833	117	0·97500
4	0·03333	42	0·35000	80	0·66667	118	0·98333
5	0·04167	43	0·35833	81	0·67500	119	0·99167
6	0·05000	44	0·36667	82	0·68333	120	1·00000
7	0·05833	45	0·37500	83	0·69167	128	1·06667
8	0·06667	46	0·38333	84	0·70000	130	1·08333
9	0·07500	47	0·39167	85	0·70833	140	1·16667
10	0·08333	48	0·40000	86	0·71667	144	1·20000
11	0·09167	49	0·40833	87	0·72500	150	1·25000
12	0·10000	50	0·41667	88	0·73333	156	1·30000
13	0·10833	51	0·42500	89	0·74167	160	1·33333
14	0·11667	52	0·43333	90	0·75000	168	1·40000
15	0·12500	53	0·44167	91	0·75833	170	1·41667
16	0·13333	54	0·45000	92	0·76667	180	1·50000
17	0·14167	55	0·45833	93	0·77500	190	1·58333
18	0·15000	56	0·46667	94	0·78333	196	1·63333
19	0·15833	57	0·47500	95	0·79167	200	1·66667
20	0·16667	58	0·48333	96	0·80000	220	1·83333
21	0·17500	59	0·49167	97	0·80833	224	1·86667
22	0·18333	60	0·50000	98	0·81667	256	2·13333
23	0·19167	61	0·50833	99	0·82500	280	2·33333
24	0·20000	62	0·51667	100	0·83333	300	2·50000
25	0·20833	63	0·52500	101	0·84167	365	3·04167
26	0·21667	64	0·53333	102	0·85000	400	3·33333
27	0·22500	65	0·54167	103	0·85833	480	4·00000
28	0·23333	66	0·55000	104	0·86667	500	4·16667
29	0·24167	67	0·55833	105	0·87500	516	4·30000
30	0·25000	68	0·56667	106	0·88333	560	4·66667
31	0·25833	69	0·57500	107	0·89167	600	5·00000
32	0·26667	70	0·58333	108	0·90000	625	5·20833
33	0·27500	71	0·59167	109	0·90833	640	5·33333
34	0·28333	72	0·60000	110	0·91667	700	5·83333
35	0·29167	73	0·60833	111	0·92500	750	6·25000
36	0·30000	74	0·61667	112	0·93333	800	6·66667
37	0·30833	75	0·62500	113	0·94167	900	7·50000

No.	£	No.	£	No.	£
1000	8·33333	1760	14·46667	6000	50·00000
1016	8·46667	2000	16·66667	7000	58·33333
1094	9·11667	2240	18·66667	7500	62·50000
1120	9·33333	2500	20·83333	10000	83·33333
1250	10·41667	3000	25·00000	15000	125·00000
1500	12·50000	4000	33·33333	20000	166·66667
1750	14·58333	5000	41·66667	30000	250·00000

No.	£	No.	£	No.	£	No.	£
1	0·00885	38	0·33646	76	0·67292	114	1·00937
1½	0·01328	39	0·34531	77	0·68177	115	1·01823
2	0·01771	40	0·35417	78	0·69062	116	1·02708
3	0·02656	41	0·36302	79	0·69948	117	1·03594
4	0·03542	42	0·37187	80	0·70833	118	1·04479
5	0·04427	43	0·38073	81	0·71719	119	1·05364
6	0·05312	44	0·38958	82	0·72604	120	1·06250
7	0·06198	45	0·39844	83	0·73490	128	1·13333
8	0·07083	46	0·40729	84	0·74375	130	1·15104
9	0·07969	47	0·41614	85	0·75260	140	1·23958
10	0·08854	48	0·42500	86	0·76146	144	1·27500
11	0·09740	49	0·43385	87	0·77031	150	1·32812
12	0·10625	50	0·44271	88	0·77917	156	1·38125
13	0·11510	51	0·45156	89	0·78802	160	1·41667
14	0·12396	52	0·46042	90	0·79687	168	1·48750
15	0·13281	53	0·46927	91	0·80573	170	1·50521
16	0·14167	54	0·47812	92	0·81458	180	1·59375
17	0·15052	55	0·48698	93	0·82344	190	1·68229
18	0·15937	56	0·49583	94	0·83229	196	1·73542
19	0·16823	57	0·50469	95	0·84115	200	1·77083
20	0·17708	58	0·51354	96	0·85000	220	1·94792
21	0·18594	59	0·52240	97	0·85885	224	1·98333
22	0·19479	60	0·53125	98	0·86771	256	2·26667
23	0·20365	61	0·54010	99	0·87656	280	2·47917
24	0·21250	62	0·54896	100	0·88542	300	2·65625
25	0·22135	63	0·55781	101	0·89427	365	3·23177
26	0·23021	64	0·56667	102	0·90312	400	3·54167
27	0·23906	65	0·57552	103	0·91198	480	4·25000
28	0·24792	66	0·58437	104	0·92083	500	4·42708
29	0·25677	67	0·59323	105	0·92969	516	4·56875
30	0·26562	68	0·60208	106	0·93854	560	4·95833
31	0·27448	69	0·61094	107	0·94740	600	5·31250
32	0·28333	70	0·61979	108	0·95625	625	5·53385
33	0·29219	71	0·62865	109	0·96510	640	5·66667
34	0·30104	72	0·63750	110	0·97396	700	6·19792
35	0·30990	73	0·64635	111	0·98281	750	6·64062
36	0·31875	74	0·65521	112	0·99167	800	7·08333
37	0·32760	75	0·66406	113	1·00052	900	7·96875

No.	£	No.	£	No.	£
1000	8·85417	1760	15·58333	6000	53·12500
1016	8·99583	2000	17·70833	7000	61·97917
1094	9·68646	2240	19·83333	7500	66·40625
1120	9·91667	2500	22·13542	10000	88·54167
1250	11·06771	3000	26·56250	15000	132·81250
1500	13·28125	4000	35·41667	20000	177·08333
1750	15·49480	5000	44·27083	30000	265·62500

No.	£	No.	£	No.	£	No.	£
1	0·00937	38	0·35625	76	0·71250	114	1·06875
1½	0·01406	39	0·36562	77	0·72187	115	1·07812
2	0·01875	40	0·37500	78	0·73125	116	1·08750
3	0·02812	41	0·38437	79	0·74062	117	1·09687
4	0·03750	42	0·39375	80	0·75000	118	1·10625
5	0·04687	43	0·40312	81	0·75937	119	1·11562
6	0·05625	44	0·41250	82	0·76875	120	1·12500
7	0·06562	45	0·42187	83	0·77812	128	1·20000
8	0·07500	46	0·43125	84	0·78750	130	1·21875
9	0·08437	47	0·44062	85	0·79687	140	1·31250
10	0·09375	48	0·45000	86	0·80625	144	1·35000
11	0·10312	49	0·45937	87	0·81562	150	1·40625
12	0·11250	50	0·46875	88	0·82500	156	1·46250
13	0·12187	51	0·47812	89	0·83437	160	1·50000
14	0·13125	52	0·48750	90	0·84375	168	1·57500
15	0·14062	53	0·49687	91	0·85312	170	1·59375
16	0·15000	54	0·50625	92	0·86250	180	1·68750
17	0·15937	55	0·51562	93	0·87187	190	1·78125
18	0·16875	56	0·52500	94	0·88125	196	1·83750
19	0·17812	57	0·53437	95	0·89062	200	1·87500
20	0·18750	58	0·54375	96	0·90000	220	2·06250
21	0·19687	59	0·55312	97	0·90937	224	2·10000
22	0·20625	60	0·56250	98	0·91875	256	2·40000
23	0·21562	61	0·57187	99	0·92812	280	2·62500
24	0·22500	62	0·58125	100	0·93750	300	2·81250
25	0·23437	63	0·59062	101	0·94687	365	3·42187
26	0·24375	64	0·60000	102	0·95625	400	3·75000
27	0·25312	65	0·60937	103	0·96562	480	4·50000
28	0·26250	66	0·61875	104	0·97500	500	4·68750
29	0·27187	67	0·62812	105	0·98437	516	4·83750
30	0·28125	68	0·63750	106	0·99375	560	5·25000
31	0·29062	69	0·64687	107	1·00312	600	5·62500
32	0·30000	70	0·65625	108	1·01250	625	5·85937
33	0·30937	71	0·66562	109	1·02187	640	6·00000
34	0·31875	72	0·67500	110	1·03125	700	6·56250
35	0·32812	73	0·68437	111	1·04062	750	7·03125
36	0·33750	74	0·69375	112	1·05000	800	7·50000
37	0·34687	75	0·70312	113	1·05937	900	8·43750

No.	£	No.	£	No.	£
1000	9·37500	1760	16·50000	6000	56·25000
1016	9·52500	2000	18·75000	7000	65·62500
1094	10·25625	2240	21·00000	7500	70·31250
1120	10·50000	2500	23·43750	10000	93·75000
1250	11·71875	3000	28·12500	15000	140·62500
1500	14·06250	4000	37·50000	20000	187·50000
1750	16·40625	5000	46·87500	30000	281·25000

$2\frac{3}{8}$d OLD PENNY SUPPLEMENTARY TABLE $2\frac{3}{8}$d

No.	£	No.	£	No.	£	No.	£
1	0·00990	38	0·37604	76	0·75208	114	1·12812
1½	0·01484	39	0·38594	77	0·76198	115	1·13802
2	0·01979	40	0·39583	78	0·77187	116	1·14792
3	0·02969	41	0·40573	79	0·78177	117	1·15781
4	0·03958	42	0·41562	80	0·79167	118	1·16771
5	0·04948	43	0·42552	81	0·80156	119	1·17760
6	0·05937	44	0·43542	82	0·81146	120	1·18750
7	0·06927	45	0·44531	83	0·82135	128	1·26667
8	0·07917	46	0·45521	84	0·83125	130	1·28646
9	0·08906	47	0·46510	85	0·84114	140	1·38542
10	0·09896	48	0·47500	86	0·85104	144	1·42500
11	0·10885	49	0·48490	87	0·86094	150	1·48437
12	0·11875	50	0·49479	88	0·87083	156	1·54375
13	0·12864	51	0·50469	89	0·88073	160	1·58333
14	0·13854	52	0·51458	90	0·89062	168	1·66250
15	0·14844	53	0·52448	91	0·90052	170	1·68229
16	0·15833	54	0·53437	92	0·91042	180	1·78125
17	0·16823	55	0·54427	93	0·92031	190	1·88021
18	0·17812	56	0·55417	94	0·93021	196	1·93958
19	0·18802	57	0·56406	95	0·94010	200	1·97917
20	0·19792	58	0·57396	96	0·95000	220	2·17708
21	0·20781	59	0·58385	97	0·95990	224	2·21667
22	0·21771	60	0·59375	98	0·96979	256	2·53333
23	0·22760	61	0·60365	99	0·97969	280	2·77083
24	0·23750	62	0·61354	100	0·98958	300	2·96875
25	0·24740	63	0·62344	101	0·99948	365	3·61198
26	0·25729	64	0·63333	102	1·00937	400	3·95833
27	0·26719	65	0·64323	103	1·01927	480	4·75000
28	0·27708	66	0·65312	104	1·02917	500	4·94792
29	0·28698	67	0·66302	105	1·03906	516	5·10625
30	0·29687	68	0·67292	106	1·04896	560	5·54167
31	0·30677	69	0·68281	107	1·05885	600	5·93750
32	0·31667	70	0·69271	108	1·06875	625	6·18490
33	0·32656	71	0·70260	109	1·07865	640	6·33333
34	0·33646	72	0·71250	110	1·08854	700	6·92708
35	0·34635	73	0·72240	111	1·09844	750	7·42187
36	0·35625	74	0·73229	112	1·10833	800	7·91667
37	0·36614	75	0·74219	113	1·11823	900	8·90625

No.	£	No.	£	No.	£
1000	9·89583	1760	17·41667	6000	59·37500
1016	10·05417	2000	19·79167	7000	69·27083
1094	10·82604	2240	22·16667	7500	74·21875
1120	11·83333	2500	24·73958	10000	98·95833
1250	12·36979	3000	29·68750	15000	148·43750
1500	14·84375	4000	39·58333	20000	197·91667
1750	17·31771	5000	49·47917	30000	296·87500

CURRENCY AND COMMERCE

The pound sterling is the major unit of currency of the United Kingdom. In £sd currency the pound is subdivided into shillings (s) and pence (d). In decimal currency the new penny (p) is the only other monetary unit besides the pound.

£sd	£p (decimal)
12d = 1s	100p = £1
20s = £1	

Coinage

£sd	£p equivalent	£p	£sd equivalent
½d	5/24 p	½p	1·2d
1d	5/12 p	1p	2·4d
3d	1¼p	2p	4·8d
6d	2½p	5p	1s
1s	5p	10p	2s
2s	10p	50p	10s
2/6	12½p		

There are £1, £5 and £10 notes in both currencies and a £20 note in the £p currency.

Conversion Tables

Only £sd amounts which end in sixpence or multiples of sixpence convert exactly into £p. Because there are differences between the odd penny amounts and the nearest decimal equivalents, conversion tables are used for orderly and consistent conversions. The new half-penny table can be used for cash transactions and the whole new penny table is needed because banking and most machine accounting work on whole new penny intervals. The following are the accepted conversion tables. Both tables round down the same number of amounts as are rounded up so if they are applied consistently debtors and creditors gains balance out.

Shoppers table Shillings are first converted (by multiplying by five) and the pence are then converted by using the table. The two amounts are then added together.

Banking and accounting table The largest even number of shillings is first converted. The remainder, which will be an amount between 1d and 1s 11d, is then converted by using the table and the two amounts are then added together.

Shoppers Table (or new half-penny table)

£sd	£p
1d	½p
2d	1p
3d	1p
4d	1½p
5d	2p
6d =	2½p
7d	3p
8d	3½p
9d	4p
10d	4p
11d	4½p
1s =	5p

Banking and Accounting Table (or whole new penny table)

£sd	£p	£sd	£p
1d	0p	1/1	5p
2d	1p	1/2	6p
3d	1p	1/3	6p
4d	2p	1/4	7p
5d	2p	1/5	7p
6d	3p	1/6	7p
7d	3p	1/7	8p
8d	3p	1/8	8p
9d	4p	1/9	9p
10d	4p	1/10	9p
11d	5p	1/11	10p
1s = 5p		2s = 10p	

Calculations in Decimal Currency

A decimal currency makes the calculations involved in cash transactions very simple. There is no need to convert the result, e.g. from pence to pounds and shillings.

Examples:

Cost of 8 articles costing 2p each = (8×2)p = 16p
= £0·16

Cost of 6 articles costing 25p each = (6×25)p
= 150p = £1·50

Cost of 3 articles costing £1·30 each = £$(3 \times 1{\cdot}30)$
= £3·90

Fractional Parts of £1

and the Percentage Equivalents of the Fractions

Parts of £1 (rounded)		Percentage equivalents (rounded)
50p	$\frac{1}{2}$	50 %
$33\frac{1}{2}$p	$\frac{1}{3}$	33 %
$66\frac{1}{2}$p	$\frac{2}{3}$	67 %
25p	$\frac{1}{4}$	25 %
75p	$\frac{3}{4}$	75 %
20p	$\frac{1}{5}$	20 %
40p	$\frac{2}{5}$	40 %
60p	$\frac{3}{5}$	60 %
80p	$\frac{4}{5}$	80 %
$12\frac{1}{2}$p	$\frac{1}{8}$	$12\frac{1}{2}$ %
10p	$\frac{1}{10}$	10 %
5p	$\frac{1}{20}$	5 %
$2\frac{1}{2}$p	$\frac{1}{40}$	$2\frac{1}{2}$ %
2p	$\frac{1}{50}$	2 %
1p	$\frac{1}{100}$	1 %

Wages Table for the Year, Quarter, Calendar Month, Week and Day

Yearly £	Yearly p	Quarterly £	Quarterly p	Monthly £	Monthly p	Weekly £	Weekly p	Daily £	Daily p
0	50	0	$12\frac{1}{2}$	0	04	0	01	0	00
1	00	0	25	0	$08\frac{1}{2}$	0	02	0	$00\frac{1}{2}$
2	00	0	50	0	$16\frac{1}{2}$	0	04	0	$00\frac{1}{2}$
3	00	0	75	0	25	0	06	0	01
4	00	1	00	0	$33\frac{1}{2}$	0	$07\frac{1}{2}$	0	01
5	00	1	25	0	$41\frac{1}{2}$	0	$09\frac{1}{2}$	0	$01\frac{1}{2}$
6	00	1	50	0	50	0	$11\frac{1}{2}$	0	$01\frac{1}{2}$
7	00	1	75	0	$58\frac{1}{2}$	0	$13\frac{1}{2}$	0	02
8	00	2	00	0	$66\frac{1}{2}$	0	$15\frac{1}{2}$	0	02
9	00	2	25	0	75	0	$17\frac{1}{2}$	0	$02\frac{1}{2}$
10	00	2	50	0	$83\frac{1}{2}$	0	19	0	$02\frac{1}{2}$
20	00	5	00	1	$66\frac{1}{2}$	0	$38\frac{1}{2}$	0	$05\frac{1}{2}$
30	00	7	50	2	50	0	$57\frac{1}{2}$	0	08
40	00	10	00	3	$33\frac{1}{2}$	0	77	0	11
50	00	12	50	4	$16\frac{1}{2}$	0	96	0	$13\frac{1}{2}$
60	00	15	00	5	00	1	$15\frac{1}{2}$	0	$16\frac{1}{2}$
70	00	17	50	5	$83\frac{1}{2}$	1	$34\frac{1}{2}$	0	19
80	00	20	00	6	$66\frac{1}{2}$	1	54	0	22
90	00	22	50	7	50	1	73	0	$24\frac{1}{2}$
100	00	25	00	8	$33\frac{1}{2}$	1	$92\frac{1}{2}$	0	$27\frac{1}{2}$
200	00	50	00	16	$66\frac{1}{2}$	3	$84\frac{1}{2}$	0	55
300	00	75	00	25	00	5	77	0	82
400	00	100	00	33	$33\frac{1}{2}$	7	69	1	$09\frac{1}{2}$
500	00	125	00	41	$66\frac{1}{2}$	9	$61\frac{1}{2}$	1	37
600	00	150	00	50	00	11	54	1	$64\frac{1}{2}$
700	00	175	00	58	$33\frac{1}{2}$	13	46	1	92
800	00	200	00	66	$66\frac{1}{2}$	15	$38\frac{1}{2}$	2	19
900	00	225	00	75	00	17	31	2	$46\frac{1}{2}$
1000	00	250	00	83	$33\frac{1}{2}$	19	23	2	74

(All entries correct to the nearest $\frac{1}{2}$p.)

Any wage can be accommodated by this table by breaking the amount down into halves of units, units, tens, hundreds and thousands, e.g.

£2345·50 = 2 × £1000 + £300 + £40 + £5 + £0·50

So £2345·50 yearly

= (2 × £19·23 + £5·77 + £0·77 + £0·09½ + £0·01) weekly

= £45·10½ weekly

Simple and Compound Interest

The term **Interest** in commerce means the money paid for the use of money lent.

Simple Interest is calculated on the original loan. The amount originally lent is called the **principal**. The simple interest which accumulates can be calculated from the formula

$$I = \frac{P \times R \times T}{100}$$

where P is the principal, R is the rate per cent and T the time.

The sum to which the principal will grow is given by the formula

$$S = P\left(1 + \frac{R \times T}{100}\right)$$

Compound Interest is the term used when interest is paid not only on the principal but also on the interest as it accumulates. The sum to which the principal will grow is given by the formula

$$S = P(1 + i)^n$$

where i is the periodic interest and n the number of periods.

Time at which Money Doubles Itself

Interest Rate	Simple Interest		Compound Interest	
1%	100 years		70 years	
2%	50 "		35 "	1 day
3%	33 "	4 months	23 "	164 days
4%	25 "		17 "	246 "
5%	20 "		14 "	75 "
6%	16 "	8 months	11 "	327 "
7%	14 "	104 days	10 "	89 "
8%	12 "	6 months	9 "	2 "
9%	11 "	40 days	8 "	16 "
10%	10 "		7 "	100 "

Currencies of the World

Country	Monetary Unit	Value of unit in British Currency (March 1970)
Australia	Dollar = 100 Cents	£0·466
Austria	Schilling = 100 Groschen	£0·016
Belgium	Franc = 100 Centimes	£0·008
Canada	Dollar = 100 Cents	£0·388
Denmark	Krone = 100 Öre	£0·055
France	Franc = 100 Centimes	£0·075
Germany	Deutsche Mark = 100 Pfennig	£0·113
Holland	Guilder = 100 Cents	£0·114
Italy	Lira = 100 Centesimi	£0·001
Japan	Yen	£0·001
Norway	Krone = 100 Öre	£0·058
Portugal	Escudo = 100 Centavos	£0·015
Spain	Peseta = 100 Céntimos	£0·006
Sweden	Krona = 100 Öre	£0·080
Switzerland	Franc = 100 Centimes	£0·097
U.S.A.	Dollar = 100 Cents	£0·417

Commercial Symbols

£	pound sterling
$	dollar
p	(new) penny
%	per cent
c/o	care of
a/c	account
@	at

WEIGHTS AND MEASURES

The **Imperial System** of measurement, based on the yard for length and the pound for weight, has been used in the United Kingdom for many centuries.

The **Metric System** was founded by the French during the French Revolution.

The **Système International d'Unités** (International System of Units) is the modern form of the metric system finally agreed at an international conference in 1960. The international symbol for this system is **SI**. SI is the result of the rationalisation of the whole structure of metric derived units. The United Kingdom decided to adopt SI as the primary system of measures and weights because almost 90% of the world's population live in countries that use SI, or are committed to use it.

The International System of Units

SI is based on six **base-units**:

Quantity	Unit	Symbol
length	metre	m
mass	kilogramme	kg
time	second	s
electric current	ampere	A
temperature	kelvin	K
luminous intensity	candela	cd

The SI units for plane angle and solid angle, the radian (rad) and steradian (sr) respectively, are called **supplementary units**.

The **derived units** are stated in terms of the base-units,

e.g., velocity is expressed in metres per second (m/s). Some derived units are given special names, e.g., the watt (W).

Note. By international agreement the United Kingdom, Europe and most other countries use the spellings *metre* and *kilogramme*. In North America the spellings are *meter* and *kilogram*.

Larger or smaller quantities are formed by multiplying or dividing the SI units by 10, 100, 1000 and so on. The names of these quantities are formed by means of prefixes to the principal units.

prefix		symbol
mega	— a million times	M
kilo	— a thousand times	k
hecto*	— a hundred times	h
deca*	— ten times	da
deci*	— a tenth part of	d
centi*	— a hundredth part of	c
milli	— a thousandth part of	m
micro	— a millionth part of	μ

* The use of these prefixes is avoided unless absolutely necessary.

Examples:

1 millimetre (mm) = $\frac{1}{10}$ centimetre (cm) = $\frac{1}{1000}$ metre (m)
1 megawatt (MW) = 1000 kilowatts (kW) = 1 000 000 watts (W)

Length

Metre (m) is the SI base-unit for length.

The metre was intended to be one ten-millionth part of the distance from the North Pole to the Equator at sea-level through Paris.

1 m = 1·094 yd = 39·37 in

1 in = 25·4 mm	
1 ft = 0·304 8 m	
= 30·48 cm	
1 yd = 0·914 4 m	
1 mile = 1·609 km	

1 mm = 0·039 4 in
1 km = 0·621 4 mile = 1093·6 yd

Examples:

Imperial Measure	SI Units (approx.)
Man's height 5 ft 11 in	180 cm or 1·8 m
Diameter of a 6-in plate	15 cm
Length of a cricket pitch: 22 yd = 1 chain	20·1 m
Distance from Dover to Calais: 22 miles	35·4 km
Distance from London to Manchester: 184 miles	296 km
Distance from London to Frankfurt: 406 miles	653 km
Distance from London to New York: 3442 miles	5539 km
Distance from the Earth to the Moon: 238 840 miles	384 380 km

Approximate Conversions:

Metres into feet: multiply by $3^1/_4$
Metres into yards: add one-tenth
Kilometres into miles: multiply by $^5/_8$

Millimetres into inches: divide by 25

Yards into metres: deduct one-tenth
Feet into metres: multiply by $^3/_{10}$
Miles into kilometres: multiply by $^8/_5$
Inches into millimetres: multiply by 25

Area

Square metre (m²) is the derived SI unit for area.

There are also two special units which can be used.

Hectare (ha) = 10 000 m²

Are (a) = 100 m²

1 m² = 1·196 yd²

1 in² = 645·16 mm²	
1 ft² = 0·092 9 m² = 929·03 cm²	
1 yd² = 0·836 1 m²	
1 acre = 4046·86 m² = 0·404 7 ha	
1 sq. mile = 2·590 km² = 258·999 ha	

1 ha = 2·471 acres
1 a = 1076 ft²
1 km² = 247·1 acres = 0·386 1 sq. mile

Examples:

Imperial Measure	SI Units (approx.)
Area of a football pitch: 120 yd × 80 yd = 9600 yd²	8027 m²
Area of a doubles tennis court: 78 ft × 36 ft = 2808 ft²	261 m²
Area of an average carpet: 4 yd × 3 yd = 12 yd²	10 m²
Area of an average house-plot: $\frac{1}{3}$ acre	0·13 ha
Surface area of a 6-in diameter plate: 28·3 in²	183 cm²

Approximate Conversions:

Square metres into square yards: add one-fifth
Hectares into acres: multiply by $\frac{5}{2}$

Acres into hectares: multiply by $\frac{2}{5}$

Volume

Cubic metre (m³) is the derived SI unit for volume.

1 m³ = 1·308 0 yd³

$1 \text{ in}^3 = 16\cdot387 \text{ cm}^3$
$1 \text{ ft}^3 = 0\cdot028\ 3 \text{ m}^3$
$1 \text{ yd}^3 = 0\cdot764\ 6 \text{ m}^3$

$1 \text{ dm}^3 = 0\cdot035\ 3 \text{ ft}^3$
$1 \text{ cm}^3 = 0\cdot061\ 0 \text{ in}^3$

Examples:

Imperial Measure	SI Units (approx.)
Volume of a 3-lb biscuit tin:	7005 cm³
9 in × 9½ in × 5 in = 427·5 in³	
Volume of an average room:	47·6 m³
12 ft × 14 ft × 10 ft = 1680 ft³	

Approximate Conversions:

Cubic metres into cubic yards: add one-third

Cubic yards into cubic metres: deduct one-third

Capacity

(For volumes of Fluids)

Litre (l) is the SI unit used for general measures of capacity but not for scientific measurements, when the cubic metre, cubic millimetre, etc., are used.

1 l = 1 dm³

There are less widely used multiples and sub-multiples, in particular the **hectolitre (hl)** and **millilitre (ml)**.

1 l = 0·220 gal = 1·760 pt = 61·026 in³

$1 \text{ gal} = 4\cdot546 \text{ l}$
$1 \text{ qt} = 1\cdot136 \text{ l}$
$1 \text{ pt} = 0\cdot568 \text{ l}$
$1 \text{ gill} = 142 \text{ ml}$
$1 \text{ fl. oz} = 28\cdot4 \text{ ml}$

1 hl = 22·00 gal

continued

Examples:

Imperial Measure	SI Units (approx.)
1 British teaspoon holds approx.	
1/25 gill = 1/5 fl. oz	5·6 ml
4 gallons of petrol	18 l
Pint of milk, beer, paint, etc.	0·57 l
40-gal drum of petrol or oil	1·8 hl

Approximate Conversions:

Litres into pints: add three-quarters

Pints into litres: multiply by 3/5

Weight

Kilogramme (kg) is the SI base-unit for weight.

The gramme was intended to be the mass of one cubic centimetre (one millilitre) of water at 0°C.

1 tonne (t) (metric ton) = 1000 kg
1 metric carat = 0·2 g

The metric carat is used for commercial transactions in diamonds, fine pearls and precious stones.

1 kg = 2·205 lb

$1 \text{ oz} = 28\cdot350 \text{ g}$
$1 \text{ lb} = 454 \text{ g}$
$1 \text{ stone} = 6\cdot350 \text{ kg}$
$1 \text{ cwt} = 50\cdot802 \text{ kg}$
$1 \text{ ton} = 1\cdot016 \text{ t}$

1 g = 0·035 oz
1 t = 0·984 ton

Examples:

Imperial Measure	SI Units (approx.)
½ lb butter	0·23 kg or 227 g
3 lb flour	1·4 kg
5 cwt coal	254 kg
A birth weight of 8½ lb	3856 g or 3·9 kg
A man weighing 13½ stone = 189 lb	85·7 kg

continued

Approximate Conversions:

Kilogrammes into pounds : add a tenth and multiply by 2
Pounds into kilogrammes : deduct a tenth and divide by 2
Ounces into grammes : multiply by 28
Hundredweights into kilogrammes : multiply by 50
The tonne and ton are *nearly* equal.

Temperature

Kelvin (K) is the SI base-unit for temperature.

Degrees Kelvin, also known as degrees **Absolute**, are mainly used for scientific measurements. The customary international unit is the degree **Celsius** which is known as **Centigrade** (°C) in the United Kingdom. (In France, Centigrade is a unit of angular measure and the name Celsius is used for temperature.) The zero of the Centigrade scale is the temperature of the ice-point (273·16°K). The units of the Centigrade and Kelvin temperature interval are the same. Another unit used in the United Kingdom is the degree **Fahrenheit** (°F).

	°C	°F
Ice point	0	32
Boiling point of water under standard pressure	100	212

To convert °F to °C deduct 32 and multiply by $\frac{5}{9}$.
To convert °C to °F multiply by $\frac{9}{5}$ and add 32.

Examples:

	°F	°C
Temperature on a very frosty day	12	−11
Temperature on a hot summer day	86	30
Normal body temperature	98·4	37

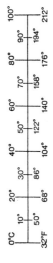

Angular Measure

Radian (rad) is the SI unit for angular measure. It is a supplementary SI Unit.

A more commonly used unit for angular measure is the **degree** which is subdivided into **minutes** and **seconds.**

60 seconds (")	= 1 minute
60 minutes (')	= 1 degree
90 degrees (°)	= 1 right angle
360 degrees (°)	= 1 full circle

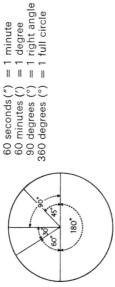

An **acute** angle is one less than 90°.

An **obtuse** angle is one between 90° and 180°.

A **reflex** angle is one between 180° and 360°.

The circumference of a circle is 3·141 59, or nearly $3\frac{1}{7}$, times its diameter. This number 3·141 59 is known as **π**, a widely used mathematical constant.
A radian is the angle between two radii of a circle which

cut off on the circumference an arc equal in length to the radius.

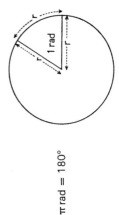

$$\pi \text{ rad} = 180°$$

The angles of a triangle added together are equal to 180°.

Velocity

Velocity can be measured in **metres per second** (m/s) or **kilometres per hour** (km/h) in SI.

1 km/h = 0·621 mile/h   1 mile/h = 1·609 km/h
1 m/s = 3·281 ft/s   1 ft/s = 0·304 8 m/s

Examples:

Imperial Measure   **SI Units** (approx.)
30 mile/h = 44 ft/s   48 km/h = 13 m/s
50 mile/h   80 km/h
70 mile/h   113 km/h

Approximate Conversions:

km/h into mile/h :   mile/h into km/h :
multiply by $\frac{5}{8}$ multiply by $\frac{8}{5}$

Force

Newton (N) is the derived SI unit of Force. It is the force which when applied to a mass of 1 kilogramme gives it an acceleration of 1 metre per second per second.

The **dyne** is a non-SI metric unit.
$$1 \text{ N} = 100\ 000 \text{ dynes}$$

Pressure

The SI unit of pressure or stress is the **newton per square metre** (N/m^2).

$1 \text{ N/m}^2 = 0·000\ 145 \text{ lbf/in}^2$ $1 \text{ lbf/in}^2 \text{ (1 p.s.i.)} = 6894·76 \text{ N/m}^2$
$1 \text{ kN/m}^2 = 0·295 \text{ inHg}$ $1 \text{ inHg} = 3383·39 \text{ N/m}^2$

The **millibar** (mb or mbar) and **millimetres of mercury** (mmHg) are non-SI metric units used to measure atmospheric pressure.

$$1 \text{ mbar} = 100 \text{ N/m}^2$$
$$1 \text{ mmHg} = 133·322 \text{ N/m}^2$$

Energy

Joule (J) is the SI unit which measures work and quantity of heat. It is the work done when the point of application of a force of 1 newton is displaced through a distance of 1 metre in the direction of the force.

1 J = 0·738 ft lbf   1 therm = 105·5 MJ
1 kJ = 0·278 Wh   1 kWh = 3·6 MJ
               1 Btu = 1·0554 kJ

The **calorie, kilo-calorie** and **Calorie** are non-SI metric units.

$$1 \text{ cal} = 4·186\ 8 \text{ J}$$

The kilo-calorie and Calorie (spelt with a capital 'C') are

equal to 1000 calories. The kilo-calorie is used for measurements of large quantities of heat. The Calorie is used for describing the energy values of foods.

Power

Watt (W) is the SI unit of power. The watt is equal to 1 joule per second.

$$1 \text{ hp} = 745{\cdot}7 \text{ W}$$

Electricity

Ampere (A) is the SI base-unit for **electric current.**

Coulomb (C) is the SI unit of **electric charge.** It is the quantity of electricity transported in 1 second by 1 ampere.

Volt. (V) is the SI unit of **electric potential.** A volt is the difference of electric potential between two points of a conducting wire carrying a constant current of 1 ampere when the power dissipated between these points is equal to 1 watt.

Ohm (Ω) is the SI unit of **electric resistance.** A resistance of 1 ohm between two points of a conductor with a constant difference of potential of 1 volt produces in the conductor a current of 1 ampere.

Farad (F) is the SI unit of **electric capacitance.** It is the capacitance of a capacitor charged to a potential of 1 volt by 1 coulomb of electricity.

Formulae :

Volts = Amperes × Ohms ($V = A \times \Omega$)
Watts = Volts × Amperes ($W = V \times A$)

THE IMPERIAL SYSTEM OF UNITS

Length

1 inch (in or ")		
1 foot (ft or ')	=	12 inches
1 yard (yd)	=	36 inches / 3 feet
1 fathom (fm)	=	6 feet / 2 yards
1 link	=	7·92 inches
1 rod, pole or perch	=	25 links / 5½ yards
1 chain (ch)	=	100 links / 22 yards / 4 poles
1 furlong (fur)	=	220 yards / 40 poles / 10 chains
1 mile	=	1760 yards / 80 chains / 8 furlongs

Area

1 square inch (sq. in or in²)		
1 square foot (sq. ft or ft²)	=	144 (12 × 12) sq. inches
1 square yard (sq. yd or yd²)	=	9 (3 × 3) sq. feet
1 square rod, pole or perch	=	625 (25 × 25) sq. links / 30¼ (5½ × 5½) sq. yards
1 square chain	=	10 000 (100 × 100) sq. links / 16 (4 × 4) sq. poles
1 rood	=	1210 sq. yards / 40 sq. rods
1 acre	=	100 000 sq. links / 10 sq. chains / 4 roods
1 square mile	=	640 acres
1 hide of land	=	100 acres
1 barony	=	40 hides

Volume

1 cubic inch (cu. in or in³)		
1 cubic foot (cu. ft or ft³)	=	1728 (12 × 12 × 12) cu. inches
1 cubic yard (cu. yd or yd³)	=	27 (3 × 3 × 3) cu. feet

Capacity

1 fluid ounce (fl. oz)	=	5 fl. oz
1 gill	=	20 fl. oz
1 pint (pt)	=	4 gills
1 quart (qt)	=	2 pints
1 gallon (gal)	=	8 pints
		4 quarts
1 peck (pk)	=	2 gallons
1 bushel	=	8 gallons
1 quarter	=	8 bushels
1 chaldron	=	36 bushels

Weight

1 grain (gr)		
1 dram (dr)	=	16 drams
1 ounce (oz)	=	7000 grains
1 pound (lb)	=	16 oz
1 stone	=	14 lb
1 quarter	=	28 lb
		2 stone
1 cental	=	100 lb
		112 lb
1 hundredweight (cwt)	=	8 stone
		4 quarters
1 ton	=	2240 lb
		20 cwt

Mathematical Signs and Symbols

+	Plus, the sign of addition
−	Minus, the sign of subtraction
×	The sign of multiplication
÷	The sign of division
. :	Is to
::	As ⎫ The signs of proportion. Thus 3 : 6 : : 4 : 8
. .	Is to ⎭
: .	Because
. :	Therefore
=	Equals, the sign of equality
>	Greater than
<	Less than
√	Square root
∛	Cube root. ∜ Fourth root. ⁵√ Fifth root, etc.
( ) [ ] { }	Indicate that the figures enclosed are to be taken together. Thus 10 × (7 + 4) : 8 − [9 ÷ 3] ;

$$30 \times \left\{ \dfrac{7 \times 3}{4 - 2} \right\}$$

° ′ ″	Degrees, minutes, seconds, (angular measure). Thus 25° 14′ 10″ represents 25 degrees, 14 minutes, 10 seconds
′ ″	Feet, inches. Thus 9′ 10″ = 9 feet 10 inches
∞	Infinity

Signs used in geometry

⊥	Perpendicular to	∟	Right angle
=	Parallel to	□	Square
○	Circle	▭	Rectangle
∠	Angle	△	Triangle

35/"